DIMENSIONS IN TIME AND SPACE

BY MARK CAMPBELL

Dimensions in Time and Space
1st Edition - Winter 2003
2nd Edition - Autumn 2005

A definitive listing and guide to Dr Who

Published by Steven Scott
The Stamp Centre, 79 The Strand, London WC2R 0DE

Printed by E.J. Rickard Ltd., Plymouth (01752) 660955

Front cover courtesy of © Canal Plus Image UK
© Mark Campbell October 2003

Copyright

The content of this book is protected by copyright. No reproduction of any part of this publication is allowed without the prior permission in writing of The Author. Any such requests must be directed via the publisher. This applies to any form of onward transmission including photocopying, scanning, E-Mail, using electrical, mechanical, computerised or other means. This catalogue is sold on the basis that under no circumstances is it lent, re-sold, circulated or otherwise disposed of, other than in its complete form. Furthermore, all the foregoing shall apply and be imposed upon any subsequent possessor of this book.

ISBN 1 871330 58 0

ACKNOWLEDGEMENTS

Many people have kindly donated their time and wisdom to help with the research for this book. In no particular order I would like to thank the following: Elaine Clarke at BBC Products and Sales, Derek and Paul at 10th Planet, Alex Loosely-Saul at The Who Shop, Paul Vanezis and Mark Ayres of the BBC's Restoration Team (you're doing a great job, chaps), and Iain Jarvis and my wife Mary for proof-reading and fact-checking chores. With regard to written materials, three sources of information have proved invaluable - *Howe's Transcendental Toybox* by David J Howe and Arnold T Blumberg (Telos), *Doctor Who on Location* by Richard Bignell (Reynolds and Hearn) and Andrew Pixley's comprehensive and exhaustive Archives in Panini's long-running *Doctor Who Magazine*, along with the respective Specials that accompany each Doctor. My especial thanks to Steven Scott for commissioning this book in the first place. And last, but certainly not least, I am eternally grateful to Jesus Christ for giving me the energy to keep on going despite the odds.

DEDICATION

This book is respectfully dedicated to the memory of Douglas Adams and John Nathan-Turner, two *Doctor Who* luminaries who gave much and died too young.

Foreword by Tom Baker

This book really might change your life. Note the cunning "might" and then you can snort if that's your taste and times being what they are. For this a book about the times of our lives. It is a book of "Allusions". For those of us who spend time and money on our nostalgia, this not so little book is a welcome bonus. I don't have to say that you know, I choose to say it. Over the past few years Steven Scott at The Stamp Centre has promoted many *Doctor Who* events without ever failing once. And at these events I have met a few, more than a few extraordinary people. I was once introduced to the last survivor of the Titanic disaster. She'd changed a little over the years but then so have I and I've been through a few adventures too.

Doctor Who fans, like all fans of cult programmes, live in the past. I'm talking of their imaginative lives of course. We can all now re-visit our childhood days at the touch of a button. And we do so, often. But this book will allow us to check the minute details of our memories. For example who said and in what episode: "Are you going to come quietly or do I have to use ear-plugs?" You will not find the answer in this book because that was a quote from *The Goon Show*. But here is a collection of detailed facts enough to sate a *Who* glutton. It will sate you without making you fat. It will make you sigh. It might make you angry too, for who can satisfy completely the appetite of a dedicated Whovian? I commend this book and hope if makes you all happy. All the best from the man who was who the fourth and enjoyed it all.

Tom Baker

Contents

Introduction

1: Television   1
*The BBC television series, the TV movie,
charity spoofs and other oddities*

2: Audio   281
LP recordings, radio programmes and Big Finish audio adventures

3: Cinema Films   305
The two 1960s Dalek films from Aaru

4: Comic Strips   309
Long-running adventures featuring all the Doctors from 1964 to the present

5: Books   361
Literary outpourings from Virgin, BBC and Telos

6: Internet Webcasts   409
The new way of watching Doctor Who

7: Stage Plays   411
Theatrical productions from 1965 to 1989

Introduction

Doctor Who has just finished its wildly successful relaunch on BBC One after fifteen years in the wilderness. Beating everything ITV1 threw against it, and often the most-watched programme of the night, *Doctor Who* has once more taken its place as the most influential family drama series ever made. Before it started, media executives across the land were muttering into their caffe lattes that "family drama was dead", that respected TV scriptwriter Russell T Davies was probably exhibiting early signs of senile dementia in shackling his name to a long-dead property. Even the fans were a little cautious. Would this be the final gasp of a once mainstream hit? Would there be a mammoth ratings tumble as viewers got over their initial nostalgia fix?

Well, we all know what happened next. To the sound of hats being furtively chewed by the great and the good in TV Land, *Doctor Who* proved a massive critical and commercial success. A mere thirteen weeks of telly pretty much put the nail into the dominance of reality TV programming and is ushering in a new era of quality drama. They're all talking about it, about how *Doctor Who* has reinvented good, solid family drama. No *Fungus the Bogeyman* this - here we have a show with much to amuse and entertain all age groups, from 3 to 103 (and possibly older). For goodness sake, even arch-villain Sir Michael Grade, who infamously tried to cancel the show back in the mid-eighties, was heard to compliment the new series! And now with David Tennant giving Season 28 a new lease of life, things look better than ever. It's a great time to be a *Doctor Who* fan. It's a great time to be six years old.

What this book intends to do is highlight *Doctor Who*'s extraordinary 42-year storytelling legacy over several key media. The bulk of the work concerns, as you would expect, the BBC television series. Following this are sections on TV spin-offs, audio stories, films, comic strips, books, webcasts and stage plays. The aim of each section is to be as comprehensive as possible without becoming just another list (although, inevitably, the nature of the book leans in that direction). Certain things you will not find within these covers - short stories (for instance, in annuals, holiday specials, magazines and books), documentaries (be they on TV, radio, CD, DVD or video), fan-produced stories (in any media) and adventures that do not (except in a few exceptional cases) feature the Doctor.

More than just another television guide, my hope is that *Dimensions in Time and Space* will be of interest to die-hard fans as well as those who just want to find out a little more about that mysterious time-traveller from Gallifrey...

Mark Campbell
Plumstead, London
August 2005

1: TELEVISION

Original and Repeat Transmissions
Original transmissions are all on BBCtv (until 1964), BBC1 (until 1996) and BBC One (from Season 27 onwards). The final figures show rating in millions followed by weekly chart position. The original transmission chart positions are for all terrestrial channels combined while repeat transmission positions are for that channel only. Where no figure is shown, the information is unavailable (usually due to negligible audience figures). Excepting BBC Three and BBC Four, non-terrestrial channels have been excluded.

BBC Archive
This lists the existing format of the episodes (where retained) prior to them being transferred to Digital Betacam for transmission or commercial release. These newly transferred prints are kept at the BBC Worldwide Tape Library, with restored versions (where relevant) reintegrated into the BBC Windmill Road Videotape Library. '71 Edits' are earlier, slightly longer, versions of the episodes prior to trimming for transmission.

Novelization
Separate entries are only given for editions with brand new artwork. The title is followed by total pages and chapters (including prologue, epilogue, introduction or conclusion) in parenthesis. Book club and foreign editions are excluded. For hardback and paperback editions, the International Standard Book Number (ISBN) and cover artist is in parenthesis. If hardback not listed, only a paperback was printed.

Non-Fiction Book
Any title that deals solely and specifically with the story in question. Details as for novelization.

Video
BBC Video catalogue numbers and cover artists are given in parenthesis, while details in square brackets, where relevant, indicate the BBC catalogue number and artist of a box set's outer case. All videos are VHS-Pal unless otherwise stated.

DVD
Certain *Doctor Who* DVDs are now given the VidFIRE™ treatment by the BBC's Restoration Team. VidFIRE is an acronym for Video Field Interpolation Restoration Effect, a process that generates an extra 25 fields of picture information for b/w and colour film recordings to mimic the smoothness of motion associated with the video look of the original recordings.

Music and Sound Effects
All LPs, audio cassettes and CDs listed, with catalogue number and cover artist in parenthesis

Telesnaps
Off-monitor b/w photographs (approximately 60 per episode) taken by John Cura in the 1960s. *DWM* = *Doctor Who Magazine*, *DWCC* = *Doctor Who Classic Comics*

Précis
The plot in a sentence.

Cast
All speaking parts and major non-speaking parts. Extras and walk-ons not listed unless relevant to the story.

DWM Index
All major *Doctor Who Magazine* references are listed (not included are questions and answers in *Matrix Data Bank*, most *Gallifrey Guardian* news items [shown as 'GG'] and brief mentions in general features). 'Archive' is a detailed synopsis of the story, 'Archive + Fact File' contains a brief 'making of' featurette, while 'Archive Feature' has concise story details and an exhaustive production feature courtesy of television archivist Andrew Pixley. 'Episode Guide' contains cliffhanger endings for each instalment. Winter and Summer Specials are shown, for example, as 'W94' or 'S91', while *Doctor Who Classic Comics* is denoted as 'CC'.

Recording Dates
For reasons of space, studio test sessions (except where the footage is used in the programme) and post-production editing has not been included. Modelwork filming is listed where known, but often information on these sessions is sketchy. 'BH' = Broadcasting House (Radio), 'EFS' = Ealing Film Studios, 'LG' = Lime Grove, 'MV' = Maida Vale (Radio), 'PM' = Pebble Mill (Birmingham), 'RS' = Riverside Studios, 'TC' = Television Centre, "Q2" = Unit 2 (Newport)

Factoids
Unusual, quirky, entertaining or informative - anything to give a flavour of the story.

Comment
Informed opinion about the story's merits or failings. My usual benchmark is whether the story is entertaining - for whatever reason. If it's not particularly interesting, even if it is well-made or held in high esteem by organized *Doctor Who* fandom, then my percentage mark will reflect this.

All merchandise is produced by the BBC unless otherwise stated. Only merchandise produced in the UK has been included in this volume.

The Television Series

First Doctor: William Hartnell

"I was born in the 49th century." ~ *Susan Foreman*

0) An Unearthly Child (Pilot)
Anthony Coburn, from an idea by CE Webber

Serial Code: A
Original Transmission
On BBC2 as part of the 'Lime Grove Studio Day': An Unearthly Child [Pilot]
Monday 26 August 1991, 14.15-14.40, 1.7m / -
BBC Archive
The episode exists as an unedited 35mm b/w film recording of the 405-line two-inch master videotape (wiped by the late 1960s).
Video
1. June 1991, as part of 'The Hartnell Years' (BBCV 4608 / Photographs)
2. May 2000, as *Dr Who: The Pilot Episode* with *The Edge of Destruction* (BBCV 6877 / Photomontage)
DVD
January 2005, in *The Beginning* box set
Music and Sound Effects
1. October 1998, Julian Knott, *Space Adventures: Music from Doctor Who 1963-1971*, CD (JPD 2CD / Photographs)
2. May 2000, *Doctor Who at the BBC Radiophonic Workshop - Volume 1: The Early Years*, CD (WMSF 6023-2 / Photographs)
Précis
Two schoolteachers follow a mysterious pupil back to her home - a police-box in a junk-yard…
Cast
William Hartnell (Doctor Who), William Russell (Ian Chesterton), Jacqueline Hill (Barbara Wright), Carole Ann Ford (Susan Foreman), Fred Rawlings (Policeman), Carole Clarke, Francesco Bertorelli, Heather Lyons, Mavis Ranson (Schoolgirls), Richard Wilson, Cedric Schoeman, Brian Thomas (Schoolboys), Leslie Bates (Shadow Double for Kal)
Crew
Visual Effects BBC Visual Effects Department, *Studio Lighting* Sam Barclay, *Studio Sound* Jack Clayton, *Film Cameraman* Robert Sleigh, *Film Editors* John Griffiths, John House, *Special Sound* Brian Hodgson, *Incidental Music* Norman Kay, *Costume Designer* Maureen Heneghan, *Make-Up Artist* Elizabeth Blattner, *Designer* Peter Brachacki, *Production Assistant* Douglas Camfield, *Assistant Floor Manager* Catherine Childs, *Story Editor* David Whitaker, *Associate Producer* Mervyn Pinfield, *Producer* Verity Lambert, *Director* Waris Hussein
DWM Index
61   Behind The Scenes: Graphic Design
167   Waris Hussein interview
177   Video review ('The Hartnell Years')
198   Dick Mills interview
199   Delia Derbyshire interview
207   The Dawn of Knowledge
208   Nothing At The End of the Lane
221   Rex Tucker interview
234   Verity Lambert interview
272   Waris Hussein interview
292   Video review
345   Waris Hussein interview
Recording Dates
19 September 1963 (EFS), 27 September 1963 (LG D)
Working Title
As broadcast
Factoids
- *Doctor Who*'s first storyline was called *The Giants*, by CE (Cecil Edwin) Webber, and concerned the Tardis occupants materializing in a school laboratory, but reduced to the size of pinheads (see *Doctor Who Magazine* 209). This story was rejected as being too ambitious, although the idea was later used for *Planet of Giants* (9). BBC staff writer Anthony Coburn was drafted in to write a new story, using much of the material in Webber's introductory episode.
- Ian Chesterton and Barbara Wright were originally called Cliff and Lola McGovern. Susan was referred to as Sue. Doctor Who was described as a refugee from the 50th century.
- The first ever *Doctor Who* recording took place on 20 August 1963 when BBC graphics designer Bernard Lodge filmed the opening titles at Ealing Film Studios. Utilising electronic 'howlround' (an effect achieved by pointing a video camera at a television screen showing its own output and filming the resultant visual feedback), he also incorporated a few seconds' worth of howlround conducted by BBC engineer Ben Palmer for the television nativity play

Amahl And The Night Visitors by Gian Carlo Menotti - this constituted the first 'comet-trail' image of the sequence.
- The familiar *Doctor Who* theme music was written by Ron Grainer. Based loosely on the visuals Bernard Lodge was providing, Grainer augmented a simple melody with expressions such as 'windbubble and clouds' to suggest an ethereal feel to the music. BBC Radiophonic Workshop composer Delia Derbyshire realized Grainer's score by creating sounds on various electronic generators and then physically chopping up tapes and looping them together to build up the various elements, with assistance by fellow Radiophonic Workshop collaborator Dick Mills. For the pilot episode, a thunderclap was inserted over the opening bars.
- The Tardis set was designed by Peter Brachacki and built by freelance modelmakers Shawcraft Models. The reason for having a hexagonal one-piece control console, reasoned Brachacki, was because the Tardis only had one operator and thus all the controls had to be close together. The wooden walls had vacuum-formed PVC roundels inlaid into them which were originally planned to pulse with light when the ship was in flight, but the idea was abandoned at an early stage due to budgetary restrictions. Other walls were simply blown-up photographs of a small piece of plastic with holes drilled into it. Above the console hung a large hexagonal unit that supposedly provided lighting for the ship, while three 'transporter pads' stood to the left of the scanner screen (a television monitor mounted on a wall-bracket).
- The episode was performed largely 'as live', with only one recording break - the cut between Ian and Barbara entering the police box prop and emerging into the Tardis interior set. The second half was recorded several times, with retakes at the start caused by an inability to close the Tardis doors properly.
- BBC's Head of Drama Sydney Newman considered the finished programme to be unsuitable for transmission, due mainly to various technical errors, but also because he considered the Doctor was too unsympathetic a character and Susan was too enigmatic. These, along with other minor points, would be altered for the remounted recording.

Comment
Hard to see why this was considered so below standard, as similar fluffed lines and technical bloopers are repeated in many a transmitted Hartnell episode. Presumably it's because everyone involved with the production wanted as near-perfect an introductory episode as possible, and certainly the remount is superior in many ways. But even so, this is still a damn good piece of television fantasy - eerie, spectacular, exciting and bold. The most obvious change from this to the 'proper' episode is the toning down of Hartnell's crabbiness and the deletion of specific references to the Doctor's homeworld and history. Both are, in hindsight, very wise moves, allowing the audience to feel more sympathy towards this strange figure, and yet be totally in the dark as to his motives and background. **84%**

Season 1

"Fear makes companions of all of us." ~ The Doctor

1) *An Unearthly Child*

Anthony Coburn (Episode 1 from an idea by CE Webber)

Serial Code: A
Original Transmission
1) *An Unearthly Child*
Saturday 23 November 1963, 17.15-17.40, 4.4m / 114
2) *The Cave of Skulls*
Saturday 30 November 1963, 17.30-17.55, 5.9m / 85
3) *The Forest of Fear*
Saturday 7 December 1963, 17.15-17.40, 6.9m / 61
4) *The Firemaker*
Saturday 14 December 1963, 17.15-17.40, 6.4m / 70
Repeat Transmissions
1) *An Unearthly Child*
Saturday 30 November 1963, 17.05-17.30, 6m / 85
On BBC2 as part of 'The Five Faces of Doctor Who':
1) *An Unearthly Child*
Monday 2 November 1981, 17.40-18.05, 4.6m / 8

2) *The Cave of Skulls*
Tuesday 3 November 1981, 17.40-18.05,
4.3m / 13
3) *The Forest of Fear*
Wednesday 4 November 1981, 17.40-18.05,
4.4m / 10
4) *The Firemaker*
Thursday 5 November 1981, 17.40-18.05,
3.9m / 15

BBC Archive
All episodes exist as 16mm b/w film recordings of the 405-line two-inch monochrome master videotapes (wiped by the late 1960s).

Novelization
Doctor Who and an Unearthly Child by Terrance Dicks (128/12)
Hardback:
October 1981, WH Allen (0491027486 / Andrew Skilleter)
Paperback:
1. October 1981, Target (0426201442 / Andrew Skilleter)
2. February 1990, Target, renamed *Doctor Who - An Unearthly Child* (0426201442 / Alister Pearson)

Video
1. February 1990, edited (BBCV 4311 / Alister Pearson)
2. September 2000 (BBCV 6959 / Photomontage)

DVD
January 2006, in *The Beginning* box set

Music and Sound Effects
May 2000, *Doctor Who at the BBC Radiophonic Workshop - Volume 1: The Early Years*, CD (WMSF 6023-2 / Photographs)

Script Book
January 1988, Titan Books [as *The Tribe of Gum*], edited by John McElroy with background notes by Jan Vincent-Rudzki (185286012X / Dave McKean)

Précis
The Tardis takes the Doctor and his new companions back to the Stone Age...

Cast
William Hartnell (Doctor Who), William Russell (Ian Chesterton), Jacqueline Hill (Barbara Wright), Carole Ann Ford (Susan Foreman), Reg Cranfield (Policeman), Carole Clarke, Francesco Bertorelli, Heather Lyons, Mavis Ranson (Schoolgirls), Richard Wilson, Cedric Schoeman, Brian Thomas (Schoolboys), Leslie Bates (Shadow Double for Kal), Derek Newark (Za), Jeremy Young (Kal), Alethea Charlton (Hur), Eileen Way (Old Mother), Howard Lang (Horg), Derek Ware (Stunt Double for Kal), Billy Cornelius (Stunt Double for Za)

Crew
Fight Arranger Derek Ware, *Studio Lighting* Geoff Shaw, *Studio Sound* Jack Clayton, *Film Cameraman* Robert Sleigh, *Special Sound* Brian Hodgson, *Incidental Music* Norman Kay, *Costume Designer* Maureen Heneghan, *Make-Up Artist* Elizabeth Blattner, *Designers* Peter Brachacki (1), Barry Newbery (2-4), *Production Assistants* Douglas Camfield, Tony Lightley, *Assistant Floor Manager* Catherine Childs, *Story Editor* David Whitaker, *Associate Producer* Mervyn Pinfield, *Producer* Verity Lambert, *Director* Waris Hussein

DWM Index
50   Episode Guide
58   'The Five Faces of Doctor Who' feature
80   Andrew Skilleter interview
83   Heather Hartnell interview
113 Season 1 Flashback
115 William Russell interview
132 Archive + Fact File
133 Script Book review
141 Sydney Newman interview
152 Barry Newbery on *The Tribe of Gum*
160 Novelization review
     Video review
167 Waris Hussein interview
     Those *Radio Times*
186 What The Papers Said
196 What The Papers Said (BBC2 repeat)
207 The Dawn of Knowledge
208 Nothing at the End of the Lane
S94 Archive Feature
221 Rex Tucker interview
226 Vox Pops
234 Verity Lambert interview
272 Waris Hussein interview
279 Time Team
295 Video review
296 Jeremy Young interview
333 The Accidental Tourist Part 1
337 The Fact of Fiction
345 Waris Hussein interview

Recording Dates
19 September 1963 (EFS), 9-11 October 1963 (EFS), 18 October 1963 (LG D), 25 October 1963 (LG D), 1 November 1963 (LG D), 8 November 1963 (LG D)

Working Titles
First Serial
The Tribe of Gum
Dr Who and a 100,000 BC
100,000 BC
Dr Who and the Tribe of Gum

Factoids
- Various changes were made to the remounted first episode, such as the omission of the thunderclap at the start of the opening music, fog swirling around the junkyard (actually, dry ice), the Tardis hum being quieter and the dematerialization sound effect more strident. The Tardis console was rebuilt with a different arrangement of switches and a modified central rotor, while some of the photographic blow-up walls were replaced with a series of panels with flashing lights.
- Production assistant Douglas Camfield directed the filmed fight scenes between Kal and Za in *The Firemaker* using stunt doubles Derek Ware and Billy Cornelius.
- The cave sets were constructed from chicken wire and expanded polystyrene, with Hessian stretched over it. Approximately one hundred and fifty vacuum formed skulls littered the set, some of which were fireproofed so that they could be placed on burning torches.

Comment
The first episode is a classic piece of television. The script is economic and elegant, Hussein makes the most of the claustrophobic settings and the mystery about 'the unearthly child' and her grandfather is beautifully portrayed. The Tardis' first dematerialization - the longest ever attempted for the programme - is a spine-chilling moment. As to the other three parts, Coburn has a good stab at depicting what life would be like for primeval cave dwellers and the production generally stands up very well. It's grim and dirty and violent, redolent of a Palaeolithic kitchen sink drama, and the schoolteachers' reactions to their hostile new environment are the most realistically conceived in the programme's history. Difficult to be objective about the birth of a legend, but even taking into account the odd technical hiccup here and there, it's still remarkably effective and a triumph for all concerned. **90%**

"If they call *us* mutations, what must *they* be like?" ~ Alydon

2) *The Daleks*
Terry Nation

Serial Code: B
Original Transmission
1) *The Dead Planet*
Saturday 21 December 1963, 17.15-17.40, 6.9m / 67
2) *The Survivors*
Saturday 28 December 1963, 17.15-17.40, 6.4m / 78
3) *The Escape*
Saturday 4 January 1964, 17.15-17.40, 8.9m / 45
4) *The Ambush*
Saturday 11 January 1964, 17.15-17.40, 9.9m / 29
5) *The Expedition*
Saturday 18 January 1964, 17.15-17.40, 9.9m / 27
6) *The Ordeal*
Saturday 25 January 1964, 17.15-17.40, 10.4m / 29
7) *The Rescue*
Saturday 1 February 1964, 17.15-17.40, 10.4m / 27

Repeat Transmission
On BBC 2 as part of 'Doctor Who Night':
7) *The Rescue* [re-edited]
Saturday 13 November 1999, 22.30-22.55, 1.6m / -

BBC Archive
All episodes exist as 16mm b/w film recordings of the 405-line two-inch master monochrome videotapes of Episodes 1, 2, 3, 5, 6 and 7 (wiped by 1969) and the 35mm film recording of Episode 4 (junked before 1976).

Novelization
Doctor Who in an Exciting Adventure with the Daleks by David Whitaker (157/10)
Hardback:
1. November 1964, Frederick Muller (- / Arnold Schwartzman)
2. May 1973, Allan Wingate, renamed *Doctor Who and the Daleks* (- / Chris Achilleos)
3. June 1975, White Lion (0856861723 / -)
Paperback:
1. October 1965, Armada (C130 / Peter Archer)
2. May 1973, Target, renamed *Doctor Who and the Daleks* (0426101103 / Chris Achilleos)
3. January 1992, Target, renamed *Doctor Who - The Daleks* (0426101103 / Alister Pearson)

Talking Book
March 2005, 1 x MP3-CD, read by William Russell (0563527293 / Chris Achilleos)
Video
1. June 1989, twin-pack, edited (BBCV 4242 / Photomontage)
2. February 2001, remastered (BBCV 6960 / Photomontage)
DVD
January 2006, in *The Beginning* box set
Music and Sound Effects
1. May 2000, *Doctor Who at the BBC Radiophonic Workshop - Volume 1: The Early Years*, CD (WMSF 6023-2 / Photographs)
2. September 2003, *Doctor Who - Devils' Planets: The Music of Tristram Cary*, CD (WMSF 6072-2 / Photograph)
Script Book
December 1989, Titan Books, edited by John McElroy with background notes by Jan Vincent-Rudski (1852861452 / Tony Clark)
Précis
The Doctor and his friends find themselves on Skaro, a desolate world inhabited by metallic creatures...
Cast
William Hartnell (Doctor Who), William Russell (Ian), Jacqueline Hill (Barbara), Carole Ann Ford (Susan), (Philip Bond (Ganatus), John Lee (Alydon), Virginia Wetherell (Dyoni), Alan Wheatley (Temmosus), Gerald Curtis (Elyon), Jonathan Crane (Kristas), Marcus Hammond (Antodus), Chris Browning (First Thal/Double for Alydon), Peter Diamond (Stunt Double for Antodus), Michael Ferguson (Alydon's Hand/Dalek Arm Operator/Dalek Hand), Robert Jewell, Kevin Manser, Peter Murphy, Michael Summerton, Gerald Taylor (Daleks), Peter Hawkins, David Graham (Dalek Voices)
Crew
Studio Lighting John Treays, Geoff Shaw, *Studio Sound* Jack Clayton, Jack Brummitt, *Film Cameraman* Stewart Farnell, *Film Editor* Ted Walter, *Special Sound* Brian Hodgson, *Incidental Music* Tristram Cary, *Costume Designer* Daphne Dare, *Make-Up Artist* Elizabeth Blattner, *Designers* Raymond Cusick (1-5,7), Jeremy Davis (6), *Production Assistant* Norman Stewart, *Assistant Floor Managers* Michael Ferguson, Jeremy Hare, *Story Editor* David Whitaker, *Associate Producer* Mervyn Pinfield, *Producer* Verity Lambert, *Directors* Christopher Barry (1-2,4-5), Richard Martin (3,6-7)

DWM Index
50	Episode Guide
83	Heather Hartnell interview
87	Chris Achilleos interview
98	Novelization review
	Whitaker's World of *Doctor Who*
99	Christopher Barry interview
105	Jacqueline Hill interview
	Raymond Cusick interview
112	Nostalgia
113	Season 1 Flashback
141	Sydney Newman interview
145	Terry Nation interview
156	Script Book review
161	Novelization review
167	Those *Radio Times*
180	Christopher Barry interview
185	Michael Ferguson interview
200	Whitaker's World
232	Richard Martin interview
235	Verity Lambert interview
274	William Russell interview
279	Time Team 1-4
280	Time Team 5-7
301	Virginia Wetherell interview
	Video review (reissue)
314	Christopher Barry interview
331	Archive Feature
340	*Devils' Planets* CD review
354	Talking Book feature
	Talking Book review

Recording Dates
28 October-1 November 1963 (EFS), 15 November 1963 (LG D), 22 November 1963 (LG D), 26 November 1963 (EFS), 29 November 1963 (LG D), 2 December 1963 (EFS), 6 December 1963 (LG D), 13 December 1963 (LG D), 20 December 1963 (LG D), 3 January 1964 (LG D), 10 January 1964 (LG D)

Working Titles
The Survivors
Doctor Who and the Mutants
The Mutants
Beyond the Sun

Factoids
- This story was originally to have been made fifth, but was moved forward after the mooted second story, *Dr Who and the Robots*/*Dr Who and the Masters of Luxor* by Anthony Coburn, could not be completed in time.
- BBC staff designer Ridley Scott - the director of such blockbuster films as *Alien*, *Blade Runner* and *Gladiator* - was originally assigned to work on this story, but was unavailable on the dates requested.

- Terry Nation's inspiration for the Daleks came from memories of watching the female members of the Georgian State Dancers, their long skirts giving them the appearance of gliding around the stage. The actual design was arrived at by Raymond Cusick, with input from Bernard Wilkie and Jack Kine of the BBC Visual Effects Department. Four Daleks were made by Bill Roberts of outside contractor Shawcraft Models. The skirt section was fibreglass atop a wooden base, the midriff was framed plywood, and the hemispherical dome was made from fibreglass. They were painted silver and grey with blue skirt balls. The dome lights and three mandibles (eyestalk, plunger and gun) were controlled by the operator, who perched on a seat and 'walked' the Dalek around with his feet.
- The first episode, *The Dead Planet*, was ruined by talkback from the production assistant's headphones being picked up by the studio cameras. A remount was scheduled for 6 December 1963, a week after the third episode had been taped. One benefit of this was that Raymond Cusick could redesign a previously unsatisfactory model of the Dalek city.
- The Dalek extermination effect was achieved by over-exposing the camera image - this resulted in the picture turning negative. At the start of *The Dead Planet*, the cameras were slightly over-exposed to suggest an irradiated atmosphere.
- David Graham and Peter Hawkins pre-recorded some of their Dalek dialogue, leaving some to be vocalised live in studio. Their voices were passed through a device called a Ring Modulator that broke up their smooth intonation into staccato vibrations at 30 cycles/second.

Comment
Following on from the realistic setting of *An Unearthly Child*, *The Daleks* is a consistently paced (if somewhat leisurely) journey into a similarly alien environment. Once again, the Doctor and his friends suffer discomfort and pain, and their weakness against the seemingly intractable Daleks adds weight to the lengthy narrative. There is a real sense that the Doctor and Susan are out of practice when it comes to travelling in the Tardis, and it is often left to Ian to take the lead. The Thals are a wet bunch, but the Daleks are every bit as impressive as they should be. Certain model shots and studio effects are found wanting, but in general the direction is solid. Far better than the Technicolor film version, only the last episode's mediocre resolution disappoints. **85%**

"Can it be possible, then, that this is the end?" ~ *The Doctor*

3) The Edge of Destruction
David Whitaker

Serial Code: C
Original Transmission
1) *The Edge of Destruction*
Saturday 8 February 1964, 17.15-17.40, 10.4m / 21
2) *The Brink of Disaster*
Saturday 15 February 1964, 17.15-17.40, 9.9m / 31
BBC Archive
Both episodes exist as 16mm b/w film recordings of the 405-line two-inch monochrome master videotapes (wiped by 1969).
Novelization
Doctor Who - The Edge of Destruction by Nigel Robinson (120/14)
Hardback:
May 1988, WH Allen (0491031483 / Alister Pearson)
Paperback:
October 1988, Target (0426203275 / Alister Pearson)
Video
May 2000, with *Dr Who: The Pilot Episode* (BBCV 6877 / Photomontage)
DVD
January 2006, in *The Beginning* box set
Music and Sound Effects
1. October 1998, Julian Knott, *Space Adventures: Music from Doctor Who 1963-1971*, CD (JPD 2CD / Photographs)
2. May 2000, *Doctor Who at the BBC Radiophonic Workshop - Volume 1: The Early Years*, CD (WMSF 6023-2 / Photographs)
Précis
The Tardis and its occupants start behaving in a very disturbing way…
Cast
William Hartnell (Doctor Who), William Russell (Ian), Carole Ann Ford (Susan), Jacqueline Hill (Barbara)

Crew
Studio Lighting Dennis Channon, *Studio Sound* Jack Brummitt, *Special Sound* Brian Hodgson, *Costume Designer* Daphne Dare, *Make-Up Artist* Ann Ferriggi, *Designer* Raymond Cusick, *Production Assistant* Tony Lightley, *Assistant Floor Manager* Jeremy Hare, *Story Editor* David Whitaker, *Associate Producer* Mervyn Pinfield, *Producer* Verity Lambert, *Directors* Richard Martin (1), Frank Cox (2)

DWM Index
50   Episode Guide
86   Carole Ann Ford interview
91   The Incredible Malcolm Hulke
98   Whitaker's World of *Doctor Who*
113 Season 1 Flashback
137 Novelization review
167 Those *Radio Times*
174 Archive + Fact File
200 Whitaker's World
221 Carole Ann Ford interview
231 William Russell interview
235 Verity Lambert interview
276 Archive Feature
280 Time Team
292 Video review

Recording Dates
17 January 1964 (LG D), 24 January 1964 (LG D)

Working Titles
Dr Who inside the Spaceship
Inside the Spaceship

Factoids
- This two-part story was designed to bring the initial run of episodes up to the probational number of 13. Due to overspending on the previous story, and *Marco Polo*'s projected expense, it was decided to set *The Edge of Destruction* entirely within the Tardis and feature no guest cast. Serendipitously, it also fulfilled the function of a 'sideways' story, one of three themes mooted for the fledging series, the other two being 'past' and 'future'.

Comment
On paper it sounds great - a chilling character piece set within a doomladen claustrophobic environment. Unfortunately, what we get on screen has very little tension or, indeed, coherence. Part of this is down to the quality of the acting, part of it is due to the extremely slow way the narrative unfolds. Much talk is made of 'something' having invaded the Ship - a very scary idea - but the eventual solution couldn't be more trivial. A botched opportunity for some top-notch drama. **55%**

"One day we'll know all the mysteries of the skies and we'll stop our wanderings." ~ Susan Foreman

4) *Marco Polo*
John Lucarotti

Serial Code: D
Original Transmission
1) *The Roof of the World*
Saturday 22 February 1964, 17.15-17.40, 9.4m / 33
2) *The Singing Sands*
Saturday 29 February 1964, 17.15-17.40, 9.4m / 33
3) *Five Hundred Eyes*
Saturday 7 March 1964, 17.15-17.40, 9.4m / 34
4) *The Wall of Lies*
Saturday 14 March 1964, 17.15-17.40, 9.9m / 31
5) *Rider from Shang-Tu*
Saturday 21 March 1964, 17.15-17.40, 9.4m / 37
6) *Mighty Kublai Khan*
Saturday 28 March 1964, 17.30-17.55, 8.4m / 49
7) *Assassin at Peking*
Saturday 4 April 1964, 17.30-17.55, 10.4m / 22

BBC Archive
None of the episodes exist in any visual medium, the master videotapes having been wiped in the mid-1960s and the 16mm b/w film recordings by 1974.

Novelization
Doctor Who - Marco Polo by John Lucarotti (144/17)
Hardback: December 1984, WH Allen (0491034938 / David McAllister)
Paperback: April 1985, Target (0426199677 / David McAllister)

Soundtrack
November 2003, 3 x CDs narrated by William Russell (0563535083 / Photomontage)

Telesnaps
1) *The Roof of the World*   DWM 342
2) *The Singing Sands*   DWM 343
3) *Five Hundred Eyes*   DWM 344
5) *Rider from Shang-Tu*   DWM 345
6) *Mighty Kublai Khan*   DWM 346
7) *Assassin at Peking*   DWM 347

Précis
The Doctor and his companions spend several months with Marco Polo on his journey to Peking...

Cast
William Hartnell (Doctor Who), William Russell (Ian), Jacqueline Hill (Barbara), Carole Ann Ford (Susan), Mark Eden (Marco Polo), Zienia Merton (Ping-Cho), Derren Nesbitt (Tegana), Jimmy

Gardner (Chenchu), Charles Wade (Malik), Philip Voss (Acomat), Michael Guest (Mongol Bandit), Gabor Baraker (Wang-Lo), Paul Carson (Ling-Tau), Tutte Lemkow (Kuiju), Peter Lawrence (Vizier), Martin Miller (Kublai Khan), Claire Davenport (Empress), Leslie Bates (Man at Lop), Basil Tang (Office Foreman)

Crew
Sword Fight Arranger Derek Ware, *Studio Lighting* Howard King, John Treays, *Studio Sound* Jack Brummitt, Hugh Barker, Derek Martin-Timmins, *Film Editors* John House, Elmer Davies, Richard Barclay, *Special Sound* Brian Hodgson, *Fight Arranger* Derek Ware, *Special Sound* Brian Hodgson, *Incidental Music* Tristram Cary, *Costume Designer* Daphne Dare, *Make-Up Artist* Ann Ferriggi, *Designer* Barry Newbery, *Production Assistants* Douglas Camfield, Penny Joy, *Floor Assistant* Catherine Childs, *Story Editor* David Whitaker, *Associate Producer* Mervyn Pinfield, *Producer* Verity Lambert, *Directors* Waris Hussein (1-3,5-7), John Crockett (4)

DWM Index
50 Episode Guide
83 Heather Hartnell interview
93 Novelization review
113 Season 1 Flashback
115 William Russell interview
124 John Lucarotti interview
151 The Fall Guys
162 Nostalgia
163 William Russell interview
167 Waris Hussein interview
    Those *Radio Times*
240 Archive Feature
    Mark Eden interview
272 Waris Hussein interview
280 Time Team 1-3
281 Time Team 4-7
317 Derek Ware interview
320 Derren Nesbitt interview
338 CD review
345 Waris Hussein interview

Recording Dates
13-17 January 1964 (EFS), 31 January 1964 (LG D), 7 February 1964 (LG D), 14 February 1964 (LG D), 21 February 1964 (LG D), 28 February 1964 (LG D), 6 March 1964 (LG D), 13 March 1964 (LG D)

Working Title
Dr Who and a Journey to Cathay

Factoids
- Author John Lucarotti had already written a 15-part radio series about Marco Polo for the Canadian Broadcasting Corporation in 1956.
- Unusually for *Doctor Who*, the events in this story straddle a period of approximately five months, from April to 1 September 1289.
  Filmed inserts of a route map and of Marco Polo writing his diary (in fact, the hand of calligrapher John Woodcock) punctuated the narrative, with voice-overs by Mark Eden.
- The serial was promoted with *Doctor Who*'s first appearance on the cover of *Radio Times* (issue dated 22-28 February 1964). William Russell was said to have complained to his agent about not being included on it.

Comment
The discovery of six episodes' worth of telesnaps in 2004 has confirmed the high reputation of this story. It may not be possible to know exactly what it's like, but judging from comments made by people who worked on it and viewers who were lucky (and old) enough to see it, by all accounts it was a thing of great beauty. Barry Newbery's sets look gorgeous and the whole production has an opulence to it that seems to outshine Lucarotti's next historical, *The Aztecs* (6). One of *Doctor Who*'s most keenly felt losses. **80%**

"For the sake of all my people, I hope you succeed." ~ Arbitan

5) The Keys of Marinus
Terry Nation

Serial Code: E
Original Transmission
1) *The Sea of Death*
Saturday 11 April 1964, 17.30-17.55, 9.9m / 22
2) *The Velvet Web*
Saturday 18 April 1964, 17.30-17.55, 9.4m / 25
3) *The Screaming Jungle*
Saturday 25 April 1964, 17.30-17.55, 9.9m / 22
4) *The Snows of Terror*
Saturday 2 May 1964, 17.30-17.55, 10.4m / 20
5) *Sentence of Death*
Saturday 9 May 1964, 17.15-17.40, 7.9m / 29
6) *The Keys of Marinus*
Saturday 16 May 1964, 17.15-17.40, 6.9m / 43

BBC Archive
All episodes exist as 16mm b/w film recordings of the 405-line two-inch monochrome master videotapes (wiped in 1967).

Novelization
Doctor Who and the Keys of Marinus by Philip Hinchcliffe (128/13)
Hardback:
August 1980, WH Allen (0491029217 / David McAllister)
Paperback:
August 1980, Target (0426201256 / David McAllister)
Video
March 1999, twin-pack (BBCV 6671 / Photomontage)
Music and Sound Effects
May 2000, *Doctor Who at the BBC Radiophonic Workshop - Volume 1: The Early Years*, CD (WMSF 6023-2 / Photographs)
Précis
The Tardis crew must search for four keys to a machine that will restore harmony to Marinus…
Cast
William Hartnell (Doctor Who), William Russell (Ian), Jacqueline Hill (Barbara), Carole Ann Ford (Susan), George Couloris (Arbitan), Robin Phillips (Altos), Katharine Schofield (Sabetha), Heron Carvic (Morpho Voice), Edmund Warwick (Darrius), Francis de Wolff (Vasor), Dougie Dean (Eprin), Henley Thomas (Tarron), Michael Allaby (Larn), Fiona Walker (Kala), Martin Cort (Aydan), Donald Pickering (Eyesen), Martin Cort (Voord/Warrior/Aydan), Peter Stenson (Voord/Ice Soldier/Second Judge), Gordon Wales (Voord), Michael Allaby (Ice Soldier/Larn), Alan James (Ice Soldier/First Judge/Guard), Anthony Verner (Ice Soldier), Raf de la Torre (Senior Judge), Stephen Dartnell (Yartek), John Beerbohm (Double for Arbitan), Veronica Thornton (Lady in Waiting/Citizen of Millenius), Faith Hines, Daphne Thomas, Sharon Young, Lynda Taylor (Ladies in Waiting), Bob Haddow (Idol), Valerie Stanton, David Kramer, Adrian Drotskie, Leslie Shannon, Patricia Anne, Desmond Cullum Jones, Billy Dean, Tony Lampton, Brian Bates, Monique Lewis, Heidi Laine, Rosina Stewart, Cecilia Johnson, Perin Lewis, Jill Howard, Yvonne Howard, Tony Hennessey, Johnny Crawford, Leslie Wilkinson (Citizens of Millenius)
Crew
Studio Lighting Peter Murray, *Studio Sound* Jack Brummitt, Tony Milton, *Special Sound* Brian Hodgson, *Incidental Music* Norman Kay, *Costume Designer* Daphne Dare, *Make-Up Artist* Jill Summers, *Designer* Raymond Cusick, *Production Assistants* David Conroy, Penny Joy, *Assistant Floor Manager* Timothy Combe, *Story Editor* David Whitaker, *Associate Producer* Mervyn Pinfield, *Producer* Verity Lambert, *Director* John Gorrie

DWM Index
50	Episode Guide
105	Raymond Cusick interview
113	Season 1 Flashback
142	Archive I
143	Archive II + Fact File
167	Those *Radio Times*
209	John Gorrie interview
276	Video review
281	Time Team 1-4
282	Time Team 5-6
310	Archive Feature

Recording Dates
March 1964 (EFS), 20 March 1964 (LG D), 27 March 1964 (LG D), 3 April 1964 (LG D), 10 April 1964 (LG D), 17 April 1964 (LG D), 24 April 1964 (LG D)
Working Title
Doctor Who and the Keys of Marinus
Factoids
- This story achieved two notable firsts: *The Sea of Death* was the first episode to show the Tardis materializing on-screen, in the form of a model shot over the opening captions, while *The Screaming Jungle* was the first *Doctor Who* episode to air on the newly renamed BBC1 (previously the BBC Television Service or simply BBC-tv).
- Three Voord costumes were made by Daphne Dare from adapted wetsuits with vulcanised rubber heads.
- William Hartnell was on leave for the middle two episodes.

Comment
The proverbial 'wobbly set' story, this is *Doctor Who*'s first real dud. Terry Nation's ambitious script can't possibly accommodate the limited resources of the time and although the production team tries its hardest (at least, one assumes they tried their hardest), there are many embarrassingly amateur moments. It looks for the most part like a dry run for the real thing. Still, the Voords are good. **33%**

"You can't rewrite history - not one line!" ~ *The Doctor*

6) The Aztecs

John Lucarotti

Serial Code: F
Original Transmission
1) *The Temple of Evil*
Saturday 23 May 1964, 17.15-17.40, 7.4m / 25
2) *The Warriors of Death*
Saturday 30 May 1964, 17.15-17.40, 7.4m / 34
3) *The Bride of Sac*rifice
Saturday 6 June 1964, 17.15-17.40, 7.9m / 19
4) *The Day of Darkness*
Saturday 13 June 1964, 17.15-17.40, 7.4m / 34

BBC Archive
All episodes exist as 16mm b/w film recordings of the 405-line two-inch monochrome master videotapes (wiped in 1967).

Novelization
Doctor Who - The Aztecs by John Lucarotti (121/15)
Hardback:
June 1984, WH Allen (0491034628 / Nick Spender)
Paperback:
1. September 1984, Target (0426195884 / Nick Spender)
2. September 1992, Target (0426195884 / Andrew Skilleter)

Video
November 1992 (BBCV 4743 / Andrew Skilleter)

DVD
October 2002, VidFIREd, Arabic soundtrack for *The Day of Darkness*, production subtitles, photo gallery, commentary by William Russell, Carole Ann Ford and Verity Lambert (BBCDVD 1099 / Clayton Hickman)

Précis
Barbara is mistaken for an Aztec deity in 15th century Mexico…

Cast
William Hartnell (Doctor Who), William Russell (Ian), Jacqueline Hill (Barbara), Carole Ann Ford (Susan), John Ringham (Tlotoxl), Keith Pyott (Autloc), Ian Cullen (Ixta), Margot Van Der Burgh (Cameca), Tom Booth (First Victim), David Anderson (Aztec Captain), Walter Randall (Tonila), Andre Boulay (Perfect Victim), David Anderson (Stunt Double for Ixta), Billy Cornelius (Stunt Double for Ian)

Crew
Fight Arrangers David Anderson, Derek Ware, *Studio Lighting* Howard King, *Studio Sound* Jack Brummitt, John Staple, *Special Sound* Brian Hodgson, *Incidental Music* Richard Rodney Bennett, *Conductor* Marcus Dods, *Costume Designers* Daphne Dare, Tony Pearce, *Make-Up Artist* Jill Summers, *Designer* Barry Newbery, *Production Assistant* Ron Craddock, *Assistant Floor Manager* Ken Howard, *Story Editor* David Whitaker, *Associate Producer* Mervyn Pinfield, *Producer* Verity Lambert, *Director* John Crockett

DWM Index
51	Episode Guide
88	Novelization review
105	Jacqueline Hill interview
113	Season 1 Flashback
124	John Lucarotti interview
151	The Fall Guys
167	Those *Radio Times*
171	Making History
194	John Ringham interview
	Ian Cullen interview
	Video review
220	Walter Randall interview
226	Vox Pops
266	Archive Feature
282	Time Team
317	Derek Ware interview
322	DVD review

Recording Dates
13-14 April 1964 (EFS), 1 May 1964 (LG D), 8 May 1964 (TC3), 15 May 1964 (TC3), 22 May 1964 (LG D)

Working Title
Doctor Who and the Aztecs

Factoids
- Carole Ann Ford was on holiday for two weeks during production of this serial, and so her brief appearances in the middle two episodes were pre-filmed at Ealing.
- *The Aztecs* was the first *Doctor Who* story to be recorded (partly) at BBC Television Centre at White City. The greater space it afforded was beneficial for designer Barry Newbery's impressive set designs and allowed his painted cyclorama to be hung further from the camera, thus creating a more convincing effect.
- The Garden of Peace set was accidentally destroyed at the end of the first episode, thus Newbery had to cobble together a replacement from a redressed cell set for the second episode, *The Warriors of Death*. The cyclorama had not been stored properly and was covered in footprints, although this is not apparent in the finished production.

Comment
Ostensibly a worthy subject with good production values, *The Aztecs* suffers from a script that thinks it's Shakespeare and an actor who thinks he's Richard III. That said, the story really belongs to Jacqueline Hill who shows a rare strength as the reincarnated priest Yetaxa battling against the weight of history. William Hartnell also gets the chance to shine in his unrequited love scenes with Cameca. **63%**

"There's not an ounce of curiosity in me, my dear boy." ~ The Doctor

7) The Sensorites
Peter R Newman

Serial Code: G
Original Transmission
1) *Strangers in Space*
Saturday 20 June 1964, 17.15-17.40, 7.9m / 17
2) *The Unwilling Warriors*
Saturday 27 June 1964, 17.40-18.05, 6.9m / 39
3) *Hidden Danger*
Saturday 11 July 1964, 17.15-17.40, 7.4m / 22
4) *A Race Against Death*
Saturday 18 July 1964, 17.15-17.40, 5.5m / 58
5) *Kidnap*
Saturday 25 July 1964, 17.15-17.40, 6.9m / 29
6) *A Desperate Venture*
Saturday 1 August 1964, 17.15-17.40, 6.9m / 39

BBC Archive
All episodes exist as 16mm b/w film recordings of the 405-line two-inch monochrome master videotapes (wiped by 1969).

Novelization
Doctor Who - The Sensorites by Nigel Robinson (143/14)
Hardback:
February 1987, WH Allen (0491034555 / Nick Spender)
Paperback:
July 1987, Target (0426202953 / Nick Spender)

Video
November 2002, VidFIREd, in 'The First Doctor Special Edition Box Set' [BBCV 7268 / Photomontage] with *The Time Meddler* and *The Gunfighters* (BBCV 7276 / Photomontage)

Music and Sound Effects
May 2000, *Doctor Who at the BBC Radiophonic Workshop - Volume 1: The Early Years*, CD (WMSF 6023-2 / Photographs)

Précis
Timid telepathic aliens are terrorizing the occupants of an Earth spaceship…

Cast
William Hartnell (Doctor Who), William Russell (Ian), Jacqueline Hill (Barbara), Carole Ann Ford (Susan), Ilona Rodgers (Carol), Stephen Dartnell (John), Lorne Cossette (Maitland), Ken Tyllsen (First Sensorite/First Scientist), Joe Greig (Second Sensorite/Second Scientist/Warrior), Peter Glaze (Third Sensorite), Arthur Newall (Fourth Sensorite), Eric Francis (First Elder), Bartlett Mullins (Second Elder), John Bailey (Commander), Martyn Huntley (First Human), Giles Phibbs (Second Human), Anthony Rogers (Sensorite Outside Ship/Sensorite), Gerry Martin (Sensorite)

Crew
Studio Lighting Peter Murray, *Studio Sound* Les Wilkins, Jack Brummitt, *Special Sound* Brian Hodgson, *Incidental Music* Norman Kay, *Costume Designer* Daphne Dare, *Make-Up Artist* Jill Summers, *Designer* Raymond Cusick, *Production Assistant* David Conroy, *Assistant Floor Managers* Val McCrimmon, Dawn Robertson, *Story Editor* David Whitaker, *Associate Producer* Mervyn Pinfield, *Producer* Verity Lambert, *Directors* Mervyn Pinfield (1-4), Frank Cox (5-6)

DWM Index
51	Episode Guide
105	Raymond Cusick interview
113	Season 1 Flashback
120	Novelization review
167	Those *Radio Times*
213	Frank Cox interview
221	Carole Ann Ford interview
248	Archive Feature
282	Time Team 1-2
284	Time Team 3-6
323	Video review

Recording Dates
May 1964 (EFS), 29 May 1964 (TC3), 5 June 1964 (TC3), 12 June 1964 (LG D), 19 June 1964 (TC4), 26 June 1964 (LG D), 3 July 1964 (LG D)

Working Title
Dr Who and the Sensorites

Factoids
- Although many early *Doctor Who* stories showed the exterior view outside the Tardis doors, *The Sensorites* is the only one to have had the camera follow the crew as they walk through the doorway and out of the ship.

- Episode three, *Hidden Danger*, was delayed a week to make way for an extended edition of *Grandstand*. Dipping well under 6 million, it received the lowest audience figures yet recorded.
- The Sensorites' feet were large circles of cardboard covered with stretched fabric. This made walking problematic for the diminutive actors chosen to play the creatures, and they often ended up standing on each other's feet.
- Peter Glaze (Third Sensorite) was famous for his 1960s *Crackerjack* appearances with Leslie Crowther, and later Don Mclean in the 1970s.
- Actress Jacqueline Hill took a fortnight's holiday during this story and was absent from the episodes *A Race Against Death* and *Kidnap*.

Comment
The scenes aboard the Earth spaceship are pleasingly spooky, and the first cliffhanger is a treat - but when the action shifts to the bland Sense-Sphere with the samey Sensorites, the story becomes very dull. It would have made a reasonable four-parter, but six is pushing it. **46%**

"Our destiny is in the stars, so let's go and search for it…" ~ The Doctor

8) The Reign of Terror
Dennis Spooner

Serial Code: H
Original Transmission
1) *A Land of Fear*
Saturday 8 August 1964, 17.15-17.40, 6.9m / 37
2) *Guests of Madame Guillotine*
Saturday 15 August 1964, 17.15-17.40, 6.9m / 35
3) *A Change of Identity*
Saturday 22 August 1964, 17.30-17.55, 6.9m / 34
4) *The Tyrant of France*
Saturday 29 August 1964, 17.15-17.40, 6.4m / 36
5) *A Bargain of Necessity*
Saturday 5 September 1964, 17.30-17.55, 6.9m / 39
6) *Prisoners of Conciergerie*
Saturday 12 September 1964, 17.30-17.55, 6.4m / 38

BBC Archive
Episodes 1, 2, 3 and 6 exist as 16mm b/w film recordings of the 405-line two-inch monochrome master videotapes (wiped by 1978). Episodes 4 and 5 do not exist in any visual medium.

Novelization
Doctor Who - The Reign of Terror by Ian Marter (160/12)
Hardback:
March 1987, WH Allen (0491037023 / Tony Masero)
Paperback:
August 1987, Target (0426202643 / Tony Masero)
Video
November 2003, VidFIREd, part of '*The Reign of Terror* Collectors' Set' [BBCV 7335 / Photomontage] with *The Web of Fear* 1 and *The Faceless Ones* 1, 3 (BBCV 7540 / Photomontage)
DVD
November 2004, 8mm off-air clips on 'Doctor Who - Lost in Time' (BBCDVD 1353 / Clayton Hickman)
Précis
The Tardis crew are caught up in the terrible events of Robespierre's Reign of Terror in 1794 Paris…
Cast
William Hartnell (Doctor Who), William Russell (Ian), Jacqueline Hill (Barbara), Carole Ann Ford (Susan), James Cairncross (Lemaitre), Jack Cunningham (Jailer), Donald Morley (Jules Renan), Peter Walker (Jean-Pierre), Laidlaw Dalling (Rouvray), Neville Smith (D'Argenson), Howard Charlton (Judge), Jeffry Wickham (Webster), Dallas Cavell (Roadworks Overseer), Roy Herrick (Jean), John Barrard (Shopkeeper), Caroline Hunt (Danielle), Edward Brayshaw (Leon Colbert), Keith Anderson (Robespierre), Ronald Pickup (Physician), John Law (Paul Barrass), Robert Hunter (Sergeant), Ken Lawrence (Lieutenant), James Hall, Terry Bale, Patrick Marley (Soldiers), Denis Cleary (Peasant), Tony Wall (Napoleon), Brian Proudfoot (Double for Doctor Who/Paris Citizen/Soldier)
Crew
Studio Lighting Howard King, *Studio Sound* Ray Angel, Chick Anthony, *Film Cameraman* Peter Hamilton, *Film Editor* Caroline Shields, *Special Sound* Brian Hodgson, *Incidental Music* Stanley Myers, *Costume Designer* Daphne Dare, *Make-Up Artists* Sonia Markham, Jill Summers, *Designer* Roderick Laing, *Production Assistant* Timothy Combe, *Assistant Floor Manager* Michael Cager, *Story Editor* David Whitaker, *Associate Producer* Mervyn Pinfield, *Producer* Verity Lambert, *Directors* Henric Hirsch (1-2,4-6), John Gorrie (5)

DWM Index
*51   Episode Guide
56   Dennis Spooner interview
113   Season 1 Flashback
115   William Russell interview
167   Those Radio Times
204   Archive Feature
284   Time Team 1-4
285   Time Team 5-6
337   Video review*

Recording Dates
15 June 1964 (Location filming), 16-18 June 1964 (EFS), 10 July 1964 (LG G), 17 July 164 (LG G), 24 July 1964 (LG G), 31 July 1964 (LG G), 7 August 1964 (TC4), 14 August 1964 (TC4)

Locations
Isle of Wight Farm, Gerrards Cross, Buckinghamshire; White Plains, Tilehouse Lane, Denham Green, Buckinghamshire

Working Title
Doctor Who and the Reign of Terror

Factoids
- The *Reign of Terror* featured the first ever location filming conducted for the show. A brief montage of silent scenes showed Brian Proudfoot, doubling for William Hartnell (who was rehearsing for the previous story, *The Sensorites*), walking down poplar-lined country lanes and across a field for insertion into the second episode, *Guests of Madame Guillotine*.
- William Russell took a fortnight's holiday during production, with his brief appearances in Episodes Two and Three consisting of pre-filmed material at Ealing.
- Composer Stanley Myers went on to produce scores for such acclaimed films as *The Deer Hunter* (1978), *My Beautiful Laundrette* (1985) and *Castaway* (1986).

Comment
One of the lesser-known Hartnell historicals, *The Reign of Terror* is a pleasing mix of humour and drama. The French locale is convincingly done and the splendid guest cast give it their all. And while the story doesn't have quite enough plot for its running time, it's a great shame that two episodes are missing. **75%**

Season 2

"Oh, it gets more horrifying every moment." ~ *Barbara*

9) *Planet of Giants*
Louis Marks

Serial Code: J
Original Transmission
1) *Planet of Giants*
Saturday 31 October 1964, 17.15-17.40, 8.4m / 37
2) *Dangerous Journey*
Saturday 7 November 1964, 17.15-17.40, 8.4m / 45
3) *Crisis*
Saturday 14 November 1964, 17.15-17.40, 8.9m / 33

BBC Archive
All episodes exist as 16mm b/w film recordings of the 405-line two-inch monochrome master videotapes of the first two episodes and a 35mm b/w film print of the final one (all wiped in 1969).

Novelization
Doctor Who - Planet of Giants by Terrance Dicks (112/14)
Hardback: None
Paperback: January 1990, Target (0426203453 / Alister Pearson)

Video
January 2002, VidFIREd (BBCV 7263 / Photomontage)

Précis
Reduced to one inch high, the Tardis crew find themselves in an English country garden...

Cast
William Hartnell (Doctor Who), William Russell (Ian), Jacqueline Hill (Barbara), Carole Ann Ford (Susan), Frank Crawshaw (Farrow), Alan Tilvern (Forester), Reginald Barratt (Smithers), Rosemary Johnson (Hilda Rowse), Fred Ferris (Bert Rowse)

Crew
Studio Lighting Howard King, *Studio Sound* Alan Fogg, *Special Sound* Brian Hodgson, *Incidental Music* Dudley Simpson, *Costume Designer* Daphne Dare, *Make-Up Artist* Sonia Markham, *Designer* Raymond Cusick, *Production Assistant* Norman Stewart, *Assistant Floor Managers* Val McCrimmon, Dawn Robertson, *Story Editor* David Whitaker, *Producer* Verity Lambert, *Directors* Mervyn Pinfield (1-3) Douglas Camfield (3)

DWM Index
51	Episode Guide
86	Carole Ann Ford interview
105	Raymond Cusick interview
115	William Russell interview
156	Novelization review
163	Terrance Dicks interview
167	Those *Radio Times*
186	What The Papers said
204	Dudley Simpson interview
226	Vox Pops
234	Verity Lambert interview
256	Louis Marks interview
	Archive Feature
285	Time Team
313	Video review
330	Dudley Simpson interview

Recording Dates
Approx 23-30 July 1964 (EFS), 13 August 1964 (EFS), 21 August 1964 (TC4), 28 August 1964 (TC4), 4 September 1964 (TC4), 11 September 1964 (TC4)

Working Title
Miniscule Story
The Planet of Giants

Factoids
- Oversize props built by Raymond Cusick included a worm, a fly, a laboratory sink and a matchbox. To achieve the effect of the Doctor and his friends standing in front of Farrow's giant face, a small caption slide of actor Frank Crawshaw was combined with a mirrored reflection of Hartnell and crew against black drapes in a distant part of the studio.
- The serial was written and recorded in four parts, but Head of Serials Donald Wilson decided that there was not sufficient material to justify a four-part story. Thus part three and part four, *The Urge to Live*, were transferred to 35mm film and edited down into a standard length episode.
- *Planet of Giants* marked the start of two notable *Doctor Who* contributors' careers. It was scored by Dudley Simpson, a regular on the series until *The Horns of Nimon* (108), while the original forth episode was directed by Douglas Camfield, who would be responsible for many stories up until *The Seeds of Doom* (85).

Comment
This naturalistic story seems at odds with much of the epic drama around it and the central premise is at once highly relevant (chemical warfare) yet also strangely dated (the *Dixon of Dock Green* characters). Ultimately, it succeeds on the strength of its excellent production values and the truthful performances of the regular cast. But the slow pace makes one thankful we haven't got the intended four-part version. **70%**

"The place is swarming with Daleks." ~ *Jenny*

10) The Dalek Invasion of Earth
Terry Nation

Serial Code: K
Original Transmission
1) *World's End*
Saturday 21 November 1964, 17.40-18.05, 11.4m / 12
2) *The Daleks*
Saturday 28 November 1964, 17.40-18.05, 12.4m / 10
3) *Day of Reckoning*
Saturday 5 December 1964, 17.40-18.05, 11.9m / 10
4) *The End of Tomorrow*
Saturday 12 December 1964, 17.40-18.05, 11.9m / 11
5) *The Waking Ally*
Saturday 19 December 1964, 17.40-18.05, 11.4m / 18
6) *Flashpoint*
Saturday 26 December 1964, 17.55-18.20, 12.4m / 12

BBC Archive
Episodes 1, 2, 3, 4 and 6 exist as 16mm b/w film recordings of the 405-line two-inch monochrome master videotapes (wiped by 1969). Episode 5 exists as the original 35mm b/w film recording.

Novelization
Doctor Who and the Dalek Invasion of Earth by Terrance Dicks (142/14)
Hardback:
1. March 1977, Allan Wingate (0491021240 / Chris Achilleos)
2. June 1983, WH Allen, as part of 'Doctor Who - Dalek Omnibus' with *Doctor Who and the Day of the Daleks* and *Doctor Who and the Planet of the Daleks* (0491034202 / Andrew Skilleter)
Paperback:
1. March 1977, Target (042611244X / Chris Achilleos)
2. August 1988, Star, as part of 'Doctor Who Classics' with *Doctor Who and the Crusaders* (0352322640 / Andrew Skilleter)
3. August 1990, Target, renamed *Doctor Who - The Dalek Invasion of Earth* (042611244X / Alister Pearson)

Video
May 1990, twin-pack, edited (BBCV 4353 / Alister Pearson)
DVD
1. June 2003, VidFIREd, optional CGI effects, trailers, 8mm colour rehearsal film, production subtitles, photo gallery, commentary by William Russell, Carole Ann Ford, Verity Lambert, Richard Martin and Gary Russell (BBCDVD 1156 / Clayton Hickman)
2. October 2003, as part of 'Dalek Collectors Edition' exclusive to WHSmith (- / Photomontage)
Précis
The Doctor arrives on a 22nd century Earth devastated by Daleks…
Cast
William Hartnell (Doctor Who), William Russell (Ian), Jacqueline Hill (Barbara), Carole Ann Ford (Susan), Peter Fraser (David Campbell), Bernard Kay (Carl Tyler), Alan Judd (Dortmun), Ann Davies (Jenny), Michael Goldie (Craddock), Graham Rigby (Larry Madison), Nicholas Smith (Wells), Michael Davis (Thomson), Richard McNeff (Baker), Patrick O'Connell (Ashton), Robert Aldous (Insurgent), Martyn Huntley, Peter Badger (Robomen), Jean Conroy, Meriel Hobson (Women in Wood), Robert Jewell, Gerald Taylor, Kevin Manser, Peter Murphy, Ken Tyllsen (Daleks), Nick Evans (Slyther/Dalek), Peter Hawkins, David Graham (Dalek Voices), Kenton Moore (Roboman in River), Peter Diamond (Stunt Double for Ian/Roboman/Freedom Fighter), Edmund Warwick (Double for Doctor Who)
Crew
Stuntman Peter Diamond, *Studio Lighting* Howard King, *Studio Sound* Jack Brummitt, *Film Cameraman* Peter Hamilton, *Film Editor* John Griffiths, *Special Sound* Brian Hodgson, *Incidental Music* Francis Chagrin, *Costume Designers* Daphne Dare (1,2,5,6), Tony Pearce (3,4), *Make-Up Artists* Sonia Markham (1,2,3,5,6), Elizabeth Blattner (4), *Designer* Spencer Chapman, *Production Assistant* Jane Shirley, *Assistant Floor Manager* Christina Lawton, *Story Editor* David Whitaker, *Associate Producer* Mervyn Pinfield, *Producer* Verity Lambert, *Director* Richard Martin

DWM Index
51	Episode Guide
105	Jacqueline Hill interview
115	William Russell interview
141	Nostalgia
145	Terry Nation interview
161	Video review
167	Those *Radio Times*
186	What The Papers Said
218	What The Censor Saw
226	Vox Pops
232	Richard Martin interview
235	Verity Lambert interview
280	Archive Feature
285	Time Team 1-3
286	Time Team 4-6
330	Preview(DVD)
331	DVD review

Recording Dates
23 August 1964 (Location filming), 25 August 1964 (Location filming), 27-28 August 1964 (Location filming), 28 August 1964 (EFS modelwork), 18 September 1964 (RS 1), 25 September 1964 (RS 1), 2 October 1964 (RS 1), 9 October 1964 (RS 1), 16 October 1964 (RS 1), 23 October 1964 (RS 1)

Locations
Kew Rail Bridge, Surrey; Butler's Wharf, Southwark, London SE1; Warehouse and wharf, St Katherine's Dock, London E1; White City Underground Station, London W12; Albert Embankment, London SE11; Westminster Bridge, Whitehall and Trafalgar Square, London SW1; Royal Albert Hall and Albert Memorial, London SW7; Palace of Industry and Third Way, Wembley, Middlesex; John's Hole Quarry, Stone, Kent

Working Titles
Doctor Who and the Daleks
The Return of the Daleks
The Daleks in Europe

Factoids
- Two new Dalek props were added to the four original ones from *The Daleks* (2). They had larger fenders and were equipped with pedals to aid movement. A dish receptor was added to their backs to indicate that they were receiving energy from their spaceship.
- Arriving at the height of 'Dalekmania', this sequel to *The Daleks* featured many location scenes in London. For the first day of filming, cast and crew assembled at Trafalgar Square at 6am one Sunday morning to capture as deserted a London as possible. (Unfortunately, a lorry is plainly visible in the background of one shot.)
- William Hartnell was written out of *The End of Tomorrow* after he sustained an injury during camera rehearsals for *Day of Reckoning*: he fell awkwardly from a stretcher and was briefly paralysed. Edmund Warwick doubled for him as the Doctor collapsed at the beginning of the fourth episode, remaining comatose throughout.

- Carole Ann Ford's departure was by mutual consent. She was dissatisfied with the treatment of her character and wanted to avoid being typecast as a 'screaming girl'. It appears that she succeeded, as her next television appearance was a prostitute in the ABC production *Public Eye*.
- The serial was promoted by a second *Radio Times* cover (issue dated 21-27 November 1964)

Comment
Any subtlety that the first Daleks' outing had (and there wasn't much) has been totally wiped away by this obvious crowd-pleaser of a sequel. Unfortunately, the production values are probably the worst yet seen on the programme, despite the impressive location footage. Performances in general are amateurish and the action sequences are clumsily directed by Richard Martin, who is clearly happier when dealing with simple dialogue scenes. Susan's departure is handled very movingly, but in every other way the cinematic version is by far the best way to enjoy this story. **46%**

"If you like adventure, my dear, I can promise you an abundance of it." ~ The Doctor

11) The Rescue
David Whitaker

Serial Code: L
Original Transmission
1) *The Powerful Enemy*
Saturday 2 January 1965, 17.40-18.05, 12m / 11
2) *Desperate Measures*
Saturday 9 January 1965, 17.40-18.05, 13m / 8
BBC Archive
Both episodes exist as 16mm b/w film recordings of the 405-line two-inch monochrome master videotapes (wiped by 1969).
Novelization
Doctor Who - The Rescue by Ian Marter (139/17)
Hardback: August 1987, WH Allen (0426203097 / Tony Clark)
Paperback: January 1988, Target (0426203089 / Tony Clark)
Video
September 1994, edited, twin-pack with *The Romans* (BBCV 5378 / Andrew Skilleter)
Précis
Survivors of a crashed spaceship live in fear of a hideous alien called Koquillion…

Cast
William Hartnell (Doctor Who), William Russell (Ian), Jacqueline Hill (Barbara), Maureen O'Brien (Vicki), Ray Barrett (Bennett/Koquillion), John Stuart, Colin Hughes (Didonians), Tom Sheridan (Space Captain Voice/Sand Monster)
Crew
Studio Lighting Howard King, *Studio Sound* Richard Chubb, *Film Cameraman* Dick Bush, *Film Editor* Jim Latham, *Special Sound* Brian Hodgson, *Incidental Music* Tristram Cary (reused from *The Daleks* [2]), *Costume Supervisor* Daphne Dare, *Make-Up Supervisor* Sonia Markham, *Designer* Raymond Cusick, *Production Assistant* David Maloney, *Assistant Floor Manager* Valerie Wilkins, *Associate Producer* Mervyn Pinfield, *Story Editor* Dennis Spooner, *Producer* Verity Lambert, *Director* Christopher Barry
DWM Index
52 Episode Guide
98 Whitaker's World of *Doctor Who*
99 Christopher Barry interview
105 Raymond Cusick interview
125 Novelization review
176 Those *Radio Times*
180 Christopher Barry interview
186 What The Papers Said
200 What The Papers Said
217 Video review
286 Time Team
314 Christopher Barry interview
325 Archive Feature
Recording Dates
16-17 November 1964 (EFS modelwork), 4 December 1964 (RS 1), 11 December 1964 (RS 1)
Working Titles
Doctor Who and Tanni
Doctor Who and the Rescue
Factoids
- The character of Vicki was originally to be called Tanni, and then Lukki (pronounced 'Lucky').
- To preserve the identity of the villain, Koquillion was named as 'Sydney Wilson' (a pseudonym for *Doctor Who* creators Sydney Newman and Donald Wilson).
- *Desperate Measures* was the most-watched *Doctor Who* episode to date.

Comment
A tightly written character piece that serves as a simple introductory story for Vicki and a welcome rest from the rigours of recent adventures, *The Rescue* is hard to criticize. That said, the central conceit of Bennett being Koquillion makes no sense - why doesn't he just drop the charade and kill Vicki? **76%**

"I've got a friend who specializes in trouble. He dives in and usually finds a way." ~ Ian Chesterton

12) The Romans
Dennis Spooner

Serial Code: M
Original Transmission
1) *The Slave Traders*
Saturday 16 January 1965, 17.40-18.05, 13m / 7
2) *All Roads Lead to Rome*
Saturday 23 January 1965, 17.40-18.05, 11.5m / 15
3) *Conspiracy*
Saturday 30 January 1965, 17.40-18.05, 10m / 28
4) *Inferno*
Saturday 6 February 1965, 17.40-18.05, 12m / 13
BBC Archive
All episodes exist as 16mm b/w film recordings of the 405-line two-inch monochrome master videotapes (wiped in 1967).
Novelization
Doctor Who - The Romans by Donald Cotton (128/31)
Hardback: April 1987, WH Allen (049103833X / Tony Masero)
Paperback: September 1987, Target (0426202880 / Tony Masero)
Video
September 1994, edited, twin-pack with *The Rescue* (BBCV 5378 / Andrew Skilleter)
Précis
In Ancient Italy, Ian is enslaved and Nero mistakes the Doctor for an accomplished musician...
Cast
William Hartnell (Doctor Who), William Russell (Ian), Jacqueline Hill (Barbara), Maureen O'Brien (Vicki), Nicholas Evans (Didius), Derek Sydney (Sevcheria), Margot Thomas (Stallholder), Derek Francis (Nero), Bart Allison (Maximus Pettulian), Barry Jackson (Ascaris), Peter Diamond (Delos), Michael Peake (Tavius), Dorothy-Rose Gribble (Woman Slave), Gertan Klauber (Galley Master), Brian Proudfoot (Tigilinus), Kay Patrick (Poppaea), Ann Tirard (Locusta), Dennis Edwards (Centurion), Edward Kelsey (Slave Buyer), Ernest Jennings (First Man in Market), John Caesar (Second Man in Market), Tony Lambden (Court Messenger)
Crew
Fight Arranger Peter Diamond, *Studio Lighting* Howard King, *Studio Sound* Richard Chubb, *Film Cameraman* Dick Bush, *Film Editor* Jim Latham,

Special Sound Brian Hodgson, *Incidental Music* Raymond Jones, *Costume Designer* Daphne Dare, *Make-Up Artist* Sonia Markham, *Designer* Raymond Cusick, *Production Assistant* David Maloney, *Assistant Floor Manager* Valerie Wilkins, *Associate Producer* Mervyn Pinfield, *Producer* Verity Lambert, *Director* Christopher Barry
DWM Index
52   Episode Guide
56   Dennis Spooner interview
99   Christopher Barry interview
105 Jacqueline Hill interview
        Raymond Cusick interview
115 William Russell interview
121 Novelization review
167 Those *Radio Times*
180 Christopher Barry interview
186 What The Papers Said
217 Video review
226 Vox Pops
235 Verity Lambert interview
251 Archive Feature
286 Time Team 1-3
287 Time Team 4
314 Christopher Barry interview
Recording Dates
16-17 November 1964 (EFS modelwork), 18 November 1964 (EFS), 18 December 1965 (RS 1), 1 January 1965 (RS 1), 8 January 1965 (RS 1), 15 January 1965 (RS 1)
Working Title
Dr Who and the Romans
Factoids
- Scriptwriter Dennis Spooner was inspired to write a humorous *Doctor Who* story set in Ancient Rome after a summer visit to Pinewood Studios in which *Carry On Cleo* was being filmed. Both projects shared the same researcher, as well as an actor in the form of Gertan Klauber (slave trader Markus in *Cleo*, opposite Warren Mitchell as Spencius). Klauber would go on to feature in *Carry On Doctor*, *Carry On Henry*, *Carry On Abroad*, *Carry On Spying* and *Carry On Emmannuelle*, the former three with Nero actor Derek Francis. Francis would also appear in *Carry On Camping*, *Carry On Loving* and *Carry On Matron*.
- Nicholas Evans, as Nick Evans, had been the Slyther and a Dalek operator in *The Dalek Invasion of Earth* (10).
- William Hartnell, William Russell and Peter Diamond all sustained minor injuries while recording fight scenes for this story.

Comment
A spoof of a parody of a cliché, *The Romans* shouldn't really be as good as it is. But thanks to a wonderful cast and a sympathetic director, this is a hugely enjoyable romp that seems a million years from the dour machismo of *The Dalek Invasion of Earth*. William Hartnell - in his only topless appearance in the programme - is priceless as the player of the invisible lyre. **85%**

"The question is: is it some natural phenomena, or is it intelligent, deliberate - or for a purpose?" ~ The Doctor

13) The Web Planet
Bill Strutton

Serial Code: N
Original Transmission
1) *The Web Planet*
Saturday 13 February 1965, 17.40-18.05, 13.5m /7
2) *The Zarbi*
Saturday 20 February 1965, 17.40-18.05, 12.5m / 12
3) *Escape to Danger*
Saturday 27 February 1965, 17.40-18.05, 12.5m / 11
4) *Crater of Needles*
Saturday 6 March 1965, 17.40-18.05, 13m / 9
5) *Invasion*
Saturday 13 March 1965, 17.40-18.05, 12m / 12
6) *The Centre*
Saturday 20 March 1965, 17.55-18.20, 11.5m / 14

BBC Archive
All episodes exist as 16mm b/w film recordings of the 405-line two-inch monochrome master videotapes (wiped by 1969).

Novelization
Doctor Who and the Zarbi by Bill Strutton (174/6)
Hardback:
1. September 1965, Frederick Muller (- / John Wood)
2. May 1973, Allan Wingate (0426113241 / Chris Achilleos)
3. September 1975, White Lion (0856861677 / -)
Paperback:
1. May 1973, Target (0426101294 / Chris Achilleos)
2. January 1991, Target, renamed *Doctor Who - The Web Planet* (0426203569 / Alister Pearson)

Video
September 1990, edited, twin-pack (BBCV 2763 / Alister Pearson)
DVD
September 2005, VidFIREd, commentary by Verity Lambert, Richard Martin, William Russell, Martin Jarvis and Gary Russell (BBCDVD 1355 / Clayton Hickman)
Précis
The Tardis lands on the craggy world of Vortis, home to the winged Menoptra and the antlike Zarbi...
Cast
William Hartnell (Doctor Who), William Russell (Ian), Jacqueline Hill (Barbara), Maureen O'Brien (Vicki), Roslyn de Winter (Vrestin), Arne Gordon (Hrostar), Martin Jarvis (Hilio), Arthur Blake (Hrhoonda), Jolyon Booth (Prapillus), Jocelyn Birdsall (Hlynia), Ian Thompson (Hetra), Barbara Joss (Nemini), Catherine Fleming (Animus Voice), Ken McGarvey (Slave Menoptra/ Menoptra), Len Russell, Jane Bowman (Optera Guards), Robert Jewell, Jack Pitt, Gerald Taylor, Hugh Lund, Kevin Manser, John Scott Martin (Zarbi)
Crew
Insect Movement Roslyn de Winter, *Studio Lighting* Ralph Walton, *Studio Sound* Ray Angel, *Film Cameraman* Peter Hamilton, *Film Editor* Gitta Zadek, *Special Sound* Brian Hodgson, *Costume Designer* Daphne Dare, *Make-Up Artist* Sonia Markham, *Make-Up Assistant* Sylvia James, *Designer* John Wood, *Production Assistant* Norman Stewart, *Assistant Floor Managers* Elisabeth Dunbar, Gillian Chardet, *Story Editor* Dennis Spooner, *Producer* Verity Lambert, *Director* Richard Martin
DWM Index
52	Episode Guide
56	Dennis Spooner interview
87	Chris Achilleos interview
114	Chris Achilleos interview
156	Archive 1
157	Archive 2 + Fact File
158	Bill Strutton interview
167	Those *Radio Times* Video review
186	What The Papers Said
201	Martin Jarvis interview
202	David Maloney interview
220	Peter Purves interview
226	Vox Pops
231	William Russell interview
233	Richard Martin interview
235	Verity Lambert interview
286	Archive Feature
287	Time Team
326	Martin Jarvis interview

19

Recording Dates
4-8 January 1965 (EFS), 11 January 1965 (EFS), 22 January 1965 (RS 1), 29 January 1965 (RS 1), 5 February 1965 (RS 1), 12 February 1965 (RS 1), 19 February 1965 (RS 1), 26 February 1965 (RS 1)
Working Title
Doctor Who and the Webbed Planet
Factoids
- The *Web Planet* has the distinction of being the only *Doctor Who* story to not feature any humanoid characters, excluding the regular cast.
- The Zarbi costumes were made by Shawcraft Models from fibreglass and worn as a three-piece suit of armour. Due to the large abdomen section, the only way the operators could stand up straight was to balance on one-foot high blocks.
- Eight Menoptra costumes were made, four with harnesses to allow flying on Kirby wires. The bodies were made from black vinyl catsuit wrapped with strips of yellow fur, some also having delicate polythene wings.
- A *Radio Times* cover for the serial, the third to date, appeared on the issue dated 13-16 February 1965, and a specially-shot trailer showing a Zarbi arriving at Ealing Studios was screened straight after the final part of the previous story, *The Romans*.
- Director Richard Martin used Vaseline-smeared lens on the film and video sequences to give the impression of an alien atmosphere on Vortis.
- Jacqueline Hill took a week's holiday during the story and thus was absent for the third episode, *Escape to Danger*.
- Stock music was provided by French *musique concrete* composers Jacques Lasry and Francois Baschet under the name Les Structures Sonores (a group originally scheduled to record the programme's title music in 1963).

Comment
The concepts here are beautiful and intriguing, and episode one starts off with a tangible sense of mystery, despite Hartnell's bonkers performance. Vortis is wonderfully realized and the Zarbi are actually pretty nifty. But what follows is five episodes of under-rehearsed, badly executed fumbling around with extras in ridiculous costumes and even more ridiculous accents. Shame. **42%**

"You must serve my purpose - or you have no purpose." ~ *Saladin*

14) *The Crusade*
David Whitaker

Serial Code: P
Original Transmission
1) *The Lion*
Saturday 27 March 1965, 17.40-18.05, 10.5m / 16
2) *The Knight of Jaffa*
Saturday 3 April 1965, 17.40-18.05, 8.5m / 29
3) *The Wheel of Fortune*
Saturday 10 April 1965, 7.40-18.05, 9m / 32
4) *The Warlords*
Saturday 17 April 1965, 17.40-18.05, 9.5m / 27
BBC Archive
Episodes 1 and 3 exist as 16mm b/w film recordings of the 405-line two-inch monochrome master videotapes (wiped by 1969). Episodes 2 and 4 do not exist in any visual medium, except for telesnaps.
Novelization
Doctor Who and the Crusaders by David Whitaker (160/9)
Hardback:
1. February 1966, Frederick Muller (- / Henry Fox)
2. May 1973, Allan Wingate (- / Chris Achilleos)
3. December 1975, White Lion (0856861626 / Unknown)
4. January 1985, WH Allen (0491036701 / Andrew Skilleter)
Paperback:
1. 1967, Green Dragon (041180670X / Unknown)
2. May 1973, Target (0426101375 / Chris Achilleos)
3. 1982, Target (0426113160 / Andrew Skilleter)
4. August 1988, Star, as part of 'Doctor Who Classics' with *Doctor Who and the Dalek Invasion of Earth* (0352322640 / Andrew Skilleter)
Video
1. June 1991, *The Wheel of Fortune* on 'The Hartnell Years' (BBCV 4608 / Photographs)
2. July 1999, *The Lion* and *The Wheel of Fortune* in a limited edition box set [BBCV 6805] with *The Space Museum* (BBCV 6888 / Photomontage)
DVD
November 2004, *The Wheel of Fortune* VT clock, *The Lion* and *The Wheel of Fortune* (VidFIREd, commentary by Julian Glover and Gary Russell on the latter) with soundtrack from *The Knight of Jaffa* and *The Warlords* on 'Doctor Who - Lost in Time' (BBCDVD 1353 / Clayton Hickman)

Soundtrack
May 2005, 2 x CDs, narrated (and with an interview) by William Russell (0563523220 / Max Ellis)
Telesnaps
2) *The Knight of Jaffa* — DWM 280
4) *The Warlords* — DWM 280
Script Book
November 1994, Titan Books, edited by John G McElroy with background notes by Stephen James Walker (1852865644 / Alister Pearson)
Précis
The Tardis lands in 12th century Palestine in the midst of a bloodthirsty holy war…
Cast
William Hartnell (Doctor Who), William Russell (Ian), Jacqueline Hill (Barbara), Maureen O'Brien (Vicki), Julian Glover (Richard the Lionheart), Jean Marsh (Joanna), John Flint (William des Preaux), Walter Randall (El Akir), Bruce Wightman (William de Tornebu), David Anderson (Reynier de Marun), Reg Pritchard (Ben Daheer), Tony Caunter (Thatcher), Roger Avon (Saphadin), Bernard Kay (Saladin), Robert Lankesheer (Chamberlain), George Little (Haroun), Zohra Segal (Sheyrah), Gabor Baraker (Luigi Ferrigo), Petra Markham (Safiya), John Bay (Earl of Leicester), Sandra Hampton (Maimuna), Viviane Sorrel (Fatima), Diana McKenzie (Hafsa), Tutte Lemkow (Ibrahim), Derek Ware, Valentino Musetti, Chris Konyils, Raymond Novak, Anthony Colby (Saracen Warriors), David Brewster (Turkish Bandit), Billy Cornelius (Man-at-Arms), Viktors Ritelis (Double for Ian's Arm), John Holmes (Falconer)
Crew
Fight Arranger Derek Ware, *Studio Lighting* Ralph Walton, *Studio Sound* Brian Hiles, *Engineer Film Cameraman* Peter Hamilton, *Film Editor* Pam Bosworth, *Special Sound* Brian Hodgson, *Incidental Music* Dudley Simpson, *Costume Designer* Daphne Dare, *Make-Up Artist* Sonia Markham, *Make-Up Assistant* Sylvia James, *Designer* Barry Newbery, *Production Assistant* Viktors Ritelis, *Assistant Floor Manager* Michael Briant, *Story Editor* Dennis Spooner, *Producer* Verity Lambert, *Director* Douglas Camfield
DWM Index
52   Episode Guide
56   Dennis Spooner interview
93   Douglas Camfield interview
98   Novelization review
     Whitaker's World of *Doctor Who*
105 Jacqueline Hill interview
     Archive + Fact File
115 William Russell interview
125 Jean Marsh interview
167 Those *Radio Times*
177 Video review ('The Hartnell Years')
200 Whitaker's World
     What The Papers Said (Novelization)
205 Julian Glover interview
220 Walter Randall interview
222 Script Book review
237 Jean Marsh interview
259 Archive Feature
275 The Reel of Fortune
279 Video review
287 Time Team 1
288 Time Team 2-4
317 Derek Ware interview
350 DVD review
357 CD review
Recording Dates
16-18 February 1965 (EFS), 5 March 1965 (RS 1), 12 March 1965 (RS 1), 19 March 1965 (RS 1), 26 March 1965 (RS 1)
Working Titles
Dr Who and the Saracen Hordes
The Lionheart
Doctor Who and the Crusaders
Factoids
- William Russell had a week's holiday during the third episode, *The Wheel of Fortune*, only appearing in pre-filmed inserts.
- For reasons unknown, the usual Tardis materialization sound effect was eschewed for a more obviously electronic version; the dematerialization sound effect was as normal.
- To add authenticity to Richard the Lionheart's hunting party in *The Lion*, a trained hawk was hired from an animal centre in Oxfordshire, along with trainer John Holmes who played the part of the falconer.
- Ants were supplied by London Zoo for the filmed sequence of them creeping towards Ian in *The Warlords*. William Russell refused to do a close-up of them running up his arm, so production assistant Viktors Ritelis acted as his body double.

Comment
The two existent episodes reveal a solid story with the sort of production values you'd associate with a BBC historical drama. The fight scenes are well choreographed and the regular cast are clearly enjoying the chance to interact with people again (rather than giant insects). Julian Glover holds the thing together while a blacked-up Bernard Kay (very non-PC) makes an intriguingly soft-spoken villain. **75%**

"You know, I don't mind admitting I've always found it extremely difficult to solve the Fourth Dimension." ~ *The Doctor*

15) *The Space Museum*
Glyn Jones

Serial Code: Q
Original Transmission
1) *The Space Museum*
Saturday 24 April 1965, 17.40-18.05, 10.5m / 16
2) *The Dimensions of Time*
Saturday 1 May 1965, 17.50-18.15, 9.3m / 23
3) *The Search*
Saturday 8 May 1965, 18.00-18.25, 8.5m / 22
4) *The Final Phase*
Saturday 15 May 1965, 17.40-18.05, 8.5m / 27
BBC Archive
All episodes exist as 16mm b/w film recordings of the 405-line two-inch monochrome master videotapes (wiped by 1969).
Novelization
Doctor Who - The Space Museum by Glyn Jones (142/6)
Hardback:
January 1987, WH Allen (0491032951 / David McAllister)
Paperback:
June 1987, Target (0426202899 / David McAllister)
Video
July 1999, in a limited edition box set [BBCV 6805] with *The Crusade* 1 and 3 (BBCV 6888 / Photomontage)
Music and Sound Effects
October 1998, Julian Knott, *Space Adventures: Music from Doctor Who 1963-1971*, CD (JPD 2CD / Photographs)
Précis
The Tardis jumps a time-track and the travellers arrive before they're supposed to…
Cast
William Hartnell (Doctor Who), William Russell (Ian), Jacqueline Hill (Barbara), Maureen O'Brien (Vicki), Peter Craze (Dako), Peter Sanders (Sita), Richard Shaw (Lobos), Jeremy Bulloch (Tor), Ivor Salter (Morok Commander), Lawrence Dean, Ken Norris (Morok Guards), Salvin Stewart (Morok Messenger/Morok Guard), Peter Diamond (Morok Technician/Morok Guard), Billy Cornelius (Morok Guard), Michael Gordon, Edward Granville, David Wolliscroft, Bill Starkey (Xerons), Peter Hawkins (Dalek Voice), Murphy Grumbar (Dalek)

Crew
Fight Arranger Peter Diamond, *Studio Lighting* Howard King, *Studio Sound* Ray Angel, *Special Sound* Brian Hodgson, *Costume Designer* Daphne Dare, *Costume Assistant* Tony Pearce, *Make-Up Artist* Sonia Markham, *Designer* Spencer Chapman, *Production Assistant* Snowy Lydiard-White, *Assistant Floor Managers* John Tait, Caroline Walmsley, *Story Editor* Dennis Spooner, *Producer* Verity Lambert, *Director* Mervyn Pinfield
DWM Index
52   Episode Guide
120   Novelization review
167   Those *Radio Times*
188   Jeremy Bulloch interview
206   Vox Pops
279   Video review
288   Time Team
316   Archive
Recording Dates
11 March 1965 (EFS), 2 April 1965 (TC 4), 9 April 1965 (TC 4), 16 April 1965 (TC 4), 23 April 1965 (TC 4)
Working Title
As broadcast
Factoids
- The Ealing pre-filming merely consisted of some model sequences and the shot of Vicki dropping the glass (which would then be played backwards for the transmitted programme).
- Stock music was used throughout the serial, most notably at the conclusion of the first episode.
- Writer Glyn Jones appeared in the Fourth Doctor story *The Sontaran Experiment* (77).

Comment
The Space Museum is one of those annoying stories that begins admirably but then completely loses its way and becomes so dull that it is almost unwatchable. The first episode postulates an intriguing (albeit ultimately ludicrous) concept that one can become 'living ghosts', but then this idea is dropped for the subsequent three episodes. The remaining storyline is insipid and predictable, featuring two of the dullest alien races yet seen on the programme. **23%**

"Don't stand there screaming, you little fool - run!" ~ Ian Chesterton

16) The Chase
Terry Nation

Serial Code: R
Original Transmission
1) *The Executioners*
Saturday 22 May 1965, 17.40-18.05, 10m / 14
2) *The Death of Time*
Saturday 29 May 1965, 17.40-18.05, 9.5m / 12
3) *Flight Through Eternity*
Saturday 5 June 1965, 17.45-18.10, 9m / 12
4) *Journey Into Terror*
Saturday 12 June 1965, 17.40-18.05, 9.5m / 8
5) *The Death of Doctor Who*
Saturday 19 June 1965, 17.40-18.05, 9m / 11
6) *The Planet of Decision*
Saturday 26 June 1965, 17.40-18.05, 9.5m / 7
BBC Archive
All episodes exist as 16mm b/w film recordings of the 405-line two-inch monochrome master videotapes (wiped by 1969).
Novelization
Doctor Who - The Chase by John Peel (144/14)
Paperback:
July 1989, Target (0426203364 / Alister Pearson)
Video
September 1993, in 'The Daleks Limited Edition Box Set' [BBCV 5005 / Photographs] with *Remembrance of the Daleks* (BBCV 5006 / Andrew Skilleter)
Soundtrack
1966, Century 21 Records, edited version of *The Planet of Decision*, LP (MA106 / Photograph)
Music and Sound Effects
May 2000, *Doctor Who at the BBC Radiophonic Workshop - Volume 1: The Early Years*, CD (WMSF 6023-2 / Photographs)
Précis
The Daleks chase the Tardis through space and time to the planet Mechanus…
Cast
William Hartnell (Doctor Who), William Russell (Ian), Jacqueline Hill (Barbara), Maureen O'Brien (Vicki), Peter Purves (Steven Taylor/Morton Dill), Robert Marsden (Abraham Lincoln), Hugh Walters (Shakespeare), Roger Hammond (Francis Bacon), Vivienne Bennett (Queen Elizabeth), The Beatles (Themselves), Ian Thompson (Malsan), Hywel Bennett (Rynian), Al Raymond (Prondyn), Arne Gordon (Guide), Dennis Chinnery (Richardson), David Blake Kelly (Briggs), Patrick Carter (Bosun), Douglas Ditta (Willoughby), John Maxim (Frankenstein's Monster), Malcolm Rogers (Dracula), Roslyn de Winter (Grey Lady), Edmund Warwick (Robot Doctor), David Graham (Mechonoid Voices), Peter Hawkins, David Graham (Dalek Voices/Mechonoid Voices), Murphy Grumbar, Jack Pitt (Mechonoids), Robert Jewell, Kevin Manser, Gerald Taylor (Daleks), John Scott Martin (Mechonoid/Dalek)
Crew
Fight Arranger Peter Diamond, *Studio Lighting* Howard King, *Studio Sound* Ray Angel, Brian Hiles, *Film Cameraman* Charles Parnell, *Film Editor* Norman Matthews, *Special Sound* Brian Hodgson, *Incidental Music* Dudley Simpson, *Costume Designer* Daphne Dare, *Make-Up Artist* Sonia Markham, *Designer* John Wood, *Production Assistants* Alan Miller, Colin Leslie, *Assistant Floor Manager* Ian Strachan, *Story Editor* Dennis Spooner, *Producer* Verity Lambert, *Director* Richard Martin
DWM Index
53	Episode Guide
105	Jacqueline Hill interview
	Raymond Cusick interview
115	William Russell interview
121	Peter Purves interview
123	Maureen O'Brien interview
144	Production Notes
145	Terry Nation interview
151	Derek Ware interview
152	Novelization review
167	Those *Radio Times*
186	What The Papers Said
191	Donald Tosh interview
S93	Archive Feature
204	Video review
220	Peter Purves interview
231	William Russell interview
233	Richard Martin interview
274	William Russell interview
	Peter Purves interview
288	Time Team 1
289	Time Team 2-6

Recording Dates
9 April 1965 (Location filming), 12-15 April 1965 (EFS), 30 April 1965 (RS 1), 6 May 1965 (Location stills photography), 7 May 1965 (RS 1), 10 May 1965 (EFS), 14 May 1965 (RS 1), 21 May 1965 (RS 1), 28 May 1965 (RS 1), 4 June 1965 (RS 1)
Locations
Camber Sands, Camber, East Sussex; Garage at Ealing Film Studios, Ealing, London W5; Houses of Parliament, Westminster Bridge, Trafalgar Square, Piccadilly Circus, Regent Street, Hyde Park, all London (Still photographs only)

Working Titles
Dr Who and the Daleks (III)
The Pursuers
Factoids
- Director Richard Martin hired two Daleks from the Aaru feature film *Dr. Who and the Daleks* for this story. They were modified, along with four BBC Daleks, with vertical slats replacing the receptor dishes from *The Dalek Invasion of Earth* (10).
- Raymond Cusick based the Mechonoids on the geometric designs of American architect Buckminster Fuller. Three fully working props were made out of fibreglass by Shawcraft, complete with flashing lights, movable arms and flamethrowers.
- The Mire Beast was made from bright orange foam rubber covered with a latex skin. Three Fungoids were constructed along similar lines, but painted green, grey and yellow. Both creatures were built by outside contractor Jack Lovell Ltd to Daphne Dare's designs.
- New companion Peter Purves also played the role of dim-witted American tourist Morton Dill in episode three.

Comment
If you didn't know any different, you'd assume this story was written by someone with a grudge against the Daleks. The plot tries to squeeze in every SF cliché under the sun and the Skarosian marauders are portrayed as feeble-minded and idiotic. Comedy worked on *The Romans* - but it doesn't here. Added to which, the six episodes drag terribly, it's full of awful comedy jazz music and there's no clear idea where the story is going. If only the whole thing had been about the Mechonoids - worthy new opponents - this might have been great. **38%**

"There's more to this time-travelling than meets the eye." ~ Steven Taylor

17) *The Time Meddler*
Dennis Spooner

Serial Code: S
Original Transmission
1) *The Watcher*
Saturday 3 July 1965, 18.55-19.20, 8.9m / 15
2) *The Meddling Monk*
Saturday 10 July 1965, 17.40-18.05, 8.8m / 19
3) *A Battle of Wits*
Saturday 17 July 1965, 17.40-18.05, 7.7m / 28
4) *Checkmate*
Saturday 24 July 1965, 17.40-18.05, 8.3m / 24
Repeat Transmission
On BBC2:
1) *The Watcher*
Friday 3 January 1992, 19.20-19.45, 2.4m / 15
2) *The Meddling Monk*
Friday 10 January 1992, 18.50-19.15, 2.8m / 21
3) *A Battle of Wits*
Friday 17 January 1992, 18.50-19.15, 2.6m / 13
4) *Checkmate*
Friday 24 January 1992, 18.50-19.15, 2.6m / 15
BBC Archive
All episodes exist as 16mm b/w film recordings of the 405-line two-inch monochrome master videotapes (wiped by 1969).
Novelization
Doctor Who - The Time Meddler by Nigel Robinson (141/13)
Hardback:
October 1987, WH Allen (0426203127 / Jeff Cummins)
Paperback:
March 1988, Target (0491033370 / Jeff Cummins)
Video
November 2002, in 'The First Doctor Special Edition Box Set' [BBCV 7268] with *The Sensorites* and *The Gunfighters* (BBCV 7275 / Photomontage)
Music and Sound Effects
October 1998, Julian Knott, *Space Adventures: Music from Doctor Who 1963-1971*, CD (JPD 2CD / Photographs)
Précis
A monk with strange 20th century gadgets intends to change the outcome of the Battle of Hastings...
Cast
William Hartnell (Doctor Who), Maureen O'Brien (Vicki), Peter Purves (Steven), Peter Butterworth (Monk), Alethea Charlton (Edith), Peter Russell (Eldred), Michael Miller (Wulnoth), Norman Hartley (Ulf), David Anderson (Sven), Geoffrey Cheshire (Viking Leader), Ronald Rich (Gunnar), Michael Guest (Saxon Hunter), Don Simons, Duggie Dean (Saxon Boys)
Crew
Fight Arranger David Anderson, *Stuntmen* Fred Hagerty, Tim Condren, *Studio Lighting* Ralph Walton, *Studio Sound* Ray Angel, Brian Hiles, *Special Sound* Brian Hodgson, *Percussion Music* Charles Botterill, *Costume Designer* Daphne Dare, *Make-Up Artists* Sonia Markham, Monica Ludkin, *Designer* Barry Newbery, *Production Assistant* David Maloney, *Assistant Floor Manager* Gillian Chardet, *Story Editor* Donald Tosh, *Producer* Verity Lambert, *Director* Douglas Camfield

DWM Index
53 Episode Guide
89 Archive
93 Douglas Camfield interview
108 David Maloney interview
128 Novelization review
167 Those *Radio Times*
184 TV review (repeat)
185 On Set
191 Donald Tosh interview
201 David Maloney interview
289 Time Team 1-3
291 Time Team 4
307 Archive Feature
323 Video review

Recording Dates
10 May 1965 (EFS modelwork), 11 June 1965 (TC4), 18 June 1965 (TC3), 25 June 1965 (TC4), 2 July 1965 (TC4)

Working Title
Dr Who and the Monk

Factoids
- William Hartnell was on holiday for the second episode, *The Meddling Monk*. Supposedly locked in a prison cell, his brief snatches of dialogue were in the form of pre-recorded voice-overs taped the previous week.
- The only specially composed music for *The Time Meddler* was a few minutes' worth of percussion drumbeats by Charles Botterill - all other music was provided from stock.
- Incoming producer John Wiles trailed this production, prior to officially taking over from Verity Lambert for *The Myth Makers* (20).

Comment
It may not feel like it, but this is a pivotal story. It marks the introduction of another rogue member of the Doctor's unnamed race - this time a baddie - and toys with the notion that time can be altered after all. *The Aztecs* it is not. However, the dearth of material and the mind-numbingly slow pace tend to induce sleepiness rather than stimulation. Peter Butterworth gives an uncharacteristically muted performance and Hartnell appears to be making most of his lines up as he goes along. Disappointing. **62%**

Season 3

"The fear! The horror! The shuddering of a planet in its last moments of life!" ~ *Maaga*

18) Galaxy 4
William Emms

Serial Code: T
Original Transmission
1) *Four Hundred Dawns*
Saturday 11 September 1965, 17.40-18.05, 9m / 23
2) *Trap of Steel*
Saturday 18 September 1965, 17.50-18.15, 9.5m / 22
3) *Air Lock*
Saturday 25 September 1965, 17.50-18.15, 11.3m / 13
4) *The Exploding Planet*
Saturday 2 October 1965, 17.50-18.15, 9.9m / 20

BBC Archive
None of the episodes exist in any visual medium, except for two brief extracts from Episode 1: a 16mm b/w film clip taken from the 405-line two-inch monochrome master videotape (wiped by 1969) and a few seconds of 8mm cine film footage taken off-screen from the same episode.

Novelization
Doctor Who -Galaxy Four by William Emms (141/4)
Hardback:
November 1985, WH Allen (0491036914 / Andrew Skilleter)
Paperback:
April 1986, Target (0426202033 / Andrew Skilleter)

Video
November 1998, *Four Hundred Dawn* excerpts on 'The Missing Years', part of 'The Ice Warriors Collection' [BBCV 6387 / Photomontage] with *The Ice Warriors* 1, 4-6 (BBCV 6766 / Photomontage)

DVD
November 2004, 8mm off-air clips and *Four Hundred Dawns* excerpt on 'Doctor Who - Lost in Time' (BBCDVD 1353 / Clayton Hickman)

Soundtrack
June 2000, 2 x CDs, narrated by Peter Purves (0563477008 / Max Ellis)

Music and Sound Effects
1. July 1993, *Doctor Who: 30 Years at the Radiophonic Workshop*, CD (BBCCD 871 / Photomontage)
2. May 2000, *Doctor Who at the BBC Radiophonic Workshop: Volume 1 - The Early Years 1963-1969*, CD (WMSF 6023-2 / Photographs)

Script Book
July 1994, Titan Books, edited by John McElroy with background notes by Stephen James Walker (1852865660 / Alister Pearson)

Précis
The Doctor finds beautiful Drahvins and ugly Rills stranded on a disintegrating planet...

Cast
William Hartnell (Doctor Who), Maureen O'Brien (Vicki), Peter Purves (Steven), Stephanie Bidmead (Maaga), Marina Martin (Drahvin One), Susanna Carroll (Drahvin Two), Lyn Ashley (Drahvin Three/Dead Drahvin), Robert Cartland (Rill Voice), Jimmy Kaye, William Shearer, Angelo Muscat, Pepi Poupee, Tommy Reynolds (Chumblies), Barry Jackson (Jeff Garvey)

Crew
Studio Lighting Ralph Walton, Derek Hobday, *Studio Sound* George Prince, *Special Sound* Brian Hodgson, *Costume Designer* Daphne Dare, *Make-Up Artist* Sonia Markham, *Designer* Richard Hunt, *Production Assistant* Angela Gordon, *Assistant Floor Manager* Marjorie Yorke, *Story Editor* Donald Tosh, *Producers* Verity Lambert, John Wiles, *Directors* Mervyn Pinfield, Derek Martinus

DWM Index
53	Episode Guide
87	Archive
105	Novelization review
121	Peter Purves interview
123	Maureen O'Brien interview
127	Season 3 Flashback
156	William Emms interview
167	Those *Radio Times*
191	Donald Tosh interview
205	William Emms Obituary
217	Script Book review
218	What The Censor Saw
243	Derek Martinus interview
274	Peter Purves interview
291	Time Team
294	CD review
299	Archive Feature

Recording Dates
21-24 June 1965 (EFS), 9 July 1965 (TC4), 16 July 1965 (TC4), 23 July 1965 (TC4), 30 July 1965 (TC3)

Working Titles
Dr Who and the Chumblies
The Chumblies

Factoids
- Mervyn Pinfield was assigned to direct this story and the next one-part *Mission to the Unknown* segment. However, while directing the pre-filmed Ealing sequences, it became apparent that he was too ill to continue, so American-trained director Derek Martinus was hurriedly employed to take over.
- The interior of the Rill spaceship used the same background sound effect as the Daleks' control room, first heard in *The Daleks* (2).
- Four fibreglass Chumbley costumes were built by Shawcraft and operated by midget actors. Two deliberately damaged dummy props were also provided.

Comment
Galaxy 4 is an intriguing (if obvious) tale about not judging by appearances. Hard to think of the Drahvins as glamorous in their PT skirts and Doc Marten boots, but the sexual issues the story raises are surprisingly adult in nature, and the surviving picture of a Rill makes them look like a scarier version of the monster in Roger Corman's 1956 film *It Conquered the World*. Which can't be bad. **60%**

"This is the most hostile planet in the Universe."
~ Marc Cory

19) *Mission to the Unknown*
Terry Nation

Serial Code: T/A
Original Transmission
1) *Mission to the Unknown*
Saturday 9 October 1965, 17.50-18.15, 8.3m / 37
BBC Archive
This episode does not exist in any visual medium. The 405-line two-inch monochrome master videotape was wiped in 1974.
Novelization
Doctor Who - The Daleks' Masterplan Part 1: Mission to the Unknown by John Peel [Chapters 1-3] (174/16)
Paperback:
September 1989, Target (0426203437 / Alister Pearson)

Soundtrack
1. October 2001, 1 x CD, narrated by Peter Purves, with *The Daleks' Master Plan* (0563535008 / Max Ellis)
2. April 2003, 1 x MP3-CD, narrated by Peter Purves, with *The Daleks' Master Plan* (0563494174 / Max Ellis)
Music and Sound Effects
May 2000, *Doctor Who at the BBC Radiophonic Workshop: Volume 1 - The Early Years 1963-1969*, CD (WMSF 6023-2 / Photographs)
Précis
Special agent Marc Cory discovers the Daleks are massing on the jungle planet of Kembel…
Cast
Barry Jackson (Jeff Garvey), Edward de Souza (Marc Cory), Robert Cartland (Malpha), Jeremy Young (Gordon Lowery), Ronald Rich (Trantis), Sam Mansary (Sentreat), Johnny Clayton (Beaus), Pat Gorman (Gearon), Len Russell (Warrien), Gerald Taylor, John Scott Martin, Kevin Manser, Robert Jewell (Daleks), David Graham, Peter Hawkins (Dalek Voices)
Crew
Studio Lighting Ralph Walton, *Studio Sound* George Prince, *Special Sound* Brian Hodgson, *Costume Designer* Daphne Dare, *Make-Up Artist* Sonia Markham, *Designers* Richard Hunt, Raymond Cusick, *Production Assistant* Angela Gordon, *Assistant Floor Manager* Marjorie Yorke, *Story Editor* Donald Tosh, *Producers* Verity Lambert, John Wiles, *Director* Derek Martinus
DWM Index
54   Episode Guide
64   Archive
127 Season 3 Flashback
145 Terry Nation interview
152 Novelization review
271 Archive Feature
279 John Wiles Tribute
291 Time Team
296 Jeremy Young interview
310 Soundtrack review
Recording Dates
25 June 1965 (EFS), 6 August 1965 (TC3)
Working Titles
Dalek Cutaway
Dalek Cut-Away
Factoids
- *Mission to the Unknown* is the only *Doctor Who* episode to not feature any regular cast members. The slot was apparently offered to producer Verity Lambert as recompense for the previous season's *Planet of Giants* (9) being cut from four episodes to three. The aim of this non-Doctor stand-alone episode was twofold: to act as a prologue to the forthcoming epic-length *The Daleks' Master Plan* and to avoid paying the regular cast extra fees on top of their normal salary.
- Three silver Daleks and one black Dalek Supreme were reused from *The Chase* (16).

Comment
This is a fascinating little oddity. Not only does it omit the title character, but the next story has nothing to do with it - viewers must have been rather confused! Judging by the soundtrack, it's a well-made little number, if a trifle melodramatic, and Edward de Souza's rich modulations are very pleasing to the ear. Great looking aliens too.
69%

"You're selfish, greedy, corrupt, cheap, horrible!"
~ *The Doctor*

20) The Myth Makers
Donald Cotton

Serial Code: U
Original Transmission
1) *Temple of Secrets*
Saturday 16 October 1965, 17.50-18.15, 8.3m / 34
2) *Small Prophet, Quick Return*
Saturday 23 October 1965, 17.50-18.15, 8.1m / 40
3) *Death of a Spy*
Saturday 30 October 1965, 17.50-18.15, 8.7m / 33
4) *Horse of Destruction*
Saturday 6 November 1965, 17.50-18.15, 8.3m / 38
BBC Archive
None of the episodes exist in any visual medium, except for 8mm off-screen clips from Episodes 1 and 2. The 405-line two-inch monochrome master videotapes were wiped by 1969.
Novelization
Doctor Who - The Myth Makers by Donald Cotton (142/28)
Hardback:
April 1985, WH Allen (0491035802) / Andrew Skilleter
Paperback:
1. September 1985, Target (0426201701 /Andrew Skilleter)
2. August 1988, Star, as part of 'Doctor Who Classics' with *Doctor Who and the Gunfighters* (0352322632 / Andrew Skilleter)

DVD
November 2004, 8mm off-air clips on 'Doctor Who - Lost in Time' (BBCDVD 1353 / Clayton Hickman)
Soundtrack
January 2001, 2 x CDs, narrated by Peter Purves (0563477776 / Max Ellis)
Précis
The Tardis deposits the Doctor and his companions in the midst of the Trojan War...
Cast
William Hartnell (Doctor Who), Maureen O'Brien (Vicki), Peter Purves (Steven), Francis de Wolff (Agamemnon), Max Adrian (King Priam), Barrie Ingham (Paris), Ivor Salter (Odysseus), Cavan Kendall (Achilles), Jack Melford (Menelaus), Tutte Lemkow (Cyclops), Frances White (Cassandra), James Lynn (Troilus), Alan Haywood (Hector), John Luxton (Messenger), Adrienne Hill (Katarina), Pat Gorman (Double for Achilles), Michael Wilder (Double for Hector)
Crew
Fight Arranger/Stuntman Derek Ware, *Studio Lighting* Ralph Walton, *Studio Sound* Dave Kitchen, Bryan Forgham, *Film Cameraman* Peter Hamilton, *Film Editor* Caroline Shields, *Special Sound* Brian Hodgson, *Incidental Music* Humphrey Searle, *Costume Designers* Daphne Dare, Tony Pearce, *Make-Up Artists* Elizabeth Blattner, Sonia Markham, *Make-Up Assistant* Sylvia James, *Designer* John Wood, *Production Assistants* David Maloney, Richard Brooks, *Assistant Floor Manager* Dawn Robertson, *Story Editor* Donald Tosh, *Producer* John Wiles, *Director* Michael Leeston-Smith

DWM Index
53   Episode Guide
73   Archive
93   Novelization review
121 Peter Purves interview
127 Season 3 Flashback
167 Those *Radio Times*
188 Michael Leeston-Smith
191 Donald Tosh interview 1
192 Donald Tosh interview 2
220 Peter Purves interview
226 Vox Pops
279 John Wiles Tribute
284 Archive Feature
291 Time Team 1-2
     Donald Cotton Obituary
292 Time Team 3-4
300 CD review
317 Derek Ware interview

Recording Dates
27 August-2 September 1965 (Location filming), 3 September 1965 (EFS), 17 September 1965 (RS 1), 24 September 1965 (RS 1), 1 October 1965 (RS 1), 8 October 1965 (RS 1)
Locations
Frensham Little Pond, Frensham, Surrey; Ham Polo Club, Ham, Middlesex
Working Titles
The Mythmakers
The Myth-Makers
Doctor Who and the Mythmakers
Factoids
- Donald Cotton had written several radio plays for the BBC's Third Programme (renamed Radio 3 in 1967), most of them based on Greek-related metaphors to tackle contemporary issues. For his *Doctor Who* assignment, Cotton brought with him regular Third Programme contributors Max Adrian and musician Humphrey Searle. The latter was a prolific composer - during his lifetime he wrote five symphonies, two piano concerti, three ballets and three operas, as well as scoring two notable horror films: *The Abominable Snowmen* (1957) and *The Haunting* (1963).
- *The Myth Makers* featured the programme's first location glass shot. A glass painting of Troy was placed in front of a locked-off camera while actors moved around in the distance, visible through the unpainted areas of the glass.

Comment
A wonderful blend of farce and fact, *The Myth Makers* is more successful than earlier comic historical *The Romans* thanks to author Donald Cotton's drier and more sophisticated sense of humour (although he's not adverse to throwing in some terrible puns). The dialogue is so entertaining that the omission of the pictures is not as disastrous as you might imagine.
85%

"There's nothing you can do to stop us now!" ~ *Mavic Chen*

21) *The Daleks' Master Plan*

Terry Nation (1-5, 7) and Dennis Spooner [from an idea by Terry Nation] (6, 8-12)

Serial Code: V
Original Transmission
1) *The Nightmare Begins*
Saturday 13 November 1965, 17.50-18.15, 9.1m / 35
2) *Day of Armageddon*
Saturday 20 November 1965, 17.50-18.15, 9.8m / 31
3) *Devil's Planet*
Saturday 27 December 1965, 17.50-18.15, 10.3m / 29
4) *The Traitors*
Saturday 4 December 1965, 17.50-18.15, 9.5m / 34
5) *Counter Plot*
Saturday 11 December 1965, 17.50-18.15, 9.9m / 26
6) *Coronas of the Sun*
Saturday 18 December 1965, 17.50-18.15, 9.1m / 40
7) *The Feast of Steven*
Saturday 25 December 1965, 18.35-19.00, 7.9m / 71
8) *Volcano*
Saturday 1 January 1966, 17.50-18.15, 9.6m / 31
9) *Golden Death*
Saturday 8 January 1966, 17.50-18.15, 9.2m / 43
10) *Escape Switch*
Saturday 15 January 1966, 17.50-18.15, 9.5m / 37
11) *The Abandoned Planet*
Saturday 22 January 1966, 17.50-18.15, 9.8m / 35
12) *Destruction of Time*
Saturday 29 January 1966, 17.50-18.15, 8.6m / 39

BBC Archive
Episode 2, 5 and 10 exist as 16mm b/w film recordings of the original 405-line two-inch monochrome master videotapes (wiped by 1969). No other episodes exist in any visual medium, excepting brief clips from Episodes 1, 3 and 4.

Novelization
Doctor Who - The Daleks' Masterplan Part I: Mission to the Unknown by John Peel [Chapters 4-16] (174/16)
Doctor Who - The Daleks' Masterplan Part II: The Mutation of Time by John Peel (157/15)

Paperbacks:
Part I - September 1989, Target (0426203437 / Alister Pearson)
Part II - October 1989, Target (0426203445 / Alister Pearson)
Video
July 1992, *Counter Plot* and *Escape Switch* on 'Daleks - The Early Years' (BBCV 4810 / Photographs)
DVD
November 2004, *Day of Armageddon* (commentary by Peter Purves, Kevin Stoney and Raymond Cusick), *Counter Plot* and *Escape Switch*, all VidFIREd, plus clips, on 'Doctor Who - Lost in Time' (BBCDVD 1353 / Clayton Hickman)
Soundtrack
October 2001, 4 x CDs, narrated by Peter Purves (0563535008 / Max Ellis)
Music and Sound Effects
1. May 2000, *Doctor Who at the BBC Radiophonic Workshop: Volume 1 - The Early Years 1963-1969*, CD (WMSF 6023-2 / Photographs)
2. September 2003, *Doctor Who - Devils' Planets: The Music of Tristram Cary*, CD (WMSF 6072-2 / Photograph)
Précis
The Doctor and his friends help secret agent Bret Vyon to stop Mavic Chen from aiding the Daleks…
Cast
William Hartnell (Doctor Who), Peter Purves (Steven), Jean Marsh (Sara Kingdom), Adrienne Hill (Katarina), Kevin Stoney (Mavic Chen), Peter Butterworth (Meddling Monk), Brian Cant (Kert Gantry), Nicholas Courtney (Bret Vyon), Pamela Greer (Lizan), Philip Anthony (Roald), Michael Guest (Interviewer), Julian Sherrier (Zephon), Roy Evans (Trantis), Douglas Sheldon (Kirksen), Geoff Cheshire (Garge), Dallas Cavell (Bors), Maurice Browning (Karlton), Jack Pitt (Gearon), Roger Avon (Daxtar), James Hall (Borkar), Bill Meilen (Froyn), John Herrington (Rhynmal), Terence Woodfield (Celation), Jeffrey Isaac (Khepren), Derek Ware (Tuthmos), Walter Randall (Hyksos), Bryan Mosley (Malpha), Roger Brierley (Trevor), Norman Mitchell, Malcolm Rogers (Policemen), Clifford Earl (Station Sergeant), Keneth Thornett (Detective Inspector), Reg Pritchard (Man in Mackintosh), Sheila Dunn (Blossom Lefavre), Leonard Grahame (Darcy Tranton), Royston Tickner (Steinberger P Green), Mark Ross (Ingmar Knopf), Conrad Monk (Assistant Director), Steve Machin (Cameraman), David James (Arab Sheik), Paula Topham (Vamp), MJ Matthews (Charlie Chaplin), Albert Barrington (Professor Webster),

Buddy Windrush [AKA Brian Mosley] (Prop Man), Bruce Wightman (Scott), May Warden (Old Sara), Robert Jewell (Bing Crosby/Dalek), Jack Pitt (Gearon/Dalek), Ian East (Celation), Brian Edwards (Malpha), Gerry Videl (Beaus), Rob Walker (Double for Kirksen), John Scott Martin, Kevin Manser, Gerald Taylor (Daleks), Peter Hawkins, David Graham (Dalek Voices)

Crew
Fight Arrangers Derek Ware, David Anderson, *Studio Lighting* Geoff Shaw, *Studio Sound* Robin Luxford, *Film Cameraman* Peter Hamilton, *Film Editor* Keith Raven, *Special Sound* Brian Hodgson, *Incidental Music* Tristram Cary, *Costume Designer* Daphne Dare, Tony Pearce, *Make-Up Artist* Sonia Markham, *Make-Up Assistant* Sylvia James, *Designers* Raymond Cusick, Barry Newbery, *Special Photographic Transparencies* George Pollock, *Production Assistants* Viktors Ritelis, Michael Briant, *Assistant Floor Managers* Catherine Childs, Caroline Walmsley, *Story Editor* Donald Tosh, *Producer* John Wiles, *Director* Douglas Camfield

DWM Index
54   Episode Guide
67   Archive
72   Nicholas Courtney interview
93   Douglas Camfield interview
105 Raymond Cusick interview
121 Peter Purves interview
125 Jean Marsh interview
     Nostalgia
127 Season 3 Flashback
145 Terry Nation interview
150 The Newbery Masterpieces
151 Derek Ware interview
152 Novelizations review
167 Those *Radio Times*
183 Set Photographs
186 What The Papers Said
189 Video review ('Daleks - The Early Years')
191 Donald Tosh interview
218 What The Censor Saw
220 Peter Purves interview
     Walter Randall interview
229 Vox Pops
237 Jean Marsh interview
263 Michael E Briant interview
272 Holding Back The Years
     Archive Feature
274 Peter Purves interview
279 John Wiles Tribute
292 Time Team 1-6
293 Time Team 7-12
310 Kevin Stoney interview
     CD review
340 GG: Episode 2 found
     Devils' Planets CD review
342 Time Team: *Day of Armageddon*
     A Delegate Situation
350 DVD review

Recording Dates
27 September-1 October 1965 (EFS), 4-8 October 1965 (EFS), 18 October 1965 (EFS), 21 October 1965 (EFS), 22 October 1965 (TC3), 29 October 1965 (TC3), 5 November 1965 (TC3), 12 November 1965 (TC3), 15 November 1965 (Ealing Film Studios), 19 November 1965 (TC4), 26 November 1965 (TC4), 3 December 1965 (TC3), 10 December 1965 (TC3), 17 December 1965 (TC3), 23 December 1965 (EFS), 31 December 1965 (TC3), 7 January 1966 (TC3), 14 January 1966 (TC3)

Working Titles
Dr Who and the Daleks Master Plan
Twelve Part Dalek Segment

Factoids
- This epic-length adventure was allegedly suggested by BBC Television's Managing Director, Huw Wheldon, on the basis that his elderly mother-in-law wished to see more Dalek stories.
- A model sequence of an exploding volcano was considered unsatisfactory during pre-filming at Ealing; it was remounted three times before director Douglas Camfield was happy with it.
- This serial saw two companions killed: Katarina in *The Traitors* and Sara Kingdom in *Destruction of Time*.
- *The Feast of Steven* was broadcast on Christmas Day. Written as a comedic break from the rest of the story, it featuring a spoof of *Z Cars* and a slapstick dash through 1920s Hollywood in the form of a speeded-up Keystone Kops chase. At the end, in a convention common to 1960s Christmas specials, the Doctor addresses the viewers directly, saying, "Incidentally, a happy Christmas to all of you at home!"
- Writing chores were split between Dalek creator Terry Nation and former story editor Dennis Spooner, with a staggered crossover in the middle so that they could set each other cliffhangers that were supposedly impossible to get out of.
- This story marked actor Nicholas Courtney's long association with the programme. Counting *Dimensions in Time*, he would appear with every television Doctor up to Sylvester McCoy.

Comment

Judging by the existing episodes and, more importantly, the CD soundtrack, this really does qualify as a genuine epic. The longest self-contained *Doctor Who* story ever attempted, it offers a whole host of characters, locales and life-and-death situations for our heroes to battle their way through. Featuring the deaths of two (alleged) companions, the reappearance of the Meddling Monk and a bizarre Christmas Day runaround in which the Doctor breaks the fourth wall and speaks to the viewers, it's a hugely enjoyable treasury of all that is uniquely eccentric about the programme. **90%**

"Now, they've all gone. All gone. None of them could understand, not even my little Susan…" ~ The Doctor

22) *The Massacre of St Bartholomew's Eve*

John Lucarotti and Donald Tosh

Serial Code: W
Original Transmission
1) *War of God*
Saturday 5 February 1966, 17.15-17.40, 8m / 45
2) *The Sea Beggar*
Saturday 12 February 1966, 17.15-17.40, 6m / 96
3) *Priest of Death*
Saturday 19 February 1966, 17.15-17.40, 5.9m / 92
4) *Bell of Doom*
Saturday 26 February 1966, 17.15-17.40, 5.8m / 94

BBC Archive
None of the episodes exist in any visual medium. The 405-line two-inch monochrome master videotapes were wiped in 1967 and the 16mm b/w film recordings were junked by 1974.

Novelization
Doctor Who - The Massacre by John Lucarotti (144/19)
Hardback:
June 1987, WH Allen (0491034237 / Tony Masero)
Paperback:
1. November 1987, Target (042620297X / Tony Masero)
2. October 1992, Target (042620297X / Alister Pearson)

Soundtrack
1. August 1999, 2 x cassettes, narrated by Peter Purves (0563552611 / Photomontage)
2. August 1999, 2 x CDs, narrated by Peter Purves (0563552565 / Photomontage)

Music and Sound Effects
October 1998, Julian Knott, *Space Adventures: Music from Doctor Who 1963-1971*, CD (JPD 2CD / Photographs)

Précis
In 1572 Paris, Steven is shocked to find that the Doctor is the spitting image of the Abbot of Amboise…

Cast
William Hartnell (Doctor Who/Abbot of Amboise), Peter Purves (Steven), Andre Morell (Marshal Tavannes), Leonard Sachs (Admiral de Coligny), David Weston (Nicholas), Annette Robinson (Anne Chaplet), John Tillinger (Simon), Eric Thompson (Gaston), Edwin Finn (Landlord), Erik Chitty (Preslin), Christopher Tranchell (Roger), Barry Justice (Charles IX), Joan Young (Catherine de Medici), Michael Bilton (Teligny), Clive Cazes (Captain of the Guard), Reginald Jessup (Servant), Cynthia Etherington (Old Woman), Norman Claridge (Priest), Will Stampe (First Man), Ernest Smith (Second Man), Jack Tarran (First Guard), Leslie Bates (Second Guard), John Slavid (Officer), Jackie Lane (Dodo Chaplet), John Clifford (Double for Steven)

Crew
Studio Lighting Dennis Channon, *Studio Sound* Gordon Mackie, *Film Cameraman* Tony Leggo, *Film Editor* Bob Rymer, *Costume Designer* Daphne Dare, *Make-Up Artist* Sonia Markham, *Designer* Michael Young, *Production Assistant* Gerry Mill, *Assistant Floor Managers* Fiona Cumming, Richard Valentine, *Story Editors* Donald Tosh, Gerry Davis, *Producer* John Wiles, *Director* Paddy Russell

DWM Index
54	Episode Guide
74	Jackie Lane interview
124	Novelization review
	John Lucarotti interview
127	Paddy Russell interview
	Season 3 Flashback
157	Jackie Lane interview
167	Those *Radio Times*
191	Donald Tosh interview
233	Archive Feature
	Michael Young interview
266	Paddy Russell interview
279	John Wiles Tribute
282	CD review
293	Time Team 1-2
294	Time Team 3-4

Recording Dates
3-6 January 1966 (EFS), 7 January 1966 (Location filming), 21 January 1966 (RS 1), 28 January 1966 (RS 1), 4 February 1966 (RS 1), 11 February 1966 (RS 1)

Location
Wimbledon Common, Wimbledon, London SW19

Working Titles
The War of God
The Massacre of St. Bartholomew

Factoids
- Paddy Russell was the first woman to direct a *Doctor Who* story. She had previously worked as an assistant floor manager on the BBC *Quatermass* serials; the final one, *Quatermass and the Pit* (1958/9), starring Andre Morrell (Tavannes) in the title role.
- The characters of the Doctor and the Abbot (both played by Hartnell) never appeared in shot together, thus avoiding the complexities of split-screen optical effects.
- Woodcuts supplied by the British Museum were used to show the Huguenot massacre at the end of *Bell of Doom*, accompanied by sound effects of screaming, rioting and burning.

Comment
Back to the serious historicals again for this bleak look at one of history's least savoury moments. The cast is fantastic - Andre Morell and Eric Thompson are especially compelling - and Hartnell shines as the doppelganger villain. On the negative side, the plot is rather confusing (one feels it could have been made simpler with no detrimental effect to the story) and the coda is a little contrived. **80%**

"If we were to tell them the story, do you think they'd believe us?" ~ *Venussa*

23) *The Ark*
Paul Erickson

Serial Code: X
Original Transmission
1) *The Steel Sky*
Saturday 5 March 1966, 17.15-17.40, 5.5m / 102
2) *The Plague*
Saturday 12 March 1966, 17.15-17.40, 6.9m / 70
3) *The Return*
Saturday 19 March 1966, 17.15-17.40, 6.2m / 85
4) *The Bomb*
Saturday 26 March 1966, 17.15-17.40, 7.3m / 71

BBC Archive
All episodes exist as 16mm b/w film recordings of the original 405-line two-inch monochrome master videotapes (wiped by 1967).

Novelization
Doctor Who - The Ark by Paul Erickson (144/8)
Hardback:
October 1986, WH Allen (0491039638 / David McAllister)
Paperback:
1. March 1987, Target (0426202538 / David McAllister)
2. December 1992, Target (0426202538 / Alister Pearson)

Video
October 1998 (BBCV 6609 / Photomontage)

Précis
The Doctor lands on a spaceship taking the last survivors of Earth to the new planet of Refusis...

Cast
William Hartnell (Doctor Who), Peter Purves (Steven), Jackie Lane (Dodo Chaplet), Inigo Jackson (Zentos), Eric Elliott (Commander), Roy Spencer (Manyak), Kate Newman (Mellium), Michael Sheard (Rhos), Ian Frost (Baccu), Terence Woodfield (Maharis), Terence Bayler (Yendom), Brian Wright (Dassuk), Eileen Helsby (Venussa), Stephanie Heesom, Paul Greenhalgh (Guardians), Edmund Coulter, Frank George, Ralph Carrigan, John Caesar (Monoids), Roy Skelton, John Halstead (Monoid Voices), Richard Beale (Refusian Voice)

Crew
Monoid Costumes Jack and John Lovell, *Monoid Statue Model* John Friedlander, *Studio Lighting* Howard King, *Studio Sound* Ray Angel, *Film Cameraman* Tony Leggo, *Film Editor* Noel Chapman, *Special Sound* Brian Hodgson, *Costume Designer* Daphne Dare, *Make-Up Artist* Sonia Markham, *Make-Up Assistant* Sylvia James, *Designer* Barry Newbery, *Production Assistant* David Maloney, *Assistant Floor Manager* Chris D'Oyly-John, *Story Editor* Gerry Davis, Donald Tosh, *Producers* John Wiles, Innes Lloyd, *Director* Michael Imison

DWM Index
54	Episode Guide
55	Archive
74	Jackie Lane interview
117	Novelization review
127	Season 3 Flashback
157	Jackie Lane interview
167	Those *Radio Times*
192	Donald Tosh interview
228	Archive Feature
241	Chris D'Oyly-John interview

270   Video review
279   John Wiles Tribute
294   Time Team
302   Michael Sheard interview

Recording Dates
31 January-3 February 1966 (EFS), 18 February 1966 (RS 1), 25 February 1966 (RS 1), 4 March 1966 (RS 1), 11 March 1966 (RS 1)

Working Title
As broadcast

Factoids
- Eight Monoid costumes were constructed, with the single eye being a painted ping-pong ball held in the actor's mouth (a yak-hair wig hiding the rest of his face).
- For the Ealing filming, a monitor lizard, a hornbill bird, a snake and a baby Indian elephant were provided by a zoo in the North of England.
- Scripts for this story have Paul Erickson's wife Lesley Scott as co-writer, although this appears to have been for contractual reasons only as she had no input in the story.

Comment
One of the earliest examples of a story being split into two distinct segments (a practice that would be applied to many six-parters in the 1970s), *The Ark* is an ambitious story brought to the screen with a certain amount of flair and ingenuity, despite wildly variable modelwork. SF clichés abound, and the invisible Refusians are undeniably silly, but scenes aboard the Ark itself possess a gravitas rare in monochrome *Doctor Who*. **63%**

"The game is not yet over." ~ The Toymaker

24) *The Celestial Toymaker*

Gerry Davis, with material by Donald Tosh from a story by Brian Hayles

Serial Code: Y
Original Transmission
1) *The Celestial Toyroom*
Saturday 2 April 1966, 17.50-18.15, 8m / 44
2) *The Hall of Dolls*
Saturday 9 April 1966, 17.50-18.15, 8m / 49
3) *The Dancing Floor*
Saturday 16 April 1966, 17.50-18.15, 9.4m / 32
4) *The Final Test*
Saturday 23 April 1966, 17.50-18.15, 7.8m / 36

BBC Archive
Episode 4 exists as a 16mm b/w film recording of the 405-line two-inch monochrome master videotape (wiped by 1976). Episodes 1-3 do not exist in any visual medium.

Novelization
Doctor Who - The Celestial Toymaker by Gerry Davis and Alison Bingeman (127/10)
Hardback:
June 1986, WH Allen (0491032323 / Graham Potts)
Paperback:
1. November 1986, Target (0426202511 / Graham Potts)
2. December 1992, Target (0426202511 / Alister Pearson)

Video
June 1991, *The Final Test* on 'The Hartnell Years' (BBCV 4608 / Photographs)

DVD
November 2004, *The Final Test*, VidFIREd, on 'Doctor Who - Lost in Time' (BBCDVD 1353 / Clayton Hickman)

Soundtrack
April 2001, 2 x CDs, narrated by Peter Purves (0563478551 / Max Ellis)

Précis
A strange world of make-believe is presided over by the Mandarin-like Celestial Toymaker…

Cast
William Hartnell (Doctor Who), Peter Purves (Steven), Jackie Lane (Dodo), Michael Gough (Toymaker), Carmen Silvera (Clara/Queen of Hearts/Mrs Wiggs), Campbell Singer (Joey/King of Hearts/Sergeant Rugg), Peter Stephens (Knave of Hearts/Kitchen Boy/Cyril), Reg Lever (Joker), Beryl Braham, Ann Harrison, Delia Lindon (Ballerina Dolls), Albert Ward (Double for The Doctor's Hand)

Crew
Choreographer Tutte Lemkow, *Studio Lighting* Frank Cresswell, *Studio Sound* Alan Fogg, *Special Sound* Brian Hodgson, *Incidental Music* Dudley Simpson, *Costume Designer* Daphne Dare, *Make-Up Artist* Sonia Markham, *Make-Up Assistant* Sylvia James, *Designer* John Wood, *Production Assistant* Snowy Lydiard White, *Assistant Floor Manager* Elisabeth Dunbar, *Story Editor* Gerry Davis, *Producer* Innes Lloyd, *Director* Bill Sellars

DWM Index
54   Episode Guide
74   Jackie Lane interview
83   Archive
94   Brian Hayles Retrospective
114   Novelization review
121   Peter Purves interview

124	Gerry Davis interview
127	Season 3 Flashback
141	Sydney Newman interview
157	Jackie Lane interview
177	Video review ('The Hartnell Years')
180	Innes Lloyd interview
192	Donald Tosh interview
196	Archive Feature
203	Carmen Silvera interview
220	Peter Purves interview
225	Sylvia James interview
229	Vox Pops
279	John Wiles Tribute
294	Time Team 1-2
295	Time Team 3-4
302	CD review
350	DVD review

Recording Dates
3 March 1966 (EFS), 18 March 1966 (RS 1), 25 March 1966 (RS 1), 1 April 1966 (RS 1), 8 April 1966 (RS 1)

Working Titles
Doctor Who and the Toymaker
Doctor Who and the Celestial Toymaker

Factoids
- William Hartnell was absent from episodes two and three. The original plan was to replace him with another actor in the final part, due to Hartnell's increasing ill health and his discomfort with the new producer and story editor. However, his contract was renewed before firm plans were set in place.
- Brian Hayles' original storyline featured the title characters from Gerald Savory's 1942 play *George and Margaret*. Like Samuel Beckett's *Waiting for Godot*, these characters were never seen by the audience, and it was Hayles' notion that they be finally revealed in the Toymaker's realm as sinister uncle and aunt figures. However, days before production was due to begin, Savory - then BBC Head of Drama - withdrew permission for his characters to be used. This necessitated frantic rewrites by incoming story editor Gerry Davis, who also changed the emphasis from the battle of wills between the Doctor and the Toymaker to Steven and Dodo playing the surreal nursery games.
- The overgrown schoolboy Cyril was originally to have been akin to the Artful Dodger from Charles Dickens' 1838 novel *Oliver Twist*. His final appearance as Billy Bunter in all but name drew complaints from the estate of Frank Richards (author of

the Bunter books). An announcement over the end titles for *The Final Test* explained that any resemblance was purely coincidental.
- *The Celestial Toyroom* featured the first use of flashbacks to previous *Doctor Who* stories: telecine inserts from *The Daleks' Master Plan* (21) and *The Massacre of St Bartholomew's Eve* (22) appeared on the giant toy robot's chest screen.

Comment
Notable as *Doctor Who*'s first tentative step into surrealism, one can't help feeling that Brian Hayles' original storyline was far more imaginative than this watered down replacement. The production values are poor and the plot is non-existent. Michael Gough does his best, but there's no real depth to his character, and the sight of Steven and Dodo solving endless clues can't help but remind modern viewers of naff Ted Rogers game show *3-2-1*. **49%**

"Shut up and sing, friend!" ~ Phineas Clanton

25) The Gunfighters
Donald Cotton

Serial Code: Z
Original Transmission
1) *A Holiday for the Doctor*
Saturday 30 April 1966, 17.50-18.15, 6.5m / 50
2) *Don't Shoot the Pianist*
Saturday 7 May 1966, 17.50-18.15, 6.6m / 45
3) *Johnny Ringo*
Saturday 14 May 1966, 17.55-18.20, 6.2m / 51
4) *The O.K. Corral*
Saturday 21 May 1966, 17.50-18.20, 5.7m / 60

BBC Archive
All episodes exist as 16mm film recordings of the 405-line two-inch master videotapes (wiped in the late 1960s).

Novelization
Doctor Who - The Gunfighters by Donald Cotton (152/25)
Hardback:
July 1985, WH Allen (049103721X / Andrew Skilleter)
Paperback:
January 1986, Target (0426201957 / Andrew Skilleter)

Video
November 2002, VidFIREd, in 'The First Doctor Special Edition Box Set' [BBCV 7268] with *The Sensorites* and *The Time Meddler* (BBCV 7277 / Photomontage)

Précis
The Doctor is mistaken for Doc Holliday in Tombstone, Arizona…

Cast
William Hartnell (Doctor Who), Peter Purves (Steven), Jackie Lane (Dodo), John Alderson (Wyatt Earp), Anthony Jacobs (Doc Holliday), William Hurndell (Ike Clanton), Laurence Payne (Johnny Ringo), Maurice Good (Phineas Clanton), David Cole (Billy Clanton), Sheena Marshe (Kate), Shane Rimmer (Seth Harper), David Graham (Charlie), Richard Beale (Bat Masterson), Reed de Rouen (Pa Clanton), Martyn Huntley (Warren Earp), Victor Carin (Virgil Earp), Lynda Baron (Ballad singer), John Raven (Savage)

Crew
Studio Lighting George Summers, *Studio Sound* Colin Dixon, *Film Cameraman* Ken Westbury, *Film Editor* Les Newman, *Ballad Music* Tristram Cary, *Costume Designer* Daphne Dare, *Make-Up Artist* Sonia Markham, *Designer* Barry Newbery, *Production Assistants* Tristan de Vere Cole, Angela Gordon, *Assistant Floor Manager* Tom O'Sullivan, *Story Editor* Gerry Davis, *Producer* Innes Lloyd, *Director* Rex Tucker

DWM Index
54 Episode Guide
74 Jackie Lane interview
82 Archive
101 Novelization review
124 Gerry Davis interview
127 Season 3 Flashback
157 Jackie Lane interview
167 Those *Radio Times*
192 Donald Tosh interview
195 Laurence Payne interview
220 Peter Purves interview
221 Rex Tucker interview
Archive Feature
229 Vox Pops
291 Donald Cotton Obituary
295 Time Team
323 Video review

Recording Dates
28-31 March 1966 (EFS), 15 April 1966 (TC4), 22 April 1966 (RS 1), 29 April 1966 (RS 1), 1 May 1966 (Location filming), 6 May 1966 (RS 1)

Location
Callow Hill Sandpit, Virginia Water, Surrey

Working Title
The Gunslingers
Dr Who and the Gun-Fighters

Factoids
- Director Rex Tucker was *Doctor Who*'s fledgling producer prior to the series being broadcast, relinquishing the role to Verity Lambert in June 1963. He was also mooted to direct the first story, *An Unearthly Child*.
- Of the cast, only three had experience of acting with American accents: Shane Rimmer (Seth Harper) and David Graham (Billy Clanton) were voice artistes on the Gerry Anderson show *Thunderbirds*, while John Alderson (Wyatt Earp) had spent some years in Hollywood and had appeared in the bona fide Western series *Bonanza* (1959-1973).
- For the only time in the programme's history, a specially commissioned 25-verse ballad punctuated the narrative at key moments. It was written by Donald Cotton and Rex Tucker, and performed off-screen by singer/actress Lynda Baron to piano accompaniment by Tom McCall and Winifred Taylor.
- *The Gunfighters* received the lowest *Doctor Who* Audience Appreciate Figures to date (an infrequent survey that measured how well a particular television programme was perceived, rather than how many people watched it). This would sound the death knell for future historical stories.

Comment
The Gunfighters may be silly and inconsequential, but it's also a charming and witty Wild West pastiche with the Tardis regulars clearly loving the change of pace. As with *The Romans* (12), it's sheer joy to watch Hartnell doing comedy (less so with Peter Purves), and the much-derided ballad is actually a great counterpoint to the action. **85%**

"I don't know what you're doing here, but whatever it is, I don't like it!" ~ *Dodo Chaplet*

26) The Savages
Ian Stuart Black

Serial Code: AA
Original Transmission
Episode 1
Saturday 28 May 1966, 17.35-18.00, 4.8m / 62
Episode 2
Saturday 4 June 1966, 17.35-18.00, 5.6m / 50
Episode 3
Saturday 11 June 1966, 17.35-18.00, 5m / 66
Episode 4
Saturday 18 June 1966, 17.35-18.00, 4.5m / 93

BBC Archive
None of the episodes exist in any visual medium, except for telesnaps of the whole serial and ten brief 8mm off-screen clips from Episodes 3 and 4. The 405-line monochrome master videotapes were wiped in 1967 and the 16mm b/w film recordings were junked in 1974.

Novelization
Doctor Who - The Savages by Ian Stuart Black (127/11)
Hardback:
March 1986, WH Allen (0491036027 / David McAllister)
Paperback:
1. September 1986, Target (0426202309 / David McAllister)
2. November 1992, Target (0426202309 / Alister Pearson)

DVD
November 2004, 8mm off-air clips on 'Doctor Who - Lost in Time' (BBCDVD 1353 / Clayton Hickman)

Soundtrack
October 2002, 2 x CDs, narrated by Peter Purves (0563535024 / Max Ellis)

Music and Sound Effects
May 2000, *Doctor Who at the BBC Radiophonic Workshop: Volume 1 - The Early Years 1963-1969*, CD (WMSF 6023-2 / Photographs)

Précis
Elders in an advanced yet sterile civilization rely on the life essences of their subjugated savages...

Cast
William Hartnell (Doctor Who), Peter Purves (Steven), Jackie Lane (Dodo), Frederick Jaeger (Jano), Ewen Solon (Chal), Patrick Godfrey (Tor), Geoffrey Frederick (Exorse), Robert Sidaway (Avon), Peter Thomas (Captain Edal), Kay Patrick (Flower), Norman Henry (Senta), Clare Jenkins (Nanina), Edward Caddick (Wylda), Andrew Lodge, Christopher Denham, Tony Holland (Assistants), John Dillon (Savage), Tim Goodman (Guard)

Crew
Studio Lighting Graham Southcott, *Studio Sound* Norman Greaves, *Special Sound* Brian Hodgson, *Incidental Music* Raymond Jones, *Costume Designer* Daphne Dare, *Make-Up Artist* Sonia Markham, *Designer* Stuart Walker, *Production Assistant* Norman Stewart, *Assistant Floor Manager* Gareth Gwenlan, *Story Editor* Gerry Davis, *Producer* Innes Lloyd, *Director* Christopher Barry

DWM Index
55	Episode Guide
74	Jackie Lane interview
80	Archive
111	Novelization review
121	Peter Purves interview
127	Season 3 Flashback
167	Those *Radio Times*
170	Ian Stuart Black interview
180	Christopher Barry interview
220	Peter Purves interview
229	Vox Pops
295	Archive Feature Time Team 1-2
296	Time Team 3-4
314	Christopher Barry interview
325	CD review

Recording Dates
27-29 April 1966 (EFS), 1 May 1966 (Location filming), 13 May 1966
(RS 1), 20 May 1966 (RS 1), 27 May 1966 (RS 1), 3 June 1966 (RS 1)

Locations
Callow Hill Sandpit, Virginia Water, Surrey; Shire Lane Quarry, Chalfont St Peter, Buckinghamshire

Working Titles
Dr Who & the White Savages
Dr Who and the Savages

Factoids
- *The Savages* was the first *Doctor Who* story to feature a quarry masquerading as an alien planet.
- From this story onwards, the practice of naming individual episodes was dropped in favour of an overall on-screen story title.
- For the ageing effect on the drained Savages, a thin layer of latex was supplied to the actors' skin. This was then stretched and blown with a hairdryer to make it wrinkle.

Comment
A sociological allegory, in a similar vein to *Galaxy 4* (18), *The Savages* (judging by the soundtrack) is a very impressive production, so it's a pity such little visual material has survived. Frederick Jaeger is always good value and here he gives a memorable impersonation of Hartnell's inflections and mannerisms when possessed by the Doctor's life force. The cello music is very effective and the central concept - the rich literally living off the poor - is a chilling one.
85%

"Further attacks on London can be expected in the next twenty-four hours." ~ Kenneth Kendall

27) The War Machines
Ian Stuart Black, based on a storyline by Pat Dunlap from an idea by Kit Pedler

Serial Code: BB
Original Transmission
Episode 1
Saturday 25 June 1966, 17.35-18.00, 5.4m / 71
Episode 2
Saturday 2 July 1966, 18.55-19.20, 4.7m / 76
Episode 3
Saturday 9 July 1966, 17.35-18.00, 5.3m / 62
Episode 4
Saturday 16 July 1966, 17.15-17.40, 5.5m / 67
BBC Archive
All episodes exist as 16mm b/w film recordings, with minor edits, of the 405-line two-inch monochrome master videotapes (wiped in 1974).
Novelization
Doctor Who - The War Machines by Ian Stuart Black (142/13)
Paperback:
February 1989, Target (0426203321 / Alister Pearson and Graeme Wey)
Video
June 1997 (BBCV 6183 / Photomontage)
Précis
A powerful computer in the Post Office Tower seeks to dominate the world…
Cast
William Hartnell (Doctor Who), Jackie Lane (Dodo), Anneke Wills (Polly), Michael Craze (Ben Jackson/Policeman's Voice), William Mervyn (Sir Charles Summer), John Harvey (Professor Brett), John Cater (Professor Krimpton), Alan Curtis (Major Green), Sandra Bryant (Kitty), John Rolfe (Captain), John Boyd-Brent (Sergeant), Frank Jarvis (Corporal), Robin Dawson (Soldier), Ewan Proctor (Flash), Roy Godfrey (Tramp), Michael Rathborne (Taxi Driver), Ric Felgate (American Journalist), Carl Conway (American Correspondent), John Doye (Interviewer), Desmond Cullum-Jones, Eddie Davis (Workers), George Cross (Minister), Edward Colliver (Garage Mechanic), John Slavid (Man in Telephone Box), Dwight Whylie (Radio Announcer), Kenneth Kendall (Himself), WOTAN (Itself), Gerald Taylor (War Machine Operator/WOTAN Voice)
Crew
Studio Lighting George Summers, *Studio Sound* David Hughes, *Film Cameraman* Alan Jonas, *Film Sound* Eric Mival, *Special Sound* Brian Hodgson, *Costume Designers* Daphne Dare, Barbara Lane, *Make-Up Artist* Sonia Markham, *Designer* Raymond London, *Production Assistant* Snowy Lidiard-White, *Assistant Floor Managers* Lovett Bickford, Margot Hayhoe, *Story Editor* Gerry Davis, *Producer* Innes Lloyd, *Director* Michael Ferguson
DWM Index
55   Episode Guide
74   Jackie Lane interview
124   Gerry Davis interview
127   Season 3 Flashback
139   Novelization review
167   Those *Radio Times*
170   Ian Stuart Black interview
185   Michael Ferguson interview
       Ian Stuart Black interview
       Archive Feature
187   Anneke Wills interview
225   Michael Craze interview
229   Vox Pops
252   Video review
253   1966 And All That
296   Time Team
322   Anneke Wills interview
Recording Dates
22 May 1966 (Location filming), 23-25 May 1966 (EFS), 26 May 1966 (Location filming), 10 June 1966 (RS 1), 17 June 1966 (RS 1), 24 June 1966 (RS 1), 1 July 1966 (RS 1)
Locations
Conway Street, Charlotte Street, Gresse Street, Berners Mews and Maple Street, Fitzrovia, London W1; Bedford Square, Bloomsbury, London WC1; Covent Garden and Royal Opera House, London WC2; Ealing Film Studios backlot, Ealing, London W5; Cornwall Gardens and Cornwall Gardens Walk, South Kensington, London SW7

Working Title
Doctor Who and the Computers
Factoids
- Story editor Gerry Davis met with several scientists with a view to making one of them a consultant to the programme. Sexologist Dr Alex Comfort, Professor Eric Laithwaite of Imperial College and astronomer Patrick Moore were all considered, but it was Dr Christopher Magnus Howard (Kit) Pedler, Head of Research at London University, who was finally chosen. Pedler's enthusiasm for science fiction and his ability to think up exciting new ideas made him the ideal candidate.
- *The War Machines* was the first story to be set entirely within a contemporary time period and subsequently featured the first use of extensive contemporary location filming. It was story editor Gerry Davis' idea to feature the newly constructed Post Office Tower (opened on 8 October 1965) as the centrepiece of the story.
- A single War Machine prop was built by Shawcraft Models to Ray London's designs, with the number on the front being changed to represent any of twelve supposed machines. A motor turned tape spools on the side and rotated a radar scanner on top, with operator Gerald Taylor operating the lights, arm rams and guns. A CO_2 fire extinguisher, located on the front panel, provided the War Machine with its main weapon.
- Episode 2 was transmitted 90 minutes later than normal to allow for the Wimbledon Finals to finish.

Comment
This is a very slick production that manages to predict the Internet revolution two decades ahead of time. The oodles of London location work and the contemporary setting (state-of-the-art Post Office Tower and 'groovy' nightclub Inferno) make a huge impact, knocking away the cobwebs of Hartnell's mainly studio-bound adventures. Speaking of Hartnell, he does appear to be rather senile here, and although one hopes he's acting, it's all too apparent that his illness is making it more and more difficult to remember his lines and stick to the script. Dodo's exit is shabby, but then as a character she wasn't much cop anyway.
75%

Season 4

"Well, Doctor, you talk sweet, but don't toy with me or ye'll rue it!" ~ *Captain Pike*

28) The Smugglers
Brian Hayles

Serial Code: CC
Original Transmission
Episode 1
Saturday 10 September 1966, 17.50-18.15, 4.3m / 96
Episode 2
Saturday 17 September 1966, 17.50-18.15, 4.9m / 77
Episode 3
Saturday 24 September 1966, 17.50-18.15, 4.2m / 96
Episode 4
Saturday 1 October 1966, 17.50-18.15, 4.5m / 109
BBC Archive
None of the episodes exist in any visual medium, except as telesnaps and brief Australian censor clips from Episodes 1, 3 and 4. The 405-line two-inch master videotapes were wiped by 1974 and the 16mm b/w film recording were junked by 1977.
Novelization
Doctor Who - The Smugglers by Terrance Dicks (128/12)
Hardback:
June 1988, WH Allen (0491031483 / Alister Pearson)
Paperback:
November 1988, Target (0426203283 / Alister Pearson)
Video
November 1998, censor clips on 'The Missing Years', part of 'The Ice Warriors Collection' [BBCV 6387 / Photomontage] with *The Ice Warriors* 1, 4-6 (BBCV 6766 / Photomontage)
DVD
November 2004, censor clips and colour location footage on 'Doctor Who - Lost in Time' (BBCDVD 1353 / Clayton Hickman)
Soundtrack
May 2002, 2 x CDs, narrated by Anneke Wills (0563535040 / Max Ellis)
Telesnaps
Episodes 1-4   *DWM* 217

Précis
The Doctor, Ben and Polly get mixed up in 17th century Cornish smuggling…

Cast
William Hartnell (Doctor Who), Michael Craze (Ben), Anneke Wills (Polly), George A Cooper (Cherub), Terence de Marney (Churchwarden), David Blake Kelly (Jacob Kewper), Mike Lucas (Tom), Paul Whitsun-Jones (Squire), Michael Godfrey (Captain Pike), Elroy Josephs (Jamaica), John Ringham (Blake), Jack Bligh (Gaptooth), Derek Ware (Spaniard/Double for Blake), Gordon Craig (Double for Doctor Who), Terence Connolly (Double for Jacob Kewper's Corpse), Buddy Windrush [AKA Bryan Mosley], Fred Windrush, Ian McKay, Valentino Musetti, Mike Horsburgh (Stunt Pirates), Bill Weston, Terry Walsh, Malcolm Douglas, Brian Mulholland, David Newman (Stunt Militiamen)

Crew
Fight Arranger Derek Ware, *Action* HAVOC, *Studio Lighting* Cyril Wilkins, *Studio Sound* Leo Sturges, *Film Cameraman* Jimmy Court, *Film Editor* Colin Eggleston, *Special Sound* Brian Hodgson, *Costume Designer* Daphne Dare, *Make-Up Artist* Gilliam James, *Designer* Richard Hunt, *Production Assistant* John Hobbs, *Assistant Floor Managers* Tony Gilbert, John Hansen, Maggie Saunders, *Story Editor* Gerry Davis, *Producer* Innes Lloyd, *Director* Julia Smith

DWM Index
55   Episode Guide
75   Michael Craze interview
79   Archive
94   Brian Hayles Retrospective
127   Season 3 Flashback
139   Novelization review
151   Derek Ware interview
167   Those *Radio Times*
194   John Ringham interview
296   Time Team 1-2
297   Time Team 3-4
317   Derek Ware interview
318   CD review
321   Archive Feature
322   Anneke Wills interview

Recording Dates
19-23 June 1966 (Location filming), 8 July 1966 (RS 1), 15 July 1966 (RS 1), 22 July 1966 (RS 1), 29 July 1966 (RS 1)

Locations
Nanjizal Bay and Bosistow Cliffs, Nanjizal, Cornwall; St Grada Church, Grade, Cornwall; Church Cove, Cornwall; Farmland between Helson and Wendron, Cornwall; Trethewey Farm, Trethewey, Cornwall; Newlyn Harbour, Newlyn, Cornwall

Working Title
Doctor Who and the Smugglers

Factoids
- This was the first time *Doctor Who* had filmed any location scenes outside the Home Counties. Director Julia Smith (later to co-create BBC soap opera *EastEnders*) knew Cornwall well and so was able to make maximum use of its picturesque scenery.
- Scenes on the pirate ship *Black Albatross* were filmed aboard a motorized fishing boat called the Bonny Mary, dressed as a 17th century privateer. Owner Donald Turtle sailed it from Newlyn Harbour to Nanjizal Bay, but heavy swells caused many of the actors and production team to become violently seasick.
- *The Smugglers* was the first *Doctor Who* story to employ the services of newly formed stunt team HAVOC, headed by regular fight arranger and stuntman Derek Ware. Ten stuntmen were used in this serial but during the studio-recorded graveyard fight in Episode 4 they would creep out of shot after being 'killed', don different hats and wigs, and carry on fighting under new guises, thereby increasing the apparent number of men.

Comment
With nothing more than telesnaps and an off-air soundtrack, one can only imagine how lovely *The Smugglers* must have been. Historical accuracy has been replaced with Hollywood cliché, and this Boys' Own adventure tale is a far cry from the grim events of, say, *The Massacre of St Bartholomew's Eve* (22); but the cast seem to be enjoying themselves hugely and it provides a bit of light (albeit violent) relief between two technological thrillers. **70%**

"It's far from being all over." ~ *The Doctor*

29) *The Tenth Planet*
Kit Pedler and Gerry Davis

Serial Code: DD
Original Transmission
Episode 1
Saturday 8 October 1966, 17.50-18.15, 5.5m / 77
Episode 2
Saturday 15 October 1966, 17.50-18.15, 6.4m / 57

Episode 3
Saturday 22 October 1966, 17.50-18.15,
7.6m / 46
Episode 4
Saturday 29 October 1966, 17.50-18.15, 7.5m /48

BBC Archive
Episodes 1-3 exist as 16mm b/w film recordings of the 405-line two-inch monochrome master videotapes (wiped in the late 1960s). Episode 4 does not exist in any visual medium, except for brief 8mm off-screen clips and a clip of the regeneration scene on 625-line two-inch PAL colour videotape taken from the 16mm b/w film recording of the 405-line two-inch monochrome master videotape (wiped in 1969).

Novelization
Doctor Who and the Tenth Planet by Gerry Davis (141/13)
Hardback:
February 1976, Allan Wingate (0855230622 / Chris Achilleos)
Paperback:
1. February 1976, Target (0426110684 / Chris Achilleos)
2. February 1993, Target, renamed *Doctor Who - The Tenth Planet* (0426110684 / Alister Pearson)

Video
November 2000, with reconstructed Episode 4 in 'Cybermen Limited Edition Tin' [BBCV 7030] with *Attack of the Cybermen* (BBCV 6874 / Photomontage with trees)

DVD
November 2004, 8mm off-air clips and Episode 4 clips on 'Doctor Who - Lost in Time' (BBCDVD 1353 / Clayton Hickman)

Soundtrack
November 2004, 2 x CDs, narrated by Anneke Wills, in 'Doctor Who - Cybermen' collectors' tin (0563525088 / Max Ellis)

Music and Sound Effects
1. October 1998, Julian Knott, *Space Adventures: Music from Doctor Who 1963-1971*, CD (JPD 2CD / Photographs)
2. May 2000, *Doctor Who at the BBC Radiophonic Workshop: Volume 1 - The Early Years 1963-1969*, CD (WMSF 6023-2 / Photographs)
3. January 2001, Ochre, *Dr Who: Music from The Tenth Planet*, CD (OCH050 / Photograph)

Telesnaps
Episode 4   *DWM* 207

Précis
At the North Pole, Cybermen arrive from Mondas to drain the Earth of its power...

Cast
William Hartnell, Patrick Troughton (Doctor Who), Michael Craze (Ben), Anneke Wills (Polly), Robert Beatty (General Cutler), Earl Cameron (Williams), David Dodimead (Barclay), Dudley Jones (Dyson), Alan White (Schultz), Steve Plytas (Wigner), Christopher Matthews (Radar Technician), Ellen Cullen (Geneva Technician), Glenn Beck (TV Announcer), Christopher Dunham (R/T Technician), Callen Angelo (Terry Cutler), Shane Shelton (Tito), John Brandon (American Sergeant), Reg Whitehead (Krail/Jarl), Harry Brooks (Talon/Krang), Gregg Palmer (Shav/Gern), Peter Hawkins (Cybermen Voices), Roy Skelton (Cybermen Voices/Snowcap Base Voices/Countdown Voice), Gordon Craig (Double for Doctor Who), Peter Pocock (Double for Ben)

Crew
Studio Lighting Howard King, *Studio Sound* Adrian Bishop-Laggett, *Vision Mixer* Shirley Coward, *Special Sound* Brian Hodgson, *Costume Designer* Sandra Reid, *Make-Up Artist* Gillian James, *Designer* Peter Kindred, *Production Assistant* Edwina Verner, *Assistant Floor Manager* Jenny McArthur, *Story Editor* Gerry Davis, *Producer* Innes Lloyd, *Director* Derek Martinus

DWM Index
55	Episode Guide
75	Michael Craze interview
78	Patrick Troughton interview
88	Who'd Have Believed It? (Colourizing *The Tenth Planet*)
108	Derek Martinus interview
124	Gerry Davis interview
131	Season 4 Flashback
167	Those *Radio Times*
180	On Set
186	What The Papers Said
214	Archive Feature
218	What The Censors Saw
225	Michael Craze interview
243	Derek Martinus interview
297	*The Tenth Planet* Restoration Time Team
298	Video review
322	Anneke Wills interview
349	CD review
352	The Fact of Fiction

Recording Dates
30 August-1 September 1966 (EFS), 17 September 1966 (RS 1), 24 September 1966 (RS 1), 1 October 1966 (RS 1), 8 October 1966 (RS 1)

Working Title
Dr. Who and the Tenth Planet
Doctor Who & The Tenth Planet

Factoids
- William Hartnell was finding it increasingly difficult to learn his lines due to the onset of arteriosclerosis, and frequent clashes with producer Innes Lloyd over what the actor claimed were inappropriate levels of evil in a children's programme meant that the time had come for him to leave. Script editor Gerry Davis suggested the Doctor could rejuvenate into a younger man, something that Head of Series Shaun Sutton was enthusiastic about.
- Sandra Reid designed the Cybermen's appearance in collaboration with Kit Pedler, and seven costumes were made in total. They consisted of full-length cloth body stockings overlaid with transparent polythene suits. The actors wore stretched grey jersey masks with crude eyeholes. Shawcraft made the heavy metal headpieces surmounted with truck headlamps (held together with adhesive tape) and chest units with battery-powered flashing mechanisms. Bare hands suggested their human roots.
- A special title sequence was designed by Bernard Lodge, comprising of computer lettering (N, X, O and Z) forming into the words of the title, author and episode. The same style was carried over onto the end credits. Kit Pedler's name was misspelt 'Kitt' on Episode 1.
- The singsong vocal delivery of the Cybermen was voice artiste Roy Skelton's attempt to emulate a computer-generated intonation.
- The closing moments of Episode 4 - the regeneration/rejuvenation sequence - was recorded first on the final studio day. This was an unusual occurrence for the programme at this stage in its development, as everything was normally recorded in running order. As this was a key scene, more than an hour's worth of studio time had been allocated to this one shot. It was achieved by mixing from Hartnell to Troughton via a faulty mixing desk that created a flared, over-exposed picture.

Comment
The Tenth Planet has a real 'end of an era' feel to it. There are hints that Hartnell's Doctor is getting weaker as the story progresses, and the Cybermen are fearsome new creations - imaginative, disturbing and vaguely sympathetic individuals; a far cry from the corporate villainy of the Daleks. For a start, these benighted creatures have names! Apart from some poor model shots, the production stands up quite well and it's nice to see a futuristic control room filled with ordinary-looking people for a change. And thanks to the marvellous reconstruction work by the BBC's Restoration Team, we can all see for ourselves just how impressive and moving the programme's first regeneration (or rejuvenation) is. **91%**

Second Doctor: Patrick Troughton

"I would like a hat like that." ~ *The Doctor*

30) *The Power of the Daleks*
David Whitaker, with rewrites by Dennis Spooner

Serial Code: EE
Original Transmission
Episode One
5 November 1966, 17.50-18.15, 7.9m / 44
Episode Two
12 November 1966, 17.50-18.15, 7.8m / 50
Episode Three
19 November 1966, 17.50-18.15, 7.5m / 52
Episode Four
26 November 1966, 17.50-18.15, 7.8m / 50
Episode Five
3 December 1966, 17.50-18.15, 8m / 48
Episode Six
10 December 1966, 17.50-18.15, 7.8m / 37
BBC Archive
No episodes exist in any visual medium, except for telesnaps, 8mm off-screen clips from Episodes One and Two, and brief film clips from Episodes Four, Five and Six. The 405-line two-inch monochrome master videotapes were wiped in the late 1960s while the 16mm b/w film recordings were junked in the early 1970s.
Novelization
Doctor Who - The Power of the Daleks by John Peel (253/29)
Paperback:
July 1993, Doctor Who (0426203909 / Alister Pearson)
Video
November 1998, clips on 'The Missing Years', part of 'The Ice Warriors Collection' [BBCV 6387 / Photomontage] with *The Ice Warriors* 1, 4-6 (BBCV 6766 / Photomontage)
DVD
November 2004, 8mm off-air clips, episode clips and trailer on 'Doctor Who - Lost in Time' (BBCDVD 1353 / Clayton Hickman)

Soundtrack
1. August 1993, 2 x cassettes, narrated by Tom Baker (056340695X / Photographs)
2. November 2003, 3 x CDs, narrated by Frazer Hines, as part of 'The Daleks Tin' with *The Evil of the Daleks* (056349476X / Photomontage)

Music and Sound Effects
May 2000, *Doctor Who at the BBC Radiophonic Workshop: Volume 1 - The Early Years 1963-1969*, CD (WMSF 6023-2 / Photographs)

Telesnaps
1990, Photonovel published by *Doctor Who Bulletin*

Script Book
March 1993, Titan Books, edited by John G McElroy with background notes by Stephen James Walker (1852863277 / Alister Pearson)

Précis
The Daleks have infiltrated an Earth colony on 21st century Vulcan…

Cast
Patrick Troughton (Doctor Who), Michael Craze (Ben), Anneke Wills (Polly), Bernard Archard (Bragen), Robert James (Lesterson), Nicholas Hawtrey (Quinn), Pamela Ann Davy (Janley), Peter Bathurst (Hensell), Richard Kane (Valmar), Steven Scott (Kebble), Martin King (Examiner), Edward Kelsey (Resno), Peter Forbes-Robertson, Robert Russell, Robert Luckham (Guards), Gerald Taylor, Kevin Manser, Robert Jewell, John Scott Martin, Alan Whibley (Daleks), Peter Hawkins (Dalek Voices)

Crew
Visual Effects Assistant Alan Whibley, *Vision Mixers* Clive Doig, Dennis Curran, *Studio Lighting* Graham Southcott, Ray Hider, *Studio Sound* Buster Cole, *Film Cameraman* Peter Sargent, *Film Editor* Jim Latham, *Special Sound* Brian Hodgson, *Grams Operator* Lance Andrews, *Costume Designer* Sandra Reid, *Make-Up Artist* Gillian James, *Designer* Derek Dodd, *Production Assistant* Michael Briant, *Assistant Floor Manager* Marjorie Yorke, *Director's Assistants* Gail Paul, Sybil Harper, Jennifer Jones, *Floor Assistants* Julian Aston, Eddie Shah, *Story Editor* Gerry Davis, *Producer* Innes Lloyd, *Director* Christopher Barry

DWM Index
55	Episode Guide
56	Dennis Spooner interview
68	Archive
75	Michael Craze interview
98	Whitaker's World of *Doctor Who*
99	Christopher Barry interview
102	Patrick Troughton interview
120	Dennis Spooner Tribute
131	Season 4 Flashback
169	Those *Radio Times*
180	Christopher Barry interview
	Innes Lloyd interview
	Archive Feature
202	Novelization review
204	Bernard Archard interview
	Edward Kelsey interview
	Robert James interview
219	What The Censor Saw
225	Michael Craze interview
336	CD review

Recording Dates
26-28 September 1966 (EFS), 22 October 1966 (RS 1), 29 October 1966 (RS 1), 5 November 1966 (RS 1), 12 November 1966 (RS 1), 19 November 1966 (RS 1), 26 November 1966 (RS 1)

Working Titles
The Destiny of Dr Who
Dr Who and the Power of the Daleks

Factoids
- Patrick Troughton was 46 years old when he accepted his new role. Various costumes ideas were mooted for this 'renewed' Doctor, including a blacked-up *Arabian Nights* figure, a Victorian parliamentarian and a pirate captain. A Harpo Marx wig was rejected at a late stage, with the Doctor's eventual look being a scruffier version of William Hartnell's costume (which regenerated along with the actor).
- Four Dalek props were augmented with several full-size hardboard photographic blow-ups to pad out background scenes. For the Dalek production line sequence, commercially sold Hertz toy Daleks were filmed moving along a twelve-foot conveyer belt.
- Episode Six was recorded straight onto 35mm film, but using 625-line studio cameras rather than 405-line ones. This was the first time *Doctor Who* had used this more advanced system, although regular 625-line recordings would not begin until Episode Three of *The Enemy of the World* (40).
- The story was promoted with a *Radio Times* cover (the fourth since the show began), dated 5-11 November 1966.

Comment
The Power of the Daleks offers a fresh look at what makes the Daleks scary, with their submissive behaviour doubly threatening because of what we know from previous adventures. Patrick Troughton, still finding his feet, couldn't

be more different to Hartnell, and although the humour is a little over-played, his lightness of touch makes a welcome change. The story itself may be nothing special - compared to previous Dalek stories, the events are positively trivial - but there are some notable moments (the production line sequence for one) and it's a solid foundation for the new incumbent. **75%**

"I'm not very expert with these things and it just might go off in your face." ~ The Doctor

31) The Highlanders
Elwyn Jones and Gerry Davis

Serial Code: FF
Original Transmission
Episode 1
Saturday 17 December 1966, 17.50-18.15, 6.7m / 67
Episode 2
Saturday 24 December 1966, 17.50-18.15, 6.8m / 89
Episode 3
Saturday 31 December 1966, 17.50-18.15, 7.4m / 68
Episode 4
Saturday 7 January 1967, 17.50-18.15, 7.3m / 66
BBC Archive
No episodes exist in any visual medium, except for telesnaps of the whole story and brief Australian censor clips from Episode 1. The 405-line two-inch monochrome master videotapes were wiped in 1967 and the 16mm b/w film recordings were junked in the late 1970s.
Novelization
Doctor Who - The Highlanders by Gerry Davis (126/17)
Paperback:
November 1984, Target (0426196767 / Nick Spender)
DVD
November 2004, clips on 'Doctor Who - Lost in Time' (BBCDVD 1353 / Clayton Hickman)
Soundtrack
August 2000, 2 x CDs, narrated by Frazer Hines (056347555 / Max Ellis)
Telesnaps
Episode 1   *DWM* 233
Episode 2   *DWM* 234
Episode 3   *DWM* 235
Episode 4   *DWM* 236

Précis
The Tardis travellers fall in with Scottish Highlanders after the Battle of Culloden in 1746...
Cast
Patrick Troughton (Doctor Who), Michael Craze (Ben), Anneke Wills (Polly), Frazer Hines (Jamie McCrimmon), Donald Bisset (Laird), William Dysart (Alexander), Hannah Gordon (Kirsty), Michael Elwyn (Lieutenant Algernon ffinch), Peter Welch (Sergeant), David Garth (Solicitor Grey), Sydney Arnold (Perkins), Dallas Cavell (Trask), Barbara Bruce (Mollie), Andrew Downie (Willie Mackay), Guy Middleton (Colonel Attwood), Tom Bowman (Sentry), Peter Diamond (Sailor/English Soldier/Stunt Double for Ben/Double for Jim Hughes' Corpse), André Cameron (Double for Kirsty)
Crew
Fight Arranger Peter Diamond, *Vision Mixer* Nola Schiff, *Studio Lighting* George Summers, Ken McGregor, John Farr, *Studio Sound* Larry Goodson, *Special Sound* Brian Hodgson, *Costume Designer* Sandra Reid, *Make-Up Artist* Gillian James, *Designer* Geoffrey Kirkland, *Production Assistant* Fiona Cumming, *Assistant Floor Manager* Nicholas John, *Director's Assistants* Shirley Coward, Evelyn Cowdrey, *Floor Assistant* Jeremy Ward, *Story Editor* Gerry Davis, *Producer* Innes Lloyd, *Director* Hugh David
DWM Index
56   Episode Guide
66   Archive
78   Patrick Troughton interview
89   Novelization review
98   Frazer Hines interview
124   Gerry Davis interview
131   Season 4 Flashback
169   Those *Radio Times*
243   Frazer Hines interview
292   Archive Feature
296   CD review
298   Time Team
306   Michael Troughton's Memories
322   Anneke Wills interview
Recording Dates
11 November 1966 (EFS), 14-15 November 1966 (Location filming), 16 November 1966 (EFS), 21 November 1966 (Location filming), 3 December 1966 (RS 1), 10 December 1966 (RS 1), 17 December 1966 (RS 1), 24 December 1966 (RS 1)
Location
Frensham Ponds, Frensham, Surrey
Working Titles
Culloden
Dr Who and the Highlanders

Factoids
- Elwyn Jones had only penned notes for this *Doctor Who* story before he was called away to reformat the 1967 revival of *Z Cars* as a twice-weekly soap opera. Story editor Gerry Davis and incoming director Hugh David wrote the scripts from scratch, based on Jones' notes, using Robert Louis Stephenson's 1886 novel *Kidnapped* as inspiration.
- When it became clear that 22-year-old Frazer Hines would become a companion, a reshoot was scheduled at Frensham Ponds on 21 November 1966 to show the actor stepping aboard the Tardis.
- More comedy was introduced into the role of the Second Doctor in this story: he calls himself 'Doctor von Wer' (German for 'Doctor Who') and disguises himself as a washerwoman.
- Because of *The Gunfighters*' disastrous audience appreciation figures, it was decided that *The Highlanders* would be the last 'straight' historical story produced (until *Black Orchid* [121] in 1982).

Comment
It's ironic that this would be the last true historical for many years, as *The Highlanders* is a perfect blend of exciting adventure story and light-hearted romp. One feels that the Tardis regulars are never in real trouble, despite their breathless life-and-death escapades, and there's a zest to the storyline that's utterly infectious. **85%**

"Nuzzink in zee vorld can stop me now!" ~ Professor Zaroff

32) *The Underwater Menace*
Geoffrey Orme

Serial Code: GG
Original Transmission
Episode 1
Saturday 14 January 1967, 17.50-18.15, 8.3m / 43
Episode 2
Saturday 21 January 1967, 17.50-18.15, 7.5m / 64
Episode 3
Saturday 28 January 1967, 17.50-18.15, 7.1m / 59
Episode 4
Saturday 4 February 1967, 17.50-18.15, 7m / 65

BBC Archive
Episode 3 exists as a 16mm b/w film recording of the 405-line two-inch monochrome master videotape (wiped in 1969). All other episodes do not exist complete in any visual medium, except for brief Australian censor clips from Episodes 1, 2 and 4.

Novelization
Doctor Who - The Underwater Menace by Nigel Robinson (137/13)
Hardback:
February 1988, WH Allen (0491034962 / Alister Pearson)
Paperback:
July 1988, Target (0426203267 / Alister Pearson)

Soundtrack
February 2005, 2 x CDs, narrated by Anneke Wills (0563535067 / Max Ellis)

Video
November 1998, Episode 3 and Australian censor clips on 'The Missing Years', part of 'The Ice Warriors Collection' [BBCV 6387 / Photomontage] with *The Ice Warriors* 1, 4-6 (BBCV 6766 / Photomontage)

DVD
November 2004, Episode 3, VidFIREd, plus clips, on 'Doctor Who - Lost in Time' (BBCDVD 1353 / Clayton Hickman)

Music and Sound Effects
1. July 1993, *Doctor Who: 30 Years at the Radiophonic Workshop*, CD (BBCCD 871 / Photomontage)
2. May 2000, *Doctor Who at the BBC Radiophonic Workshop: Volume 1 - The Early Years 1963-1969*, CD (WMSF 6023-2 / Photographs)

Telesnaps
Episode 1	*DWM* 220
Episode 2	*DWM* 221
Episode 3	*DWM* 222
Episode 4	*DWM* 223

Précis
In Atlantis, Professor Zaroff has a mad plan to drain the seas into the molten core of the Earth…

Cast
Patrick Troughton (Doctor Who), Michael Craze (Ben), Anneke Wills (Polly), Frazer Hines (Jamie), Joseph Furst (Professor Zaroff), Catherine Howe (Ara), Tom Watson (Ramo), Colin Jeavons (Damon), Gerald Taylor (Damon's Assistant/Laboratory Assistant), Peter Stephens (Lolem), Graham Ashley (Overseer), Paul Anil (Jacko), PG Stephens (Sean), Noël Johnson (King Thous), Roma Woodnutt (Nola), Tony Handy (Zaroff's Guard)

Crew
Fight Arranger Derek Ware, *Vision Mixer* Bruce Milliard, *Studio Lighting* George Summers, John Farr, David Hare, *Studio Sound* Bryan Forgham, *Special Sound* Brian Hodgson, *Incidental Music* Dudley Simpson, Brian Hodgson, *Costume Designers* Sandra Reid, Juanita Waterson, *Make-Up Artist* Gillian James, *Designer* Jack Robinson, *Production Assistant* Norman Stewart, *Assistant Floor Manager* Gareth Gwenlan, *Director's Assistant* Betty Coatts, *Floor Assistants* Quintin Mann, Steven Clark-Hall, *Story Editor* Gerry Davis, *Producer* Innes Lloyd, *Director* Julia Smith

DWM Index
56	Episode Guide
78	Archive
131	Season 4 Flashback
135	Novelization review
169	Those *Radio Times*
187	What The Papers Said
209	Archive Feature
219	What The Censor Saw
225	Michael Craze interview
271	Video review
299	Time Team
306	Michael Troughton's Memories
317	Derek Ware interview
322	Anneke Wills interview
350	DVD review
353	CD review

Recording Dates
12-13 December 1966 (Location filming), 14-16 December 1966 (EFS), 7 January 1967 (RS 1), 14 January 1967 (RS 2), 21 January 1967 (RS 1), 28 January 1967 (RS 1)

Location
Winspit Quarry, Worth Matravers, Dorset

Working Titles
Dr Who Under the Sea
Doctor Who and the Fish People
Doctor Who and the Underwater Menace

Factoids
- Episode 1's recording was delayed a week so it did not fall on New Year's Eve. This meant that *Doctor Who* was now being recorded only one week before transmission.
- Joseph Furst (Zaroff) was a Viennese-born actor, usually billed as Joseph Fürst, who made a career of playing larger-than-life characters in such films as *Theatre of Death* (1966) and *Diamonds are Forever* (1971). Noël Johnson (Thous) had been famous on the radio as *Dick Barton - Special Agent* on the BBC Light Programme from 1946 to 1949.
- After watching Episode 4, playwright Joe Orton telephoned Peter Willes, the producer of the BBC's forthcoming adaptation of his 1964 play *Entertaining Mr Sloane* (directed by future *Doctor Who* director Peter Moffatt), and suggested that Frazer Hines would be perfect as the title character.
- A complaint was received from a spokeswoman for the National Society for the Welfare of Children in Hospitals complaining that the hypodermic syringe cliffhanger to Episode 1 might put children off undergoing routine operations.

Comment
Okay, so it's a terrible piece of old tat, but I can't help liking it. Joseph Furst is absolutely hilarious in a scenery-chewing part that demands over-acting (and gets it), and the sets and costumes actually aren't *that* bad. The Fish People are no worse than, say, the Cryons (*Attack of the Cybermen*, 138) or the Aridians (*The Chase*, 16) and anything with Colin Jeavons in has got to be worth a look. It may be bad, but at least it's not dull. **62%**

"It's you! The Phantom Piper!" ~ *Jamie*

33) The Moonbase
Kit Pedler

Serial Code: HH
Original Transmission
Episode 1
Saturday 11 February 1967, 17.50-18.15, 8.1m / 56
Episode 2
Saturday 18 February 1967, 17.50-18.15, 8.9m / 36
Episode 3
Saturday 25 February 1967, 17.50-18.15, 8.2m / 49
Episode 4
Saturday 4 March 1967, 17.50-18.15, 8.1m / 44
BBC Archive
Episodes 2 and 4 exist as 16mm b/w film recordings of the 405-line two-inch monochrome master videotapes (wiped in 1969). Episodes 1 and 3 do not exist in any visual medium.
Novelization
Doctor Who and the Cybermen by Gerry Davis (150/11)

Hardback:
July 1981, WH Allen (0426029152 / Bill Donohoe)
Paperback:
1. February 1975, Target (0426105753 / Chris Achilleos)
2. 1981, Target (0426114639 / Bill Donohoe)

Video
July 1992, Episodes 2 and 4 (edited) on 'Cybermen - The Early Years' (BBCV 4813 / Photographs)

DVD
November 2004, Episodes 2 and 4, VidFIREd, with soundtracks of Episodes 1 and 3, on 'Doctor Who - Lost in Time' (BBCDVD 1353 / Clayton Hickman)

Soundtrack
April 2002, 2 x CDs, narrated by Frazer Hines (0563478543 / Max Ellis)

Music and Sound Effects
October 1998, Julian Knott, *Space Adventures: Music from Doctor Who 1963-1971*, CD (JPD 2CD / Photographs)

Précis
The Cybermen plan to take control of an Earth weather station on the Moon…

Cast
Patrick Troughton (Doctor Who), Michael Craze (Ben), Anneke Wills (Polly), Frazer Hines (Jamie), Andre Maranne (Benoit), Patrick Barr (Hobson), John Rolfe (Sam), Michael Wolf (Nils), Mark Heath (Ralph), Alan Rowe (Dr Evans/Voice from Space Control), Victor Pemberton (Jules), Ron Pinnell (Jim), Edward Phillips (Bob), Robin Scott (Charlie), Alan Wells (Joe), Derek Calder (Peter/Double for John), Leon Maybank (Ted), Barry Ashton (Franz), Arnold Chazen (John), Denis McCarthy (Voice of Controller Rinberg), Sonnie Willis, John Wills, Peter Greene, Keith Goodman, Reg Whitehead, Bernard Reid, Terry Wallis, Decland Cuffe, Derek Schafer, John Levine, Barry Noble, Ronald Lee (Cybermen), Peter Hawkins (Cybermen Voices)

Crew
Graphics Peter Netley, *Vision Mixer* Ian Easterbrook, *Studio Lighting* Dave Sydenham, Brian Clemett, *Studio Sound* Gordon Mackie, *Special Sound* Brian Hodgson, *Grams Operators* Alan Boyd, Dave Baumber, *Costume Designers* Sandra Reid (film), Mary Woods (1-2), Daphne Dare (3-4), *Make-Up Artist* Gilliam James, Jeanne Richmond, *Designer* Colin Shaw, *Production Assistant* Desmond McCarthy, *Assistant Floor Manager* Lovett Bickford, *Director's Assistant* Glenys Williams, *Floor Assistants* Peter Campbell, Mike Healy, *Story Editor* Gerry Davis, *Producer* Innes Lloyd, *Director* Morris Barry

DWM Index
54	Morris Barry interview
56	Episode Guide
75	Michael Craze interview
102	Patrick Troughton interview
108	Victor Pemberton interview
131	Season 4 Flashback
138	Archive + Fact File
169	Those *Radio Times*
181	On Set
187	What The Papers Said Anneke Wills interview
189	Video review ('Cybermen - The Early Years')
239	Vox Pops
243	Frazer Hines interview
299	Time Team
303	CD review
306	Michael Troughton's Memories
318	Victor Pemberton interview
322	Archive Feature Anneke Wills interview
350	DVD review

Recording Dates
17-20 January 1967 (EFS), 4 February 1967 (RS 1), 11 February 1967 (RS 1), 17 February 1967 (EFS), 18 February 1967 (RS 1), 25 February 1967 (LG D)

Working Titles
Dr Who and the Return of the Cybermen
The Return of the Cybermen
Return of the Cybermen
Doctor Who and the Moonbase

Factoids
- Eleven new Cybermen costumes were designed by Sandra Reid, with input from John and Jack Lovell. They were simpler than those seen in *The Tenth Planet* (29), with two-piece fibreglass masks equipped with battery-powered lights. The body was a silver vinyl jumpsuit with three fingers, topped off with silver laced army boots, over which hung an aluminium chest unit with flashing lights and a rod weapon that could light up on cue. To create the impression of hydraulic limbs, vacuum cleaner tubes with practice golf balls were fixed along the arms and legs.
- The Cybermen's voices became less sing-song for this story, with voice artiste Peter Hawkins making use of an uncomfortable medical device that allowed you to speak if your larynx had been removed. He was fitted with a dental plate housing a tiny loudspeaker, and when this vibrated he would silently mouth his dialogue - the result was an electronic-sounding form of speech.

- The Tardis crew wore quilted spacesuits with clear goldfish-bowl helmets for their Moonwalk in Episode 1. The camera was set to film at a higher than normal speed so that the finished scenes would be in slow-motion, and in addition Anneke Wills was rigged up to Kirby wires so that she could appear to float in the low gravity.
- The spread of the Cybermen's neurotrope was animated on photographs of its victim, Derek Calder, by BBC graphics designer Peter Netley. Episode 4's sequence of the Cybermen attacking the Moonbase with a laser-beam weapon was the first use of a filmed optical effect in *Doctor Who*: the ray of light was matted onto the live action in an optical printer.
- John Levene, later to play Sergeant Benton in many of the UNIT stories, was contracted to play a Cyberman. Victor Pemberton (Jules) went on to write *Fury From The Deep* (42) and was story editor for *The Tomb Of The Cybermen* (37).

Comment
The Moonbase is a reworking of *The Tenth Planet* spoilt by clichéd characters and too many Tardis crewmembers. Eschewing the earlier story's realism, we have such quaint ideas as plugging a hole into space with a tea-tray and allowing a Cyberman to hide under a sheet in full view of the entire cast for a whole episode. One of those odd situations when the soundtrack is probably scarier than the episode itself. **50%**

"Well, this is gay!" ~ The Doctor

34) *The Macra Terror*
Ian Stuart Black

Serial Code: JJ
Original Transmission
Episode 1
Saturday 11 March 1967, 17.50-18.15, 8m / 37
Episode 2
Saturday 18 March 1967, 17.50-18.15, 7.9m / 42
Episode 3
Saturday 25 March 1967, 17.50-18.15, 8.5m / 45
Episode 4
Saturday 1 April 1967, 17.50-18.15, 8.4m / 39

BBC Archive
None of the episodes exist in any visual medium, except for telesnaps of the whole story, 8mm film off-screen clips from Episode 3 and Australian censor clips from Episodes 2 and 3. The 405-line two-inch monochrome master videotapes were wiped in 1974 and the 16mm b/w film recordings were junked by 1977.

Novelization
Doctor Who - The Macra Terror by Ian Stuart Black (139/12)
Hardback:
July 1987, WH Allen (0491032277 / Tony Masero)
Paperback:
December 1987, Target (0426203070 / Tony Masero)

Video
November 1998, Australian censor clips on 'The Missing Years' (BBCV 6766 / Photomontage), part of 'The Ice Warriors Collection' [BBCV 6387 / Photomontage]

DVD
1. January 2002, new title sequence test footage on *The Tomb of the Cybermen* (BBCDVD 1032 / Clayton Hickman)
2. November 2004, 8mm off-air clips, episode clips on 'Doctor Who - Lost in Time' (BBCDVD 1353 / Clayton Hickman)

Soundtrack
1. July 1992, 2 x cassettes, narrated by Colin Baker (0563366826 / Photographs)
2. August 2000, 2 x CDs (remastered), narrated by Colin Baker (0563477563 / Max Ellis)

Music and Sound Effects
1. July 1993, *Doctor Who: 30 Years at the Radiophonic Workshop*, CD (BBCCD 871 / Photographs)
2. May 2000, *Doctor Who at the BBC Radiophonic Workshop: Volume 1 - The Early Years 1963-1969*, CD (WMSF 6023-2 / Photographs)

Telesnaps
Episode 1   DWM 251
Episode 2   DWM 252
Episode 3   DWM 253
Episode 4   DWM 254

Précis
Huge crablike Macra creatures have taken over an Earth colony run like a holiday camp...

Cast
Patrick Troughton (Doctor Who), Michael Craze (Ben), Anneke Wills (Polly), Frazer Hines (Jamie), Peter Jeffrey (Pilot), Graham Armitage (Barney), Ian Fairbairn (Questa), Jane Enshawe (Sunnaa), Sandra Bryant (Chicki, 1), Karol Keyes (Chicki, 2),

47

Terence Lodge (Medok), Gertan Klauber (Ola), Graham Leaman (Controller), Denis Goacher (Control Voice), Richard Beale (Broadcast Voice/Propaganda Voice), Maureen Lane (Drum Majorette), Anthony Gardner (Alvis), Robert Jewell (Macra Operator), John Harvey (Official), John Caesar, Steve Emerson, Danny Rae (Guards), Roger Jerome (Cheerleader Leader), Terry Wright, Ralph Carrigan (Cheerleaders)

Crew
Vision Mixer Bruce Milliard, *Studio Lighting* Frank Cresswell, Terry Wild, *Studio Sound* Gordon Mackie, Hugh Barker, *Special Sound* Brian Hodgson, *Grams Operator* Chris Pocock, *Incidental Music* Dudley Simpson, John Baker, *Costume Designer* Vanessa Clarke, *Make-Up Artist* Gillian James, *Designer* Kenneth Sharp, *Production Assistant* Chris D'Oyly-John, *Assistant Floor Manager* Ann Faggetter, *Director's Assistant* Marianne Willison, *Floor Assistant* Charles Wallace, *Story Editor* Gerry Davis, *Producer* Innes Lloyd, *Director* John Davies

DWM Index
56	Episode Guide
67	Archive
75	Michael Craze interview
78	Patrick Troughton interview
122	Novelization review
124	Gerry Davis interview
131	Season 4 Flashback
169	Those *Radio Times*
170	Ian Stuart Black interview
187	What The Papers Said
189	Cassette review
241	Chris D'Oyly-John interview
243	Frazer Hines interview
254	John Davies interview
288	Peter Jeffrey interview
295	CD review
301	Time Team
306	Michael Troughton's Memories
308	Archive Feature
322	Anneke Wills interview

Recording Dates
15 February 1967 (Location filming), 17 February 1967 (Location filming), 4 March 1967 (LG D), 11 March 1976 (LG D), 18 March 1967 (LG D), 25 March 1967 (LG D)

Location
Associated Portland Cement Manufacturers Quarry, Dunstable, Bedfordshire

Working Titles
Dr Who & The Spidermen
Doctor Who and the Spidermen!
The Spidermen
Doctor Who and the Insect-Men
Dr Who & The Macras
Dr Who and the Macras

Factoids
- The titular creatures were originally to have been arachnid, until designer Kenneth Sharpe visited the Natural History Museum in London and saw a display of large South American crabs.
- Constructed by Shawcraft, one ten-feet tall wooden Macra prop was built at a cost of £500. A person inside could move the two huge pincers and the glove-like claws and could switch the eyes - which were mounted on long stalks - on or off to show whether the monster was awake or not.
- A new version of the title sequence debuted with Episode 1. Utilising the same howlround technique as the previous sequence, Bernard Lodge (under the supervision of engineer Ben Palmer) began by incorporating a photo caption of Patrick Troughton as part of this effect, making it 'bleed' into view. This then disappeared via an optical wipe (formed using a brightly lit piece of rough polystyrene) and a revised *Doctor Who* logo, in a New Times Roman font, was seen to 'bleed' in, and then out, of the howlround background.

Comment
What 1980s producer John Nathan-Turner would have called an "oddball" story, *The Macra Terror* makes great play of the horrors that lurk beneath the seemingly happy-go-lucky surface of a glorified holiday camp. The Macra itself, looming out of its dark caves amid swirls of dry ice, is a superb creation, although its limited manoeuvrability becomes quickly apparent. The perfect story to illustrate the Second Doctor's rebellious and non-conforming nature, his railing against bland homogeneity is a character-defining moment. **88%**

"Your friends are worried about you. Well, then we shall have to do something to *stop* them worrying…" ~ Captain Blade

35) *The Faceless Ones*
David Ellis and Malcolm Hulke

Serial Code: KK
Original Transmission
Episode 1
Saturday 8 April 1967, 17.50-18.15, 8m / 47
Episode 2
Saturday 15 April 1967, 17.50-18.15, 6.4m / 70

Episode 3
Saturday 22 April 1967, 17.50-18.15, 7.9m / 43
Episode 4
Saturday 29 April 1967, 17.50-18.15, 6.9m / 62
Episode 5
Saturday 6 May 1967, 17.50-18.15, 7.1m / 39
Episode 6
Saturday 13 May 1967, 17.50-18.15, 8m / 33

BBC Archive
Episode 1 exists as a b/w 16mm film recording of the 405-line two-inch monochrome master videotape; Episode 3 likewise, except for several missing segments caused by damaged frames being removed. The other Episodes do not survive in any visual medium, except for telesnaps for the whole serial and a very brief off-screen 8mm home movie clip from Episode 2. The 405-line two-inch monochrome master videotapes were wiped in 1969 and the 16mm b/w film recordings were junked in the early 1970s.

Novelization
Doctor Who - The Faceless Ones by Terrance Dicks (140/15)
Hardback:
December 1986, WH Allen (0491036922 / David McAllister)
Paperback:
May 1987, Target (0426202945 / David McAllister)

Video
November 2003, Episodes 1 and 3, VidFIREd, as part of '*The Reign of Terror* Collectors' Set' [BBCV 7335 / Photomontage] with *The Web of Fear* 1 (BBCV 7539 / Photomontage)

DVD
November 2004, 8mm off-air clips, Episodes 1 and 3, VidFIREd, on 'Doctor Who - Lost in Time' (BBCDVD 1353 / Clayton Hickman)

Soundtrack
February 2002, 2 x CDs, narrated by Frazer Hines (0563535016 / Max Ellis)

Music and Sound Effects
May 2000, *Doctor Who at the BBC Radiophonic Workshop: Volume 1 - The Early Years 1963-1969*, CD (WMSF 6023-2 / Photographs)

Telesnaps
Episode 1   *DWM* 260
Episode 2   *DWM* 261
Episode 3   *DWM* 262
Episode 4   *DWM* 263
Episode 5   *DWM* 264
Episode 6   *DWM* 266

Précis
Teenage holidaymakers travelling with Chameleon Tours are disappearing into thin air...

Cast
Patrick Troughton (Doctor Who), Michael Craze (Ben), Anneke Wills (Polly), Frazer Hines (Jamie), Wanda Ventham (Jean Rock), Colin Gordon (Commandant), Bernard Kay (Inspector Crossland), Donald Pickering (Captain Blade), Pauline Collins (Samantha Briggs), George Selway (George Meadows), Victor Winding (Spencer), Chris Tranchell (Stephen Jenkins), Madalena Nicol (Nurse Pinto), Gilly Fraser (Ann Davidson), Barry Wilshere (Heslington), James Appleby (Policeman), Peter Whitaker (Inspector Gascoigne), Brigit Paul (Announcer), Michael Ladkan (RAF Pilot), Leonard Trolley (Superintendent Reynolds), Barrie Du Pre, Robin Dawson, Pat Leclere (Chameleons), Roy Pearce (Chameleon/Airport Policeman), Terence Denville (Double for Blade), Elizabeth Smith (Double for Nurse Pinto)

Crew
Technical Manager Fred Wright, *Vision Mixer* Clive Doig, *Studio Lighting* Howard King, *Studio Sound* Gordon Mackie, *Film Cameraman* Tony Imi, *Film Editor* Chris Haydon, *Special Sound* Brian Hodgson, *Grams Operators* Dave Thompson, Pat Heigham, *Costume Designers* Daphne Dare, Sandra Reid, *Make-Up Artist* Gillian James, *Designer* Geoffrey Kirkland, *Production Assistant* Richard Brooks, *Assistant Floor Manager* Sue Marlborough, *Director's Assistants* Pamela Lintern, Pat Harrington, *Floor Assistant* Peter Hebbes, *Story Editor* Gerry Davis, *Associate Producer* Peter Bryant, *Producer* Innes Lloyd, *Director* Gerry Mill

DWM Index
56	Episode Guide
61	Behind The Scenes: Graphic Design
71	Archive
91	The Incredible Malcolm Hulke
115	Novelization review
131	Season 4 Flashback
169	Those *Radio Times*
180	Innes Lloyd interview
187	What The Papers Said
192	Crossing the Line
212	Archive Feature
	Pauline Collins interview
243	Frazer Hines interview
260	Behind The Scenes
266	Donald Pickering interview
	Wanda Ventham interview
301	Time Team 1-4
302	Time Team 5-6
306	Michael Troughton's Memories
314	CD review
322	Anneke Wills interview
337	Video review

Recording Dates
10 March 1967 (Location filming), 13-14 March 1967 (Location Filming), 15-16 March 1967 (EFS modelwork), 17 March 1967 (Location filming), 1 April 1967 (LG D), 8 April 1967 (LG D), 11 April 1967 (EFS modelwork remount), 15 April 1967 (LG D), 22 April 1967 (LG D), 29 April 1967 (LG D), 6 May 1967 (LG D)

Location
Gatwick Airport, Gatwick, Surrey

Working Titles
Doctor Who & The Chameleons
The Chameleons

Factoids
- Writing partners Malcolm Hulke and David Ellis originally proposed a four-part story called *The Big Store*, concerning an alien invasion via a 1973 department store. They were asked to change the locale to an airport by producer Innes Lloyd and story editor Gerry Davis, and extend the story to six parts.
- Due to problems with the model VC10 and Chameleon satellite built by outside contractor Shawcraft, this would be the last *Doctor Who* story they would contribute to. From the next story, special effects were handled by the BBC's own Visual Effects Department.
- The Chameleons' hands and heads were covered in a blobby layer of latex covered with Vaseline. Barring their appearance in the telesnaps, only one photograph of them is known to survive.
- Anneke Wills and Michael Craze were not needed beyond their second studio recording session; their appearance in Episode 6 had been pre-filmed at Gatwick a month earlier. Pauline Collins, playing chirpy Liverpudlian Samantha Briggs, was asked to stay on as a regular companion by Innes Lloyd. She declined the offer.
- To accompany the new title sequence for *The Macra Terror*, Delia Derbyshire and the BBC Radiophonic Workshop revised the theme music, which debuted on Episode 2 of this serial. To the original arrangement was added rising arpeggiated patterns ('electronic spangles'), while a delayed echo with feedback gave the bass line greater weight. The closing music remained the same.

Comment
From the existing episodes, telesnaps and soundtrack, this appears to be a well-made production of an ambitious script. The scenes shot at Gatwick Airport do much to broaden the scope of the show and Pauline Collins and Frazer Hines make a wonderful double-act. The Chameleons - *Doctor Who*'s most mysterious alien species due to the dearth of reference photos - look surprisingly scary with their melted faces. The only thing that disappoints is the lame ending in which the Doctor vaguely promises to help the Chameleons and everyone lives happily ever after. **80%**

"It's no use having a conscience now." ~ *The Doctor*

36) *The Evil of the Daleks*
David Whitaker

Serial Code: LL
Original Transmission
Episode 1
Saturday 20 May 1967, 18.00-18.25, 8.1m / 37
Episode 2
Saturday 27 May 1967, 17.50-18.15, 7.5m / 37
Episode 3
Saturday 3 June 1967, 17.45-18.10, 6.1m / 61
Episode 4
Saturday 10 June 1967, 17.45-18.10, 5.3m / 51
Episode 5
Saturday 17 June 1967, 17.45-18.10, 5.1m / 62
Episode 6
Saturday 24 June 1967, 17.45-18.10, 6.8m / 38
Episode 7
Saturday 1 July 1967, 18.25-18.50, 6.1m / 50
Repeat Transmission
Episode 1 (with voice-over)
Saturday 8 June 1968, 17.15-17.40, 6.3m / 31
Episode 2
Saturday 15 June 1968, 17.15-17.40, 5m / 63
Episode 3
Saturday 22 June 1968, 17.15-17.40, 6.3m / 49
Episode 4
Saturday 13 July 1968, 17.15-17.40, 5m / 68
Episode 5
Saturday 20 July 1968, 17.15-17.40, 5.1m / 67
Episode 6
Saturday 27 July 1968, 17.15-17.40, 4.2m / 74
Episode 7
Saturday 3 August 1968, 17.15-17.40, 5.5m / 57
BBC Archive
Episode 2 exists as a 16mm b/w film recording of the 405-line two-inch monochrome master videotape (wiped by 1969). The other episodes do not exist in any visual medium, except for telesnaps of the whole serial and 8mm home movie footage of the filming of Episode 7.

Novelization
Doctor Who - The Evil of the Daleks by John Peel (288/35)
Paperback:
August 1993, Doctor Who (0426203895 / Alister Pearson)

Video
1. July 1992, Episode 2 on 'Daleks - The Early Years' (BBCV 4810 / Photographs)
2. November 1998, excerpts of 8mm home movie footage on 'The Missing Years', part of 'The Ice Warriors Collection' [BBCV 6387] with *The Ice Warriors* 1, 4-6 (BBCV 6766 / Photomontage)

DVD
1. January 2002, 'The Final End' (edited 8mm home movie footage of Episode 7) on *The Tomb of the Cybermen* (BBCDVD 1032 / Clayton Hickman)
2. February 2003, 'The Last Dalek' (complete 8mm home movie footage of Episode 7) on *The Seeds of Death* (BBCDVD 1151 / Clayton Hickman)
3. November 2004, Episode 2, VidFIREd, commentary by Deborah Watling and Gary Russell, and 'The Last Dalek' on 'Doctor Who - Lost in Time' (BBCDVD 1353 / Clayton Hickman)

Soundtrack
1. July 1992, 2 x cassettes, edited, narrated by Tom Baker (0563366834 / Photographs)
2. November 2003, 3 x CDs (remastered), narrated by Frazer Hines, as part of 'The Daleks Tin' with *The Power of the Daleks* (056349476X / Max Ellis)

Music and Sound Effects
1. July 1993, *Doctor Who: 30 Years at the Radiophonic Workshop*, CD (BBCCD 871 / Photomontage)
2. October 1998, Julian Knott, *Space Adventures: Music from Doctor Who 1963-1971*, CD (JPD 2CD / Photographs)

Telesnaps

Episode 1	*DWM* 237
Episode 2	*DWM* 238
Episode 3	*DWM* 239
Episode 4	*DWM* 240
Episode 5	*DWM* 241
Episode 6	*DWM* 242
Episode 7	*DWM* 243

Précis
In Victorian England, the Daleks are experimenting with the 'Human Factor'…

Cast
Patrick Troughton (Doctor Who), Frazer Hines (Jamie), Deborah Watling (Victoria Waterfield), John Bailey (Edward Waterfield), Marius Goring (Theodore Maxtible), Windsor Davies (Toby), Alec Ross (Bob Hall), Griffith Davies (Kennedy), Geoffrey Colville (Perry), Jo Rowbottom (Mollie Dawson), Brigit Forsyth (Ruth Maxtible), Gary Watson (Arthur Terrall), Sonny Caldinez (Kemel), Robert Jewell, Gerald Taylor, John Scott Martin, Murphy Grumbar, Ken Tyllsen (Daleks), Roy Skelton, Peter Hawkins (Dalek Voices), Barry Ashton (Double for The Doctor/Policeman at Antique Shop)

Crew
Fight Arranger Peter Diamond, *Visual Effects Designers* Michaeljohn Harris, Peter Day, *Technical Managers* Tommy Dawson, Neil Campbell, *Vision Mixers* Bruce Milliard, John Barclay, *Studio Lighting* Wally Whitmore, *Studio Sound* Bryan Forgham, *Film Cameraman* John Baker, *Film Editor* Ted Walters, *Special Sound* Brian Hodgson, *Grams Operator* Dave Thompson, *Incidental Music* Dudley Simpson, *Costume Designer* Sandra Reid, *Make-Up Artist* Gillian James, *Designer* Chris Thompson, *Production Assistant/Dalek Fight Film Sequence Director* Timothy Combe, *Assistant Floor Managers* David Tilley, Margaret Rushton, *Director's Assistant* Jenny Huddleston, *Floor Assistants* Stephen Withers, Graham Hoosem, *Story Editors* Gerry Davis, Peter Bryant, *Assistant Story Editor* Victor Pemberton, *Producer* Innes Lloyd, *Director* Derek Martinus

DWM Index

57	Episode Guide
78	Patrick Troughton interview
87	Deborah Watling interview
98	Frazer Hines interview
	Whitaker's World of *Doctor Who*
108	Derek Martinus interview
128	Nostalgia
131	Season 4 Flashback
146	Victor Pemberton interview
169	Those *Radio Times*
187	What The Papers Said
189	CD review
	Video review ('Daleks - The Early Years')
200	Whitaker's World
	Archive Feature
203	Novelization review
212	Deborah Watling interview
237	TV review
239	Vox Pops
243	Derek Martinus interview
265	*DWM* Awards (9th)
302	Time Team 1-6
303	Time Team 7
306	Michael Troughton's Memories
308	Deborah Watling interview
318	Victor Pemberton interview

336 CD review
342 The Fact of Fiction
350 DVD review

Recording Dates
20-21 April 1967 (Location filming), 24-25 April 1967 (Location filming), 26-27 April 1967 (EFS modelwork), 28 April 1967 (EFS), 13 May 1967 (RS D), 16-17 May 1967 (EFS), 20 May 1967 (LG D), 27 May 1967 (LG D), 3 June 1967 (LG D), 10 June 1967 (LG D), 17 June 1967 (LG D), 24 June 1967 (LG D)

Locations
Grim's Dyke House, Old Redding, Harrow-Weald, Middlesex; BBC's Outside Broadcast Transport Base, Kendal Avenue, London W3; Warehouse Lane, Shepherd's Bush, London W12

Working Titles
Daleks
The Daleks

Factoids
- Because of a week's holiday, Patrick Troughton was absent from the studio scenes of Episode 4.
- Incoming producer Peter Bryant took over as story editor during pre-production, as a preliminary measure to him taking on fully-fledged producership with the next story, *The Tomb of the Cybermen* (37).
- Deborah Watling had previously auditioned for the role of Polly. When it came to casting Victoria, Gerry Davis remembered seeing a photograph of the actress on the cover of *Radio Times*, dressed in Victorian garb for her appearance in Dennis Potter's play *Alice* (broadcast 13 October 1965).
- Five Daleks were employed, incorporating body parts from previous serials as well as the 1965 stage play *The Curse of the Daleks*. From this story onward, the BBC's Visual Effects Department would handle all the programme's special effects. Toy Louis Marx Daleks were used in the civil war sequences for Episode 7. They were packed with Swarfega (a gelatinous industrial hand cleaner) and detonated on cue. Lifesize dummy props made of wood, plastic and polystyrene were also blown up in the Ealing live action studio.
- The following year, *The Evil of the Daleks* was chosen as the first scheduled *Doctor Who* repeat. It was transmitted in the form of a 'thought pattern' that the Doctor shows to new companion Zoe, beginning with a brief excerpt from Episode 2 at the end of her first story, *The Wheel in Space* (43). It

bridged the gap between Seasons 5 and 6 (with a fortnight's gap in the middle for Wimbledon) with Episode 1 starting with a specially recorded voiceover as the Doctor introduces the story to Zoe.

Comment
Inexplicably adulated as a classic adventure, *The Evil of the Daleks* is just as silly, contrived and nonsensical as the much-derided 1984 story *Resurrection of the Daleks* (134). The Victorian stuff, with all the waffle about distilling the 'Dalek Factor', Troughton playing 'trains' on Daleks, and mirrors being used as a means of time travelling is as unconvincing as it is naïve. As the programme's first foray into Victorian cliché it may be of some interest, but other than the scenes set on Skaro, there is little here to excite the intellect. **40%**

Season 5

"Our lives are different to anybody else's - that's the exciting thing. There's nobody in the Universe can do what we're doing." ~ The Doctor

37) *The Tomb of the Cybermen*
Kit Pedler and Gerry Davis

Serial Code: MM
Original Transmission
Episode 1
Saturday 2 September 1967, 17.50-18.15, 6m / 57
Episode 2
Saturday 9 September 1967, 17.50-18.15, 6.4m / 57
Episode 3
Saturday 16 September 1967, 17.50-18.15, 7.2m / 38
Episode 4
Saturday 23 September 1967, 17.50-18.15, 7.4m / 34

BBC Archive
All episodes exist as 16mm b/w film recordings taken from the 405-line two-inch monochrome master videotapes (wiped in 1969).

Novelization
Doctor Who and the Tomb of the Cybermen by Gerry Davis (141/14)
Hardback:
March 1978, WH Allen (049102262X / Jeff Cummins)

Paperback:
1. March 1978, Target (0426110765 / Jeff Cummins)
2. October 1992, Target, renamed *Doctor Who - The Tomb of the Cybermen* (0426110765 / Alister Pearson)

Video
May 1992 (BBCV 4772 / Alister Pearson)

DVD
January 2002, VidFIREd clip of Episode 3, clean title sequence, title sequence tests, *The Abominable Snowmen* audio trailer, production subtitles, photo gallery, commentary by Frazer Hines and Deborah Watling (BBCDVD 1032 / Clayton Hickman)

Soundtrack
June 1993, 2 x cassettes, narrated by Jon Pertwee (0563401478 / Photomontage)

Music and Sound Effects
1. October 1998, Julian Knott, *Space Adventures: Music from Doctor Who 1963-1971*, CD (JPD 2CD / Photographs)
2. May 1997, Via Satellite, *Music from The Tomb of the Cybermen*, CD (V-Sat ASTRA 3967 / Photograph)

Script Book
August 1989, Titan Books, edited by John McElroy with background notes by Jan Vincent Rudski (1852861460 / Tony Clark)

Précis
The Doctor helps an archaeological team to reanimate some dormant Cybermen from their tomb…

Cast
Patrick Troughton (Doctor Who), Frazer Hines (Jamie), Deborah Watling (Victoria), Aubrey Richards (Professor Parry), George Pastell (Eric Klieg), Cyril Shaps (John Viner), Roy Stewart (Toberman), Clive Merrison (Jim Callum), Shirley Cooklin (Kaftan), George Roubicek (Captain Hopper), Alan Johns (Ted Rogers), Bernard Holley (Peter Haydon), Ray Grover (Crewman), Frankie Dunn (Bio-projector Operator), Michael Kilgarriff (Cyberman Controller), Reg Whitehead, Hans de Vries, Tony Harwood, John Hogan, Richard Kerley, Ronald Lee, Charles Pemberton, Kenneth Seeger, (Cybermen), Peter Hawkins (Cybermen Voices)

Crew
Visual Effects Designers Michaeljohn Harris, Peter Day, *Technical Manager* Ray Hider, *Vision Mixer* Ian Easterbrook, *Studio Lighting* Graham Southcott, *Studio Sound* Brian Hiles, *Film Cameraman* Peter Hamilton, *Film Editor* Alan Martin, *Special Sound* Brian Hodgson, *Grams Operator* Laurie Taylor, *Costume Designers* Sandra Reid, Dorothea Wallace, *Make-Up Artist* Gillian James, *Designer* Martin Johnson, *Production Assistant* Snowy Lidiard-White, *Assistant Floor Managers* Sue Willis, Catherine Sykes, *Director's Assistant* Pat Harrington, *Floor Assistant* Bob Haines, *Story Editor* Victor Pemberton, *Producer* Peter Bryant, *Director* Morris Barry

DWM Index
54	Archive
	Morris Barry interview
57	Episode Guide
108	Victor Pemberton interview
116	Season 5 Flashback
124	Gerry Davis interview
146	Victor Pemberton interview
150	Nostalgia
154	Script Book review
169	Those *Radio Times*
184	On Set
	Victor Pemberton interview
	Morris Barry interview
187	Lost Tapes
	Video review
	What The Papers Said
212	Deborah Watling interview
219	What The Censor Saw
243	Frazer Hines interview
265	*Doctor Who Magazine* Awards (8th)
281	Archive Feature
303	Time Team
307	Michael Troughton's Memories
308	Clive Merrison interview
313	DVD review
318	Victor Pemberton interview

Recording Dates
12-16 June 1967 (Location filming), 19 June 1967 (TC Puppet Theatre), 1 July 1967 (LG D), 8 July 1967 (LG D), 15 July 1967 (LG D), 22 July 1967 (LG D)

Location
Gerrards Cross Quarry, Wapsey's Wood, Gerrards Cross, Buckinghamshire

Working Title
Doctor Who and the Cybermen Planet

Factoids
- Michaeljohn Harris built about ten Cybermats, basing his design on a paper snake toy with a wriggly tail. Some were pulled along on wire, some had motors, and two were operated by a primitive radio control system.
- Cybermen costumes from *The Moonbase* (33) were reused with slight modifications, while a brand-new costume for the Controller was built, featuring a larger

cranium with no 'handles' and no chest unit. 6' 5" actor Michael Kilgarriff was chosen to play the part.
- On 26 September 1967, the BBC's new viewer comment programme *Talkback* included an item on violence in *Doctor Who*. Writer Kit Pedler attempted to defend *The Tomb of the Cybermen*'s perceived violence against vociferous criticisms by members of the public.
- Innes Lloyd stepped aside to let Peter Bryant take on the chores of producing this story - fresh from story editing the previous serial, *The Evil of the Daleks* - as a stand-alone experiment prior to his permanent position from *The Enemy of the World* (40) onward.
- The serial was promoted with a *Radio Times* cover (dated 2-8 September 1967) showing a montage of shots from the story.

Comment
For many years, this story was considered one of the untouchable classics of *Doctor Who*. That all changed in 1992 when a copy of it turned up in Hong Kong. Everyone discovered (or rediscovered) that it was good, but not *that* good. That said, the sets are wonderful, the plotting is dynamically paced and there are sterling efforts to turn the large cast into a collection of individual characters. On the downside, some of the acting is rather wooden and the dummy Controller on wires appears to have escaped from an episode of *The Goodies*. But Troughton's Doctor is uncharacteristically manipulative, which adds an extra dimension to the proceedings. **75%**

"The great hairy beastie - it's the Doctor!" ~ *Jamie*

38) *The Abominable Snowmen*
Mervyn Haisman and Henry Lincoln

Serial Code: NN
Original Transmission
Episode One
Saturday 30 September 1967, 17.25-17.50, 6.3m / 57
Episode Two
Saturday 7 October 1967, 17.25-17.50, 6m / 71
Episode Three
Saturday 14 October 1967, 17.25-17.50, 7.1m / 51
Episode Four
Saturday 21 October 1967, 17.25-17.50, 7.1m / 60

Episode Five
Saturday 28 October 1967, 17.25-17.50, 7.2m / 61
Episode Six
Saturday 4 November 1967, 17.25-17.50, 7.4m / 56

BBC Archive
Episode Two exists as a 16mm b/w film recording of the 405-line two-inch monochrome master videotape (wiped in 1969). No other episode exists in any visual medium, except for telesnaps of the whole serial and 16mm film clips of Episode Four from BBC2 programme *Late Night Line-Up* (transmitted 25 November 1967)

Novelization
Doctor Who and the Abominable Snowmen by Terrance Dicks (142/12)
Hardback:
January 1985, WH Allen (0491036604 / Andrew Skilleter)
Paperback:
1. November 1974, Target (0426105834 / Chris Achilleos)
2. 1983, Target (0426105834 / Andrew Skilleter)

Video
June 1991, Episode Two, edited, on 'The Troughton Years' (BBCV 4609 / Photographs)

DVD
1. January 2002, *Late Night Line-Up* clips on *The Tomb of the Cybermen* (DVD 1032 / Clayton Hickman)
2. November 2004, Episode 2, VidFIREd, commentary by Deborah Watling and Gary Russell, plus clips and colour location footage on 'Doctor Who - Lost in Time' (BBCDVD 1353 / Clayton Hickman)

Soundtrack
July 2001, 2 x CDs, narrated by Frazer Hines (056347856X / Photomontage)

Telesnaps
Episode One	DWM 224
Episode Two	DWM 225
Episode Three	DWM 226
Episode Four	DWM 227
Episode Five	DWM 228
Episode Six	DWM 229

Précis
In 1930s Tibet, strange creatures are massing in the Himalayas...

Cast
Patrick Troughton (Doctor Who), Frazer Hines (Jamie), Deborah Watling (Victoria), Jack Watling (Professor Travers), David Spenser (Thonmi), Wolfe Morris (Padmasambhava), Norman Jones (Khrisong), David Grey (Rinchen), Raymond Llewellyn (Sapan), Charles Morgan (Songsten),

David Baron (Ralpachan), Reg Whitehead (Yeti/Corpse of John), Tony Harwood, Richard Kerley, John Hogan (Yeti)
Crew
Visual Effects Designers Ron Oates, Ulrich Grosser, *Visual Effects Assistants* Alan Bond, Bernard Wilkie, Jack Kine, *Technical Managers* Lance Wood, Fred Wright, *Vision Mixer* Shirley Coward, *Studio Lighting* Howard King, *Studio Sound* Alan Edmonds, Norman Bennett, *Film Cameramen* Peter Bartlett, Ken Westbury, *Film Editor* Peter Barnikel, *Special Sound* Brian Hodgson, *Grams Operator* John Howell, *Costume Designer* Martin Baugh, *Make-Up Artist* Sylvia James, *Designer* Malcolm Middleton, *Production Assistant* Marjorie Yorke, *Assistant Floor Manager* Roselyn Parker, *Director's Assistant* Judy Shears, *Floor Assistant* Bernard Doe, *Story Editor* Peter Bryant, *Assistant Story Editor* Victor Pemberton, *Producer* Innes Loyd, *Director* Gerald Blake

DWM Index
57   Episode Guide
87   Deborah Watling interview
98   Frazer Hines interview
102   Archive + Fact File
107   Andrew Skilleter interview
116   Season 5 Flashback
117   Mervyn Haisman interview
169   Those *Radio Times*
177   Video review ('The Troughton Years')
180   Innes Lloyd interview
224   Archive Feature
225   Sylvia James interview
243   Frazer Hines interview
268   Mervyn Haisman interview
303   Time Team 1-3
304   Time Team 4-6
307   Michael Troughton's Memories CD review
308   Deborah Watling interview
314   Henry Lincoln interview
318   Victor Pemberton interview

Recording Dates
23-25 August 1967 (EFS), 4-9 September 1967 (Location filming), 15 September 1967 (LG D), 16 September 1967 (LG D), 23 September 1967 (LG D), 30 September 1967 (LG D), 7 October 1967 (LG D), 14 October 1967 (LG D)

Location
Nant Ffrancon Pass, Gwynedd, North Wales

Working Title
Dr Who and the Abominable Snowmen

Factoids
- Extensive filming was conducted in Snowdonia. The valley chosen to represent Tibet had also featured in the Ingrid Bergman film *The Inn of the Sixth Happiness* (1958), doubling as China when permission to shoot in that country had been denied. It would feature again as Tibet in 1968 for the perennial comedy classic *Carry On…Up The Khyber*. For its *Doctor Who* appearance, the locale proved very cold and rainy, although there was unfortunately no snow to create the illusion of the Tibetan foothills.
- Four Yeti costumes were made. They stood almost seven feet high and were made of fur skins draped over a bamboo frame. A small patch of gauze at head-height enabled the operator inside to see out.
- A filmed sequence of Padmasambhava's head dissolving was dropped from the finished programme because it was considered too unpleasant. It consisted of a latex bust of Wolfe Morris with acid poured over it, achieving an effect presumably not dissimilar to Kane's demise in *Dragonfire* (148).
- The Yeti spheres were made to move by pulling them along on a wire or guiding them from underneath a thin layer of soil. One prop was fitted with caterpillar tracks and operated by radio control.
- For the first time on the series, two studio sessions were scheduled back-to-back (rather than weekly) to help widen the gap between recording and broadcast of the episodes.
- The serial saw the first use of the BBC's foam generating machine, a device that would be used again for *Fury from the Deep* (42) and *The Seeds of Death* (48) amongst others.

Comment
Judging from the existing instalment and the soundtrack, this is a gloomy production with rather more episodes than it needs. It's certainly atmospheric, but at times it can also be rather slow. The regulars are all excellent and there is a rich vein of humour running through the story, but the Monks are a dour lot and the whole thing seems a little monotonous. **47%**

"Suddenly, one year, there was no spring." ~ *Clent*

39) The Ice Warriors
Brian Hayles

Serial Code: OO
Original Transmission
One
Saturday 11 November 1967, 17.10-17.35, 6.7m / 68
Two
Saturday 18 November 1967, 17.25-17.50, 7.1m / 71
Three
Saturday 25 November 1967, 17.25-17.50, 7.4m / 64
Four
Saturday 2 December 1967, 17.25-17.50, 7.3m / 63
Five
Saturday 9 December 1967, 17.25-17.50, 8m / 44
Six
Saturday 16 December 1967, 17.25-17.50, 7.5m / 59
BBC Archive
One, Four, Five and Six exist as 16mm b/w film recordings of the 405-line two-inch master videotapes (wiped in 1969). Two and Three do not exist in any visual medium, except as telesnaps.
Novelization
Doctor Who and the Ice Warriors by Brian Hayles (144/10)
Hardback:
March 1976, Allan Wingate (855230665 / Chris Achilleos)
Paperback:
March 1976, Target (0426108663 / Chris Achilleos)
Video
November 1998, *The Ice Warriors* One, Four, Five and Six as part of 'The Ice Warriors Collection' [BBCV 6387] with 'The Missing Years' (BBCV 6755 / Photomontage)
Telesnaps
One	DWCC 24
Two	DWM 217
Three	DWCC 25
Four	DWM 218
Five	DWCC 26
Six	DWM 219

Précis
A frozen Martian warrior is defrosted at a scientific base during Earth's second Ice Age…
Cast
Patrick Troughton (Doctor Who), Frazer Hines (Jamie), Deborah Watling (Victoria), Peter Barkworth (Clent), Wendy Gifford (Miss Garrett), George Waring (Arden), Peter Diamond (Davis), Angus Lennie (Storr), Peter Sallis (Penley), Roy Skelton (Computer Voice), Bernard Bresslaw (Varga), Malcolm Taylor (Walters), Roger Jones (Zondal), Sonny Caldinez (Turoc), Tony Harwood (Rintan), Michael Attwell (Isbur), Tony Harwood (Double for Varga)
Crew
Visual Effects Bernard Wilkie, Ron Oates, *Technical Manager* Tommy Dawson, *Vision Mixer* Jim Stevens, *Studio Lighting* Sam Neeter, *Studio Sound* Bryan Forgham, *Film Cameraman* Brian Langley, *Film Editor* Malcolm Lockey, *Special Sound* Brian Hodgson, *Grams Operator* Pat Heigham, *Incidental Music* Dudley Simpson, *Costume Designer* Martin Baugh, *Make-Up Artist* Sylvia James, *Designer* Jeremy Davies, *Production Assistant* Snowy Lidiard-White, *Assistant Floor Manager* Quenton Annis, *Director's Assistant* Sheenagh Tuckwell, *Floor Assistant* Alan Benson, *Story Editors* Peter Bryant, Victor Pemberton, *Producer* Innes Lloyd, *Director* Derek Martinus
DWM Index
57	Episode Guide
87	Deborah Watling interview
94	History of the Ice Warriors
	Novelization review
	Brian Hayles Retrospective
108	Derek Martinus interview
116	Season 5 Flashback
143	Innes Lloyd interview
149	Archive 1
150	Archive 2 + Fact File
169	Those *Radio Times*
210	Angus Lennie interview
225	Sylvia James interview
243	Frazer Hines interview
	Derek Martinus interview
271	Coming In From The Cold
	Video review
303	Archive Feature
304	Time Team 1-5
305	Time Team 6
318	Victor Pemberton interview

Recording Dates
25-29 September 1967 (EFS), 2 October 1967 (EFS), 21 October 1967 (LG D), 28 October 1967 (LG D), 4 November 1967 (LG D), 11 November 1967 (LG D), 18 November 1967 (LG D), 25 November 1967 (LG D)

Working Title
Doctor Who and the Ice Warriors
Factoids
- *Carry On* star Bernard Bresslaw appeared as the Ice Warrior leader Varga, but shooting for *Carry On Doctor* (1967) - in which he played patient Ken Biddle - prevented him from being present during the Ealing filming session. Tony Harwood, one of the non-speaking Warriors, doubled for him.
- The reptilian Ice Warrior costumes consisted of a two-part fibreglass shell for the torso with latex rubber arms and legs. Lighter versions of the helmets were requested for the studio sessions as they had proved too uncomfortable during the Ealing pre-filming.
- The serial was promoted after the final episode of *The Abominable Snowman* (38) with a specially shot 75-second trailer featuring actors Peter Barkworth and Peter Sallis addressing the viewers in character.

Comment
Despite being ostensibly a character piece, *The Ice Warriors* offers little character development. Although the Ice Warriors are impressive creations, the production suffers from an extremely slow pace and endless dialogue scenes. Clent argues with the Doctor (and just about everyone else) all through the story, while the hermit-like Penley offers up nothing much useful more than a ragtag of snide and cynical remarks. Hayles' script is often extremely articulate, but unfortunately it's also very dull.
35%

"Why did I ever leave Woolamaloo?" ~ *Griffin the Chef*

40) The Enemy of the World
David Whitaker

Serial Code: PP
Original Transmission
Episode 1
Saturday 23 December 1967, 17.25-17.50, 6.8m / 89
Episode 2
Saturday 30 December 1967, 17.25-17.50, 7.6m / 75
Episode 3
Saturday 6 January 1968, 17.25-17.50, 7.1m / 79
Episode 4
Saturday 13 January 1968, 17.25-17.50, 7.8m / 66
Episode 5
Saturday 20 January 1968, 17.25-17.50, 6.9m / 73
Episode 6
Saturday 27 January 1968, 17.25-17.50, 8.3m / 55

BBC Archive
Episode 3 exists as a 16mm b/w film recording of the 625-line two-inch monochrome master videotape (wiped in 1969). The other episodes do not exist in any visual medium, except for telesnaps (excluding Episode 4).

Novelization
Doctor Who and the Enemy of the World by Ian Marter (127/10)
Hardback:
March 1981, WH Allen (0491029721 / Bill Donohoe)
Paperback:
1. April 1981, Target (0426201264 / Bill Donohoe)
2. May 1993, Target, renamed *Doctor Who - The Enemy of the World* (0426201264 / Alister Pearson)

Video
June 1991, Episode 3 on 'The Troughton Years' (BBCV 4609 / Photographs)

DVD
November 2004, Episode 3, VidFIREd, on 'Doctor Who - Lost in Time' (BBCDVD 1353 / Clayton Hickman)

Soundtrack
August 2002, 2 x CDs, narrated by Frazer Hines (0563535032 / Max Ellis)

Telesnaps
Episode 1	DWM 273
Episode 2	DWM 274
Episode 3	DWM 275
Episode 5	DWM 276
Episode 6	DWM 277

Précis
In Australia of the near future, the Doctor bears an uncanny resemblance to mad dictator Salamander…

Cast
Patrick Troughton (Doctor Who/Salamander), Frazer Hines (Jamie), Deborah Watling (Victoria), Bill Kerr (Giles Kent), Colin Douglas (Donald Bruce), Mary Peach (Astrid), Henry Stamper (Anton), Rhys McConnochie (Rod), Simon Cain (Curly), Milton Johns (Benik), George Pravda (Denes), David Nettheim (Fedorin), Carmen Munroe (Fariah), Reg Lye (Griffin the Chef),

Christopher Burgess (Swann), Adam Verney (Colin), Margaret Hickey (Mary), Gordon Faith, Elliott Cairnes (Guard Captains), Andrew Staines (Sergeant to Benik), Bill Lyons (Denes' Guard), Bob Anderson (Fighting Guard), William McGuirk (Corridor Guard), Dibbs Mather (Caravan Guard), Peter Diamond (Double for Doctor Who/Double for Salamander), KR Morgan (Double for Doctor Who), Richard Halifax (Double for Jamie), Sarah Lisemore (Double for Victoria/Shelter Person), David Troughton (Guard)

Crew
Technical Manager Fred Wright, *Vision Mixer* Clive Halls, *Studio Lighting* Howard King, *Studio Sound* Tony Millier, *Film Cameraman* Fred Hamilton, *Film Editor* Philip Barnikel, *Special Sound* Brian Hodgson, *Grams Operators* Pat Heigham, Bruce Englefield, Laurie Taylor, *Costume Designer* Martin Baugh, *Make-Up Artist* Sylvia James, *Designer* Christopher Pemsel, *Production Assistant* Martin Lisemore, *Assistant Floor Manager* Edwina Verner, *Director's Assistant* Patricia Stern, *Floor Assistant* Roger Singleton-Turner, *Story Editor* Peter Bryant, *Assistant Story Editor* Derrick Sherwin, *Associate Story Editor* Terrance Dicks, *Producer* Innes Lloyd, *Director* Barry Letts

DWM Index
57	Episode Guide
93	Ian Marter interview
98	Archive + Fact File
	Frazer Hines interview
	Whitaker's World of *Doctor Who*
116	Season 5 Flashback
121	Ian Marter Tribute
125	Novelization review
169	Those *Radio Times*
177	Video review ('The Troughton Years')
200	Whitaker's World
	Whitaker's novelization proposal
219	Archive Feature
	Milton Johns interview
270	Barry Letts interview
273	TV review
305	Time Team
307	Michael Troughton's Memories
321	CD review

Recording Dates
5-9 November 1967 (Location filming), 10-11 November 1967 (EFS), 13 November 1967 (EFS), 2 December 1967 (LG D), 9 December 1967 (LG D), 16 December 1967 (LG D), 23 December 1967 (LG D), 30 December 1967 (LG D), 6 January 1968 (LG D)

Locations
Climping Beach, Littlehampton, West Sussex; BBC Villiers House and Walpole Park, Ealing, London W5

Working Title
Dr Who and the Enemy of the World

Factoids
- Tardis scenes for Episode 6 were filmed at Ealing Studios. To combine Salamander and the Doctor in the same shot, it was planned to film half the picture with Troughton as the Doctor, rewind the film, and then shoot the other half with him playing the villain. However, the film jammed inside the camera and so only a small portion of the footage was usable. (During studio recordings, Salamander and the Doctor never meet, necessitating much out-of-sequence recording but no complex split-screen effects.)
- For the first time on the series a helicopter was used, alongside a four-seater hovercraft, to add excitement to the beach scenes in Episode 1.
- Episode 3 was the first *Doctor Who* instalment to be recorded on 625-line videotape. BBC2 had been broadcasting on 625-lines since its launch on 20 April 1964, but most televisions were still only capable of receiving the inferior 405-line signal.
- Frazer Hines and Deborah Watling took a week's holiday halfway through the story and so were absent during Episode 4.
- To coincide with Episode 5, the *Radio Times* (dated 20-26 January) ran a feature entitled 'The Monstrous World of Doctor Who' and promoted it with its first colour *Doctor Who* cover (using a photograph of Troughton from *The Ice Warriors*, 39).

Comment
More Len Deighton than Ian Fleming, *The Enemy of the World* is a brave stab at a credible futuristic thriller with political machinations replacing the monsters. Unusually, nothing much is made of the Australian background to the story, and this adds to the 'ordinary' feeling of much of the narrative. The only OTT element is Salamander himself, with Troughton giving a masterclass in villainy complete with outrageous Mexican accent and fake tan. As if to contrast this, his performance as the Doctor is especially charming. **68%**

"All these tunnels look the same to me." ~
Victoria Waterfield

41) *The Web of Fear*
Mervyn Haisman and Henry Lincoln

Serial Code: QQ
Original Transmission
Episode 1
Saturday 3 February 1968, 17.25-17.50, 7.2m / 82
Episode 2
Saturday 10 February 1968, 17.15-17.40, 6.8m / 80
Episode 3
Saturday 17 February 1968, 17.25-17.50, 7m / 71
Episode 4
Saturday 24 February 1968, 17.25-17.50, 8.4m / 52
Episode 5
Saturday 2 March 1968, 17.25-17.50, 8m / 48
Episode 6
Saturday 9 March 1968, 17.25-17.50, 8.3m / 36
BBC Archive
Episode 1 exists as a 16mm b/w film recording of the 625-line two-inch monochrome master videotape (wiped in 1969). The other episodes do not exist in any visual medium, except for telesnaps of the whole serial and New Zealand censor clips from Episodes 2, 4 and 5.
Novelization
Doctor Who and the Web of Fear by Terrance Dicks (127/14)
Hardback:
1. August 1976, Allan Wingate (0855230738 / Chris Achilleos)
Paperback:
1. August 1976, Target (0426110846 / Chris Achilleos)
2. 1983, Target (0426110846 / Andrew Skilleter)
3. December 1993, Target, renamed *Doctor Who - The Web of Fear* (0426110846 / Alister Pearson)
Video
November 2003, Episode 1 as part of *'The Reign of Terror* Collectors' Set' [BBCV 7335 / Photomontage] with *The Faceless Ones* 1, 3 (BBCV 7539 / Photomontage)
DVD
1. February 2003, New Zealand censor cuts on *The Seeds of Death* (BBCDVD 1151 / Clayton Hickman)
2. November 2004, Episode 1, VidFIREd, commentary by Deborah Watling, Derrick Sherwin and Gary Russell, plus clips on 'Doctor Who - Lost in Time' (BBCDVD 1353 / Clayton Hickman)

Soundtrack
1. March 2000, 3 x CDs, narrated by Frazer Hines (0563553820 / Max Ellis)
2. August 2002, trailer on CD2 of *The Enemy of the World* (0563535032 / Max Ellis)
Music and Sound Effects
1. October 1998, Julian Knott, *Space Adventures: Music from Doctor Who 1963-1971*, CD (JPD 2CD / Photographs)
2. May 2000, *Doctor Who at the BBC Radiophonic Workshop: Volume 1 - The Early Years 1963-1969*, CD (WMSF 6023-2 / Photographs)
Stage Play
May-June 2000, adapted by Rob Thrush, performed by Bedlam Theatre Company and Dramatis Personae (Portsmouth Arts Centre)
Telesnaps
Episode 1   *DWCC* 18
Episode 2   *DWM* 211
Episode 3   *DWCC* 19
Episode 4   *DWM* 212
Episode 5   *DWCC* 20
Episode 6   *DWM* 213
Précis
The abominable snowmen are at large in the London Underground…
Cast
Patrick Troughton (Doctor Who), Frazer Hines (Jamie), Deborah Watling (Victoria), Jack Watling (Professor Travers), Tina Packer (Anne Travers), Nicholas Courtney (Colonel Lethbridge-Stewart), Jack Woolgar (Staff Sergeant Arnold/Great Intelligence Voice), Frederick Schrecker (Silverstein), Rod Beacham (Corporal Lane), Richardson Morgan (Corporal Blake), Ralph Watson (Captain Knight), Jon Rollason (Harold Chorley), Derek Pollitt (Driver Evans), Stephen Whittaker (Craftsman Weams), James Jordan, Joseph O'Connell (Soldiers), John Levene, Gordon Stothard, Colin Warman, John Lord, Jeremy King, Roger Jacombs (Yeti), Bert Sims (Corpse of Newspaper Seller)
Crew
Fight Arranger Derek Ware, *Stuntmen* Douglas Kirk, Tim Condren, Terry Walsh, Derek Martin, *Visual Effects Designer* Ron Oates, *Technical Manager* Clive Leighton, *Vision Mixer* John Barclay, *Studio Lighting* Geoff Shaw, *Studio Sound* Ray Angel, *Film Cameramen* Alan Jonas, Jimmy Court, *Film Editors* Philip Barnikel, Colin Hobson, *Special Sound* Brian Hodgson, *Grams Operator* Brian Duffett, *Costume Designer* Martin Baugh, *Make-Up Artist* Sylvia James, *Designer* David Myerscough-Jones, *Production Assistant* Gareth Gwenlan, *Assistant Floor Manager*

Roselyn Parker, *Director's Assistant* Evelyn Cowdrey, *Floor Assistant* Paul Cole, *Story Editor* Derrick Sherwin, *Producer* Peter Bryant, *Director* Douglas Camfield

DWM Index
58   Episode Guide
72   Nicholas Courtney interview
82   John Levene interview
87   Deborah Watling interview
93   Douglas Camfield interview
98   Frazer Hines interview
115   Nostalgia
116   Season 5 Flashback
117   Mervyn Haisman interview
151   Derek Ware interview
169   Those *Radio Times*
187   What The Papers Said
      AJ Mitchell interview
235   Archive Feature
243   Frazer Hines interview
265   *Doctor Who Magazine* Awards (10th place)
268   Mervyn Haisman interview
291   CD review
294   Stage Play review
305   Time Team 1
306   Time Team 2-6
307   Michael Troughton's Memories
308   Deborah Watling interview
314   Henry Lincoln interview
317   Derek Ware interview
337   Video review

Recording Dates
15 December 1967 (EFS), 17 December 1967 (Location filming), 18 December 1967 (EFS), 20 December 1967 (EFS), 3 January 1968 (EFS remount), 8 January 1968 (TC Puppet Theatre), 13 January 1968 (LG D), 14 January 1968 (Location filming remount), 15 January 1968 (Location stills photography), 20 January 1968 (LG D), 27 January 1968 (LG D), 3 February 1968 (LG D), 10 February 1968 (LG D), 17 February 1968 (LG D)

Locations
Covent Garden, London WC2; Ealing Film Studios backlot, Ealing, London W5

Working Title
Dr Who and the Web of Fear

Factoids
- Even before *The Abominable Snowmen* (38) aired, Mervyn Haisman and Henry Lincoln had been commissioned to provide a Yeti sequel set in the present day.
- Nicholas Courtney was originally given the part of Captain Knight. But when David Langton - the actor playing Corporal Lethbridge-Stewart (originally just Lethbridge) - had to back out of the story at short notice, Courtney was given this larger role instead. John Levene, who would play UNIT's Sergeant Benton, was a Yeti operator.
- Four new Yetis were made by freelance prop manufacturers Jack and John Lovell. Their bodies were made of grey yak hair with a band of skin around the waist. To make them scarier than their predecessors, they were given larger claws and glowing eyes; a modulated electronic roar was added by Brian Hodgson of the Radiophonic Workshop.
- Patrick Troughton recorded a special trailer for this story during the Episode 1 studio session, in which he warned the viewers that the Yeti would be more frightening than the last time they had seen them. It was transmitted after Episode 6 of the previous story, *The Enemy of the World*.
- Patrick Troughton was absent for Episode 2 due to a planned holiday.

Comment
Iconic *Doctor Who* - dark tunnels, soldiers, hairy monsters, a deserted London, a traitor in the fold, mind possession, disembodied voices...it's all here. And if Episode 1 is anything to go by, this adventure must have been one of the best-looking yet. As a gripping story in its own right, as well as a template for future Jon Pertwee UNIT stories, this really is unbeatable. **92%**

"It's down there... in the darkness...in the pipeline.... ...waiting..." ~ *Van Lutyens*

42) Fury from the Deep
Victor Pemberton

Serial Code: RR
Original Transmission
Episode 1
Saturday 16 March 1968, 17.15-17.40, 8.2m / 46
Episode 2
Saturday 23 March 1968, 17.15-17.40, 7.9m / 40
Episode 3
Saturday 30 March 1968, 17.15-17.40, 7.7m / 47
Episode 4
Saturday 6 April 1968, 17.15-17.40, 6.6m / 62
Episode 5
Saturday 13 April 1968, 17.15-17.40, 5.9m / 73

Episode 6
Saturday 20 April 1968, 17.15-17.40, 6.9m / 42
BBC Archive
None of the episodes exist in any visual medium, except for telesnaps of the whole serial, Australian 16mm b/w film recorded censor clips of Episodes 2, 4 and 5, 16mm b/w film footage from Episode 1 reused in *The War Games* Episode Ten, and 16mm b/w unused 'trims' from Episode 6. The 625-line two-inch monochrome master videotapes were wiped in 1974, and the 16mm b/w film recordings were junked the same year.
Novelization
Doctor Who - Fury from the Deep by Victor Pemberton (189/12)
Hardback:
May 1986, WH Allen (0491036523 / David McAllister)
Paperback:
October 1986, Target (0426202597 / David McAllister)
Video
November 1998, Australian censor clips on 'The Missing Years', part of 'The Ice Warriors Collection' [BBCV 6387 / Photomontage] with *The Ice Warriors* 1, 4-6 (BBCV 6766 / Photomontage)
DVD
November 2004, clips and colour studio footage on 'Doctor Who - Lost in Time' (BBCDVD 1353 / Clayton Hickman)
Soundtrack
October 1993, 2 x cassettes, narrated by Tom Baker (0563401079 / Photomontage)
Music and Sound Effects
May 2000, *Doctor Who at the BBC Radiophonic Workshop: Volume 1 - The Early Years 1963-1969*, CD (WMSF 6023-2 / Photographs)
Stage Play
March 2002, adapted by Rob Thrush, performed by Bedlam Theatre Company and Dramatis Personae (New Theatre Royal, Portsmouth)
Telesnaps
Episode 1	*DWCC* 15
Episode 2	*DWM* 208
Episode 3	*DWCC* 16
Episode 4	*DWM* 209
Episode 5	*DWCC* 17
Episode 6	*DWM* 210

Précis
A terrifying seaweed creature is possessing the inhabitants of a North Sea gas refinery...
Cast
Patrick Troughton (Doctor Who), Frazer Hines (Jamie), Deborah Watling (Victoria), John Abineri (Van Lutyens), Victor Maddern (Robson), Roy Spencer (Harris), June Murphy (Maggie Harris), Graham Leaman (Price), John Garvin (Carney), Hubert Rees (Chief Engineer), Richard Mayes (Chief Baxter), John Gill (Oak), Bill Burridge (Quill), Margaret John (Megan Jones), Brian Cullingford (Perkins), Peter Ducrow (Guard), Peter Day (Weed Monster)
Crew
Visual Effects Designers Peter Day, Len Hutton, *Technical Manager* Reg Callaghan, *Vision Mixers* Derek Kibble, Clive Doig, *Studio Lighting* Sam Neeter, *Studio Sound* David Hughes, *Film Cameraman* Ken Westbury, *Film Editor* Colin Hobson, *Special Sound* Brian Hodgson, *Grams Operator* Laurie Taylor, *Incidental Music* Dudley Simpson, *Costume Designer* Martin Baugh, *Make-Up Artist* Sylvia James, *Designer* Peter Kindred, *Production Assistant* Michael Briant, *Assistant Floor Manager* Margot Hayhoe, *Director's Assistant* Pat Hughes, *Floor Assistant* Barry Martin, *Story Editor* Derrick Sherwin, *Producer* Peter Bryant, *Director* Hugh David
DWM Index
58	Episode Guide
87	Deborah Watling interview
108	Victor Pemberton interview
112	Novelization review
116	Season 5 Flashback
133	Target Survey Winner
145	Archive 1
146	Archive 2 + Fact File
	Victor Pemberton interview
169	Those *Radio Times*
187	What The Papers Said
206	Victor Maddern interview
	John Abineri interview
208	CD review
263	Michael E Briant interview
277	Archive Feature
306	Time Team 1-3
307	Michael Troughton's Memories
308	Time Team 4-6
	Deborah Watling interview
318	Victor Pemberton interview
	Stage Play review
341	CD review (remastered)

Recording Dates
4-6 February 1968 (Location filming), 7-9 February 1968 (EFS), 12 February 1968 (Location filming), 24 February 1968 (LG D), 2 March 1968 (LG D), 5-6 March 1968 (EFS), 9 March 1968 (LG D), 16 March 1968 (LG D), 23 March 1968 (LG D), 29 March 1968 (TC1)
Locations
Botony Bay, Kingsgate, Kent; Red Sand Fort, Thames Estuary; Denham Aerodrome, Denham Green, Buckinghamshire

Working Titles
Doctor Who and the Colony of Devils
The Colony of Devils
Doctor Who and Fury from the Deep
Factoids
- Victor Pemberton's storyline borrowed heavily from his seven-part BBC radio play *The Slide*. Starring Maurice Denham and Roger Delgado (later to appear as The Master in *Doctor Who*), the chilling story of sentient mud oozing from an earthquake site was broadcast on the BBC Light Programme from 13 February to 27 March 1966.
- The means of defeating the Weed Creature was originally to have been the wailing of Jamie's bagpipes, but this was rewritten to become Victoria's screams, a not-so-subtle dig at her loud reaction to most of the alien threats she encountered in the series.
- The location for the gas rig was Red Sand Fort, a cluster of seven towers rising on concrete legs in the middle of the Thames Estuary. Designed by Guy Maunsell in 1943 as defence against German bombing raids, they housed 1230 men in total and successfully destroyed 22 planes, 30 flying bombs and even a German U-boat. By the 1960s they were occupied by pirate radio stations, such as Screaming Lord Sutch's Radio Sutch. Several towers have since collapsed or been demolished, but English Heritage (subject to funding) is planning to restore the remaining forts to their former glory.
- Two helicopters were hired for this story. One, a two-man Hughes 300, was used to suspend the quarter-sized Tardis model onto the surface of the sea at Botony Bay, near Margate. It was also used to perform the dangerous stunt of flying between the legs of a sea fort; pilot Mike Smith performed the feat with only five feet clearance either side of his rotor blades. Foam was pumped onto Botony Bay beach from the other helicopter, an Alouette, which also captured footage of the Red Sand Fort stunt and the Doctor's dinghy being paddled to the shore in Episode 1.
- The sonic screwdriver makes its first appearance in Episode 1. Victor Pemberton's script referred to it as a normal screwdriver, but producer Peter Bryant thought a futuristic one that used sound waves would be more suitable. The prop itself was constructed by Peter Day along the lines of a simple pen-torch.

Comment
With no episodes surviving, *Fury from the Deep* lives on in the spine-chilling soundtrack. And what a soundtrack it is! As the impeller shaft echoes to the deep throb of the Weed Creature's terrifying heartbeat, this is undeniably *Doctor Who* at its most spooky. The cadaverous double-act of Oak and Quill are wonderful (despite Dudley Simpson's ridiculous music) and every actor gives of their all, especially Victor Maddern as the psychotic boss Robson - one in a long line of borderline insane directors, scientists or commanders that seems to be the programme's stock-in-trade. Strange though, considering the morbid nature of the story, that there are no on-screen deaths. **92%**

"I imagine you have orders to destroy me." ~ The Doctor

43) *The Wheel in Space*
David Whitaker, from a story by Kit Pedler

Serial Code: SS
Original Transmission
Episode 1
Saturday 27 April 1968, 17.15-17.40, 7.2m / 40
Episode 2
Saturday 4 May 1968, 17.15-17.40, 6.9m / 59
Episode 3
Saturday 11 May 1968, 17.15-17.40, 7.5m / 40
Episode 4
Saturday 18 May 1968, 18.00-18.25, 8.6m / 28
Episode 5
Saturday 25 May 1968, 17.15-17.40, 6.8m / 44
Episode 6
Saturday 1 June 1968, 18.05-18.30, 6.5m / 51
BBC Archive
Episode 3 exists as a 16mm b/w film recording of the 625-line two-inch monochrome videotape master (wiped in 1969), and Episode 6 exists as a 35mm film recording of the same (with two versions of the soundtrack - one with music and sound effects, and one without). The other episodes do not exist in any visual medium, except for telesnaps of the whole serial, a brief clip of Episode 1 from *The War Games* Episode Ten and an Australian censor clip from Episode 4.
Novelization
Doctor Who - The Wheel in Space by Terrance Dicks (143/18)
Hardback:
March 1988, WH Allen (0491033567 / Ian Burgess)

Paperback:
August 1988, Target (0426203216 / Ian Burgess)
Video
July 1992, Episodes 3 and 6 on 'Cybermen - The Early Years' (BBCV 4813 / Photographs)
DVD
1. February 2003, Australian censor clip on *The Seeds of Death* (BBCDVD 1151 / Clayton Hickman)
2. November 2004, Episodes 3 and 6, VidFIREd, commentary by Derrick Sherwin and Tristan de Vere Cole on the latter, plus clips, on 'Doctor Who - Lost in Time' (BBCDVD 1353 / Clayton Hickman)
Music and Sound Effects
1. July 1993, *Doctor Who: 30 Years at the Radiophonic Workshop*, CD (BBCCD 871 / Photomontage)
2. May 2000, *Doctor Who at the BBC Radiophonic Workshop: Volume 1 - The Early Years 1963-1969*, CD (WMSF 6023-2 / Photographs)
Telesnaps
Episode 1	*DWCC* 21
Episode 2	*DWM* 214
Episode 3	*DWCC* 22
Episode 4	*DWM* 215
Episode 5	*DWCC* 23
Episode 6	*DWM* 216

Précis
Cybermen and their Cybermats invade a space station to spearhead an attack on Earth…
Cast
Patrick Troughton (Doctor Who), Frazer Hines (Jamie), Wendy Padbury (Zoe), Deborah Watling (Victoria), Eric Flynn (Leo Ryan), Michael Turner (Jarvis Bennett), Anne Ridler (Dr Gemma Corwyn), Clare Jenkins (Tanya Lernov), Donald Sumpter (Enrico Casali), Michael Goldie (Elton Laleham), Kenneth Watson (Bill Duggan), Derrick Gilbert (Armand Vallance), Kevork Malikyan (Kemel Rudkin), Peter Laird (Chang), James Mellor (Sean Flannigan), Freddie Foote (Servo Robot), Jerry Holmes, Gordon Stothard, Tony Harwood (Cybermen), Peter Hawkins (Cybermen Voices/Earth Control Voice), Roy Skelton (Cybermen Voices/Wheel Voice), Chris Jeffries (Double for Doctor Who), Ken Gibson (Double for Jamie), Dorothy Ford (Double for Gemma Corwyn)
Crew
Visual Effects Designer Bill King (Trading Post), *Technical Manager* Peter Valentine, *Vision Mixers* Clive Doig, Shirley Coward, *Studio Lighting* Mike Jefferies, *Studio Sound* John Holmes, *Film Cameraman* Jimmy Court, *Film Editor* Ron Fry, *Special Sound* Brian Hodgson, *Grams Operators* Laurie Taylor, Dave Thompson, *Incidental Music* Brian Hodgson, *Costume Designer* Martin Baugh, *Make-Up Artist* Sylvia James, *Designer* Derek Dodd, *Production Assistant* Ian Strachan, *Assistant Floor Manager* Marcia Wheeler, *Director's Assistant* Rita Dunn, *Floor Assistant* Tony Hare, *Story Editor* Derrick Sherwin, *Producer* Peter Bryant, *Director* Tristan de Vere Cole

DWM Index
58	Episode Guide
74	Archive
98	Whitaker's World of *Doctor Who*
135	Novelization review
169	Those *Radio Times*
187	What The Papers Said
189	Video review ('Cybermen - The Early Years')
208	Wendy Padbury interview
239	Vox Pops
254	Archive Feature
308	Time Team 1-5 Michael Troughton's Memories
309	Time Team 6
343	CD review
350	DVD review

Recording Dates
18-22 March 1968 (EFS), 5 April 1968 (LG D), 12 April 1968 (TC3), 19 April 1968 (TC1), 26 April 1968 (TC3), 3 May 1968 (RS 1), 10 May 1968 (RS 1)
Working Titles
The Space Wheel
Dr Who and the Wheel in Space
Doctor Who and the Wheel in Space
Factoids
- Susan George, then girlfriend of Frazer Hines, auditioned for the part of new companion Zoe. Pauline Collins was again asked to consider joining the series (see *The Faceless Ones*, 35) but once more declined. The successful actress, 20-year-old Wendy Padbury, auditioned at Lime Grove during recording of *The Web of Fear* (41).
- Two new Cybermen costumes were constructed by Martin Baugh. The body was now a silver wetsuit, rather than a jumpsuit, and the helmet and chest unit (worn upside-down) were modified versions of the ones seen in *The Moonbase* (33). A third one, from *The Tomb of the Cybermen* (37), was used in the background of the filmed space-walking sequence in Episode 6. Four new radio-controlled Cybermats were built by outside contractor Bill King and Trading Post.

- *The Wheel in Space* was shot in five different studios (including Ealing) - a record number.
- The end of Episode 6 led into a repeat showing of *The Evil of the Daleks* (36), as the Doctor showed Zoe what sort of dangers she might be up against. It was transmitted from the 405-line master videotape.

Comment
After a terrifying tale of formless horrors under the sea, we come down to earth with a bang with this insipid, time-wasting exercise in rehashing old ideas and padding them to interminable length. The setting of Station Three is blandly-lit and uninspiring, while the Cybermen are rather obviously not much of a threat, seeing as there's only two of them. The Cybermats are as effective as before, although the Servo Robot looks unconvincing and is hardly necessary to the plot (such as it is). Judging by the existing episodes, I'm not in any hurry for the others to be found. **25%**

Season 6

"Haste is not in the Dulcian tradition." ~ *Councillor*

44) The Dominators

Norman Ashby (pen-name n for Mervyn Haisman and Henry Lincoln), rewritten by Derrick Sherwin and Terrance Dicks

Serial Code: TT
Original Transmission
Episode 1
Saturday 10 August 1968, 17.15-17.40, 6.1m / 54
Episode 2
Saturday 17 August 1968, 17.15-17.40, 5.9m / 61
Episode 3
Saturday 24 August 1968, 17.15-17.40, 5.4m / 65
Episode 4
Saturday 31 August 1968, 17.15-17.40, 7.5m / 33
Episode 5
Saturday 7 September 1968, 17.15-17.40, 5.9m / 64

BBC Archive
Episodes 1, 2, 4 and 5 exist as 16mm b/w film recordings of the 625-line two-inch monochrome master videotapes (wiped in 1969), while Episode 3 exists as a 35mm b/w film recording of the same.

Novelization
Doctor Who - The Dominators by Ian Marter (126/10)
Hardback:
April 1984, WH Allen (0491032927 / Andrew Skilleter)
Paperback:
1. July 1984, Target (0426195531 / Andrew Skilleter)
2. September 1988, Star, as part of 'Doctor Who Classics' with *Doctor Who - The Krotons* (0352322659 / Andrew Skilleter)
3. February 1991, Target (0426195531 / Alister Pearson)

Video
September 1990, edited (BBCV 4406 / Alister Pearson)

Music and Sound Effects
1. July 1993, *Doctor Who: 30 Years at the Radiophonic Workshop*, CD (BBCCD 871 / Photomontage)
2. May 2000, *Doctor Who at the BBC Radiophonic Workshop: Volume 1 - The Early Years 1963-1969*, CD (WMSF 6023-2 / Photographs)

Précis
War-hungry Dominators attempt to enslave the peaceful inhabitants of Dulkis...

Cast
Patrick Troughton (Doctor Who), Frazer Hines (Jamie), Wendy Padbury (Zoe), Ronald Allen (Rago), Kenneth Ives (Toba), Walter Fitzgerald (Senex), Arthur Cox (Cully), Philip Voss (Wahed), Malcolm Terris (Etnin), Nicolette Pendrell (Tolata), Felicity Gibson (Kando), Giles Block (Teel), Alan Gerrard (Bovem), Brian Cant (Tensa), Johnson Bayly (Balan), Ronald Mansell, John Cross (Council Members), John Hicks, Gary Smith, Freddie Wilson (Quarks), Sheila Grant (Quark Voices/Intercom Voice), Chris Jeffries (Double for Doctor Who), John Tucker (Double for Balan's Corpse)

Crew
Visual Effects Designer Ron Oates, *Graphics* Peter Netley, *Technical Manager* Reg Jones, *Vision Mixer* Bill Morton, *Studio Lighting* Sam Neeter, *Studio Sound* Richard Chubb, *Film Cameraman* Peter Hamilton, *Film Editor* Chris Hayden, *Special Sound* Brian Hodgson, *Grams Operator* Dave Thompson, *Incidental Music* Brian Hodgson (stock), *Costume Designer* Martin Baugh, *Make-Up Artist* Sylvia James, *Designer* Barry Newbery, *Production Assistant* John Bruce, *Assistant Floor Manager* Barbara Stuart, *Director's Assistant* Joan Elliott, *Floor Assistants* David Smith, Guy Francis, *Script Editor* Derrick Sherwin, *Assistant Script Editor* Terrance Dicks, *Producer* Peter Bryant, *Director* Morris Barry

DWM Index

58	Episode Guide
98	Frazer Hines interview
117	Mervyn Haisman interview
120	Wendy Padbury interview
121	Ian Marter Tribute
125	Novelization review
166	Derrick Sherwin interview
167	Video review
169	Those *Radio Times*
173	Comic Assassins
239	Vox Pops
243	Frazer Hines interview
262	Archive Feature
268	Mervyn Haisman interview
308	Michael Troughton's Memories
309	Time Team
314	Henry Lincoln interview

Recording Dates
25-26 April 1968 (Location filming), 28-29 April 1968 (Location filming), 30 April-1 May 1968 (EFS), 2-3 May 1968 (Location filming), 17 May 1968 (TC4), 24 May 1968 (TC4), 31 May 1968 (TC3), 7 June 1968 (TC3), 14 June 1968 (TC3)

Locations
Gerrards Cross Sand and Gravel Quarry, Wapsey's Wood, Gerrards Cross, Buckinghamshire; Olley Sand Pit, Trottiscliffe, Kent

Working Title
Dr Who and the Dominators

Factoids
- Mervyn Haisman and Henry Lincoln were upset with producer Peter Bryant because their six-part morality play had had one of its episodes cut and its emphasis changed from intellectual discussion to physical violence. They were also concerned about not having sole ownership of the Quarks (the BBC offered them 25%), especially as the BBC had allowed them to be used in a *TV Comic* strip without the authors' permission. At the last minute, they withdrew their names from this story and ceased work on their third Yeti tale, *The Laird of McCrimmon*, intended to close Season 6 and write out Jamie.
- Episode 3, recorded on 35mm b/w film from a 625-line monitor, omitted the title caption in error.
- Three Quarks were built by outside contractors John and Jack Lovell from fibreglass and Perspex and operated by drama school pupils.
- Ronald Allen would become famous for playing the character of David Hunter in the original series of *Crossroads* (1964-1988)

Comment
A thought-provoking morality tale about a Fascist takeover of a 'hippy' peace-loving civilization - a remake of *The Daleks* in other words - is let down by plodding direction, *Flash Gordon* effects and a linear narrative. The two hunchbacked Dominators are mildly diverting, although their constant bickering is a distinct turn-off. Worth seeing, though, for Wendy Padbury wrapped in a see-through curtain. **40%**

"We're nowhere. It's as simple as that." ~ The Doctor

45) The Mind Robber
Derrick Sherwin (1) and Peter Ling (2-5)

Serial Code: UU
Original Transmission
Episode 1
Saturday 14 September 1968, 17.20-17.40, 6.6m / 55
Episode 2
Saturday 21 September 1968, 17.20-17.40, 6.5m / 54
Episode 3
Saturday 28 September 1968, 17.20-17.40, 7.2m / 45
Episode 4
Saturday 5 October 1968, 17.20-17.40, 7.3m / 44
Episode 5
Saturday 12 October 1968, 17.20-17.40, 6.7m / 84

Repeat Transmission
On BBC2:
Episode 1
Friday 31 January 1992, 18.50-19.10, 2.5m / 16
Episode 2
Friday 7 February 1992, 18.50-19.10, 2.6m / 20
Episode 3
Friday 14 February 1992, 19.40-20.00, 1.5m / -
Episode 4
Friday 21 February 1992, 19.40-20.00, 1.5m / -
Episode 5
Friday 28 February 1992, 18.50-19.10, 3.5m / 10

BBC Archive
All episodes exist as 16mm b/w film recordings of the 625-line two-inch monochrome master videotapes (wiped in 1969). Episode 5 also exists as a 35mm b/w film recording of the same.

Novelization
Doctor Who - The Mind Robber by Peter Ling (144/10)

Hardback:
November 1986, WH Allen (0491036825 / David McAllister)
Paperback:
1. April 1987, Target (0426202864 / David McAllister)
2. August 1990, Target (0426202864 / Alister Pearson)
Video
May 1990, edited (BBCV 4352 / Alister Pearson)
DVD
March 2005, VidFIREd, BBC2 continuity announcements, production subtitles, photo gallery, commentary by Frazer Hines, Wendy Padbury, David Maloney and Hamish Wilson (BBCDVD 1358 / Clayton Hickman)
Music and Sound Effects
1. July 1993, *Doctor Who: 30 Years at the Radiophonic Workshop*, CD (BBCCD 871 / Photomontage)
2. May 2000, *Doctor Who at the BBC Radiophonic Workshop: Volume 1 - The Early Years 1963-1969*, CD (WMSF 6023-2 / Photographs)
Précis
The Tardis is destroyed and the Doctor, Zoe and Jamie find themselves in a bizarre world of fiction...
Cast
Patrick Troughton (Doctor Who), Frazer Hines, Hamish Wilson (Jamie), Wendy Padbury (Zoe), Bernard Horsfall (Lemuel Gulliver), Emrys Jones (The Master), Christine Pirie (Princess Rapunzel/Woman's Voice), Sue Pulford (The Medusa), Christopher Robbie (The Karkus), David Cannon (Cyrano de Bergerac), Gerry Wain (Blackbeard), John Greenwood (D'Artagnan/Sir Lancelot), John Atterbury, Ralph Carrigan, Bill Wiesener, Terry Wright (White Robots), Philip Ryan (Redcoat), Barbara Loft, Martin Langley, David Reynolds, Christopher Reynolds, Timothy Horton, Sylvestra Le Tozel (Children), Goldy the Wonder Horse (Unicorn), Paul Alexander, Ian Hines (Soldiers), Richard Ireson (Soldier/Minotaur), Richard Halifax (Double for Jamie)
Crew
Fight Arrangers BH Barry, John Greenwood, *Visual Effects Designers* Jack Kine, Bernard Wilkie, *Medusa Head* John Friedlander, *Technical Managers* Fred Wright, Neil Campbell, *Vision Mixer* Geoff Walmsley, *Studio Lighting* Howard King, *Studio Sound* John Holmes, *Film Cameraman* Jimmy Court, *Film Editor* Martyn Day, *Special Sound* Brian Hodgson, *Grams Operator* Pat Heigham, *Costume Designers* Martin Baugh, Susan Wheal, *Make-Up Artist* Sylvia James, *Horse Trainer* Joan Rosaire,

Designer Evan Hercules, *Production Assistant* John Lopes, *Assistant Floor Manager* Edwina Verner, *Director's Assistant* Judy Shears, *Floor Assistant* Gavin Birkett, *Script Editor* Derrick Sherwin, *Assistant Script Editor* Terrance Dicks, *Producer* Peter Bryant, *Director* David Maloney

DWM Index
58	Episode Guide
78	Patrick Troughton interview
98	Frazer Hines interview
102	Patrick Troughton interview
108	David Maloney interview
119	Peter Ling interview
	Novelization review
120	Wendy Padbury interview
124	Archive + Fact File
162	Video review
166	Derrick Sherwin interview
169	Those *Radio Times*
177	Peter Ling interview
185	TV review (BBC2 repeat)
187	What The Papers Said
201	David Maloney interview
208	Wendy Padbury interview
239	Vox Pops
243	Frazer Hines interview
245	Archive Feature
308	Michael Troughton's Memories
309	Time Team 1-2
311	Time Team 3-5
354	DVD preview
355	DVD review

Recording Dates
9 June 1968 (Location filming), 10-11 June 1968 (TC Puppet Theatre), 12-14 June 1968 (EFS), 21 June 1968 (TC3), 28 June 1968 (TC3), 5 July 1968 (LG D), 12 July 1968 (LG D), 19 July 1968 (TC3)
Locations
Harrison's Rocks, Groombridge, Tunbridge Wells, East Sussex; Kenley Aerodrome, Kenley, Surrey
Working Titles
The Fact of Fiction
Man Power
Manpower
Factoids
- Peter Ling, the creator of ATV soap opera *Crossroads* (1964-1998, 2001-2003), based his six-part *Doctor Who* storyline around his experience of viewers thinking that fictional TV characters were real people. Cut down to four short episodes, editor Derrick Sherwin then penned a new opening instalment (gained from the previous, shortened, story *The Dominators*) using just the Tardis set, the regular characters and a white studio cyclorama.

- The four White Robots were reused from *The Prophet*, an episode of BBC2 science fiction anthology series *Out of the Unknown* broadcast on 1 January 1967.
- The make-up team covered Goldy, the horse chosen to be the unicorn in Episodes 2 and 3, with blanco (armed forces boot whitener) to turn it from light brown to white. A polystyrene horn was stuck to his forehead, as well as hair to his chin, with the scenes involving him filmed from a moving car at midnight at Kenley Aerodrome.
- The snakes in the Medusa's hair were made to move by stop-motion animation - a rare occurrence for the programme.
- Frazer Hines - whose cousin, Ian, was playing a soldier - contracted chicken pox from his neighbours and so was absent for Episode 2's recording. His appearance at the start was done out-of-sequence with Episode 3. The plot was reworked slightly to have the Doctor messing up the photofit picture so that another actor, Hamish Wilson, would play Jamie. Wilson had previously appeared in the Walt Disney film *Greyfriar's Bobby* (1961).

Comment
A beautifully realised production that has not dated in any way, *The Mind Robber* has a great many amusing, disturbing and witty moments liberally scattered throughout its oh-so-brief episodes. A postmodern take on the craft of storytelling and the role of the reader/viewer, the whole thing manages to be subversive, gripping and funny in equal measure. Easily the finest Troughton, and certainly the best in a lacklustre season. **95%**

"So this is your great vision, Vaughn - to be master of a dead world." ~ The Doctor

46) The Invasion
Derrick Sherwin, from a story by Kit Pedler

Serial Code: VV
Original Transmission
Episode 1
Saturday 2 November 1968, 17.15-17.40, 7.3m / 55
Episode 2
Saturday 9 November 1968, 17.15-17.40, 7.1m / 55
Episode 3
Saturday 16 November 1968, 17.15-17.40, 7.1m / 66
Episode 4
Saturday 23 November 1968, 17.15-17.40, 6.4m / 73
Episode 5
Saturday 30 November 1968, 17.15-17.40, 6.7m / 67
Episode 6
Saturday 7 December 1968, 17.15-17.40, 6.5m / 72
Episode 7
Saturday 14 December 1968, 17.15-17.40, 7.2m / 51
Episode 8
Saturday 21 December 1968, 17.15-17.40, 7m / 80

BBC Archive
Episodes 2, 3 and 5-8 exist as 16mm b/w film recordings of the 625-line two-inch monochrome master videotapes (wiped in 1971). Episodes 1 and 4 do not exist in any visual medium.

Novelization
Doctor Who - The Invasion by Ian Marter (159/11)
Hardback:
May 1985, WH Allen (0491033249 / Andrew Skilleter)
Paperback:
1. October 1985, Target (0426201698 / Andrew Skilleter)
2. September 1993, Target (0426201698 / Alister Pearson)

Video
June 1993, twin-pack, presented by Nicholas Courtney (BBCV 4974 / Andrew Skilleter)

Soundtrack
November 2004, 2 x CDs, narrated by Anneke Wills, in 'Doctor Who - Cybermen' collectors' tin (0563525088 / Max Ellis)

Music and Sound Effects
May 2000, *Doctor Who at the BBC Radiophonic Workshop: Volume 1 - The Early Years 1963-1969*, CD (WMSF 6023-2 / Photographs)

Précis
The Doctor helps UNIT defeat a Cyberman invasion via London's sewers...

Cast
Patrick Troughton (Doctor Who), Frazer Hines (Jamie), Wendy Padbury (Zoe), Nicholas Courtney (Brigadier Lethbridge-Stewart), Kevin Stoney (Tobias Vaughn), Peter Halliday (Packer/Cyberplanner Voice/Cybermen Voices), Sally Faulkner (Isobel), John Levene (Corporal Benton), Geoffrey Cheshire (Tracy), Ian Fairbairn (Gregory), James Thornhill (Sergeant Walters), Robert Sidaway (Captain Turner), Edward Burnham (Professor Watkins), Edward Dentith (Major

General Rutlidge), Clifford Earl (Major Branwell), Norman Hartley (Sergeant Peters), Murray Evans (Lorry Driver), Walter Randall (Patrolman), Dominic Allan (Policeman), Sheila Dunn (Phone Operator/Computer Voice), Peter Thompson (Workman/Computer Voice), Stacy Davies (Private Perkins), Douglas Camfield (Car Driver), Charles Finch (Cyberman/UNIT Soldier/Bunker Man), Pat Gorman, Derek Chaffer, John Spradbury, Terence Denville, Ralph Carrigan, Richard King, Peter Thornton (Cybermen)

Crew
Stuntmen Billy Horrigan, Alan Chuntz, Terry Walsh, *Visual Effects Designer* Bill King (Trading Post), *Technical Managers* Don Babbage, Peter Valentine, *Studio Lighting* Robbie Robinson, *Studio Sound* Alan Edmonds, Bryan Forgham, *Film Cameraman* Alan Jonas, *Film Sound* Bill Chesneau, *Film Editor* Martyn Day, *Special Sound* Brian Hodgson, *Grams Operators* Ron Arnett, Bryan Forgham, *Incidental Music* Don Harper (with Brian Hodgson and John Baker), *Costume Designer* Bobi Bartlett, *Make-Up Artist* Sylvia James, *Designer* Richard Hunt, *Production Assistant* Chris D'Oyly-John, *Assistant Floor Manager* Sue Willis, *Director's Assistant* Sue Sly, *Floor Assistant* Michael Ward, *Script Editor* Terrance Dicks, *Assistant Script Editor/Assistant Producer* Derrick Sherwin, *Producer* Peter Bryant, *Director* Douglas Camfield

DWM Index
59	Episode Guide
72	Nicholas Courtney interview
82	John Levene interview
93	Douglas Camfield interview
	Ian Marter interview
96	Novelization review
102	Patrick Troughton interview
121	Ian Marter Tribute
125	Novelization overview
166	Derrick Sherwin interview
169	Those *Radio Times*
179	Case Studies: Tobias Vaughn
189	Archive Feature
201	Video review
202	Park Royal Invaded!
226	Nicholas Courtney interview
241	Chris D'Oyly-John interview
243	Frazer Hines interview
308	Michael Troughton's Memories
310	Kevin Stoney interview
311	Time Team 1-5
312	Time Team 6-8
321	Peter Halliday interview
349	CD review

Recording Dates
31 August 1968 (EFS modelwork), 3-13 September 1968 (Location filming), 13 September 1968 (EFS) mid-September 1968 (Location filming), 20 September 1968 (LG D), 27 September 1968 (LG D), 4 October 1968 (LG D), 11 October 1968 (LG D), 18 October 1968 (LG D), 25 October 1968 (LG D), 1 November 1968 (LG D), 8 November 1968 (LG D)

Locations
RAF Fairford, Fairford, Gloucestershire; Williamstrip Farm and Hatherop Road, Coln St Aldwyn, Gloucestershire; Kingston Minerals, Kempsford, Gloucestershire; Associated British Maltsters, Wallingford, Oxfordshire; St James' Gardens, Kensington, London W8; Princedale Road, Heathfield Street and Walmer Road, Notting Hill, London W12; Peter's Hill, Knightrider Street, Distaff Lane, Queen Victoria Street, St Paul's Churchyard, City, London EC4; Moor Lane, Fore Street, City, London EC2; TCC Condensers, Ealing, London W3; Millbank Tower, Millbank, London SW1; Guinness Brewery, Park Royal, London NW10; Maida Hill Tunnel, Regent's Canal, London NW8; Cumberland Terrace, Regents Park, London NW1; Australia House, Strand, London WC2; Denham Aerodrome, Denham Green, Buckinghamshire

Working Titles
Return of the Cybermen
Dr Who and the Invasion
Doctor Who and the Invasion

Factoids
- A fortnight's gap preceded this story to allow for *Grandstand*'s coverage of the 1968 Olympic Games from Mexico.
- Professor Travers and his daughter Anne (from *The Web of Fear*, 41) were intended to return in this story. Neither actor being available, the identikit characters of Professor Watkins and his niece Isobel were created.
- Ex-army director Douglas Camfield persuaded the Ministry of Defence to loan him the 2nd Battalion of the Coldstream Guards to pad out the extras playing UNIT soldiers. These featured prominently in the battle scenes in Episode 8, along with bazookas, Land Rovers and a military lorry. The MoD also made available a Hercules transporter aircraft to represent UNIT's new mobile HQ.

- The BBC's Outside Broadcast helicopter made its first appearance in the programme in Episode 3 as a UNIT vehicle - it would feature in many more UNIT stories in the early 1970s.
- Six new Cybermen costumes were constructed, again based on two-piece rubber wetsuits as in *The Wheel in Space* (43). Larger fibreglass helmets were made by Bill King of Trading Post - these now sported the familiar 'headphones' design and had powerful army torches imbedded in the top. Jack and John Lovell built the bodies, which were equipped with lighter chest units with battery-powered sequencer lights as before. The Cyberplanner was an augmented version of the one seen in *The Wheel in Space*.
- Wendy Padbury was absent for Episode 3's recording because of a week's holiday. Frazer Hines was absent for the same reason in Episode 8 (his last sequences was pre-filmed weeks before).
- Extensive filming in and around London began early on a Sunday morning to capture the deserted streets of the capital. Unfortunately, despite Camfield's rigidly planned shooting script, time was lost with inquisitive bystanders interrupting the filming. For this reason, sequences at Tower Bridge, the Houses of Parliament and Hyde Park had to be abandoned.

Comment
Despite copious amounts of location work and the niftiest Cybermen ever seen, *The Invasion* turns out to be one long bore. This is down to a variety of factors, not the least being that the story can't possibly sustain eight episodes and almost every time there is an exciting setpiece, it tends to happen off-screen. The special effects are truly awful and the horribly repetitive incidental music is irritating in the extreme. Mavic Chen - sorry, I mean Tobias Vaughn - is a wonderful villain, brought to life so well by Kevin Stoney, but this is probably the dullest story in a disappointing season. **22%**

"An atomic laser? Is that better than an axe?" ~ *Thara*

47) The Krotons
Robert Holmes

Serial Code: WW
Original Transmission
Episode One
Saturday 28 December 1968, 17.15-17.40, 9m / 55
Episode Two
Saturday 4 January 1969, 17.15-17.40, 8.4m / 54
Episode Three
Saturday 11 January 1969, 17.15-17.40, 7.5m / 61
Episode Four
Saturday 18 January 1969, 17.15-17.40, 7.1m / 68

Repeat Transmission
On BBC2 as part of 'The Five Faces of Doctor Who':
Episode One
Monday 9 November 1981, 17.40-18.05, 4.4m / 12
Episode Two
Tuesday 10 November 1981, 17.40-18.05, 4.6m / 9
Episode Three
Wednesday 11 November 1981, 17.40-18.05, 4.6m / 9
Episode Four
Thursday 12 November 1981, 17.40-18.05, 4.4m / 11

BBC Archive
Episode One exists as a 35mm b/w film recording and Episodes Two, Thee and Four exist as 16mm b/w film recordings, all taken from the 625-line two-inch monochrome master videotapes (wiped in 1969).

Novelization
Doctor Who - The Krotons by Terrance Dicks (121/12)
Hardback:
June 1985, WH Allen (0491035500 / Andrew Skilleter)
Paperback:
1. November 1985, Target (0426201892 / Andrew Skilleter)
2. September 1988, Star, as part of 'Doctor Who Classics' with *Doctor Who - The Dominators* (0352322659 / Andrew Skilleter)
3. July 1991, Target (0426201892 / Alister Pearson)

69

Video
February 1991, edited (BBCV 4452 / Alister Pearson)

Music and Sound Effects
1. July 1993, *Doctor Who: 30 Years at the Radiophonic Workshop*, CD (BBCCD 871 / Photomontage)
2. May 2000, *Doctor Who at the BBC Radiophonic Workshop: Volume 1 - The Early Years 1963-1969*, CD (WMSF 6023-2 / Photographs)

Précis
The Doctor comes to the aid of the Gonds, a primitive race under the thrall of the crystalline Krotons…

Cast
Patrick Troughton (Doctor Who), Frazer Hines (Jamie), Wendy Padbury (Zoe), Philip Madoc (Eelek), Gilbert Wynne (Thara), James Copeland (Selris), Terence Brown (Abu), Madeleine Mills (Vana), Richard Ireson (Axus), James Cairncross (Beta), Maurice Selwyn (Custodian), Bronson Shaw (Student), Robert La'Bassiere, Miles Northover (Krotons), Roy Skelton, Patrick Tull (Kroton Voices)

Crew
Visual Effects Designer Bill King (Trading Post), *Technical Manager* Fred Wright, *Vision Mixer* David Langford, *Studio Lighting* Howard King, *Studio Sound* John Holmes, *Film Cameraman* Alan Jonas, *Film Editor* Martyn Day, *Special Sound* Brian Hodgson, *Grams Operator* Ron Arnett, *Costume Designer* Bobi Bartlett, *Make-Up Artist* Sylvia James, *Designer* Raymond London, *Production Assistant* Edwina Verner, *Assistant Floor Manager* David Tilley, *Director's Assistant* Raquel Ebbutt, *Floor Assistant* Maurice Gallagher, *Script Editor* Terrance Dicks, *Producer* Peter Bryant, *Director* David Maloney

DWM Index
58   'The Five Faces of Doctor Who' feature
59   Episode Guide
85   Archive
98   Frazer Hines interview
100   Robert Holmes interview
102   Novelization review
108   David Maloney interview
171   Video review
239   Vox Pops
243   Frazer Hines interview
308   Michael Troughton's Memories
312   Time Team
318   Archive Feature

Recording Dates
10-11 November 1968 (Location filming), 12-13 November 1968 (EFS), 22 November 1968 (LG D), 29 November 1968 (LG D), 6 December 1968 (LG D), 13 December 1968 (LG D)

Locations
West of England Quarry and Tank Quarry, Malvern, Hereford and Worcestershire

Working Titles
Dr Who and the Space-Trap
The Trap
Doctor Who and the Space Trap
Doctor Who and the Krotons

Factoids
- *The Krotons* was the fourth attempt at producing a story for this particular slot. In March 1968, Paul Wheeler had been commissioned to write *Dr Who and the Dreamspinners*, but this was written off as being unsuitable. After another abandoned storyline, comedy writer Dick Sharples proposed gender-swap satire *Doctor Who and the Amazons*. Retitled *The Prison in Space*, the story came very close to being produced, but continual rewrites led to Sharples abandoning it. The only other storyline available to plug the gap at such short notice was by Robert Holmes (an early draft of which was submitted to story editor Donald Tosh in 1965).
- *The Krotons* was the first *Doctor Who* story not to overlap its pre-filming with the previous story's production.
- Episode One, which was recorded directly onto 35mm film, achieved the highest audience rating of Patrick Troughton's entire period in *Doctor Who*.
- Two Kroton costumes were made from fibreglass and perspex by Jack and John Lovell to Bobi Bartlett's specifications. They had fully rotating heads and a rubber skirt to hide the operators' legs.

Comment
A watertight, if clichéd, story that perfectly fits its four episodes, *The Krotons* has many a pleasing moment in its unsophisticated plot. While James Copeland exhibits the acting skills of an oak tree, the regulars are on fine form with some particularly charming business from Troughton as he fumbles the Krotons' intelligence tests. Interesting direction from David Maloney (especially the eerie scenes inside the Dynatrope) goes a long way to making the workaday story feel more special than it is. **71%**

"You can't kill me - I'm a genius!" ~ *The Doctor*

48) The Seeds of Death

Brian Hayles (1-2) and Terrance Dicks (3-6, based on a story by Brian Hayles)

Serial Code: XX
Original Transmission
Episode One
Saturday 25 January 1969, 17.15-17.40, 6.6m / 68
Episode Two
Saturday 1 February 1969, 17.15-17.40, 6.8m / 72
Episode Three
Saturday 8 February 1969, 17.15-17.40, 7.5m / 65
Episode Four
Saturday 15 February 1969, 17.15-17.40, 7.1m / 74
Episode Five
Saturday 22 February 1969, 17.15-17.40, 7.6m / 65
Episode Six
Saturday 1 March 1969, 17.15-17.40, 7.7m / 59

BBC Archive
Episodes One, Two, Three, Four and Six exist as 16mm b/w film recordings of the 625-line two-inch monochrome master videotapes (wiped in 1969), and Episode Five exists as a 35mm b/w film recording of the same.

Novelization
Doctor Who - The Seeds of Death by Terrance Dicks (149/15)
Hardback:
July 1986, WH Allen (0491036620 / David McAllister)
Paperback:
December 1986, Target (042620252X / David McAllister)

Video
1. July 1985, compilation (BBCV 2019 / Photomontage)
2. July 1985, compilation, Betamax (BBCB 2019 / Photomontage)

DVD
February 2003, 2 x discs, VidFIREd, *The Web of Fear* and *The Wheel in Space* censor clips, 'The Last Dalek' (8mm home movie footage of *The Evil of the Daleks* Episode 7), production subtitles, photo gallery, commentary by Frazer Hines, Wendy Padbury, Michael Ferguson and Terrance Dicks (BBCDVD 1151 / Clayton Hickman)

Précis
Ice Warriors sabotage a transmat station on the Moon, spreading a deadly virus worldwide…

Cast
Patrick Troughton (Doctor Who), Frazer Hines (Jamie), Wendy Padbury (Zoe), Ronald Leigh-Hunt (Commander Radnor), Philip Ray (Eldred), Louise Pajo (Gia Kelly), Terry Scully (Fewsham), Harry Towb (Osgood), Ric Felgate (Brent), Martin Cort (Locke), Christopher Coll (Phipps), Hugh Morton (Sir James Gregson), Derek Slater (Security Guard), Alan Bennion (Slaar), Steve Peters, Tony Harwood, Sonny Caldinez (Ice Warriors), Graham Leaman (Grand Marshall), John Witty (Computer Voice), Tommy Laird (Double for Doctor Who), Michael Wisher (Voice), Alan Chuntz (Harvey)

Crew
Stuntman Alan Chuntz, *Visual Effects Designer* Bill King (Trading Post), *Visual Effects Assistant* John Friedlander, *Vision Mixer* Chris Griffin, *Studio Lighting* Fred Wright, *Studio Sound* Bryan Forgham, *Film Cameraman* Peter Hall, *Film Editor* Martyn Day, *Special Sound* Brian Hodgson, *Grams Operator* John Lloyd, *Incidental Music* Dudley Simpson, *Costume Designer* Bobi Bartlett, *Make-Up Artist* Sylvia James, *Designer* Paul Allen, *Assistant Floor Manager* Trina Cornwell, *Director's Assistants* Tricia Warrington, Raquel Ebbutt, *Floor Assistant* John Norton, *Script Editor* Terrance Dicks, *Producer* Peter Bryant, *Director* Michael Ferguson

DWM Index
57	John Friedlander interview
59	Episode Guide
94	History of the Ice Warriors Brian Hayles Retrospective
104	Video review
115	Novelization review
120	Wendy Padbury interview
185	Michael Ferguson interview
203	Alan Bennion interview
239	Vox Pops
243	Frazer Hines interview
274	Archive Feature
312	Time Team 1
314	Time Team 2-6
326	Preview(DVD)
327	DVD review
330	Dudley Simpson interview

Recording Dates
13 December 1968 (EFS modelwork), 16-18 December 1968 (EFS), 19 December 1968 (Location filming), 20 December 1968 (EFS modelwork), 23 December 1968 (EFS modelwork), 3 January 1969 (LG D), 10 January

1969 (LG D), 17 January 1969 (LG D), 24 January 1969 (LG D), 31 January 1969 (LG D), 7 February 1969 (LG D)
Location
Hampstead Heath, Hampstead, London NW3
Working Titles
The Lords of the Red Planet
Dr Who and the Seeds of Death
Doctor Who and the Seeds of Death
Factoids
- A new character called Nik was to be introduced in this story, as it had been arranged that Frazer Hines would be leaving in the previous adventure (planned to be *The Prison in Space*). But when Hines agreed to stay on, the character was dropped. Rewrites caused by this change and a dissatisfaction with how the story was progressing led script editor Terrance Dicks paying Hayles off for his work and writing the last four parts himself, based loosely on Hayles' originally storyline.
- The Ice Warriors had new latex mouthpieces sculpted by John Friedlander. The body of Ice Lord Slaar was constructed by Jack and John Lovell out of rubber (as were the pincers), with the fibreglass helmet and latex half-mask designed by Friedlander.
- To show the effect of the Ice Warriors' sonic weapons, the victim was reflected on a thin sheet of mirrored material called mirrorlon (captured by a camera that reversed the resulting picture), which was then pushed from behind by a studio hand, creating a distorting effect.
- The BBC's foam generator was used on Hampstead Heath and at the Ealing studios to represent the Ice Warriors' fungus. The spores were white balloons filled with talcum powder.
- Patrick Troughton was absent for Episode Four, with Tommy Laird doubling for his unconscious body.

Comment
Hard to know where this story goes wrong, as individually it's full of good things. Michael Ferguson's direction is striking, the special effects are reasonable, acting is generally good, and the Ice Lord Slaar - brilliantly played by Alan Bennion - is a welcome addition to the Martian hierarchy. What lets the production down are the drab and uninteresting sets and the rather repetitive nature of the plotting, rather neatly summed up by Patrick Troughton virtually running on the spot in Episode Three's peculiar chase sequence. Workmanlike but overlong (which could be said for much of this season's output). **35%**

"Is it all right if I blow my nose, or is that another offence?" ~ Milo Clancey

49) The Space Pirates
Robert Holmes

Serial Code: YY
Original Transmission
Episode One
Saturday 8 March 1969, 17.15-17.40, 5.8m / 96
Episode Two
Saturday 15 March 1969, 17.15-17.40, 6.8m / 74
Episode Three
Saturday 22 March 1969, 17.15-17.40, 6.4m / 75
Episode Four
Saturday 29 March 1969, 17.15-17.40, 5.8m / 83
Episode Five
Saturday 5 April 1969, 17.15-17.40, 5.5m / 70
Episode Six
Saturday 12 April 1969, 17.15-17.40, 5.3m / 98
BBC Archive
Episode Two exists as a 35mm b/w film recording of the 625-line two-inch monochrome master videotape (wiped in 1969). The other episodes do not exist in any visual medium.
Novelization
Doctor Who - The Space Pirates by Terrance Dicks (132/14)
Paperback:
March 1990, Target (0426203461 / Tony Clark)
Video
June 1991, Episode Two on 'The Troughton Years' (BBCV 4609 / Photographs)
DVD
November 2004, Episode Two, VidFIREd, model film footage, on 'Doctor Who - Lost in Time' (BBCDVD 1353 / Clayton Hickman)
Soundtrack
February 2003, 2 x CDs, narrated by Frazer Hines (0563535059 / Max Ellis)
Music and Sound Effects
May 2000, *Doctor Who at the BBC Radiophonic Workshop: Volume 1 - The Early Years 1963-1969*, CD (WMSF 6023-2 / Photographs)
Précis
The Doctor and his friends team up with the International Space Corps to track a gang of pirates...

Cast
Patrick Troughton (Doctor Who), Frazer Hines (Jamie), Wendy Padbury (Zoe), Gordon Gostelow (Milo Clancey), Jack May (General Hermack), Donald Gee (Major Ian Warne), Dudley Foster (Caven), Edmond Knight (Dom Issigri), Lisa Daniely (Madeleine Issigri), Brian Peck (Dervish), George Layton (Technician Penn), Nik Zaran (Lieutenant Sorba), Anthony Donovan (Space Guard), Steve Peters (Pirate Guard), Valerie Stantion (Madeleine's Secretary)

Crew
Visual Effects Designer John Wood, *Visual Effects Assistant* John Horton, *Technical Manager* Derek Martin, *Vision Mixer* David Hanks, Clive Halls, *Studio Lighting* Peter Winn, *Studio Sound* David Hughes, *Film Cameraman* Peter Hall, *Film Editor* Martyn Day, *Special Sound* Brian Hodgson, *Grams Operator* David Silk, Ron Arnett, *Incidental Music* Dudley Simpson, *Vocals* Mary Thomas, *Costume Designer* Nicholas Bullen, *Make-Up Artists* Sylvia James, Sallie Evans, Liz Rowell, *Designer* Ian Watson, *Production Assistant* Snowy Lidiard-White, *Assistant Floor Manager* Liam Foster, *Director's Assistant* Marianne Willison, *Floor Assistant* John Turner, *Script Editor/Acting Producer* Derrick Sherwin, *Producer* Peter Bryant, *Director* Michael Hart

DWM Index
59 Episode Guide
63 Archive
78 Patrick Troughton interview
100 Robert Holmes interview
158 Novelization review
163 Terrance Dicks interview
177 Video review ('The Troughton Years')
187 What The Papers Said
190 Ian Scoones interview
233 The John Nathan-Turner Memoirs
242 Archive Feature
308 Michael Troughton's Memories
314 Time Team 1-3
315 Time Team 4-6
316 CD review

Recording Dates
February 1969 (TC Puppet Theatre), 7 February 1969 (EFS), 10-14 February 1969 (EFS), 19 February 1969 (EFS), 21 February 1969 (LG D), 28 February 1969 (TC4), 7 March 1969 (TC4), 14 March 1969 (TC4), 21 March 1969 (TC6), 28 March 1969 (TC4)

Working Title
Dr Who and the Space Pirates

Factoids
- Because Terrance Dicks was working on the ten-part finale to the season, incoming producer Derrick Sherwin took back his old job as script editor for this one story. Robert Holmes was asked to tap into the huge public interest in the Apollo Moon program, which at that time was at its peak. (The first alleged Moon landing occurred approximately a month after the last episode of Season 6 finale *The War Games*, 50).
- Extensive model filming was conducted by outside contractor Bowie Films Ltd. Supervised by visual effects designer John Wood, the spacecraft models were built by Magna Models and BBC visual effects assistant John Horton, who had worked on the Stanley Kubrick film *2001: A Space Odyssey* (1968). Bowie Films had shot miniatures for Gerry Anderson's *Thunderbirds* series, and for their *Doctor Who* assignment Ian Scoones and Nick Alder filmed the model sequences. Scoones joined the BBC a few months later, and found himself working on many more *Doctor Who* stories.
- Episode One was the final one recorded at Lime Grove, while Episode Two was the last monochrome episode to be recorded onto 35mm film. Episode Six only featured the regulars on pre-filmed material - the studio recording was conducted entirely by the guest cast.
- Peter Bryant was now producer in name only, Derrick Sherwin having unofficially taken up most of the producing chores himself by this stage.
- Future producer John Nathan-Turner began his *Doctor Who* career working on this story as floor assistant, under the name John Turner.

Comment
If the surviving episode is anything to go by, this is one of the dullest Troughton stories ever. Replacing monsters with squabbles about mineral smuggling in space may have seemed like a good idea at the time, but it's hard to see why. From the plummy intonations of General Hermack to the rootin' tootin' Western drawl of Milo Clancey, this isn't funny enough to be a comedy, nor dramatic enough to be exciting. **25%**

"You asked me to justify my actions - I am doing so!" ~ The Doctor

50) *The War Games*
Terrance Dicks and Malcolm Hulke

Serial Code: ZZ
Original Transmission
Episode One
Saturday 19 April 1969, 17.15-17.40, 5.5m / 88
Episode Two
Saturday 26 April 1969, 17.15-17.40, 6.3m / 68
Episode Three
Saturday 3 May 1969, 17.15-17.40, 5.1m / 81
Episode Four
Saturday 10 May 1969, 17.15-17.40, 5.7m / 63
Episode Five
Saturday 17 May 1969, 17.15-17.40, 5.1m / 87
Episode Six
Saturday 24 May 1969, 17.15-17.40, 4.2m / 91
Episode Seven
Saturday 31 May 1969, 17.15-17.40, 4.9m / 83
Episode Eight
Saturday 7 June 1969, 17.15-17.40, 3.5m / 96
Episode Nine
Saturday 14 June 1969, 17.15-17.40, 4.1m / 91
Episode Ten
Saturday 21 June 1969, 17.15-17.40, 5m / 66
BBC Archive
All episodes exist as 16mm b/w film recordings of the 625-line two-inch monochrome master videotapes (wiped in 1971).
Novelization
Doctor Who and the War Games by Malcolm Hulke (143/11)
Hardback:
October 1979, WH Allen (0491024282 / John Geary)
Paperback:
1. September 1979, Target (0426200829 / John Geary)
2. February 1990, Target, renamed *Doctor Who - The War Games* (0426200829 /Alister Pearson)
Video
1. February 1990, twin-pack (BBCV 4310/Alister Pearson)
2. September 2002, twin-pack, in 'The Time Lord Collection' [BBCV 7346 / Photomontage] with *The Three Doctors* and *The Deadly Assassin* (BBCV 7363 / Photomontage)
Music and Sound Effects
May 2000, *Doctor Who at the BBC Radiophonic Workshop: Volume 1 - The Early Years 1963-1969*, CD (WMSF 6023-2 / Photographs)

Précis
The Doctor finds himself up against a foe too great for him to defeat alone...
Cast
Patrick Troughton (Doctor Who), Frazer Hines (Jamie), Wendy Padbury (Zoe), Jane Sherwin (Lady Jennifer Buckingham), John Livesey, Bernard Davies (German Soldiers), David Savile (Lieutenant Carstairs), Terence Bayler (Major Barrington), Brian Forster (Sergeant Willis), Noel Coleman (General Smythe), Hubert Rees (Captain Ransom), Esmond Webb (Sergeant Major Burns), Richard Steele (Commandant Gorton), David Valla (Lieutenant Crane), Peter Stanton (Military Chauffer), Pat Gorman (Military Policeman), Gregg Palmer (Lieutenant Lucke), Tony McEwan (Redcoat), David Garfield (Von Weich), Bill Hutchinson (Sergeant Thompson), Terry Adams (Corporal Riley), Edward Brayshaw (War Chief), Leslie Schofield (Leroy), Vernon Dobtcheff (Scientist), Rudolph Walker (Harper), Michael Lynch (Spencer), John Atterbury (Alien Guard), Graham Weston (Russell), James Bree (Security Chief), David Troughton (Moor), Philip Madoc (War Lord), Peter Craze (Du Pont), Michael Napier-Brown (Arturo Villar), Stephen Hubay (Petrov), Clare Jenkins (Tanya Lernov), Bernard Horsfall, Trevor Martin, Clyde Pollitt (Time Lords), Freddie Wilson (Quark), John Levene (Yeti), Tony Harwood (Ice Warrior), Roy Pearce (Cyberman), Robert Jewell (Dalek)
Crew
Fight Arrangers Peter Diamond, Arthur Howell, *Visual Effects Designer* Michaeljohn Harris, *Graphics* Alan Jeapes, *Technical Managers* David Hare, Fred Wright, *Vision Mixer* David Langford, *Studio Lighting* Howard King, *Studio Sound* John Staple, *Film Cameraman* Alan Jonas, *Film Editor* Chris Hayden, *Special Sound* Brian Hodgson, *Grams Operator* Ron Arnett, *Incidental Music* Dudley Simpson, *Costume Designer* Nick Bullen, *Make-Up Artists* Sylvia James, Elizabeth Rowell, *Designer* Roger Cheveley, *Production Assistant* Edwina Verner, *Assistant Floor Manager* Marion McDougall, *Director's Assistant* Carole Bissett, *Floor Assistant* Don Ross, *Producer* Derrick Sherwin, *Director* David Maloney
DWM Index
50	Archive 1
51	Archive 2
59	Episode Guide
78	Patrick Troughton interview
91	The Incredible Malcolm Hulke Novelization review
95	Terrance Dicks interview
98	Frazer Hines interview

102	Patrick Troughton interview
108	David Maloney interview
120	Wendy Padbury interview
126	Patrick Troughton - A Tribute
160	Video review
164	Philip Madoc interview
166	Case Studies: The War Lord and the War Chief
169	Those *Radio Times*
171	Jane Sherwin interview
187	What The Papers Said
201	David Maloney interview
215	David Troughton interview
225	Sylvia James interview
232	Archive Feature
	Roger Cheveley interview
239	Vox Pops
243	Frazer Hines interview
272	Terrance Dicks interview
315	Time Team 1-5
316	Time Team 6-10
325	Video ('Time Lord Collection')

Recording Dates
23-28 March 1969 (Location filming), 30 March-1 April 1969 (Location filming), 3 April 1969 (EFS), 11 April 1969 (TC4), 18 April 1969 (TC4), 25 April 1969 (TC4), 2 May 1969 (TC4), 8 May 1969 (TC4), 15 May 1969 (TC8), 22 May 1969 (TC1), 29 May 1969 (TC8), 5 June 1969 (TC6), 12 June 1969 (TC8)

Locations
Sheepcote Rubbish Tip, Brighton, East Sussex; Seven Sisters Country park, Seaford, East Sussex; bridle path, Clayton, West Sussex; roads in West Dean, East Sussex; High Park Farm, Exceat, Seaford, East Sussex; Birling Manor Farm, East Dean, East Sussex

Working Titles
Doctor Who and the War Games
Doctor Who & The War Games

Factoids
- *The War Games* replaced two aborted storylines, the six-part *Doctor Who and the Impersonators* by Malcolm Hulke and an unnamed four-part story by Derrick Sherwin.
- The decision to reveal the Doctor's Time Lord identity was twofold - either the series could reach a natural conclusion, or a new format could be considered for the next season.
- When the Doctor was trying to escape the Time Lords, excerpts from two previous stories were shown - *Fury from the Deep* (42) had the Tardis landing on the sea, while *The Web of Fear* (41) showed it hanging in space.
- Troughton, Hines and Padbury made their last appearance - along with the final monochrome appearances of a Cyberman, Ice Warrior, Yet, Quark and Dalek - on the final studio day, 12 June 1969.
- Jon Pertwee was announced as the new Doctor on 17 June, a few days before *The War Games*' final episode.

Comment
By rights this should be the television equivalent of watching paint dry. But somehow, somewhere along the line, some magic spark has entered the production and - a few *longueurs* aside - this mammoth-length story is really rather engaging. There's far less story than in the twelve-part *The Daleks' Master Plan* (21), yet it never feels as slow and padded as, say, *The Wheel in Space* (43). Director David Maloney keeps the whole thing moving, and there's some great eye candy in the psychedelic sets and the authentically re-enacted battle scenes. And rather neatly, the final episode is virtually a stand-alone story in its own right, a neat coda to the six-year ongoing story of *Doctor Who*, in just the same way that the first episode of the first story, *An Unearthly Child*, acted as a prologue to the whole series. **85%**

Third Doctor: Jon Pertwee

Season 7

"We deal with the odd, the unexplained. Anything on Earth - or even beyond." ~ *Brigadier Lethbridge-Stewart*

51) Spearhead from Space
Robert Holmes

Serial Code: AAA
Original Transmission
Episode 1
Saturday 3 January 1970, 17.15-17.40, 8.4m / 54
Episode 2
Saturday 10 January 1970, 17.15-17.40, 8.1m / 57
Episode 3
Saturday 17 January 1970, 17.15-17.40, 8.3m / 49

Episode 4
Saturday 24 January 1970, 17.15-17.40, 8.1m / 51
Repeat Transmissions
Episode 1
Friday 9 July 1971, 18.20-18.45, 2.9m / 115
Episode 2
Friday 16 July 1971, 18.20-18.45, 3m / 102
Episode 3
Friday 23 July 1971, 18.20-18.45, 3.4m / 98
Episode 4
Friday 30 July 1971, 18.20-18.45, 3.9m / 83
On BBC2:
Episode 1
Tuesday 16 November 1999, 18.00-18.25, 2.7m / -
Episode 2
Tuesday 16 November 1999, 18.25-18.50, 2.9m / -
Episode 3
Tuesday 23 November 1999, 18.00-18.25, 2.4m / -
Episode 4
Tuesday 30 November 1999, 18.00-18.25, 2.2m / -
BBC Archive
All episodes exist as the original 16mm colour film master prints.
Novelization
Doctor Who and the Auton Invasion by Terrance Dicks (156/10)
Hardback:
1. January 1974, Allan Wingate (0855230355 / Chris Achilleos)
2. November 1981, WH Allen (0491028954 / Andrew Skilleter)
Paperback:
1. January 1974, Target (0426103130 / Chris Achilleos)
2. 1982, Target (0426112954 / Andrew Skilleter)
3. March 1991, Target, renamed *Doctor Who - The Auton Invasion* (0426112954 / Alister Pearson)
Video
1. February 1988, compilation (BBCV 4107 / Photomontage)
2. February 1995 (BBCV 5509 / Photomontage)
DVD
February 2001, title sequence tests, BBC2 trailers, production subtitles, photo gallery, commentary by Nicholas Courtney and Caroline John (BBCDVD 1033 / Photograph)
Précis
A regenerated Doctor teams up with UNIT to deal with a Nestene invasion of Earth…

Cast
Jon Pertwee (Doctor Who), Caroline John (Liz Shaw), Nicholas Courtney (Brigadier Lethbridge-Stewart), Hugh Burden (Channing), John Woodnutt (Hibbert), Neil Wilson (Sam Seeley), Betty Bowden (Meg Seeley), Derek Smee (Ransome), John Breslin (Captain Munro), Antony Webb (Dr Henderson), Hamilton Dyce (Major General Scobie), Talfryn Thomas (Mullins), Ellis Jones (Technician/Voice of Dr Lomax), Tessa Shaw (UNIT Officer), Helen Dorward (Nurse), George Lee (Corporal Forbes), Iain Smith (UNIT Soldier), Allan Mitchell (Wagstaffe), Prentis Hancock (Second Reporter), Henry McCarthy (Dr Beavis), Clifford Cox (Sergeant), Edmund Bailey (Attendant), Derrick Sherwin (Commissionaire), Michael Horsburgh (Stunt Double for the Doctor), Ivan Orton (Double for Channing)
Crew
Stuntman Derek Martin, *Visual Effects Designer* John Horton, *Visual Effects Assistant* Alan Whibley, *Film Cameramen* Stan Speel, Robert McDonnell, *Film Sound* Derek Medus, *Film Editors* William Symon, Adam Dawson, *Special Sound* Brian Hodgson, *Incidental Music* Dudley Simpson, *Costume Designer* Christine Rawlins, *Make-Up Artist* Cynthia Goodwin, *Designer* Paul Allen, *Production Assistant* Peter Grimwade, *Script Editor* Terrance Dicks, *Assistant Script Editor* Trevor Ray, *Producer* Derrick Sherwin, *Director* Derek Martinus
DWM Index
52	Cry HAVOC
53	Peter Grimwade interview
60	Episode Guide
61	Behind The Scenes: Graphic Design
76	Archive
108	Derek Martinus interview
113	Jon Pertwee interview
114	Caroline John interview
136	Video review
166	Derrick Sherwin interview
170	Jon Pertwee interview
172	Those *Radio Times*
181	John Woodnutt interview Archive Feature
188	What The Papers Said
219	Caroline John interview
226	Nicholas Courtney interview
243	Derek Martinus interview
250	Vox Pops
286	Cutting A Dash Trevor Ray interview
287	DVD Restoration (Gallifrey Guardian)
300	DVD review
322	Time Team

327 The Mary Whitehouse Experience
354 Time Team

Recording Dates
13-19 September 1969 (Location filming), 8-17 October 1969 (Location filming), 20-31 October 1969 (Location filming), 3-4 November 1969 (Van Arden Ealing Studios), 5 November 1969 (Location filming), 19 November 1969 (EFS modelwork), 22 November 1969 (EFS)

Locations
Favourite Doll Factory, Holloway, London N7; Euston Road and Midland Road, London NW1; Rear of St Pancras Station, London NW1; John Sanders Ltd, Ealing, London W5; High Street and Lancaster Road, Ealing, London W5; Royal Horticultural Society, Wisley, Surrey; Hatchford Park School, Hatchford, Surrey; TCC Condensers, Ealing, London W3; Wood Norton Estate, Evesham, Hereford and Worcestershire; Mansion House Hotel, Evesham, Worcestershire; Wheelbarrow Castle Cottage, Radford, Worcestershire; Madame Tussaud's, Marylebone, London NW1

Working Title
Facsimile

Factoids
- Ron Moody was producer Derrick Sherwin's original choice for the role of the Doctor.
- A new title sequence was devised by Bernard Lodge. It consisted of monochrome howlround as before, but this time tinted with colour gels via an optical printer. The closing credit sequence also had a howlround background added, and the captions were now flashed on and off rather than scrolled vertically. Accompanying this was a slightly amended version of Ron Grainer's theme music which would last, with occasional changes, until *The Horns of Nimon* (109). As a one-off experiment, the story title zoomed towards the viewer.
- Because of a scene-shifters' strike at BBC Television Centre, video studio allocation for *Spearhead from Space* was cancelled. Producer Derrick Sherwin decided that it would be economically viable to shoot the whole story on 16mm film (the first time this had happened), in colour, and for the most part on location. Some inserts were later conducted at an Ealing film studio.
- For Pertwee's first photo session in costume, he wore a selection of his grandfather's eveningwear, including a long flowing cape and frilly shirt. This look inspired his eventual television appearance.

- Robert Holmes' script borrowing heavily from *Quatermass II* (1955) and his own 1965 film *Invasion*, starring Edward Judd.
- Several Auton masks and fake gun-hands were made from vacuum-formed plastic and fibreglass by John Horton. Climactic scenes of the writhing, tentacled Nestene creature were not thought convincing enough, though, and were remounted during recording of the next story, *Doctor Who and the Silurians*, with Ivan Orton standing in for Hugh Burden.
- A *Radio Times* cover with Jon Pertwee (dated 3-9 January 1970) heralded the new series, but due to an editorial oversight, there was no accompanying feature within.

Comment
Much-overrated, *Spearhead from Space* has more bad points than good. Okay, so it's shot on film, but that doesn't excuse the general blandness of the production and the terrible acoustics of many of the interiors - this is a story in which all the actors speak very LOUDLY in order to be picked up on the BBC's primitive boom mikes. The climactic appearance of the Nestene monster is, frankly, pathetic, as is Pertwee's embarrassingly inappropriate attempts at gurning. Also, the plot moves along at a snail's pace (nothing happens in Episode 1) and the repetitive music cues are very irritating. On the plus side, the Autons are terrifying - is this really a kids' programme anymore? -and the reanimated shop dummies sequence is beautifully executed. **45%**

"You say these creatures have infected us with a plague, but do you still want us to *negotiate* with them?" ~ *Masters*

52) Doctor Who and the Silurians
Malcolm Hulke

Serial Code: BBB
Original Transmission
Episode 1
Saturday 31 January 1970, 17.15-17.40, 8.8m / 41
Episode 2
Saturday 7 February 1970, 17.15-17.40, 7.3m / 68
Episode 3
Saturday 14 February 1970, 17.15-17.40, 7.5m / 59

Episode 4
Saturday 21 February 1970, 17.15-17.40, 8.2m / 46
Episode 5
Saturday 28 February 1970, 17.15-17.40, 7.5m / 52
Episode 6
Saturday 7 March 1970, 17.15-17.40, 7.2m / 63
Episode 7
Saturday 14 March 1970, 17.15-17.40, 7.5m / 54

Repeat Transmission
On BBC2:
Episode 1
Tuesday 7 December 1999, 18.00-18.25, - / -
Episode 2
Tuesday 14 December 1999, 18.00-18.25, - / -
Episode 3
Tuesday 21 December 1999, 18.00-18.25, - / -
Episode 4
Tuesday 4 January 2000, 18.00-18.25, - / -
Episode 5
Tuesday 11 January 2000, 18.00-18.25, 1.7m / -
Episode 6
Tuesday 18 January 2000, 18.00-18.25, - / -
Episode 7
Tuesday 25 January 2000, 18.00-18.25, - / -

BBC Archive
All episodes exist as a combination of 16mm b/w film recordings and 525-line NTSC colour U-Matic off-air videotapes. The 625-line two-inch colour PAL master videotapes were wiped in the mid-1970s.

Novelization
Doctor Who and the Cave-Monsters by Malcolm Hulke (158/1)
Hardback:
February 1974, Allan Wingate (0855230363 / Chris Achilleos)
Paperback:
1. January 1974, Target (0426102924 / Chris Achilleos)
2. August 1992, Target, renamed *Doctor Who - The Silurians* (0426203828 / Alister Pearson)

Video
July 1993, twin-pack, recoloured (BBCV 4990 / Andrew Skilleter)

Music and Sound Effects
July 1999, Upbeat Classics, *Sherlock Holmes Meets Dr Who*, CD (URCD148 / -)

Précis
Cave-dwelling Silurians threaten the safety of an underground atomic research centre…

Cast
Jon Pertwee (Doctor Who), Caroline John (Liz), Nicholas Courtney (Brigadier Lethbridge-Stewart), John Newman (Spencer), Bill Matthews (Davis), Peter Miles (Dr Lawrence), Norman Jones (Major Baker), Fulton Mackay (Dr Quinn), Thomasine Heiner (Miss Dawson), Roy Branigan (Roberts), Ian Cunningham (Dr Meredith), Paul Darrow (Captain Hawkins), Nancie Jackson (Doris Squire), Gordon Richardson (Squire), Richard Steele (Sergeant Hart), Ian Talbot (Travis), Geoffrey Palmer (Masters), Harry Swift (Private Robins), Derek Pollitt (Private Wright), Alan Mason (Corporal Nutting), Peter Halliday (Silurian Voices), Brendan Barry (Hospital Doctor), Dave Carter (Old Silurian/Silurian/Ambulance Man), Nigel Johns (Young Silurian), Pat Gorman (Silurian/Silurian Scientist), Paul Barton, Simon Cain (Silurian/Private Upton), John Churchill (Silurian), Bertram A Collacott (Dinosaur)

Crew
Visual Effects James Ward, *Visual Effects Assistants* Gerry Abouaf, Anna Braybrooke, *Videotape Editor* Sam Upton, *Studio Lighting* Ralph Walton, *Studio Sound* John Staple, *Film Cameraman* Fred Hamilton, *Film Editor* Bill Huthert, *Special Sound* Brian Hodgson, *Incidental Music* Carey Blyton, *Costume Designer* Christine Rawlins, *Make-Up Artists* Marion Richards, Teresa Wright, *Designer* Barry Newbery, *Production Manager* Chris D'Oyly-John, *Script Editor* Terrance Dicks, *Assistant Script Editor* Trevor Ray, *Producer* Barry Letts, *Director* Timothy Combe

DWM Index
60	Episode Guide
91	Archive + Fact File The Incredible Malcolm Hulke Novelization review
111	Nicholas Courtney interview
114	Caroline John interview
172	Those *Radio Times*
188	What The Papers Said
192	Crossing the Line
196	Rebuilding the Classics
202	Video review
219	Caroline John interview
222	Archive Feature
226	Nicholas Courtney interview
241	Chris D'Oyly-John interview
250	Vox Pops
286	Cutting a Dash Trevor Ray interview
321	Peter Halliday interview
322	Time Team (1-4)
323	Time Team (5-7)
335	Peter Miles interview

Recording Dates
12-14 November 1969 (Location filming), 17-20 November 1969 (Location filming), 24 November 1969 (Location filming remount), 8 December

1969 (TC3), 15 December 1969 (TC1), 21 December 1969 (TC1), 22 December 1969 (TC1), 5 January 1970 (TC1), 12 January 1970 (TC1), 19 January 1970 (TC8), 26 January 1970 (TC8)
Locations
Hog's Back Transmitter Station, Hog's Back, Guildford, Surrey; High Street, Godalming, Surrey; Milford Chest Hospital, Milford, Surrey; Hankley Common, Rushmoor, Surrey; Sheephatch Farm, Tilford, Surrey; Marylebone Station, London NW1; Melcombe Place, Marylebone, London NW1; Dorset Square and Balcombe Street, Marylebone, London NW1; Edward Woods Estate, Shepherd's Bush, London, W12
Working Title
Doctor Who and the Monsters
Factoids
- For plague scenes in Marylebone Station, director Timothy Combe called on members of his production team to swell the number of extras, including former script editor Victor Pemberton, current script editor Terrance Dicks, producer Barry Letts and assistant script editor Trevor Ray as the ticket inspector. Unfortunately, the film was ruined in the development lab and the sequence had to be remounted.
- Six Silurian costumes were made by James Ward, consisting of thin PVC bodysuits with latex hands. Latex masks with 12v battery-powered lights in their foreheads were made by Gerry Abouaf.
- To show the Silurians' trained Tyrannosaurus Rex, the story marked the first use of Colour Separation Overlay (CSO), in which two or more images from different camera sources were combined electronically to produce one composite picture.
- Fulton Mackay would become more familiar to viewers as the chief prison warder Mr Mackay in BBC sitcom *Porridge* (1973-1977).
- The Doctor's newly acquired car Bessie appeared for the first time in Episode 1. The vehicle was a limited edition four-seater Edwardian 'kit car' made by Siva/Neville Trickett (Design) Ltd of Blandford, Dorset.

Comment
To fans, there is a lot to enjoy in this long, but complex, story. For a start, there are the convincing power station interiors and the bleak, moorland location photography. Then there is the quality of the cast, one of the strongest line-ups in any *Doctor Who* story. Special mention should go to Norman Jones and Peter Miles, who both give performances above and beyond the level of realism normally expected on such a programme. The general viewer, however, might be more inclined to laugh at the wobbly-headed Brummie Silurians, the childish kazoo music and Pertwee's unfortunate facial expression at the end of Episode 6. **80%**

"I don't know what we've brought down in Mars Probe 7 - but it certainly wasn't human." ~ The Doctor

53) *The Ambassadors of Death*
David Whitaker (and Malcolm Hulke, 4-7)

Serial Code: CC
Original Transmission
Episode 1
Saturday 21 March 1970, 17.15-17.40, 7.1m / 60
Episode 2
Saturday 28 March 1970, 17.15-17.40, 7.6m / 59
Episode 3
Saturday 4 April 1970, 17.20-17.45, 8m / 60
Episode 4
Saturday 11 April 1970, 17.45-18.10, 9.3m / 46
Episode 5
Saturday 18 April 1970, 17.15-17.40, 7.1m / 57
Episode 6
Saturday 25 April 1970, 17.15-17.40, 6.9m / 70
Episode 7
Saturday 2 May 1970, 17.15-17.40, 5.4m / 80
BBC Archive
Episode 1 exists as a 625-line two-inch colour PAL master videotape. Episodes 2, 3, 4 and 7 exist as 16mm b/w film recordings, and Episodes 5 and 6 exist as a combination of the 16mm b/w film recordings and 525-line NTSC colour U-Matic off-air videotapes. The 625-line master videotapes of Episodes 2 to 7 were wiped by 1977.
Novelization
Doctor Who - The Ambassadors of Death by Terrance Dicks (144/16)
Hardback:
May 1987, WH Allen (0491037120 / Tony Masero)
Paperback:
1. October 1987, Target (0426203054 / Tony Masero)
2. March 1991, Target (0426203054 / Alister Pearson)

Video
May 2002, partly recoloured, with trailer (BBCV 7265 / Photomontage)
Précis
Astronauts from a British Mars probe have been replaced by hostile aliens…
Cast
Jon Pertwee (Doctor Who), Caroline John (Liz), Nicholas Courtney (Brigadier Lethbridge-Stewart), John Levene (Sergeant Benton), Ronald Allen (Ralph Cornish), Michael Wisher (John Wakefield), Robert Cawdron (Taltalian), John Abineri (General Carrington), Ric Felgate (Van Lyden/Astronaut), Steve Peters (Lefee/Astronaut), Neville Simons (Michaels/Astronaut), Dallas Cavell (Quinlan), Gordon Sterne (Heldorf), William Dysart (Reegan), Cyril Shaps (Lennox), Geoffrey Beevers (Private Johnson), Cheryl Molineaux (Miss Rutherford), Ray Armstrong (Grey), Robert Robinson (Collinson), Juan Moreno (Dobson), James Haswell (Corporal Champion), Bernard Martin, Joanna Ross, Carl Conway (Control Room Assistants), Derek Ware (Sergeant), John Lord (Masters), Max Faulkner (Soldier), Tony Harwood (Flynn), James Clayton (Private Parker), Roy Scammell (Technician/Double for Liz Shaw), Peter Noel Cook (Alien Captain), Peter Halliday (Aliens' Voices)
Crew
Action HAVOC, *Visual Effects Designers* Peter Day, Ian Scoones, *Visual Effects Assistant* Rhys Jones, *Inlay Operators* AJ Mitchell, Alan Gomery, *Technical Manager* Bernard Fox, *Vision Mixer* John Barclay, *Studio Lighting* Geoff Shaw, Dave Sydenham, Ralph Walton, *Studio Sound* Gordon Mackie, Brian Hiles, *Film Cameramen* AA Englander, Tony Leggo, *Film Editors* Don Godden, Chris Wimble, *Special Sound* Brian Hodgson, *Grams Operators* Andy Stacey, Tony Philpot, *Incidental Music* Dudley Simpson, *Costume Designer* Christine Rawlins, *Make-Up Artist* Marion Richards, *Designer* David Myerscough-Jones, *Assistant Floor Manager* Margot Hayhoe, *Director's Assistants* Pauline Silcock, Michael Jackley, Kate Nemet, *Floor Assistant* John Turner, *Script Editor* Terrance Dicks, *Producer* Barry Letts, *Director* Michael Ferguson

DWM Index
52	Cry HAVOC
60	Episode Guide
77	Archive
91	The Incredible Malcolm Hulke
98	Whitaker's World of *Doctor Who*
114	Caroline John interview
122	Novelization review
151	Terry Walsh interview
185	Michael Ferguson interview
187	A J Mitchell interview
188	What The Papers Said
219	Caroline John interview
227	Nicholas Courtney interview
233	The John Nathan-Turner Memoirs
252	Archive Feature
286	Cutting A Dash
311	Geoffrey Beevers interview
317	Derek Ware interview
318	Video review
323	Time Team 1-5
324	Time Team 6-7

Recording Dates
Unknown date (Modelwork), 23 January 1970 (Location filming), 26-31 January 1970 (Location filming), 2-4 February 1970 (Location filming), 13 February 1970 (TC3), 20 February 1970 (TC3), 27 February 1970 (TC3), 6 March 1970 (TC3), 13 March 1970 (TC3), 20 March 1970 (TC4), 27 March 1970 (TC1)

Locations
Southall Gas Works, Southall, Middlesex; TCC Condensers, Ealing, London W3; Claycart Bottom, Puckeridge Hill Road Bridge and Farnborough Airfield, Aldershot, Hampshire; Wycombe Air Park, High Wycombe, Buckinghamshire; Folley's Gravel Pit and Little Marlow Sewage Treatment Works, Little Marlow, Buckinghamshire; Gossmore Lane and Marlow Weir, Marlow, Buckinghamshire; Beacon Hill, near Ewshot, Hampshire; Blue Circle Cement Plant, Northfleet, Kent

Working Titles
The Invaders from Mars
The Carriers of Death
Doctor Who and the Carriers of Death
Doctor Who and the Ambassadors of Death
The Ambassadors

Factoids
- A 90-second trailer of scenes from this story featured Jon Pertwee directly addressing the viewer. It was recorded during the Episode 3 studio session and shown immediately after the final part of *Doctor Who and the Silurians*.
- An unusual experiment was attempted with the title sequence for *The Ambassadors of Death*. Just before the story credits came up, the sequence gave way to the cliffhanger of the previous episode (a précis in the case of Episode 1), and then began again with title ('The Ambassadors' zooming up, followed by 'Of Death' accompanied by an electronic 'thunderclap' sound), writer and episode number. The cliffhanger resolution then followed.

- The Recovery 7 capsule interior was shared by the BBC thriller series *Doomwatch* - it was used for the episode *Re-Entry Forbidden* (broadcast 16 March 1970).
- During filming of the hijack scene in Episode 2, a motorbike crashed into director's assistant Pauline Silcock, seriously wounding her leg and leading to her being rushed into hospital. Michael Jackley replaced her.
- UNIT Sergeant West was renamed 'Benton', allowing John Levene to make his second, promoted, appearance in UNIT, following on from *The Invasion* (46).
- CSO was used extensively in the Space Control set to feed images onto the large video screen and desk monitor, and to add a (miniature) girdered roof seen in Episodes 1 and 7.
- Episode 4, scheduled to begin at 17.15, was delayed by 30 minutes to allow for an overrunning FA Cup Final broadcast.

Comment
An impressively mounted production that does a good job of distracting the viewer from the repetitious and illogical nature of the plot. The futuristic background is convincing, although some of the technical detail (such as a successful British rocket programme) now seems quaint. But there are excellent action set-pieces courtesy of HAVOC and the direction is never less than enthusiastic. The closing moments are beautifully underplayed.
80%

"The world's going up in flames and they're still playing at tin soldiers!" ~ Greg Sutton

54) Inferno
Don Houghton

Serial Code: DDD
Original Transmission
Episode 1
Saturday 9 May 1970, 17.15-17.40, 5.7m / 72
Episode 2
Saturday 16 May 1970 17.15-17.40, 5.9m / 66
Episode 3
Saturday 23 May 1970, 17.15-17.40, 4.8m / 85
Episode 4
Saturday 30 May 1970, 17.15-17.40, 6m / 54
Episode 5
Saturday 6 June 1970, 17.15-17.40, 5.4m / 54
Episode 6
Saturday 13 June 1970, 17.15-17.40, 5.7m / 73
Episode 7
Saturday 20 June 1970, 17.15-17.40, 5.5m / 79
BBC Archive
All episodes exist as a combination of 16mm b/w film recordings and 525-line NTSC colour two-inch master videotapes. The 625-line two-inch colour PAL master videotapes were wiped circa 1977.
Novelization
Doctor Who - Inferno by Terrance Dicks (126/15)
Hardback:
June 1984, WH Allen (0491031432 / Nick Spender)
Paperback:
October 1984, Target (0426196171 / Nick Spender)
Video
May 1994, twin-pack (BBCV 5269 / Colin Howard)
Music and Sound Effects
May 2000, *Doctor Who at the BBC Radiophonic Workshop: Volume 2 - New Beginnings 1970-1980*, CD (WMSF 6024-2 / Photographs)
Précis
Professor Stahlman' dangerous drilling experiment could destroy the world...
Cast
Jon Pertwee (Doctor Who/Radio Voice), Caroline John (Liz/Section Leader Elizabeth Shaw), Nicholas Courtney (Brigadier Lethbridge-Stewart/Brigade Leader Lethbridge-Stewart), John Levene (Sergeant Benton/Platoon Under Leader Benton/Primord), Olaf Pooley (Professor Stahlman/Director Stahlman), Sheila Dunn (Petra Williams/Dr Petra Williams), Derek Newark (Greg Sutton), Christopher Benjamin (Sir Keith Gold), Walter Randall (Harry Slocum), Ian Fairbairn (Bromley/Loudspeaker Voice), David Simeon (Private Latimer), Derek Ware (Private Wyatt), Roy Scammell (RSF Sentry/RSF Soldier/Disaster Crewmember), Dave Carter, Pat Gorman, Philip Ryan, Peter Thompson, Walter Henry (Primords), Keith James (Patterson), Terry Walsh (Stunt Double for The Doctor)
Crew
Action HAVOC, *Visual Effects Designer* Len Hutton, *Visual Effects Assistant* Tony Harding, *Technical Managers* Ray Hider, Lance Wood, *Vision Mixer* John Gorman, *Studio Lighting* John Green, *Studio Sound* John Staple, *Film Cameraman* Fred Hamilton, *Film Sound* Graham Hare, *Film Editor* Martyn Day, *Special Sound* Brian Hodgson, *Grams Operator* Tony Philpott, Gerry Burrows, *Costume Designer* Christine Rawlins, *Costume Assistant* Jean Ellis, *Make-Up Artist* Marion Richards, *Make-Up Assistants* Irena

Walls, Sue Duckworth, Judy Cain, *Designer*
Jeremy Davies, *Production Assistant* Chris
D'Oyly-John, *Assistant Floor Manager* Sue
Hedden, *Director's Assistants* Hugh Miles, Sue
Upton, *Floor Assistant* Frank Mullan, *Script Editor*
Terrance Dicks, *Producer* Barry Letts, *Directors*
Douglas Camfield, Barry Letts

DWM Index

52	Barry Letts interview
	Cry HAVOC
60	Episode Guide
72	Nicholas Courtney interview
82	John Levene interview
88	Novelization review
93	Douglas Camfield interview
113	Jon Pertwee interview
114	Archive + Fact File
	Caroline John interview
151	Derek Ware interview
172	Those *Radio Times*
190	Ian Scoones interview
212	Video review
217	Public Image
219	Caroline John interview
220	Walter Randall interview
227	Nicholas Courtney interview
230	John Levene interview
241	Chris D'Oyly-John interview
286	Cutting A Dash
305	Archive Feature
317	Derek Ware interview
324	Time Team 1-6
325	Time Team 7

Recording Dates
31 March-3 April 1970 (Location filming), 6-7 April 1970 (EFS modelwork), 24 April 1970 (TC3), 7-8 April 1970 (TC3), 21-22 May 1970 (TC6), 29 May 1970 (TC3)

Location
Berry Wiggins and Co Ltd, Hoo St Werburgh, Kent

Working Titles
Doctor Who and the Mo-Hole Project
Operation: Mole-Bore
Dr Who and the Mole-Bore
Project Inferno

Factoids
- Don Houghton's storyline was based on a genuine American drilling project called Project Mo-Hole. Scheduled for 1964/5, the idea was to penetrate the Earth's crust and drill into the mantle itself. After much publicity, the outcome of the project was hushed up, which led Houghton to wonder what dangers might have been caused by such an experiment.
- Although credited as director of *Inferno*, Douglas Camfield collapsed with a heart murmur after the first studio session, and so the bulk of the directing was done by producer Barry Letts. Camfield's wife, actress Sheila Dunn (playing Petra Williams) persuaded him not to work on *Doctor Who* again, a promise he kept until *Terror of the Zygons* (80).
- Six Primords (originally called 'Primeords') featured in the serial. The actors were made-up with dental appliances, wigs, facial make-up and humped backs, emitting blood-curdling Radiophonic screams courtesy of Brian Hodgson.
- Stuntman Roy Scammell, doubling as Sergeant Wyatt for colleague Derek Ware, performed a spectacular 45-feet fall from the top of one of the gasometers. A wide-angle lens was used to make the drop seem even higher.
- Caroline John, who had just discovered she was pregnant, was told during recording of *Inferno* that she would not be contracted to appear for Season 8. It was felt by producer Barry Letts that her character was too intelligent for the programme and didn't fulfil the same empathetic role that previous companions had.
- From this story onwards, a regular policy of recording two episodes every two weeks was adopted. Previously, individual episodes had been recorded on a weekly basis, meaning that sets often became damaged after being struck and rebuilt five or six times.

Comment
Quite possibly the most visceral *Doctor Who* ever made, this looks like a million dollars right from the start. The fantastic location filming gives the whole story a real sense of place, and the atmosphere is doomladen and oppressive throughout. From the moment you get the hammer 'jump cut' in Episode 1, you know this is going to be a particularly stylish production, and Camfield's directorial touch is present in every scene, despite illness preventing him from being on-set for much of the production. The constant noise is almost hypnotic, and the monsters are suitably frightening. (Note the first use of green slime as an alien menace.) Superb modelwork and exemplary performances, especially by Nicholas Courtney, and the greatest cliffhanger in the show's history, all adds up to Episode 6 being the most riveting instalment of *Doctor Who* to date. In comparison, the final part feels a little redundant. **95%**

Season 8

"Death is always more frightening when it strikes invisibly." ~ The Master

55) Terror of the Autons
Robert Holmes

Serial Code: EEE
Original Transmission
Episode One
Saturday 2 January 1971, 17.15-17.40, 7.3m / 78
Episode Two
Saturday 9 January 1971, 17.15-17.40, 8m / 71
Episode Three
Saturday 16 January 1971, 17.15-17.40, 8.1m / 58
Episode Four
Saturday 23 January 1971, 17.15-17.40, 8.4m / 59

BBC Archive
All episodes exist as a combination of 16mm b/w film recordings and 525-line colour NTSC U-Matic domestic video recordings. The 625-line two-inch colour PAL master videotapes were wiped by 1977. In addition, a brief clip from Episode One exists on 625-line colour two-inch PAL videotape.

Novelization
Doctor Who and the Terror of the Autons by Terrance Dicks (128/12)
Hardback:
February 1981, WH Allen (0491028644 / Alun Hood)
Paperback:
1. May 1975, Target (0426106393 / Peter Brookes)
2. 1979, Target (0426115007/ Alun Hood)

Video
April 1993, recoloured (BBCV 4957 / Alister Pearson)

DVD
October 2002, 625-line colour PAL videotape clip of Episode One on *The Aztecs* (BBCDVD 1099 / Clayton Hickman)

Music and Sound Effects
October 1998, Julian Knott, *Space Adventures: Music from Doctor Who 1963-1971*, CD (JPD 2CD / Photographs)

Précis
The Nestene Consciousness returns to dominate the world with its Auton-infected plastic products...

Cast
Jon Pertwee (Doctor Who), Katy Manning (Jo Grant), Nicholas Courtney (Brigadier Lethbridge-Stewart), Richard Franklin (Captain Mike Yates), John Levene (Sergeant Benton), Roger Delgado (The Master), Michael Wisher (Rex Farrel), Harry Towb (McDermott), Stephen Jack (John Farrel), Barbara Leake (Mrs Farrel), Roy Stewart (Tony the Strong Man), Dermot Tuohy (Brownrose), John Baskcomb (Luigi Rossini), Christopher Burgess (Professor Phillips), Dave Carter (Museum Attendant), Andrew Staines (Goodge), Frank Mills (Radio Telescope Director), David Garth (Pinstripe Time Lord), Terry Walsh (Auton Policeman/Stunt Double for The Doctor), Pat Gorman (Auton Leader), Haydn Jones (Auton Voice), Norman Stanley (Telephone Mechanic/The Master), Bill McGuirk (Policeman), Tommy Reynolds (Troll Doll), Dinny Powell (Stunt Double for Captain Yates)

Crew
Action HAVOC, *Visual Effects Designer* Michaeljohn Harris, *Effects Sculptor* John Friedlander, *Inlay Operators* Alan Rixon, John McPherson, *Technical Managers* Ray Hider, Graham Southcott, *Vision Mixer* Shirley Coward, *Studio Lighting* Eric Monk, *Studio Sound* Colin Dixon, *Circus Sequences* Robert Brothers, *Film Cameraman* John Baker, *Film Editor* Geoffrey Botterill, *Special Sound* Brian Hodgson, *Grams Operator* Linton Howell Hughes, *Incidental Music* Dudley Simpson, *Costume Designer* Ken Trew, *Make-Up Artist* Jan Harrison, *Designer* Ian Watson, *Production Assistant* Nicholas Howard John, *Assistant Floor Manager* Bruce Best, *Director's Assistant* Rita Dunn, *Floor Assistant* Edward Pugh, *Script Editor* Terrance Dicks, *Producer/Director* Barry Letts

DWM Index
52	Barry Letts interview
	Cry HAVOC
60	Episode Guide
95	Richard Franklin interview
117	Michael Wisher interview
121	Season 8 Flashback
151	Stuart Fell interview
	Terry Walsh interview
160	Barry Letts interview
164	Archive 1
165	Archive 2 + Fact File
172	Those *Radio Times*
188	What The Papers Said
199	Rebuilding The Classics II
	Video review
220	What The Censor Saw
227	Nicholas Courtney interview

256 Katy Manning interview
270 Barry Letts interview
311 Archive Feature
317 Derek Ware interview
325 Time Team

Recording Dates
17-18 September 1970 (Location filming), 21-23 September 1970 (Location filming), 9-10 October 1970 (TC8), 23 October 1970 (TC6), 24 October 1970 (TC8)

Locations
St Peter's Court Shopping Centre and Car Park, Church Lane, Chalfont St Peter, Buckinghamshire; Hedgemoor Woods, Chalfont St Giles, Buckinghamshire; Queen's Wharf, Hammersmith, London W6; Robert Brothers Circus, Leyton, London E10; Totternhoe Lime and Stone Co Ltd, Totternhoe, Dunstable, Bedfordshire; GPO Relay Station, Caddington, Bedfordshire; Thermo Plastics Ltd, Dunstable, Bedfordshire

Working Title
The Spray of Death

Factoids
- Producer Barry Letts introduced the characters of Jo Grant and Captain Mike Yates in a bid to mirror the success of the Jamie and Victoria relationship from *The Enemy of the World* (40), the Patrick Troughton story he had directed. The Master was conceived as a returning villain in the style of Arthur Conan Doyle's Moriarty character. The actor chosen to play him, Roger Delgado (full name: Roger Caesar Marius Bernard de Delgado Torres Castillo Roberto) worked mainly in the film industry and had appeared in several Hammer horror movies.
- Various problems plagued the location shoot. Katy Manning twisted her ankle and had to walk with a limp (explained in the script by her jumping badly from the coach). Nicholas Courtney suffered an attack of depression and was replaced by a double for some scenes, and stuntman Terry Walsh was injured performing an impressive fall down a slope after being hit by Captain Yates in his UNIT jeep (doubled by fellow stuntman Dinny Powell).
- A climactic special effects shot of the materializing Nestene Consciousness in Episode Four was deemed unconvincing and was dropped from the final edit. For the Beacon Hill radio telescopes, models of the two dishes were placed in front of the location cameras and aligned with the horizon.

- Sequences involving the plastic chair that suffocates McDermott and the telephone cord that wraps itself around the Doctor's neck were acted out in reverse and recorded onto videodisc, which was then played backwards. Videodisc was also used to speed up the movement of the Troll doll (played by Tommy Reynolds), whose scenes were recorded in front of blue drapes and CSOed into the main sets. In order to save money, CSO was used for many backgrounds, such as the woods outside the telephone box, the Space Centre museum, the Auton factory and Mrs Farrel's kitchen.
- To herald the new series, the *Radio Times* (dated 2-8 January 1971) featured a front cover of the Doctor, Jo, the Brigadier and the Master outside the Tardis.

Comment
A comic strip version of *Spearhead from Space* (51), this Auton sequel succeeds by virtue of its frenetic pace and well-honed script. Roger Delgado brings instant gravitas to a clichéd villain, while Jo Grant and Mike Yates, although both equally wet, are nonetheless likeable new additions to the so-called 'UNIT family'. *Terror of the Autons* relaunches the Pertwee era as if the events of Season 7 never happened - everything is gaudier, tackier and fringed with CSO shimmer, the action is more outlandish and the characterization riper, yet amazingly the whole thing works better than it has any right to. Naff ending aside, it's a far more entertaining story than *Spearhead* and, for once, depicts an alien menace that uses cunning instead of brute force. **75%**

"I remember this place. Something happened here...something terrible." ~ *Barnham*

56) The Mind of Evil
Don Houghton

Serial Code: FFF
Original Transmission
Episode One
Saturday 30 January 1971, 17.15-17.40, 6.1m / 61
Episode Two
Saturday 6 February 1971, 17.15-17.40, 8.8m / 54

Episode Three
Saturday 13 February 1971, 17.15-17.40, 7.5m / 70
Episode Four
Saturday 20 February 1971, 17.15-17.40, 7.4m / 63
Episode Five
Saturday 27 February 1971, 17.15-17.40, 7.6m / 58
Episode Six
Saturday 6 March 1971, 17.15-17.40, 7.3m / 65

BBC Archive
All episodes exist as 16mm b/w film recordings of the 625-line two-inch PAL colour master videotapes (wiped in the mid-1970s). Colour clips exist from Episode Six on 525-line NTSC colour U-Matic domestic videotape.

Novelization
Doctor Who - The Mind of Evil by Terrance Dicks (144/16)
Hardback:
March 1985, WH Allen (0491033338 / Andrew Skilleter)
Paperback:
1. July 1985, Target (0426201663 / Andrew Skilleter)
2. March 1989, Star, part of 'Doctor Who Classics' with *Doctor Who - The Claws of Axos* (0352323817 / Andrew Skilleter)

Video
May 1998, plus colour clips from Episode Six, twin-pack (BBCV 6361 / Photomontage)

Music and Sound Effects
1. October 1973, 'The World of Doctor Who' on B-side of *Moonbase 3*, single (RESL 13)
2. April 1975, *BBC Radiophonic Workshop 21*, LP (REC 354 / Photograph)
3. April 1975, *BBC Radiophonic Workshop 21*, cassette (ZCM 354 / Photograph)
4. December 1992, Silva Screen, *Doctor Who - Earthshock*, CD (FILMCD 709 / Alister Pearson)
5. December 1992, Silva Screen, *Doctor Who - Earthshock*, cassette (FILMC 709 / Alister Pearson)
6. May 2000, *Doctor Who at the BBC Radiophonic Workshop: Volume 2 - New Beginnings 1970-1980*, CD (WMSF 6024-2 / Photographs)

Précis
An experimental new machine that drains criminals of their violent tendencies goes on the rampage…

Cast
Jon Pertwee (Doctor Who), Katy Manning (Jo), Nicholas Courtney (Brigadier Lethbridge-Stewart), Richard Franklin (Captain Yates), John Levene (Sergeant Benton), Neil McCarthy (Barnham), William Marlowe (Henry Mailer), Roger Delgado (Keller/The Master), Pik-Sen Lim (Captain Chin Lee), Michael Sheard (Dr Summers), Tommy Duggan (Senator Alcott), Simon Lack (Professor Kettering), Haydn Jones (Vosper), Patrick Godfrey (Major Cosworth), Eric Mason (Senior Prison Officer Green), Roy Purcell (Chief Prison Officer Powers), Raymond Westwell (Prison Governor), Bill Matthews, Barry Wade, Dave Carter, Martin Gordon (Prison Officers), Clive Scott (Linwood), Fernanda Marlowe (Corporal Bell), Kristopher Kum (Fu Peng), David Calderisi (Charlie), Johnny Barrs (Fuller), Matthew Walters (Main Gates Prisoner)

Crew
Fight Arranger Derek Martin, *Action* HAVOC, *Visual Effects Designer* Jim Ward, *Visual Effects Assistant* Dave Havard, *Technical Manager* Graham Southcott, *Vision Mixers* Mike Catherwood, Shirley Coward, *Videotape Editors* Sam Upton, Roger Harvey, *Studio Lighting* Eric Monk, *Studio Sound* Chick Anthony, *Film Cameramen* Max Samett, Fred Hamilton, *Film Editor* Howard Billingham, *Special Sound* Brian Hodgson, *Grams Operator* Gerry Burrows, *Incidental Music* Dudley Simpson, *Costume Designer* Bobi Bartlett, *Make-Up Artist* Jan Harrison, *Designer* Ray London, *Production Assistant* John Griffiths, *Assistant Floor Manager* Sue Hedden, *Director's Assistant* Joan Elliott, *Floor Assistant* June O'Shaunessy, *Script Editor* Terrance Dicks, *Producer* Barry Letts, *Director* Timothy Combe

DWM Index
45	Jon Pertwee interview
61	Episode Guide
65	Archive
82	John Levene interview
95	Richard Franklin interview
96	Novelization review
121	Season 8 Flashback
187	AJ Mitchell interview
208	Archive Feature
227	Nicholas Courtney interview
230	John Levene interview
264	Video review
302	Michael Sheard interview
317	Derek Ware interview
325	Time Team 1-3
326	Time Team 4-6

Recording Dates
26-31 October 1970 (Location filming), 2-4 November 1970 (Location filming), 20-21 November 1970 (TC3), 4-5 December 1970 (TC6), 11-12 December 1970 (TC3)

Locations
Dover Castle, Dover, Kent; Archers Court Road, Whitfield, Kent; RAF Manston, Manston, Kent; RAF Swingate, Dover, Kent; Pineham Road, Pineham, Kent; Cornwall Gardens, South Kensington, London SW7; Commonwealth Institute, Kensington, London W8

Working Titles
The Pandora's Box
Doctor Who and the Pandora Machine
Pandora Machine

Factoids
- Barry Letts used a genuine Bloodhound missile, loaned by the 36th Heavy Air Defence Regiment at Shoeburyness, Essex. The MoD also supplied eight soldiers to go with it.
- Fight sequences at Dover Castle had to be reshot because of a scratch on the film negative. For the remount, director Timothy Combe assumed the role of a prisoner to swell the meagre number of extras allotted for the day.
- Much of the footage shot at RAF Swingate was cut from the story due to problems with over-running. Also cut were scenes inside the Commonwealth Institute as Timothy Combe was unhappy with Andy Ho's performance as Chinese delegate Fu Peng. He was replaced in studio recordings with Kristopher Kum. Because of these problems, the high film quotient and the large amount of extras and stuntmen required, *The Mind of Evil* was a very expensive serial to make and ended up considerably over-budget.
- Still photographs of a Dalek (*The Dalek Invasion of Earth*, 10), Koquillion (*The Rescue*, 11), a Zarbi (*The Web Planet*, 13), Slaar and an Ice Warrior (both *The Seeds of Death*, 48), a War Machine (*The War Machines*, 27), a Silurian (*Doctor Who and the Silurians*, 52) and a Cyberman (*The Invasion*, 46) were superimposed over Episode Three's cliffhanger ending as the Keller Machine conjures up the Doctor's worst nightmares. Other planned images were the Slyther (*The Dalek Invasion of Earth*, 10), Servo-Robot (*The Wheel in Space*, 43) and a Sensorite (*The Sensorites*, 7).

Comment
This is a grim, *Clockwork Orange*-inspired story that benefits greatly from being left to posterity in black and white - knowing the overuse of colour in this period of *Doctor Who*'s life, some of the doomladen atmosphere would surely be lost amidst a swelter of garish hues. The prison setting is very believably presented, and the riots and fighting are particularly violent. In many ways, this is a throwback to the previous season and echoes the seriousness of the author's first story, *Inferno* (54) - plotwise it's perhaps a little disjointed, but there's no denying the gusto with which director Timothy Combe has assembled his material. William Marlow makes an effectively ruthless gangster, and the sight of the Master suavely smoking a cigar in the back of a chauffer-driven limousine seems somehow terribly *right*.
85%

"I doubt if even Axonite could increase the growth of human commonsense." ~ The Doctor

57) *The Claws of Axos*
Bob Baker and Dave Martin

Serial Code: GGG
Original Transmission
Episode One
Saturday 13 March 1971, 17.15-17.40, 7.3m / 57
Episode Two
Saturday 20 March 1971, 17.15-17.40, 8m / 43
Episode Three
Saturday 27 March 1971, 17.15-17.40, 6.4m / 70
Episode Four
Saturday 3 April 1971, 17.15-17.40, 7.8m / 49

BBC Archive
Episodes One and Four exist as 625-line two-inch PAL colour master videotapes. Episodes Two and Three exist as 525-line NTSC two-inch colour videotapes converted to 625-line PAL. 16mm b/w film recordings of each episode also exist.

Novelization
Doctor Who and the Claws of Axos by Terrance Dicks (141/12)
Hardback:
April 1977, Allan Wingate (0855231815 / Chris Achilleos)
Paperback:
1. April 1977, Target (0426117034 / Chris Achilleos)
2. June 1979, Target (0426117034 / John Geary)
3. March 1989, Star, part of 'Doctor Who Classics' with *Doctor Who - The Mind of Evil* (0352323817 / Andrew Skilleter)

Video
May 1992 (BBCV 4742 / Andrew Skilleter)

DVD
April 2005, studio footage, commentary by Barry Letts, Katy Manning and Richard Franklin (BBCDVD 1354 / Clayton Hickman)
Music and Sound Effects
1. 1972, Electronic Music Studio, *Sounds From…EMS*, EP (- / -)
2. 1972, Electronic Music Studio, *Sounds From…EMS*, Flexidisc (- / -)
3. October 1973, 'The World of Doctor Who' on B-side of *Moonbase 3*, single (RESL 13)
4. May 2000, *Doctor Who at the BBC Radiophonic Workshop: Volume 2 - New Beginnings 1970-1980*, CD (WMSF 6024-2 / Photographs)
Précis
Inhabitants of an organic spaceship offer the world a miraculous answer to food shortages…
Cast
Jon Pertwee (Doctor Who), Katy Manning (Jo), Nicholas Courtney (Brigadier Lethbridge-Stewart), John Levene (Sergeant Benton), Richard Franklin (Captain Yates), Paul Grist (Filer), Donald Hewlett (Hardiman), Roger Delgado (The Master), Peter Bathurst (Chinn), David Savile (Winser), Derek Ware (Pigbin Josh), Fernanda Marlowe (Corporal Bell), Bernard Holley (Axon Man), Patricia Gordino (Axon Woman), John Hicks (Axon Boy), Debbie Lee London (Axon Girl), Tim Pigott-Smith (Captain Harker), Michael Walker, David G March (Radar Operators), Kenneth Benda (The Minister), Nick Hobbs (Nuton Driver), Royston Farrell (Technician), Gloria Walker (Secretary/Nurse), Nick Hobbs (Stunt Double for Axon Man), Sue Crossland (Stunt Double for Axon Woman), Jack Cooper (Stunt Double for The Master), Derek Ware (Stunt Double for Filer), Peter Holmes, Steve Smart, Pierce McAvoy, George Howse, Stuart Fell, Clinton Morris, Marc Boyle, Jack Cooper (Axon Monsters), Mildred Brown (Double for Aged Jo), Jack Cooper (Stunt Double for Hardiman)
Crew
Fight Arranger Derek Ware, *Action* HAVOC, *Visual Effects Designer* John Horton, *Visual Effects Assistant* Dave Havard, Colin Mapson, James Ward, *Technical Manager* Bernard Fox, *Vision Mixer* Mike Catherwood, *Studio Lighting* Ralph Walton, *Studio Sound* Dave Kitchen, *Senior Studio Engineer, Film Cameraman* AA Englander, *Film Editor* Bob Rymer, *Special Sound* Brian Hodgson, *Grams Operator* Linton Howell-Hughes, *Incidental Music* Dudley Simpson, *Costume Designer* Barbara Lane, *Make-Up Artists* Jan Harrison, Rhian Davies, *Designer* Kenneth Sharp, *Production Assistant* Marion McDougall, *Assistant Floor Manager* Roselyn Parker, *Director's Assistant* Sue Stapely, *Floor Assistant* Chris Fox, *Script Editor* Terrance Dicks, *Producer* Barry Letts, *Director* Michael Ferguson

DWM Index
61	Episode Guide
95	Richard Franklin interview
121	Season 8 Flashback
142	Bob Baker interview
151	Derek Ware interview
172	Those *Radio Times*
185	Michael Ferguson interview
187	Tim Pigott-Smith interview
	Donald Hewlett interview
	Bernard Holley interview
	Video review
227	Nicholas Courtney interview
235	Bob Baker and Dave Martin interview
256	Katy Manning interview
264	Archive Feature
317	Derek Ware interview
326	Time Team
355	DVD preview
356	DVD review

Recording Dates
22 December 1970 (TC7), 4-8 January 1971 (Location filming), January 1971 (unknown studio modelwork), 22-23 January 1971 (TC3), 5-6 February 1971 (TC4)
Locations
Dungeness Nuclear Power Station and Dungeness Road, Dungeness, Kent; Dengemarsh Road, Lydd, Kent; St Martin's Plain Camp, Cheriton High Street, Shorncliffe, Kent
Working Titles
Doctor Who and the Gift
The Friendly Invasion
Gift
The Axons
Vampire from Space
The Vampire from Space
Factoids
- *The Claws of Axos* began life as a seven-part Patrick Troughton story, before being rewritten as a six-part Pertwee story. The revised storyline still contained too many ideas, and was subsequently trimmed down to four parts with the character of the Master added to the mix.
- The first studio session was used to conduct CSO experiments for the serial. Sequences inside Axos were recorded with front and back projection, and a psychedelic light projector (of the kind seen prominently in the Thames TV series *The Tomorrow People*) was 'borrowed' from *Top of the*

Pops. Some scenes made it to the final production, such as CSO shots of Axos in space (a fibreglass model covered with unlubricated condoms) and the Axons writhing inside it.
- Extreme weather conditions on location included rain, fog, snow and sunshine. A line was inserted in the first studio session to explain away these inconsistencies, claiming the "freak weather" was caused by the Axons' arrival.
- The Tardis interior - seen for the first time since *The War Games* (50) - was redesigned by Kenneth Sharp. The roundelled wall flat was simplified (although the old photographic blow-up wall remained the same) while the console was repaired and updated slightly with colourful new neon lights added to the central column.
- Opening titles reading '*The Vampire from Space*' were recorded for Episodes One and Two. It was only by the final recording session that Barry Letts had decided to lose the 'Hammer Horror' tag and change it to *The Claws of Axos*, necessitating the titles being reshot.
- Pigbin Josh's death scene, in which his face crumbles away, was considered too horrific, and so a whiteout effect was superimposed over the top.

Comment
If you could sum up the whole Pertwee era in one story, then *The Claws of Axos* would have to be a strong contender. Continuing the trend started with *Terror of the Autons* (55), there's a definite comic strip feel to the action and the characters are all larger-than-life. Like *Terror*, there's a riot of colour on show, and the Axon's awesome organic spaceship is one of the programme makers' most impressive attempts at 'alienness' yet. The Axons are excellent in their many stages of 'blobbiness', the Dungeness locations have a quiet, eerie quality unlike anything yet seen in the series, and the many stunt scenes are done with verve and energy. Okay, so it's often cheap-looking and silly (and the acting is often woeful), but for sheer inventiveness and creativity, and ignoring some of the more dodgy effects (such as the exploding Nuton complex and the sleeping-bag Axon), *The Claws of Axos* - the dictionary definition of 'psychedelic' - is an absolute treat. **90%**

"All that talk of your about travelling in time and space - it's true!" ~ *Jo Grant*

58) Colony in Space
Malcolm Hulke

Serial Code: HHH
Original Transmission
Episode One
Saturday 10 April 1971, 18.10-18.35, 7.6m / 41
Episode Two
Saturday 17 April 1971, 18.10-18.35, 8.5m / 28
Episode Three
Saturday 24 April 1971, 18.10-18.35, 9.5m / 26
Episode Four
Saturday 1 May 1971, 18.10-18.35, 8.1m / 28
Episode Five
Saturday 8 May 1971, 18.10-18.35, 8.8m / 23
Episode Six
Saturday 15 May 1971, 18.10-18.35, 8.7m / 23
BBC Archive
All episodes exist as 525-line two-inch colour NTSC videotapes converted to 625-line PAL. 16mm b/w film recordings exist for every episode, but the 625-line two-inch PAL colour master videotapes were wiped by 1978.
Novelization
Doctor Who and the Doomsday Weapon by Malcolm Hulke (166/21)
Hardback:
March 1982, WH Allen (0491027079 / Jeff Cummins)
Paperback:
1. April 1974, Target (0426103726 / Chris Achilleos)
2. August 1979, Target (0426103726 / Jeff Cummins)
Video
November 2001, in the 'Master Limited Edition Tin' [BBCV 7175] with *The Time Monster* (BBCV 7176 / Photomontage)
Précis
On the planet Uxarieus, colonists are fighting for their rights against a vicious mining company…
Cast
Jon Pertwee (Doctor Who), Katy Manning (Jo), Nicholas Courtney (Brigadier Lethbridge-Stewart), Roger Delgado (Adjudicator/The Master), David Webb (Leeson), Sheila Grant (Jane Leeson), John Tordoff (Alec Leeson), John Ringham (Ashe), Helen Worth (Mary Ashe), Nicholas Pennell (Winton), Roy Skelton (Norton), Morris Perry (Dent), Tony Caunter (Morgan), Bernard Kay (Caldwell), John Herrington (Holden), Norman Atkyns (The Guardian), Roy Heymann (Alien

Priest), Peter Forbes-Robertson (First Time Lord), John Baker (Second Time Lord), Graham Leaman (Third Time Lord), John Scott Martin (IMC Robot), John Line (Martin), Mitzi Webster (Mrs Martin), Pat Gorman (Primitive/Long/Colonist), Stanley McGeach (Allen), Michael Briant (IMC Console Voices), Terry Walsh (IMC Guard Rogers)

Crew
Action HAVOC, *Visual Effects Designer* Bernard Wilkie, *Visual Effects Assistants* John Friedlander, Ian Scoones, *Technical Manager* Bernard Fox, *Vision Mixer* Jim Stephens, *Studio Lighting* Ralph Walton, *Studio Sound* David Hughes, Tony Millier, *Film Cameraman* Peter Hall, *Film Editor* William Symon, *Special Sound* Brian Hodgson, *Grams Operator* Gordon Phillipson, *Incidental Music* Dudley Simpson, *Costume Designer* Michael Burdle, *Make-Up Artist* Jan Harrison, *Designer* Tim Gleeson, *Production Assistant* Nicholas John, *Assistant Floor Manager* Graeme Harper, *Director's Assistant* Pauline Silcock, *Floor Assistant* John Turner, *Script Editor* Terrance Dicks, *Producer* Barry Letts, *Director* Michael Briant

DWM Index
52	Barry Letts interview
61	Episode Guide
67	Archive
90	Graeme Harper interview
91	The Incredible Malcolm Hulke Novelization review
97	Michael Briant interview
121	Season 8 Flashback
172	Those *Radio Times*
184	Graeme Harper interview
188	What The Papers Said
190	Ian Scoones interview
192	Crossing the Line
194	John Ringham interview
220	What The Censor Saw
233	The John Nathan-Turner Memoirs
238	Archive Feature
256	Katy Manning interview
263	Michael E Briant interview
311	Video review
326	Time Team 1
328	Time Team 2-6

Recording Dates
10-12 February 1971 (Location filming), 15-16 February 1971 (Location filming), unknown date (EFS modelwork), 5-6 March 1971 (TC4), 19-20 March 1971 (TC3), 2-3 April 1971 (TC3)

Location
Old Baal Clay Pit, Carclaze, near St Austell, Cornwall

Working Title
Colony

Factoids
- The IMC Servo Robot was carried along by effects assistant Ian Scoones on location, as its caster wheels jammed on the muddy terrain. Made from blockboard and card by Magna Models, it was damaged after being left out in the rain overnight and its use was kept to a minimum during studio recordings.
- The Tardis materialized and dematerialised as a jump-cut instead of a gradual fade - director Michael Briant claiming this was due to the Time Lords' controlling the craft. However, as this also happens with the Master's Tardis, it seems more likely to be a simple continuity error.
- A fight between stuntman Terry Walsh and Nicholas Pennell was filmed with two cameras in one take, as it was conducted in one of the muddiest areas of the pit and the actors didn't have spare costumes for a retake.
- On 3 March, during rehearsals for the first studio block, Eamonn Andrews surprised Jon Pertwee by presenting him with the big red book for *This Is Your Life*. The programme was broadcast on 14 April 1971.
- Modelwork was conducted on location and at Ealing. The IMC spaceship was a redressed aeroplane from the Gerry Anderson series *Joe 90*, bought by the BBC as part of a job lot of miniatures when Anderson's Century 21 studios closed circa 1970.
- This serial saw the last appearance of the photographic blow-up Tardis wall flats, in use since the *An Unearthly Child* (1).

Comment
A workaday story that, although on the slow side, is pleasingly constructed and has a fascinating story to tell about the clash of individualism vs corporatism. As with all of Hulke's work, shades of grey predominate, and the baddies (mostly) exhibit believable motivations for their actions. Caldwell, played with much conviction by Bernard Kay, is an especially strong character whose changing opinion about his own loyalties adds much drama to the story. Visually the story is weak, with little of the panache of previous Pertwee adventures, but at least the grim and authentically muddy location scenes give the colonists' dilemma some veracity. The Master's inclusion, though, is superfluous. **67%**

"Jenkins, chap with wings there - five round rapid!" ~ *Brigadier Lethbridge-Stewart*

59) The Dæmons

Guy Leopold (pen-name for Robert Sloman and Barry Letts)

Serial Code: JJJ
Original Transmission
Episode One
Saturday 22 May 1971, 18.15-18.40, 9.2m / 26
Episode Two
Saturday 29 May 1971, 18.10-18.35, 8m / 23
Episode Three
Saturday 5 June 1971, 18.10-18.35, 8.1m / 34
Episode Four
Saturday 12 June 1971, 18.10-18.35, 8.1m / 24
Episode Five
Saturday 19 June 1971, 18.10-18.35, 8.3m / 17
Repeat Transmissions
Omnibus
Tuesday 28 December 1971, 16.20-17.50, 10.5m / 38
On BBC2:
Episode One
Friday 20 November 1992, 19.15-19.40, 2.5m / 27
Episode Two
Friday 27 November 1992, 19.15-19.40, 3m / 23
Episode Three
Friday 4 December 1992, 19.15-19.40, 2.3m / -
Episode Four
Friday 11 December 1992, 19.15-19.40, 2.2m / 26
Episode Five
Friday 18 December 1992, 19.15-19.40, 2.3m / 24
BBC Archive
Episodes One, Two, Three and Five exist as composites of 16mm b/w film recordings, taken from the 625-line two-inch PAL colour master videotapes, with 525-line NTSC colour U-Matic domestic videotapes. Episode Four exists as the 625-line two-inch PAL colour master videotape (the others having being wiped by 1977).
Novelization
Doctor Who and the Dæmons by Barry Letts (172/15)
Hardback:
January 1982, WH Allen, renamed *Doctor Who - Doctor Who and the Dæmons* (0491026870 / Andrew Skilleter)

Paperback:
1. October 1974, Target (0426104447 / Chris Achilleos)
2. January 1980, Target (0426113322 / Andrew Skilleter)
3. March 1989, Star, part of 'Doctor Who Classics' with *Doctor Who - The Time Monster* (0352323825 / Andrew Skilleter)
4. October 1993, Target, renamed *Doctor Who - The Dæmons* (0426113322 / Alister Pearson)
Video
March 1993, recoloured (BBCV 4950 / Alister Pearson)
Script Book
October 1992, Titan Books, edited by John McElroy with background notes by Stephen James Walker (1852863242 / Alister Pearson)
Précis
The villagers of Devil's End are trapped when an archaeological dig uncovers seemingly occult forces...
Cast
Jon Pertwee (Doctor Who), Katy Manning (Jo), Nicholas Courtney (Brigadier Lethbridge-Stewart/BBC3 Announcer), Richard Franklin (Captain Mike Yates), John Levene (Sergeant Benton), Damaris Hayman (Miss Hawthorne), Roger Delgado (The Master /Reverend Magister), Robin Wentworth (Professor Horner), David Simeon (Alistair Fergus), Don McKillop (Bert the Landlord), Jon Croft (Tom Girton), Christopher Wray (PC Groom), John Joyce (Garvin), Eric Hillyard (Dr Reeves), James Snell (Harry), Rollo Gamble (Winstanley), Alec Linstead (Sergeant Osgood), John Owens (Thorpe), Gerald Taylor (Baker's Man), The Headington Quarry Men (Morris Dancers), Matthew Corbett (Jones), Stanley Mason (Bok), Stephen Thorne (Azal), John Holmes (Man With Dog), John Scott Martin (Charlie), Mike Smith (Helicopter Pilot/Double for Mike Yates and Tom Girton), Peter Diamond (Double for Mike Yates/Morris Dancer), John Crane (Motorbike Double for Mike Yates), Pamela Deveraux (Double for Jo Grant), Jack Silk (Double for Doctor Who), Christopher Barry (RAF Pilot Voice)
Crew
Fight Arranger Peter Diamond, *Stuntmen* Peter Diamond, Jack Silk, *Visual Effects Designer* Peter Day, *Visual Effects Assistants* Peter Day, Ricky Grosser, *Studio Lighting* Ralph Walton, *Studio Sound* Tony Millier, *Film Cameraman* Fred Hamilton, *Film Sound* Dick Manton, *Film Editor* Chris Wimble, *Special Sound* Brian Hodgson, *Incidental Music* Dudley Simpson, *Costume Designer* Barbara Lane, *Make-Up Artist* Jan

Harrison, *Designer* Roger Ford, *Production Assistant* Peter Grimwade, *Assistant Floor Manager* Sue Hedden, *Script Editor* Terrance Dicks, *Producer* Barry Letts, *Director* Christopher Barry

DWM Index
52 Barry Letts interview
54 Peter Grimwade interview
57 Archive
61 Episode Guide
82 John Levene interview
95 Richard Franklin interview
99 Christopher Barry interview
111 Nicholas Courtney interview
113 Jon Pertwee interview
119 Nostalgia
121 Season 8 Flashback
160 Barry Letts interview
172 Those *Radio Times*
180 Christopher Barry interview
194 Script Book review
195 Christopher Barry interview
196 Rebuilding The Classics
197 *Return to Devil's End* video review
    Return to Devil's End location report
198 Video review
220 What The Censor Saw
230 John Levene interview
241 Archive Feature
256 Katy Manning interview
276 Robert Sloman interview
315 Christopher Barry interview
328 Time Team 1-3
329 Time Team 4-5

Recording Dates
19-24 April 1971 (Location filming), 26-30 April 1971 (Location filming), 11 May 1971 (TC4), 19 May 1971 (TC4), 26 May 1971 (TC4)

Locations
Aldbourne village and Four Barrows, Aldbourne, Wiltshire; Membury Airfield, Membury, Wiltshire; Oaken Coppice, Knighton, Wiltshire; Airfields, Darrells Farm, Ramsbury, Wiltshire

Working Title
The Demons

Factoids
- Scenes of the heat barrier were hampered by a late snowfall which had to be cleared away by hand. The heat barrier itself was a metal hoop covered with tinsel which was then filmed through a lens applied with Vaseline to blur the image.
- The exploding church in Episode Five was a filmed model insert, although some viewers complained that the BBC had actually destroyed a real building.
- The pen-name 'Guy Leopold' was used for two reasons - partly because Barry Letts wasn't officially allowed to write and produce for the same series, and partly so that Robert Sloman could disguise the fact that he was not working with his usual writing partner.
- Matthew Corbett, in a minor role, went on to become famous as Sooty and Sweep's right-hand man.

Comment
A ripped-off *Quatermass and the Pit*, this is the story that everyone in the 'UNIT family' remembers with affection. The village location is smashing, there are some chilling moments early on, and characterization throughout is strong.
 Just a few things mar the enjoyment, such as the odd bit of bargain-basement acting, some lame effects, and the illogical ending, but otherwise this is a heady, albeit over-rated, brew.
79%

Season 9

"Frankly, I don't know whether I can stand much more of your hospitality." ~ The Doctor

60) *Day of the Daleks*
Louis Marks

Serial Code: KKK
Original Transmission
Episode One
Saturday 1 January 1972, 17.50-18.15, 9.8m / 38
Episode Two
Saturday 8 January 1972, 17.50-18.15, 10.4m / 29
Episode Three
Saturday 15 January 1972, 17.50-18.15, 9.1m / 38
Episode Four
Saturday 22 January 1972, 17.50-18.15, 9.1m / 40
Repeat Transmission
Omnibus
Monday 3 September 1973, 19.00-20.00, 7.4m / 32
BBC Archive
All episodes exist as 625-line two-inch colour PAL master videotapes.

Novelization
Doctor Who and the Day of the Daleks by Terrance Dicks (140/14)
Hardback:
1. August 1981, WH Allen (0491029756 / Andrew Skilleter)
2. June 1983, WH Allen, part of 'Doctor Who - Dalek Omnibus' with *Doctor Who and the Dalek Invasion of Earth* and *Doctor Who and the Planet of the Daleks* (0491034202 / Andrew Skilleter)
Paperback:
1. April 1974, Target (0426103807 / Chris Achilleos)
2. 1982, Target (0426103807 / Andrew Skilleter)
3. January 1994, Target, renamed *Doctor Who - The Day of the Daleks* (0426103807 / Alister Pearson)

Video
1. July 1986, compilation, renamed *The Day of the Daleks* (BBCV 2036 / Photomontage)
2. July 1986, compilation, renamed *The Day of the Daleks*, Betamax (BBCB 2036 / Photomontage)
3. February 1988, renamed *The Day of the Daleks* (BBCV 5216 / Photomontage)
4. February 1994, renamed *The Day of the Daleks* (BBCV 5219 / Photomontage)

Laserdisc
April 1997, Encore Entertainment (EE1202 / Pete Wallbank)

Précis
Rebels from the 22nd century try and avert a Dalek-controlled future Earth…

Cast
Jon Pertwee (Doctor Who), Katy Manning (Jo), Nicholas Courtney (Brigadier Lethbridge-Stewart), Richard Franklin (Captain Yates), John Levene (Sergeant Benton), Jean McFarlane (Miss Paget), Wilfrid Carter (Sir Reginald Styles), Tim Condren (Guerrilla), Aubrey Woods (Controller), Deborah Brayshaw (Girl Technician), Gypsie Kemp (UNIT Radio Operator), Anna Barry (Anat), Jimmy Winston (Shura), Scott Fredericks (Boaz), Valentine Palmer (Monia), Rick Lester, Maurice Bush, David Joyce, Frank Menzies, Bruce Wells, Geoffrey Todd (Ogrons), Andrew Carr (Senior Guard), George Raistrick (Work Centre Guard), Peter Hill (Manager), Alex MacIntosh (Himself), John Scott Martin, Ricky Newby, Murphy Grumbar (Daleks), Oliver Gilbert, Peter Messaline (Dalek Voices/Secretary's Voice/Minister's Voice/Radio Voices), Sue Farebrother (Stunt Double for Jo)

Crew
Fight Arranger Rick Lester, *Visual Effects Designer* Jim Ward, *Special Graphics* Sid Lomax, *Ogron Mask* John Friedlander, *Technical Managers* Derek Martin, Alan Arbuthnott, *Vision Mixer* Mike Catherwood, *Studio Lighting* Alan Horne, *Studio Sound* Tony Millier, *Film Cameraman* Fred Hamilton, *Film Editor* Dan Rae, *Special Sound* Brian Hodgson, *Grams Operator* Gordon Phillipson, *Incidental Music* Dudley Simpson, *Costume Designer* Mary Husband, *Make-Up Artist* Heather Stewart, *Designer* David Myerscough-Jones, *Production Assistant* Norman Stewart, *Assistant Floor Manager* Sue Hedden, *Director's Assistant* Carolyn Driver, *Floor Assistant* John O'Shaughnessy, *Script Editor* Terrance Dicks, *Producer* Barry Letts, *Director* Paul Bernard

DWM Index
57	John Friedlander interview
61	Episode Guide
82	John Levene interview
111	Archive + Fact File
113	Jon Pertwee interview
135	Season 9 Flashback
168	Paul Bernard interview
172	Those *Radio Times*
188	What The Papers Said
227	Nicholas Courtney interview
246	Laserdisc review
250	Vox Pops
256	Katy Manning interview
	Louis Marks interview
301	Archive Feature
307	Scott Fredericks interview
329	Time Team

Recording Dates
13-16 September 1971 (Location filming), 4-5 October 1971 (TC4), 18-19 October 1971 (TC8)

Locations
United States International University, Dropmore Park, Burnham, Buckinghamshire; Railway bridge and wasteland near Bulls Bridge, Hayes, Middlesex; Harvey House, Green Dragon Lane, Brentford, Middlesex

Working Title
Ghost Hunters
Years of Doom
The Time Warriors
The Day of the Daleks
Ghosts

Factoids
- Louis Marks' *Ghost Hunters* serial began life as a non-Dalek story - guerrillas were trying to avert a future world overtaken by a military dictatorship. Robert Sloman was then asked to formulate a Dalek story, and this was initially planned as a six-part season finale called *The Daleks in London*.

Finally it was decided that the Daleks could make a dramatic impact in the first story with minimal reworking of Marks' existing script.

- Three 1960s Dalek props featured in this story, taken from storage at Pinewood Studios. Two were repainted dark grey and the other was given a gold colour scheme to suggest its Chief Dalek rank. New dome lights, castors and a 'pupil' on their eyestalks were added. The Ogrons (originally 'Ogorons') had half-masks sculpted by effects assistant John Friedlander.
- A *Radio Times* cover heralded the return of the Daleks and the debut of Season 9 courtesy of a stunning painting by Frank Bellamy (dated 1-7 January 1972).
- Black and white captions of the first two Doctors were overlaid against the Pertwee title sequence background and CSOed onto a screen as the Third Doctor is brainwashed at the end of Episode Three. The screen also incorporated the closing title sequence, with Jon Pertwee's title card superimposed over his recumbent form in the manner of an epitaph.
- Alex MacIntosh was a BBC in-vision television announcer from 1955 to 1961. He presented *Come Dancing* for nearly a decade (1957-1966) and also the London news magazine *Town and Around* in 1961. Later he worked for a television company in Sydney, Australia.
- A primitive form of 'scene-synch' (see *Meglos*, 111) was introduced with this story, in which one camera could exactly copy the movement of another. It was used for CSO scenes of the scanner screen in the Dalek control room and allowed the main camera to zoom back while retaining the same image proportions on screen.
- The final scene of the story was to have been of the Doctor and Jo meeting their earlier selves in the UNIT lab (as seen in Episode One). However, this was cut late in the day when it was discovered that Episode Four was over-running.

Comment

Ironically, *Doctor Who* had never touched a 'time paradox' story before, and so *Day of the Daleks*, a cleverly scripted and handsomely produced story anyway, is thus especially satisfying. The future Earth scenario is believably downbeat (although I would've liked to see the Daleks in front of a shattered Big Ben), and the polished metallic sets are excellent. Acting is top-drawer too, with honours going to Aubrey Woods as the oily Controller, a scheming puppet dictator with a vestige of humanity in his heart. The gradual realization that the rebels are trapped in a time loop of their own making is extremely effective and leads to all sorts of weighty questions about cause and effect that would be revisited years later with the *Terminator* film trilogy. The letdowns, of course, are the Daleks. Static, poorly vocalised, and few in number, they are a pale shadow of their 1960s selves. Still, the Ogrons are good. **80%**

"The future you set so much store by is yours now." ~ *Hepesh*

61) The Curse of Peladon
Brian Hayles

Serial Code: MMM
Original Transmission
Episode One
Saturday 29 January 1972, 17.50-18.15, 10.3m / 36
Episode Two
Saturday 5 February 1972, 17.50-18.15, 11m / 20
Episode Three
Saturday 12 February 1972, 17.50-18.15, 7.8m / 49
Episode Four
Saturday 19 February 1972, 17.50-18.15, 8.4m / 27
Repeat Transmission
As part of 'Doctor Who and the Monsters' season:
Episode 1 (One & Two)
Monday 12 July 1982, 19.20-20.10, - / -
Episode 2 (Three & Four)
Monday 19 July 1982, 19.20-20.10, - / -
BBC Archive
All episodes exist as 525-line two-inch NTSC colour videotapes converted to 625-line PAL, as well as 16mm b/w film recordings of the 625-line two-inch PAL colour master videotapes (wiped circa 1975).
Novelization
Doctor Who and the Curse of Peladon by Brian Hayles (142/11)
Hardback:
July 1980, WH Allen (0491027834 / Bill Donohoe)

Paperback:
1. January 1975, Target (0426104528 / Chris Achilleos)
2. June 1992, Target, renamed *Doctor Who - The Curse of Peladon* (0426114981 / Alister Pearson)

Video
August 1993, close-captioned (BBCV 4978 / Andrew Skilleter)

Audio Book
July 1995, 1 x cassette, abridged, read by Jon Pertwee (0563388218 / Photomontage)

Précis
Visions of a giant beast threaten King Peladon's entry to the Galactic Federation…

Cast
Jon Pertwee (Doctor Who), Katy Manning (Jo), David Troughton (Peladon), Geoffrey Toone (Hepesh), Stuart Fell (Alpha Centauri), Ysanne Churchman (Alpha Centauri Voice), Murphy Grumbar (Arcturus), Terry Bale (Arcturus Voice), Alan Bennion (Izlyr), Sonny Caldinez (Ssorg), Henry Gilbert (Torbis), Gordon St Clair (Grun), Nick Hobbs (Aggedor), George Giles (Guard Captain), Wendy Danvers (Amazonia), Terry Walsh (Double for Doctor Who)

Crew
Fight Arranger Terry Walsh, *Fight Profile*, *Visual Effects Designers* Ian Scoones, Bernard Wilkie, *Visual Effects Assistants* Mat Irvine, Brian Marsh, Tony Harding, *Technical Manager* Fred Wright, *Senior Cameraman* Ron Peverall, *Vision Mixer* Michael Turner, *Studio Lighting* Howard King, *Studio Sound* Tony Millier, *Miniatures Cameraman* Mike Wilson, *Film Cameramen* Fred Hamilton, Peter Sargent, *Film Editor* Michael Sha-Dyan, *Special Sound* Brian Hodgson, *Grams/Tape Operator* Gerry Burrows, *Incidental Music* Dudley Simpson, *Costume Designer* Barbara Lane, *Make-Up Artist* Sylvia James, *Designer* Gloria Clayton, *Production Assistant* Chris D'Oyly-John, *Assistant Floor Manager* Ros Anderson, *Director's Assistant* Sue Stapely, *Floor Assistant* Michael Throne, *Script Editor* Terrance Dicks, *Producer* Barry Letts, *Director* Lennie Mayne

DWM Index
59	Mat Irvine interview
62	Episode Guide
69	'Doctor Who and the Monsters' feature
	Archive
	Novelization review
94	Brian Hayles Retrospective
129	Archive + Fact File
135	Season 9 Flashback
151	Stuart Fell interview
190	Ian Scoones interview
203	Alan Bennion interview
	Video review
204	Dudley Simpson interview
215	Archive Feature
	David Troughton interview
220	What The Censor Saw
227	Chris Wallace (Talking Book)
229	Talking Book review
241	Chris D'Oyly-John interview
256	Katy Manning interview
329	Time Team 1-2
330	Time Team 3-4

Recording Dates
15-17 December 1971 (TC Puppet Theatre), 16-17 December (EFS), 17-18 January 1972 (TC4), 31 January-1 February 1972 (TC3)

Working Titles
The Curse
Curse of the Peladons

Factoids
- *The Curse of Peladon* was the first of only two Pertwee stories to be allocated no location filming (*The Monster of Peladon* being the second).
- On first seeing the Alpha Centauri costume, Australian director Lennie Mayne was shocked at its resemblance to "a one-eyed penis" and asked for a cape to be draped around its body to disguise its phallic appearance.
- Alan Bennion's Ice Lord costume was new (although almost identical to that featured in *The Seeds of Death*, 48), while Sonny Caldinez wore Varga's costume from *The Ice Warriors* (39). Bennion wore a more free-moving rubber mouthpiece than he had done in the former story, and was able to speak all his lines live rather than miming them to a pre-recording.
- *The Curse of Peladon* was the first story to feature stunts from Profile, an organization run by Terry Walsh after he'd left Derek Ware's HAVOC team.
- Episode Three and Four's low ratings were due to nationwide blackouts caused by ongoing industrial disputes.
- It was Jon Pertwee's idea to chant his Venusian lullaby 'Klokleda Partha Mennin Klatch' to the tune of 'God Rest Ye Merry Gentlemen'. The spinning hypnotism device was another of Ian Scoones' reused props from Gerry Anderson's Century 21 studios.

Comment
Doctor Who meets *Star Trek* with this stylish tale about a feudal oligarchy signing up to the all-powerful Galactic Federation. Peladon is a wonderfully realised civilization and it really does seem to have a life outside its television appearance. The night-time studio setting adds to the claustrophobia and director Lennie Mayne milks his darkened passages and low-ceilinged tunnels for all they're worth. David Troughton's King is drippy (but then again, so is Jo, so they'd make a perfect couple), but Pertwee is in commanding performance as bogus Earth delegate and his scenes with Alan Bennion as sibilant Ice Lord Izlyr are beautifully played. Alpha Centauri is an outrageous creation, but utterly charming, thanks to Ysanne Churchman's high-pitched wittering and Stuart Fell's dithering body language. The most ridiculous-looking monster yet, but oddly, also one of the most believable. **91%**

"We shall be the victors in the war against Mankind." ~ *Chief Sea Devil*

62) *The Sea Devils*
Malcolm Hulke

Serial Code: LLL
Original Transmission
Episode One
Saturday 26 February 1972, 17.50-18.15, 6.4m / 76
Episode Two
Saturday 4 March 1972, 17.50-18.15, 9.7m / 26
Episode Three
Saturday 11 March 1972, 17.50-18.15, 8.3m / 45
Episode Four
Saturday 18 March 1972, 17.50-18.15, 7.8m / 40
Episode Five
Saturday 25 March 1972, 17.50-18.15, 8.3m / 39
Episode Six
Saturday 1 April 1972, 17.50-18.15, 8.5m / 47
Repeat Transmissions
Omnibus
Wednesday 27 December 1972, 15.05-16.35, 8.7m / 51

Omnibus (unscheduled)
Monday 27 May 1974, 11.15-12.45, 4.6m / 99
On BBC2:
Episode One
Friday 6 March 1992, 18.50-19.15, 3.1m / 14
Episode Two
Friday 13 March 1992, 18.50-19.15, 3.6m / 13
Episode Three
Friday 20 May 1992, 18.50-19.15, 3m / 15
Episode Four
Friday 27 May 1992, 18.50-19.15, 3.4m / 12
Episode Five
Friday 3 April 1992, 18.20-18.45, 3.1m / 13
Episode Six
Friday 10 April 1992, 18.50-19.15, 3m / 15
BBC Archive
Episodes One, Two and Three exist as 525-line two-inch NTSC colour videotapes converted to 625-line PAL. Episodes Four, Five and Six exist as 625-line two-inch PAL colour master videotapes (the others having been wiped by the late 1970s). 16mm b/w film recordings also exist for all the episodes.
Novelization
Doctor Who and the Sea-Devils by Malcolm Hulke (139/13)
Hardback:
June 1981, WH Allen (0491029543 / John Geary)
Paperback:
1. October 1974, Target (0426105168 / Chris Achilleos)
2. April 1979, Target (042611308X / John Geary)
Non-Fiction Book
April 1972, Piccolo, 'Diary of a Production' in *The Making of Doctor Who* by Malcolm Hulke and Terrance Dicks, Paperback (0330232037 / Photograph)
Video
September 1995, twin-pack (BBCV 5667 / Colin Howard)
Music and Sound Effects
1. March 1983, *Doctor Who - The Music*, LP (REH 462 / Iain McCaig)
2. March 1983, *Doctor Who - The Music*, cassette (ZCR 462 / Iain McCaig)
3. May 2000, *Doctor Who at the BBC Radiophonic Workshop: Volume 2 - New Beginnings 1970-1980*, CD (WMSF 6024-2 / Photographs)
Précis
Undersea cousins of the Silurians threaten to wage war against Mankind...
Cast
Jon Pertwee (Doctor Who), Katy Manning (Jo), Roger Delgado (Master), Clive Morton (Trenchard), Edwin Richfield (Hart), June Murphy (Third Officer Jane Blythe), Hugh Futcher (Hickman), Declan Mulholland (Clark), Donald Sumpter (Commander Ridgeway), Martin Boddey (Walker), David Griffin (Lieutenant Commander Mitchell), Christopher Way (Leading Seaman

Lovell), Colin Bell (CPO Summers), Brian Vaughan (Lieutenant Commander Watts), Neil Seiler (Radio Operator), Alec Wallis (Leading Telegraphist Bowman), Royston Tickner (Robbins), Eric Mason (GPO Smedley), Terry Walsh (Castle Guard Barclay), Brian Justice (Castle Guard Wilson), Stanley McGeagh (Castle Guard Drew), Norman Atkyns (Rear Admiral), Rex Rowland (A/B Girton), John Caesar (CPO Myers), Pat Gorman, Brian Nolan, Steve Ismay, Jeff Witherick, Frank Seton, Billy Horrigan, Alan Chuntz (Sea Devils), Mike Stephens (Sea Devil/Castle Guard/HMS Seaspite Sailor), Mike Horsborough (Sea Devil/Castle Guard/HMS Seaspite Sailor), Marc Boyle (Sea Devil/Castle Guard/HMS Seaspite Sailor), Peter Brace (Sea Devil/Castle Guard/HMS Seaspite Sailor), Peter Forbes-Robertson (Chief Sea Devil), Terry Walsh (Double for Doctor Who/Double for The Master/Sea Devil), Derek Ware (Double for The Master/Sailor), Stuart Fell (Double for Jo/Sea Devil/Castle Guard), Michael Briant (DJ Voice)

Crew
Swordfight Arranger Derek Ware, *Action HAVOC*, *Visual Effects Designer* Peter Day, *Visual Effects Assistants* Len Hutton, Jack Kine, *Sea Devil Masks* John Friedlander, *Technical Manager* Peter Valentine, *Vision Mixer* John Gorman, *Studio Lighting* Mike Jefferies, *Studio Sound* Tony Millier, Colin Dixon, *Film Cameraman* Peter Sargent, *Film Editor* Martyn Day, *Special Sound* Brian Hodgson, *Grams Operators* Gordon Phillipson, Barry Bonner, *Incidental Music* Malcolm Clarke, *Costume Designer* Maggie Fletcher, *Make-Up Artist* Sylvia James, *Designer* Tony Snoaden, *Production Assistant* Colin Dudley, *Assistant Floor Manager* John Bradburn, *Director's Assistant* Pauline Silcock, *Floor Assistant* Tony Cox, *Script Editor* Terrance Dicks, *Producer* Barry Letts, *Director* Michael Briant

DWM Index
52   Cry HAVOC
57   John Friedlander interview
62   Episode Guide
70   Archive
91   The Incredible Malcolm Hulke Novelization review
97   Michael Briant interview
133 Nostalgia
135 Season 9 Flashback
151 Derek Ware interview
     Terry Walsh interview
172 Those *Radio Times*
186 TV review (repeat)
192 Archive Feature
     Crossing The Line
195 Malcolm Clarke interview
230 Video review
250 Vox Pops
256 Katy Manning interview
263 Michael E Briant interview
317 Derek Ware interview
330 Time Team

Recording Dates
21-22 October 1971 (Location filming), 25-29 October 1971 (Location filming), 15-16 November 1971 (TC8), 29-30 November 1971 (TC8), 13-14 December 1971 (TC8)

Locations
Fraser Gunnery Range, HMS St George, Southsea, Portsmouth, Hampshire; HMS Reclaim, Portsmouth Harbour, Hampshire; No Man's Land Fort, Solent; Red Cliff, Sandown, Isle of Wight; Whitecliff Bay, Isle of Wight; Bembridge Sailing Club and Harbour, Bembridge, Isle of Wight; Norris Castle, East Cowes, Isle of Wight; Priory Bay, Seaview, Isle of Wight

Working Title
The Sea Silurians

Factoids
- The Royal Navy were keen to provide as many resources for the story as possible (although they couldn't stretch to a helicopter, proffering an SRN5 hovercraft instead). Various shots of vessels and explosions were taken from Royal Navy training films. After the show was broadcast, the Navy's Director of Public Relations wrote to the BBC to suggest any royalty fee be waived in lieu of the good publicity the organization had received.
- Because *The Sea Devils* required a lot of location work, it was made before the preceding story in transmission order, *The Curse of Peladon*, to maximum daylight filming hours. This would be the first instance of a *Doctor Who* story being made and shown out of sequence.
- Six Sea Devil costumes were constructed out of latex-covered overalls by Maggie Fletcher, with turtlelike heads sculpted by John Friedlander and worn as hats on top of the actors' heads. Air bubbles inside these heads caused problems when the actors had to emerge from the water in Episode Four - they would 'pop up' unexpectedly, rather than emerge *en masse* at the same moment.
- *The Rock Collector* episode of *The Clangers* (1969-72), originally transmitted on 25 April

1971, was shown on the Master's television screen in Episode One.
- The Silurians were retroactively renamed 'Eocenes' in this story, though neither are accurate periods for these creatures to hail from.
- The Naval submarine was copied from plans observed on a visit to Admiralty House in London. Peter Day built it from polystyrene and dressed it with plastic model kit parts. Disliking the original propeller, he added one of his own design which coincidentally copied an attachment being developed for the new Polaris nuclear submarine by Naval Intelligence. This led to representatives of the MoD visiting the BBC to check whether any footage of real vessels in operation had been obtained in breach of the Official Secrets Act.

Comment
An empty excuse for gung-ho action set-pieces, *The Sea Devils* replaces the complex political power plays of *Doctor Who and the Silurians* with a two and a half hour promotional film for the Royal Navy. The scene of the Sea Devils emerging from the sea is iconic, but there is much in the story that is unintentionally amusing and the production ultimately outstays its welcome. That said, Roger Delgado gives a rich, multifaceted performance as the Master and introduces a welcome note of sardonic humour into the part. But as the final credits roll, this author feels he's seen enough ships and explosions to last him a lifetime. **65%**

"We'd all become unpeople, undoing unthings untogether. Fascinating." ~ The Doctor

63) The Mutants
Bob Baker and Dave Martin

Serial Code: NNN
Original Transmission
Episode One
Saturday 8 April 1972, 17.50-18.15, 9.1m / 29
Episode Two
Saturday 15 April 1972, 17.50-18.15, 7.8m / 38
Episode Three
Saturday 22 April 1972, 17.50-18.15, 7.9m / 36
Episode Four
Saturday 29 April 1972, 17.50-18.15, 7.5m / 44
Episode Five
Saturday 6 May 1972, 17.50-18.15, 7.9m / 44
Episode Six
Saturday 13 May 1972, 17.50-18.15, 6.5m / 67
BBC Archive
Episodes One and Two exist as 525-line two-inch colour NTSC videotapes converted to 625-line PAL. Episodes Three, Four, Five and Six exist as 625-line two-inch colour PAL master videotapes. All episodes also exist as 16mm b/w film recordings taken from the 625-line two-inch colour PAL master videotapes (Episodes One and Two wiped in the mid-1970s).
Novelization
Doctor Who and the Mutants by Terrance Dicks (127/15)
Hardback:
October 1977, Allan Wingate (0855234717 / Jeff Cummins)
Paperback:
September 1977, Target (0426116909 / Jeff Cummins)
Video
February 2003 (BBCV 7347 / Photomontage)
Music and Sound Effects
September 2003, *Doctor Who - Devils' Planets: The Music of Tristram Cary*, CD (WMSF 6072-2 / Photograph)
Précis
On the dismal planet Solos, the power-mad Marshall is wiping out the natives...
Cast
Jon Pertwee (Doctor Who), Katy Manning (Jo), Paul Whitsun-Jones (Marshal), Rick James (Cotton), Christopher Coll (Stubbs), Geoffrey Palmer (Administrator), James Mellor (Varan), Jonathan Sherwood (Varan's son), Garrick Hagon (Ky/Skybase Tannoy Voice), George Pravda (Jaeger), John Hollis (Sondergaard/Voice of Hyperion), David J Grahame (Old Man, 1), Sidney Johnson (Old Man, 3), Roy Pearce, Damon Sanders (Solos Guards), David Arlen (Warrior Guard), Martin Taylor (Skybase Guard), John Scott Martin, Mike Torres, Eddie Sommer, Laurie Goode, Nick Thompson Hill, Mike Mungarven, Rick Newby, Bill Gosling (Mutts), Peter Howell (Investigator)
Crew
Stunt Advisor Terry Walsh, *Visual Effects Designer* John Horton, *Technical Manager* Clive Leighton, *Vision Mixer* Mike Turner, *Studio Lighting* Frank Creswell, *Studio Sound* Tony Millier, *Film Cameraman* Fred Hamilton, *Film Sound* Dick Manton, *Film Editor* Dave King, *Special Sound* Brian Hodgson, Dick Mills, *Grams Operator* Gordon Phillipson, *Incidental Music* Tristram Cary (1-5), Dudley Simpson (6), *Costume Designer* James Acheson, *Make-Up Artist* Joan

Barrett, *Designer* Jeremy Bear, *Production Assistants* Fiona Cumming, Chris D'Oyly-John, *Assistant Floor Manager* Sue Hedden, *Assistant* Joan Elliott, *Floor Assistant* Philip Hill, *Script Editor* Terrance Dicks, *Producer* Barry Letts, *Director* Christopher Barry

DWM Index
62   Episode Guide
99   Christopher Barry interview
135   Season 9 Flashback
141   Archive + Fact File
142   Bob Baker interview
180   Christopher Barry interview
230   Jeremy Bear interview
      Archive Feature
235   Bob Baker and Dave Martin interview
241   Chris D'Oyly-John interview
315   Christopher Barry interview
326   Video review
331   Time Team
340   *Devils' Planets* CD review

Recording Dates
7-12 February 1972 (Location filming), unknown date (modelwork), 28-29 February 1972 (TC4), 13-14 March 1972 (TC8), 27-28 March 1972 (TC3)

Locations
Western Quarry, Northfleet, Kent; Stone House Farm, Lower Rochester Road, Frindsbury, Kent; Chislehurst Caves, Chislehurst, Kent

Working Titles
Independence
The Emergents

Factoids
- Six Mutt costumes were built by freelance prop maker Alistair Bowtell Effects, based on designs by Jim Acheson. They consisted of wire frames with fabric stretched across them, with latex claws and heads with movable mandibles.
- Dry ice was pumped across the quarry location to suggest poisonous fumes, while any plant life was sprayed silver. For the Chislehurst Caves filming, red and green lighting and hexagonal symbols painted onto the walls gave a suitably alien effect.
- Two state-of-the-art technological tools debuted with this story - a colour synthesiser and a multiple-feed mixing desk. The new mixing desk enabled the output of five camera images to be combined - rather than the usual two - while the colour synthesiser allowed for a myriad of changing colour patterns to be created and added to a chosen picture. For Ky's transformation into 'Super-Ky' at the

end of Episode Six, and his subsequent shooting down of the Marshall, a composite combination of five camera images was blended together live in the studio, with the addition of swirling colours courtesy of the colour synthesiser. It was considered the most technically demanding shot yet undertaken for the programme (and, by definition, for UK television in general).

Comment
Somewhere along the way, a promising story about colonialism and apartheid became a dull, meandering runaround in boring, dimly lit caves and boring, brightly lit corridors. Paul Whitsun-Jones makes a crass villain, but he's no worse than the bizarre John Hollis, the wooden George Pravda and the totally miscast Rick James. Model effects are consistently terrible and there's no reality about any of the studio sets. Even the location filming is grey and uninspiring (presumably deliberately so, but it doesn't help an already bland production). The one bright spot is the Mutts, who look stunning. Such a pity they didn't have a decent story to go with them. **37%**

"I'm sorry about your coccyx too, Miss Grant." ~ *The Master*

64) *The Time Monster*
Robert Sloman

Serial Code: OOO
Original Transmission
Episode One
Saturday 20 May 1972, 17.50-18.15, 7.6m / 37
Episode Two
Saturday 27 May 1972, 17.50-18.15, 7.4m / 60
Episode Three
Saturday 3 June 1972, 17.50-18.15, 8.1m / 36
Episode Four
Saturday 10 June 1972, 17.50-18.15, 7.6m / 28
Episode Five
Saturday 17 June 1972, 17.45-18.10, 6m / 67
Episode Six
Saturday 24 June 1972, 17.45-18.10, 7.6m / 39
BBC Archive
Episodes One to Five exist as 525-line NTSC two-inch colour videotape copies converted to 625-line PAL. Episode Six exists as a combination of 525-line NTSC two-inch colour videotape and monochrome 625-line videotape. The 625-line PAL two-inch colour master videotapes were wiped circa 1976.

Novelization
Doctor Who - The Time Monster by Terrance Dicks (151/15)
Hardback:
September 1985, WH Allen (0491038704 / Andrew Skilleter)
Paperback:
1. February 1986, Target (042620221X / Andrew Skilleter)
2. March 1989, Star, part of 'Doctor Who Classics' with *Doctor Who - The Daemons* (0352323825 / Andrew Skilleter)

Video
November 2001, in the 'Master Limited Edition Tin' [BBCV 7175] with *Colony in Space* (BBCV 7177 / Photomontage)

Précis
The Master travels to ancient Atlantis to unleash the terrible power of Kronos the Chronovore...

Cast
Jon Pertwee (Doctor Who), Katy Manning (Jo), Nicholas Courtney (Brigadier Lethbridge-Stewart), Richard Franklin (Captain Yates), John Levene (Sergeant Benton), Roger Delgado (Thascalos/The Master), Wanda Moore (Dr Ruth Ingram), Ian Collier (Stuart Hyde), John Wyse (Dr Percival), Donald Eccles (Krasis), Aidan Murphy (Hippias), George Cormack (Dalios), Ingrid Pitt (Galleia), Susan Penhaligon (Lakis), Dave Prowse (Minotaur), Marc Boyle (Kronos), Ingrid Bower (Face of Kronos), Terry Walsh (Window Cleaner/Stunt Double for Minotaur), Neville Barber (Dr Cook), Barry Ashton (Proctor), Keith Dalton (Neophite), Gregory Powell (Knight), Dave Carter (Roundhead Officer), George Lee (Farmworker), Simon Legree (UNIT Sergeant), Derek Murcott (Crito), Michael Walker (Miseus), Melville Jones (Guard), Darren Plant (Baby Benton), Val Musetti (Stunt Double for Hippias)

Crew
Visual Effects Designers Michaeljohn Harris, Peter Pegrum, *Technical Manager* Frank Rose, *Vision Mixers* Shirley Coward, Fred Law, *Studio Lighting* Derek Hobday, *Studio Sound* Tony Millier, *Film Cameraman* Peter Hamilton, *Film Sound* Derek Medus, *Film Editor* Martyn Day, *Special Sound* Brian Hodgson, *Grams Operator* Gordon Phillipson, *Incidental Music* Dudley Simpson, *Costume Designer* Barbara Lane, *Make-Up Artist* Joan Barrett, *Aged Make-Up Artist* Alan Boyle, *Designer* Tim Gleeson, *Production Assistant* Marion McDougall, *Assistant Floor Manager* Rosemary Hester, *Director's Assistant* Sue Upton, *Floor Assistant* Stephen Morris, *Script Editor* Terrance Dicks, *Producer* Barry Letts, *Director* Paul Bernard

DWM Index
52	Archive
62	Episode Guide
102	Novelization review
135	Season 9 Flashback
168	Paul Bernard interview
199	Ingrid Pitt interview
227	Nicholas Courtney interview
230	John Levene interview
250	Vox Pops
256	Katy Manning interview
261	Ian Collier interview
268	Archive Feature
276	Robert Sloman interview
311	Video review
331	Time Team 1-2
333	Time Team 3-6

Recording Dates
29-30 March 1972 (EFS), 4-7 April 1972 (Location filming), unknown date (modelwork), 25-26 April 1972 (TC3), 9-10 May 1972 (TC4), 23-24 May 1972 (TC3)

Locations
Swallowfield Park, Swallowfield, Berkshire; Stratfield Saye Park and roads, Stratfield Saye, Hampshire; Mortimer Lane, Mortimer, Berkshire; School Lane, Heckfield Heath, Hampshire; Road near Old Church Farm, Hartley Wintney, Hampshire

Working Title
As broadcast

Factoids
- The Minotaur was played by Somerset-born actor Dave Prowse. He had appeared as the monster in the Hammer film *The Horror of Frankenstein* (1970), a bodybuilder/servant in Stanley Kubrick's *A Clockwork Orange* (1971) and would become famous as The Green Cross Code Man for various television advertisements in the mid-1970s (a campaign to which Jon Pertwee would also contribute). In 1977 he donned the black PVC costume of Darth Vader for *Star Wars*, although his voice was dubbed by American actor James Earl Jones.
- A brand-new Tardis interior was designed by Tim Gleeson featuring tessellated 'washing up bowls' lining the walls instead of the traditional inset roundels. Barry Letts didn't think it was as effective as the original set, and *The Time Monster* would see its first and only appearance.
- Dick Mills assisted with special sound requirements, as a prelude to him taking over from Brian Hodgson for the next recorded story, *Carnival of Monsters* (66).

Comment
A *Doctor Who* spoof gone horribly wrong, *The Time Monster* is a nightmare if watched in one go (at least without the aid of mind-altering drugs). In weekly instalments it's not quite so bad, but still seems full of the most clichéd situations and lame dialogue imaginable. The first four episodes are superfluous, with UNIT appearing as comic relief and Roger Delgado forced to make the best of a ridiculously hammy script, and when the viewer eventually arrives at Atlantis it isn't a patch on its 1967 counterpart in *The Underwater Menace* (32). **39%**

Season 10

"Oh, so you're my replacements - a dandy and a clown." ~ The First Doctor

65) The Three Doctors
Bob Baker and Dave Martin

Serial Code: RRR
Original Transmission
Episode One
Saturday 30 December 1972, 17.50-18.15, 9.6m / 41
Episode Two
Saturday 6 January 1973, 17.50-18.15, 10.8m / 22
Episode Three
Saturday 13 January 1973, 17.50-18.15, 8.8m / 44
Episode Four
Saturday 20 January 1973, 17.50-18.15, 11.9m / 17
Repeat Transmission
On BBC2 as part of 'The Five Faces of Doctor Who' season:
Episode One
Monday 23 November 1981, 17.40-18.05, 5m / 12
Episode Two
Tuesday 24 November 1981, 17.35-18.00, 4.5m / 16
Episode Three
Wednesday 25 November 1981, 17.40-18.05, 5.7m / 9
Episode Four
Thursday 26 November 1981, 17.40-18.05, 5.8m / 8

BBC Archive
All episodes exist on 625-line two-inch PAL colour master videotapes.
Novelization
Doctor Who - The Three Doctors by Terrance Dicks (127/11)
Hardback:
November 1975, Allan Wingate (0855230533 / Chris Achilleos)
Paperback:
1. November 1975, Target (0426109384 / Chris Achilleos)
2. April 1978, Target, renamed *Doctor Who and the Three Doctors* (0426115783 / Jeff Cummins)
3. August 1991, Target (0426115783 / Alister Pearson)
Video
1. August 1991 (BBCV 4650 / Alister Pearson)
2. September 2002, as part of 'The Time Lord Collection' [BBCV 7346 / Photomontage] with *The War Games* and *The Deadly Assassin* (BBCV 7364 / Photomontage)
DVD
November 2003, commentary by Nicholas Courtney, Katy Manning and Barry Letts (BBCDVD 1144 / Clayton Hickman)
Précis
Three incarnations of the Doctor team up to battle mad Time Lord Omega...
Cast
Jon Pertwee, Patrick Troughton, William Hartnell (Doctor Who), Katy Manning (Jo), Nicholas Courtney (Brigadier Lethbridge-Stewart), John Levene (Sergeant Benton), Rex Robinson (Dr Tyler), Denys Palmer (Corporal Palmer) Stephen Thorne (Omega), Laurie Webb (Mr Ollis), Patricia Prior (Mrs Ollis), Roy Purcell (President of the Council), Graham Leaman (Time Lord), Clyde Pollitt (Chancellor), Cy Town, Rick Newby, Murphy Grumbar, John Scott Martin (Gell Guards), Terry Walsh (Double for Doctor Who), Alan Chuntz (Omega's Champion)
Crew
Visual Effects Designer Michaeljohn Harris, Len Hutton, *Technical Manager* John Fane, *Vision Mixer* Tony Rowe, Shirley Coward, *Studio Lighting* Clive Thomas, *Studio Sound* Derek Miller-Timmins, *Film Cameraman* John Baker, *Film Sound* Bob Roberts, *Film Editor* Jim Walker, *Properties Buyer* Magda Oleander, *Special Sound* Dick Mills, *Grams Operator* Gerry Burrows, *Incidental Music* Dudley Simpson, *Costume Designer* James Acheson, *Make-Up Artist* Ann Rayment, *Designer* Roger Liminton, *Production Assistant* David Tilley, *Assistant Floor Manager* Trina Cornwell, *Floor Assistant* Paul Braithwaite,

Director's Assistant Rita Dunn, *Script Editor* Terrance Dicks, *Producer* Barry Letts, *Director* Lennie Mayne

DWM Index
- *52* Barry Letts interview
- *58* 'The Five Faces of Doctor Who' feature
- *62* Episode Guide
- *72* Nicholas Courtney interview
- *82* John Levene interview
- *83* Heather Hartnell interview
- *111* Nicholas Courtney interview
- *118* Archive + Fact File
- *142* Bob Baker interview
- *151* Alan Chuntz interview
- *172* Those *Radio Times*
- *174* Nostalgia
- *177* Video review
- *190* What The Papers Said
- *227* Nicholas Courtney interview
- *230* John Levene interview
- *235* Bob Baker and Dave Martin interview
- *256* Katy Manning interview
- *260* Archive Feature
- *325* Video review (Time Lord Box Set)
- *333* Time Team
- *336* Preview(DVD)
- *338* DVD review

Recording Dates
6 November 1972 (EFS), 7-10 November 1972 (Location filming), 14-15 November 1972 (TC Puppet Theatre), 27-28 November 1972 (TC1), 11-12 December 1972 (TC6)

Locations
Summerfield Bungalow, Springwell Quarry and Springwell Reservoir, all Rickmansworth, Hertfordshire; Halings House, Denham Green, Buckinghamshire

Working Title
The Black Hole

Factoids
- William Hartnell's role was originally to have been more extensive; however, arteriosclerosis had affected his memory to such a degree that he was no longer able to learn his lines, and would not be able to cope with the pressures of a month-long production period. As a result, his speaking chores were limited to one day's shooting at Ealing with his lines written out on large cue-cards positioned just off-camera (in the story, he can be seen glancing at these as he speaks). This would be his last professional acting engagement.
- The black and white sequence of Patrick Troughton in Episode One was specially filmed at Springwell Quarry on 9 November 1972, the same day that William Hartnell visited the quarry for a photocall and was filmed in the garden of nearby Summerfield Bungalow for his black and white appearance in the same episode.
- Four Gell Guard costumes were built by Alistair Bowtell Effects (as was Omega's mask), consisting of a latex skirt section - worn like a barrel with shoulder straps - and a hard fibreglass headpiece. A single claw was operated from inside, with sequencer lights flashing along it whenever it 'fired'. All close-ups of the claw were done at Springwell Quarry, leading to inconsistencies when inserts were used for non-quarry scenes.
- Another new Tardis set was designed for this story. Designer Roger Liminton sought inspiration from Peter Brachaki's first Tardis set for the pilot episode, *An Unearthly Child* (0), and so he enlarged the room, re-incorporated the 'transporter pad' and put the monitor back onto a gimballed television screen, rather than on a CSOed roundel.
- The blobby gel organism seen in Episode One was a furry rod puppet, defocused, electronically coloured, and CSOed into the live-action. For UNIT HQ's disappearance, a cross-fade was performed between two still photographs taken on location.
- A new rendition of the theme music was commissioned for this Tenth Anniversary season. Delia Derbyshire, the arranger of the original score, recorded an updated version on an electronic synthesiser called the Delaware, assisted by Paddy Kingsland. Although it was dubbed onto this story, as well as *Carnival of Monsters* (66) and *Frontier in Space* (67), it was generally considered much less effective than its predecessor and was hurriedly replaced with the original prior to transmission. The only time it was heard in the UK was in a trailer for *The Three Doctors* on 27 December 1972, although overseas copies were accidentally sent out with the Delaware version still appended.
- Dick Mills of the BBC Radiophonic Workshop officially took over the responsibility of providing special sounds for the series from this story onwards (although *Carnival of Monsters* would revert to Brian Hodgson as it was recorded before *The Three Doctors*).

- The new series was promoted by an atmospheric photograph of the first three Doctors on the cover of the *Radio Times* (dated 30 December 1972 - 5 January 1973).

Comment
An obvious crowd-pleaser, *The Three Doctors* is let down by bargain-basement effects and humdrum direction. Troughton is lovely - his scenes with Pertwee are a joy - and it's a shame that Hartnell is never physically present, although his on-screen appearances are surprisingly effective, bestowing upon this incarnation an almost Godlike wisdom and authority. But there's too much standing around and pontificating about things, the quarry location is uninteresting, and Omega's palace is one of the cheapest sets ever to appear on the programme - ironic, considering it's supposed to be a fantastic edifice conjured up from the villain's own imagination. The story may be important historically, but in televisual terms it leaves a lot to be desired. **45%**

"Give them a hygiene chamber and they store fossil fuel in it." ~ *Orum*

66) *Carnival of Monsters*
Robert Holmes

Serial Code: PPP
Original Transmission
Episode One
Saturday 27 January 1973, 17.50-18.15, 9.5m / 29
Episode Two
Saturday 3 February 1973, 17.50-18.15, 9m / 36
Episode Three
Saturday 10 February 1973, 17.50-18.15, 9m / 44
Episode Four
Saturday 17 February 1973, 17.50-18.15, 9.2m / 38
Repeat Transmission
On BBC2 as part of 'The Five Faces of Doctor Who':
Episode One
Monday 16 November 1981, 17.40-18.05, 4.9m / 12
Episode Two
Tuesday 17 November 1981, 17.40-18.05, 4.5m / 14
Episode Three
Wednesday 18 November 1981, 17.40-18.05, 5.6m / 8

Episode Four
Thursday 19 November 1981, 17.40-18.05, 6m / 5
BBC Archive
All episodes exist on 625-line two-inch PAL colour master videotapes. In addition, a 71 edit exists of Episode Two in the same format.
Novelization
Doctor Who and the Carnival of Monsters by Terrance Dicks (125/12)
Hardback:
January 1977, Allan Wingate (049102114 / Chris Achilleos)
Paperback:
1. January 1977, Target (0426110250 / Chris Achilleos)
2. May 1993, Target, renamed *Doctor Who - Carnival of Monsters* (0426110250 / Alister Pearson)
Video
March 1995, 71 edit of Episode Two, edited (BBCV 5556 / Colin Howard)
DVD
July 2002, clean title sequence, extended and deleted scenes, director's amended ending, Delaware opening and closing titles, 'The Five Faces of Doctor Who' trailer, visual effects test film, production subtitles, photo gallery, commentary by Katy Manning and Barry Letts (BBCDVD 1098 / Clayton Hickman)
Précis
The Doctor and Jo arrive on a ship in the Indian Ocean, but appearances can be deceptive...
Cast
Jon Pertwee (Doctor Who), Katy Manning (Jo), Peter Halliday (Pletrac), Michael Wisher (Kalik), Terence Lodge (Orum), Leslie Dwyer (Vorg), Cheryl Hall (Shirna), Tenniel Evans (Major Daly), Ian Marter (First Officer John Andrews), Jenny McCracken (Claire Daly), Andrew Staines (Captain), Terry Walsh (Double for Doctor Who), Linda Regan (Double for Jo Grant)
Crew
Fight Arranger/Stuntman Terry Walsh, *Visual Effects Designer* John Horton, *Visual Effects Assistant* Colin Mapson, *Technical Manager* Reg Hutchins, *Vision Mixer* Bill Morton, *Studio Lighting* Clive Thomas, *Studio Sound* Gordon Mackie, *Film Cameraman* Peter Hamilton, *Film Sound* Derek Medus, *Film Editor* Peter Evans, *Special Sound* Brian Hodgson, *Grams Operator* Gordon Phillipson, *Incidental Music* Dudley Simpson, *Costume Designer* James Acheson, *Make-Up Artist* Angela Seyfang, *Production Assistant* Chris D'Oyly-John, *Assistant Floor Manager* Karilyn Collier, *Director's Assistant*

Frances Alcock, *Floor Assistant* Ian Pleeth, *Script Editor* Terrance Dicks, *Producer/Director* Barry Letts

DWM Index

58	'The Five Faces of Doctor Who' feature
63	Episode Guide
93	Ian Marter interview
100	Robert Holmes interview
113	Archive + Fact File
117	Michael Wisher interview
190	What The Papers Said
193	Brian Hodgson interview
W94	Archive Feature
224	Video review
241	Chris D'Oyly-John interview
270	Barry Letts interview
320	DVD review
321	Peter Halliday interview
335	Time Team

Recording Dates

30 May-2 June 1972 (Location filming), 19-20 June 1972 (TC4), 3-4 July 1972 (TC6)

Locations

Tillingham Marshes, Tillingham, Essex; Carwoods Quarry, Asheldham, Essex; Royal Fleet Auxiliary Ship Robert Dundas, Chatham Dockyard to Sheerness Docks, Kent

Working Title

Peepshow

Factoids

- Location filming was conducted aboard the coastal storage tanker *Robert Dundas* on its final three-hour journey down the River Medway to Sheerness to be broken up for scrap.
- Ian Marter, playing First Officer Andrews, had previously auditioned for the part of Captain Yates in 1970. He would go on to play the Fourth Doctor's assistant Harry Sullivan, starting in *Robot* (75).
- *Carnival of Monsters* would be the last story for which Brian Hodgson would provide special sounds. Starting with the pilot episode (0), he had worked on virtually ever adventure since 1963. Hodgson later formed his own sound studio company Electrophon.
- Three Drashigs (each two-and-a-half feet long) were constructed, one of which was a fully articulated rod puppet. The heads were made from terrier skulls, while the bodies were latex covered frames fleshed out with strips of foam rubber. The Plesiosaurus was a simple glove puppet with another fox skull forming the head.
- A fuzzy picture of a Cybermen (wearing a helmet from *The Invasion*, 46) was CSOed onto the Miniscope in Episode Two. The 'scope itself was a light prop made from Styrofoam and plastic sheeting. A melted version was also made for the end of Episode Four

Comment

A deeply satisfying, witty and complex 'story within a story', *Carnival of Monsters* is a joy from start to finish. The mind-expanding idea of being outside, yet inside a small machine, never ceases to excite the imagination, and Robert Holmes' gifted ear for dialogue has rarely been bettered than with the double act of Vorg and Shirna, or the triumvirate of grey-faced officials. The cast is exceptionally strong, with nary a duff performance to distract the viewer. By turns hilarious and frightening, there's almost nothing to fault in this perfectly paced four parter. The special effects are good, and the Drashigs are positively terrifying. **94%**

"Your health is very precious to me - for the moment." ~ *The Master*

67) *Frontier in Space*

Malcolm Hulke

Serial Code: QQQ

Original Transmission

Episode One
Saturday 24 February 1973, 17.50-18.15, 9.1m / 32
Episode Two
Saturday 3 March 1973, 17.50-18.15, 7.8m / 53
Episode Three
Saturday 10 March 1973, 17.50-18.15, 7.5m / 57
Episode Four
Saturday 17 March 1973, 17.50-18.15, 7.1m / 55
Episode Five
Saturday 24 March 1973, 17.50-18.15, 7.7m / 57
Episode Six
Saturday 31 March 1973, 17.50-18.15, 8.9m / 40

BBC Archive

All episodes exist on 625-line two-inch PAL colour master videotapes. In addition, a 71 edit exists of Episode Five in the same format.

Novelization

Doctor Who and the Space War by Malcolm Hulke (142/12)

Hardback:
September 1976, Allan Wingate (0855230770 / Chris Achilleos)
Paperback:
September 1976, Target (0426110331 / Chris Achilleos)
Video
1. March 1992, Episode Six on 'The Pertwee Years' (BBCV 4756 / Photographs)
2. August 1995, with 71 edit of Episode Five (BBCV 5640 / Colin Howard)
Précis
In the 26th century, the vast empires of Earth and Draconia are struggling for supremacy…
Cast
Jon Pertwee (Doctor Who), Katy Manning (Jo), Michael Hawkins (General Williams), Roger Delgado (The Master/Sirius 4 Commissioner), John Woodnutt (Draconian Emperor), Peter Birrel (Draconian Prince), Vera Fusek (President of Earth), Richard Shaw (Cross), Harold Goldblatt (Professor Dale), John Rees (Hardy), James Culliford (Stewart), Roy Pattison (Draconian Space Pilot), Lawrence Davidson (Draconian First Secretary), Timothy Craven (Cell Guard), Louise Mahoney (Newscaster, 1), Bill Mitchell (Newscaster, 6), Karol Hagar (Secretary), Roy Lonnen (Gardiner), Barry Ashton (Kemp), Luan Peters (Sheila), Caroline Hunt (Technician), Laurence Harrington (Lunar Guard), Madhav Sharma (Patel), Dennis Bowen (Prison Governor), Bill Wilde (Draconian Captain), Stephen Thorne (First Ogron), Michael Kilgarriff (Second Ogron), Rick Lester (Third Ogron), Ian Frost (Draconian Messenger), Clifford Elkin (Earth Cruiser Captain), Ramsay Williams (Congressman Brook), Stanley Price (Spaceship Pilot), John Scott Martin (Chief Dalek/Mutant), Murphy Grumbar, Cy Town (Daleks), Michael Wisher (Dalek Voices), John Bradburn (Ogron Eater), Kathy Jones (Stunt Double for Jo Grant), Terry Walsh (Stunt Double for Doctor Who), Bill Burridge (Doctor Who as Draconian).
Crew
Visual Effects Designers Bernard Wilkie, Rhys Jones, *Visual Effects Assistants* Mat Irvine, Ian Scoones, *Draconian Masks* John Friedlander, *Technical Manager* Tommy Dawson, Ron Bristow, *Vision Mixers* Mike Turner, Shirley Coward, *Studio Lighting* Ralph Walton, *Studio Sound* Brian Hiles, *Film Cameraman* John Tiley, *Special Sound* Dick Mills, *Grams Operator* Gordon Phillipson, *Incidental Music* Dudley Simpson, *Costume Designer* Barbara Kidd, *Make-Up Artist* Sandra Shepherd, *Designer* Cynthia Kljuco, *Production Assistant* Nick John, *Assistant Floor Manager* John Bradburn, *Director's Assistant* Kay Stephens, *Floor Assistant* Christopher Moss, *Script Editor* Terrance Dicks, *Producer* Barry Letts, *Director* Paul Bernard, *Additional Scenes Director* David Maloney

DWM Index
57	John Friedlander interview
59	Mat Irvine interview
63	Episode Guide
91	The Incredible Malcolm Hulke Novelization review
114	Chris Achilleos interview
168	Paul Bernard interview
181	John Woodnutt interview
192	Crossing The Line
193	Brian Hodgson interview
201	Archive Feature
229	Video review
250	Vox Pops
270	Barry Letts interview
335	Time Team 1-4
336	Time Team 5-6

Recording Dates
14 August 1972 (Bray Studios modelwork), 18 August 1972 (Bray Studios modelwork), 22 August 1972 (Bray Studios modelwork), 10-13 September 1972 (Location filming), 14 September 1972 (EFS), 2-3 October 1972 (TC4), 16-17 October 1972 (TC4), 31 October-1 November 1972 (TC3), 22 January 1973 (TC4)
Locations
Hayward Gallery, Lambeth, London SE1; 8a Fitzroy Park, Highgate, London N6; Beachfields Quarry, Redhill, Surrey
Working Title
Frontiers in Space
Factoids
- *Frontier in Space* formed the first half of a 'Dalek double bill' with *Planet of the Daleks*. It was the production team's attempt to emulate the success and longevity of the 1965/6 adventure *The Daleks' Master Plan* (21).
- Ian Scoones, unhappy with the standard of model filming at the BBC, supervised the various model sequences at Bray Studios with a freelance lighting crew. Models were plundered from Gerry Anderson's Century 21 studios, including spacecraft from *UFO* (1970-3) and *Thunderbirds* (1965-66).
- The same three Daleks from *Day of the Daleks* (60) were used at the end of Episode Six. AFM John Bradburn donned a glorified sleeping bag to play the 'fearsome' Ogron Eater in that same episode.

- As in the previous story, *Frontier in Space* featured several specially shot monster cameos - the Master transformed into a Drashig, a Mutt and a Sea Devil when he tried to hypnotise Jo.
- This story would see Roger Delgado's final appearance as the Master. There were suggestions that he would return the following season in a story called *The Final Game* by Robert Sloman and sacrifice his life to save the Doctor. But tragically the actor was killed in a car crash in Turkey in June 1973, shelving any plans for a rematch until 1976's *The Deadly Assassin* (88).
- To tie-in more closely with *Planet of the Daleks*, the ending of this story was reshot by director David Maloney. Utilising a plain wall flat and the Tardis, a short scene with the injured Doctor and Jo was recorded during the first session of the following Dalek story. Unfortunately, the result of this modified ending was that the Master apparently vanished without explanation.
- The Shogun-influenced Draconian costumes were designed by director Paul Bernard and costume designer Barbara Kidd. The latex half-masks were sculpted by John Friedlander.

Comment

Worthy but dull, *Frontier in Space* is a brave attempt to tackle the 'space opera' genre, ending up as a well-produced, although arguably slow-moving, political thriller characterized by endless escapes and recaptures. The Draconians are another race of excellently conceived aliens, second only to the Ice Warriors in terms of their detailed culture and history. Modelwork is variable, but the futuristic 1970s sets are impressive, as is the grand sweep of the storyline. The Episode Six revelation is hardly surprising, considering the Ogrons accompanied the Daleks on their previous outing, and Episode Five's 'cliffhanger' has to be the weakest in the show's history. It's also a terrible shame that Roger Delgado is not given a decent send-off, and the last few minutes of the story are very garbled. But despite its faults, *Frontier in Space* is a superior tale dealing with (relatively) grown-up issues.
60%

"We have been delayed, not defeated. Daleks are never defeated!" ~ *Dalek Supreme*

68) *Planet of the Daleks*
Terry Nation

Serial Code: SSS
Original Transmission
Episode One
Saturday 7 April 1973, 18.10-18.35, 11m / 9
Episode Two
Saturday 14 April 1973, 17.50-18.15, 10.7m / 18
Episode Three
Saturday 21 April 1973, 17.50-18.15, 10.1m / 26
Episode Four
Saturday 28 April 1973, 17.50-18.15, 8.3m / 29
Episode Five
Saturday 5 May 1973, 17.50-18.15, 9.7m / 21
Episode Six
Saturday 12 May 1973, 17.50-18.15, 8.5m / 24
Repeat Transmission:
Episode One
Friday 5 November 1993, 19.35-20.00, 3.6m / -
Episode Two
Friday 12 November 1993, 19.35-20.00, 4m / -
Episode Three
Friday 19 November 1993, 19.35-20.00, 3.9m / -
Episode Four
Friday 3 December 1993, 19.35-20.00, 3.3m / -
Episode Five
Friday 10 December 1993, 19.35-20.00, 3.3m / -
Episode Six
Friday 17 December 1993, 19.35-20.00, 3.5m / -
BBC Archive
Episodes One, Two, Four, Five and Six exist on 625-line two-inch PAL colour master videotapes. Episode Three exists as a 16mm b/w film recording of the 625-line master videotape.
Novelization
Doctor Who and the Planet of the Daleks by Terrance Dicks (125/12)
Hardback:
1. September 1976, Allan Wingate (0855230762 / Chris Achilleos)
2. June 1983, WH Allen, as part of 'Doctor Who - Dalek Omnibus' with *Doctor Who and the Dalek Invasion of Earth* and *Doctor Who and the Day of the Daleks* (0491034202 / Andrew Skilleter)
Paperback:
1. October 1976, Target (0426112520 / Chris Achilleos)
2. July 1992, Target, renamed *Doctor Who - Planet of the Daleks* (0426112520 / Alister Pearson)

Talking Book
June 1995, 1 x cassette, abridged, read by Jon Pertwee (0563388269 / Photomontage)
Video
November 1999, in 'Dalek Limited Edition Tin' [BBCV 6875 / Photomontage] with *Revelation of the Daleks* (BBCV 6928 / Photomontage)
Music and Sound Effects
October 1973, 'The World of Doctor Who' on B-side of *Moonbase 3*, single (RESL 13)
Précis
The Doctor tracks the Daleks to Spiridon where a vast army lies dormant under a volcano...
Cast
Jon Pertwee (Doctor Who), Katy Manning (Jo), Bernard Horsfall (Taron), Tim Preece (Codal), Prentis Hancock (Vaber), Roy Skelton (Wester/Dalek Voices/Spiridon Voices), Jane How (Rebec), Alan Tucker (Latep), Hilary Minster (Marat), Michael Wisher (Dalek Voices/Spiridon Voices), John Scott Martin, Cy Town, Murphy Grumbar (Daleks), Tony Starr (Dalek Supreme), Alan Casley (Thal Corpse)
Crew
Visual Effects Designer Clifford Culley, *Technical Manager* Ron Bristow, *Vision Mixer* Michael Turner, *Studio Lighting* Derek Slee, *Studio Sound* Tony Millier, *Special Sound* Dick Mills, *Grams Operator* Gerry Burrows, *Incidental Music* Dudley Simpson, *Costume Designer* Hazel Pethig, *Make-Up Artist* Jean McMillan, *Designer* John Hurst, *Production Assistant* George Gallaccio, *Assistant Floor Managers* Sue Hedden, Graeme Harper, John Cook, *Director's Assistant* Carole Bisset, *Floor Assistant* Ken Dodds, *Script Editor* Terrance Dicks, *Producer* Barry Letts, *Director* David Maloney
DWM Index
63   Episode Guide
72   Archive
108   David Maloney interview
168   Paul Bernard interview
190   What The Papers Said
202   David Maloney interview
     Archive Feature
209   Jane How interview
     TV review (repeat)
256   Katy Manning interview
280   George Gallaccio interview
284   Video review
293   Clifford Culley interview
303   Prentis Hancock interview
336   Time Team
Recording Dates
2-3 January 1973 (Location filming), 4-5 January 1973 (EFS), 8-9 January 1973 (EFS), 16 January 1973 (unknown studio modelwork), 22-23 January 1973 (TC4), 27 January 1973 (unknown studio modelwork), 29 January 1973 (unknown studio modelwork), 5-6 February 1973 (TC6), 8 February 1973 (unknown studio modelwork), 19-20 February 1973 (TC1)
Location
Beachfields Quarry, Redhill, Surrey
Working Titles
Destination: Daleks
Destination Daleks
Factoids
- Script editor Terrance Dicks restructured the start of this story and the end of *Frontier in Space* in order to link them together more closely.
- The three Daleks were reused from *Frontier in Space* (with the gold one painted grey), while four new, simplified wood and plywood 'goon' Daleks were made for background scenes.
- The molten ice that erupts from the ice volcano was actually wallpaper paste mixed with green gelatine.
- Approximately one hundred 4-inch Louis Marx toy Daleks were used for the vast Dalek army, as they had been before on *The Evil of the Daleks* (36). Painted grey, they were attached to strips of cardboard and moved by off-screen effects technicians.
- The Dalek Supreme, seen in Episode Six, was a prop built for the 1966 Aaru film *Daleks' Invasion Earth 2150AD*. Owned by Terry Nation, it was loaned to the BBC for this story and augmented with jam jars over its randomly flashing indicator lights and a torch stuck to the end of its eyestalk.

Comment
An old-fashioned Dalek adventure scripted by an old-fashioned storyteller, *Planet of the Daleks* is great fun from start to finish. The Daleks are at their manipulative best, the special effects are generally very good (especially the invisible Spiridons), and the jungle is suitably creepy. Episode One is particularly atmospheric, with Katy Manning holding centre-stage as she gives the viewer a quick recap of events so far. Bernard Horsfall is excellent as always, although the other Thals are not so engaging (Prentis Hancock giving his usual one-note performance). The only thing that jars is Pertwee's reaction to the excellent Episode One cliffhanger - he acts as if he's shocked, whereas that's the reason he came to the planet in the first place. **84%**

"Cheap petrol and lots of it. Exactly what the world needs." ~ Brigadier Lethbridge-Stewart

69) The Green Death
Robert Sloman

Serial Code: TTT
Original Transmission
Episode One
Saturday 19 May 1973, 17.50-18.15, 9.2m / 18
Episode Two
Saturday 26 May 1973, 17.50-18.15, 7.2m / 38
Episode Three
Saturday 2 June 1973, 17.50-18.15, 7.8m / 29
Episode Four
Saturday 9 June 1973, 17.50-18.15, 6.8m / 32
Episode Five
Saturday 16 June 1973, 17.50-18.15, 8.3m / 15
Episode Six
Saturday 23 June 1973, 17.50-18.15, 7m / 30
Repeat Transmissions
Omnibus
Thursday 27 December 1973, 16.00-17.30, 10.5m / 44
On BBC2:
Episode One
Sunday 2 January 1994, 12.00-12.25, 1.3m / -
Episode Two
Sunday 9 January 1994, 12.00-12.25, 1.1m / -
Episode Three
Sunday 16 January 1994, 12.00-12.25, 0.8m / -
Episode Four
Sunday 23 January 1994, 12.00-12.25, 1.1m / -
Episode Five
Sunday 30 January 1994, 12.00-12.25, 1.3m / -
Episode Six
Sunday 6 February 1994, 12.00-12.25, 1.3m / -
BBC Archive
All episodes exist on 625-line two-inch PAL colour master videotapes.
Novelization
Doctor Who and the Green Death by Malcolm Hulke (142/12)
Hardback:
April 1981, WH Allen (0491028741 / Alun Hood)
Paperback:
1. August 1975, Target (0426106474 / Peter Brookes)
2. March 1979, Target (0426115430 / Alun Hood)
Video
October 1996, twin-pack (BBCV 5816 / Colin Howard)
DVD
May 2004, original and BBC1 continuity announcements, production subtitles, photo gallery, commentary by Barry Letts, Terrance Dicks and Katy Manning (BBCDVD 1142 / Clayton Hickman)
Précis
Chemical waste is creating deadly green maggots down a Welsh mine...
Cast
Jon Pertwee (Doctor Who), Katy Manning (Jo), Nicholas Courtney (Brigadier Lethbridge-Stewart), Richard Franklin (Captain Yates), John Levene (Sergeant Benton), Jerome Willis (Stevens), Stewart Bevan (Clifford Jones), Tony Adams (Elgin), John Dearth (BOSS Voice/UNIT Radio/Tannoy Voices), Ben Howard (Hinks), Mostyn Evans (Dai Evans), Talfryn Thomas (Dave), John Scott Martin (Hughes), Ray Handy (Jones the Milk), Mitzi McKenzie (Nancy), Roy Evans (Bert), John Rolfe (Fell), Richard Beale (Minister of Ecology), Jean Burgess (Cleaner), Brian Justice (Yates' Guard), Terry Walsh (Guard/Stunt Double for Doctor Who/Stunt Double for Captain Yates), Billy Horrigan, Alan Chuntz (Security Guards), Roy Skelton (James), Brychan Powell (Prime Minister, Sir Jeremy), Jean Channon (Lotus Position Girl), Jessica Stanley-Clarke (Flautist)
Crew
Fight Arranger Terry Walsh, *Stuntmen* Terry Walsh, Billy Horrigan, Alan Chuntz, *Visual Effects Designer* Ron Oates, *Visual Effects Sculptor* John Friedlander, *Visual Effects Assistants* Colin Mapson, Richard Conway, Tony Harding, *Inlay Operators* Nick Rodgers, Geoff Vian, *Technical Managers* Fred Wright, Terry Wild, Tommy Dawson, *Senior Cameraman* Peter Granger, *Vision Mixer* John Gorman, *Studio Lighting* Mike Jefferies, *Studio Sound* Richard Chubb, *Film Cameramen* Bill Matthews, Ken Lowe, *Film Sound* Simon Wilson, *Film Editor* Alistair Mackay, *Special Sound* Dick Mills, *Grams Operator* Gerry Burrows, *Incidental Music* Dudley Simpson, *Costume Designer* Barbara Kidd, *Make-Up Artist* Ann Rayment, *Designer* John Burrowes, *Production Assistants* John Harris, Michael McDermott, *Assistant Floor Manager* Karilyn Collier, *Director's Assistant* Brenda Loader, *Floor Assistant* James Piner, *Script Editor* Terrance Dicks, *Producer* Barry Letts, *Director* Michael Briant
DWM Index
52	Barry Letts interview
63	Episode Guide
82	John Levene interview
91	Novelization review
95	Richard Franklin interview
97	Michael Briant interview
120	Archive + Fact File
172	Those *Radio Times*

190 What The Papers Said
192 Crossing The Line
204 Dudley Simpson interview
210 Video review (delayed)
245 Video review
256 Katy Manning interview
263 Michael E Briant interview
276 Robert Sloman interview
320 Archive Feature
330 Dudley Simpson interview
337 Time Team
342 Preview(DVD)
343 DVD review

Recording Dates
12-16 February 1973 (Location filming), 17 February 1973 (unknown studio modelwork), 19-20 February 1973 (Location filming), 2-3 April 1973 (TC3), 16-17 April 1973 (TC3), 29-30 April 1973 (TC3)

Locations
Ogilvie Colliery and Quarry, Deri, Glamorgan; Troed-y-Rhiw-Jestyn, Deri, Glamorgan; RCA International factory, Brynmawr, Powys

Working Title
As broadcast

Factoids
- An article entitled *A Blueprint for Survival* in environmental magazine *The Ecologist* prompted Barry Letts to commission a story that would tackle the growing menace of pollution. The article formed the basis of a book published in August 1972, which launched the People Party in the UK, latterly the Green Party.
- The industrial complex was originally named Universal Chemicals, then changed to United Chemicals, then once more to Global Chemicals for broadcast (in Hulke's novelization it became Panorama Chemicals). Charles Bell was changed to Ralph Fell because in real-life a Douglas Bell was chief executive of ICI.
- The maggots were created in various different ways - glove puppets, rod puppets (operated from under a raised set), inert props pulled along on wires, live maggots in miniature sets and water-filled condoms. The maggot that threatens Jo at the end of Episode Three was a rod puppet inlaid with CSO.
- Keen to deflect criticism that *The Green Death* promoted anti-Conservative views, Barry Letts made sure that the unseen future Prime Minister would be called 'Sir Jeremy' after the then-leader of the Liberal Party, Jeremy Thorpe.

- The same Hughes 300 helicopter used for *The Enemy of the World* (40) was hired for shots of UNIT dropping bombs (in actuality, toilet ballcocks) onto the slagheap, and also for establishing shots of the mine in Episode One.
- The end credits film sequences for Episodes Two, Five and Six were recorded backwards and upside-down in error.
- Katy Manning and Stewart Bevan were a couple in real life, adding to the emotional impact of Jo's departure. For her leaving scene in Episode Six (recorded first thing on the final studio day), guests included extras and studio visitors.

Comment
Glorious location photography adds authenticity to this frightening tale of poison-spitting venomous grubs. The maggots are gruesomely believable, and even when the CSO isn't quite up to it, they never fail to make this particular viewer squirm. The whole ecology angle is very pleasing, but doesn't swamp the storyline - this may be a story with a message, but we're never hit over the head with it. *The Green Death* even has room for comedy, with the silly Metebelis 3 sequences, after-dinner jokes at the Wholeweal community and the Doctor dressing up in drag. But its main function is to scare the kiddies, which it does with aplomb - Episode Two's cliffhanger, where maggots burst from the mine tunnel walls, is one of *Doctor Who*'s all-time best. And, of course, it contains one of the saddest farewell scenes in the history of the programme. **95%**

Season 11

"My people are very keen to stamp out unlicensed time travel - you can look upon them as galactic ticket inspectors if you like." ~ The Doctor

70) *The Time Warrior*
Robert Holmes

Serial Code: UUU
Original Transmission
Part One
Saturday 15 December 1973, 17.10-17.35, 8.7m / 34

Part Two
Saturday 22 December 1973, 17.45-18.10, 7m / 75
Part Three
Saturday 29 December 1973, 17.10-17.35, 6.6m / 89
Part Four
Saturday 5 January 1974, 17.30-17.55, 10.6m / 22

BBC Archive
All episodes exist on 625-line two-inch PAL colour master videotapes.

Novelization
Doctor Who and the Time Warrior by Terrance Dicks, with a prologue by Robert Holmes (144/18)
Hardback:
June 1978, WH Allen (0491024134 / Roy Knipe)
Paperback:
1. June 1978, Target (0426200233 / Roy Knipe)
2. June 1993, Target, renamed *Doctor Who - The Time Warrior* (0426200233 / Alister Pearson)

Video
June 1989, compilation (BBCV 4245 / Photomontage)

Précis
A Sontaran stuck in the 13th century is abducting present-day scientists to fix its spacecraft...

Cast
Jon Pertwee (Doctor Who), Elisabeth Sladen (Sarah Jane Smith), Kevin Lindsay (Linx), David Daker (Irongron), John J Carney (Bloodaxe), Donald Pelmear (Professor Rubeish), June Brown (Lady Eleanor), Jeremy Bulloch (Hal), Alan Rowe (Edward of Wessex), Sheila Fay (Meg), Nicholas Courtney (Brigadier Lethbridge-Stewart), Gordon Pitt (Eric), Steve Brunswick (Sentry), Bella Emberg, Mary Rennie (Kitchen Hags)

Crew
Fight Arrangers/Stuntmen Marc Boyle, Terry Walsh, *Visual Effects Designer* Jim Ward, *Visual Effects Sculptor* John Friedlander, *Senior Cameraman* Paul Kay, *Vision Mixer* John Barclay, *Studio Lighting* Mike Jefferies, *Studio Sound* Tony Millier, *Film Cameraman* Max Samett, *Film Sound* John Gatland, *Film Editor* William Symon, *Special Sound* Dick Mills, *Grams Operator* Barry Bonner, *Incidental Music* Dudley Simpson, *Costume Designer* James Acheson, *Costume Assistant* Robin Stubbs, *Make-Up Artist* Sandra Exelby, *Designer* Keith Cheetham, *Production Assistant* Marcia Wheeler, *Assistant Floor Manager* Rosemary Webb, *Floor Assistants* Chris Brossard, John O'Shaughnessy, *Director's Assistant* Judith Harris, *Script Editor* Terrance Dicks, *Producer* Barry Letts, *Director* Alan Bromly

DWM Index
57	John Friedlander interview
63	Episode Guide
88	Archive
163	Elisabeth Sladen interview
172	Those *Radio Times*
188	Jeremy Bulloch interview
246	Archive Feature
250	Elisabeth Sladen interview Vox Pops
337	Time Team 1-2
339	Time Team 3-4

Recording Dates
7-10 May 1973 (Location filming), 28-29 May 1973 (TC6), 11-12 June 1973 (TC1)

Location
Peckforton Castle, Peckforton, Cheshire

Working Titles
The Fugitive
The Time Survivor

Factoids
- Linx' toadlike mask was sculpted from heavy-duty latex by John Friedlander. The suit was made from heavily padded lurex with leather boots and an equipment belt, while the helmet was made from fibreglass. Actor Kevin Lindsay found the costume very uncomfortable to wear and the mask gave him difficulty breathing.
- This was Elisabeth Sladen's first story as companion Sarah Jane Smith. The idea was to contrast this new 'Women's Libber' journalist with the more demure Jo Grant who had left at the end of the previous season. However, Sarah's feminist beliefs were only mentioned here and in *The Monster of Peladon* (73).
- A new title sequence to celebrate the programme's tenth anniversary was commissioned from graphic designer Bernard Lodge, utilising a laborious and time-consuming technique of rostrum animation called 'slit scan' (as used in the stargate sequences of Stanley Kubrick's 1968 film *2001: A Space Odyssey*). Consisting of stretched plastic bags sandwiched between sheets of glass, the sequence was shot with polarized filters and took three months to complete. For the first time, the Tardis, the 'time tunnel' and the Doctor's whole body made an appearance in the title sequence.
- A *Radio Times* cover photograph of Jon Pertwee surrounded by fans Michael Parkinson, Vanessa Miles and Paul and David Jones promoted the new season (dated 15-21 December 1973).

Comment
Linx the Sontaran is a brilliantly realized creation, brought to evil life by the late, great Kevin Lindsay. Sladen makes a promising new companion and there's a vigour about the story that makes the whole thing seem much more fresh and exciting than many of the rather ponderous tales of the previous season. On the other hand, Linx' inventions seem more preposterous than scary, and there's a sense that, having invented this wonderful character, Robert Holmes doesn't quite know what to do with him. David Daker and John J Carney make hissable villains, but Professor Rubeish is, well, frankly rubbish. **78%**

"Take the world that you've got and try and make something of it. It's not too late." ~ The Doctor

71) Invasion of the Dinosaurs
Malcolm Hulke

Serial Code: WWW
Original Transmission
Part One ('Invasion')
Saturday 12 January 1974, 17.30-17.55, 11m / 24
Part Two
Saturday 19 January 1974, 17.30-17.55, 10.1m / 26
Part Three
Saturday 25 January 1974, 17.30-17.55, 11m / 27
Part Four
Saturday 2 February 1974, 17.30-17.55, 9m / 34
Part Five
Saturday 9 February 1974, 17.30-17.55, 9m / 23
Part Six
Saturday 16 February 1974, 17.30-17.55, 7.5m / 54
BBC Archive
Episodes Two, Three, Four, Five and Six exist on 625-line two-inch PAL colour master videotapes. Episode One exists as a 16mm b/w film recording taken from the same source (the master videotape being wiped in 1974). In addition, Episode Three also exists as a 71 edit on 625-line two-inch Pal colour master videotape.
Novelization
Doctor Who and the Dinosaur Invasion by Malcolm Hulke (141/10)
Hardback:
February 1976, Allan Wingate (0855230614 / Chris Achilleos)

Paperback:
1. February 1976, Target (0426108744 / Chris Achilleos)
2. June 1978, Target (0426108744 / Jeff Cummins)
3. November 1993, Target, renamed *Doctor Who - Invasion of the Dinosaurs* (0426108744 / Alister Pearson)
Video
October 2003 (BBCV 7333 / Photomontage)
Précis
The Doctor and Sarah arrive in a deserted London only to find dinosaurs wandering the streets...
Cast
Jon Pertwee (Doctor Who), Elisabeth Sladen (Sarah), Nicholas Courtney (Brigadier Lethbridge-Stewart), Richard Franklin (Captain Yates), John Levene (Sergeant Benton), Gordon Reid (Phillips), George Bryson (Private Ogden), Noel Johnson (Charles Grover), Peter Miles (Professor Whitaker/Grover's Secretary's Voice), Martin Jarvis (Butler), John Bennett (General Finch), Terence Wilton (Mark), Brian Badcoe (Adam), Carmen Silvera (Ruth), Terry Walsh, Alan Bull (Warehouse Looters), Martin Taylor (Corporal Norton), Dave Carter (Sergeant Duffy), Trevor Lawrence (Lodge), John Caesar (R/T Soldier), Ben Aris (Lieutenant Shears), James Marcus (Peasant), Pat Gorman (UNIT Corporal), Colin Bell (Private Bryson), Timothy Craven (Robinson), Stuart Myers (Army Photographer), Heidi (UNIT Tracker Dog)
Crew
Stuntman Terry Walsh, *Visual Effects Designer* Clifford Culley, *Dinosaur Models* Rodney Fuller, *Inlay Operators* Phil Nixon, Alan Holey, *Back Projection Operator* Len Thurlow, *Technical Manager* Terry Wild, *Senior Cameraman* Colin Reid, *Vision Mixer* Michael Turner, *Videotape Editor* Barry Stevens, *Studio Lighting* Alan Horne, *Studio Sound* Trevor Webster, *Film Cameramen* Tony Leggo, Keith Hopper, *Assistant Film Cameraman* Fred Bagwell, *Film Sound* Andrew Boulton, *Film Editor* Robert Rymer, *Special Sound* Dick Mills, *Grams Operators* Gordon Phillipson, Mike Pinchin, *Incidental Music* Dudley Simpson, *Costume Designer* Barbara Kidd, *Make-Up Artist* Jean McMillan, *Designer* Richard Morris, *Production Assistant* George Gallaccio, *Assistant Floor Manager* John Wilcox, *Director's Assistant* Brenda Loader, *Floor Assistant* Malcolm Hamilton, *Script Editor* Terrance Dicks, *Assistant Script Editor* Robert Holmes, *Producer* Barry Letts, *Director* Paddy Russell

DWM Index
64   Episode Guide
75   Whomobile feature
82   John Levene interview
87   Chris Achilleos interview
91   The Incredible Malcolm Hulke
      Novelization review
95   Richard Franklin interview
111   Nicholas Courtney interview
127   Paddy Russell interview
192   Crossing The Line
201   Martin Jarvis interview
203   Carmen Silvera interview
      Archive Feature
222   Richard Franklin interview
250   Elisabeth Sladen interview
266   Paddy Russell interview
280   George Gallaccio interview
293   Clifford Culley interview
335   The Fact of Fiction
      Peter Miles interview
336   Video review
339   Time Team

Recording Dates
2 September 1973 (Location filming), 23-27 September 1973 (Location filming), 29 September 1973 (Location filming), 8-9 October 1973 (unknown studio modelwork), 15-16 October 1973 (TC6), 18-20 October 1973 (unknown studio modelwork), 22 October 1973 (unknown studio modelwork), 29-30 October 1973 (TC8), 1 November 1973 (unknown studio modelwork), 6 November 1973 (Pinewood Studios modelwork), 12-13 November 1973 (TC3)

Locations
Albert Embankment, London SE11; Westminster Bridge, Whitehall, Trafalgar Square, Margaret Street and Haymarket, London SW1; Billingsgate Market, London EC3; Covent Garden, London WC2; Outer Circle, Regent's Park, London NW1; Claypons Avenue, Brentford, Middlesex; Wilmer Close, Canbury Gardens, Lower Ham Road, GPO Sorting Office, Palmer Crescent, Kingston Meat Market, South Lane and Parkfield Road, Kingston-upon-Thames, Surrey; Southall Gas Works, White Street and The Straight, Southall, Middlesex; Moorfields, New Union Street and Moorgate Underground Station, London EC2; Northfields School, Balfour Road, London W13; Pickfords Depositories and Chamberlain Road, Ealing, London W13; CEGB Sub Station, Ealing, London W5; Long Lane and Lindsay Street, Smithfield, London EC1; Wimbledon Common, Wimbledon, London SW19; Riverside Drive, Ham, Middlesex.

Working Title
Timescoop
Factoids
- The first episode was entitled *Invasion* in order to keep the Episode One cliffhanger a surprise. Malcolm Hulke was upset about this, insisting that more viewers would have tuned in had they known that dinosaurs were to have been featured (although the *Radio Times* spoilt the surprise anyway by printing a drawing of a pterodactyl next to the cast list).
- The serial saw the debut of the Doctor's futuristic car. Nicknamed the Whomobile, its 'official' appellation was The Alien, although it was never given an on-screen name. Owned by Pertwee himself, the vehicle took six months to build and was powered by a 975cc Hillman Imp sports unit on a three-wheeled Bond Bug chassis. 14 feet long and seven feet wide, the body was made up of two pieces of fibreglass while a rubber skirt section gave it the appearance of hovering. Despite being able to reach a speed of 100mph, it was classified by the DVLO as an invalid tricycle (registration number WVO 2M).
- To capture shots of a deserted London, director Paddy Russell, film cameraman Tony Leggo and assistant Fred Bagwell made an unauthorised trip into the centre of town on 2 September 1973, three weeks before planned location filming. All the opening shots in Episode One were captured that day, although when their sojourn was discovered Russell was told off by her superiors for not alerting the police or the BBC. Barry Letts, though, applauded her ingenuity.
- The story saw the first use of a gallery-only day, in which editing and CSO effects took place after live action videoing and filming had been completed.
- Five dinosaurs were made by freelance contractor Rodney Fuller at Pinewood Studios. They consisted of a tyrannosaurus rex (full model and a head), stegosaurus, brontosaurus, triceratops and pterodactyl (full-size version flown on wires and a glove-puppet) and were made out of solid latex. All - apart from the pterodactyl - were controlled off-screen by rods and cables. Generally filmed on 16mm and 35mm on model London sets (although they were also used in studio recordings), the creatures were occasionally inserted into the live-

action pictures with CSO, although differences in picture stability between film and video often made them appear to be 'floating' above the ground.

Comment
A tremendous fuss is always made about how bad the dinosaurs are in this story. Well, perhaps it's just me being brought up on episodes of *The Goodies* featuring oversize animals and objects, but I find them perfectly acceptable for the most part. Some scenes are positively enthralling, such as the tyrannosaurus rex that slumbers behind Sarah in the warehouse or the stegosaurus that appears at the end of an alley in Part Two. The story itself is brilliantly perceptive, satirizing the naïve beliefs of sad *Daily Mail* reading nostalgia-junkies and showing that we have to sort out our world problems *now* rather than lock ourselves away in a perceived 'perfect age'. Professor Whitaker has a logical, workable plan and an ultimate goal that will, as he sees it, benefit Mankind by wiping away thousands of years of immorality to make a fresh start. A fabulous idea, and one of Hulke's most impassioned pleas for sanity in a mad world. Operation Golden Age is wonderfully postmodern (the spaceship set is really a spaceship set) and the whole production glistens with confidence, wit and style. And as if that wasn't enough, we have the Whomobile (or whatever it's called), Yates as a traitor and a well-executed chase sequence. Hard to fault. **96%**

"I think we're the flies in a jar of very nasty ointment." ~ *The Doctor*

72) *Death to the Daleks*
Terry Nation

Serial Code: XXX
Original Transmission
Part One
Saturday 23 February 1974, 17.30-17.55, 8.1m / 49
Part Two
Saturday 2 March 1974, 17.30-17.55, 9.5m / 30
Part Three
Saturday 9 March 1974, 17.30-17.55, 10.5m / 20
Part Four
Saturday 16 March 1974, 17.30-17.55, 9.5m / 21
BBC Archive
All episodes exist on 625-line two-inch PAL colour master videotapes.

Novelization
Doctor Who - Death to the Daleks by Terrance Dicks (125/15)
Hardback:
July 1978, WH Allen (0491024339 / Roy Knipe)
Paperback:
1. July 1978, Target (042620042X / Roy Knipe)
2. April 1991, Target (042620042X / Alister Pearson)
Video
1. July 1987, compilation (BBCV 4073 / Photomontage)
2. February 1995, edited (BBCV 5520 / Photomontage)
Music and Sound Effects
July 1999, Upbeat Classics, *Sherlock Holmes Meets Dr Who*, CD (URCD148 / -)
Précis
Drained of power, The Tardis lands on Exxilon, followed by the Daleks...
Cast
Jon Pertwee (Doctor Who), Elisabeth Sladen (Sarah), Duncan Lamont (Dan Galloway), John Abineri (Richard Railton), Julian Fox (Peter Hamilton), Joy Harrison (Jill Tarrant), Neil Seiler (Commander Stewart), Mostyn Evans (High Priest), Arnold Yarrow (Bellal), Terry Walsh (Jack/Zombie/Burning Exxilon/Stunt Double for Doctor Who), Roy Heymann (Gotal), John Scott Martin, Cy Town, Murphy Grumbar (Daleks), Michael Wisher (Dalek Voices), Steven Ismay (Zombie/Exxilon)
Crew
Fight Arranger Terry Walsh, *Stuntmen* Terry Walsh, Marc Boyle, Max Faulkner, *Visual Effects Designer* Jim Ward, *Visual Effects Assistants* Colin Mapson, Peter Pegrum, Mat Irvine, *Masks* John Friedlander, *Technical Manager* Eric Wallis, *Vision Mixer* Nick Lake, *Studio Lighting* Derek Slee, *Studio Sound* Richard Chubb, *Film Cameraman* Bill Matthews, *Assistant Film Cameramen* Martin Patmore, Ian Pugsley, *Film Sound* Bill Chesneau, *Assistant Film Sound Recordists* Chris Lovelock, Clive Derbyshire, *Grips* Alan Woods, *Film Lighting* Dave Smith, *Film Editor* Bob Rymer, Larry Toft, *Special Sound* Dick Mills, *Grams Operator* Gordon Phillipson, *Incidental Music* Carey Blyton and the London Saxophone Quartet, *Costume Designer* L Rowland-Warne, *Make-Up Artists* Magdalen Gaffney, Cynthia Goodwin, *Designer* Colin Green, *Production Assistant* Chris D'Oyly-John, *Assistant Floor Manager* Richard Leyland, *Director's Assistant* Michael Lewty, *Floor Assistant* Malcolm Hamilton, *Script Editor* Terrance Dicks, *Assistant Script Editor* Robert Holmes, *Producer* Barry Letts, *Director* Michael Briant

DWM Index
56 Archive
64 Episode Guide
97 Michael Briant interview
241 Chris D'Oyly-John interview
250 Elisabeth Sladen interview
264 Michael E Briant interview
278 Archive Feature
340 Time Team

Recording Dates
13-16 November 1973 (Location filming), 19 November 1973 (Location filming), 4 December 1973 (TC4), 17-18 December 1973 (TC4)

Location
ARC Sand Pit, Gallows Hill, Dorset

Working Titles
Four Part Dalek Story
Doctor Who and the Exilons

Factoids
- Four Daleks were used in total for this serial, repainted gun-metal grey with black dots. One Dalek had no operator and was only used in the background of certain shots. For the sandpit location shoot, the creatures were propelled by the cast (rather too swiftly on occasion) along camera dolly rails. The rails can sometimes be seen on the finished programme, as can the wires that hold up the Exxilon root in Part Three (a prop controlled by the visual effects technicians from a scaffolding on top of the lake cliff). A dummy Dalek prop was seen to blow up in Part Two.
- Ten Exxilon costumes were made from calico and terylene wadding which were dipped into latex and silica to give them a stone-like appearance. The three subterranean Exxilons had tightly fitting latex body stockings on which were painted stratified lines. These lines were intended to glow with the aid of Front Axial Projection lighting (reflected off a mirror placed at a 45º degree angle in front of the camera). FAP was also used to make the Exxilon City wall symbols and the interior maze puzzle appear on cue.
- The Exxilon city was carved from polystyrene and made to liquefy by spraying it with acetone through an atomiser.
- To emphasise the electrical power losses in the story, Michael Briant opted to use conventional saxophone music rather than a Radiophonic Workshop-modified score.

Comment
Terrible music aside, this is a run-of-the-mill Dalek story - their last before Davros came along and ended their independent supremacy - with some good design work and very atmospheric location filming. Unfortunately, much of the studio footage is too brightly lit and the Exxilon city interiors are utterly bland. The model exterior, however, is very impressive and contrasts nicely with the bleakness of the quarry surroundings. As for the cast, Joy Harrison is a treat for the eyes and John Abineri takes it all as seriously as ever. The Exxilons are genuinely creepy, especially when one sneaks into the Tardis in Part One. But at the end of the day, though, the whole thing feels rather dated and lacking in excitement. *Dearth of the Daleks* would be a better title. **70%**

"There's nothing 'only' about being a girl, your majesty." ~ *Sarah Jane Smith*

73) The Monster of Peladon
Brian Hayles

Serial Code: YYY
Original Transmission
Part One
Saturday 23 March 1974, 17.30-17.55, 9.2m / 23
Part Two
Saturday 30 March 1974, 17.30-17.55, 6.8m / 55
Part Three
Saturday 6 April 1974, 17.30-17.55, 7.4m / 42
Part Four
Saturday 13 April 1974, 17.30-17.55, 7.2m / 37
Part Five
Saturday 20 April 1974, 17.30-17.55, 7.5m / 42
Part Six
Saturday 27 April 1974, 17.30-17.55, 8.1m / 30

BBC Archive
All episodes exist on 625-line two-inch PAL colour master videotapes.

Novelization
Doctor Who and the Monster of Peladon by Terrance Dicks (124/12)
Hardback:
November 1980, WH Allen (0491028237 / Steve Kyte)
Paperback:
1. December 1980, Target (0426201329 / Steve Kyte)
2. June 1992, Target, renamed *Doctor Who - The Monster of Peladon* (0426201329 / Alister Pearson)

Video
December 1995, twin-pack (BBCV 5781 / Colin Howard)
Music and Sound Effects
May 2000, *Doctor Who at the BBC Radiophonic Workshop: Volume 2 - New Beginnings 1970-1980*, CD (WMSF 6024-2 / Photographs)
Précis
The Doctor returns to Peladon to find the Ice Warriors up to their usual tricks...
Cast
Jon Pertwee (Doctor Who), Elisabeth Sladen (Sarah), Frank Gatliff (Ortron), Nina Thomas (Queen Thalira), Donald Gee (Eckersley), Ralph Watson (Ettis), Michael Crane (Blor), Sonny Caldinez (Sskel), Alan Bennion (Azaxyr), David Cleeve, Kevin Moran, Alan Lenoir, Terence Denville (Ice Warriors), Nick Hobbs (Aggedor), Stuart Fell (Alpha Centauri), Ysanne Churchman (Alpha Centauri Voice), Gerald Taylor (Vega Nexos), Rex Robinson (Gebek), Terry Walsh (Guard/Guard Captain/Double for Doctor Who), Graeme Eton (Preba), Roy Evans, Ifor Owen (Miners), Max Faulkner (Miner/Double for Ettis)
Crew
Fight Arranger Terry Walsh, *Stuntmen* Terry Walsh, Max Faulkner, *Visual Effects Designers* Peter Day, Ian Scoones, *Technical Managers* Jack Walsh, Tommy Dawson, *Vision Mixers* Michael Turner, Nick Lake, *Studio Lighting* Ralph Walton, *Studio Sound* Tony Millier, *Film Cameraman* Keith Hopper, *Film Sound* John Gatland, *Film Editor* William Symon, *Special Sound* Dick Mills, *Grams Operator* Gordon Phillipson, *Incidental Music* Dudley Simpson, *Costume Designer* Barbara Kidd, *Make-Up Artist* Elizabeth Moss, *Designer* Gloria Clayton, *Production Assistant* Marcia Wheeler, *Assistant Floor Manager* Roselyn Parker, *Director's Assistant* Carole Bisset, *Floor Assistants* Esther Nordin, Tom Kingdon, *Script Editor* Terrance Dicks, *Assistant Script Editor* Robert Holmes, *Producer* Barry Letts, *Director* Lennie Mayne
DWM Index
64 Episode Guide
94 Archive + Fact File
 Brian Hayles Retrospective
203 Alan Bennion interview
216 Archive Feature
234 Video review
250 Elisabeth Sladen interview
340 Time Team 1-4
341 Time Team 5-6
Recording Dates
14-18 January 1974 (EFS), 28-29 January 1974 (TC8), 11-12 February 1974 (TC6), 26-27 February 1974 (TC6)

Working Titles
Return to Peladon
Monster of Peladon
Factoids
- As this studio-bound serial was a direct sequel to *The Curse of Peladon* (61), producer Barry Letts tried to assemble the same key technical personnel who had worked on the earlier serial, including designer Gloria Clayton and director Lennie Mayne. Monster costumes were reused, as well as model footage of the Peladon citadel, with three other Ice Warrior costumes coming from stock - one from their original story, *The Ice Warriors* (39) and two from *The Seeds of Death* (48).
- During rehearsals for this story, Pertwee decided that this would be his last season in *Doctor Who*. His main reason was that since Roger Delgado's sudden death in April 1973, many of his friends had, or were going to, move on from the series and he felt it was time that he himself moved on to new projects. Shortly after leaving, he would take on the chairman's role in ITV's popular 1970s panel game *Whodunnit?*
- In 1995, John Tulloch and Henry Jenkins' media studies book *Science Fiction Audiences: Watching Doctor Who and Star Trek* (Routledge) used *The Monster of Peladon* as a test case with which to monitor fan reactions to the programme.

Comment
Whereas *The Curse of Peladon* was an atmospheric, well-produced political thriller/whodunit, its sequel is a flabby, overlit exercise in poor acting and bland direction. Having the Ice Warriors turn out to be the baddies again ruins their sophisticated character development in the early story; unless you can add a new twist, reusing old monsters and stock characters is a sure sign that the programme-makers are running out of new ideas. Although there are occasional moments of contemporary social comment (miners' strikes, feminism), they make the story seem dated and don't add anything of dramatic relevance to it. Pertwee looks bored and the whole thing's as flat as a pancake. **25%**

"You are free - you don't have to be dominated."
~ K'anpo Rimpoche

74) *Planet of the Spiders*
Robert Sloman

Serial Code: ZZZ
Original Transmission
Part One
Saturday 4 May 1974, 17.45-18.10, 10.1m / 17
Part Two
Saturday 11 May 1974, 17.40-18.05, 8.9m / 26
Part Three
Saturday 18 May 1974, 17.40-18.05, 8.8m / 22
Part Four
Saturday 25 May 1974, 17.30-17.55, 8.2m / 24
Part Five
Saturday 1 June 1974, 17.35-18.00, 9.2m / 19
Part Six
Saturday 8 June 1974, 17.35-18.00, 8.9m / 25
Repeat Transmission
Omnibus
Friday 27 December 1974, 14.45-16.30, 8.6m / 49
BBC Archive
All episodes exist on 625-line two-inch PAL colour master videotapes.
Novelization
Doctor Who and the Planet of the Spiders by Terrance Dicks (121/14)
Hardback:
October 1975, Allan Wingate (0855230525 / Peter Brookes)
Paperback:
1. November 1975, Target (0426106555 / Peter Brookes)
2. September 1978, Target (0426106555 / Alun Hood)
3. August 1991, Target, renamed *Doctor Who - Planet of the Spiders* (0426106555 / Alister Pearson)
Video
April 1991, twin-pack (BBCV 4491 / Andrew Skilleter)
Music and Sound Effects
May 2000, *Doctor Who at the BBC Radiophonic Workshop: Volume 2 - New Beginnings 1970-1980*, CD (WMSF 6024-2 / Photographs)
Précis
Giant spiders from Metebelis 3 want to invade Earth through the weak minds of meditating humans...

Cast
Jon Pertwee, Tom Baker (Doctor Who), Elisabeth Sladen (Sarah), Nicholas Courtney (Brigadier Lethbridge-Stewart), Richard Franklin (Mike Yates), John Levene (Sergeant Benton), John Dearth (Lupton), Cyril Shaps (Professor Clegg), Kevin Lindsay (Cho-je), John Kane (Tommy), Ysanne Churchman, Kismet Delgado (Spider Voices), Maureen Morris (Spider Voices/The Great One Voice), George Cormack (K'Anpo), Carl Forgione (Land), Terence Lodge (Moss), Geoffrey Morris (Sabor), Andrew Staines (Keaver), Christopher Burgess (Barnes), George Cormack (K'anpo Rimpoche), Gareth Hunt (Arak), Ralph Arliss (Tuar), Jenny Laird (Neska), Pat Gorman (Soldier), Chubby Oates (Policeman), Terry Walsh (Man With Boat), Michael Pinder (Hopkins), Stuart Fell (Tramp), Joanna Monro (Rega), Walter Randall, Max Faulkner (Guard Captains)
Crew
Fight Arranger/Stunt Coordinator Terry Walsh, *Stuntmen* Terry Walsh, Alan Chuntz, Billy Horrigan, Stuart Fell, *Visual Effects Designer* Bernard Wilkie, *Visual Effects Assistants* Ian Scoones, Richard Conway, Steve Bowman, Mat Irvine, *Puppeteer* Barry Smith, *Inlay Operator* Dave Chapman, *Vision Mixer* Nick Lake, *Studio Lighting* Ralph Walton, Tommy Dawson, *Studio Sound* John Holmes, *Film Cameraman* Fred Hamilton, *Film Sound* John Gatland, *Film Editor* Bob Rymer, *Special Sound* Dick Mills, *Grams Operator* Andrew Hunter, *Incidental Music* Dudley Simpson, *Costume Designer* L Rowland-Warne, *Make-Up Artist* Deanne Turner, *Designer* Rochelle Selwyn, *Production Unit Manager* George Gallaccio, *Production Assistant* Marion McDougall, *Assistant Floor Manager* Graeme Harper, *Floor Assistant* Geoff Posner, *Director's Assistant* Heather Dunthorne, *Script Editor* Terrance Dicks, *Producer* Barry Letts, *Director* Barry Letts
DWM Index
52	Barry Letts interview
60	Archive
64	Episode Guide
75	Bessie and the Whomobile
82	John Levene interview
90	Graeme Harper interview
95	Richard Franklin interview
151	Terry Walsh interview
	Stuart Fell interview
172	Those *Radio Times*
173	Video review
184	Graeme Harper interview
187	AJ Mitchell interview

191 What The Papers Said
Ian Scoones interview
220 Walter Randall interview
What The Censor Saw
222 Richard Franklin interview
250 Elisabeth Sladen interview
Vox Pops
270 Barry Letts interview
276 Robert Sloman interview
314 Archive Feature
341 Time Team
Recording Dates
11-15 March 1974 (Location filming), 2-3 April 1974 (TC1), 16-17 April 1974 (TC8), 30 April-1 May 1974 (TC6)
Locations
Tidmarsh Manor, Tidmarsh, Berkshire; Mortimer Railway Station and environs, Stratfield Mortimer, Berkshire; Le Marchant Barracks, Devizes, Wiltshire; Membury Airfield, Membury, Wiltshire; River Severn, near Westbury-on-Seven, Gloucestershire
Working Titles
The Final Game
The Planet of the Spiders
Factoids
- Clips of Drashigs from *Carnival of Monsters* (66) were shown as Clegg 'mind reads' the sonic screwdriver.
- Because Part Five was running short, several minutes from Part Six were included at the end, and a new cliffhanger was edited in from later in the final episode: thus the recap for Part Six is substantially different to the conclusion of Part Five.
- Approximately twenty latex-covered puppet spiders were made by Ian Scoones and Steve Bowman, while the Queen Spider was a more complex marionette controlled by cables hidden beneath its platform. Scoones designed a five-foot-long black, hairy version of the Great One, but it was deemed too frightening by producer Barry Letts and was replaced with the Queen prop. A self-propelling spider running on a Meccano motor, christened Boris, was built by Scoones and Mat Irvine for brief shots in Part Five.

Comment
A witty, thought-provoking and disturbing script by Robert Sloman is complemented by imaginative, and occasionally avant-garde, direction by Barry Letts. There's a real sense of an era coming to a close, and it is especially brave that amidst the celebration and reflection, the Doctor is shown to be fatally flawed in his obsessive quest for knowledge. On the negative side, some of the acting is less than convincing (hello, Jenny Laird) and there are some very dodgy CSO Metebelis background slides. But on the whole, this is a supremely confident *fin de siècle* epic that manages to scare and delight in equal measure. **97%**

Fourth Doctor: Tom Baker

Season 12

"If the square on the hypotenuse equals the sum of the square on the other two sides, why is a mouse when it spins?" ~ The Doctor

75) *Robot*
Terrance Dicks

Serial Code
4A
Original Transmission
Part One
Saturday 28 December 1974, 17.35-18.00, 10.8m / 25
Part Two
Saturday 4 January 1974, 17.30-17.55, 10.7m / 17
Part Three
Saturday 11 January 1974, 17.30-17.55, 10.1m / 22
Part Four
Saturday 18 January 1974, 17.30-17.55, 9m / 30
BBC Archive
All episodes exist on 625-line two-inch PAL colour master videotapes.
Novelization
Doctor Who and the Giant Robot by Terrance Dicks (124/12)
Hardback:
April 1986, WH Allen (0491036639 / Jeff Cummins)
Paperback:
1. March 1975, Target (0426108582 / Peter Brookes)
2. April 1979, Target (0426112792 / Jeff Cummins)
3. May 1992, Target, renamed *Doctor Who - Robot* (0426203712 / Alister Pearson)

Junior Novelization
Junior Doctor Who and the Giant Robot (94/12)
Hardback:
May 1979, WH Allen (0491024975 / Harry Hants)
Paperback:
1980, Target (0426200640 / Harry Hants)

Non-Fiction Book
December 1976, Target, 'The Diary of a Production' in *The Making of Doctor Who* by Terrance Dicks and Malcolm Hulke, Paperback (0426116151 / Chris Achilleos)

Video
January 1992 (BBCV 4714 / Alister Pearson)

Script
November 2001, *Doctor Who: The Scripts - Tom Baker 1974/5* with additional text by Justin Richards and Andrew Pixley, Hardback (0563538155 / Photomontage)

Précis
A fascist group of scientists is using a powerful robot to hold the world to ransom…

Cast
Tom Baker (Doctor Who), Elisabeth Sladen (Sarah), Ian Marter (Surgeon Lieutenant Harry Sullivan), Nicholas Courtney (Brigadier Lethbridge-Stewart), John Levene (RSM Benton), Alec Linstead (Arnold Jellicoe), Patricia Maynard (Hilda Winters), Edward Burnham (Professor JP Kettlewell), Michael Kilgarriff (K1 Robot), Timothy Craven (Short), John Scott Martin (MoD Guard), Pat Gorman (Thinktank Guard), Elizabeth Cassidy (Double for Sarah Jane Smith), Terry Sartain, Terry Walsh (SRC Bouncers), Walter Goodman (Joseph Chambers MP)

Crew
Visual Effects Designer Clifford Culley, *Inlay Operator* Dave Jervis, *Technical Manager* Derek Thompson, *Senior Cameraman* Colin Reid, *Vision Mixer* Graham Giles, *Studio Lighting* Nigel Wright, *Studio Sound* John Holmes, *OB Lighting* John Mason, *OB Sound* Vic Godrich, Trevor Webster, *Special Sound* Dick Mills, *Grams Operator* Gordon Phillipson, *Incidental Music* Dudley Simpson, *Costume Designers* James Acheson, Begonia Pope, *Make-Up Artist* Judy Clay, *Make-Up Assistants* Ann Edwards, Gail Glaser, *Designer* Ian Rawnsley, *Production Unit Manager* George Gallaccio, *Production Assistant* Peter Grimwade, *Assistant Floor Manager* David Tilley, *Director's Assistant* Joy Sinclair, *Floor Assistant* Geoffrey Posner, *Script Editor* Robert Holmes, *Producer* Barry Letts, *Director* Christopher Barry

DWM Index
54   Peter Grimwade interview
64   Episode Guide
72   Nicholas Courtney interview
82   John Levene interview
89   Elisabeth Sladen interview
92   Archive + Fact File
99   Christopher Barry interview
100 Robert Holmes interview
179 Tom Baker interview
180 Christopher Barry interview 1
181 Christopher Barry interview 2
     Video review
191 What The Papers Said
250 Elisabeth Sladen interview
260 Vox Pops
261 Nuts And Bolts
272 Terrance Dicks interview
290 Archive Feature
293 Clifford Culley interview
315 Christopher Barry interview
344 Time Team

Recording Dates
28 April-2 May 1974 (Location videotaping), 5-6 May 1974 (Location videotaping), 22 May 1974 (TC3), 1-2 June 1974 (TC3), 6-7 June 1974 (TC3), 24 October 1974 (TC7)

Location
BBC Engineering Training Centre, Wood Norton, Evesham, Worcestershire

Working Title
As broadcast

Factoids
- Actors considered for the role of the Fourth Doctor included Ron Moody, Richard Hearne, Graham Crowden, Michael Bentine, Jim Dale, Bernard Cribbins and Fulton Mackay. At the time of being cast, Tom Baker was working on a building site in Ebury Street in central London.
- Script editor Robert Holmes described the new Doctor as being a cross between Sherlock Holmes, Professor Bernard Quatermass and George Bernard Shaw. His costume was deliberately chosen to contrast with the elegance of Jon Pertwee and was partly inspired by a famous 1892 poster by Henri de Toulouse-Lautrec. The long, multicoloured scarf was knitted by Begonia Pope out of a huge amount of wool given to her by James Acheson.
- New producer Philip Hinchcliffe, fresh from ATV, trailed Barry Letts for this story before taking over properly with *The Ark in Space* (76).

- All previous *Doctor Who* stories had required certain sequences - and always location scenes - to be shot on 16mm or 35mm film. *Robot* would be the first serial to be recorded entirely on videotape, mainly because it would make CSO overlays of the giant Robot more seamless. (The combination of film and video on previous 'large monster' tale, *Invasion of the Dinosaurs* [71], had been all too obvious.) The chosen location was the same as for *Spearhead from Space* - the BBC's training centre at Wood Norton.
- Two remounts were undertaken for this story. One because industrial action had plagued the first studio session (21 May was abandoned, and much of the material on 22 May was deemed unsatisfactory), and the second was to restage the giant Robot sequences for Part Four, which Barry Letts had been unhappy with.
- Alistair Bowtell Effects constructed the large K1 Robot out of aluminium sheeting over a framework of metal and balsawood. Its transparent 'brain case' was illuminated with flashing battery-powered lights, but these were not bright enough to show up on location. Michael Kilgarriff found wearing the top-heavy, claustrophobic costume very exhausting, and afterwards suffered nightmares about the experience.
- A new title sequences was created by Bernard Lodge. He retaining the previous season's slit-scan 'time tunnel', to which he added a Tardis silhouette and Tom Baker's face. The closing credits sequence remained unchanged.

Comment
Robot manages the clever trick of being markedly different from *Planet of the Spiders* and yet not so different as to alienate loyal viewers. Tom Baker makes a big impression, and it's nice to see Elisabeth Sladen getting the lion's share of the action (although she ends up as just another screaming heroine at the end). Ian Marter makes a pleasing new addition to the muster of male companions, and the villains are suitably villainous. It's also nice to see a non-extraterrestrial threat, one of only a handful of times this has occurred in the programme. But the star of the show is the fantastic K1 Robot itself - a masterpiece of design that overshadows every other aspect of the production. **85%**

"Keep back! No, don't touch me!" ~ *Libri*

76) The Ark in Space
Robert Holmes, from an idea by John Lucarotti

Serial Code: 4C
Original Transmission
Part One
Saturday 25 January 1975, 17.35-18.00, 9.4m / 27
Part Two
Saturday 1 February 1975, 17.30-17.55, 13.6m / 5
Part Three
Saturday 8 February 1975, 17.30-17.55, 11.2m / 17
Part Four
Saturday 15 February 1975, 17.30-17.55, 10.2m / 24
Repeat Transmission
Omnibus
Wednesday 20 August 1975, 18.35-19.45, 8.2m / 29
BBC Archive
All episodes exist on 625-line two-inch PAL colour master videotapes.
Novelization
Doctor Who and the Ark in Space by Ian Marter (140/9)
Hardback:
April 1977, Allan Wingate (0855231912 / Chris Achilleos)
Paperback:
1. May 1977, Target (0426116313 / Chris Achilleos)
2. May 1991, Target, renamed *Doctor Who - The Ark in Space* (0426116313 / Alister Pearson)
Video
1. June 1989, compilation (BBCV 4244 / Photomontage)
2. February 1994 (BBCV 5218 / Photomontage)
DVD
April 2002, optional CGI effects, unused title sequence, original trailer, model footage, Blackpool Exhibition trailer, production subtitles, photo gallery, commentary by Tom Baker, Elisabeth Sladen and Philip Hinchcliffe (BBCDVD 1097 / Clayton Hickman)
Laserdisc
1996, Encore Entertainment (EE1158 / Pete Wallbank)
Music and Sound Effects
1. October 1993, Silva Screen, *Doctor Who - Pyramids of Mars*, CD (FILMCD 134 / Alister Pearson)

2. May 2000, *Doctor Who at the BBC Radiophonic Workshop: Volume 2 - New Beginnings 1970-1980* , CD (WMSF 6024-2 / Photographs)
Script
November 2001, *Doctor Who: The Scripts - Tom Baker 1974/5* with additional text by Justin Richards and Andrew Pixley, Hardback (0563538155 / Photomontage)
Précis
A swarm of giant parasitic insects threaten the lives of the last surviving inhabitants of Earth…
Cast
Tom Baker (Doctor Who), Elisabeth Sladen (Sarah), Ian Marter (Harry), Kenton Moore (Noah), Wendy Williams (Vira), Christopher Masters (Libri), Richardson Morgan (Rogin), John Gregg (Lycett), Gladys Spencer (Voice of High Minister), Peter Tuddenham (Voices), Stuart Fell (Wirrn Grub Operator/Wirrn Operator), Nick Hobbs (Wirrn Operator), Brian Jacobs (Dune)
Crew
Visual Effects Designers John Friedlander, Tony Oxley, *Technical Manager* Tommy Dawson, *Senior Cameraman* Peter Granger, *Vision Mixer* Mary Kellehar, *Studio Lighting* Nigel Wright, *Studio Sound* John Lloyd, *Special Sound* Dick Mills, *Grams Operator* Gordon Phillipson, *Incidental Music* Dudley Simpson, *Costume Designer* Barbara Kidd, *Make-Up Artist* Sylvia James, *Make-Up Assistants* Martha Livesley, Leri O'Gorman, *Designer* Roger Murray-Leach, *Production Unit Manager* George Gallaccio, *Production Assistant* Marion McDougall, *Assistant Floor Manager* Russ Karel, *Floor Assistant* John Smith, *Director's Assistant* Pauline Silcock, *Script Editor* Philip Hinchcliffe, *Producer* Philip Hinchcliffe, *Director* Rodney Bennett
DWM Index
57	John Friedlander interview
65	Episode Guide
92	Tom Baker interview
93	Ian Marter interview
100	Robert Holmes interview
114	Chris Achilleos interview
121	Ian Marter Tribute
125	Novelization review
152	Stuart Fell interview
177	Those *Radio Times*
179	Tom Baker interview
191	What The Papers Said
210	Philip Hinchcliffe interview
218	Archive Feature
221	What The Censor Saw
225	Sylvia James interview
246	Laserdisc review
250	Elisabeth Sladen interview
268	Rodney Bennett interview
280	George Gallaccio interview
317	DVD review
344	Time Team

Recording Dates
28-29 October 1974 (TC3), 11-12 November 1974 (TC1)
Working Title
As broadcast
Factoids
- This *Quatermass Experiment*-inspired story and the following one, *The Sontaran Experiment*, were hastily written substitutes for an unsuitable six-part serial by writer John Lucarotti. (His overall title is unknown, although individual episodes bore such names as *Puffball* and *Golfball*). Lucarotti's storyline was itself a replacement for an unused story by Christopher Langley called *Space Station*.
- The Wirrn larvae were made from bubble-wrap packing material, while the full-size Wirrn were build from latex over a bamboo frame with a fibreglass head section. 16mm modelwork of puppet Wirrn crawling across the surface of the Ark was trimmed back radically in the transmitted story as it was deemed unconvincing.
- A sequence of Noah begging to be killed was edited out from the finished programme at producer Hinchcliffe's insistence - he considered it too horrifying to be broadcast in an early evening timeslot.
- For reasons unknown, the title sequence of Part One was tinted green and pink.

Comment
This is a chilling tale of possession, in many ways the precursor of the 1979 film *Alien*, with wonderful sets by designer Roger Murray-Leach and a carefully structured plot that gets more and more tense as the story progresses. Unusually, the harsh studio lighting adds to the horror by creating a clinical white 'hospital-style' visual look that contrasts disturbingly with the grotesque Wirrn infection. **87%**

"I just love clocks. Atomic clocks, quartz clocks, grandfather clocks...cuckoo clocks." ~ *The Doctor*

77) *The Sontaran Experiment*
Bob Baker and Dave Martin

Serial Code: 4B
Original Transmission
Part One
Saturday 22 February 1975, 17.30-17.55, 11m / 18
Part Two
Saturday 1 March 1975, 17.30-17.55, 10.5m / 17
Repeat Transmission
Omnibus
Friday 9 July 1976, 18.25-19.15, 8.2m / 25
BBC Archive
All episodes exist as 625-line two-inch PAL colour master videotapes.
Novelization
Doctor Who and the Sontaran Experiment by Ian Marter (127/8)
Hardback:
November 1978, WH Allen (0491020465 / Roy Knipe)
Paperback:
December 1978, Target (0426200497 / Roy Knipe)
Video
October 1991, twin-pack with *The Genesis of the Daleks* [sic] (BBCV 4643 / Andrew Skilleter)
Music and Sound Effects
1. May 1978, *Doctor Who Sound Effects*, LP (REC 316 / Photomontage)
2. May 1978, *Doctor Who Sound Effects*, cassette (ZCM 316 / Photomontage)
3. July 1993, *Doctor Who: 30 Years at the Radiophonic Workshop*, CD (BBCCD 871 / Photomontage)
Script
November 2001, *Doctor Who: The Scripts - Tom Baker 1974/5* with additional text by Justin Richards and Andrew Pixley, Hardback (0563538155 / Photomontage)
Précis
The Doctor, Sarah and Harry find a lone Sontaran conducting obscene experiments on Earth colonists...
Cast
Tom Baker (Doctor Who), Elisabeth Sladen (Sarah), Ian Marter (Harry), Kevin Lindsay (Styre/The Marshall), Donald Douglas (Vural), Terry Walsh (Zake), Peter Walshe (Erak), Glyn Jones (Krans), Peter Rutherford (Roth), Brian Ellis (Prisoner), Terry Walsh (Stunt Double for Doctor Who/Stunt Double for Harry Sullivan), Stuart Fell (Double for Styre)
Crew
Fight Arranger Terry Walsh, *Stuntmen* Terry Walsh, Stuart Fell, *Visual Effects Designers* John Friedlander, Tony Oxley, *Visual Effects Assistant* Peter Pegrum, *OB Lighting* Tommy Thomas, *OB Sound* Vic Godrich, *OB VT Editor* Ian Rutter, *Engineering Manager* George Jakins, *Special Sound* Dick Mills, *Incidental Music* Dudley Simpson, *Costume Designer* Barbara Kidd, *Costume Assistant* Richard Winter, *Make-Up Artist* Sylvia James, *Make-Up Assistant* Martha Livesley, *Designer* Roger Murray-Leach, *Production Unit Manager* George Gallaccio, *Production Assistant* Marion McDougall, *Assistant Floor Manager* Russ Karel, *Director's Assistant* Pauline Silcock, *Script Editor* Robert Holmes, *Producer* Philip Hinchcliffe, *Director* Rodney Bennett
DWM Index
57	John Friedlander interview
65	Episode Guide
93	Ian Marter interview
121	Ian Marter Tribute
125	Novelization review
133	Archive + Fact File
152	Stuart Fell interview
	Terry Walsh interview
179	Tom Baker interview
	Video review
235	Bob Baker and Dave Martin interview
237	Archive Feature
250	Elisabeth Sladen interview
268	Rodney Bennett interview
280	George Gallaccio interview
346	Time Team

Recording Dates
26 September-2 October 1974 (Location videotaping)
Locations
Hound Tor, near Manaton, Dartmoor, Devon; Headland Warren Farm, Postbridge, Devon
Working Title
The Destructors
Factoids
- Following *Robot*'s example as the first *Doctor Who* story shot entirely on video, *The Sontaran Experiment* was the first serial shot entirely on video *and* on location. There were various problems with the antiquated Outside Broadcast equipment provided for the serial and some planned CSO work had to be scrapped.

- A new mask was sculpted by John Friedlander for Styre (also used for the Marshall). The rest of the costume was the same as in *The Time Warrior* (70), but with the Sontaran now sporting five, rather than three, fingers. Styre's robot was a lightweight aluminium prop pulled along on camera dolly tracks.
- Due to slippery conditions caused by sleet and rain, Tom Baker slipped and broke his collar bone on the fourth day of taping. After a visit to Torquay Hospital, he was back at work the next day although he was only able to perform stationary close-up shots. Terry Walsh subsequently doubled for him in long shots and fight sequences.

Comment
The Sontaran Experiment is a slick, atmospheric two-parter that still looks fresh and vibrant three decades on. The obvious reality of the setting adds enormously to the plot (which actually makes little sense) and the scenes of torture, both mental and physical, are surprisingly sadistic. The GalSec colonists are a bit of a bland bunch but Kevin Lindsay gives another chilling performance as a Sontaran (Linx in all but name). My one criticism is that the plot doesn't really kick in until Part Two, but it's all so engaging the viewer hardly notices. **88%**

"Why must we always destroy beauty? Why kill another creature because it is not in our image? ~ Sevrin

78) Genesis of the Daleks
Terry Nation

Serial Code: 4E
Original Transmission
Part One
Saturday 8 March 1975, 17.30-17.55, 10.7m / 23
Part Two
Saturday 15 March 1975, 17.30-17.55, 10.5m / 15
Part Three
Saturday 22 March 1975, 17.30-17.55, 8.5m / 42
Part Four
Saturday 29 March 1975, 17.30-17.55, 8.8m / 36
Part Five
Saturday 5 April 1975, 17.30-17.55, 9.8m / 30
Part Six
Saturday 12 April 1975, 17.55-18.20, 9.1m / 26

Repeat Transmissions
Omnibus
Saturday 27 December 1975, 15.00-16.25, - / - Compilation as part of 'Doctor Who and the Monsters' season:
Part One   (Parts One - Three)
Monday 26 July 1982, 19.25-20.10, 4.9m / 76
Part Two (Parts Four - Six)
Monday 2 August 1982, 19.25-20.10, 5m / 69
On BBC2:
Part One
Friday 8 January 1993, 19.15-19.40, 2.2m / 22
Part Two
Friday 15 January 1993, 19.15-19.40, 2.2m / 25
Part Three
Friday 22 January 1993, 19.15-19.40, 2.3m / 25
Part Four
Friday 29 January 1993, 19.15-19.40, 2.1m / 30
Part Five
Friday 5 February 1993, 19.15-19.40, 2.3m / 28
Part Six
Friday 12 February 1993, 19.15-19.40, 2.3m / -
On BBC2:
Part One
Tuesday 1 February 2000, 18.00-18.25, - / -
Part Two/Three
Tuesday 8 February 2000, 18.00-18.50, - / -
Part Four
Tuesday 15 February 2000, 18.00-18.25, - / -
Part Five
Tuesday 22 February 2000, 18.00-18.25, - / -
Part Six
Tuesday 29 February 2000, 18.00-18.25, 1.5m / -
BBC Archive
All episodes exist on 625-line two-inch PAL colour master videotapes.
Novelization
Doctor Who and the Genesis of the Daleks by Terrance Dicks (140/12)
Hardback:
July 1976, Allan Wingate (085523072X / Chris Achilleos)
Paperback:
1. July 1976, Target (0426112601 / Chris Achilleos)
2. September 1991, Target, renamed *Doctor Who - Genesis of the Daleks* (0426112601 / Alister Pearson)
Video
1. October 1991, twin-pack with *The Sontaran Experiment* (BBCV 4643 / Andrew Skilleter)
2. September 2001, in 'The Davros Collection' box set [BBCV 7241 / Photomontage] with the other four Davros stories (BBCV 7251 / Photomontage)

Soundtrack
1. October 1979, LP, narrated by Tom Baker (REH 364 / Photomontage)
2. October 1979, cassette, narrated by Tom Baker (ZCR 364 / Photomontage)
3. November 1988, 2 x cassettes, narrated by Tom Baker, with *Slipback* (0563225572 / Photomontage)
4. July 2001, CD, narrated by Tom Baker, with *Exploration Earth* (0563478578 / Photomontage)

Script
November 2001, *Doctor Who: The Scripts - Tom Baker 1974/5* with additional text by Justin Richards and Andrew Pixley, Hardback (0563538155 / Photomontage)

Précis
The Time Lords send the Doctor on a mission to destroy the Daleks at their birth…

Cast
Tom Baker (Doctor Who), Elisabeth Sladen (Sarah), Ian Marter (Harry), Peter Miles (Nyder), Michael Wisher (Davros/Dalek Voices), Dennis Chinnery (Gharman), Guy Siner (Ravon), Richard Reeves (Kaled Leader), Stephen Yardley (Sevrin), James Garbutt (Ronson), Tom Georgeson (Kavell), Ivor Roberts (Mogran), Harriet Philpin (Bettan), John Franklyn-Robbins (Time Lord), Drew Wood (Tane), Jeremy Chandler (Gerrill), Andrew Johns (Kravos), Dod Watson (Thing), Tracey Eddon (Double for Sarah Jane), John Scott Martin, Cy Town, Keith Ashley (Daleks), Roy Skelton (Dalek Voices)

Crew
Stuntmen Alan Chuntz, Terry Walsh, Max Faulkner, Jim Dowdall, Dinny Powell, Paddy Ryan, *Stuntwoman* Tracey Eddon, *Armourers* Alf Trustrum, Jack Wells, *Visual Effects Designer* Peter Day, *Davros Mask* John Friedlander, *Inlay Operators* Dave Jervis, Dave Chapman, *Technical Manager* Dicky Ashman, *Senior Cameraman* Peter Granger, *Vision Mixers* John Gorman, Jim Stephens, *Studio Lighting* Duncan Brown, *Studio Sound* Tony Millier, *Film Cameraman* Elmer Cossey, *Film Sound* Bill Meekums, *Film Editor* Larry Toft, *Special Sound* Dick Mills, *Grams Operator* Gordon Phillipson, *Incidental Music* Dudley Simpson, *Costume Designer* Barbara Kidd, *Costume Assistant* Doreen James, *Make-Up Artist* Sylvia James, *Make-Up Assistant* Carolyn Perry, *Designer* David Spode, *Production Unit Manager* George Gallaccio, *Production Assistant* Rosemary Crowson, *Assistant Floor Manager* Karilyn Collier, *Floor Assistant* Val Birch, *Script Editor* Robert Holmes, *Producer* Philip Hinchcliffe, *Director* David Maloney

DWM Index
57	John Friedlander interview
65	Episode Guide
69	Repeat review
89	Elisabeth Sladen interview
92	Tom Baker interview
108	David Maloney interview
114	Chris Achilleos interview
117	Michael Wisher interview
145	Terry Nation interview
152	Terry Walsh interview
163	Elisabeth Sladen interview
177	Those *Radio Times*
179	Nostalgia feature
	Michael Wisher interview
	Peter Miles interview
	Tom Baker interview
	Video review
191	What The Papers Said
197	TV review (repeat)
201	Stephen Yardley interview
202	David Maloney interview
210	Philip Hinchcliffe interview
221	What The Censor Saw
250	Elisabeth Sladen interview
	Peter Miles interview
	Archive Feature
260	Vox Pops
265	*Doctor Who Magazine* Awards (1st)
280	George Gallaccio interview
308	CD review
309	Video review ('The Davros Collection')
327	The Mary Whitehouse Experience
335	Peter Miles interview
346	Time Team

Recording Dates
6-10 January 1975 (Location filming), 13-14 January 1975 (EFS), 27-28 January 1975 (TC1), 10-11 February 1975 (TC8), 24-25 February 1975 (TC6)

Location
Betchworth Quarry, Pebblehill Road, Betchworth, Surrey

Working Title
Daleks - Genesis of Terror

Factoids
- Terry Nation's storyline was commissioned by outgoing producer Barry Letts and confirmed the notion that the Daleks represented fascism, specifically the Nazi regime under Adolf Hitler. To emphasise this, Peter Miles, playing Nyder, wore an Iron Cross during the first studio recording session. Considered as too obvious a motif by director David Maloney, it was removed for subsequent sessions.

- The three 1960s Dalek props previously seen in *Death to the Daleks* (72) were used for this story, along with the four 'goon' shells made for *Planet of the Daleks* (68). Learning from his mistakes on this latter story, David Maloney opted not to use any Daleks at the quarry location. Davros' wheelchair was constructed by Peter Day, and the mask sculpted by John Friedlander, based loosely on the large-headed Mekon from the 1950s *Dan Dare* comic strips in the *Eagle* comic. Like the Daleks, Michael Wisher's voice was treated with a ring modulator to echo his creations' vocal inflections.
- Unusually, Part Two began without a reprise, and for its cliffhanger utilized a freeze-frame ending. It was the first time this technique had been tried on *Doctor Who* and would become a semi-regular feature of the show for the next few years. (It was last seen in 1985 on Part Two of *Revelation of the Daleks*, 143).
- The body of an Ice Warrior costume formed the carapace of a large, sluglike mutant seen in the cave, while the Thals' guns previously saw service in *Galaxy 4* (18). Silent footage of a Saturn V rocket take-off was used for the Thal missile (and was also seen in the following story, *Revenge of the Cybermen*).

Comment
So much has been written about this most-repeated of *Doctor Who* stories that it hardly seems worthwhile to add anything. Suffice it to say that the dialogue is razor-sharp, the filmwork is lovely and Michael Wisher and Peter Miles are the programme's best villainous double act. On the negative side, there are at least two episodes of padding, the Daleks aren't in it enough and the giant clams are very silly. It's also sad that from this story onwards, the Daleks would always be shackled to their creator Davros and would never exhibit the same independent cunning as they had done in previous adventures. **75%**

"You're just a pathetic bunch of tin soldiers skulking about the Universe in an ancient spaceship." ~ The Doctor

79) *Revenge of the Cybermen*
Robert Holmes, based on a storyline by Gerry Davis

Serial Code: 4D
Original Transmission
Part One
Saturday 19 April 1975, 17.35-18.00, 9.5m / 24
Part Two
Saturday 26 April 1975, 17.30-17.55, 8.3m / 28
Part Three
Saturday 3 May 1975, 17.50-18.15, 8.9m / 25
Part Four
Saturday 10 May 1975, 17.30-17.55, 9.4m / 22
BBC Archive
All episodes exist as 625-line two-inch PAL colour master videotapes.
Novelization
Doctor Who and the Revenge of the Cybermen by Terrance Dicks (128/12)
Hardback:
May 1976, Allan Wingate (0855230711 / Chris Achilleos)
Paperback:
1. May 1976, Target, first edition cover renamed *Doctor Who - The Revenge of the Cybermen* (042610997X / Chris Achilleos)
2. May 1991, Target, renamed *Doctor Who - The Revenge of the Cybermen* (042610997X / Alister Pearson)
Video
1. October 1983, compilation (BBCV 2003 / Photomontage)
2. October 1983, compilation, Betamax (BBCB 2003 / Photomontage)
3. October 1983, compilation, Video 2000 (- / Photomontage)
4. December 1986, compilation (BBCV 4013 / Photomontage)
5. April 1999 (BBCV 6773 / Photomontage)
Laserdisc
1983 (BBCL 2003 / Photomontage)
Script
November 2001, *Doctor Who: The Scripts - Tom Baker 1974/5* with additional text by Justin Richards and Andrew Pixley, Hardback (0563538155 / Photomontage)
Music and Sound Effects
1. July 1999, Upbeat Classics, *Sherlock Holmes Meets Dr Who*, CD (URCD148 / -)
2. 2003, Apollo Sound, *Carey Blyton - The Film Production Music*, CD (APSCD 225 / -)

Précis
The Doctor and friends return to Nerva Beacon in the past to find the Cybermats waiting for them…

Cast
Tom Baker (Doctor Who), Elisabeth Sladen (Sarah), Ian Marter (Harry), Jeremy Wilkin (Kellman), Ronald Leigh-Hunt (Commander Stevenson), William Marlowe (Lester), Alec Wallis (Warner), David Collings (Vorus), Michael Wisher (Magrik/Voice of Colville/Voice of Vogan Radio Operator), Kevin Stoney (Tyrum), Brian Grellis (Sheprah), Christopher Robbie (Cyberleader), Melville Jones (Cyberman), Tony Lord (Cyberman/Nerva Beacon Corpse), Pat Gorman (Cybermen/Nerva Beacon Corpse), Michael E Briant (Monitor Voice), Terry Walsh (Stunt Double for Doctor Who), Alan Chuntz (Stunt Double for Commander Stevenson/Stunt Double for Harry Sullivan)

Crew
Armourer Jack Wells, *Stuntmen* Terry Walsh, Alan Chuntz, *Visual Effects Designer* James Ward, *Visual Effects Assistant* Tony Harding, *Vogan Masks* John Friedlander, *Inlay Operator* Dave Jervis, *Technical Manager* John Farr, *Senior Cameraman* Peter Granger, *Vision Mixer* Nick Lake, *Studio Lighting* Derek Slee, *Studio Sound* Norman Bennett, *Film Cameraman* Elmer Cossey, *Film Sound* John Gatland, *Film Editor* Sheila S Tomlinson, *Special Sound* Dick Mills, *Grams Operator* Paul Graydon, *Incidental Music* Carey Blyton, Peter Howell, *Costume Designer* Prue Handley, *Make-Up Artist* Cecile Hay-Arthur, *Make-Up Assistants* Jane Boak, Martha Fisher, Martha Livesley, Kerin Carswell, Vanessa Poulton, *Designer* Roger Murray-Leach, *Production Unit Manager* George Gallaccio, *Production Assistant* John Bradburn, *Assistant Floor Managers* Russ Karel, *Director's Assistant* Sue Mansfield, *Floor Assistant* Steve Haggard, *Script Editor* Robert Holmes, *Producer* Philip Hinchcliffe, *Director* Michael E Briant

DWM Index
65	Episode Guide
89	Elisabeth Sladen interview
97	Archive + Fact File
99	Video review
117	Michael Wisher interview
124	Gerry Davis interview
152	Terry Walsh interview
177	David Collings interview
210	Philip Hinchcliffe interview
250	Elisabeth Sladen interview
264	Michael E Briant interview
277	Video review (reissue)
280	George Gallaccio interview
297	Archive Feature
329	David Collings interview
347	Time Team

Recording Dates
12 November 1974 (TC Puppet Theatre), 18-21 November 1974 (Location filming), 3 December (TC1), 17 December 1974 (TC3)

Location
Wookey Hole Caves, Wells, Somerset

Working Titles
The Revenge of the Cybermen
Doctor Who and the Return of the Cybermen

Factoids
- Gerry Davis was asked to make his Cyberman story a studio-bound adventure reusing the same sets as Christopher Langley's *Space Station*, in order to minimise costs. *Space Station* was then junked in favour of *The Ark in Space* (76), and Davis' original idea of the station as an intergalactic casino was amended to a navigation beacon. His storyline bore individual episode titles in the style of 1960s *Doctor Who* - they were *The Beacon in Space*, *The Plague Carriers*, *The Gold Miners* and *The Battle for Nerva*. Robert Holmes rewrote much of the storyline (with input from Philip Hinchcliffe), adding all the material in the newly scheduled location scenes and changing the human miners to aliens.
- Four new Cybermen costumes were made by Alistair Bowtell Effects. Similar to the ones seen in *Invasion* (46), they had flared trousers and weapons incorporated into their 'middle eye'. These weapons consisted of four flash-charges, each one only able to fire once before being reloaded (as with the handheld discs in *The Sea Devils*, 62). James Ward redesigned the Cybermats, making them larger and more elongated than their appearances in the 1960s. They were moved with a combination of CSO, rod puppets and actors manipulating them by hand.
- During filming at Wookey Hole Caves, various accidents occurred which were allegedly the result of dressing up the Witch rock formation with a cloak and broomstick. An electrician fell and broke his leg and Elisabeth Sladen was nearly drowned in a lake after her hired motorboat went out of control. Stuntman Terry Walsh dived in and rescued her.

- Shop dummies were used as corpses in Part One, while Front Axial Projection material in the form of veins was fixed to plague victims' faces to make them pulse under the correct lighting conditions.
- Carey Blyton's music was felt to be unnecessarily comical in nature, and so Peter Howell of the Radiophonic Workshop augmented it electronically to give it greater dramatic weight.

Comment
Extraordinary to think that this was the first ever BBC Video release, as it's almost the worst story in Philip Hinchcliffe's three-year producership, and certainly the cheapest-looking story in Tom Baker's first season. The location filming is effective and Jeremy Wilkin makes a suitably smug villain, but in many ways the story is very poor. The impressive *Ark in Space* sets now look tacky, the Cybermen are emotional, ineffectual hunchbacks, the special effects are universally *appalling* and the Vogans look like a vast army of Barbara Cartland clones. Thank goodness Carey Blyton's music has been improved though. **40%**

Season 13

"His eyes...his eyes were terrible to see." ~ Angus MacRanald

80) Terror of the Zygons
Robert Banks Stewart

Serial Code: 4F
Original Transmission
Part One
Saturday 30 August 1975, 17.45-18.10, 8.4m / 29
Part Two
Saturday 6 September 1975, 17.45-18.10, 6.1m / 61
Part Three
Saturday 13 September 1975, 17.45-18.10, 8.2m / 32
Part Four
Saturday 20 September 1975, 17.20-17.45, 7.2m / 45
BBC Archive
All episodes exist as 625-line two-inch PAL colour master videotapes.

Novelization
Doctor Who and the Loch Ness Monster by Terrance Dicks (127/12)
Hardback:
January 1976, Allan Wingate (0855230541 / Chris Achilleos)
Paperback:
1. January 1976, Target (0426110412 / Chris Achilleos)
2. March 1993, Target, renamed *Doctor Who - Terror of the Zygons* (0426203917 / Alister Pearson)
Video
1. November 1988, compilation (BBCV 4186 / Photomontage)
2. June 1999 (BBCV 6774 / Photomontage)
Music and Sound Effects
1. May 1978, *Doctor Who Sound Effects*, LP (REC 316 / Photomontage)
2. May 1978, *Doctor Who Sound Effects*, cassette (ZCM 316 / Photomontage)
3. January 2000, *Doctor Who: Terror of the Zygons*, CD (WMSF 6020-2 / Photomontage)
Précis
Something strange is happening under the surface of Loch Ness...
Cast
Tom Baker (Doctor Who), Elisabeth Sladen (Sarah), Ian Marter (Harry), Nicholas Courtney (Brigadier Lethbridge-Stewart), John Levene (RSM Benton), John Woodnutt (Duke of Forgill/Broton), Angus Lennie (Angus MacRanald), Tony Sibbald (Huckle), Robert Russell (The Caber/Zygon Voice), Lillias Walker (Sister Lamont/Zygon Voice), Hugh Martin (Munro), Bruce Wightman (Radio Operator), Keith Ashley, Ronald Gough, David Selby (Zygons), Bernard G High (Corporal), Peter Symonds (Soldier), Douglas Camfield (Angus' Singing Voice)
Crew
Visual Effects Designers John Horton, John Friedlander, *Visual Effects Assistant* Steve Bowman, *Inlay Operator* Dave Jervis, *Technical Manager* Henry Barber, *Senior Cameraman* Paul Kay, *Vision Mixer* Nick Lake, *Studio Lighting* John Dixon, *Studio Sound* Michael McCarthy, *Film Cameraman* Peter Hall, *Film Sound* John Tellick, *Film Editor* Ian McKendrick, *Special Sound* Dick Mills, *Grams Operator* Gordon Phillipson, *Incidental Music* Geoffrey Burgon, *Bagpipes* Angus Lennie, *Costume Designer* James Acheson, *Make-Up Artist* Sylvia James, *Make-Up Assistants* Martha Livesley, Suzanne Jansen, *Designer* Nigel Curzon, *Production Unit Manager* George Gallaccio, *Production Assistant* Edwina Craze, *Assistant Floor Manager* Rosemary Webb,

Director's Assistant Joy Sinclair, *Floor Assistant* Carol Scott, *Script Editor* Robert Holmes, *Producer* Philip Hinchcliffe, *Director* Douglas Camfield

DWM Index
57	John Friedlander interview
65	Episode Guide
72	Nicholas Courtney interview
82	John Levene interview
93	Archive + Fact File
	Douglas Camfield interview
	Ian Marter interview
111	Nicholas Courtney interview
114	Chris Achilleos interview
124	Season 13 Flashback
177	Those *Radio Times*
181	John Woodnutt interview
191	What The Papers Said
210	Archive Feature
	Angus Lennie interview
221	What The Censor Saw
235	First Impressions: Class 4G on *Terror of the Zygons*
250	Elisabeth Sladen interview
273	Robert Banks Stewart interview
280	Video review
289	Music CD review
345	The Fact of Fiction
347	Time Team

Recording Dates
March 1975 (Unknown studio modelwork), 17-21 March 1975 (Location filming), 7-8 April 1975 (TC3), 22-23 April 1975 (TC4)

Locations
Climping Beach, Climping, West Sussex; Ambersham Common, South Ambersham, West Sussex; Hall Aggregates Quarry, Storrington, West Sussex; Charlton, West Sussex; Furnace Pond, Crabtree, West Sussex; Millbank Tower, London SW1

Working Titles
Loch Ness
The Secret of Loch Ness
The Loch Ness Monster
Doctor Who and the Zygons

Factoids
- Three Zygons were made, their foetal appearance suggested by their reliance on the Skarasen's lactic fluid for survival. Using a pregnancy book for reference, costume designer James Acheson designing the bodies, and visual effects sculptor John Friedlander made the heads. The torso was constructed from thin fibreglass, and the arms and legs from latex. The whole ensemble was then sprayed orange. Two Skarasen miniatures were built, one a glove puppet and the other a fully jointed model for stop-motion-animation work. Little was seen of this later model, as the animation was felt to be unconvincing.
- Two models of the doomed oilrig seen in Part One were made. The second one - a standby in case the first one did not break up convincingly - was featured in Huckle's office in the same episode. Two three-feet diameter plasticard and polystyrene models of the Zygons' ship were made, one of which was taken to location filming and placed in the foreground of the Episode Four quarry scenes to create a false perspective shot.
- Douglas Camfield attempted to shoot an invisible Tardis scene - as he done before in *The Invasion* (46). To show the Doctor and his companions appearing from mid-air, the film was exposed in two halves, but during editing it was found that the daylight had changed dramatically between shots and the material was therefore unusable.
- *Terror of the Zygons* was the final story recorded for *Doctor Who*'s twelfth recording block. When the BBC decided to bring Season 13 forward from winter to autumn, the story was held in reserve for several months to give the production team breathing space as they attempted to bring the new stories in ahead of the earlier transmission dates.

Comment
In many ways this is a totally formulaic story and in essence extremely similar to *The Android Invasion* (83), the season's third 'body double' story (of which *The Pyramids of Mars* is the second). But what makes *Terror of the Zygons* so immensely watchable is Douglas Camfield's energetic and powerful direction, coupled with excellent design work and the unique appearance of the title creatures. The Scottish atmosphere is splendidly evoked - albeit relying on stereotyped clichés - and there are some fine moments of suspense, in particular the greatest cliffhanger we never had, Sarah's run-in with the copied 'Harry' in the barn in Part Two. Unfortunately, despite all the good work, the whole thing comes unravelled in the final ten minutes as the action switches inexplicably to London and we're treated to laughable effects and a conspicuously cheap resolution. Pity. **87%**

"Pure energy in physical form - it's incredible!" ~ Professor Sorenson

81) Planet of Evil
Louis Marks

Serial Code: 4H
Original Transmission
Part One
Saturday 27 September 1975, 17.45-18.10, 10.4m / 19
Part Two
Saturday 4 October 1975, 17.45-18.10, 9.9m / 24
Part Three
Saturday 11 October 1975, 18.05-18.30, 9.1m / 29
Part Four
Saturday 18 October 1975, 17.45-18.10, 10.1m / 26
Repeat Transmission
Part One
Monday 5 July 1976, 18.35-19.00, 5m / 61
Part Two
Tuesday 6 July 1976, 18.25-18.50, 5m / 63
Part Three
Wednesday 7 July 1976, 18.20-18.55, 4.3m / 87
Part Four
Thursday 8 July 1976, 18.25-18.50, 3.9m / 99
BBC Archive
All episodes exist as 625-line two-inch PAL colour master videotapes.
Novelization
Doctor Who and the Planet of Evil by Terrance Dicks (126/11)
Hardback:
July 1977, Allan Wingate, cover renamed *Doctor Who - The Planet of Evil* (0855232315 / Mike Little)
Paperback:
1. August 1977, Target, cover renamed *Doctor Who - The Planet of Evil* (0426116828 / Mike Little)
2. 1982, Target (0426116828 / Andrew Skilleter)
Video
January 1994 (BBCV 5180 / Colin Howard)
Précis
On Zeta Minor, a Morestran expedition is being annihilated by a mysterious antimatter energy force…
Cast
Tom Baker (Doctor Who), Elisabeth Sladen (Sarah), Frederick Jaeger (Sorenson), Ewen Solon (Vishinsky), Michael Wisher (Morelli/Voice of Ranjit), Prentis Hancock (Salamar), Graham Weston (De Haan), Louis Mahoney (Ponti), Terence Brook (Braun), Tony McEwan (Baldwin), Haydn Wood (O'Hara), Melvyn Bedford (Reig), Mike Lee Lane (Antimatter Monster), Terry Walsh (Double for Doctor Who/Double for Sorenson), Alan Chuntz (Stunt Double for Doctor Who), Ray Knight, Douglas Stark (Antimatter Men)
Crew
Stuntmen Terry Walsh, Max Faulkner, Alan Chuntz, *Visual Effects Designer* Dave Havard, *Visual Effects Assistants* Janine Killick, Stephen Scott, *Inlay Operator* Richard Broadhurst, *Technical Manager* Fred Wright, *Vision Mixer* Nick Lake, *Studio Lighting* Brian Clemett, *Studio Sound* Tony Millier, Brendan Shaw, *Film Cameramen* Kenneth MacMillan, Stan Speel, *Film Sound* Colin March, *Film Editor* Mike [MAC] Adams, *Special Sound* Peter Howell, *Grams Operators* Paul Graydon, Gordon Phillipson, *Incidental Music* Dudley Simpson, *Costume Designer* Andrew Ross, *Make-Up Artist* Jenny Shircore, *Make-Up Assistants* Dorka Nieradzik, Suzanne Jansen, Derry Hawes, Caroline O'Neill, *Designer* Roger Murray-Leach, *Production Unit Manager* Janet Radenkovic, *Production Assistant* Malachy Shaw Jones, *Assistant Floor Manager* Karilyn Collier, *Floor Assistant* Jim Burge, *Director's Assistant* Maggie Lewty, *Script Editor* Robert Holmes, *Producer* Philip Hinchcliffe, *Director* David Maloney
DWM Index
66	Episode Guide
89	Elisabeth Sladen interview
117	Michael Wisher interview
124	Season 13 Flashback
163	Elisabeth Sladen interview
183	Archive Feature
203	David Maloney interview
208	Video review
250	Elisabeth Sladen interview
256	Louis Marks interview
260	Vox Pops
303	Prentis Hancock interview
348	Time Team

Recording Dates
Mid-June 1975 (EFS), 30 June-1 July 1975 (TC6), 14-15 July 1975 (TC1)
Working Title
As broadcast
Factoids
- Designer Roger Murray-Leach's jungle set was an enormous creation consisting of jabolite trees, rock pools, and flora, such as vines and creepers, of all shapes and sizes. A false perspective backdrop made it seem larger than it was and a wind-machine was used to convey the movement of the

Antimatter Monster through the jungle. Due to the size and complexity of the set it was hard to position boom microphones, so much of the Doctor and Sarah's dialogue was redubbed later.
- The Antimatter Monster was based on the Id Monster from the 1956 film *Forbidden Planet*. Extra Mike Lee Lane wore a silver costume under harsh lighting, whose outline was then keyed electronically by CSO into the studio jungle scenes.

Comment
A visually stunning *Jekyll and Hyde* pastiche with a remarkably realized alien jungle; scientifically, however, it is slightly less accurate than a Brothers Grimm fairytale. But there are many frightening sequences, and by dint of some neat throwaway lines and decent characterization, the Morestrans are one of the more believable cultures the Doctor has encountered. **80%**

"I bring Sutekh's gift of death to all humanity..." ~ *Sutekh's Servant*

82) *Pyramids of Mars*
Stephen Harris (pen-name for Robert Holmes, from a story by Lewis Greifer)

Serial Code: 4G
Original Transmission
Part One
Saturday 25 October 1975, 17.45-18.10, 10.5m / 28
Part Two
Saturday 1 November 1975, 17.45-18.10, 11.3m / 15
Part Three
Saturday 8 November 1975, 17.45-18.10, 9.4m / 37
Part Four
Saturday 15 November 1975, 17.45-18.10, 11.7m / 22
Repeat Transmissions
Omnibus
Saturday 27 November 1976, 17.50-18.50, 13.7m / 7
On BBC2:
Part One
Sunday 6 March 1994, 12.00-12.25, 1.1m / -
Part Two
Sunday 13 March 1994, 12.00-12.25, 1.1m / -
Part Three
Sunday 20 March 1994, 12.00-12.25, 0.8m / -
Part Four
Sunday 27 March 1994, 12.00-12.25, 1m / -

BBC Archive
All episodes exist as 625-line two-inch PAL colour master videotapes.
Novelization
Doctor Who and the Pyramids of Mars by Terrance Dicks (122/14)
Hardback:
December 1976, Allan Wingate (0855431416 / Chris Achilleos)
Paperback:
1. December 1976, Target (0426116666 / Chris Achilleos)
2. 1982, Target (0426116666 / Andrew Skilleter)
2. March 1993, Target, renamed *Doctor Who - Pyramids of Mars* (0426116666 / Alister Pearson)
Video
1. March 1985, compilation, edited (BBCV 2014 / Photomontage)
2. March 1985, compilation, edited, Betamax (BBCB 2014 / Photomontage)
3. February 1994 (BBCV 5220 / Photomontage)
DVD
March 2004, original and BBC2 continuity announcements, deleted scenes, production subtitles, photo gallery, commentary by Philip Hinchcliffe, Elisabeth Sladen and Michael Sheard (BBCDVD 1350 / Clayton Hickman)
Music and Sound Effects
1. May 1978, *Doctor Who Sound Effects*, LP (REC 316 / Photomontage)
2. May 1978, *Doctor Who Sound Effects*, cassette (ZCM 316 / Photomontage)
Précis
In Edwardian England, a possessed Egyptologist plans to release Sutekh from his Martian tomb...
Cast
Tom Baker (Doctor Who), Elisabeth Sladen (Sarah), Peter Maycock (Ibrahim Namin), Bernard Archard (Marcus Scarman), Peter Copley (Dr Warlock), Michael Sheard (Laurence Scarman), George Tovey (Ernie Clements), Gabriel Woolf (Sutekh/Horus Voice), Michael Bilton (Collins), Vic Tablian (Ahmed), Nick Burnell, Melvyn Bedford, Kevin Selway (Mummies), Tony Alless, Oscar Charles (Egyptian Labourers)
Crew
Visual Effects Designer Ian Scoones, *Visual Effects Assistants* John Friedlander, Mat Irvine, Ken Bomphray, Peter Logan, *Inlay Operator* Dave Jervis, *Technical Manager* Harry Bradley, *Vision Mixer* James Gould, *Studio Lighting* Ron Koplick, *Studio Sound* Brian Hiles, *Film Cameraman* John McGlashan, *Film Sound* Andrew Boulton, *Film Editor* MAC Adams, *Special Sound* Dick Mills, *Grams Operator* Gordon Phillipson, *Incidental Music* Dudley Simpson, *Organist* Leslie Pearson,

Costume Designer Barbara Kidd, *Make-Up Artist* Jean Steward, *Make-Up Assistants* M Wade, Carolyn Greaves, *Designer* Christine Ruscoe, *Production Unit Managers* George Gallaccio, Janet Radenkovic, *Production Assistant* Peter Grimwade, *Assistant Floor Manager* Paul Braithwaite, *Director's Assistants* Val Hodgkinson, Caroline Rogers, *Floor Assistant* James Burge, *Script Editor* Robert Holmes, *Producer* Philip Hinchcliffe, *Director* Paddy Russell

DWM Index
54	Peter Grimwade interview
59	Archive
	Mat Irvine interview
66	Episode Guide
100	Robert Holmes interview
	Video review
122	Nostalgia
124	Season 13 Flashback
127	Paddy Russell interview
179	Tom Baker interview
191	Ian Scoones interview
193	What The Papers Said
204	Bernard Archard interview
221	What The Censor Saw
250	Elisabeth Sladen interview
265	*Doctor Who Magazine* Awards (4th)
266	Paddy Russell interview
300	Archive Feature
302	Michael Sheard interview
330	Dudley Simpson interview
340	Preview(DVD)
341	DVD review
348	Time Team

Recording Dates
29 April-2 May 1975 (Location filming), 19-20 May 1975 (TC3), 22-23 May 1975 (TC Puppet Theatre), 2-3 June 1975 (TC6)

Location
Stargroves Manor, East End, Hampshire

Working Title
Dr Who & The Pyramids of Mars

Factoids
- Lewis Greifer's original storyline was deemed totally unsuitable, but circumstances prevented him from rewriting it himself, so Robert Holmes (assisted by director Paddy Russell) did the necessary chores. Such was the radically altered script, Greifer took his name off the credits and a pseudonym was substituted instead.
- Three Mummy costumes were designed by Barbara Kidd. A hollow fibreglass head and chest shell, sculpted by John Friedlander, was worn over the actor's body, on top of which were wound elasticised fabric bandages. Despite protestations, Tom Baker had to wear a full costume for Part Two's film scenes, as director Paddy Russell believed that his distinctive body language could not be copied by another actor.
- A new Tardis interior set, sans scanner screen, was designed by Christine Ruscoe. Replacing the old one last seen in *Death to the Daleks* (72), it featured simplified roundels and serrated door edges. The console panels were also modified, but because they were no longer numbered underneath, they would appear in random combinations for subsequent stories.
- For Scarman's miraculous recovery from a bullet wound, Bernard Archard acted the scene in reverse, up to the point an explosive charge detonated on the harness he was wearing. This was recorded onto videodisc and then played backwards, resulting in the smoke from the charge appearing to be sucked back into his body.

Comment
The first three parts of this story look and sound magnificent. The Gothic horror that Holmes and Hinchcliffe so desperately wanted is evident in every shot, with some commendably tense sequences filmed in the grounds of Stargroves as the Mummies lumber through the undergrowth. The mixture of science and fantasy is very seductive, and the performances by all the cast are surprisingly restrained. It becomes readily apparent, however, that the antagonist is going to do nothing more than sit on a chair throughout the proceedings, and the dull and obviously cheap traipse past some painted scenery flats that is Part Four is a total let-down. An average story with distractingly good visuals (for the most part). **75%**

"That small phial contains a death sentence for the entire human race." ~ *Styggron*

83) *The Android Invasion*
Terry Nation

Serial Code: 4J
Original Transmission
Part One
Saturday 22 November 1975, 17.45-18.10, 11.9m / 17
Part Two
Saturday 29 November 1975, 17.45-18.10, 11.3m / 24

Part Three
Saturday 6 December 1975, 17.45-18.10,
12.1m / 14
Part Four
Saturday 13 December 1975, 17.55-18.20,
11.4m / 15

BBC Archive
All episodes exist as 625-line two-inch PAL colour master videotapes.

Novelization
Doctor Who and the Android Invasion by Terrance Dicks (126/12)
Hardback:
November 1978, WH Allen (0491020260 / Roy Knipe)
Paperback:
November 1978, Target (0426200373 / Roy Knipe)

Video
March 1995 (BBCV 5526 / Colin Howard)

Music and Sound Effects
1. May 1978, *Doctor Who Sound Effects*, LP (REC 316 / Photomontage)
2. May 1978, *Doctor Who Sound Effects*, cassette (ZCM 316 / Photomontage)

Précis
The eerie village of Devesham is not quite what it seems…

Cast
Tom Baker (Doctor Who), Elisabeth Sladen (Sarah), Ian Marter (Harry), John Levene (RSM Benton), Milton Johns (Guy Crayford), Patrick Newell (Colonel Faraday), Dave Carter (Grierson), Heather Emmanuel (Tessa), Hugh Lund (Matthews), Martin Friend (Styggron), Roy Skelton (Marshal Chedaki), Max Faulkner (Corporal Adams), Peter Welch (Morgan), Stuart Fell (Kraal Chargehand/Double for Styggron), Terry Walsh (Double for Doctor Who/Double for Doctor Who's Double), Joan Woodgate (Double for Sarah)

Crew
Fight Arranger Terry Walsh, *Stuntmen* Max Faulkner, Stuart Fell, Terry Walsh, Peter Brace, *Visual Effects Designers* Len Hutton, *Visual Effects Assistant* Lauri Warburton, *Inlay Operators* Richard Broadhurst, AJ Mitchell, *Technical Managers* Dickie Ashman, Alan Arbuthnott, *Senior Cameraman* Peter Ware, *Vision Mixer* Nick Lake, *Studio Lighting* Duncan Brown, *Studio Sound* Alan Machin, *Film Cameraman* Len Newson, *Film Sound* Doug Mawson, *Film Editor* Mike Stoffer, *Special Sound* Dick Mills, *Grams Operators* Gerry Burrows, Gordon Phillipson, *Incidental Music* Dudley Simpson, *Costume Designer* Barbara Lane, *Make-Up Artist* Sylvia Thornton, *Make-Up Assistants* Sandra Bircham, Jocelyn Cox, *Designer* Philip Lindley, *Production Unit Manager* Janet Radenkovic, *Production Assistant* Marion McDougall, *Assistant Floor Manager* Felicity Trew, *Director's Assistant* Joy Sinclair, *Floor Assistants* Steven Fuller, Peter Sofronioux, *Script Editor* Robert Holmes, *Producer* Philip Hinchcliffe, *Director* Barry Letts

DWM Index
66	Episode Guide
82	John Levene interview
93	Ian Marter interview
124	Season 13 Flashback
145	Terry Nation interview
193	Archive Feature
219	Milton Johns interview
224	Video review
230	John Levene interview
250	Elisabeth Sladen interview
270	Barry Letts interview
349	Time Team

Recording Dates
22-25 July 1975 (Location filming), 11-12 August 1975 (TC3), 25-26 August 1975 (TC8)

Locations
National Radiological Protection Board, Harwell, Oxfordshire; East Hagbourne, Oxfordshire; Worsham Quarry, Witney, Oxfordshire; Tubney Wood, Tubney, Oxfordshire

Working Title
The Enemy Within
The Kraals

Factoids
- Three Kraal costumes were made for this serial, their rhinocerotic masks sculpted by Lauri Warburton out of thick latex. Only one, Styggron (Martin Friend), featured on location.
- *The Android Invasion* was to feature the final appearances of two notable UNIT members: Harry Sullivan (Ian Marter) and RSM Benton (John Levene). Nicholas Courtney was unable to reprise his Brigadier Lethbridge-Stewart role due to theatre commitments and so Patrick Newell, famous as Mother from the popular ABC series *The Avengers* (1961-69), appeared as Colonel Faraday.
- Keen to perform as many of his own stunts as possible, Tom Baker immersed himself in cold, dirty pond water in Tubney Woods for Part Two's chase sequence - despite already suffering from a sore throat which made him noticeably hoarse during the location filming.

Comment
Standing apart from the other stories in this season by dint of its non-Gothic Horror influences, *The Android Invasion* is a smartly directed mystery with some excellent location work and a tangible sense of dislocation: everything is as it should be - and yet it's not quite 'right'. Production standards are high, and it's a nice surprise to see two more large sets unveiled in Parts Three and Four (normally we've seen everything there is to see by Part Two). The Kraals are impressive creations - with more than a hint of the Sontaran about them - and their 'patchwork' base is as alien as the Zygons' ship in the previous but one story. Flaws: the title undermines the 'shock' revelation in Part Two, and the Doctor's handy 'android detector' could've proved quite useful earlier on in the proceedings. But it's a lively story, well paced, with many good moments. **82%**

"What a magnificent head!" ~ *Dr Mehendri Solon*

84) The Brain of Morbius
Robin Bland (pen-name for Terrance Dicks and Robert Holmes)

Serial Code: 4K
Original Transmission
Part One
Saturday 3 January 1976, 17.55-18.20, 9.5m / 30
Part Two
Saturday 10 January 1976, 17.45-18.10, 9.3m / 32
Part Three
Saturday 17 January 1976, 17.45-18.10, 10.1m / 23
Part Four
Saturday 24 January 1976, 17.55-18.20, 10.2m / 28
Repeat Transmission
Omnibus
Saturday 4 December 1976, 17.50-18.50, 10.9m / 17
BBC Archive
All episodes exist as 625-line two-inch PAL colour master videotapes.
Novelization
Doctor Who and the Brain of Morbius by Terrance Dicks (140/12)
Hardback:
May 1977, Allan Wingate (0855232013 / Mike Little)

Paperback:
1. June 1977, Target (0426116747 / Mike Little)
2. January 1991, Target, renamed *Doctor Who - The Brain of Morbius* (0426116747 / Alister Pearson)
Video
1. July 1984, one-hour compilation (BBCV 2012 / Photograph)
2. July 1984, one-hour compilation, Betamax (BBCB 2012 / Photograph)
3. July 1990, edited (BBCV 4388 / Alister Pearson)
Music and Sound Effects
1. May 1978, *Doctor Who Sound Effects*, LP (REC 316 / Photomontage)
2. May 1978, *Doctor Who Sound Effects*, cassette (ZCM 316 / Photomontage)
3. May 2000, *Doctor Who at the BBC Radiophonic Workshop: Volume 2 - New Beginnings 1970-1980*, CD (WMSF 6024-2 / Photographs)
Précis
On the storm lashed planet of Karn, a mad professor is attempting to resurrect his Time Lord hero…
Cast
Tom Baker (Doctor Who), Elisabeth Sladen (Sarah), Philip Madoc (Dr Mehendri Solon), Colin Fay (Condo), Cynthia Grenville (Maren), Gilly Brown (Ohica), Stuart Fell (Complete Monster), Michael Spice (Morbius Voice), John Scott Martin (Kriz), Sue Bishop, Janie Kells, Gabrielle Mowbray, Veronica Ridge (Sisters), Alan Crisp (Headless Monster), Jennie Le Fre (Stunt Double for Sarah Jane Smith), Martine Holland (Double for Young Maren)
Crew
Movement Geraldine Stephenson, *Visual Effects Designer* John Horton, *Inlay Operator* Dave Chapman, *Stills Photographer* J Allan, *Technical Manager* Norman Brierley, *Vision Mixer* Fred Law, *Studio Lighting* Peter Catlett, *Studio Sound* Tony Millier, *Special Sound* Dick Mills, *Grams Operator* Gordon Phillipson, *Incidental Music* Dudley Simpson, *Costume Assistant* L Rowland-Warne, *Make-Up Artist* Jean McMillan, *Make-Up Assistants* Joan Stribling, Daphne Barker, Maureen Hannaford-Naisbett, Leri Misselbrook, *Designer* Barry Newbery, *Design Assistant* Les McCallum, *Production Unit Manager* Janet Radenkovic, *Production Assistant* Carol Wiseman, *Assistant Floor Manager* Felicity Trew, *Director's Assistant* Pauline Silcock, *Floor Assistant* John Green, *Script Editor* Robert Holmes, *Producer* Philip Hinchcliffe, *Director* Christopher Barry

DWM Index
66	Episode Guide
89	Renegade Time Lords: Morbius
99	Video review
	Christopher Barry interview
100	Robert Holmes interview
124	Season 13 Flashback
152	Stuart Fell interview
164	Philip Madoc interview
	Video review (reissue)
179	Tom Baker interview
180	Christopher Barry interview
221	What The Censor Saw
250	Elisabeth Sladen interview
272	Terrance Dicks interview
280	George Gallaccio interview
316	Christopher Barry interview
327	The Mary Whitehouse Experience
329	Archive Feature
349	Time Team

Recording Dates
6-7 October 1975 (TC1), 20-21 October 1975 (TC3)

Working Title
As broadcast

Factoids
- Terrance Dicks' initial storyline concerned a robot piecing together the once-handsome Morbius from alien body parts after his spaceship crashes. Elements of the story (the desolate planet Karn, a monster with a crablike claw, a mind battle) were lifted directly from Dicks' 1974 stage play *Doctor Who and the Daleks in Seven Keys to Doomsday*. When Robert Holmes restructured the story to reflect a more obvious horror film interpretation, Dicks - feeling that any subtlety had been excised from his script - asked for a 'bland' pseudonym to be appended to the story.
- Designer Barry Newbery based the Morbius castle set on the work of Spanish architect Antonio Gaudi, who never used right angles in any of his structures. The Sisterhood of Karn wore costumes decorated with gold-painted plastic teaspoons from the BBC canteen.
- The monster costume was made from a foam-covered cotton body suit overlaid with terylene wadding dipped into latex to form the muscles. It was deliberately designed by L Rowland-Warne to suggest disparate lumps of flesh haphazardly sewn together. Hair was glued to the back of the costume to hide the zipper. Morbius' brain was an internally lit silicone prop made by Steve Bowman.

- In Part Four, the faces seen on the mind-bending device were as follows: Jon Pertwee, Patrick Troughton, William Hartnell, production unit manager George Gallaccio, script editor Robert Holmes, production assistant Graeme Harper, director Douglas Camfield, producer Philip Hinchcliffe, production assistant Chris Baker, scriptwriter Robert Banks Stewart and director Christopher Barry. The photos appeared against looped film of the programme's title sequence.
- Because the Sisterhood's sacred flame had been fixed with the aid of a firework, as a joke Christopher Barry decided that the Tardis would disappear in a puff of smoke at the end, accompanied by a speeded-up dematerialization sound. (Ironically, this links in with the sudden appearance and disappearance of the Time Lord-controlled Tardis in *Colony in Space*, 58).

Comment
A shameless rip-off of the 1930s Universal Frankenstein films, *The Brain of Morbius* lays it on so thick you have trouble seeing the plot for the cliché. All the Hollywood Gothic trademarks are there, from the crashing chandelier to the torch-wielding lynch mob, via the grotesquely ugly monster, the hunchbacked assistant and the craggy lightning-silhouetted rocks. Star of the show is Philip Madoc, who makes the most of his over-ripe dialogue with a perfectly judged performance that blends fanaticism and amoral cunning to great effect. The Sisterhood are less interesting, but the sheer unrepentant cheek of the unmodified subject matter - and the production's relish for blood and gore - makes this hugely enjoyable, if unoriginal, fare. **95%**

"You know, Doctor, I could play all day in my green cathedral." ~ Harrison Chase

85) *The Seeds of Doom*
Robert Banks Stewart

Serial Code: 4L
Original Transmission
Part One
Saturday 31 January 1976, 18.00-18.25, 11.4m / 16
Part Two
Saturday 7 February 1976, 17.30-17.55, 11.4m / 30

Part Three
Saturday 14 February 1976, 17.55-18.20, 10.3m / 32
Part Four
Saturday 21 February 1976, 17.45-18.10, 11.1m / 23
Part Five
Saturday 28 February 1976, 17.45-18.10, 9.9m / 26
Part Six
Saturday 6 March 1976, 17.45-18.10, 11.5m / 15

BBC Archive
All episodes exist as 625-line two-inch PAL colour master videotapes.

Novelization
Doctor Who and the Seeds of Doom by Philip Hinchcliffe (128/12)
Hardback:
March 1977, Allan Wingate (0855231610 / Chris Achilleos)
Paperback:
1. February 1977, Target (0426116585 / Chris Achilleos)
2. May 1989, Star, as part of 'Doctor Who Classics' with *Doctor Who and the Deadly Assassin* (0352324163 / Chris Achilleos)

Video
August 1994, twin-pack (BBCV 5377 / Colin Howard)

Music and Sound Effects
January 2000, *Doctor Who: Terror of the Zygons*, CD (WMSF 6020-2 / Photomontage)

Précis
Insane botanist Harrison Chase wants to wipe out human life with a deadly Krynoid pod…

Cast
Tom Baker (Doctor Who), Elisabeth Sladen (Sarah), Tony Beckley (Harrison Chase), John Challis (Scorby), Kenneth Gilbert (Richard Dunbar), Michael McStay (Derek Moberley), John Gleeson (Charles Winlett), Hubert Rees (John Stevenson), Seymour Green (Hargreaves), Michael Barrington (Sir Colin Thackeray), Mark Jones (Arnold Keeler/Krynoid Voice), Sylvia Coleridge (Amelia Ducat), John Acheson (Major Beresford), Ray Barron (Sergeant Henderson), Ian Fairbairn (Dr Chester), Alan Chuntz (Chauffeur), David Masterman (Guard Leader), Harry Fielder (Guard), Terry Walsh (Stunt Double for Doctor Who), Ronald Gough, Keith Ashley (Krynoid)

Crew
Fight Arranger Terry Walsh, *Visual Effects Designer* Richard Conway, *Visual Effects Assistant* John Brace, *Electronic Effects* Dave Jervis, *Technical Manager* Bernard Fox, *Senior Cameraman* Paul Kay, *Vision Mixers* Sue Thorne, Graham Giles, *Studio Lighting* John Dixon, *Studio Sound* John Holmes, *Film Cameraman* Keith Hopper, *Film Editor* MAC Adams, *OB Lighting* Clive Potter, *OB Sound* Vic Godrich, *OB Engineering Manager* Bert Robinson, *OB Vision Mixer* Paul Jackson, *Artist Booker* Nansi Davies, *Properties Buyer* Maurice Watson, *Special Sound* Dick Mills, *Grams Operator* Andrew Hunter, *Incidental Music* Geoffrey Burgon, *Costume Designer* Barbara Lane, *Make-Up Artist* Ann Briggs, *Make-Up Assistants* Catherine Cary-Elwes, Janet Gilpin, Gillain Thomas, *Designer* Jeremy Bear (1-2), Roger Murray-Leach (3-6), *Production Unit Managers* Janet Radenkovic (1-2), George Gallaccio (3-6), *Production Assistant* Graeme Harper, *Assistant Floor Manager* Sue Shearman, *Director's Assistant* Briony Brown, *Floor Assistants* Robin Burman, Steve Haggard, *Script Editor* Robert Holmes, *Producer* Philip Hinchcliffe, *Director* Douglas Camfield

DWM Index
66	Episode Guide
67	Archive
90	Graeme Harper interview
92	Tom Baker interview
93	Douglas Camfield interview
124	Season 13 Flashback
152	Alan Chuntz interview
184	Graeme Harper interview
191	What The Papers Said
216	John Challis interview
	Kenneth Gilbert interview
	Growing The Seeds (omnibus version)
	Video review
221	What The Censor Saw
250	Elisabeth Sladen interview
263	Archive Feature
273	Robert Banks Stewart interview
289	CD review
327	The Mary Whitehouse Experience
351	Time Team

Recording Dates
Unknown date (Bray Studios modelwork), 30 October-3 November 1975 (Location videotaping), 17-18 November 1975 (TC4), 1-2 December 1975 (TC4), 7-8 December 1975 (Location videotaping), 15-16 December 1975 (TC8)

Locations
Buckland Sand and Silica Co Ltd, Buckland, Surrey; Athelhampton House, Athelhampton, Dorset; BBC Television Centre, Shepherd's Bush, London W12

Working Title
As broadcast

Factoids
- Designer Jeremy Bear was taken ill after completing the Antartic base sets for Parts One and Two and was replaced by Roger Murray-Leach for the two final studio sessions (consisting of interiors of Chase's unnamed mansion).
- As with *The Android Invasion* (83) earlier in the season, Nicholas Courtney was unavailable to play the Brigadier and so the character of Major Beresford was created to fulfil his role.
- The Krynoid in its early stage of transformation was a reused Axon costume from *The Claws of Axos* (57), sprayed green. The larger version, seen in later episodes, was operated like a tent with two extras walking it along and operating the breathing mechanism and tentacles.
- The location shoot was conducted on OB videotape to help make CSO effects of the giant Krynoid in Parts Five and Six more realistic. A similar technique had proven successful on *Robot* (75).
- Buckland Quarry stood in for a real quarry in Part Three as well as for the Antarctic seen in the first three parts. For this latter role, a large area was sprayed with granulated polystyrene and foam, which dried to give a snowlike 'crunchy' consistency. High contrast film of a snow blizzard was superimposed onto the picture in post-production, in the same way that rainfall had been added to studio exteriors in *The Brain of Morbius* (84).
- The original 1963 Police Box prop would be seen for the last time in this story. Extremely battered after 13 years of service, the final straw came when its roof fell onto Elisabeth Sladen when waiting inside for her cue to emerge in Episode Six. A new prop was budgeted for the following season.

Comment
A compelling and brilliantly made ecological spinechiller. Tony Beckley manages the trick of delivers his campy dialogue dead straight, while John Challis plays a convincing psychopathic killer who enjoys genuine character development over the course of the six parts. Location filming is glorious, the Antarctic modelwork is stunning and the set design is better than anything seen previously on the series. All in all, *The Seeds of Doom* is a virtually critic-proof story that manages to blend strong violence with wit and humour, without damaging either. Tom Baker plays it with a sharp edge and Sylvia Coleridge gives a delightful turn as the dotty Amelia Ducat. Don't worry if it's more *The Avengers* than *Doctor Who*, it's still a fantastic story and just beats *The Brain of Morbius* as the best story of the season, despite the unfunny ending. **97%**

Season 14

"Keep an open mind. That's the secret." ~ The Doctor

86) The Masque of Mandragora
Louis Marks

Serial Code: 4M
Original Transmission
Part One
Saturday 4 September 1976, 18.10-18.35, 8.3m / 40
Part Two
Saturday 11 September 1976, 18.05-18.30, 9.8m / 22
Part Three
Saturday 18 September 1976, 18.10-18.35, 9.2m / 29
Part Four
Saturday 25 September 1976, 18.10-18.35, 10.6m / 23
BBC Archive
All episodes exist as 625-line two-inch PAL colour master videotapes.
Novelization
Doctor Who and the Masque of Mandragora by Philip Hinchcliffe (123/12)
Hardback:
January 1978, WH Allen (0491022727 / Mike Little)
Paperback:
1. December 1977, Target (0426118936 / Mike Little)
2. September 1991, Target, renamed *Doctor Who - The Masque of Mandragora* (0426118936 / Alister Pearson)
Video
August 1991 (BBCV 4642 / Alister Pearson)
Music and Sound Effects
1. May 1978, *Doctor Who Sound Effects*, LP (REC 316 / Photomontage)
2. May 1978, *Doctor Who Sound Effects*, cassette (ZCM 316 / Photomontage)

3. July 1993, *Doctor Who: 30 Years at the Radiophonic Workshop*, CD (BBCCD 871 / Photomontage)

4. May 2000, *Doctor Who at the BBC Radiophonic Workshop: Volume 2 - New Beginnings 1970-1980*, CD (WMSF 6024-2 / Photographs)

Précis
Mind-controlling Mandragora energy is let loose in Renaissance Italy…

Cast
Tom Baker (Doctor Who), Elisabeth Sladen (Sarah), Gareth Armstrong (Giuliano), Jon Laurimore (Count Federico), Tim Pigott-Smith (Marco), Norman Jones (Hieronymous), Antony Carrick (Captain Rossini), Robert James (High Priest), Pat Gorman (Soldier), Brian Ellis (Brother), John Clamp, James Appleby (Guards), Peter Walshe, Jay Neill (Pikemen), Stuart Fell (Entertainer/Soldier/Peasant at Lake), Peter Tuddenham (Titan Voice), Peggy Dixon, Jack Edwards, Michael Reid, Alistair Fullerton, Kathy Wolff (Dancers), Terry Walsh, Roy Street (Stunt Doubles for Doctor Who), Tex Fuller (Executioner)

Crew
Armourer Jack Wells, *Stuntmen* Stuart Fell, Terry Walsh, Paddy Ryan, Bruno McLoughlin, Billy Horrigan, Roy Street, Peter Pocock, *Visual Effects Designer* Ian Scoones, *Visual Effects Assistant* Mat Irvine, *Inlay Operator* Dave Chapman, *Technical Manager* Henry Barber, *Vision Mixer* Graham Giles, *Studio Lighting* Dennis Channon, *Studio Sound* Colin Dixon, *Film Cameraman* John Baker, *Film Sound* Hugh Cleverley, *Film Editor* Clare Douglas, *OB Cameramen* Dave White, Peter Granger, *Special Sound* Dick Mills, *Grams Operator* Don Slater, *Incidental Music* Dudley Simpson, *Costume Designer* James Acheson, *Make-Up Artist* Jan Harrison, *Make-Up Assistants* Hadsera Coouadia, Vivian Riley, Carolyn Buisuinne, Suzanne Jansen, Christine Wheeler, *Designer* Barry Newbery, *Design Assistant* Les McCallum, *Production Unit Manager* Chris D'Oyly-John, *Production Assistant* Thea Murray, *Assistant Floor Manager* Linda Graeme, *Director's Assistant* Hazel Marriott, *Floor Assistant* Jim Burge, *Script Editor* Robert Holmes, *Producer* Philip Hinchcliffe, *Director* Rodney Bennett

DWM Index
68	Episode Guide
92	Tom Baker interview
138	Season 14 Flashback 1
139	Season 14 Flashback 2
152	Stuart Fell interview
161	Archive + Fact File
	Barry Newbery interview
163	Elisabeth Sladen interview
177	Video review
187	Tim Pigott-Smith interview
191	Ian Scoones interview
204	Robert James interview
250	Elisabeth Sladen interview
256	Louis Marks interview
260	Vox Pops
268	Rodney Bennett interview
287	Archive Feature
352	Time Team

Recording Dates
3-6 May 1976 (Location filming), May 1976 (unknown studio modelwork), 24-25 May 1976 (TC3), 6-7 June 1976 (TC3)

Location
Portmeirion, Penrhyndeudraeth, Gwynedd

Working Titles
Catacombs of Death
Secret of the Labyrinth
The Curse of Mandragora

Factoids
- A new Police Box prop was built by Barry Newbery, featuring a simplified, flatter roof. The console room (referred to in the script as the Secondary Control Room) was also totally designed by Newbery for this one season, eschewing the previous white, high-tech look for a darker, Edwardian feel. The walls were made from plywood lined with wood veneer wallpaper, and the smaller console was made from wood-effect plywood and had a shaving mirror in the middle rather than a transparent rotor. The scanner was now a large CSO screen behind horizontally opening shutters, while a black-draped exit replaced the traditional double-doors.
- A new serif font for the opening and closing credits made its debut with this story.
- The Palace state room was a redressed version of a set used in a BBC2 programme to celebrate Yehudi Menuhin's 70th birthday, while the various 15th century costumes were reused from the 1954 film *Romeo and Juliet*, starring Laurence Harvey and Susan Shentall.
- For sequences requiring the Brethren's ruined temple to become magically restored to its former glory, Rodney Bennett decided to do it 'live' in studio rather than electronically - painted gauze drapes were hung across the black background curtains and then slowly illuminated with red lights to reveal their details.

- The Welsh coastal town of Portmeirion was chosen for its medieval Italianate architecture (although it had actually opened to the public in 1926). It famously featured as the Village in the 1966/67 Patrick McGoohan series *The Prisoner*.

Comment
At its core, this is an intriguing story about Free Will versus Predeterminism. Portmeirion looks sumptuous and the guest cast act as if they're in a serious BBC historical drama rather than some kids' programme shoved out after *Grandstand*. Jon Laurimore giving a particularly vivid performance as Count Federico. But although it has many good points, *The Masque of Mandragora* ultimately fails to impress. Perhaps it's the lack of hideous monsters - those masks are really rather boring - or perhaps the acting is just a little too mannered to impart a sense of tension or excitement to the proceedings. As an exercise in style it's undoubtedly successful, and the central concept is strong, but it sometimes seems stagy and soulless when it should really be going for the jugular. **64%**

"I'm going to pack my goodies and I'm going home!" ~ Sarah Jane Smith

87) The Hand of Fear
Bob Baker and Dave Martin

Serial Code: 4N
Original Transmission
Part One
Saturday 2 October 1976, 18.10-18.35, 10.5m / 24
Part Two
Saturday 9 October 1976, 17.50-18.15, 10.2m / 29
Part Three
Saturday 16 October 1976, 18.05-18.30, 11.1m / 20
Part Four
Saturday 23 October 1976, 18.00-18.25, 12m / 19
BBC Archive
All episodes exist as 625-line two-inch PAL colour master videotapes.
Novelization
Doctor Who and the Hand of Fear by Terrance Dicks (127/15)

Hardback:
January 1979, WH Allen (0491022565 / Roy Knipe)
Paperback:
January 1979, Target (0426200330 / Roy Knipe)
Video
February 1996 (BBCV 5789 / Colin Howard)
Music and Sound Effects
1. May 1978, *Doctor Who Sound Effects*, LP (REC 316 / Photomontage)
2. May 1978, *Doctor Who Sound Effects*, cassette (ZCM 316 / Photomontage)
3. May 2000, *Doctor Who at the BBC Radiophonic Workshop: Volume 2 - New Beginnings 1970-1980*, CD (WMSF 6024-2 / Photographs)
Précis
Sarah is possessed by the fossilised hand of a Kastrian criminal called Eldrad...
Cast
Tom Baker (Doctor Who), Elisabeth Sladen (Sarah), Roy Pattison (Zazzka), Rex Robinson (Dr Carter), Glyn Houston (Professor Watson), Judith Paris, Stephen Thorne (Eldrad), Roy Skelton (King Rokon/Command Dome Voice), David Purcell (Tom Abbott), Renu Setna (Doctor), Robin Hargrave (Guard), Frances Pidgeon (Miss Jackson), Roy Boyd (Driscoll), John Cannon (Elgin), Peter Roy (Technik Obarl)
Crew
Fight Arranger/Stuntman Max Faulkner, *Visual Effects Designer* Colin Mapson, *Visual Effects Assistants* Steve Drewett, Charlie Lumm, *Inlay Operator* Dave Chapman, *Technical Manager* Fred Wright, *Senior Cameraman* Ronnie Peverall, *Vision Mixer* Nick Lake, *Studio Lighting* Derek Slee, *Studio Sound* Brian Hiles, *Film Cameraman* Max Sammett, *Film Sound* Graham Bedwell, *Film Editor* Christopher Rowlands, *Special Sound* Dick Mills, *Grams Operators* Martin Ridout, Andy Stacey, *Incidental Music* Dudley Simpson, *Costume Designer* Barbara Lane, *Make-Up Artist* Judy Neame, *Make-Up Assistants* Caroline O'Neill, Jennifer Hughes, Janet Gilpin, *Designer* Christine Ruscoe, *Production Unit Manager* Chris D'Oyly-John, *Production Assistant* Marion McDougall, *Assistant Floor Manager* Terry Winders, *Director's Assistant* Joy Sinclair, *Floor Assistant* Philip Livingstone, *Script Editor* Robert Holmes, *Producer* Philip Hinchcliffe, *Director* Lennie Mayne
DWM Index
68	Episode Guide
138	Season 14 Flashback 1
139	Season 14 Flashback 2
193	What The Papers Said

235   Video review
236   Bob Baker and Dave Martin interview
250   Elisabeth Sladen interview
302   On The Other Hand…(Original storyline)
352   Time Team

Recording Dates
14-17 June 1976 (Location filming), June 1976 (unknown studio modelwork), 5-6 July 1976 (TC8), 19-20 July 1976 (TC8).

Locations
Cromhall Quarry, Wotton-under-Edge, Gloucestershire; Oldbury Power Station, Oldbury Naite, Thornbury, Gloucestershire; Stokefield Close, Thornbury, Gloucestershire

Working Title
As broadcast

Factoids
- Bob Baker and Dave Martin's original six-part storyline had been intended to conclude Season 13 and kill off the Brigadier. The Bristol-based writers had scouted out their local power station - Oldbury, near the River Severn - as a possible filming venue, and the establishment had been very enthusiastic about the BBC using it. However, script editor Robert Holmes thought the script too ambitious and replaced it with *The Seeds of Doom* (85).
- Because Kastrian architecture was based on three-sided shapes akin to the Martians in HG Wells' novel *The War of the Worlds* (1898), visual effects designer Colin Mapson deliberately designed Eldrad's obliteration module as a copy of the manta-ray spaceships from George Pal's 1953 film adaptation.
- There were three versions of Eldrad's hand. Two were made of plaster - one without a third finger, one with - and were both static, used for shots of it being carried by an actor. The third was a glove with a severed wrist section, worn by effects assistant Steve Drewett. This latter prop was either CSOed into the action, if it was required to move along, or else manipulated 'live' in the studio by the operator sticking his hand through a hole in a specially made prop, such as the Tupperware box or the radiation cabinet (in which Drewett's arm can be clearly seen). During recording, the main prop hand was stolen by a disgruntled BBC employee, so another one was hurriedly fashioned for the final studio session.
- Elisabeth Sladen and Tom Baker largely rewrote their final Tardis scene. The Croydon shots were actually filmed in Thornbury, near Oldbury Power Station.
- Eldrad's costume was a tight bodysuit onto which were glued hundreds of fibreglass crystalline shapes, which also covered the actor's hands and face. Judith Paris' voice was deepened by the use of a vocoder.

Comment
This is a stylish story that avoids the garishness of much of Bob Baker and Dave Martin's other *Doctor Who* output. By concentrating on a tightly written story set in a recognisably contemporary locale, many of the more fantastic elements seem almost feasible, and Judith Paris is sensational as the single-minded first incarnation of Eldrad. (The less said about Stephen Thorne the better.) The power station location adds immeasurable weight to the story, while Elisabeth Sladen at last gets a chance to show us what a good actress she is. The BBC reactor room set is a bit of a joke, and Part Four looks shockingly cheap, but generally this is a classy production, slickly directed by Lennie Mayne, with two of the most poignant moments in *Doctor Who* history. The first is Professor Watkins' final 'phone-call to his family (a beautifully played character piece, totally irrelevant to the plot), and the second, of course, is Sarah's wonderfully underplayed departure scene. If that's not a tear in the corner of your eye, check yourself for a pulse. **81%**

"As I believe I told you long ago, Doctor, you will never amount to anything in the galaxy while you retain your propensity for vulgar facetiousness" ~ Cardinal Borusa

88) The Deadly Assassin
Robert Holmes

Serial Code: 4P
Original Transmission
Part One
Saturday 30 October 1976, 18.05-18.30, 11.8m / 15
Part Two
Saturday 6 November 1976, 18.05-18.30, 12.1m / 11
Part Three
Saturday 13 November 1976, 18.05-18.30, 13m / 12
Part Four
Saturday 20 November 1976, 18.05-18.30, 11.8m / 12

Repeat Transmission
Part One
Thursday 4 August 1977, 18.20-18.45, 4.4m / 72
Part Two
Thursday 11 August 1977, 18.20-18.45,
2.6m / 139
Part Three
Thursday 18 August 1977, 18.20-18.45,
3.8m / 99
Part Four
Thursday 25 August 1977, 18.20-18.45,
3.5m / 104

BBC Archive
All episodes (including the edited Part Three) exist as 625-line two-inch PAL colour master videotapes. The unedited Part Three exists as a 625-line two-inch PAL colour U-Matic viewing copy.

Novelization
Doctor Who and the Deadly Assassin by Terrance Dicks (122/12)
Hardback:
October 1977, Allan Wingate (0855231203 / Mike Little)
Paperback:
1. October 1977, Target (0426119657 / Mike Little)
2. May 1989, Star, as part of 'Doctor Who Classics' with *Doctor Who and the Seeds of Doom* (0352324163 / Mike Little)

Video
1. October 1991 (BBCV 4645 / Andrew Skilleter)
2. September 2002, as part of 'The Time Lord Collection' [BBCV 7346 / Photomontage] with *The War Games* and *The Three Doctors* (BBCV 7365 / Photomontage)

Music and Sound Effects
1. May 1978, *Doctor Who Sound Effects*, LP (REC 316 / Photomontage)
2. May 1978, *Doctor Who Sound Effects*, cassette (ZCM 316 / Photomontage)

Précis
The Doctor is summoned back to Gallifrey and immediately framed for the murder of the President…

Cast
Tom Baker (Doctor Who), Angus Mackay (Cardinal Borusa), Bernard Horsfall (Chancellor Goth/Samurai), Derek Seaton (Commander Hilred), George Pravda (Castellan Spandrell), Erik Chitty (Coordinator Engin), Hugh Walters (Commentator Runcible), Peter Pratt (The Master), Llewellyn Rees (The President), Helen Blatch (Voice), Maurice Quick (Gold Usher), Peter Mayock (Solis), John Dawson, Michael Bilton (Time Lords), Brian Nolan (Camera Technician), Dave Goody (Gas-Masked Soldier), David Smith (Train Driver), Chris Jesson (Biplane Pilot), Terry Walsh (Stunt Double for Goth/Stunt Double for Doctor Who), Eddie Powell (Stunt Double for Doctor Who/Stunt Double for The Master)

Crew
Armourer Dave Goody, *Fight Arranger/Stunt Adviser* Terry Walsh, *Armourer* Dave Goody, *Stuntmen* Terry Walsh, Eddie Powell, *Visual Effects Designers* Peter Day, Len Hutton, *Inlay Operator* AJ Mitchell, *Technical Manager* Peter Valentine, *Senior Cameraman* Peter Granger, *Vision Mixer* Angela Beveridge, *Studio Lighting* Brian Clemett, *Studio Sound* Clive Gifford, *Film Cameraman* Fred Hamilton, *Film Sound* Graham Bedwell, *Film Editor* Ian McKendrick, *Special Sound* Dick Mills, *Grams Operator* John Cadman, *Incidental Music* Dudley Simpson, *Organ Music* Leslie Pearson, *Costume Designers* James Acheson, Joan Ellacott, *Make-Up Artist* Jean Williams, *Make-Up Assistants* Hadsera Coouadia, Judith Dalton, *Designer* Roger Murray-Leach, *Design Assistant* John Price Jones, *Production Unit Manager* Chris D'Oyly-John, *Production Assistant* Nicholas Howard John, *Assistant Floor Manager* Linda Graeme, *Floor Assistant* Philip Livingstone, *Director's Assistant* Joan Elliott, *Script Editor* Robert Holmes, *Producer* Philip Hinchcliffe, *Director* David Maloney

DWM Index
68	Episode Guide
100	Robert Holmes interview
108	David Maloney interview Archive + Fact File
136	Louise Jameson interview
138	Season 14 Flashback 1
139	Season 14 Flashback 2
179	Video review
187	Archive Feature AJ Mitchell interview Roger Murray-Leach interview James Acheson interview
203	David Maloney interview
210	Philip Hinchcliffe interview
222	What The Censor Saw
224	Peter Pratt Obituary
242	Chris D'Oyly John interview
325	Video review (Time Lord box set)
327	The Mary Whitehouse Experience
332	The Fact of Fiction
353	Time Team

Recording Dates
26-30 July 1976 (Location filming), 15-17 August 1976 (TC3), 1-2 September 1976 (TC8)

Locations
Betchworth Quarry, Betchworth, Surrey; Royal Alexandra and Albert School, Merstham, Surrey; Wycombe Air Park, High Wycombe, Buckinghamshire

Working Title
The Dangerous Assassin

Factoids
- D'Oyly Carte Opera Company actor Peter Pratt portrayed a transitional, ravaged version of the Master under a cadaverous-looking mask made by Alistair Bowtell Effects. It was intended that coloured liquids would be pumped through tubes running over his ravaged face, but this never materialized.
- David Maloney shot Part Three's Matrix scenario on 16mm film in the style of a pacific war movie. A puppet spider crawling up Tom Baker's arm was cut from the episode for fear it was too frightening.
- Costume designer James Acheson (later to receive several Oscars™ for his film work) left the production halfway through, citing tiredness and overwork as his chief reasons. He was replaced by Joan Ellacott. The Time Lords' high collars were cast from coloured fibreglass by Alistair Bowtell Effects, with help from Acheson.
- Part Three's freeze-frame cliffhanger of the Doctor's head being held underwater was cut from the 1977 repeat after complaints from Mary Whitehouse, spokesperson for the National Viewers and Listeners Association (NVALA). It was reinstated from a BBC Enterprises viewing copy (with a noticeable drop in picture quality) for its video release.

Comment
At the time, *The Deadly Assassin* put the cat amongst the pigeons with regard to *Doctor Who*'s fragile continuity, portraying a decrepit, inward-looking race of institutionalised politicians and hangers-on, rather than the previously glimpsed race of superior Godlike beings, as seen in *The War Games* (50) and *Colony in Space* (58). However, this story should be seen as presenting the 'real' Time Lords, rather than their rose-tinted 'public face' - and as such, it makes perfect sense as to why the Doctor would want to escape from such a stifling existence and go and explore the Universe. Production values on the story are extremely high, with the location work in Part Three reaching dizzying heights of professionalism. The ever-dependable Bernard Horsfall is a worthy opponent, and although the Master's presence is limited, the grim mask and Peter Pratt's 'from beyond the grave' voice combine to make a truly memorable villain. With its surreal imagery and companionless Doctor, *The Deadly Assassin* breaks new ground and introduces a whole raft of new Gallifreyan continuity that is still making its presence felt today. **94%**

"An omniscient computer with schizophrenia - not a very pretty thought, is it?" ~ The Doctor

89) The Face of Evil
Chris Boucher

Serial Code: 4Q
Original Transmission
Part One
Saturday 1 January 1977, 18.20-18.45, 10.7m / 23
Part Two
Saturday 8 January 1977, 18.30-18.55, 11.1m / 19
Part Three
Saturday 15 January 1977, 18.20-18.45, 11.3m / 20
Part Four
Saturday 22 January 1977, 18.20-18.45, 11.7m / 19

BBC Archive
All episodes exist as 625-line two-inch PAL colour master videotapes.

Novelization
Doctor Who and the Face of Evil by Terrance Dicks (126/15)
Hardback:
January 1978, WH Allen (049102214X / Jeff Cummins)
Paperback:
1. January 1978, Target (0426200063 / Jeff Cummins)
2. May 1989, Star, as part of 'Doctor Who Classics' with *Doctor Who and the Sunmakers* (0352324171 / Jeff Cummins)
3. April 1993, Target, renamed *Doctor Who - The Face of Evil* (0426200063 / Alister Pearson)

Video
May 1999 (BBCV 6672 / Photomontage)

Music and Sound Effects
1. May 1978, *Doctor Who Sound Effects*, LP (REC 316 / Photomontage)
2. May 1978, *Doctor Who Sound Effects*, cassette (ZCM 316 / Photomontage)

Précis
The Doctor helps the Sevateem tribe face up to their strangely familiar God…

Cast
Tom Baker (Doctor Who/Xoanon), Louise Jameson (Leela), Leslie Schofield (Calib), David Garfield (Neeva), Victor Lucas (Andor), Brendan Price (Tomas), Colin Thomas (Sole), Leon Eagles (Jabel), Mike Elles (Gentek), Lloyd McGuire (Lugo), Tom Kelly, Brett Forrest (Guards), Anthony Frieze, Rob Edwards, Pamela Salem, Roy Herrick (Xoanon's Voices), Peter Baldock (Acolyte), Terry Walsh (Double for Doctor Who)

Crew
Fight Arranger Terry Walsh, *Stuntmen* Terry Walsh, Max Faulkner, Alan Chuntz, Stuart Fell, *Visual Effects Designer* Mat Irvine, *Visual Effects Assistant* Steve Drewett, *Electronic Effects* Dave Chapman, *Technical Manager* Ron Bristow, *Senior Cameraman* Colin Reid, *Vision Mixer* Nick Lake, *Studio Lighting* Derek Slee, *Studio Sound* Colin Dixon, *Film Cameraman* John McGlashan, *Film Sound* Stan Nightingale, *Film Editors* Pam Bosworth, Tariq Anwar, *Special Sound* Dick Mills, *Grams Operator* Gordon Phillipson, *Incidental Music* Dudley Simpson, *Costume Designer* John Bloomfield, *Make-Up Artist* Ann Ailes, *Make-Up Assistants* Jennifer Hughes, Sue Frear, Karen Bryan, Carol Wilson, *Designer* Austin Ruddy, *Production Unit Manager* Chris D'Oyly-John, *Production Assistant* Marion McDougall, *Assistant Floor Manager* Linda Graeme, *Director's Assistant* Sue Ward, *Floor Assistants* Ellen Grech, James Gould, *Script Editor* Robert Holmes, *Producer* Philip Hinchcliffe, *Director* Pennant Roberts

DWM Index
59	Mat Irvine
68	Episode Guide
116	Archive + Fact File
138	Season 14 Flashback 1
139	Season 14 Flashback 2
180	Tom Baker interview
215	Louise Jameson interview
229	John Bloomfield interview
	Archive Feature
242	Chris D'Oyly-John interview
246	Pennant Roberts interview
261	Chris Boucher interview
278	Video review
353	Time Team

Recording Dates
20-24 September 1976 (EFS), 27 September 1976 (EFS), 11-12 October 1976 (TC3), 25-26 October 1976 (TC3)

Working Titles
The Prime Directive
The Tower of Imelo
The Day God Went Mad

Factoids
- Louise Jameson, 25, was chosen from sixty hopefuls for the part of Leela (named by Chris Boucher after a Palestinian terrorist called Leila Khaled). John Bloomfield designed her costume from different leather skins and she was given red contact lenses in order to turn her naturally blue eyes brown. For early make-up tests, her skin colour was darkened, but this was not done on recording. Jameson based her body language on her dog Bosie, characterized by a tilt of her head when she sensed danger.
- To offset overspends on the previous story and an expensive season finale, *The Face of Evil* and *The Robots of Death* (coincidentally both by Chris Boucher) would be granted no location filming.
- *Doctor Who* went off-air for five weeks following *The Deadly Assassin* (88). The delay was due to script problems with the final story, *The Talons of Weng-Chiang* (91), linked to a pause in production during early September when Philip Hinchcliffe had asked for, and got, a funding increase to complete the season. To help bridge the transmission gap, two sixty-minute compilation repeats were shown: *Pyramids of Mars* (82) and *The Brain of Morbius* (84). A third repeat, of *The Seeds of Doom* (85), was planned but never shown.
- Visual effects assistant Steve Drewett made the Horda seen in Parts One and Two. One Horda was a radio-controlled prop, another was a rod puppet operated off-screen with cables, and the rest were rubber dummies, as seen in the pit in Part Two.
- Seven-year old Anthony Frieze visited the studio on 24 October 1976 as the winner of a BBC Design-A-Monster competition and was allowed to record one line of dialogue as Xoanon ("Who am I?"), which was added to the cacophony of noises at the end of Part Three.

Comment
It's hard to like *The Face of Evil*. The Sevateem are clichéd savages in clichéd costumes and the Tesh, dressed in Greek national costume, are just plain silly. The jungle set, both in Ealing and the studio, is rather artificial-looking (you can see the black drapes where the foliage abruptly ends), the

spaceship interior consists of boring white corridors and nondescript rooms, and the special effects are cheap and tacky. Nothing is made of the promising Horda. The sight of David Garfield (so chilling in the 1975 children's series *The Changes*) with a cricket glove on his head is too stupid to engender anything other than derision. There's an awful lot of technobabble, and the production team seems to have forgotten how to scare their viewers.. Neither witty nor diverting, Leela's introductory story is a definite damp squib. **36%**

"We will be irresistible!" ~ *Taren Capel*

90) The Robots of Death
Chris Boucher

Serial Code: 4R
Original Transmission
Part One
Saturday 29 January 1977, 18.20-18.45, 12.8m / 14
Part Two
Saturday 5 February 1977, 18.20-18.45, 12.4m / 17
Part Three
Saturday 12 February 1977, 18.20-18.45, 13.1m / 15
Part Four
Saturday 19 February 1977, 18.25-18.50, 12.6m / 18
Repeat Transmission
Part One (Part One & Part Two)
Saturday 31 December 1977, 18.25-19.15, 10m / 29
Part Two (Part Three & Part Four)
Sunday 1 January 1978, 16.45-17.30, 7m / 80
BBC Archive
All episodes exist as 625-line two-inch PAL colour master videotapes.
Novelization
Doctor Who and the Robots of Death by Terrance Dicks (108/14)
Hardback:
May 1979, WH Allen (0491024363 / John Geary)
Paperback:
1. May 1979, Target (0426200616 / John Geary)
2. February 1994, Target, renamed *Doctor Who - The Robots of Death* (0426200616 / Alister Pearson)

Video
1. April 1986, compilation (BBCV 2030 / Photomontage)
2. April 1986, compilation, Betamax (BBCB 2030 / Photomontage)
3. February 1995 (BBCV 5521 / Photomontage)
DVD
October 2002, continuity announcement, unmixed studio footage, model film footage, studio plan, production subtitles, photo gallery, commentary by Chris Boucher and Philip Hinchcliffe (BBCDVD 1012 / Photograph)
Music and Sound Effects
1. May 1978, *Doctor Who Sound Effects*, LP (REC 316 / Photomontage)
2. May 1978, *Doctor Who Sound Effects*, cassette (ZCM 316 / Photomontage)
Précis
The Doctor fears that murders aboard a sandminer are caused by the crew's robotic helpers…
Cast
Tom Baker (Doctor Who), Louise Jameson (Leela), Russell Hunter (Uvanov), Pamela Salem (Toos), Brian Croucher (Borg), David Bailie (Dask), Tania Rogers (Zilda), Tariq Yunus (Cass), David Collings (Poul), Miles Fothergill (SV7), Gregory de Polnay (D84), Rob Edwards (Chub), Mark Blackwell Baker, John Bleasdale, Mark Cooper, Peter Langtry, Jeremy Ranchev, Richard Seager (Robots), Peter Sax (Kerril's Corpse)
Crew
Visual Effects Designer Richard Conway, *Electronic Effects* AJ Mitchell, *Technical Manager* Dickie Ashman, *Vision Mixer* John Duncan, *Studio Lighting* Duncan Brown, *Studio Sound* Tony Millier, *Film Cameraman* Peter Chapman, *Special Sound* Dick Mills, *Grams Operator* Andy Stacey, *Incidental Music* Dudley Simpson, *Costume Designer* Elizabeth Waller, *Make-Up Artist* Ann Briggs, *Make-Up Assistants* Anne Spiers, Heather Squires, Judith Dalton, *Designer* Kenneth Sharp, *Production Unit Manager* Chris D'Oyly-John, *Production Assistant* Peter Grimwade, *Assistant Floor Manager* David Tilley, *Director's Assistant* Maggie Lewty, *Floor Assistant* Tony Vanden Ende, *Script Editor* Robert Holmes, *Producer* Philip Hinchcliffe, *Director* Michael E Briant
DWM Index
54   Peter Grimwade interview
68   Episode Guide
97   Michael Briant interview
113 Video review
136 Nostalgia
138 Season 14 Flashback 1

141

139	Season 14 Flashback 2
177	David Collings interview
187	AJ Mitchell interview
215	Louise Jameson interview
261	Chris Boucher interview
264	Michael E Briant interview
265	*Doctor Who Magazine* Awards (5th)
271	Pamela Salem interview
296	Archive Feature
297	DVD launch report
	DVD review
324	Russell Hunter interview
329	David Collings interview
354	Time Team

Recording Dates
2-5 November 1976 (EFS modelwork), 23 November 1976 (TC8), 6-7 December 1976 (TC1)

Working Titles
The Storm-Mine Murders
Planet of the Robots

Factoids
- Chris Boucher named one character Taren Capel, after Czech writer Karel Capek, whose 1920 play *RUR* ('Rossum's Universal Robots') gave the world the word 'robot' (*robata* being Czech for state labour). Poul was named after American SF writer Poul Anderson.
- In Part Four a reference is made to one of the Three Laws of Robotics, a system worked out in 1941 by another SF writer, Isaac Asimov, and used extensively in his two science fiction murder mysteries, *The Caves of Steel* (1952) and *The Naked Sun* (1956). 'Grimwade's Syndrome' was a late in-joke referring to production assistant (and future director and writer) Peter Grimwade.
- Nine robots were made (five green Vocs, two olive Dums, a dummy Voc and a Supervoc), with changeable numbers on their chests to indicate many more than were actually shown. Based on Art Deco designs - as were all the Sandminer interiors - the quilted green linen costumes were made by Elizabeth Waller while the heads were modelled by set designer Kenneth Sharp and sculpted by Rose Garrard. The actors playing the robots post-dubbed their lines in calm, monotonous voices (it had been planned to have them electronically modulated, but the equipment broke down).

Comment
Something that *Doctor Who* does very well - an Agatha Christie-style whodunit in space. The drawback, though, is that it's clear quite early on who is controlling the robots, and there's a real problem with maintaining the tension through the last half hour. Many moments are beautifully staged though, with Dudley Simpson's musical score standing out as one of his very best, and of course the robots themselves are a design classic. Some of the macho posturing by the guest cast is a little forced (Boucher's greatest flaw is his inability to write anything other than endless put-downs), but David Collings and Pamela Salem overcome the material to give performances of great depth. Louise Jameson is also very strong, although there's little chemistry between her and the Doctor. Overall, an iconic *Doctor Who* story that lives on in the mind long after you've seen it. **84%**

"I may have had a bang on the head, but this is a dashed queer story." ~ *Professor Litefoot*

91) *The Talons of Weng-Chiang*
Robert Holmes, from a story by Robert Banks Stewart

Serial Code: 4S
Original Transmission
Part One
Saturday 26 February 1977, 18.30-18.55, 11.2m / 16
Part Two
Saturday 5 March 1977, 18.35-19.00, 9.8m / 28
Part Three
Saturday 12 March 1977, 18.30-18.55, 10.2m / 22
Part Four
Saturday 19 March 1977, 18.30-18.55, 11.4m / 21
Part Five
Saturday 26 March 1977, 18.30-18.55, 10.1m / 18
Part Six
Saturday 2 April 1977, 18.30-18.55, 9.3m / 32

BBC Archive
All episodes exist as 625-line two-inch PAL colour master videotapes.

Novelization
Doctor Who and the Talons of Weng-Chiang by Terrance Dicks (140/15)
Hardback:
December 1977, Allan Wingate (085523170X / Jeff Cummins)
Paperback:
1. November 1977, Target (0426119738 / Jeff Cummins)

2. March 1984, Target, renamed *Doctor Who - The Talons of Weng-Chiang* (0426119738 / Alister Pearson)

Video
November 1988, compilation (BBCV 4187 / Photomontage)

DVD
April 2003, 2 x discs, clean title sequence, continuity announcement, *Whose Doctor Who* documentary and trailers, b/w studio footage, production subtitles, photo gallery, commentary by Louise Jameson, Philip Hinchcliffe, David Maloney, John Bennett and Christopher Jago (BBCDVD 1152 / Clayton Hickman)

Script
November 1989, Titan Books, edited by John McElroy with background notes by Jan Vincent-Rudski (1852861444 / Duncan Fegredo)

Music and Sound Effects
1. May 1978, *Doctor Who Sound Effects*, LP (REC 316 / Photomontage)
2. May 1978, *Doctor Who Sound Effects*, cassette (ZCM 316 / Photomontage)

Précis
In Victorian London, a 51st century war criminal is abducting young virgins to keep himself alive…

Cast
Tom Baker (Doctor Who), Louise Jameson (Leela), John Bennett (Li H'sen Chang), Michael Spice (Weng-Chiang/Magnus Greel), Trevor Baxter (Professor George Litefoot), Christopher Benjamin (Henry Gordon Jago), Deep Roy (Mr Sin), Tony Then (Lee), John Wu (Coolie), Vincent Wong (Ho), Chris Gannon (Casey), Alan Butler (Joseph Buller), Conrad Asquith (PC Quick), David McKall (Sergeant Kyle), Patsy Smart (Old Woman), Judith Lloyd (Teresa), Vaune Craig-Raymond (Cleaner), Penny Lister (Singer), Dudley Simpson (Conductor), Stuart Fell (Giant Rat/Stunt Double for Doctor Who/Stunt Double for Magnus Greel), Debbie Cumming, Helen Simnet (Young Girls)

Crew
Fight Arranger Stuart Fell, *Stuntmen* Alan Chuntz, Max Faulkner, Stuart Fell, *Magic Advisors* Larry Barnes, Ali Bongo, *Visual Effects Designer* Michael John Harris, *Visual Effects Assistant* Andrew Lazell, *Studio Lighting* Mike Jefferies, *Studio Sound* Clive Gifford, *Film Cameraman* Fred Hamilton, *Film Sound* John Gatland, *Film Editor* David Lee, *OB Lighting* John Mason, *OB Sound* Vic Godrich, *Special Sound* Dick Mills, *Incidental Music* Dudley Simpson, *Costume Designer* John Bloomfield, *Costume Assistant* Alan Hughes, *Make-Up Artist* Heather Stewart, *Make-Up Assistants* Christine Baker, Jennifer Hughes, Martha Livesley, *Designer* Roger Murray-Leach, *Design Assistant* Gerry Scott, *Production Unit Managers* Chris D'Oyly-John, John Nathan-Turner, *Production Assistant* Ros Anderson, *Assistant Floor Manager* Linda Graeme, *Floor Assistant* Sue Box, *Director's Assistant* Rosemary Parsons, *Script Editor* Robert Holmes, *Producer* Philip Hinchcliffe, *Director* David Maloney

DWM Index
69	Episode Guide
85	Louise Jameson interview
92	Tom Baker interview
100	Robert Holmes interview
108	David Maloney interview
136	Louise Jameson interview
138	Season 14 Flashback 1
139	Season 14 Flashback 2
152	Alan Chuntz interview
154	Script Book review
171	David Jackson interview (BBC Video)
193	What The Papers Said
203	David Maloney interview
204	Dudley Simpson interview
210	Philip Hinchcliffe interview
215	Louise Jameson interview
W94	Archive Feature
222	What The Censor Saw
229	John Bloomfield interview
233	The John Nathan-Turner Memoirs
242	Chris D'Oyly-John interview
265	*Doctor Who Magazine* Awards (2nd)
328	Preview(DVD)
329	DVD review
330	Dudley Simpson interview *Whose Doctor Who* Archive Feature
331	*Whose Doctor Who*: the unedited interviews
354	Time Team 1-4
355	Time Team 5-6

Recording Dates
13-17 December 1976 (Location filming), 8-13 January 1977 (Location videotaping), 24-25 January 1977 (TC8), 8-10 February 1977 (TC1)

Locations
Northampton Repertory Theatre, St Crispin's Hospital, Rate Office, Fish Street, all Northampton; Wapping Pier Head, Bridewell Place, all Wapping, London E1; Clink Street, London SE1; St Mary Overy's Wharf, Bankside, Southwark, London SE1; St Katherine's Dock, East Smithfield, London E1; 24 Cambridge Park, Twickenham, Middlesex

Working Title
The Talons of Greel

Factoids
- *The Talons of Weng-Chiang* replaced a mooted six-part story by Robert Banks Stewart entitled *The Foe from the Future*. When Banks Stewart was poached by Thames Television to script edit *The Sweeney*, it fell to Robert Holmes, returning from a much-needed holiday, to rewrite the storyline to his own requirements. Little survived of the original treatment, except for the notion of a cadaverous time-travelling villain in a leather mask.
- Incidental musician Dudley Simpson appeared as the Palace Theatre conductor in Part One, with extras miming to pre-recorded music.
- The giant rat sequences were achieved with a real rat in a miniature set and, for scenes where it interacts with people, a large prop constructed by John Bloomfield and Michaeljohn Harris. Covered with fake fur and equipped with sprung jaws moved by operator Stuart Fell, the creature was considered one of the few weak areas of the production.
- Exterior location work was conducted as usual on 16mm film, whilst location interiors, specifically the theatre, were captured with Outside Broadcast video. The OB shoot replaced one of the three studio sessions that would normally be required for a six-part story.
- Leela wore three costumes in this story - a knickerbockers suit, an evening dress for the theatre trip and Victorian underwear for her encounter with the giant rat. Unfortunately (or fortunately, depending on your point of view), the underwear became transparent when wet.
- On Sunday 3 April 1977, the day after the final episode was shown, an hour-long documentary entitled *Whose Doctor Who* (part of the *Lively Arts* strand) was shown on BBC2 at 20.20. Presented by Melvyn Bragg, it featured clips from *Doctor Who* stories, interviews with children, students, psychologists, teachers and doctors, and behind-the-scenes footage from *The Talons of Weng-Chiang*.

Comment
For once, a *Doctor Who* story that looks like it's had a few quid spent on it. The night-time Victorian locations are beautifully photographed, the sets are gorgeous and the mix of genuine and studio interiors is virtually seamless. Tom Baker gives a measured and (for the most part) understated performance while the criminally underrated Louise Jameson steals every scene she's in. The late John Bennett as Greel's naïve lackey Chang deserves a special mention too, displaying great pathos after being chewed by the giant rat in Part Four. On the negative side (and there always is one), the story is utterly bereft of originality, milking dry every penny dreadful Victorian cliché that has ever existed. Borrowing liberally from Sherlock Holmes, Dr Fu-Manchu, the Phantom of the Opera and Jack the Ripper, *The Talons of Weng-Chiang* is really nothing more than one long chase. But taken as a colourful finale to one of the most professionally produced three years in *Doctor Who*'s history, the self-congratulatory tone is perhaps forgivable.
84%

Season 15

"I thought I'd locked the enemy out. Instead, I've locked it in - with us." ~ The Doctor

92) *Horror of Fang Rock*
Terrance Dicks

Serial Code: 4V
Original Transmission
Part One
Saturday 3 September 1977, 18.15-18.40, 6.8m / 52
Part Two
Saturday 10 September 1977, 19.15-18.40, 7.1m / 51
Part Three
Saturday 17 September 1977, 18.15-18.40, 9.8m / 28
Part Four
Saturday 24 September 1977, 19.15-18.40, 9.9m / 28
BBC Archive
All episodes exist as 625-line two-inch PAL colour master videotapes.
Novelization
Doctor Who and the Horror of Fang Rock by Terrance Dicks (126/13)
Hardback:
1978, WH Allen (0491022522 / Jeff Cummins)
Paperback:
March 1978, Target (0426200098 / Jeff Cummins)

Video
July 1998, close-captioned (BBCV 6536 / Photomontage)
DVD
January 2005, Part Three VT clock, production subtitles, photo gallery, commentary by Louise Jameson, Terrance Dicks and John Abbott (BBCDVD 1356 / Clayton Hickman)
Précis:
A shape-changing Rutan terrorizes the inhabitants of an isolated lighthouse…
Cast
Tom Baker (Doctor Who), Louise Jameson (Leela), John Abbott (Vince), Colin Douglas (Reuben/Rutan/Rutan Voice), Ralph Watson (Ben), Sean Caffrey (Lord Palmerdale), Alan Rowe (Skinsale), Annette Woollett (Adelaide), Rio Fanning (Harker)
Crew
Visual Effects Designer Peter Pegrum, *Video Effects* AJ Mitchell, *Technical Manager* John Jevons, *Senior Cameraman* Tony Wigley, *Vision Mixer* Roger Sutton, *Film Cameraman* John Walker, *Studio Lighting* Bob Gell, *Studio Sound* David Hughes, *Special Sound* Dick Mills, *Grams Operator* Gerry Burrows, *Incidental Music* Dudley Simpson, *Costume Designer* Joyce Hawkins, *Make-Up Artist* Jackie Hodgson, *Designer* Paul Allen, *Production Unit Manager* John Nathan-Turner, *Production Assistant* Peter Grimwade, *Assistant Floor Manager* Bill Hartley, *Floor Assistant* Carolyn Smith, *Director's Assistant* Pauline Silcock, *Script Editor* Robert Holmes, *Producer* Graham Williams, *Director* Paddy Russell

DWM Index
69	Episode Guide
85	Louise Jameson interview
92	Tom Baker interview
95	Terrance Dicks interview
127	Paddy Russell interview
136	Louise Jameson interview
167	Graham Williams - A Tribute
180	Tom Baker interview
188	AJ Mitchell interview
193	What The Papers Said
215	Louise Jameson interview
233	The John Nathan-Turner Memoirs
266	Paddy Russell interview
	Video review
272	Terrance Dicks interview
319	Archive
351	Preview(DVD)
352	DVD review
355	Time Team

Recording Dates
4-6 May 1977 (Ealing Film Studios), 26, 28 May 1977 (PM A), 7-9 June 1977 (PM A)
Working Titles
Rocks of Doom
The Monster of Fang Rock
The Beast of Fang Rock
Factoids
- New producer Graham Williams was brought in to replace Phillip Hinchcliffe, who was moved onto the BBC drama series *Target* (1977-78). Specifically told to reduce the levels of violence in the series by BBC bosses, he had little choice but to increase the humour and fantasy elements and downplay the horror - although not with this story.
- *Horror of Fang Rock* was a hurried replacement for Terrance Dicks' *The Vampire Mutation* (aka *The Witch Lords*), a tale about vampirism that was pulled because the BBC Drama Department were making a big budget adaptation of Bram Stoker's *Dracula* and were worried that a 'spoof' *Doctor Who* version might dent its critical reception.
- No studio was available in London and so, for the first time, the *Doctor Who* studio sessions were conducted outside the capital at the BBC's Birmingham studio Pebble Mill.
- As well as reference books, Designer Paul Allen looked at the Needles Lighthouse on the Isle of Wight and Southwold Lighthouse, Suffolk. The finished design included curved walls, doors and specially constructed furniture. The cramped stairwell set proved very difficult to shoot in.
- At the end, Louise Jameson (Leela) was allowed to discontinue using her red contact lenses - worn since her debut story *The Face of Evil* (89) - due to the discomfort they caused.

Comment
Despite new producer Graham Williams' remit to 'clean up' the horrific nature of the programme, this first story in the new season is actually a whole lot scarier than anything the previous one came up with, mainly because of the intensely claustrophobic location and the shadowy nature of the monster. There is nothing quite so nerve-jangling as the mournful sound of a foghorn at night, and *Horror of Fang Rock* taps into this eerie, desolate atmosphere brilliantly. The quality of the acting is very good, with particularly fine

performances from Louise Jameson and new young actor John Abbott (Vince) who both excel at making the situation entirely believable. Ralph Watson as Ben appears to have been trained in the Ronnie Corbett School of Acting, but thankfully his character is the first to die. *Doctor Who* was never quite this scary again until Season 27. **90%**

"I've never been inside anybody's head before." ~ *Leela*

93) The Invisible Enemy
Bob Baker and Dave Martin

Serial Code: 4T
Original Transmission
Part One
Saturday 1 October 1977, 18.20-18.45, 8.6m / 40
Part Two
Saturday 8 October 1977, 18.05-18.30, 7.3m / 55
Part Three
Saturday 15 October 1977, 18.10-18.35, 7.5m / 65
Part Four
Saturday 22 October 1977, 18.10-18.35, 8.3m / 50
Repeat Transmission
Part One
Thursday 13 July 1978, 19.00-19.25, 4.9m / 60
Part Two
Thursday 20 July 1978, 19.00-19.25, 5.5m / 76
Part Three
Thursday 27 July 1978, 19.00-19.25, 5.1m / 81
Part Four
Thursday 3 August 1978, 19.00-19.25, 6.8m / 35
BBC Archive
All episodes exist as 625-line two-inch PAL colour master videotapes.
Novelization
Doctor Who and the Invisible Enemy by Terrance Dicks (110/12)
Hardback:
March 1979, WH Allen (0491024371 / Roy Knipe)
Paperback:
March 1979, Target (0426200543 / Roy Knipe)
Video
September 2002 (BBCV 7267 / Photomontage)
Music and Sound Effects
1. 1977, *Sound Effects No.16 - "Disasters"*, LP (REC 295 / Andrew Prewett)
1. May 1978, *Doctor Who Sound Effects*, LP (REC 316 / Photomontage)
2. May 1978, *Doctor Who Sound Effects*, cassette (ZCM 316 / Photomontage)
3. July 1993, *Doctor Who: 30 Years at the Radiophonic Workshop*, CD (BBCCD 871 / Photomontage)
Précis
Possessed by a sentient virus, the Doctor has to go inside his own brain to get rid of it…
Cast
Tom Baker (Doctor Who), Louise Jameson (Leela), John Leeson (K-9 Voice/Nucleus Voice), Brian Grellis (Safran), Jay Neill (Silvey), Edmund Pegge (Meeker), Michael Sheard (Lowe), Frederick Jaeger (Professor Marius), Elizabeth Norman (Marius' Nurse), Roy Herrick (Parsons), John Scott Martin (Nucleus), Anthony Rowlands (Crewman/Computer Voice), Nell Curran (Reception Nurse), John McManus (Ophthalmologist), Kenneth Waller (Hedges), Roderick Smith (Cruikshank), Pat Gorman (Medic)
Crew
Visual Effects Designers Ian Scoones, Tony Harding, *Visual Effects Assistants* Mat Irvine, Steve Bowman, Christopher Lawson, Roger Perkins, Charlie Lumm, Andy Lazell, *K-9 Operators* Tony Harding, Andy Lazell, *Video Effects* AJ Mitchell, *Technical Manager* Dickie Bird, *Senior Cameraman* Peter Hider, *Vision Mixer* Shirley Coward, *Studio Lighting* Brian Clemett, *Studio Sound* Michael McCarthy, *Film Cameraman* Nick Allder, *Film Editor* Glenn Hyde, *Film Operations Manager* Ian Brindle, *Special Sound* Dick Mills, *Grams Operator* Dave Thomson, *Incidental Music* Dudley Simpson, *Costume Designer* Raymond Hughes, *Make-Up Artist* Maureen Winslade, *Make-Up Assistants* Eve Barker, Carolyn Buissine, *Designer* Barry Newbery, *Design Assistant* Les McCallum, *Draughtsmen* Les McCallum, Shelagh Lawson, Murray Picknett, *Production Unit Manager* John Nathan-Turner, *Production Assistant* Norman Stewart, *Assistant Floor Managers* Tony Garrick, Christabel Albery, *Director's Assistant* Pat Harrington, *Floor Assistant* Lindsay Trenholme, *Script Editor* Robert Holmes, *Assistant Script Editor* Anthony Read, *Producer* Graham Williams, *Director* Derrick Goodwin
DWM Index
69   Episode Guide
116 John Leeson interview
118 Anthony Read interview
134 Archive + Fact File
177 Those *Radio Times*
188 AJ Mitchell interview
191 Ian Scoones interview

193 What The Papers Said
215 Louise Jameson interview
222 What The Censor Saw
228 John Leeson interview
233 The John Nathan-Turner Memoirs
236 Bob Baker and Dave Martin interview
248 Graham Williams interview
271 Archive Feature
302 Michael Sheard interview
322 Video review
355 Time Team 1-2
357 Time Team 3-4

Recording Dates
Late March/Early April (Bray Studios modelwork), 10-12 April 1977 (TC6), 24-26 April 1977 (TC6)

Working Titles
The Invader Within
Invisible Invader
The Enemy Within

Factoids
- The radio-controlled K-9 prop was designed by Tony Harding. Moulded in fibreglass, it was powered by motorcycle batteries and could move backwards and forwards, as well as turn, wag its tail, wave its ears, extend an antenna probe and gun, and emit tickertape from its mouth. The radio frequency would often interfere with the camera signals, causing K-9 to veer uncontrollably in the wrong direction. It was also found that he was very noisy and could not get over the lip of the Tardis doors.
- Phonetic spelling was employed on the signage in this story - thus 'Imurjinsee Egsit' (Emergency Exit) and 'Kazyulti' (Casualty).
- This was the most effects intensive story yet conducted for *Doctor Who*, so much so that two visual effects designers worked on it - Ian Scoones for the modelwork and Tony Harding for the studio sessions. A week's filming took place at Bray Studios, heavily storyboarded by Scoones. The 35mm filming featuring approximately 80 sequences of spaceship effects and surreal images seen inside the Doctor's mind.
- The Nucleus was based on a prawn and was made of latex and fibreglass over a bamboo and metal frame. Operator John Scott Martin knelt on a trolley inside and was wheeled along by helpers. The two lower pairs of arms were linked to the top pair (operated by Martin) by wires, and thus moved when he waggled them.
- This serial saw a return to the white, futuristic console room set seen before the previous season. Corinthian-style columns now linked the wall flats and the scanner was a large CSO screen with horizontal sliding doors. This design would remain largely unchanged until *The Greatest Show in the Galaxy* (152).
- K-9's inclusion as a companion was only decided upon at a very late stage. If the robot had not joined the Tardis crew, the final scene on the Bi-Al Foundation (in which K-9 joins) would simply have been cut from the transmitted story.

Comment
A typical Baker and Martin script, brimful of the most unlikely situations and heaving with unexplored ideas, colourful characters and florid dialogue. Visually *The Invisible Enemy* is a treat - the special effects are often impressive and the extensive modelwork contains some of the most convincing images yet seen in the show. The quality of the Titan Base sets is similarly impressive - lots of scaffolding and long, dark corridors a la *Warriors Gate* (114). The Bi-Al Foundation is where everything starts looking a bit cheap and artificial and the 1970s NHS take on a space research centre is hysterical. K-9 makes an underwhelming debut, his various appearances slowing down the narrative intolerably. In hindsight, allowing K-9 to become a regular companion was a big mistake: action scenes would have to take into account his snail-like pace, while the noise of his motors would stretch credulity when he was required to sneak up on someone from behind. **75%**

"I look forward to your terror." ~ *Maximillian Stael*

94) *Image of the Fendahl*
Chris Boucher

Serial Code: 4X
Original Transmission
Part One
Saturday 29 October 1977, 18.10-18.35, 6.7m / 70
Part Two
Saturday 5 November 1977, 18.10-18.35, 7.5m / 64
Part Three
Saturday 12 November 1977, 18.05-18.30, 7.9m / 63

147

Part Four
Saturday 19 November 1977, 18.10-18.35,
9.1m / 46
BBC Archive
All episodes exist as 625-line two-inch PAL colour master videotapes.
Novelization
Doctor Who and the Image of the Fendahl by Terrance Dicks (109/12)
Hardback:
May 1979, WH Allen (0491021275 / John Geary)
Paperback:
July 1979, Target (0426200772 / John Geary)
Video
March 1993 (BBCV 4941 / Andrew Skilleter)
Précis
A 12-million-year-old skull provides a channel for the malevolent Fendahl to destroy the world…
Cast
Tom Baker (Doctor Who), Louise Jameson (Leela), John Leeson (K-9 Voice), Denis Lill (Dr Fendelman), Wanda Ventham (Thea Ransome/Fendahl Core), Scott Fredericks (Maximillian Stael), Edward Arthur (Adam Colby), Edward Evans (Ted Moss), Derek Martin (David Mitchell), Geoffrey Hinsliff (Jack Tyler), Daphne Heard (Martha Tyler), Graham Simpson (Hiker), Peter Wragg (Fendahleen Operator), Alf Trustrum (Double for Ted Moss)
Crew
Armourer Des Stewart, *Visual Effects Designer* Colin Mapson, *Visual Effects Assistant* Peter Wragg, *Electronic Effects* Dave Jervis, *Technical Manager* Peter Granger, *Senior Cameraman* Peter Hider, *Vision Mixers* Fred Law, Sue Thorne, *Studio Lighting* Jim Purdie, *Studio Sound* Alan Fogg, *Film Cameraman* Elmer Cossey, *Film Sound* Bill Meekums, *Special Sound* Dick Mills, *Grams Operator* Gordon Phillipson, *Incidental Music* Dudley Simpson, *Costume Designer* Amy Roberts, *Make-Up Artist* Pauline Cox, *Make-Up Assistants* Wendy Freeman, Liz Walsh, *Designer* Anna Ridley, *Production Unit Manager* John Nathan-Turner, *Production Assistant* Prue Saenger, *Assistant Floor Manager* Karry Collier, *Director's Assistant* Di Clark, *Floor Assistant* Barbara Simonin, *Script Editor* Robert Holmes, *Assistant Script Editor* Anthony Read, *Producer* Graham Williams, *Director* George Spenton-Foster
DWM Index
53   Archive
69   Episode Guide
85   Louise Jameson interview
118   Anthony Read interview
197   Archive Feature
198   Video review

222   What The Censor Saw
233   The John Nathan-Turner Memoirs
261   Chris Boucher interview
266   Wanda Ventham interview
307   Scott Fredericks interview
357   Time Team
Recording Dates
1-5 August 1977 (Location filming), August 1977 (Unknown studio modelwork), 20-21 August 1977 (TC6), 4-6 September 1977 (TC6)
Locations
Stargrove Manor, East End, Hampshire
Working Title
As broadcast
Factoids
- Louise Jameson's hairdresser had accidentally cut her hair too short, so it was gathered up on top of her head to disguise this fact. She also wore a new, lighter-coloured chamois leather costume. This came with leather armbands, but omitted the modesty-preserving front and back flaps from the original one.
- The seven-feet-high Fendahleen was sculpted from foam rubber and covered with latex, and operated in the studio by effects assistant Peter Wragg. An oxygen cylinder hidden inside made the tendrils quiver, a similar technique employed on the small glove puppet Fendahleen props used in the final cellar sequence and on top of Thea Ransome's prone body in Part Two.
- K-9 was not included in the scripted storyline for *Image of the Fendahl* (his companion status being a late decision in *The Invisible Enemy*, 93), and so the prop was written out, with John Leeson not being contracted to do the voice either.

Comment
A workmanlike story with some deliciously scary moments (mainly in Part One), *Image of the Fendahl* is perhaps not quite so convincing as the other horror story this season - *Horror of Fang Rock* - because of the clumsy realization of its alien protagonist. More frightening in photographs than on screen, the lifesize Fendahleen wipes away any tension by focusing the fear onto a clichéd rubber monster. Far more successful are the earlier scenes of an unseen terror stalking through the woods, accompanied by the shrieking noise of the Time Scanner. The Fendahl Core is also a grave disappointment, featuring a statuesque Wanda Ventham with big eyes painted onto her eyelids. The grown-up aspects of the story (the Doctor helping Fendelman to kill himself) sit uneasily beside the

more childish elements (such as Granny and Jack Tyler as a couple of comic country bumpkins), and the story is ultimately not as unified in production or concept as the season opener. Sadly, it would mark the last time a *Doctor Who* horror story would be attempted for many a year. **72%**

"Perhaps everyone runs from the taxman." ~ *Leela*

95) The Sun Makers
Robert Holmes

Serial Code: 4W
Original Transmission
Part One
Saturday 26 November 1977, 18.05-18.30, 8.5m / 48
Part Two
Saturday 3 December 1977, 18.05-18.30, 9.5m / 36
Part Three
Saturday 10 December 1977, 18.05-18.30, 8.9m / 35
Part Four
Saturday 17 December 1977, 18.05-18.30, 8.4m / 42
Repeat Transmission
Part One
Thursday 10 August 1978, 18.20-18.45, 3.2m / 117
Part Two
Thursday 17 August 1978, 19.10-19.35, 6.5m / 50
Part Three
Thursday 24 August 1978, 19.10-19.35, 6.5m / 49
Part Four
Thursday 31 August 1978, 18.45-19.10, 7.1m / 53
BBC Archive
All episodes exist as 625-line two-inch PAL colour master videotapes.
Novelization
Doctor Who and the Sunmakers by Terrance Dicks (127/12)
Hardback:
November 1982, WH Allen (0491027583 / Andrew Skilleter)
Paperback:
1. November 1982, Target (0426200594 / Andrew Skilleter)
2. May 1989, Star, as part of 'Doctor Who Classics' with *Doctor Who and the Face of Evil* (0352324171 / Jeff Cummins)
Video
July 2001 (BBCV 7133 / Photomontage)
Précis
On Pluto, the money-grabbing Company are taxing the populace into an early grave…
Cast
Tom Baker (Doctor Who), Louise Jameson (Leela), John Leeson (K-9 Voice/Computer Voice), Richard Leech (Gatherer Hade), Michael Keating (Goudry), Roy Macready (Cordo), Jonina Scott (Marn), William Simons (Mandrel), Adrienne Burgess (Veet), Henry Woolf (Collector), David Rowlands (Bisham), Derek Crewe (Synge), Colin McCormack (Commander), Carole Hopkin (Nurse), Tom Kelly (Guard)
Crew
Stuntmen Max Faulkner, Stuart Fell, *Visual Effects Designers* Peter Day, Peter Logan, *Electronic Effects* AJ Mitchell, *Technical Manager* Lance Wood, *Senior Cameraman* Peter Hider, *Vision Mixer* Nick Lake, *Studio Lighting* Derek Slee, *Studio Sound* Michael McCarthy, *Film Cameraman* John Tiley, *Film Sound* Dave Brinicombe, *Film Editor* Tariq Anwar, *Special Sound* Paddy Kingsland, *Grams Operator* Dave Thomson, Andrew Hunter, *Incidental Music* Dudley Simpson, *Costume Designer* Christine Rawlings, *Make-Up Artist* Janis Gould, *Make-Up Assistants* Sinikka Ikaheimo, Valerie Keen, Caroline O'Neill, *Designer* Tony Snoaden, *Production Unit Manager* John Nathan-Turner, *Production Assistant* Leon Arnold, *Assistant Floor Manager* Linda Graeme, *Director's Assistant* Gwen Foyle, *Floor Assistant* Barbara Simonin, *Script Editor* Anthony Read, *Producer* Graham Williams, *Director* Pennant Roberts
DWM Index
69   Episode Guide
85   Louise Jameson interview
116   John Leeson interview
118   Anthony Read interview
122   Pennant Roberts interview
123   Archive + Fact File
188   AJ Mitchell interview
215   Louise Jameson interview
246   Pennant Roberts interview
248   Graham Williams interview
260   Vox Pops interview
278   Anthony Read interview
306   Archive Feature
307   Video
357   Time Team 1-2
358   Time Team 3-4

149

Recording Dates
13-15 June 1977 (Location filming), 17 June 1977 (Location filming), 20 June 1977 (Location filming), 4-5 July 1977 (TC3), 17-19 July 1977 (TC6)
Locations
WD & HO Wills Tobacco Factory, Hartcliffe, Bristol, Avon; Camden Town Deep Tube Shelters, Camden Town, London NW1
Working Title
As broadcast
Factoids
- Originally written as a story about anti-colonialism, Robert Holmes' frustrations with the Inland Revenue about his freelance earnings led to him producing a script that lampooned the UK tax system. In-jokes such as "corridor P45" and the "Inner Retinue", and the protagonists being a Gatherer and a Collector, all reflected Holmes' desire to satirise what he considered an unwieldy, complex and overly bureaucratic system.
- On the recommendation of director Pennant Roberts, Michael Keating (Goudry) went on to play Vila in the entire run of BBC science fiction series *Blake's 7* (1978-81).
- Henry Woolf, playing the Collector, sat in a modified electronic wheelchair and wore a pinstriped kaftan, a cross between a City stockbroker and a wealthy Middle East businessman.
- A specially made prop called a 'Consumcard' was copied from a standard Barclaycard, in line with the general tone of the production. Fearful of advertising the bank, Graham Williams asked for coloured tape to be stuck over it to disguise its similarity.

Comment
There had been isolated examples of *Doctor Who* 'doing' comedy - *The Romans* (12) or *The Myth Makers* (20) spring to mind - but nothing had been attempted like this for many a year. *The Sun Makers* has some serious points to be made about the dangers of capitalism and the financial exploitation of the masses, but of course most people don't get past the jokes. And yes, there are some great jokes - most of them fairly black - but the undisciplined way in which Robert Holmes shoves them down the viewers' throats can be a little enervating. This isn't helped by a guest cast who feel it their job to wring as much humour out of the script as they possibly can. Generally this is acceptable for this sort of satire, but there are some that think Richard Leech and Henry Woolf should have been drummed out of Equity for delivering performances that makes a Clacton-on-Sea panto look like *The Cherry Orchard*. Personally, as a one-off, I think it's all rather fun.
85%

"I feel just like a goldfish looking out upon a new world." ~ The Doctor

96) *Underworld*
Bob Baker and Dave Martin

Serial Code: 4Y
Original Transmission
Part One
Saturday 7 January 1978, 18.25-18.50, 8.9m / 50
Part Two
Saturday 14 January 1978, 18.25-18.50, 9.1m / 37
Part Three
Saturday 21 January 1978, 18.30-18.55, 8.9m / 37
Part Four
Saturday 28 January 1978, 18.25-18.50, 11.7m / 27
BBC Archive
All episodes exist as 625-line two-inch PAL colour master videotapes.
Novelization
Doctor Who and the Underworld by Terrance Dicks (123/15)
Hardback:
January 1980, WH Allen (0491022298 / Bill Donohoe)
Paperback:
January 1980, Target (0426200683 / Bill Donohoe)
Video
March 2002 (BBCV 7264 / Photomontage)
Précis
A group of Minyans are hunting for their lost colony ship P7E which is now the core of a new planet...
Cast
Tom Baker (Doctor Who), Louise Jameson (Leela), John Leeson (K-9 Voice), Imogen Bickford-Smith (Tala), James Maxwell (Jackson), Jonathan Newth (Orfe), Alan Lake (Herrick), Jimmy Gardner (Idmon), Norman Tipton (Idas), James Marcus (Rask), Godfrey James (Tarn), Frank Jarvis (Ankh), Richard Shaw (Lakh), Stacey Tendeter (Naia), Christine Pollon (Oracle Voice), Jay Neill (Guard Klimt),

Crew
Visual Effects Designer Richard Conway, *Electronic Effects* AJ Mitchell, *Technical Manager* Mike Chislett, *Vision Mixer* Shirley Coward, *Studio Lighting* Mike Jefferies, *Studio Sound* Richard Chubb, *Film Editor* Richard Trevor, *Properties Buyer* Bob Warans, *Special Sound* Dick Mills, *Grams Operator* Gerry Burrows, *Incidental Music* Dudley Simpson, *Costume Designer* Rupert Jarvis, *Make-Up Artist* Cecile Hay-Arthur, *Make-Up Assistants* Jane Berry, Sinikka Ikaheimo, Margaret Magee, Dandra Powell, *Designer* Dick Coles, *Design Assistant* Jane Shepherd, *Production Unit Manager* John Nathan-Turner, *Production Assistant* Mike Cager, *Assistant Floor Manager* Gary Downie, *Director's Assistant* Sue Mansfield, *Floor Assistant* Sue Williams, *Script Editor* Anthony Read, *Producer* Graham Williams, *Director* Norman Stewart

DWM Index
70 Episode Guide
92 Tom Baker interview
142 Bob Baker interview
167 Graham Williams Tribute
168 Anthony Read interview
188 AJ Mitchell interview
215 Louise Jameson interview
233 The John Nathan-Turner Memoirs
236 Bob Baker and Dave Martin interview
243 Archive Feature
248 Graham Williams interview
278 Anthony Read interview
315 Video review
358 Time Team

Recording Dates
September 1977 (Bray Studios modelwork), 3-4 October 1977 (TC4), 15-18 October 1977 (TC4)

Working Title
Underground

Factoids
- A thinly-disguised retread of the Jason and the Argonauts story, *Underworld* had characters with very similar names to those found in the Greek legend: for instance, Herrick (Heracles), Orf (Orpheus), Idas (Midas) and Tala (Atalanta), while the daughter of Zeus and Demeter, Persephone, gave her name to the Minyans' spaceship P7E.
- With inflation running at an all-time high and an expensive season finale planned, director Norman Stewart and set designer Dick Coles saved money on *Underworld* by using model sets of the cave system which the actors would then be CSOed into. Because of the complexity of this technique, electronic effects operator AJ Mitchell storyboarded a 66-page document outlining what compositions could be achieved within the time limit. Normally, one minute of CSO material was achieved per hour, but for this story, the director would have to accomplish eight or nine minutes. Some of the more complex shots involved a model background, an actor (on a blue-draped set) and a foreground object, such as a model rock. Lighting had to be carefully matched and the whole process was very slow and stressful for the actors. The results, although commendably ambitious by the standards of the day, were not thought to be particularly successful.
- Imogen Bickford-Smith was made to look old by the application of cotton wool and latex paint to her face. Unfortunately, the actress (touted erroneously as a new companion in some newspapers) suffered an allergic reaction to this and had to be treated by a doctor.
- Producer Graham Williams was particularly keen for the modelwork to be as good as possible, because a new film called *Star Wars* (of which he had seen a sneak preview) was due to open in the UK at the same time as *Underworld* and he didn't want any negative comparisons.

Comment
One of those stories that can't be as bad as everyone says it is. It's actually quite engaging for some of the time, with a particularly striking Part One. The modelwork is, thanks to *Star Wars*, conspicuously excellent and there are some genuinely stylish visual effects throughout the story. The problem - and the cause of the story's bad reputation - is, of course, the overuse of CSO. As a budget-saving technique, it got a lot of work-out in *Doctor Who*, but most of the time it appeared unconvincing, and if there was too much then it just looked laughable. Unfortunately, *Underworld* has much too much of the stuff, and it's not even as if it's trying to do anything new. It's just caves, one of the programme's enduring locations. It's not even psychedelic caves like in *The Mutants* (63) - it's boring old caves like, well, every other *Doctor Who* story. Hard to enthuse about it, but certainly not the worst story ever made. **60%**

"It's so undignified! I haven't run like this for centuries!" ~ *Chancellor Borusa*

97) *The Invasion of Time*
David Agnew (pen-name for Graham Williams and Anthony Read)

Serial Code: 4Z
Original Transmission
Part One
Saturday 4 February 1978, 18.25-18.50, 11.2m / 28
Part Two
Saturday 11 February 1978, 18.25-18.50, 11.4m / 29
Part Three
Saturday 18 February 1978, 18.25-18.50, 9.5m / 47
Part Four
Saturday 25 February 1978, 18.25-18.50, 10.9m / 28
Part Five
Saturday 4 March 1978, 18.25-18.50, 10.3m / 32
Part Six
Saturday 11 March 1978, 18.25-18.50, 9.8m / 35
BBC Archive
All episodes exist as 625-line two-inch PAL colour master videotapes.
Novelization
Doctor Who and the Invasion of Time by Terrance Dicks (142/15)
Hardback:
February 1980, WH Allen (0491024398 / Andrew Skilleter)
Paperback:
February 1980, Target (0426200934 / Andrew Skilleter)
Video
March 2000 (BBCV 6876 / Photomontage)
Music and Sound Effects
1. May 1978, *Doctor Who Sound Effects*, LP (REC 316 / Photomontage)
2. May 1978, *Doctor Who Sound Effects*, cassette (ZCM 316 / Photomontage)
3. July 1993, *Doctor Who: 30 Years at the Radiophonic Workshop*, CD (BBCCD 871 / Photomontage)
Précis
The Doctor appears to be in league with the Sontarans to invade Gallifrey…
Cast
Tom Baker (Doctor Who), Louise Jameson (Leela), John Leeson (K-9 Voice), John Arnatt (Chancellor Borusa), Milton Johns (Castellan Kelner), Dennis Edwards (Lord Gomer), Reginald Jessup (Lord Savar), Christopher Tranchell (Andred), Stan McGowan (Vardan Leader), Charles Morgan (Gold Usher), Hilary Ryan (Rodan), Max Faulkner (Nesbin), Ray Callaghan (Ablif), Gai Smith (Presta), Michael Mundell (Jasko), Derek Deadman (Stor), Tom Kelly (Vardan), Christopher Christou (Guard), Michael Harley (Bodyguard), Eric Danot (Castellan Guard), Stuart Fell (Sontaran)
Crew
Visual Effects Designers Colin Mapson, Richard Conway, *K-9 Operator* Nigel Brackley, *Electronic Effects* Dave Chapman, *Technical Manager* Errol Ryan, *Senior Cameraman* Jim Atkinson, *Vision Mixer* Shirley Coward, *Studio Lighting* Mike Jefferies, *Studio Sound* Anthony Philpott, *Film Cameraman* Ken Westbury, *Film Camera Assistant* John Sennett, *Film Sound* Graham Ware, *Film Sound Assistant* Patrick Quirke, *Film Operations Manager* Ian Brindle, *Film Editor* Chris Wimble, *OB Lighting* John Stirling, Tommy Thomas, *OB Sound* Ian Leiper, *OB Cameramen* David Goutier, Alan Hayward, *Engineering Manager* Bob Wade, *Special Sound* Dick Mills, *Grams Operator* Gerry Burrows, *Incidental Music* Dudley Simpson, *Costume Designer* Dee Kelly, *Costume Assistant* Dennis Brack, Richard Winter, *Make-Up Artist* Maureen Winslade, *Make-Up Assistants* Karen Sherrie-Morton, Vicky Pocock, Vanessa Poulton, *Designer* Barbara Gosnold, *Production Unit Manager* John Nathan-Turner, *Production Assistant* Colin Dudley, *Assistant Floor Managers* Terry Winders, Romey Allison, *Director's Assistant* Joy Sinclair, *Floor Assistants* Sue Williams, Renny Tasker, *Script Editor* Anthony Read, *Producer* Graham Williams, *Director* Gerald Blake
DWM Index
70	Episode Guide
85	Louise Jameson interview
118	Anthony Read interview
136	Louise Jameson interview
152	Stuart Fell interview
167	Graham Williams Tribute
168	Anthony Read interview
193	What The Papers Said
W92	Archive Feature
215	Louise Jameson interview
219	Milton Johns interview
233	The John Nathan-Turner Memoirs
248	Graham Williams interview
278	Anthony Read interview
289	Video review
336	The Accidental Tourist Part 2
358	Time Team 1-2

Recording Dates
1-2 November 1977 (Bray Studios modelwork), 6-8 November 1977 (TC8), 14-15 November 1977 (Location filming), 16-17 November 1977 (Location videotaping), 18 November 1977 (Location filming), 5-9 December 1977 (Location videotaping), 12-16 December 1977 (Location videotaping)

Locations
St Anne's Hospital, Redhill, Surrey; British Oxygen, Blacks Road, Hammersmith Broadway, London W6; Beachfields Quarry, Redhill, Surrey

Working Title
The Invaders of Time

Factoids
- Season 15 was to have ended on a six-part story by David Weir entitled *Killers of the Dark*, but Weir was finding it hard to complete his scripts, and what he had written - Wembley Stadium filled with cat people - would have proved impossible to visualise on the BBC's limited resources. It was left to script editor Anthony Read to write an alternative Gallifrey-based adventure (a loose sequel to the previous season's popular story *The Deadly Assassin*, 88) in a fortnight. This done, producer Graham Williams spent a further four days and nights redrafting it still further. (The 'four part/two part' structure was recommended by former script editor Robert Holmes.)
- An electricians' strike meant the loss of two out of the three studio sessions normally allotted a six-part *Doctor Who* story. Producer Graham Williams had two choices - abandon the story or use a proffered OB unit to shoot 10 days' worth of location material to make up for the lost studio time. He plumped for the latter, choosing an abandoned Victorian hospital in Redhill, now demolished, to house the Tardis and Gallifrey interiors (excepting the console room and Panopticon sets, which was erected at Television Centre).
- Louise Jameson (Leela) went on to teach drama to prison inmates, including one Leslie Grantham, later to appear in *Resurrection of the Daleks* (134) before rising to fame as Dirty Den in BBC soap *EastEnders* (1984 - present).
- A new Sontaran mask, made from a lighter latex rubber than earlier ones, was created for Derek Deadman to wear as Stor. A new polyurethane foam collar and helmet were also provided. The whole ensemble was far more comfortable than the headgear that the late Kevin Lindsay had worn in earlier serials, although Deadman's dialogue when wearing his helmet had to be dubbed on afterwards as it was too muffled to be picked up by the OB sound equipment.
- The opening shot of the Vardan spaceship flying overhead was a direct lift from the newly opened *Star Wars* (1977).

Comment
Most *Doctor Who* stories stand or fall on their own merits, but with *The Invasion of Time* it's actually beneficial to know a little about the problems the production team faced when making it. A discordant mix of film, studio and OB video, the finished production is a real hodge-podge of styles - and although the location work is at times quite imaginatively conducted, the overall impression is one of cheapness. The Gallifrey sets - bar the Panopticon - are all very poorly realized, while the choice of a 19th century hospital to film/video the Tardis interiors is a very odd one. Acting is universally dire, with Derek Deadman standing out as a particularly feeble Cockney Sontaran. There's also a dearth of incidental music to cover up all the cracks in the production, with great swathes of bland dialogue played out to a silent soundtrack. On the positive side, Tom Baker gives a charismatic - albeit unhinged - performance, while the shock ending to Part Four is rightly considered one of the show's best. The worst aspect of the story, though, is the insistence that every dramatic moment be undercut by a comic line or facial expression - it makes it appear that no-one involved with the production has any real faith in it, a feeling inevitably passed onto the viewer. **65%**

Season 16

"To put it very simply, Doctor, you're suffering from a massive compensation complex." ~ Romana

98) *The Ribos Operation*
Robert Holmes

Serial Code: 5A
Original Transmission
Part One
Saturday 2 September 1978, 17.45-18.10, 8.3m / 42
Part Two
Saturday 9 September 1978, 18.20-18.45, 8.1m / 36

Part Three
Saturday 16 September 1978, 18.30-18.55, 7.9m / 38
Part Four
Saturday 23 September 1978, 18.20-18.45, 8.2m / 36

BBC Archive
All episodes exist as 625-line two-inch PAL colour master videotapes.

Novelization
Doctor Who and the Ribos Operation by Ian Marter (143/10)
Hardback:
December 1979, WH Allen (0491024290 / John Geary)
Paperback:
December 1979, Target (0426200926 / John Geary)

Video
April 1995 (BBCV 5607 / Colin Howard [cover] & Andrew Skilleter [spine])

Music and Sound Effects
July 1993, *Doctor Who: 30 Years at the Radiophonic Workshop*, CD (BBCCD 871 / Photomontage)

Précis
The Doctor and Romana search for the first Key to Time on the wintry planet of Ribos…

Cast
Tom Baker (Doctor Who), Mary Tamm (Romana), John Leeson (K-9 II Voice), Iain Cuthbertson (Garron), Nigel Plaskitt (Unstoffe), Paul Seed (Graff Vynda-K), Robert Keegan (Sholakh), Prentis Hancock (Captain), Cyril Luckham (White Guardian), Ann Tirard (The Seeker), Timothy Bateson (Binro the Heretic), Oliver Maguire (Shrieves), Nick Wilkinson, Stuart Fell (Shrivenzale)

Crew
Visual Effects Designer Dave Havard, *Visual Effects Assistants* Roger Turner, Steve Drewett, *K-9 Operator* Nigel Brackley, *Electronic Effects* Dave Chapman, *Technical Manager* Peter Granger, *Vision Mixers* Fred Law, Sue Thorne, *Senior Vision Engineer, Videotape Editor* John Turner, *Studio Lighting* Jimmy Purdie, *Studio Sound* Richard Chubb, *Special Sound* Dick Mills, *Grams Operator* Martin Ridout, *Incidental Music* Dudley Simpson, *Costume Designer* June Hudson, *Costume Assistant* Roger Oldhamstead, *Make-Up Artist* Christine Walmsley-Cotham, *Make-Up Assistants* Juliette Mayer, Suzanne Jansen, Denise Baron, *Designer* Ken Ledsham, *Production Unit Manager* John Nathan-Turner, *Production Assistant* Jane Shirley, *Assistant Floor Manager* Richard Cox, *Director's Assistant* Wendy Plowright, *Floor Assistant* Peter Leslie, *Script Editor* Anthony Read, *Producer* Graham Williams, *Director* George Spenton-Foster

DWM Index
70 Episode Guide
84 Archive
99 Mary Tamm interview
121 Ian Marter Tribute
125 Novelization review
152 Stuart Fell interview
159 Case Studies: Graff Vynda-K
177 Those *Radio Times*
178 Mary Tamm interview
194 What The Papers Said
225 Video review
S95 Archive Feature
233 The John Nathan-Turner Memoirs
249 Graham Williams interview
260 Vox Pops
262 Mary Tamm interview
278 Anthony Read interview
303 Prentis Hancock interview

Recording Dates
9-11 April 1978 (TC4), 23-25 April 1978 (TC4)

Working Titles
The Galactic Conman
Operation

Factoids
- The Key to Time umbrella theme for this season was worked out by producer Graham Williams in a three-page document he had written in 1976, intending it to apply to Season 15. For this first story, script editor Anthony Read added all the Key to Time references to Robert Holmes' script (including the entire White Guardian prologue). For continuity purposes, each story of the Key to Time sequence would have to be made in transmission order, something not attempted since 1972.
- K-9, in his supposed Mark II version, was equipped with a quieter motor and larger tyres and was painted charcoal grey (rather than greenish-gold, as previously).
- 27-year-old Mary Tamm was picked out of 120 hopefuls auditioning for the role of Romana. She had previously appeared in ITV soap *Coronation Street*, television play *The Girls of Slender Means* and 1974 spy thriller *The Odessa File*.
- Many of the Russian-influenced sets and costumes for this studio-bound story came from a ten-part BBC/Time-Life co-production of *Anna Karenina*, broadcast in 1978.

- Two identical copies of the six segments of the Key to Time were made by visual effects designer Dave Havard. Based on an interlocking wooden puzzle, each piece was made by pouring clear resin into individually-shaped hollow moulds.
- The Shrivenzale was operated by two people in the manner of a pantomime horse. They communicated to each other via a radio system normally fixed to the helmets of motorbike couriers.

Comment
After the gaudy, hectic, and sometimes not entirely successful adventures of the previous season, it makes a nice change to settle down with this delightfully written character piece by series stalwart Robert Holmes. The guest cast is excellent, especially Iain Cuthbertson and Nigel Plaskitt as the incompetent conmen, with Mary Tamm making her mark as a refreshingly aloof new companion. *The Ribos Operation* smacks of class, with beautifully designed and lit (second-hand) settings and sumptuous (second-hand) costumes. Most pleasing of all is the contrast between the all-important search for the Key to Time and the small-scale, almost trivial events on the planet Ribos. A delight from start to finish.
94%

"Destroy everything!" ~ The Captain

99) The Pirate Planet
Douglas Adams

Serial Code: 5B
Original Transmission
Part One
Saturday 30 September 1978, 18.20-18.45, 9.1m / 30
Part Two
Saturday 7 October 1978, 18.20-18.45, 7.4m / 52
Part Three
Saturday 14 October 1978, 18.20-18.45, 8.2m / 44
Part Four
Saturday 21 October 1978, 18.20-18.45, 8.4m / 46
Repeat Transmission
Part One
Thursday 12 July 1979, 18.55-19.20, 2.8m / 123
Part Two
Thursday 19 July 1979, 18.55-19.20, 4m / 91
Part Three
Thursday 26 July 1979, 18.55-19.20, 3.3m / 104
Part Four
Thursday 2 August 1979, 18.55-19.20, 3.9m / 103
BBC Archive
All episodes exist as 625-line two-inch PAL colour master videotapes.
Novelization
None
Video
April 1995 (BBCV 5608 / Colin Howard [cover] & Andrew Skilleter [spine])
Music and Sound Effects
July 1993, *Doctor Who: 30 Years at the Radiophonic Workshop*, CD (BBCCD 871 / Photomontage)
Précis
On Zanak, the Doctor meets a mad half-cyborg Captain who destroys whole planets…
Cast
Tom Baker (Doctor Who), Mary Tamm (Romana), John Leeson (K-9 II Voice), Bruce Purchase (The Captain), Rosalind Lloyd (Nurse), Andrew Robertson (Mr Fibuli), Vi Delmar (Queen Xanxia), David Sibley (Pralix), Ralph Michael (Balaton), Primi Townsend (Mula), David Warwick (Kimus), Adam Kurakin (Guard), Bernard Finch (Mentiad)
Crew
Visual Effects Designer Colin Mapson, *Visual Effects Assistants* Peter Wragg, Charlie Lumm, Chris Lawson, John Brace, *Electronic Effects* Dave Chapman, *Technical Manager* Tony Bate, *Senior Cameraman* Spence Payne, *Vision Mixer* Sue Thorne, *Videotape Editor* Rod Waldron, *Studio Lighting* Mike Jefferies, *Studio Sound* Mike Jones, *Film Cameraman* Elmer Cossey, *Film Sound* Doug Mawson, *Film Editor* John Dunstan, *Special Sound* Dick Mills, *Grams Operator* Ian Tomlin, *Incidental Music* Dudley Simpson, *Costume Designer* L Rowland-Warne, *Make-Up Artist* Janice Gould, *Make-Up Assistants* Linda Burr, Miranda Davidson, Sally Millican, Catherine Whitfield, *Designer* Jon Pusey, *Production Unit Manager* John Nathan-Turner, *Production Assistant* Michael Owen Morris, *Assistant Floor Manager* Ruth Mayorcas, *Director's Assistant* Hazel Marriott, *Floor Assistant* Peter Leslie, *Script Editor* Anthony Read, *Producer* Graham Williams, *Director* Pennant Roberts
DWM Index
70	Episode Guide
75	Archive
99	Mary Tamm interview
118	Anthony Read interview
122	Pennant Roberts interview

168 Anthony Read interview
225 Video review
233 The John Nathan-Turner Memoirs
246 Pennant Roberts interview
253 Archive Feature
262 Mary Tamm interview
278 Anthony Read interview

Recording Dates
1-5 May 1978 (Location filming), 22-23 May 1978 (TC6), 4-6 June 1978 (TC6)

Locations
Disused railway tunnel, Daren-felen, Gwent, Wales; Big Pit, Blaenavon, Gwent, Wales; Monmothshire Golf Course, Llanfoist, Gwent, Wales; Coity Mountain, Gwent, Wales; Bwlch y Garn, Ebbw Vale, Gwent, Wales; Dan-yr-Ogof Showcaves, Dan-yr-Ogof, Powys, Wales; Berkeley Power Station, Berkely, Gloucestershire

Working Title
The Pirates

Factoids
- Aspiring new writer Douglas Adams had previously sent a (rejected) storyline entitled *Dr Who and the Krikkitmen* to script editor Robert Holmes in 1976. For this new attempt, he found himself writing the final five episodes of popular radio series *The Hitch-Hiker's Guide to the Galaxy* alongside his (accepted) story *The Pirate Planet*.
- The Captain's pet, the Polyphase Avatron, was made by former visual effects assistant Tony Oxley, now a freelance props builder. With a head modelled on a Trojan soldier's helmet, two versions were constructed - a dummy and a cable-controlled working prop that would sit on the Captain's shoulder. CSO was used for scenes of it flying in Part Three.
- Whilst in a pub, Tom Baker had had his lip bitten by a small terrier belonging to actor Paul Seed during the end of production on the previous story, *The Ribos Operation*. His injury was clearly visible during the Welsh location filming for *The Pirate Planet*, explained away by a script addition to Part One's Tardis scene in which the Doctor bangs his mouth on the console.

Comment
A clever story let down by mediocre direction, *The Pirate Planet* is a curate's egg that should make far more of an impression than it actually does. A major weakness is the predilection of the guest cast to play the whole thing as a particularly lame comedy; Bruce Purchase is the worst offender, but everyone has his or her particular moment. The design work is impressive - less so the bland location filming - and the special effects are imaginative, if not entirely convincing. But above all, this is a concept-driven story that needs a far more dynamic directorial style than Pennant Roberts can offer. Even so, Tom Baker gives one of his straighter performances of the season and the scene in which he lambastes the Captain for sucking the life force from helpless planets is very powerful. **63%**

"All change at Venus for the Brighton line!" ~ The Doctor

100) The Stones of Blood
David Fisher

Serial Code: 5C
Original Transmission
Part One
Saturday 28 October 1978, 18.25-18.50, 8.6m / 38
Part Two
Saturday 4 November 1978, 18.20-18.45, 6.6m / 75
Part Three
Saturday 11 November 1978, 18.20-18.45, 9.3m / 38
Part Four
Saturday 18 November 197, 18.20-18.45, 7.6m / 66

BBC Archive
All episodes exist as 625-line two-inch PAL colour master videotapes. In addition, a 71 edit also exists for Part Two in the same format.

Novelization
Doctor Who and the Stones of Blood by Terrance Dicks (124/12)
Hardback:
March 1980, WH Allen (0491026803 / Andrew Skilleter)
Paperback:
March 1980, Target (0426200993 / Andrew Skilleter)

Video
May 1995, containing 71 edit of Part Two (BBCV 5610 / Colin Howard [cover] & Andrew Skilleter [spine])

Music and Sound Effects
July 1993, *Doctor Who: 30 Years at the Radiophonic Workshop*, CD (BBCCD 871 / Photomontage)

Précis
The third Key to Time seems to lie somewhere in the vicinity of a stone circle in present-day England…

Cast
Tom Baker (Doctor Who), Mary Tamm (Romana), John Leeson (K-9 II Voice), Beatrix Lehmann (Professor Rumford), Susan Engel (Vivien Fay), Nicholas McArdle (De Vries), Elaine Ives-Cameron (Martha), Gerald Cross (Guardian/Megara Voice), David McAlister (Megara Voice), James Murray, Shirin Taylor (Campers)

Crew
Visual Effects Designer Mat Irvine, *Visual Effects Assistants* Charlie Lumm, Roger Perkins, *K-9 Operator* Nigel Brackley, *Electronic Effects* AJ Mitchell, *Technical Manager* Bob Warman, *Senior Cameraman* Reg Poulter, *Vision Mixer* Fred Law, *Videotape Editor* Malcolm Banthorpe, *Studio Lighting* Warwick Fielding, *Studio Sound* Richard Chubb, *OB Lighting* Hugh Cartwright, *OB Sound* Vic Godrich, *OB Cameramen* Trevor Wimlett, Mike Windsor, *OB Scene Crew Supervisor* Bob Hare, *Properties Buyer* Robert Flemming, *Special Sound* Elizabeth Parker, *Grams Operator* Andrew Hunter, *Incidental Music* Dudley Simpson, *Costume Designer* Rupert Jarvis, *Dressers* Alice Gilbert, Liz Pembroke, Andre Salut, *Make-Up Artist* Ann Briggs, *Make-Up Assistant* Eve Barker, *Designer* John Stout, *Design Assistant* Kassie Pusey, *Production Unit Manager* John Nathan-Turner, *Production Assistant* Carolyn Montagu, *Assistant Floor Managers* Carol Scott, Nigel Taylor, *Floor Assistant* Peter Leslie, *Director's Assistant* Carol Kane, *Script Editor* Anthony Read, *Producer* Graham Williams, *Director* Darrol Blake

DWM Index
70	Episode Guide
99	Mary Tamm interview
116	John Leeson interview
118	Anthony Read interview
154	David Fisher interview
168	Anthony Read interview
182	Darrol Blake interview
188	AJ Mitchell interview
203	Elizabeth Parker interview
222	What The Censor Saw
226	Video review
228	John Leeson interview
S95	Archive Feature
233	The John Nathan-Turner Memoirs
249	Graham Williams interview
262	Mary Tamm interview
269	David Fisher interview
278	Anthony Read interview

Recording Dates
12-15 June 1978 (Location videotaping), 3-4 July 1978 (TC3), 16-18 July 1978 (TC3)

Locations
The King's Men, Rollright Stones, Little Rollright, Oxfordshire; Reed College, Little Compton, Warwickshire; Manor Farm field and Little Rollright Quarry, Oakham Road, Little Rollright, Oxfordshire

Working Titles
The Nine Maidens
Stones of Time

Factoids
- For this centenary story a scene, proposed by Tom Baker or Mary Tamm, was scripted and rehearsed in which the Doctor receives a cake from Romana and K-9 on the occasion of his 751st birthday. It was vetoed on the day of recording by producer Graham Williams as being too self-congratulatory.
- OB video equipment was used on the location shoot, instead of 16mm film, in order to more seamlessly match studio and location scenes.
- The story saw the first use of microchip electronics for the digital read-outs on the Beam Machine prop and the lighting in Vivien Fay's wand.
- John Stout provided three extra 'real' stones for the Rollright Stones location (made from expanded polystyrene), while Mat Irvine and Roger Perkins manufactured three Ogri creatures from transparent fibreglass lit from within. They were moved along on trolleys by Visual Effects assistants.

Comment
The first two parts are very atmospherically directed by Darrol Blake, with the omnipresent cawing of the ravens and the eerie, glowing Ogri gliding about everywhere. However, the final two episodes turn their back on this carefully orchestrated menace and slip into standard SF clichés; the scenes with Tom Baker hamming it up in the hyperspace ship are extremely tiresome. On the plus side, Beatrix Lehmann and Susan Engel both enliven the proceedings enormously and it is a rare pleasure to have such well-written female characters. **69%**

"Next time I shall not be so lenient!" ~ Count Grendel of Gracht

101) The Androids of Tara
David Fisher

Serial Code: 5D
Original Transmission
Part One
Saturday 25 November 1978, 18.20-18.45, 8.5m / 45
Part Two
Saturday 2 December 1978, 18.20-18.45, 10.1m / 30
Part Three
Saturday 9 December 1978, 18.20-18.45, 8.9m / 38
Part Four
Saturday 16 December 1978, 18.20-18.45, 9m / 45
Repeat Transmission
Part One
Thursday 9 August 1979, 18.55-19.20, 6.2m / 49
Part Two
Thursday 16 August 1979, 18.55-19.20, 10.4m / 43
Part Three
Thursday 23 August 1979, 18.55-19.20, 10.5m / 43
Part Four
Thursday 30 August 1979, 18.55-19.20, 9.6m / 41
BBC Archive
All episodes exist as 625-line two-inch PAL colour master videotapes.
Novelization
Doctor Who and the Androids of Tara by Terrance Dicks (128/12)
Hardback:
April 1980, WH Allen (049102651X / Andrew Skilleter)
Paperback:
April 1980, Target (0426201086 / Andrew Skilleter)
Video
May 1995 (BBCV 5611 / Colin Howard [cover] & Andrew Skilleter [spine])
Précis
Landing on Ruritanian-styled Tara, Romana is immediately mistaken for Princess Strella…
Cast
Tom Baker (Doctor Who), Mary Tamm (Romana/Princess Strella), John Leeson (K-9 II Voice), Peter Jeffrey (Count Grendel), Neville Jason (Prince Reynart/Android Duplicate), Paul Lavers (Farrah), Simon Lack (Zadek), Lois Baxter (Lamia), Declan Mulholland (Till), Cyril Shaps (Archimandrite), Martin Matthews (Kurster), Roy Lavender (Taran Wood Beast), Roberta Gibbs (Stunt Double for Romana), Terry Walsh (Stunt Double for Doctor Who/Stunt Double for Count Grendel)
Crew
Fight Arranger Terry Walsh, *Visual Effects Designer* Len Hutton, *Electronic Effects* AJ Mitchell, *Technical Manager* Peter Valentine, *Senior Cameraman* Ron Green, *Vision Mixer* Nigel Finnis, *Videotape Editor* Alan Goddard, *Studio Lighting* Brian Clemmett, *Studio Sound* Richard Chubb, *Film Cameraman* John Walker, *Film Sound* Don Lee, *Film Editor* David Yates, *Special Sound* Dick Mills, *Grams Operator* Andy Stacey, *Incidental Music* Dudley Simpson, *Costume Designer* Doreen James, *Make-Up Artist* Jill Hagger, *Make-Up Assistants* Leslie Roovray, Elizabeth Gray, *Designer* Valerie Warrender, *Design Assistant* Paul Wright, *Production Unit Manager* John Nathan-Turner, *Production Assistant* Teresa-Mary Winders, *Assistant Floor Manager* Rosemary Webb, *Director's Assistant* Wendy Plowright, *Floor Assistant* Julie Mann, *Script Editor* Anthony Read, *Producer* Graham Williams, *Director* Michael Hayes
DWM Index
71   Episode Guide
99   Mary Tamm interview
118   Anthony Read interview
154   David Fisher interview
178   Mary Tamm interview
188   AJ Mitchell interview
205   Doreen James interview
223   Michael Hayes interview
226   Video review
233   The John Nathan-Turner Memoirs
249   Graham Williams interview
262   Mary Tamm interview
269   David Fisher interview
278   Anthony Read interview
288   Peter Jeffrey interview
293   Archive Feature
Recording Dates
24-28 July 1978 (Location filming), 14-15 August 1978 (TC6), 28-29 August 1978 (TC1)
Locations
Leeds Castle, Maidstone, Kent
Working Titles
Androids of Zenda
The Androids of Zend
The Seeds of Time

Factoids
- *The Androids of Tara* replaced an unnamed submission by scriptwriter Ted Lewis, author of the novel *Jack's Return Home*, the basis for cult 1971 film *Get Carter* starring Michael Caine.
- Opening captions ran in a different order to normal - title, part number and then author's name.
- The electro-rapiers were standard hired props modified with dials and knobs. Due to the loss of a gallery only session because of wildcat strikes at the BBC, many electronic sparkles and flashes were missing from the swordfights. Specifically affected was the main duel between the Doctor and Grendel in Part Four.
- Leeds Castle had been used for a Middle East peace conference shortly before the *Doctor Who* film crew arrived. For establishing shots, the castle was made to seem more dramatic by the addition of a glass painting showing extra turrets.

Comment
Blend the well-drawn characters of *The Ribos Operation* (98) with the daring-do of Anthony Hope's 1894 novel *The Prisoner of Zenda*, stir well with some picturesque location filming and add a pinch of breezy comic banter and you have the gem that is *The Androids of Tara*. Whilst the lack of monsters or aliens may be initially off-putting (the pathetic bear doesn't count), this is a deeply satisfying plunder of all things *Boys' Own*, set in a perpetually summery landscape of hunting lodges, summer pavilions and turreted castles. Peter Jeffrey is brilliant as the moustache-twirling villain (pity there were no railway tracks in sight) while Neville Jason gives a studied and convincing performance as the belittled Prince Reynart. Good to see Mary Tamm getting the lion's share of the action too. There are some lovely jokes (apparently adlibbed by Tom Baker) and the plot moves along at a pleasant pace, helped enormously by the best - and longest - swordfight you're ever likely to see in the programme. All in all, rather wonderful. **95%**

"All life is sacred!" ~ Dugeen

102) The Power of Kroll
Robert Holmes

Serial Code: 5E
Original Transmission
Part One
Saturday 23 December 1978, 18.15-18.40, 6.5m / 85
Part Two
Saturday 30 December 1978, 18.30-18.55, 12.4m / 26
Part Three
Saturday 6 January 1979, 18.25-18.50, 8.9m / 51
Part Four
Saturday 13 January 1979, 18.25-18.50, 9.9m / 31
BBC Archive
All episodes exist as 625-line two-inch PAL colour master videotapes.
Novelization
Doctor Who and the Power of Kroll by Terrance Dicks (128/14)
Hardback:
WH Allen, May 1980 (0491027214 / Andrew Skilleter)
Paperback:
Target, May 1980 (0426201019 / Andrew Skilleter)
Video
June 1995 (BBCV 5612 / Colin Howard [cover] & Andrew Skilleter [spine])
Précis
On a moon of Delta Magna, a mile-wide squid is causing problems for the inhabitants...
Cast
Tom Baker (Doctor Who), Mary Tamm (Romana), Neil McCarthy (Thawn), Philip Madoc (Fenner), John Leeson (Dugeen), Glyn Owen (Rohm-Dutt), John Abineri (Ranquin), Carl Rigg (Varlik), Grahame Mallard (Harg), Terry Walsh (Mensch/Stunt Double for Nual), Frank Jarvis (Skart)
Crew
Visual Effects Designer Tony Harding, *Visual Effects Assistant* Steve Drewett, *Electronic Effects* Dave Jervis, *Technical Manager* Tony Bate, *Senior Cameraman* Alec Wheal, *Vision Mixer* Shirley Coward, *Videotape Editor* Rod Waldron, *Studio Lighting* Warwick Fielding, *Studio Sound* Richard Chubb, *Film Cameraman* Martin Patmore, *Film Sound* Stan Nightingale, *Film Editor* Michael Goldsmith, *Properties Buyer* Monica Boggust, *Special Sound* Dick Mills, *Grams Operator* Ian

Tomlin, *Incidental Music* Dudley Simpson, *Costume Designer* Colin Lavers, *Make-Up Artist* Kezia Dewinne, *Make-Up Assistants* Wendy Freeman, Caroline Marston, Vicky Pocock, Joanna Nettleton, *Designer* Don Giles, *Design Assistant* Mike Williams, *Production Unit Manager* John Nathan-Turner, *Production Assistant* Kate Nemet, *Assistant Floor Manager* Chris Moss, *Floor Assistant* Ann Healy, *Director's Assistant* Sue Mansfield, *Script Editor* Anthony Read, *Producer* Graham Williams, *Director* Norman Stewart

DWM Index
71   Episode Guide
99   Mary Tamm interview
116   John Leeson interview
152   Terry Walsh interview
164   Philip Madoc interview
177   Those *Radio Times*
227   Video review
228   John Leeson interview
233   The John Nathan-Turner Memoirs
249   Graham Williams interview
260   Vox Pops
262   Mary Tamm interview
278   Anthony Read interview
312   Archive Feature

Recording Dates
18-22 September 1978 (Location filming), 25-29 September 1978 (Location Filming), 9-11 October 1978 (TC6), 19-20 October 1978 (Bray Studios modelwork)

Locations
The Maltings, Snape, Suffolk; Iken Cliff, Iken, Suffolk.

Working Titles
Moon of Death
The Horror of the Swamp

Factoids
- Most of the location filming was conducted on 16mm as normal, whilst scenes later to be merged with 35mm modelwork of Kroll were shot on 35mm. Unfortunately, cameraman Martin Patmore was wrongly advised to mask off half his film when shooting those scenes. The resultant sharp lines that divided live action from model film meant that these composite images did not appear as convincing as was hoped.
- *The Power of Kroll*'s ratings offer an unusually polarised picture: Part Two achieved the highest viewing figures for the season (12.4m), while Part One (6.5m) achieved the lowest.
- Philip Madoc was offered, and accepted, the main role of Thawn. However, director

Norman Stewart then gave this role to actor Neil McCarthy (who had played Barnham in Pertwee story *The Mind of Evil*, 56) without notifying Madoc's agent. When Madoc was offered the secondary part of Fenner, he assumed this was still the main villain and accepted the job. By the time the mistake was discovered, it was too late for Madoc to decline.
- Kroll was a latex and foam model with a twelve-foot tentacle span, designed by Steve Drewett. It was operated with wires and air pumps in a model tank at Bray Studios.

Comment
The wide-open grassy marshland is an impressive location for the programme, and director Norman Stewart makes the most of this unusual backdrop. However, the scenes set on the refinery are all unremittingly dull and Neil McCarthy makes a boorish, one-note villain. The Swampies are your standard 'extras in a loincloth' stock cliché (see *Kinda*, 119), although John Abineri, playing their leader, is thankfully incapable of giving a poor performance. Kroll is really rather a good monster, more convincing in some scenes than the giant Krynoid from *The Seeds of Doom* (85), but poorly merged matte shots spoil its best moments. **48%**

"Any second now, beautiful mushrooms will blossom and burst!" ~ The Marshal

103) *The Armageddon Factor*
Bob Baker and Dave Martin

Serial Code: 5F
Original Transmission
Part One
Saturday 20 January 1979, 18.25-18.50, 7.5m / 93
Part Two
Saturday 27 January 1979, 18.25-18.50, 8.8m / 49
Part Three
Saturday 3 February 1979, 18.25-18.50, 7.8m / 76
Part Four
Saturday 10 February 1979, 18.25-18.50, 8.6m / 60
Part Five
Saturday 17 February 1979, 18.25-18.50, 8.6m / 66

Part Six
Saturday 24 February 1979, 18.30-18.55,
9.6m / 36
BBC Archive
All episodes exist as 625-line two-inch PAL colour master videotapes.
Novelization
Doctor Who and the Armageddon Factor by Terrance Dicks (127/14)
Hardback:
June 1980, WH Allen (0491026609 / Bill Donohoe)
Paperback:
June 1980, Target (0426201043 / Bill Donohoe)
Video
June 1995 (BBCV 5613 / Colin Howard [cover] & Andrew Skilleter [spine])
Music and Sound Effects
July 1993, *Doctor Who: 30 Years at the Radiophonic Workshop*, CD (BBCCD 871 / Photomontage)
Précis
A mysterious Shadow is manipulating the long-running war between Atrios and Zeus…
Cast
Tom Baker (Doctor Who), Mary Tamm (Romana), John Leeson (K-9 II Voice), John Woodvine (Marshal), Lalla Ward (Princess Astra), Davyd Harries (Shapp), William Squire (The Shadow), Ian Saynor (Merak), Barry Jackson (Drax), Valentine Dyall (Black Guardian), Ian Liston (Hero/Voice of Damage Control/Voice of Pilot), Susan Skipper (Heroine/Voice of Damage Control), John Cannon, Harry Fielder (Guards), Iain Armstrong (Technician), Pat Gorman (Pilot), Stephen Calcutt (Mute)
Crew
Visual Effects Designer John Horton, *Visual Effects Assistants* Jim Francis, Steve Lucas, *Graphics* Charles McGee, *K-9 Operator* Nigel Brackley, *Electronic Effects* Dave Chapman, *Technical Manager* Tony Bate, *Senior Cameraman* Alec Wheal, *Vision Mixer* James Gould, Graham Giles, *Videotape Editor* Rod Waldron, *Studio Lighting* Mike Jefferies, *Studio Sound* Richard Chubb, *Film Editor* Richard Trevor, *Properties Buyer* Shirley Spriggs, *Special Sound* Dick Mills, *Grams Operator* Andy Hunter, *Incidental Music* Dudley Simpson, *Costume Designer* Michael Burdle, *Make-Up Artist* Ann Briggs, *Make-Up Assistants* Elizabeth Hardiman, Ann McEwan, Lesley Bond, Dorey Cilia, *Designer* Richard McManan-Smith, *Design Assistant* Sarah Parkinson, *Production Unit Manager* John Nathan-Turner, *Production Assistant* Ann Aronsohn, *Assistant Floor Managers* Steve Goldie, Rosemary Padvaiskas, *Director's Assistant* Sue Upton, *Floor Assistant* Tony Bebbington, *Script Editor* Anthony Read, *Assistant Script Editor* Douglas Adams, *Producer* Graham Williams, *Director* Michael Hayes

DWM Index
71   Episode Guide
99   Mary Tamm interview
142 Bob Baker interview
178 Mary Tamm interview
194 What The Papers Said
223 Michael Hayes interview
     Archive Feature
227 Video review
233 The John Nathan Turner Memoirs
236 Bob Baker and Dave Martin interview
262 Mary Tamm interview
278 Anthony Read interview
340 Lalla Ward interview

Recording Dates
October 1978 (EFS modelwork), 3-7 November 1978 (TC3), 20-22 November 1978 (TC3), 3-5 December 1978 (TC3)

Working Title
Armageddon

Factoids
- Cast as Princess Astra was Lalla Ward (real name Lady Sarah Ward, daughter of Viscount Sir Edward Ward of Bangor) who would go on to become a regular companion the following season, in the form of a regenerated Romana.
- The Tardis police box prop was given a new light that flashed much faster than previous versions.
- Valentine Dyall, famous as BBC radio's 'Man in Black' in the 1940s, appeared as the Black Guardian in Part Six, as work commitments prevented Cyril Luckham reprising his role as the White Guardian.
- A short technical breakdown occurred at the end of Part Five. After half a minute's music accompanied by a standard caption slide apologizing for the breakdown, the episode resumed from a point a few seconds before it had stopped. Ironically, the episode was given a 30-minute slot in the *Radio Times*, as if the error had been predicted.
- This story saw Mary Tamm and John Leeson leave the programme (although Leeson would return for Season 18). Along with many companions before her, Tamm had become dissatisfied with the way her character had been watered down over the course of her adventures, while Leeson wanted to move back into live acting.

- Douglas Adams trailed outgoing script editor Anthony Read from October 1978. Graham Williams had initially offered the post to Robert Holmes, but the veteran script editor had declined his old job back. Adams' first job was to clarify the ending to Part Six.

Comment
Director Michael Hayes does the best he can, but *The Armageddon Factor* is a messy, unfocused hotchpotch of ideas that quickly loses it way after a promising start. The lack of location filming draws attention to the low-budget nature of the story, which is stretched too thinly over its six parts, and the endless dark sets (although well designed) become rather monotonous. John Woodvine gives his usual workmanlike performance, but Davyd Harries, fresh from the Terry Scott School of Acting, is often embarrassing. The last few episodes are characterized by futile running around, while a time-loop sub-plot is an obvious attempt at padding (as it would be in the later story *Meglos*, 111). As to the climax of the story - and, of course, the whole season - it's all very logical and everything, but you can't help feeling it's something of an anticlimax after 26 weeks of build-up. **35%**

Season 17

"I cannot allow myself the luxury of death." ~ *Davros*

104) *Destiny of the Daleks*
Terry Nation

Serial Code: 5J
Original Transmission
Episode One
Saturday 1 September 1979, 18.10-18.35, 13m / 28
Episode Two
Saturday 8 September 1979, 18.10-18.35, 12.7m / 39
Episode Three
Saturday 15 September 1979, 18.10-18.35, 13.8m / 28
Episode Four
Saturday 22 September 1979, 18.15-18.40, 14.4m / 27

Repeat Transmission
Episode One
Tuesday 5 August 1980, 18.25-18.50, 4.9m / 91
Episode Two
Wednesday 6 August 1980, 18.20-18.45, 5.8m / 59
Episode Three
Thursday 7 August 1980, 18.25-18.50, 7.1m / 33
Episode Four
Friday 8 August 1980, 18.25-18.50, 6.5m / 41
BBC Archive
All episodes exist as 625-line two-inch PAL colour master videotapes.
Novelization
Doctor Who and the Destiny of the Daleks by Terrance Dicks (110/14)
Hardback:
WH Allen, November 1979 (Andrew Skilleter)
Paperback:
1. Target, November 1979 (Andrew Skilleter)
2. Target, July 1992 (Alister Pearson)
Video
1. July 1994 (BBCV 5350 / Colin Howard)
2. September 2001, in 'The Davros Collection' box set [BBCV 7241 / Photomontage] with the other four Davros stories (BBCV 7252 / Photomontage)
Music and Sound Effects
May 2000, *Doctor Who at the BBC Radiophonic Workshop: Volume 2 - New Beginnings 1970-1980*, CD (WMSF 6024-2 / Photographs)
Précis
The Movellans and Daleks are both hunting for Davros on the barren wastes of Skaro...
Cast
Tom Baker (Doctor Who), Lalla Ward (Romana II), David Gooderson (Davros/Dalek Voices), Tim Barlow (Tyssan), Peter Straker (Commander Sharrel), Suzanne Danielle (Agella), Tony Osoba (Lan), Penny Casdagli (Jall), David Yip (Veldan), Cassandra, Peter Coleclough (Movellan Guards), Cy Town, Mike Mungarvan, Toby Byrne, Tony Starr (Daleks), Roy Skelton (Dalek Voices/ K-9 II Voice), Lee Richards (Short Romana), Maggie Armitage (Tall Romana), Yvonne Gallagher (Buxom Romana)
Crew
Visual Effects Designer Peter Logan, *Visual Effects Assistants* Steve Lucas, George Reed, *K-9 Operators* Nigel Brackley, Steve Cambden, *Electronic Effects* Dave Jervis, *Technical Manager* John Dean, *Senior Cameraman* Alec Wheal, *Vision Mixer* Nigel Finnis, *Videotape Editor* Alan Goddard, *Studio Lighting* John Dixon, *Studio Sound* Clive Gifford, *Film Cameramen* Phil Law, Kevin Rowley, *Film Camera Assistant* Roger

Twyman, *Steadicam* Fred Hamilton, *Film Lighting Gaffer* Monty Smart, *Film Sound* Graham Bedwell, *Film Editor* Dick Allen, *Special Sound* Dick Mills, *Grams Operator* Gordon Phillipson, *Incidental Music* Dudley Simpson, *Costume Designer* June Hudson, *Costume Assistant* Roger Oldhamstead, *Make-Up Artist* Cecile Hay-Arthur, *Make-Up Assistants* Margaret McGreen, Catherine Whitfield, Lesley Bond, Caroline Becker, *Designer* Ken Ledsham, *Design Assistant* Rob Harris, *Production Unit Manager* John Nathan-Turner, *Production Assistant* Henry Foster, *Assistant Floor Managers* David Tilley, Antony Root, *Floor Assistant* Barbara Jones, *Director's Assistant* Roz Berrystone, *Script Editor* Douglas Adams, *Producer* Graham Williams, *Director* Ken Grieve

DWM Index

71	Episode Guide
86	Archive
111	David Gooderson interview
117	Michael Wisher interview
145	Terry Nation interview
177	Those *Radio Times*
194	What The Papers Said
215	Video review
249	Graham Williams interview
280	Vox Pops
270	Ken Grieve interview
283	Archive Feature
309	Video review ('The Davros Collection')
313	Douglas Adams interview
340	Lalla Ward interview

Recording Dates
11-15 June 1979 (Location filming), 20-21 June 1979 (Acton Studios modelwork), 2-3 July 1979 (TC3), 15-17 July 1979 (TC1)

Locations
Winspit Quarry, Worth Matravers, Dorset; Binnegar Heath Sand Pit, Wareham, Dorset

Factoids
- Terry Nation's script was heavily rewritten by new script editor Douglas Adams. The manner of Romana's regeneration was entirely down to Adams, as was much of the humour, including a direction reference to his successful radio series *The Hitch-Hiker's Guide to the Galaxy* in the form of a book by Oolon Coluphid that the Doctor is seen reading.
- Four mobile Dalek props were used in this serial, while for the location shoot, hollow vacuum-formed plastic dummies were carried along by extras. The Kaled mutant found by the Doctor was a slimy children's toy called 'Worms'.
- Michael Wisher was unavailable to resume the role of Davros and was replaced by David Gooderson. The original Davros mask and wheelchair had been on display since 1975 in the BBC Enterprises exhibitions at Longleat and Blackpool and were thus in a considerable state of disrepair.
- Various members of the guest cast were famous, or went on to become famous, in other productions: Suzanne Danielle in *Carry On Emmannuelle* (1978), David Yip as *The Chinese Detective* (1981) and Tony Osoba in *Porridge* (1973-77). Tim Barlow, an actor with profound hearing loss, went on to work for disabled theatre company Graeae, founded by Nabil Shaban (Sil from *Vengeance on Varos*, 139, and the second segment of *The Trial of a Time Lord*, 144b).
- Pioneering use was made of a camera mounting system called a Steadicam (of which only three existed at the time), which allowed a very smooth tracking shot with a handheld camera. The camera received worldwide recognition when it was used the following year to brilliant effect in Stanley Kubrick's film *The Shining* (1980).
- During the Dorset location filming, merchandiser/publisher Denis Alan took photographs of Tom Baker, the Tardis and a Dalek for a range of badges, posters and greetings cards he produced under the name Denis Alan Print.
- A one-page interview with costume designer June Hudson appeared in the *Radio Times* of 1-7 August 1979, in which she discussed the appearance of the Movellans

Comment
Much maligned for its bargain basement Daleks and ineffectual Davros, this is actually a bright and breezy adventure, beautifully directed, with some great location work and sturdy, expensive-looking sets (with ceilings!). Tom Baker and Lalla Ward have a wonderful rapport and the script is fast moving and witty. The absence of music is an oddity, although much of Dudley Simpson's recent output had been very unmemorable, so it's probably no bad thing. Far better than its reputation suggests. **82%**

"I say, what a wonderful butler - he's so violent!"
~ The Doctor

105) City of Death

David Agnew (pen-name for Douglas Adams and Graham Williams, from an idea by David Fisher)

Serial Code: 5H
Original Transmission
Part One
Saturday 29 September 1979, 18.05-18.30, 12.4m / 50
Part Two
Saturday 6 October 1979, 18.15-18.40, 14.1m / 44
Part Three
Saturday 13 October 1979, 18.00-18.25, 15.4m / 34
Part Four
Saturday 20 October 1979, 18.15-18.40, 16.1m / 16
Repeat Transmission
Part One
Tuesday 12 August 1980, 18.25-18.50, 6.3m / 57
Part Two
Wednesday 13 August 1980, 18.25-18.50, 5.5m / 81
Part Three
Tuesday 19 August 1980, 18.25-18.50, - / -
Part Four
Wednesday 20 August 1980, 18.25-18.50, - / -
BBC Archive
All episodes exist as 625-line two-inch PAL colour master videotapes.
Novelization
None
Video
1. April 1991 (BBCV 4492 / Andrew Skilleter)
2. May 2001 (BBCV 7132 / Photomontage)
DVD
November 2005 (BBCDVD TBA / Clayton Hickman)
Précis
The world is at risk from a splintered creature called Skaroth who wants to destroy Mankind...
Cast
Tom Baker (Doctor Who), Lalla Ward (Romana II), Julian Glover (Count Scarlioni/Scaroth/Tancredi), Catherine Schell (Countess Scarlioni), David Graham (Kerensky), Kevin Flood (Hermann), Tom Chadbon (Duggan/Jagaroth Voice/Gendarme Voice), Pamela Stirling (Louvre Guide), Peter Halliday (Soldier/Jagaroth Voice/Television Reporter's Voice), James Charlton (Café Artist), Pat Gorman, Peter Kodak, Anthony Powell, Mike Finbar (Thugs), Richard Sheekey (Double for Scaroth), Jane Bough (Maid), John Cleese, Eleanor Bron (Art Gallery Visitors), Michael Hayes (Man in Metro/Gendarme Voice)
Crew
Visual Effects Designer Ian Scoones, *Scaroth Mask* John Friedlander, *Electronic Effects* Dave Jervis, *Technical Manager* John Dean, *Senior Cameraman* Alec Wheal, *Vision Mixer* Nigel Finnis, *Videotape Editor* Rod Waldron, *Studio Lighting* Mike Jefferies, *Studio Sound* Anthony Philpott, *Film Cameraman* John Walker, *Film Camera Assistant* Niall Kennedy, *Film Sound* Graham Bedwell, *Film Sound Assistant* John Crossland, *Film Editor* John Gregory, *Special Sound* Dick Mills, *Grams Operator* Ian Tomlin, Scott Talbot, *Incidental Music* Dudley Simpson, *Costume Designers* Doreen James, Jan Wright, *Make-Up Artist* Jean Steward, *Make-Up Assistants* Sally Woodlee, Margaret Holding, Viv Riley, *Designer* Richard McManan-Smith, *Design Assistant* Sandy Garfield, *Production Unit Manager* John Nathan-Turner, *Production Assistant* Rosemary Crowson, *Assistant Floor Manager* Carol Scott, *Floor Assistant* Sally Bates, *Director's Assistant* Jane Wellesley, *Script Editor* Douglas Adams, *Producer* Graham Williams, *Director* Michael Hayes
DWM Index
57   John Friedlander interview
61   Archive
65   Richard McManan-Smith interview
71   Episode Guide
88   Lalla Ward interview
154 David Fisher interview
158 Kevin O'Shea interview
164 John Nathan-Turner interview
165 The Doctor Abroad
173 Video review
177 Those *Radio Times*
192 Ian Scoones interview
194 What The Papers Said 1
195 What The Papers said 2
204 Dudley Simpson interview
205 Doreen James interview
     Julian Glover interview
     Archive Feature
217 Lalla Ward interview
224 Michael Hayes interview
233 The John Nathan-Turner Memoirs
251 Graham Williams interview
265 *Doctor Who Magazine* Awards (7th)
269 David Fisher interview
304 Eleanor Bron interview
     Video review (reissue)

313 Douglas Adams interview
321 Peter Halliday interview
340 Lalla Ward interview
350 The Fact of Fiction

Recording Dates
30 April-3 May 1979 (Paris location filming), 8-10 May 1979 (Bray Studios modelwork), 21-22 May 1979 (TC3), 3-5 June 1979 (TC6)

Locations
Eiffel Tower; Dupleix Metro Platform, Rue August Bartoldi; Trocadéro Metro Platform, Place du Trocadéro; Avenue Kléber; Rue de Rivoli; Louvre Museum; Le Notre Dame Brasserie; Place de la Concorde; Denise Rene Gallery, Boulevard St Germain; Avenue des Champs Elysées; 47 Rue Vielle du Temple - all Paris, France

Working Title
Curse of Sephiroth

Factoids
- *City of Death* used elements from a discarded storyline by David Fisher called *A Gamble with Time*. This was set in Las Vegas - subsequently Monte Carlo - and concerned a splintered being called Scarlioni who funded his time travel experiments by cheating gamblers at his casino.
- Various problems were encountered with the Paris location filming (the first time the series had ventured overseas). Due to a Parisian Bank Holiday, many of the chosen locations were closed, including the gallery that the Doctor and Romana were supposed to enter. Clever camera angles disguised the closure, although Tom Baker accidentally set off the burglar alarm by crashing into the closed door too hard.
- The appearance of John Cleese and Eleanor Bron was a last-minute addition to the story. On 22 May, during the first studio block for *City of Death*, Cleese was filming the delayed *Fawlty Towers* episode 'Basil the Rat' in another studio while Bron, a friend from their Cambridge Footlights days, was appearing in a satirical programme with John Fortune. Discovering this, Douglas Adams invited them to appear briefly as art lovers in Part Four and hastily wrote a scene for them during his lunch-break.
- Although the late Douglas Adams declined to novelise his story, or allow it to be novelized by another writer, he did reuse many of its ideas in his 1987 novel, *Dirk Gently's Holistic Detective Agency*.

Comment
One of the finest moments in *Doctor Who*'s long and chequered history, *City of Death* only takes itself seriously when it's absolutely necessary (which is about twice). It works best as a light drawing-room comedy with the Doctor and Romana as carefree lovers entangled in the machinations of a suave, power-mad millionaire criminal who probably cheats at Patience - the fact that he wears a mask made of spaghetti is irrelevant. Glorious music, cosmopolitan settings, the Mona Lisa, medieval thumbscrews, fantastic modelwork, John Cleese, Julian Glover, Catherine Schell, no K-9....it's got something for everyone. And it's also one of the few *Doctor Who*s in which Tom Baker's manic performance actually adds to the story. Sublime. **95%**

"I couldn't see a man of your obvious talents in a subordinate position." ~ *Adrasta*

106) The Creature from the Pit
David Fisher

Serial Code: 5G
Original Transmission
Part One
Saturday 27 October 1979, 18.00-18.25, 9.3m / 43
Part Two
Saturday 3 November 1979, 18.05-18.30, 10.8m / 23
Part Three
Saturday 10 November 1979, 18.00-18.25, 10.2m / 36
Part Four
Saturday 17 November 1979, 18.00-18.25, 9.6m / 36

BBC Archive
All episodes exist as 625-line two-inch PAL colour master videotapes. In addition, a 71 edit exists of Part Three in the same format.

Novelization
Doctor Who and the Creature from the Pit by David Fisher (121/11)
Hardback:
January 1981, WH Allen (0491029918 / Steve Kyte)
Paperback:
January 1981, Target (042620123X / Steve Kyte)
Video
July 2002 (BBCV 7266 / Photomontage)

Précis
Appearances can be deceptive when it comes to a hideous green monster in a pit...
Cast
Tom Baker (Doctor Who), Lalla Ward (Romana II), David Brierley (K-9 II Voice), Myra Frances (Adrasta), Eileen Way (Karela), Geoffrey Bayldon (Organon), John Bryans (Torvin), Edward Kelsey (Edu), Tim Munro (Ainu), Morris Barry (Tollund), David Telfer (Huntsman), Terry Walsh (Doran/Stunt Double for Doctor Who), Tommy Wright (Guardmaster), Philip Denyer, Dave Redgrave (Guards), Gail Hunter (Handmaiden)
Crew
Fight Arranger Terry Walsh, *Stuntmen* Max Faulkner, Dinny Powell, *Visual Effects Designer* Mat Irvine, *Visual Effects Assistants* Roger Perkins, Morag McLean, Steve Bowman, Charlie Lumm, Steve Lucas, *K-9 Operator* Nigel Brackley, *Electronic Effects* Dave Chapman, *Technical Manager* Mike Chislett, *Senior Cameraman* Rodney Taylor, *Vision Mixer* James Gould, *Videotape Editor* Rod Waldron, *Studio Lighting* Warwick Fielding, *Studio Sound* Anthony Philpott, *Film Cameraman* David Feig, *Film Camera Assistant* Tony Bragg, *Film Sound* Doug Mawson, *Film Sound Assistant* Stuart Moser, *Film Lighting* Des O'Brien, *Film Editor* MAC Adams, *Properties Buyer* Eric Baker, *Special Sound* Dick Mills, *Incidental Music* Dudley Simpson, *Costume Designer* June Hudson, *Costume Assistant* Roger Oldhamstead, *Make-Up Artist* Gillian Thomas, *Make-Up Assistants* Sandra Powell, Janice Sewell, Tina Baker, Sally Milligan, Lisa Pickering, *Designer* Valerie Warrender, *Design Assistant* David Laskey, *Production Unit Manager* John Nathan-Turner, *Production Assistant* Romey Allison, *Assistant Floor Managers* David Tilley, Kate Osborne, *Director's Assistant* Carol Snook, *Floor Assistant* Ed Bye, *Script Editor* Douglas Adams, *Producer* Graham Williams, *Director* Christopher Barry

DWM Index
72   Episode Guide
99   Christopher Barry interview
154 David Fisher interview
180 Christopher Barry interview
204 Edward Kelsey interview
222 What The Censor Saw
231 David Brierley interview
233 The John Nathan-Turner Memoirs
269 David Fisher interview
304 Archive Feature
316 Christopher Barry interview
319 Video review
327 The Mary Whitehouse Experience
340 Lalla Ward interview
341 Lalla Ward interview

Recording Dates
21-23 March 1979 (EFS), 26 March 1979 (EFS), 9-10 April 1979 (TC6), 22-24 April 1979 (TC6), 17-18 April 1979 (Acton Studios modelwork)

Working Title
The Creature in the Pit

Factoids
- Visual effects designer Mat Irvine and director Christopher Barry were concerned about the realization of giant blob creature Erato. Irvine recommended shooting the main version as a model on a miniature set, CSOed into live action scenes, but Barry told him to create a lifesize one instead. Made from meteorological balloons covered with a latex skin and operated by five members of the Visual Effects department, Erato had a flexible proboscis which the production crew considered distinctly phallic-looking (and was made to look less penile by the second studio session). A miniature was also made for some shots, equipped with glowing lights and an air-filled bladder to suggest breathing.
- The five wolf weeds were radio-controlled props designed by Mat Irvine. Experiencing similar problems to K-9, they were affected by signals from the production crew's equipment, as well as having problems with their gears burning out.
- Model sequences of the Tardis and Erato in space, done on the last day of the Ealing film shoot, were considered unacceptable by Christopher Barry (wires were visible and the perspective was wrong). An expensive remount was conducted after the studio sessions had been recorded.
- Playing Tollund in Part One was Morris Barry, distant relative of Christopher Barry and director of *The Moonbase* (33), *Tomb of the Cybermen* (37) and *The Dominators* (44).

Comment
A far worthier contender than *The Horns of Nimon* for the title of worst-ever *Doctor Who* story, *The Creature from the Pit* is an unmitigated disaster from the word go. The fake-bearded bandits, rejects from *Monty Python's Life of Brian* (1979), are not in the least bit funny, the dialogue teeters on the verge of schoolboy humour at every moment and Geoffrey Bayldon delivers one of the most misguided performances of his career. Obviously writing the whole thing off as a bad

joke (and one can see why), he is content to play Organon as a lazy, patronising and vaguely comedic 'mad scientist' - to watch him is an excruciating experience. The only character to emerge with her reputation intact is Myra Francis as the steel-hearted Lady Adrasta. She brings a touch of class to the witless proceedings. The title monster should never have been attempted, although its resemblance to a giant male member is perhaps an apt comment on the story itself.
24%

"Of course we should interfere! Always do what you're best at." ~ The Doctor

107) Nightmare of Eden
Bob Baker

Serial Code: 5K
Original Transmission
Part One
Saturday 24 November 1979, 18.00-18.25,
 8.7m / 41
Part Two
Saturday 1 December 1979, 18.00-18.25,
 9.6m / 31
Part Three
Saturday 8 December 1979, 18.00-18.25,
 9.6m / 32
Part Four
Saturday 15 December 1979, 18.00-18.25,
 9.4m / 32
BBC Archive
All episodes exist as 625-line two-inch PAL colour master videotapes.
Novelization
Doctor Who and the Nightmare of Eden by Terrance Dicks (111/14)
Hardback:
September 1980, WH Allen (0491021186 / Andrew Skilleter)
Paperback:
August 1980, Target (0426201302 / Andrew Skilleter)
Video
January 1999 (BBCV 6610 / Photomontage)
Précis
Two spaceships become locked together in hyperspace while monsters stalk the corridors…
Cast
Tom Baker (Doctor Who), Lalla Ward (Romana II), David Brierley (K-9 II Voice), David Daker (Rigg), Stephen Jenn (Secker), Geoffrey Bateman (Dymond), Lewis Fiander (Tryst), Jennifer Lonsdale (Della), Barry Andrews (Stott), Geoffrey Hinsliff (Fisk/PA announcer), Peter Craze (Costa), David Cole (Computer Voice), James Muir, Derek Suthern, David Korff, Jan Murzynowski, Robert Goodman (Mandrels)
Crew
Visual Effects Designer Colin Mapson, *Visual Effects Assistant* Chris Lawson, *K-9 Operator* Nigel Brackley, *Video Effects* AJ Mitchell, *Technical Manager* Terry Brett, *Senior Cameraman* Peter Hider, *Vision Mixer* Nigel Finnis, *Videotape Editor* Rod Waldron, *Studio Lighting* Warwick Fielding, *Studio Sound* Anthony Philpott, *Properties Buyer* Robert Fleming, *Special Sound* Dick Mills, *Incidental Music* Dudley Simpson, *Costume Designer* Rupert Jarvis, *Make-Up Artist* Joan Stribling, *Make-Up Assistants* Elizabeth Hardiment, Sinikka Ikaheimo, *Designer* Roger Cann, *Design Assistant* Carol Smith, *Production Unit Manager* John Nathan-Turner, *Production Assistant* Carolyn Montagu, *Assistant Floor Manager* Val McCrimmon, *Floor Assistant* Alison Barnett, *Director's Assistant* Monica Rodger, *Script Editor* Douglas Adams, *Producer* Graham Williams, *Directors* Alan Bromly, Graham Williams
DWM Index
72   Episode Guide
142   Bob Baker interview
188   AJ Mitchell interview
231   David Brierley interview
233   The John Nathan-Turner Memoirs
273   Video review
         Archive Feature
Recording Dates
12-14 August 1979 (TC6), 26-28 August 1979 (TC6)
Working Title
Nightmare of Evil
Factoids
- The spaceship scenes were all recorded electronically in studio (rather than pre-filmed) as a cost-cutting exercise.
- Five Mandrel suits were made out of textured latex rubber backed with foam. Bob Baker's script described them as fungoid and so Rupert Jarvis gave them top-heavy mushroom-like silhouettes. The heads contained battery-powered lights for their eyes.
- A trailer for the new season was recorded on the Eden jungle set during the first recording session.
- Tensions during studio recording were fraught. During the last studio day director

Alan Bromly walked out of the recording due to his inability to cope with the hectic schedule, and producer Graham Williams took over the final few hours' taping.

Comment
A sort of *Van der Valk* in space, *Nightmare of Eden* has an extremely strong storyline spoilt by some dodgy effects and silly monsters with flares. The combination of Tom Baker going overboard with seemingly ad-libbed comedy moments and Lewis Fiander's patronising performance as Tryst also does the story an injustice. Still, there are some atmospheric - almost scary - moments and the central concept of two ships locked together during warp manoeuvres is an intriguing one. Also exemplary is the treatment of Rigg's drug addiction and subsequent withdrawal symptoms.
62%

"You meddlesome hussy!" ~ Soldeed

108) The Horns of Nimon
Anthony Read

Serial Code: 5L
Original Transmission
Part One
Saturday 22 December 1979, 18.10-18.35,
6m / 100
Part Two
Saturday 29 December 1979, 17.50-18.15,
8.8m / 56
Part Three
Saturday 5 January 1980, 18.20-18.45, 9.8m / 40
Part Four
Saturday 12 January 1980, 18.05-18.35,
10.4m / 26
BBC Archive
All episodes exist as 625-line two-inch PAL colour master videotapes.
Novelization
Doctor Who and the Horns of Nimon by Terrance Dicks (111/13)
Hardback:
October 1980, WH Allen (0491022786 / Steve Kyte)
Paperback:
October 1980, Target (0426201310 / Steve Kyte)
Video
June 2003 (BBCV 7234 / Photomontage)
Music and Sound Effects
May 2000, *Doctor Who at the BBC Radiophonic Workshop: Volume 2 - New Beginnings 1970-1980*, CD (WMSF 6024-2 / Photographs)

Précis
On Skonnos, the bull-headed Nimons are ready to receive their young sacrifices...
Cast
Tom Baker (Doctor Who), Lalla Ward (Romana II), David Brierley (K-9 II Voice), Graham Crowden (Soldeed), Simon Gipps-Kent (Seth), Janet Ellis (Teka), Michael Osborne (Sorak), Bob Hornery (Pilot), Malcolm Terris (Co-Pilot), John Bailey (Sezom), Robin Sherringham, Bob Appleby, Trevor St John Hacker (Nimons), Clifford Norgate (Nimons' Voices)
Crew
Visual Effects Designer Peter Pegrum, *Visual Effects Assistants* George Reed, Dave Barton, Simon McDonald, *K-9 Operators* Nigel Brackley, Steve Cambden, *Electronic Effects* Dave Jervis, *Technical Manager* Derek Thompson, *Senior Cameraman* Alec Wheal, *Vision Mixer* James Gould, *Videotape Editor* Rod Waldron, *Studio Lighting* Nigel Wright, *Studio Sound* John Hartshorn, *Special Sound* Dick Mills, *Grams Operator* Gordon Phillipson, *Incidental Music* Dudley Simpson, *Costume Designer* June Hudson, *Costume Assistant* Roger Oldhamstead, *Make-Up Artist* Christine Walmesley-Cotham, *Make-Up Assistants* Francoise Cresson, Jenny Hughes, Christine Greenwood, *Designer* Graeme Story, *Design Assistant* Rorie Mitchell, *Production Unit Manager* John Nathan-Turner, *Production Assistant* Henry Foster, *Assistant Floor Manager* Rosemary Chapman, *Floor Assistant* Sally Bates, *Director's Assistant* Elizabeth Sherry, *Script Editor* Douglas Adams, *Producer* Graham Williams, *Director* Kenny McBain
DWM Index
72	Episode Guide
118	Anthony Read interview
168	Anthony Read interview
231	David Brierley interview
233	The John Nathan-Turner Memoirs
247	Archive Feature
278	Anthony Read interview
332	Video review
334	Janet Ellis interview

Recording Dates
24-26 September 1979 (TC3), 7-9 October 1979 (TC6)
Working Title
Horns of Nimon
Factoids
- *The Horns of Nimon* marked the final contributions for the following *Doctor Who* personnel: Graham Williams (producer), Douglas Adams (script editor), Dudley Simpson (incidental music composer) and

David Brierley (K-9 voice). It was also the last time that the Bernard Lodge title sequence and diamond logo was seen (until the 1999 spoof *The Curse of Fatal Death*), and the last outing for the Doctor's old costume and multicoloured scarf.

- *The Horns of Nimon* was inspired by the Greek legend of the Minotaur and his labyrinth. This is reflected in the choice of names: Seth (Theseus), Aneth (Athens), Skonnos (Knossos), Crinoth (Corinth) and the Nimon (Minotaur).
- Janet Ellis (Teka) went on to become a presenter of *Blue Peter* in the early 1980s and is the mother of pop star Sophie Ellis Bexter.
- Three Nimon costumes were built. The masks was made from thin fake leather, imported from Germany, stretched over a shell until it looked black and sweaty, with battery-powered glowing horns controlled by the wearer. The torso was a padded frame worn underneath a basic black bodysuit, with twelve-inch high platform sandals to make the creatures tower over the rest of the cast. Ballet dancers were hired to play them, but found it hard to move gracefully in the high platforms.
- Soldeed actor Graham Crowden is visibly seen to laugh during his death scene, but with studio time running out, a retake was not possible.

Comment
I find it impossible to dislike this story. It's the last gasp of the 1970s, a time when good storytelling and a light-hearted script was enough to provide four episodes of simple pleasure. It's nowhere near as bad as reputation suggests - in fact, some of it is rather *good* - and Tom Baker has given far worse performances than he gives here. It's always interesting, amusing (intentionally or otherwise), and even, very occasionally, thought-provoking. But never dull. I personally find the Nimons quite effective, and it would take a heart of stone not to join in with Graham Crowden's laughter at his own comedy death scene. 81%

"Think of me as a paradox in an anomaly and get on with your tea." ~ Professor Chronotis

109) Shada
Douglas Adams

Serial Code: 5M
Original Transmission
Six parts, unfinished and untransmitted (mooted transmission dates: 19 January - 23 February 1980)
BBC Archive
All studio recordings exist as 625-line two-inch PAL colour master videotapes. The 16mm colour location film also survives, as does the 16mm colour film modelwork in private hands.
Novelization
None
Video
July 1992, with complete script, narrated by Tom Baker (BBCV 4814 / Photomontage)
Webcast
March 2003, six parts (BBCi/Big Finish)
Soundtrack
December 2003, Big Finish, expanded webcast, 2 x CDs (1844350398 / Clayton Hickman)
Précis
Scientist Skagra seeks a special book that will unlock the prison of Time Lord criminal Salyavin...
Cast
Tom Baker (Doctor Who), Lalla Ward (Romana II), David Brierley (K-9 II Voice), Christopher Neame (Skagra), Denis Carey (Professor Chronotis), Victoria Burgoyne (Clare Keightley), Daniel Hill (Chris Parsons), Gerald Campion (Wilkin), James Coombes (Krarg Voices), David Strong (Driver), Derek Pollitt (Caldera), John Hallett (Constable), Shirley Dixon (Ship Voice), Colin Thomas (Don), The St John's Choristers (Themselves)
Crew
Visual Effects Designer Dave Havard, *Visual Effects Assistants* Stuart Brisdon, Roger Turner, *K-9 Operators* Nigel Brackley, Steve Cambden, *Electronic Effects Operator* Dave Chapman, *Technical Manager* Tony Bate, *Senior Cameraman* Alec Wheal, *Vision Mixer* James Gould, *Studio Lighting* Mike Jefferies, *Studio Sound* John Hartshorn, *Film Cameraman* Fintan Sheehan, *Film Camera Assistant* Colin Chase, *Film Sound* Ron Blight, *Film Operations Manager* Ian Brindle, *Film Editor* Tariq Anwar, *Properties Buyer* Helen Mackenzie, *Grams Operator* Gordon Phillipson, *Costume Designer* Rupert Roxburghe-Jarvis, *Make-Up Artist* Kim Burns,

Make-Up Assistants Sinikka Ikaheimo, Blaize Bettinson, Kim Vines, Christine Greenwood, *Designer* Victor Meredith, *Design Assistant* Les McCallum, *Production Unit Managers* John Nathan-Turner (film), Kathleen Bidmead (studio), *Production Assistant* Ralph Wilton, *Assistant Floor Manager* Val McCrimmon, *Floor Assistant* Barbra Jones, *Director's Assistants* Jenny Doe, Olivia Bazalgette, *Script Editor* Douglas Adams, *Producer* Graham Williams, *Director* Pennant Roberts

DWM Index

81	Archive
88	Lalla Ward interview
92	Tom Baker interview
122	Pennant Roberts interview
189	Behind The Scenes
	Tom Baker interview
	On The *Shada* Trail
	Video review
231	David Brierley interview
233	The John Nathan-Turner Memoirs
251	Graham Williams interview
257	Christopher Bidmead interview
267	Archive Feature
313	Douglas Adams interview
330	Webcast studio report
335	Webcast review
341	Lalla Ward interview

Recording Dates
15-17, 19 October 1979 (Location filming), 22 October 1979 (EFS modelwork), 3-5 November 1979 (TC3)

Locations
King's Parade, Emmanuel College, The Backs, Clare Bridge, Bridge Street, Blackmoor Head Yard, St Edward's Passage, Botolph Lane, Silver Street, Trumpington Street, Portugal Place, Portugal Street, Trinity Lane, Garret Hostel Lane and Bridge, all Cambridge, Cambridgeshire; High Street and Grantchester Meadows, Grantchester, Cambridgeshire

Working Title
Sunburst

Factoids
- *Shada* was intended as the climax to Season 17, and the final story of script editor Douglas Adams and producer Graham Williams. Unfortunately, industrial action caused the second studio block to be cancelled. By the time the strike had finished on 1 December, *Doctor Who* was a low priority show for the BBC - instead, *The Morecambe and Wise Show* Christmas special was recorded in its place. Despite all the location filming having been done and the first studio block recorded, the story was formally abandoned on 10 December, although extracts from the Cambridge filming turned up in the 1983 special *The Five Doctors* (130).
- Five Krarg costumes were made from dark grey PVC slats sewn onto a fabric body. The heads was made from lighter-coloured slats so that a fire effect could be keyed onto them for the ending of Part Four.
- Part Two's bicycle chase was originally to have been filmed at night but industrial action prevented the lighting operator from being present, so it was rescheduled for a daytime shoot. The inclusion of the St John's Choristers singing 'Chattanooga Choo-Choo' was a last minute addition, Tom Baker being approached by a student asking if they could be involved.
- Twelve years later, a BBC video was released that featured the surviving studio and film footage, together with animated slides of the modelwork. Incidental music was provided by Keff McCulloch and special sound by Dick Mills, with Tom Baker recording a first person narration for the missing segments from the 'Behind the Sofa' *Doctor Who* exhibition at London's Museum of the Moving Image in February 1992.
- In May 2003, BBCi/Big Finish Productions released a webcast of the story in six 20-minute segments, adapted by Gary Russell. Paul McGann starred as the Doctor, accompanied by Lalla Ward and John Leeson in their original roles as Romana and K-9 respectively. Also featuring were James Fox (Chronotis), Andrews Sachs (Skagra), Melvyn Hayes (Wilkin), Susannah Harker (Claire), Sean Biggerstaff (Chris) and Hannah Gordon (Skagra's spaceship).
- Many of the concepts used in this story and *City of Death* (105) were reused by Douglas Adams for his 1987 novel *Dirk Gently's Holistic Detective Agency*.

Comment
Hard to judge properly on the basis of what's left, but a reading of the scripts for the later episodes indicate the story's ambitious concepts might have been beyond the resources of the production team and could have led to an unsatisfactory finish to the season. As it is, we'll never know. But the story is clever, Baker and Ward are lovely together, the Cambridge setting is utterly charming and the dialogue sparkles. Just try and ignore the over-emphatic music on the video release. **75%**

Season 18

"Don't worry, ladies and gentlemen, everything is under control - or nearly everything." ~ *Pangol*

110) The Leisure Hive
David Fisher

Serial Code: 5N
Original Transmission
Part One
Saturday 30 August 1980, 18.15-18.40, 5.9m / 77
Part Two
Saturday 6 September 1980, 18.20-18.40, 5m / 103
Part Three
Saturday 13 September 1980, 17.55-18.20, 5m / 111
Part Four
Saturday 20 September 1980, 18.15-18.40, 4.5m / 111
BBC Archive
All episodes exist as 625-line two-inch PAL colour master videotapes.
Novelization
Doctor Who and the Leisure Hive by David Fisher (127/9)
Hardback:
WH Allen, July 1982 (0491027273 / Andrew Skilleter)
Paperback:
1. Target, July 1982 (0426201477 / Andrew Skilleter)
2. Target, October 1993, renamed *Doctor Who - The Leisure Hive* (0426201477 / Alister Pearson)
Non-Fiction Book
November 1980, Wayland, *A Day With a TV Producer* by Graham Rickard, Hardback (0853407932 / Photograph)
Video
January 1997 (BBCV 5821 / Colin Howard)
DVD
July 2004, isolated music score, optional Dolby 5.1 surround mix, trailer and continuity announcements, production subtitles, photo gallery, commentary by Lalla Ward, Lovett Bickford and Christopher H Bidmead (BBCDVD 1351 / Clayton Hickman)
Music and Sound Effects
1. October 1982, *Space Invaded: BBC Space Themes*, LP (REH 412 / Photograph)
2. March 1983, *Doctor Who - The Music*, LP (REH 462 / Iain McCaig)
3. March 1983, *Doctor Who - The Music*, cassette (ZCR 462 / Iain McCaig)
4. March 2002, *Doctor Who at the BBC Radiophonic Workshop: Volume 3: The Leisure Hive*, CD (WMSF 6052-2 / Photographs)
Précis
The leisure planet of Argolis is under threat from the scaly Foamasi...
Cast
Tom Baker (Doctor Who), Lalla Ward (Romana II), John Leeson (K-9 II Voice), Laurence Payne (Morix), David Haig (Pangol), John Collin (Brock), Ian Talbot (Klout), Adrienne Corri (Mena), Martin Fisk (Vargos), Nigel Lambert (Hardin), Roy Montague (Guide), David Allister (Stimson), Harriet Reynolds (Tannoy Voice), Clifford Norgate (Generator voice), Andrew Lane (Foamasi), Fred Redford (Earth Visitor Loman), Alys Dyer (Baby Pangol)
Crew
Visual Effects Designer Andrew Lazell, *Visual Effects Assistants* Stuart Brisdon, Perry Brahan, *K-9 Operator* Nigel Brackley, *Video Effects* Robin Lobb, *Technical Manager* Bob Hignett, *Senior Cameraman* Alec Wheal, *Vision Mixer* Paul del Bravo, *Videotape Editor* Rod Waldron, *Studio Lighting* Duncan Brown, *Studio Sound* John Howell, *Film Cameraman* Keith Burton, *Film Sound* Bill Chesneau, *Film Editor* Chris Wimble, *Properties Buyer* Tricia Ridell, *Special Sound* Dick Mills, *Grams Operator* Gordon Phillipson, *Incidental Music* Peter Howell, *Costume Designer* June Hudson, *Costume Assistant* Sarah Leigh, *Costume Assistant* Roger Oldhamstead, *Make-Up Artist* Dorka Nieradzik, *Make-Up Assistants* Lesley Holmes, Cathy Burczak, Benita Barrell, Sally Warren, Monica Lindford, Tina Baker, Nicola Bellamy, Sharon Broshett, *Designer* Tom Yardley-Jones, *Design Assistant* Steve Fawcett, *Production Unit Manager* Angela Smith, *Production Assistant* Romey Allison, *Assistant Floor Manager* Val McCrimmon, *Floor Assistant* Lydia Vaughn-Lake, *Director's Assistant* Carole Bisset, *Script Editor* Christopher Bidmead, *Executive Producer* Barry Letts, *Producer* John Nathan-Turner, *Director* Lovett Bickford
DWM Index
45	Preview
46	TV review
51	John Nathan-Turner interview
61	Behind the Scenes: Graphic Design
68	Dorka Nieradzik interview
72	Episode Guide
117	Archive + Fact File
154	David Fisher interview
177	Those *Radio Times*

185	June Hudson interview
	Change And Decay
191	Archive Feature
	Lovett Bickford interview
194	Peter Howell interview
195	Laurence Payne interview
234	The John Nathan-Turner Memoirs
247	Video review
257	Christopher H Bidmead interview
260	Vox Pops
269	David Fisher interview
318	Music CD review
345	Preview(DVD)
346	DVD review

Recording Dates
20-21 March 1980 (Location filming), 2-4 April 1980 (TC1), 18-20 April 1980 (TC3)

Locations
Brighton Beach, Brighton, East Sussex

Working Titles
The Argolins
Avalon

Factoids
- New producer John Nathan-Turner had been a Production Unit Manager on *Doctor Who* since *The Invisible Enemy* (93), but had worked as a Floor Assistant before that, his first assignment being the 1969 Patrick Troughton story *The Space Pirates* (49). Veteran *Doctor Who* producer Barry Letts was assigned to oversee Nathan-Turner's work on this season.
- A brand new title sequence was commissioned for *The Leisure Hive*. Designed by Sid Sutton, it used a more primitive version of the old 'slit scan' animated technique first seen on *The Time Warrior* (70). A 35mm rostrum camera would zoom slowly down to a backlit sheet of black acetate pricked with holes, and then be rewound and repeat the movement at a fractionally closer distance - thus creating the impression of stars sweeping past the viewer. Multiple exposures were used to split the new neon logo above and below the centre of the screen, in a style reminiscent of the ITV series *The Tomorrow People* (1973-79).
- A new arrangement of the theme music was conducted by Peter Howell of the BBC Radiophonic Workshop, replacing the *musique concrète* elements of the original score with a more obviously electronic arrangement.

- The Doctor's clothes received a major overhaul from June Hudson, replacing the changeable ensemble from previous seasons with a rigidly defined 'uniform'. Tom Baker now wore a burgundy overcoat (based on a 1914 Russian cavalry coat), a burgundy scarf, a shirt with question mark lapels, a velvet waistcoat, breeches, Argyll socks with brogues, and a burgundy trilby.
- A revolutionary new device called Quantel 5000 was first used in this serial. It enabled a pre-shot picture to be digitally manipulated in post-production. A notable use of this was when the camera appears to zoom back as the Tardis materialized in Part One, an effect impossible to achieve using the standard 'roll back and mix' approach.
- A new Tardis prop debuted in this story. Built out of fibreglass instead of wood, it replaced the one first built for *The Masque of Mandragora* (86) and featured a more authentically stacked roof section.
- Director Lovett Bickford chose to shoot most of his studio scenes using a start/stop single camera technique, rather than the traditional multi-camera set-up. This proved extremely time consuming and the story ran vastly over budget. Added to this, Bickford pruned his already tightly-paced narrative down even further in post-production, with Part Two coming in at just over 20 minutes in duration, a far cry from the 24'30" ideal running time.
- Most ITV regions ran the 'new' SF series *Buck Rogers in the 25th Century* (US premier: 20 September 1979) directly against *Doctor Who*, meaning that *The Leisure Hive* lost a third of its viewers compared to the previous season.

Comment
Doctor Who's 1980 makeover probably cost it several million casual viewers alienated by the new look. Although fans were blown away by it all, myself included, the wisdom of the idea, in hindsight, is debatable. Why change a popular format? Okay, so *The Leisure Hive* is a stunning tour-de-force of images accompanied by razor-sharp editing and a driving music score, but in casting off all the old cobwebs, it also loses a great deal of the charm and wit prevalent throughout the previous season. Cold, clinical and undeniably professional, *The Leisure Hive* is always worth watching, but under the gloss there is a hollowness that's hard to ignore. **79%**

"He sees the threads that join the Universe together and mends them when they break." ~ Zastor

111) Meglos
John Flanagan and Andrew McCulloch

Serial Code: 5Q
Original Transmission

Part One
Saturday 27 September 1980, 18.15-18.40,
5m / 105
Part Two
Saturday 4 October 1980, 18.15-18.40,
4.2m / 139
Part Three
Saturday 11 October 1980, 17.40-18.05,
4.7m / 129
Part Four
Saturday 18 October 1980, 17.45-18.05,
4.7m / 127
BBC Archive
All episodes exist as 625-line two-inch PAL colour master videotapes.
Novelization
Doctor Who - Meglos by Terrance Dicks (126 / 12)
Hardback:
February 1983, WH Allen (0491031505 / Andrew Skilleter)
Paperback:
1. May 1983, Target (0426201361 / Andrew Skilleter)
2. April 1993, Target (0426201361 / Alister Pearson)
Video
March 2003 (BBCV 7332 / Photomontage)
Music and Sound Effects
1. 1981, *Sci-Fi Sound Effects*, LP (REC 420 / Photomontage)
2. 1981, *Sci-Fi Sound Effects*, cassette (ZCM 420 / Photomontage)
3. March 1983, *Doctor Who - The Music*, LP (REH 462 / Iain McCaig)
4. March 1983, *Doctor Who - The Music*, cassette (ZCR 462 / Iain McCaig)
5. 1991, *Essential Science Fiction Sound Effects Volume 1*, CD (BBCCD 847 / Photomontage)
6. December 1992, Silva Screen, *Doctor Who - Earthshock*, CD (FILMCD 709 / Alister Pearson)
7. December 1992, Silva Screen, *Doctor Who - Earthshock*, cassette (FILMC 709 / Alister Pearson)
8. July 1993, *Doctor Who: 30 Years at the Radiophonic Workshop*, CD (BBCCD 871 / Photomontage)
9. May 1994, Silva Screen, *The Worlds of Doctor Who*, CD (FILMCD 715 / Alister Pearson)
10. March 2002, *Doctor Who at the BBC Radiophonic Workshop: Volume 3: The Leisure Hive*, CD (WMSF 6052-2 / Photographs)
11. March 2002, *Doctor Who at the BBC Radiophonic Workshop: Volume 4: Meglos and Full Circle*, CD (WMSF 6053-2 / Photographs)
Précis
On Tigella, the Doctor is accused of stealing the holy Dodecahedron relic...
Cast
Tom Baker (The Doctor/Meglos), Lalla Ward (Romana II), John Leeson (K-9 II Voice), Jacqueline Hill (Lexa), Crawford Logan (Deedrix), Edward Underdown (Zastor), Bill Fraser (General Grugger), Colette Gleeson (Caris), Frederick Treves (Lieutenant Brotadac), Christopher Owen (Earthling/Meglos Voice), Simon Shaw (Tigellan Guard)
Crew
Visual Effects Designer Steve Drewett, *Visual Effects Assistants* Mike Kelt, Roger Perkins, *K-9 Operators* Nigel Brackley, Steve Cambden, *Video Effects* Dave Jervis, *Technical Manager* Brendan Carr, *Senior Cameraman* Alec Wheal, *Vision Mixer* Graham Giles, *Videotape Editors* Ian Williams, Sam Upton, *Studio Lighting* Bert Postlethwaite, *Studio Sound* John Holmes, *Special Sound* Dick Mills, *Grams Operator* Andrew Hunter, *Incidental Music* Paddy Kingsland (1), Peter Howell (1-4), *Costume Designer* June Hudson, *Costume Assistant* Sarah Leigh, *Make-Up Artist* Cecile Hay-Arthur, *Make-Up Assistant* Catherine Whitefield, Margaret Magee, Jan Lee, Janet Philips, *Designer* Philip Lindley, *Design Assistant* Mary Greaves, *Production Unit Manager* Angela Smith, *Production Assistant* Marilyn Gold, *Assistant Floor Managers* Val McCrimmon, Karen Loxton, *Director's Assistants* Hermione Stewart, Alex Bridcut, *Floor Assistant* Alan Sandbrook, *Script Editor* Christopher H Bidmead, *Executive Producer* Barry Letts, *Producer* John Nathan-Turner, *Director* Terence Dudley
DWM Index
46	Preview
51	John Nathan-Turner interview
52	Season 18 review
72	Episode Guide
	Novelization review
105	Jacqueline Hill interview
185	Change And Decay
194	Peter Howell interview
205	Paddy Kingsland interview
234	The John Nathan-Turner Memoirs
257	Christopher H Bidmead interview

285 Archive Feature
318 CD review
328 Video review

Recording Dates
25-27 June 1980 (TC8), 10-12 July 1980 (TC3)

Working Titles
The Last Zolfa-Thuran
The Golden Star
The Golden Pentangle
The Golden Pentagram

Factoids
- Lexa was played by the actress Jacqueline Hill, who had portrayed one of the very first companions in *Doctor Who* - the schoolteacher Barbara Wright - in the first 16 stories.
- *Meglos* saw the first use of Scene-Sync, a technique developed in American in which two video cameras recording a composite image could, by means of an electronic link, track and tilt in unison. This had been attempted manually in the past with some success (*Day of the Daleks*, 60), although when the movement was not matched properly, the effect could be disorientating (*Horror of Fang Rock*, 92). The equipment was loaned to the *Doctor Who* production team for free as a trial run to iron out any problems prior to it being used for the BBC's big-budget (and critically derided) historical serial *The Borgias* (1981).
- Brotadac was a deliberate anagram for 'bad actor'.
- Peter Howell fell ill with flu while composing music for Part One, so fellow Radiophonic Workshop musician Paddy Kingsland took over to complete the score for that instalment. The remainder of the score was composed by Howell.
- As with the last three parts of *The Leisure Hive*, *Meglos*' final three parts ran several minutes short of the normal 25-minute slot. Parts Three and Four were moved forward to begin before the audience-grabbing ITV series *Buck Rogers in the 25th Century* in a bid to increase *Doctor Who*'s ratings. Unfortunately, this rescheduling did little to alter their downward trend.

Comment
Meglos is a queer beast. While the story itself is a gaudy, lightweight runaround of the style favoured by Season 17, the way it is presented on screen falls very much into the portentous, 'hard science' ethos of script editor Christopher H Bidmead's Season 18. The easiest way to view the serial is as a science-fiction take on the standard 'comedy thriller' cliché of mistaken identity caused by lookalike characters (for example, *Corpse!* by Gerald Moon). An ill-looking Tom Baker is clearly relishing playing the baddie; although in many instances during this season his Doctor persona is prone to bitterness, so the contrast is not as great as it could be. The guest cast are a faceless bunch, Bill Frazer excepted, while the production design is a mixture of the good (the Dodecahedron chamber) and the bad (the bell plants). The chief fault of the story is that having hit upon the concept of the Doctor's evil double, the writers don't really know where to take it. **60%**

"You can't fight Time Lords, Romana." ~ The Doctor

112) Full Circle
Andrew Smith

Serial Code: 5R
Original Transmission
Part One
Saturday 25 October 1980, 17.40-18.05, 5.9m / 106
Part Two
Saturday 1 November 1980, 17.40-18.05, 3.7m / 170
Part Three
Saturday 8 November 1980, 17.40-18.05, 5.9m / 115
Part Four
Saturday 15 November 1980, 17.40-18.05, 5.5m / 127
Repeat Transmission
Part One
Monday 3 August 1981, 18.30-18.55, 4.9m / 85
Part Two
Tuesday 4 August 1981, 18.20-18.45, 4.2m / 101
Part Three
Wednesday 5 August 1981, 18.20-18.45, 4.6 / 92
Part Four
Thursday 6 August 1981, 18.20-18.45, 6.4m / 60
BBC Archive
All episodes exist as 625-line two-inch PAL colour master videotapes.
Novelization
Doctor Who - Full Circle by Andrew Smith (123/13)
Hardback:
September 1982, WH Allen (0491027389 / Andrew Skilleter)

Paperback:
September 1982, Target (0426201507 / Andrew Skilleter)
Video
November 1997, as part of 'The E-Space Trilogy' [BBCV 6229 / Photomontage] with *State of Decay* and *Warriors' Gate* (BBCV 6230 / Photomontage)
Music and Sound Effects
1. 1981, *Sci-Fi Sound Effects*, LP (REC 420 / Photomontage)
2. 1981, *Sci-Fi Sound Effects*, cassette (ZCM 420 / Photomontage)
3. March 1983, *Doctor Who - The Music*, LP (REH 462 / Iain McCaig)
4. March 1983, *Doctor Who - The Music*, cassette (ZCR 462 / Iain McCaig)
5. 1991, *Essential Science Fiction Sound Effects Volume 1*, CD (BBCCD 847 / Photomontage)
6. December 1992, Silva Screen, *Doctor Who - Earthshock*, CD (FILMCD 709 / Alister Pearson)
7. December 1992, Silva Screen, *Doctor Who - Earthshock*, cassette (FILMC 709 / Alister Pearson)
8. July 1993, *Doctor Who: 30 Years at the Radiophonic Workshop*, CD (BBCCD 871 / Photomontage)
9. May 1994, Silva Screen, *The Worlds of Doctor Who*, CD (FILMCD 715 / Alister Pearson)
10. March 2002, *Doctor Who at the BBC Radiophonic Workshop: Volume 3: The Leisure Hive*, CD (WMSF 6052-2 / Photographs)
11. March 2002, *Doctor Who at the BBC Radiophonic Workshop: Volume 4: Meglos and Full Circle*, CD (WMSF 6053-2 / Photographs)
Viewmaster Slides
1981, GAF Corporation (3 reels, 21 pictures)
Précis
Sucked into E-Space, the Tardis lands on Alzarius where Mistfall is returning once more…
Cast
Tom Baker (Doctor Who), Lalla Ward (Romana II), John Leeson (K-9 II Voice), Matthew Waterhouse (Adric), George Baker (Login), James Bree (Nefred), Leonard Maguire (Draith), Tony Calvin (Dexeter), Richard Willis (Varsh), Bernard Padden (Tylos), Andrew Forbes (Omril), June Page (Keara), Alan Rowe (Garif), Adrian Gibbs (Rysik), Steve Kelly (Marsh Leader), Barney Lawrence, Graham Cole, Keith Guest, James Jackson, Stephen Watson, Stephen Calcutt (Marshmen), Norman Bacon (Marshchild), Stuart Fell (Stunt Double for Draith)
Crew
Visual Effects Designer John Brace, *Visual Effects Assistants* Steve Keates, Charles Jeanes, Simon Taylor, Simon McDonald, Charlie Lumm, *K-9 Operators* Nigel Brackley, Steve Cambden, *Video Effects* AJ Mitchell, *Technical Manager* Jeff Jeffery, *Senior Cameramen* Alan Kerridge, Reg Poulter, *Vision Mixer* Carol Johnson, *Videotape Editor* Rod Waldron, *Studio Lighting* Mike Jefferies, *Studio Sound* John Holmes, *Film Cameraman* Max Samett, *Film Camera Assistant* Ian Dabbs, *Film Sound* Mervyn Broadway, *Film Sound Assistant* Patricia Quirk, *Film Editor* Mike Houghton, *Properties Buyer* John Bush, *Special Sound* Dick Mills, *Grams Operator* James Cadman, *Incidental Music* Paddy Kingsland, *Costume Designer* Amy Roberts, *Make-Up Artist* Frances Needham, *Make-Up Assistants* Julie Shepherd, Caroline Gibbs, Eve Barker, Christine Vidler, *Designer* Janet Budden, *Design Assistant* Clare Tinsley, *Production Unit Manager* Angela Smith, *Production Assistant* Susan Box, *Assistant Floor Managers* Lynn Richards, Alex Bridcut, *Director's Assistant* Patricia Greenland, *Floor Assistant* Stephen Jones, *Script Editor* Christopher H Bidmead, *Executive Producer* Barry Letts, *Producer* John Nathan-Turner, *Director* Peter Grimwade

DWM Index
47	Preview
51	John Nathan-Turner interview
52	Season 18 review
53	Peter Grimwade interview
68	Novelization review
73	Episode Guide
118	Anthony Read interview
135	Archive + Fact File
152	Stuart Fell interview
177	Those *Radio Times*
185	Change And Decay
188	AJ Mitchell interview
202	Matthew Waterhouse interview
205	Paddy Kingsland interview
234	The John Nathan-Turner Memoirs
257	Christopher H Bidmead interview Video review
318	CD review
327	Archive Feature

Recording Dates
23-25 July 1980 (Location filming), 7-8 August 1980 (TC3), 21-23 August 1980 (TC6)
Locations
Black Park, Fulmer, Buckinghamshire
Working Title
The Planet That Slept
Factoids
- Exo-Space (E-Space) was the invention of script editor Christopher H Bidmead. He devised a theory that there were pockets of space that were 'charged vacuums' containing an infinite number of ever-

smaller universes one inside the other, like Russian Dolls. The Charged Vacuum Emboitment (CVE) was a gateway whereby one could travel into one of these 'pocket' universes. E-Space was much smaller than our own Universe, containing only two galaxies.
- Andrew Smith was only 18 years old when he submitted his storyline to Bidmead. Although he had submitted material to *Not The Nine O'Clock News* and radio shows *Week Ending* and *Naked Radio*, *Full Circle* would be his first work for television.
- The actor chosen to play new companion Adric was 17-year-old Matthew Waterhouse. Waterhouse was a member of the *Doctor Who* Appreciation Society and had no formal acting training. *Doctor Who* would be only his second television appearance, his debut being in two episodes of the acclaimed 13-part 1980 series *To Serve Them All My Days*. The name 'Adric' is an anagram of English physicist Paul Dirac.
- Eight Marshmen costumes were made for the serial, consisting of wetsuits covered with textured latex to suggest scales or seaweed. The heads were made from fibreglass and the actors wore surgical gloves and rubber slippers.
- Location filming at Black Park was enhanced by covering the vegetation with brightly coloured artificial flowers and illuminating scenes with arc lamps covered in red and green gels. Pigeons painted with non-toxic coloured paint were released for an establishing shot in Part One, while dry ice fanned by a wind machine represented the start of Mistfall by the lakeside.
- Various prop spiders were used, including one pulled along on nylon, a rod puppet that emerged from the river fruit at the end of Part Two, string puppets, and three models that appeared to walk along with the aid of a battery-powered Meccano mechanism (similar to Boris the Spider from *Planet of The Spiders*, 74).

Comment
One of the most polished scripts this season, *Full Circle* benefits enormously from Paddy Kingsland's emotive music score, Peter Grimwade's strong direction and the conviction of all the key performers. The filming at Black Park is luscious and helps portray a tangible sense of reality to the Terradonians' culture. There are some good shock moments, and the high concept plot-twist - although rushed in execution - is undeniably powerful. In a story full of good scenes, the Doctor's anger at Dexter's immoral experiments on the Marshchild stands out - indeed, its tragic ending provides one of the programme's few genuine moments of pathos. As to Matthew Waterhouse, he is no worse than the other young actors in his group, with Bernard Paddern as the steely Tylos the best of a bland bunch. The Part One cliffhanger is fantastic (although seen close-up, the Marshmen costumes leave a lot to be desired) and the story is dripping with atmosphere. **83%**

"This is no time for fairy tales." ~ *Romana II*

113) *State of Decay*
Terrance Dicks

Serial Code: 5P
Original Transmission
Part One
Saturday 22 November 1980, 17.40-18.05, 5.8m / 119
Part Two
Saturday 29 November 1980, 17.40-18.05, 5.3m / 136
Part Three
Saturday 6 December 1980, 17.40-18.05, 4.4m / 145
Part Four
Saturday 13 December 1980, 17.40-18.05, 5.4m / 125
BBC Archive
All episodes exist as 625-line two-inch PAL colour master videotapes.
Novelization
Doctor Who and the State of Decay by Terrance Dicks (125/14)
Hardback:
September 1981, WH Allen (0491029535 / Andrew Skilleter)
Paperback:
January 1982, Target (0426201337 / Andrew Skilleter)
Talking Book
1. June 1981, Pickwick International, 1 x cassette, abridged, read by Tom Baker (PTB 607 / Photograph)
2. 1985, Pickwick International, 2 x cassettes, abridged, read by Tom Baker (DTO 10517 / Photograph)

Video
November 1997, as part of 'The E-Space Trilogy' [BBCV 6229 / Photomontage] with *Full Circle* and *Warriors' Gate* (BBCV 6231 / Photomontage)
Music and Sound Effects
1. 1981, *Sci-Fi Sound Effects*, LP (REC 420 / Photomontage)
2. 1981, *Sci-Fi Sound Effects*, cassette (ZCM 420 / Photomontage)
3. 1991, *Essential Science Fiction Sound Effects Volume 1*, CD (BBCCD 847 / Photomontage)
Précis
A planet is ruled by vampires who are on the verge of resurrecting the Great Vampire himself…
Cast
Tom Baker (Doctor Who), Lalla Ward (Romana II), John Leeson (K-9 II Voice), Matthew Waterhouse (Adric), Emrys James (Aukon), William Lindsay (Zargo), Rachel Davies (Camilla), Clinton Greyn (Ivo), Iain Rattray (Habris), Thane Bettany (Tarak), Rhoda Lewis (Marta), Dean Allen (Karl), Arthur Hewlett (Kalmar), Stacy Davies (Veros), Stuart Fell (Roga), Stuart Blake (Zoldaz), Alan Chuntz (Stuntman/Guard), Chris Lawson (Hand of Great Vampire)
Crew
Fight Arranger Stuart Fell, *Stuntman* Alan Chuntz, *Visual Effects Designer* Tony Harding, *Visual Effects Assistants* Chris Lawson, Stuart Murdoch, *K-9 Operators* Nigel Brackley, Steve Cambden, Mat Irvine, *Video Effects* Dave Chapman, *Technical Manager* Errol Ryan, *Senior Cameraman* Alec Wheal, *Vision Mixers* Carol Johnson, Paul del Bravo, *Videotape Editor* Rod Waldron, *Studio Lighting* Bert Postlethwaite, *Studio Sound* John Howell, *Film Cameraman* Fintan Sheehan, *Film Sound* Bryan Showell, *Film Editor* John Lee, *Properties Buyer* Al Huxley, *Special Sound* Dick Mills, *Grams Operator* Gordon Phillipson, *Incidental Music* Paddy Kingsland, *Costume Designer* Amy Roberts, *Make-Up Artist* Norma Hill, *Make-Up Assistants* Lesley Smith, Charlotte Norman, Lesley Rouvrey, Sula Loizoo, Gail McAlee, Kim Vines, Cathy Burczak, *Designer* Christine Ruscoe, *Design Assistant* Sheelagh Lawson, *Production Unit Manager* Angela Smith, *Production Assistant* Rosalyn Wolfes, *Assistant Floor Manager* Lynn Richards, *Director's Assistant* Jane Wellesley, *Floor Assistant* Allison Stewart, *Script Editor* Christopher H Bidmead, *Executive Producer* Barry Letts, *Producer* John Nathan-Turner, *Director* Peter Moffatt
DWM Index
48 Preview
51 John Nathan-Turner interview
52 Season 18 review
73 Episode Guide
88 Lalla Ward interview
95 Terrance Dicks interview
107 Matthew Waterhouse interview
109 Christopher H Bidmead interview
185 Change And Decay
195 What The Papers Said
202 Matthew Waterhouse interview
205 Paddy Kingsland interview
234 The John Nathan-Turner Memoirs
253 Peter Moffatt interview
257 Christopher H Bidmead interview Video
272 Terrance Dicks interview
288 Archive Feature
340 Lalla Ward interview
Recording Dates
30 April-1 May 1980 (Location filming), 2 May 1980 (EFS), 15-16 May 1980 (TC3), 20-21 May 1980 (Visual Effects Studio modelwork), 29-31 May 1980 (TC6)
Location
Burnham Beeches, Burnham, Buckinghamshire
Working Titles
The Witch Lords
The Vampire Mutation
The Vampire Mutations
The Wasting
Factoids
- Under its original title of *The Witch Lords*, this vampire story was mooted as the opener for Season 15, but because the BBC were planning a prestigious adaptation of *Dracula*, it was hastily replaced by *Horror of Fang Rock* (92). When John Nathan-Turner took over as producer in December 1979, *The Witch Lords* was one of the few usable scripts available to him.
- Matthew Waterhouse's hair was cut short from having appeared in *To Serve Them All My Days* and so he wore a wig for this story.
- Tom Baker had become ill while on a trip to Australia and had grown worse since recording *The Leisure Hive* (110); his naturally curly hair had to be permed for this story. His relationship with Lalla Ward had broken down and they were no longer on speaking terms. (However, this state of affairs didn't last - they married on 13 December 1980). To compound the tense atmosphere, the inexperienced Matthew Waterhouse began giving acting tips to Baker, a fact that led to the star avoiding contact with him whenever possible.
- Stock film of bats was combined with mechanical toys, some of which were

pulled on wires. Questions were raised in the House of Lords about the serial's implication that bats were vampires, with complaints also received from the RSCPA and the Institute for Terrestrial Ecology.
- Two versions of the Great Vampire arising were recorded. One was provided by costume designer Amy Roberts, consisting of an actor wearing a wide cloak which was flapped by off-screen assistants. The second was a rod puppet with a two-feet wingspan operated by Tony Harding. The latter shot was chosen for its brief appearance in Part Four.

Comment
Like *Meglos*, *State of Decay* shows all the signs of being pulled in two different thematic directions. On the one hand, the story bears all the hallmarks of a standard Gothic horror tale circa Season 13; while on the other, the production team consistently try to downplay the more horrific aspects and provide wafer-thin scientific explanations for much of the action. The strong nature of the subject material usually wins over the technobabble, but there is a sense that the archetypal Hammer-influenced *State of Decay* has been inserted uneasily into a new format that now espouses scientific rationalism as its core belief. Thus the story never quite achieves the level of melodrama it so clearly needs and is left a pale shadow of what it should be. That said, individual elements are good - the Three Who Rule are beautifully stylised in look and movement, and there are some chilling revelations, such as the fuel tanks being full of blood - but the final result lacks coherence. **63%**

"Do nothing?" ~ Rorvik

114) Warriors' Gate
Steve Gallagher

Serial Code: 5S
Original Transmission
Part One
Saturday 3 January 1981, 17.20-17.45, 7.1m / 88
Part Two
Saturday 10 January 1981, 17.10-17.35, 6.7m / 93
Part Three
Saturday 17 January 1981, 17.10-17.35, 8.3m / 59
Part Four
Saturday 24 January 1981, 17.10-17.3, 7.8m / 69

BBC Archive
All episodes exist as 625-line two-inch PAL colour master videotapes. A 71 edit also exists for Part Two.
Novelization
Doctor Who and Warriors' Gate by John Lydecker [pen-name for Steve Gallagher] (124/0)
Hardback:
April 1982, WH Allen (049102746X / Andrew Skilleter)
Paperback:
April 1982, Target (0426201469 / Andrew Skilleter)
Non-Fiction Book
August 1986, Beaver Books, *Doctor Who Special Effects* by Mat Irvine (Hardback: 0091679206, Paperback: 0099426307 / Photomontage)
Video
November 1997, as part of 'The E-Space Trilogy' [BBCV 6229 / Photomontage] with *Full Circle* and *State of Decay* (BBCV 6232 / Photomontage)
Music and Sound Effects
1. 1981, *Sci-Fi Sound Effects*, LP (REC 420 / Photomontage)
2. 1981, *Sci-Fi Sound Effects*, cassette (ZCM 420 / Photomontage)
3. March 1983, *Doctor Who - The Music*, LP (REH 462 / Iain McCaig)
4. March 1983, *Doctor Who - The Music*, cassette (ZCR 462 / Iain McCaig)
5. 1991, *Essential Science Fiction Sound Effects Volume 1*, CD (BBCCD 847 / Photomontage)
6. December 1992, Silva Screen, *Doctor Who - Earthshock*, CD (FILMCD 709 / Alister Pearson)
7. December 1992, Silva Screen, *Doctor Who - Earthshock*, cassette (FILMC 709 / Alister Pearson)
8. July 1993, *Doctor Who: 30 Years at the Radiophonic Workshop*, CD (BBCCD 871 / Photomontage)
Précis
The Tardis lands in a shrinking white void next to the gateway into the normal Universe...
Cast
Tom Baker (Doctor Who), Lalla Ward (Romana II), John Leeson (K-9 II Voice), Matthew Waterhouse (Adric), Clifford Rose (Rorvik), Kenneth Cope (Packard), Freddie Earlle (Aldo), Harry Waters (Royce), Vincent Pickering (Sagan), David Weston (Biroc), Jeremy Gittins (Lazlo), David Kincaid (Lane), Robert Vowles, Derek Schafer, Pat Gorman, Carl More, George Gordon, Terry Sartaine, Brian Moorhead, Maurice Connor, John Blackman, Chris Michelle, Tony Pryor (Gundan), Mike Mungarvan (Kilroy), Marianne Lawrence (Servant), Mat Irvine (Double for Sagan), Simon Taylor (Double for Lazlo), Joe Santo, Carl Bohun,

Andy Hart, James Muir, Michael Gordon-Browne, Laurie Goode, Stephen Frost, Mark Arden (Tharils), Erika Spotswood (Child Tharil)

Crew
Visual Effects Designer Mat Irvine, *Visual Effects Assistants* Simon Taylor, Steve Lucas, Bryony Keating, *Visual Effects Cameraman* Eugene Carr, *K-9 Operator* Nigel Brackley, Mat Irvine, *Video Effects* Robin Lobb, *Technical Manager* John Dean, *Senior Cameraman* Alec Wheal, *Vision Mixers* Jim Stephens, Paul del Bravo, *Videotape Editor* Rod Waldron, *Studio Lighting* John Dixon, *Studio Sound* Alan Fogg, *Properties Buyer* Gill Meredith, *Special Sound* Dick Mills, *Grams Operator* Gerry Burrows, *Incidental Music* Peter Howell, *Costume Designer* June Hudson, *Costume Assistant* Sarah Leigh, *Make-Up Artist* Pauline Cox, *Make-Up Assistants* Lisa Pickering, Heather Squires, Helen Johnson, Wendy Holmes, Lesley Holmes, Penny Fergusson, Caroline Gibbs, Jan Lee, *Designer* Graeme Story, *Design Assistant* Roger Harris, *Production Unit Manager* Angela Smith, *Production Assistant* Graeme Harper, *Assistant Floor Manager* Val McCrimmon, *Director's Assistant* Joyce Stansfield, *Floor Assistants* Laura Gilbert, Kate Marshall, *Script Editor* Christopher H Bidmead, *Executive Producer* Barry Letts, *Producer* John Nathan-Turner, *Director* Paul Joyce

DWM Index
51   John Nathan-Turner interview
52   Season 18 review
59   Mat Irvine interview
73   Episode Guide
88   Lalla Ward interview
139   Archive + Fact File
        Stephen Gallagher interview
184   Graeme Harper interview
185   Change And Decay
194   Peter Howell interview
195   What The Papers Said
202   Matthew Waterhouse interview
234   The John Nathan-Turner interview
257   Christopher H Bidmead interview
295   Stephen Gallagher interview
315   Archive Feature

Recording Dates
1-2 September 1980 (Location photography), September 1980 (Visual Effects Studio modelwork), 24-26 September 1980 (TC6), 2-4 October 1980 (TC1)

Locations
Powis Castle, Welshpool, Powys, Wales

Working Titles
Dream Time
The Dream Time
Gateway

Factoids
- *Warriors' Gate* was a replacement for an abandoned storyline by science fiction author Christopher Priest entitled *Sealed Orders*. Fellow science fiction author Stephen Gallagher's new story was heavily influenced by the 1946 film *La Belle et la Bête* by French filmmaker Jean Cocteau. Gallagher's scripts were reworked by incoming director Paul Joyce and script editor Christopher H Bidmead, who attempted to emphasise the visual elements more.
- Director Paul Joyce was late delivering his camera plans, and studio time was lost when a dispute arose between Joyce and lighting engineer John Dixon about showing the studio lighting as part of the Privateer spaceship set. Problems were also caused by safety checks on the on-screen scaffolding, which had several loose bolts.
- The complex technical nature of the story and Joyce's slow working style, coupled with friction between the two co-stars, meant that the final studio day was very rushed, with production assistant Graeme Harper and producer John Nathan-Turner helping out to get all the material in the can.
- Quantel 5000 was used in post-production to superimpose an image of the Tardis onto Biroc's retina (actually a rotating balsawood model filmed against a dark background), add the spinning coin in Part One, and create a repeating 'trail' for the Tharils' journeys into the Time Winds.
- The Tharils were first called Tharks, before changing to Thars and then Tharls. Record producer and fan Ian Levine, an unofficial continuity adviser on the series, suggested this latter name might be confused with the Thals, blonde-haired opponents of the Daleks, and so a final change to Tharils was made just prior to recording.

Comment
At the time, *Warrior's Gate* was a slap in the face for anyone used to a cosy, linear narrative in *Doctor Who*. The first real story for the video age, repeated viewings are necessary to fully appreciate everything going on in this surreal and visually stunning story. The shrinking nature of the Gateway world, the flitting back and forth in

time via the mirrors and the subjugation of the Tharils are all fascinating concepts, which Paul Joyce makes the most of in his electrifying direction. However, unlike *Ghost Light* (154), it is still possible to enjoy the story without knowing exactly what's what, thanks to the accessible performances of the guest cast. Clifford Rose, fresh from playing a Nazi boss in *Secret Army* (1977-79), makes a wonderfully dysfunctional villain, and Kenneth Cope and David Kincaid share some pleasingly humorous banter. Never before have bog-standard spaceship crewmembers like these been given such characterful personas and it benefits the story enormously, allowing the viewer to get a handle on the strange dreamlike events that fill the narrative. The ending is a little cryptic though, and Romana and K-9's departure is far too rushed. While avoiding any mawkish sentiment, it also denies the viewer an emotive leaving scene, something that would have made the story more accessible and thus more memorable. Thought-provoking, visually gorgeous and at times disturbing (Lazlo's electrocution of Sagan is one of the most chilling images *Doctor Who* has ever thrown up), *Warriors' Gate* is a clever one-off. **84%**

"So - a new body...at last." ~ The Master

115) *The Keeper of Traken*
Johnny Byrne

Serial Code: 5T
Original Transmission
Part One
Saturday 31 January 1981, 17.10-17.35, 7.6m / 72
Part Two
Saturday 7 February 1981, 17.10-17.35, 6.1m / 106
Part Three
Saturday 14 February 1981, 17.10-17.35, 5.2m / 112
Part Four
Saturday 21 February 1981, 17.10-17.35, 6.1m / 103
Repeat Transmission
Part One
Monday 10 August 1981, 18.30-18.55, 5.2m / 71
Part Two
Tuesday 11 August 1981, 18.20-18.45, 4.4m / 93

Part Three
Wednesday 12 August 1981, 18.30-18.55, 5.2m / 71
Part Four
Thursday 13 August 1981, 18.20-18.45, 5m / 74
BBC Archive
All episodes exist as 625-line two-inch PAL colour master videotapes.
Novelization
Doctor Who and the Keeper of Traken by Terrance Dicks (124/12)
Hardback:
May 1982, WH Allen (0491027176 / Andrew Skilleter)
Paperback:
1. May 1982, Target (0426201485 / Andrew Skilleter)
2. June 1993, Target, renamed *Doctor Who - The Keeper of Traken* (0426201485 / Alister Pearson)
Video
June 1993 (BBCV 4973 / Andrew Skilleter)
Music and Sound Effects
1. 1981, *Sci-Fi Sound Effects*, LP (REC 420 / Photomontage)
2. 1981, *Sci-Fi Sound Effects*, cassette (ZCM 420 / Photomontage)
3. March 1983, *Doctor Who - The Music*, LP (REH 462 / Iain McCaig)
4. March 1983, *Doctor Who - The Music*, cassette (ZCR 462 / Iain McCaig)
5. 1991, *Essential Science Fiction Sound Effects Volume 1*, CD (BBCCD 847 / Photomontage)
6. December 1992, Silva Screen, *Doctor Who - Earthshock*, CD (FILMCD 709 / Alister Pearson)
7. December 1992, Silva Screen, *Doctor Who - Earthshock*, cassette (FILMC 709 / Alister Pearson)
Précis
On the peaceful world of Traken, a sinister statue spells disaster...
Cast
Tom Baker (Doctor Who), Matthew Waterhouse (Adric), Anthony Ainley (Tremas/The Master), Sarah Sutton (Nyssa), John Woodnutt (Seron), Denis Carey (The Keeper), Sheila Ruskin (Kassia), Anthony Ainley (Tremas), Margot Van Der Burgh (Katura), Robin Soans (Luvic), Roland Oliver (Neman), Geoffrey Beevers (Melkur Voice/The Master), Philip Bloomfield, Liam Prendergast (Fosters), Graham Cole (Melkur).
Crew
Visual Effects Designer Peter Logan, *Video Effects* Dave Chapman, *Technical Manager* Bob Hignett, *Senior Cameramen* Alec Wheal, Roger Fenner, *Vision Mixers* Carol Johnson, Nigel Finnis, Hilary Briegel, *Videotape Editor* Rod Waldron, *Studio Lighting* Don Babbage, *Studio Sound* John

Holmes, Alan Fogg, *Properties Buyer* Robert Fleming, *Special Sound* Dick Mills, *Grams Operators* Andrew Hunter, John Relph, *Incidental Music* Roger Limb, *Costume Designer* Amy Roberts, *Make-Up Artist* Norma Hill, *Make-Up Assistants* Christine Vidler, Sallie Jaye, Sally Warren, Vanessa Poulton, Diana Roberts, *Designer* Tony Burrough, *Design Assistant* Jane Clement, *Production Unit Manager* Angela Smith, *Production Assistant* Alan Wareing, *Assistant Floor Manager* Lynn Richards, *Director's Assistant* Jean Davis, *Floor Assistants* Laura Gilbert, Jacqueline Morrish, *Script Editor* Christopher H Bidmead, *Executive Producer* Barry Letts, *Producer* John Nathan-Turner, *Director* John Black

DWM Index

50	Preview
51	John Nathan-Turner interview
52	Season 18 review
66	Sarah Sutton interview
73	Episode Guide
107	Matthew Waterhouse interview
	Archive + Fact File
109	Christopher H Bidmead interview
169	Johnny Byrne interview
	A Producer's Eye: John Nathan-Turner
177	Those *Radio Times*
181	John Woodnutt interview
185	Change And Decay
196	Roger Limb interview
201	Video review
202	Matthew Waterhouse interview
234	The John Nathan-Turner Memoirs
236	Archive Feature
	Sheila Ruskin interview
258	Christopher H Bidmead interview
311	Geoffrey Beevers interview

Recording Dates
5-7 November 1980 (TC6), 21-23 November 1980 (TC8), 17 December 1980 (TC6)

Working Title
As broadcast

Factoids
- It was producer John Nathan-Turner's idea to bring back the Master, last seen in wizened form in *The Deadly Assassin* (88). The character was written into Byrne's original script, with Hellas renamed Tremas, an anagram of 'Master'. Continuity was maintained with the earlier serial by reusing the Master's cadaverous mask, albeit with the fake eyes removed, while the grandfather clock was the same prop, its interior modified to allow actors to get in and out.
- Anthony Ainley was chosen to play the final regeneration of the Master by John Nathan-Turner who recalled him appearing as Emelius in the BBC's 1974 adaptation of *The Pallisers* by Anthony Trollope, a series the producer had previously worked on. Ainley had also appeared in *Elizabeth R* (1971), *Target* (1977-78) - overseen by former *Doctor Who* producer Philip Hinchcliffe - and films such as *Oh What a Lovely War* (1969) and *The Land That Time Forgot* (1974).
- 18-year-old Sarah Sutton, playing Nyssa, had also appeared in *Alice Through the Looking Glass* (1973) and *The Moon Stallion* (1978), both produced by the BBC. One of her mooted characteristics was that would have a sixth sense, almost like ESP, but this was never seen on screen.
- The Melkur statue was made of moulded plastic. Its design was inspired by a 1913 Futurist sculpture entitled 'Unique Forms of Continuity in Space' by Umberto Boccioni.
- Peter Logan had planned and rehearsed a tornado effect for the climactic scenes in Part Four in which the Source becomes unstable, using the same water whirlpool device as seen in *The Masque of Mandragora* (86) filled with polystyrene chips. Unfortunately this broke down before recording, and there wasn't enough time to repair it. In the final sequence, the actors crept along the floor while wind-machines blew debris around the set.

Comment
Stylistically, this is a beautiful, if rather artificial-looking, production that owes much to the early Hartnell days of exploring exotic worlds and meeting well-defined historical cultures. Most alien worlds seen in recent years of the programme had been dangerous places, but here is a quiet, peaceful haven slowly overpowered by an inexplicable decay. It is the ideal backdrop to Byrne's powerful evocation of the insidious reality of evil, the staginess of the production somehow adding to the metaphorical nature of the narrative. In this sense, the theatricality of the opening prologue suits the story perfectly. The introduction of the Master is done with much style and integrity and it is good to see Anthony Ainley delivering a performance of some depth and subtlety before his character is taken over by the evil Time Lord and he is forced to ham it up for the rest of his *Doctor Who* career. Sarah Sutton also exhibits great charm as waiflike soon-to-be companion Nyssa. **80%**

"The Universe is hanging on a thread..." ~ The Master

116) Logopolis
Christopher H Bidmead

Serial Code: 5V
Original Transmission
Part One
Saturday 28 February 1981, 17.10-17.35, 7.1m / 84
Part Two
Saturday 7 March 1981, 17.10-17.35, 7.7m / 57
Part Three
Saturday 14 March 1981, 17.10-17.35, 5.8m / 102
Part Four
Saturday 21 March 1981, 17.10-17.35, 6.1m / 97
Repeat Transmission
On BBC2 as part of 'The Five Faces of Doctor Who':
Part One
Monday 30 November 1981, 17.40-18.05, 5.5m / 11
Part Two
Tuesday 1 December 1981, 17.35-18.00, 5m / 15
Part Three
Wednesday 2 December 1981, 17.40-18.05, 6m / 7
Part Four
Thursday 3 December 1981, 17.40-18.05, 5.4m / 12
BBC Archive
All episodes exist as 625-line two-inch PAL colour master videotapes.
Novelization
Doctor Who - Logopolis by Christopher H Bidmead (127/12)
Hardback:
October 1982, WH Allen (0491028571 / Andrew Skilleter)
Paperback:
1. October 1982, Target (0426201493 / Andrew Skilleter)
2. December 1991, Target (0426201493 / Alister Pearson)
Video
March 1992 (BBCV 4736 / Andrew Skilleter)
Music and Sound Effects
1. 1981, *Sci-Fi Sound Effects*, LP (REC 420 / Photomontage)
2. 1981, *Sci-Fi Sound Effects*, cassette (ZCM 420 / Photomontage)
3. 1991, *Essential Science Fiction Sound Effects Volume 1*, CD (BBCCD 847 / Photomontage)
4. December 1992, Silva Screen, *Doctor Who - Earthshock*, CD (FILMCD 709 / Alister Pearson)
5. December 1992, Silva Screen, *Doctor Who - Earthshock*, cassette (FILMC 709 / Alister Pearson)
6. July 1993, *Doctor Who: 30 Years at the Radiophonic Workshop*, CD (BBCCD 871 / Photomontage)
7. May 1994, Silva Screen, *The Worlds of Doctor Who*, CD (FILMCD 715 / Alister Pearson)
Précis
The Doctor goes to Logopolis to repair the Tardis but finds the Universe is on the point of collapse...
Cast
Tom Baker, Peter Davison (Doctor Who), Matthew Waterhouse (Adric), Sarah Sutton (Nyssa), Janet Fielding (Tegan Jovanka), Anthony Ainley (The Master), Dolore Whiteman (Aunt Vanessa), Tom Georgeson (Detective Inspector), John Fraser (The Monitor), Adrian Gibbs (Watcher), Christopher Hurst (Security Guard), Ray Knight (Policeman with Bicycle), Robin Squire (Pharos Technician)
Crew
Visual Effects Designer John Horton, *Video Effects* Dave Chapman, *Technical Manager* Terry Brett, *Senior Cameraman* Reg Poulter, *Vision Mixer* Carol Johnson, *Videotape Editor* Rod Waldron, *Studio Lighting* Henry Barber, *Studio Sound* John Holmes, *Film Cameraman* Peter Hall, *Film Camera Assistant* John Daly, *Film Sound* Jim McAlister, *Film Sound Assistant* Tim Humphries, *Film Editor* Paul Humfress, *Properties Buyer* John Stevens, *Special Sound* Dick Mills, *Grams Operator* Gordon Phillipson, *Incidental Music* Paddy Kingsland, *Costume Designer* June Hudson, *Make-Up Artist* Dorka Nieradzik, *Make-Up Assistants* Blaize Bettinson, Demelza Rogers, Viv Riley, Karen Waite, Karen Turner, Suzanne O'Mahoney, Sarah Grispo, Jayne Buxton, Charlotte Norman, *Designer* Malcolm Thornton, *Design Assistant* Jo Day, *Production Manager* Margot Hayheo, *Production Associate* Angela Smith, *Assistant Floor Manager* Val McCrimmon, *Director's Assistant* Patricia Greenland, *Floor Assistant* Sandra Wynne, *Script Editor* Christopher H Bidmead, *Executive Producer* Barry Letts, *Producer* John Nathan-Turner, *Director* Peter Grimwade
DWM Index
51	Preview
53	TV review
	Peter Grimwade interview
58	'The Five Faces of Doctor Who' feature
60	Season 18 review
68	Dorka Nieradzik interview

73	Episode Guide
80	Andrew Skilleter interview
91	Janet Fielding interview
107	Matthew Waterhouse interview
109	Christopher Bidmead interview
	Novelization review
	Archive + Fact File
110	Sarah Sutton interview
180	Tom Baker interview
185	Video review
	June Hudson interview
	Change And Decay
202	Matthew Waterhouse interview
205	Paddy Kingsland interview
218	Sarah Sutton interview
234	The John Nathan-Turner interview
257	Archive Feature
258	Christopher H Bidmead interview
353	Janet Fielding interview

Recording Dates
16 December 1980 (Location filming), 18 December 1980 (Location filming), 22 December 1980 (Location filming), 8-9 January 1981 (TC3), 22-24 January 1981 (TC6)

Locations
43 Ursula Street, Battersea, London SW11; Albert Bridge, Kensington and Chelsea, London SW3; Cadogan Pier, Chelsea, London SW3; BBC Receiving Station, Blountscourt Road, Sonning Common, Berkshire; Lay-by, A413, Denham, Buckinghamshire

Working Title
As broadcast

Factoids
- Tegan's surname came about as a misunderstanding between Christopher H Bidmead and John Nathan-Turner. Bidmead wasn't sure whether to call the character Tegan or Jovanka, so had written "Tegan (Jovanka)" - on seeing this, the producer assumed that this was her full name. Actress Janet Fielding (real name Janet Mahoney) was one of 109 hopefuls to be seen for the role. She lied about her age, claiming to be 20 instead of 23, and said that her height of five feet two would qualify her as an air stewardess on Qantas and other Eastern airlines (it wouldn't).
- Location filming was to have been conducted along the Barnet Bypass on the A6 near South Mimms because it still boasted a genuine Police Box. In the event, the box had been demolished by the time production manager Margot Hayhoe visited the site, and so filming was relocated to a similar lay-by on the A134. The old Police Box prop, last seen in *The Horns of Nimon* (108) was dusted off and used as the supposedly real item, next to which the new prop was seen to dematerialize.
- The Watcher was explained by Bidmead as being the Doctor's next body brought into being as a partially formed, embryonic figure triggered by the impending cataclysm brought about by the Master and forewarned by the sounding of the Tardis cloister bell. Adrian Gibbs - who had previously played Rysik in *Full Circle* (112) - was chosen to play this non-speaking character, wearing a cobweb-covered latex rubber mask and a costume made of white bandaging which gave the figure an unfinished, half-formed appearance.
- Logopolis itself was a large tabletop model sculpted to look like the surface of a brain. To emphasise the Logopolitans' mathematical skills, wedge-shaped brain appliances were attached to the back of the actors' heads.
- Two extensive flashback sequences were edited on 3 January 1981 to be shown during the Fourth Doctor's final moments of life in Part Four. The enemies sequence was as follows: The Master (*The Deadly Assassin*), a Dalek (*Destiny of the Daleks*), the Captain (*The Pirate Planet*), the Cyberleader (*Revenge of the Cybermen*), Davros (*Genesis of the Daleks*), Stor (*The Invasion of Time*), Broton (*Terror of the Zygons*) and the Black Guardian (*The Armageddon Factor*). For the companions sequence, the following were used: Sarah Jane Smith (*Terror of the Zygons*), Harry Sullivan (*The Sontaran Experiment*), Brigadier Lethbridge-Stewart (*Invasion of the Dinosaurs*), Leela (*The Robots of Death*), K-9 (*The Armageddon Factor*), Romana (*The Stones of Blood*) and Romana II (*Full Circle*).
- Part Four's closing titles were altered so that Tom Baker's face was hidden by stars.

Comment
The culmination of Christopher H Bidmead's scientific rationalism, *Logopolis* remains a milestone in the series' evolution. It manages to be dramatic and exciting despite exploiting a number of abstract concepts and possessing a dearth of conventional plotting. It comes as a surprise to find that Tom Baker and Matthew Waterhouse work very well together in Part One, but less successful is Tegan's debut, in which she appears rather condescending. Nyssa's inclusion

also seems somewhat unnecessary, her presence merely cluttering an already companion-heavy narrative. Anthony Ainley is already a little melodramatic, although not as much as he would become in later stories. But the story is really Tom Baker's. He gives a faultless performance, swinging from doomladen prophecies to insouciant aphorisms in the twinkling of an eye. His 'death scene', although somewhat clinically executed, hits all the right notes and provides an atypically emotive ending to this most apocalyptic of stories. Indeed, considering the nature of the threat - the end of the Universe as we know it - subsequent stories seem merely like a coda to the main event. **94%**

Fifth Doctor: Peter Davison

Season 19

"If we could cook your memories, Ruther, we should feast indeed." ~ *Shardovan*

117) *Castrovalva*
Christopher H Bidmead

Serial Code: 5Z
Original Transmission
Part One
Monday 4 January 1982, 18.55-19.20, 9.1m / 54
Part Two
Tuesday 5 January 1982, 19.00-19.25, 8.6m / 84
Part Three
Monday 11 January 1982, 18.55-19.20, 10.2m / 47
Part Four
Tuesday 12 January 1982, 19.05-19.30, 10.4m / 46
BBC Archive
All episodes exist as 625-line two-inch PAL colour master videotapes.
Novelization
Doctor Who - Castrovalva by Christopher H Bidmead (118/12)
Hardback:
March 1983, WH Allen (0491033303 / Photograph)
Paperback:
1. June 1983, Target (0426193261 / Photograph)
2. June 1991, Target (0426193261 / Alister Pearson)

Video
March 1992 (BBCV 4737 / Andrew Skilleter)
Music and Sound Effects
1990, Julian Knott, *Doctor Who - The Corridor of Eternity*, cassette (JPD1)
Viewmaster Slides
April 1983, View-Master International (3 reels, 21 pictures)
Précis
The new Doctor hides out in the seemingly restful hillside town of Castrovalva...
Cast
Peter Davison (The Doctor), Matthew Waterhouse (Adric), Janet Fielding (Tegan), Sarah Sutton (Nyssa), Anthony Ainley (Portreeve/The Master), Dallas Cavell (Head of Security), Michael Sheard (Mergrave), Derek Waring (Shardovan), Frank Wylie (Ruther), Souska John (Child), Harry Fielder, Kenneth Lawrie (Security Guards), Peter Roy, Derek Matt (Ambulance Men), David Ellis (Ambulance Driver), Ken Barker (Stunt Double for Shardovan), Stuart Fell (Stuntman/Castrovalvan Warrior)
Crew
Visual Effects Designer Simon McDonald, *Visual Effects Assistants* Malcolm James, Ron Thornton, George Reed, *Graphic Designer* Ian Hewitt, *Video Effects* Dave Chapman, *Technical Manager* Clive Gulliver, *Senior Cameraman* Alec Wheal, *Vision Mixer* Carol Johnson, *Videotape Editor* Rod Waldron, *Studio Lighting* Ron Bristow, *Studio Sound* Laurie Taylor, *Film Cameraman* John Baker, *Film Sound* Jim McAlister, *Film Editors* Mike Houghton, Robin Jackman, *Properties Buyer* Helen MacKenzie, *Special Sound* Dick Mills, *Grams Operator* John Downes, *Incidental Music* Paddy Kingsland, *Costume Designer* Odile Dicks-Mireaux, *Dressers* Liz Dixon, Tim Williamson, Ray Greenhill, *Make-Up Artist* Marion Richards, *Make-Up Assistants* Sula Loizou, Marilyn MacDonald, Lucie Wiles, Charlotte Norman, Lesley Bond, *Designer* Janet Budden, *Design Assistant* Rod McLean, *Production Manager* Margot Hayheo, *Production Associate* Angela Smith, *Production Assistant* Olivia Cripps, *Assistant Floor Manager* Renny Tasker, *Director's Assistant* Sarah Woodside, *Script Editor* Eric Saward, *Producer* John Nathan-Turner, *Director* Fiona Cumming
DWM Index
61   Preview
63   TV review
64   Janet Fielding interview
66   Sarah Sutton interview
68   John Nathan-Turner interview
69   Season Survey results

72	Imagineering interview
74	Episode Guide
90	Archive + Fact File
91	Janet Fielding interview
107	Matthew Waterhouse interview
109	Christopher H Bidmead interview
	Novelization review
110	Sarah Sutton interview
129	Fiona Cumming interview
152	Ken Barker interview
173	Fiona Cumming interview
182	Those *Radio Times*
185	Video review
	Change And Decay
196	What The Papers Said
202	Matthew Waterhouse interview
205	Paddy Kingsland interview
213	Peter Davison interview
214	Janet Fielding interview
235	The John Nathan-Turner Memoirs
258	Christopher H Bidmead interview 1
	Archive Feature
259	Christopher H Bidmead interview 2
302	Michael Sheard interview
346	Eric Saward interview

Recording Dates
1-4 September 1981 (Location filming), 15-16 September 1981 (TC3), 29 September-1 October 1981 (TC6)

Locations
Crowborough Wireless Telegraph Station, Duddleswell, East Sussex; Buckhurst Park, Hartfield, East Sussex; Harrison's Rocks, Groombridge, Tunbridge Wells, East Sussex

Working Title
The Visitor

Factoids
- 29-year-old Peter Davison (real name Peter Moffat) was cast in October 1980. His cricketing image was thought up by producer John Nathan-Turner, with the actual costume being designed by Colin Lavers as part of his work on *Four to Doomsday* (118). The question mark collars were retained from Tom Baker's costume, while it was Nathan-Turner who dreamt up the celery fixed to his lapel.
- *Castrovalva* was recorded fourth but shown first, in order to allow Peter Davison to feel his way into the part before his television debut.
- *Doctor Who* was shifted to a bi-weekly slot from this story until the end of Season 21. The reasons were twofold: the programme had had disastrous ratings when it was shown in the traditional Saturday teatime slot the previous year, and the BBC wanted to use the show to test which week nights would be most successful for airing a home-created soap opera, namely *EastEnders*. Despite fierce opposition from many quarters, the viewing figures were double those of the previous season.
- The visual look for the story came from producer John Nathan-Turner. He had often been distracted by monochrome prints of Dutch artist MC Escher (1898-1972) hanging in the office of Graeme McDonald, Head of Serials at the BBC. One, *Ascending and Descending* (1960), showed an eternally looping flight of stairs, tying in with the recursive and illusory nature of Bidmead's story. The title was subsequently lifted directly from a 1930 picture, *Castrovalva*, showing a walled town on the edge of a steep cliff. Other images that inspired the disorientating nature of the town were *Up and Down* (1947), *Relativity* (1953), *Convex and Concave* (1955) and *Belvedere* (1958).
- Part One began with a pre-title sequence, a revised version of the closing moments of *Logopolis*. The first time this technique had been used on *Doctor Who*, it would be featured extensively from Season 27 onwards.
- To keep the Master's disguise secret, the role of Portreeve was credited to 'Neil Toynay', an anagram of Tony Ainley.

Comment
Whilst *Logopolis* was a concept-heavy drama, *Castrovalva* seems far more of an aimless runaround. The direction is limp and Paddy Kingsland's music, although harmonious enough, is stylistically too similar to test card music to add much excitement. Part One appears to be 100% padding, and the story - such as it is - only really gets going in Part Three. In terms of plot, the idea of the Master fabricating a whole alien culture just to trap the Doctor seems faintly ludicrous, especially as he already had a seemingly foolproof method of despatch by sucking the Tardis back to the (feebly realized) Big Bang. On the positive side, Peter Davison gives one of his very best performances as the Doctor here, creating a wonderful picture of a man with the heart and mind of a child but the brain of a frustrated genius. The studio sets for Castrovalva are fabulous, but the split-screen effects as the town breaks down are, it has to be said, pretty rubbish. All in all, a shaky start for this promising new Doctor. **55%**

"We've got to get off this ship. We must, or we'll all die!" ~ Tegan

118) Four To Doomsday
Terence Dudley

Serial Code: 5W
Original Transmission
Part One
Monday 18 January 1982, 18.55-19.20, 8.4m / 66
Part Two
Tuesday 19 January 1982, 19.05-19.30, 8.8m / 61
Part Three
Monday 25 January 1982, 18.55-19.30, 8.9m / 63
Part Four
Tuesday 26 January 1982, 19.05-19.30, 9.4m / 53
BBC Archive
All episodes exist as 625-line two-inch PAL colour master videotapes.
Novelization
Doctor Who - Four to Doomsday by Terrance Dicks (128/12)
Hardback:
April 1983, WH Allen (0491034504 / Photomontage)
Paperback
1. July 1983, Target (0426193342 / Photomontage)
2. June 1991, Target (0426193342 / Alister Pearson)
Video
September 2001 (BBCV 7134 / Photomontage)
Précis
The froglike alien Monarch is planning to travel back in time to meet himself and become God…
Cast
Peter Davison (The Doctor), Janet Fielding (Tegan), Sarah Sutton (Nyssa), Matthew Waterhouse (Adric), Stratford Johns (Monarch), Paul Shelley (Persuasion), Annie Lambert (Enlightenment), Philip Locke (Bigon), Burt Kwouk (Lin Futu), Illarrio Bisi Pedro (Kurkutji), Nadia Hammam (Villagra).
Crew
Fight Arranger BH Barry, *Choreographer* Sue Lefton, *Visual Effects Designer* Mickey Edwards, *Video Effects* Dave Chapman, *Technical Manager* Robert Hignett, *Senior Cameraman* Alec Wheal, *Vision Mixer* Carol Johnson, *Videotape Editor* Rod Waldron, *Studio Lighting* Don Babbage, *Studio Sound* Alan Machin, *Properties Buyer* Helen MacKenzie, *Special Sound* Dick Mills, *Grams Operator* Gordon Phillipson, *Incidental Music* Roger Limb, *Costume Designer* Colin Lavers, *Make-Up Artist* Dorka Nieradzik, *Designer* Tony Burrough, *Design Assistant* Jane Clement, *Production Manager* Henry Foster, *Production Associate* Angela Smith, *Production Assistant* Jean Davis, *Assistant Floor Manager* Val McCrimmon, *Floor Assistant* Ian Strachan, *Script Editor* Antony Root, *Producer* John Nathan-Turner, *Director* John Black
DWM Index
61	Preview
64	TV review
68	John Nathan-Turner interview
	Dorka Nieradzik interview
74	Episode Guide
91	Janet Fielding interview
106	Peter Davison interview
108	Matthew Waterhouse interview
196	What The Papers Said
	Roger Limb interview
202	Matthew Waterhouse interview
213	Peter Davison interview
	Archive Feature
235	The John Nathan-Turner Memoirs
271	Antony Root interview
308	Video review

Recording Dates
13-15 April 1981 (TC6), 28-30 April 1981 (TC6)
Working Title
Day of Wrath
Factoids
- This was Peter Davison's first recorded story, but the second to be transmitted. By this time, Barry Letts' executive producership was virtually over and this was the final story to which he would contribute (in an uncredited capacity).
- The space walk sequence used five separate images blended with Quantel 5000 and CSO. A post-production effect was added to show a red spot (the Doctor's cricket ball) arcing through space and bouncing off Monarch's ship.
- Unusually, shots of Monarch's spaceship (a six-foot-long model designed by props firm Unit 22) were recorded on video in the studio, rather than in advance on film.
- Peter Davison's first press photocall in costume was held on 15 April 1981 (before recording commenced on the third studio day), in a park at the rear of BBC Television Centre.
- Script editor Antony Root was on a three-month secondment to the programme and worked on only two stories: this one and *The Visitation* (120). He received a token credit on *Earthshock* (122) to avoid Saward being credited twice.

Comment
Tony Burrough's magnificent sets are the star of this show. If there is a plot, it is hidden behind a wall of technobabble and monotonous scenes of ethnic dancing (where were the Morris Dancers, I'd like to know?). Davison's debut performance is fine, although his voice is rather more high-pitched than in other stories. As to his companions, their dialogue and body language is distinctly wooden, but Stratford Johns makes the most of his gargantuan villain and Paul Shelley can always be counted on to 'do' snide well. On the production side, the music is ghastly and the video effects are poor (except the Monopticon, which is very convincing), and the whole story lacks impetus. **45%**

"An apple a day keeps the er…no, never mind." ~ The Doctor

119) Kinda
Christopher Bailey

Serial Code: 5Y
Original Transmission
Part One
Monday 1 February 1982, 18.55-19.20, 8.4m / 78
Part Two
Tuesday 2 February 1982, 19.05-19.30, 9.4m / 45
Part Three
Monday 8 February 1982, 18.55-19.20, 8.5m / 67
Part Four
Tuesday 9 February 1982, 19.05-19.30, 8.9m / 56
Repeat Transmission
Part One
Monday 22 August 1983, 18.25-18.50, 4.2m / 96
Part Two
Tuesday 23 August 1983, 18.25-18.50, 4.3m / 91
Part Three
Wednesday 24 August 1983, 18.35-19.00, 3.9m / 103
Part Four
Thursday 25 August 1983, 18.30-18.55, 5m / 107
BBC Archive
All episodes exist as 625-line two-inch PAL colour master videotapes.
Novelization
Doctor Who - Kinda by Terrance Dicks (126/12)

Hardback:
December 1983, WH Allen (0491031211 / Photomontage)
Paperback:
1. March 1984, Virgin (0426195299 / Photomontage)
2. February 1992, Virgin (0426195299 / Alister Pearson)
Non-Fiction Book
November 1983, Macmillan, '*Kinda*: Conditions of Production and Performance' in *Doctor Who - The Unfolding Text* by John Tulloch and Manuel Alvarado, Paperback (0330348486 / Photograph and cartoon)
Talking Book
August 1997, 1 x cassette, abridged, read by Peter Davison (ZBBC 1770 / Photomontage)
Video
October 1994 (BBCV 5432 / Colin Howard)
Music and Sound Effects
1. March 1983, *Doctor Who - The Music*, LP (REH 462 / Iain McCaig)
2. March 1983, *Doctor Who - The Music*, cassette (ZCR 462 / Iain McCaig)
3. December 1992, Silva Screen, *Doctor Who - Earthshock*, CD (FILMCD 709 / Alister Pearson)
4. December 1992, Silva Screen, *Doctor Who - Earthshock*, cassette (FILMC 709 / Alister Pearson)
Précis
There's a particularly deadly serpent in the paradise world of Deva Loka…
Cast
Peter Davison (The Doctor), Matthew Waterhouse (Adric), Janet Fielding (Tegan), Sarah Sutton (Nyssa), Simon Rouse (Hindle), Richard Todd (Sanders), Nerys Hughes (Todd), Mary Morris (Panna), Adrian Mills (Aris), Sarah Prince (Karuna), Anna Wing (Anatta), Jeffrey Stewart (Dukkha), Roger Milner (Anicca), Lee Cornes (Trickster), Michael Mungarven, Barney Lawrence (Kinda Hostages), Stephen Calcutt (Mara Operator), Graham Cole (Kinda)
Crew
Visual Effects Designer Peter Logan, *Graphic Designer* Ian Hewitt, *Video Effects* Dave Chapman, *Technical Manager* David Hare, Alan Jeffery, *Senior Cameraman* Alec Wheal, *Vision Mixers* James Gould, Carol Johnson, *Videotape Editor* Steve Murray, *Studio Lighting* Mike Jefferies, Fred Wright, *Studio Sound* Alan Machin, *Properties Buyer* Chris Faraday, *Special Sound* Dick Mills, *Grams Operators* Gordon Phillipson, Andy Stacey, *Incidental Music* Peter Howell, *Costume Designer* Barbara Kidd, Dinah Collin, *Dressers* Jean Clark, Sheila Price, Leslie Hallam, Mark Connolly, Spencer Dickson, Janice Booth,

Mark Creed, *Make-Up Artist* Suzan Broad, Joan Stribling, *Make-Up Assistants* Caroline O'Neill, Joanna Nettleton, Lisa Pickering, Jennifer Boost, Petrona Wilson, *Designers* Malcolm Thornton, Bernard Lloyd-Jones, *Design Assistant* Martin Methven, *Production Managers* Ann Faggetter, Geoffrey Manton, Elinor Carruthers, *Production Associate* Angela Smith, *Production Assistants* Rosemary Parsons, Sue Plumb, Jane Ashford, *Assistant Floor Manager* Val McCrimmon, Nicholas Laughland, *Floor Assistant* Charles Beeson, *Script Editor* Eric Saward, *Producer* John Nathan-Turner, *Director* Peter Grimwade

DWM Index

62	Preview
64	Janet Fielding interview
	TV review
68	John Nathan-Turner interview
69	Season Survey results
74	Episode Guide
104	Archive + Fact File
107	Matthew Waterhouse interview
110	Sarah Sutton interview
194	Peter Howell interview
202	Matthew Waterhouse interview
214	Peter Davison interview
219	Video review
226	Archive Feature
235	The John Nathan-Turner Memoirs
259	Christopher H Bidmead interview
269	Nerys Hughes interview
	Simon Rouse interview
271	Antony Root interview
313	Peter Davison interview
327	Christopher Bailey interview
338	Gary Downie interview
346	Eric Saward interview
353	Janet Fielding interview

Recording Dates

29-31 July 1981 (TC8), 12-14 August 1981 (TC8), 11 November 1981 (TC8)

Working Title

The Kinda

Factoids

- The Buddhist overtones in the story were reflected in characters' names: Anicca (impermability), Anatta (egolessness), Dukkha (pain), Panna (wisdom) and Karuna (compassion). The box of Jhana meant 'meditation' and the Mara itself was the Buddhist term for 'temptation'.
- Many of the guest actors went on to appear in other long-running series. Anna Wing appeared as Lou Beale in *EastEnders*, while Jeffrey Stewart and Simon Rouse, joined by long-time *Doctor Who* extra Graham Cole, featured in *The Bill*. Lee Cornes became a regular in *Grange Hill*, Nerys Hughes would soon be the *District Nurse* and Adrian Mills would end up behind a desk as one of Esther Rantzen's 'boys' on consumer programme *That's Life*.
- The giant snake in Part Four was built by outside contractor Stephen Greenfield and suspended on the studio's lighting rig with wires (which post-production video effects attempted to hide). Actor Stephen Calcutt stood inside the costume and manipulated the jaws. The mirrors were made of mirrorlon, and careful camera angles had to be used to avoid seeing the reflection of the studio and production personnel.
- Part Four under-ran by four minutes and so Bailey was commissioned to write extra scenes involving Adric, Tegan and the Doctor in the Dome airlock. These were recorded in November 1981 as part of *Earthshock*'s first studio session.
- Due to Sarah Sutton's late addition to the Tardis line-up, she was largely written out of this story, allowing Tegan and Adric to share the bulk of the narrative. Her contract was only for 24 episodes (out of a 26 episode season), and so the production team did not lose any money by not employing her for Parts Three and Four.

Comment

On the surface, *Kinda* is not easy to like. The brightly-lit fake jungle, the white English actors with towels around them pretending to be natives, Tegan dropping apples on someone's head, Richard Todd over-acting like mad, the pretentious dream sequences, Part Three's cliffhanger resolution, the snake…and yet…and yet. In a nutshell, *Kinda* is one of those stories that grows on you, that matures over time and, most importantly, in the memory. Each new viewing will bring new insights and new surprises. The extraordinarily detailed and convincing Dome set, Simon Rouse' stunning performance as a man on the verge of a breakdown, Peter Davison's subtle and understated playing of a conventionally weak secondary character, the terrifying images at the end of Part Three, the haunting music, the articulate and thought-provoking script…how can one have possibly missed all this first time round? But the strangest thing of all is that *Kinda* has a reputation for complexity, and yet ultimately the story is about a giant snake that goes around taking people over. What's not to understand?

99%

"Why not smile and let me live?" ~ The Doctor

120) The Visitation
Eric Saward

Serial Code: 5X
Original Transmission
Part One
Monday 15 February 1982, 18.55-19.20,
9.1m / 54
Part Two
Tuesday 16 February 1982, 19.05-19.30,
9.3m / 48
Part Three
Monday 22 February 1982, 18.55-19.20,
9.9m / 41
Part Four
Tuesday 23 February 1982, 19.05-19.30,
10.1m / 40
Repeat Transmission
Part One
Monday 15 August 1983, 18.25-18.50, 4.3m / 85
Part Two
Tuesday 16 August 1983, 18.30-18.55, 4.6m / 79
Part Three
Wednesday 17 August 1983, 18.25-18.50,
3.6m / 104
Part Four
Thursday 18 August 1983, 18.25-18.50,
4.8m / 75
BBC Archive
All episodes exist as 625-line two-inch PAL colour master videotapes.
Novelization
Doctor Who and the Visitation by Eric Saward (121/11)
Hardback:
August 1982, WH Allen (0491028474 / Photograph)
Paperback:
1. August 1982, Target (0426201353 / Photograph)
2. February 1992, Target (0426201353 / Alister Pearson)
Non-Fiction Book
Doctor Who - The Making of a Television Series by Alan Road
Hardback: July 1982, Andre Deutsch (023397444X / Photograph)
Paperback: 1983, Puffin (0140316876 / Photograph)
Video
July 1994, twin-pack with *Black Orchid* (BBCV 5349 / Pete Wallbank)

DVD
January 2004, repeat continuity announcements, isolated music score, extended and deleted scenes, production subtitles, photo gallery, commentary by Peter Davison, Janet Fielding, Sarah Sutton, Matthew Waterhouse and Peter Moffatt (BBCDVD 1329 / Clayton Hickman)
Précis
A stranded alien Terileptil in 1666 releases plague-carrying rats...
Cast
Peter Davison (The Doctor), Matthew Waterhouse (Adric), Sarah Sutton (Nyssa), Janet Fielding (Tegan), John Savident (Squire John), Anthony Calf (Charles), John Baker (Ralph), Valerie Fyfer (Elizabeth), Michael Robbins (Richard Mace), Michael Melia (Terileptil Leader), David Sumner, Michael Leader (Terileptils), Peter Van Dissel (Android), Richard Hampton (Villager), James Charlton (Miller), Neil West (Poacher), Eric Dodson (Headman), Thomas Knox (Woodcutters), James Tye (Farmhand), Jeff Wayne (Scythe Man), Don Paul (Nightwatchman)
Crew
Stunt Arranger Alan Chuntz, *Stuntmen* Stuart Fell, Alan Chuntz, *Visual Effects Designer* Peter Wragg, *Visual Effects Assistants* Dave Barton, Peter Litten, *Video Effects* Dave Jervis, *Technical Manager* Derek Martin, *Senior Cameraman* Alec Wheal, *Vision Mixer* Carol Johnson, *Videotape Editor* Rod Waldron, *Studio Lighting* Henry Barber, *Studio Sound* Alan Machin, *Film Cameraman* Peter Chapman, *Film Sound* Stan Nightingale, *Film Editor* Ken Bilton, *Properties Buyer* Ruth Hyde, *Special Sound* Dick Mills, *Grams Operator* Gordon Phillipson, *Incidental Music* Paddy Kingsland, *Costume Designer* Odile Dicks-Mireaux, *Make-Up Artist* Carolyn Perry, *Designer* Ken Starkey, *Production Manager* Roselyn Parker, *Production Associate* Angela Smith, *Production Assistant* Julia Randall, *Assistant Floor Manager* Alison Symington, *Script Editor* Antony Root, *Producer* John Nathan-Turner, *Director* Peter Moffatt
DWM Index
62	Preview
65	TV review
66	Sarah Sutton interview
68	John Nathan-Turner interview
	Novelization review
69	Eric Saward interview
	Season Survey results
72	Imagineering interview
74	Episode Guide
116	Eric Saward - A Retrospective Review
148	Eric Saward interview

177	Nostalgia
202	Matthew Waterhouse interview
205	Paddy Kingsland interview
213	Peter Davison interview
215	Video review
235	The John Nathan-Turner Memoirs
253	Peter Moffatt interview
275	Archive Feature
338	Preview(DVD)
339	The Fact of Fiction DVD review
346	Eric Saward interview

Recording Dates
1 May 1981 (EFS), 5-8 May 1981 (Location filming), 20-21 May 1981 (TC3), 3-5 June 1981 (TC3)

Locations
Black Park, Fulmer, Buckinghamshire; Tithe Barn, Hurley, Berkshire

Working Titles
Invasion of the Plague Men
Plague Rats

Factoids
- Drunken Victorian actor and master of disguise Richard Mace had featured in three BBC Radio 4 plays written by Eric Saward in the 1970s: *The Assassin* (1 June 1974), *Pegasus* (21 May 1975) and *The Nemesis Machine* (13 August 1976). He was played by Geoffrey Matthews.
- The Terileptil leader's mask was the first time animatronics had been used in *Doctor Who*. Made out of rubber by outside contractor Imagineering, it had radio-controlled lips and gills. The three Terileptil costumes - consisting of latex arms and legs and fibreglass chests - were based on the scaly bodies of tropical fish. A latex dummy was seen to melt in Part Four, with Swarfega oozing from its nose and mouth.
- *The Visitation* saw the last appearance of the Doctor's sonic screwdriver until *Doctor Who* (157). Rather than destroy the real prop, a vacuum-formed plastic version was fitted with a pyrotechnic charge and melted on cue.
- Two glass paintings were used on the production. One featured in the Ealing Film Studios set to create the upper floors and skyline of Pudding Lane in Part Four, and another was used in the electronic studio to show the roof of Mace's barn in Part One.
- A six-week break followed completion of *The Visitation* to allow Peter Davison to star in the second series of his BBC sitcom *Sink or Swim* (1980-2).

Comment
The Visitation is a bog-standard historical alien invasion plot, directed in a workmanlike way by Peter Moffatt. The dialogue is often clunky and unrealistic (a major flaw in all of Eric Saward's stories), and Michael Robbins' portrayal of Richard Mace is as wooden as the character. The Terileptils - much vaunted at the time - are feeble-looking monsters that look as if they're about to fall to pieces at any moment. The production design is generally strong, but the narrative is too slow to create any real excitement. Blocking and acting generally is awkward, although Michael Melia gives a refreshingly naturalistic performance under his unconvincing mask. The ending started an unfortunate trend for attributing major historical disasters to *Doctor Who* monsters. **45%**

"Why do I always let my curiosity get the better of me?" ~ The Doctor

121) Black Orchid
Terence Dudley

Serial Code: 6A
Original Transmission
Part One
Monday 1 March 1982, 18.55-19.20, 9.9m / 57
Part Two
Tuesday 2 March 1982, 19.05-19.30, 10.1m / 55
Repeat Transmission
Part One
Wednesday 31 August 1983, 18.35-19.00, 4.4m / 94
Part Two
Thursday 1 September 1983, 18.25-18.50 5m / 79
BBC Archive
All episodes exist as 625-line two-inch PAL colour master videotapes.
Novelization
Doctor Who - Black Orchid by Terence Dudley (143/11)
Hardback:
September 1986, WH Allen (0491038232 / Tony Masero)
Paperback:
February 1987, Target (0426202546 / Tony Masero)
Video
July 1994, twin-pack with *The Visitation* (BBCV 5349 / Pete Wallbank)

Précis
The Doctor is accused of murdering a guest at an Edwardian fancy dress party…

Cast
Peter Davison (The Doctor), Matthew Waterhouse (Adric), Sarah Sutton (Nyssa/Ann Talbot), Janet Fielding (Tegan), Michael Cochrane (Lord Cranleigh), Barbara Murray (Lady Cranleigh), Gareth Milne (The Unknown/George Cranleigh/Stunt Double for Lord Cranleigh), Moray Watson (Sir Robert Muir), Ahmed Khalil (Latoni), Timothy Block (Tanner), Brian Hawksley (Brewster), Ivor Salter (Sergeant Markham), Andrew Tourell (Constable Cummings), David Wilde (Digby), Jim Morris (Station Master), Vanessa Paine (Double for Nyssa/Double for Ann), Caron Heggie (Ann's Maid), Amanda Carlson (Maid), Derek Hunt (Footman James), Frederick Wolfe (Footman Henry), Jimmy Muir (Police Driver)

Crew
Visual Effects Designer Tony Auger, *Graphic Designer* Ian Hewitt, *Video Effects* Dave Chapman, *Technical Manager* Alan Jeffery, *Senior Cameraman* Alec Wheal, *Vision Mixer* Carol Johnson, *Videotape Editor* Rod Waldron, *Studio Lighting* Fred Wright, *Studio Sound* Alan Machin, *Film Cameraman* Peter Chapman, *Film Sound* Ron Blight, *Film Editor* Mike Houghton, *Properties Buyer* Helen MacKenzie, *Special Sound* Dick Mills, *Grams Operator* Tony Revell, *Incidental Music* Roger Limb, *Costume Designer* Rosalind Ebbutt, *Dressers* Kathy Hall, Terry Pettigrew, John Padgen, Sheila Cullen, *Make-Up Artist* Lisa Westcott, *Make-Up Assistants* Mary Liddell, Lesley Bond, Christine Greenwood, Nicola Bellamy, *Designer* Tony Burrough, *Production Manager* Jim Capper, *Production Associate* Angela Smith, *Production Assistant* Juley Harding, *Assistant Floor Manager* Val McCrimmon, *Director's Assistant* Sarah Newman, *Floor Assistant* Sarah Woodside, *Script Editor* Eric Saward, *Producer* John Nathan-Turner, *Director* Ron Jones

DWM Index
63 Preview
65 TV review
66 Sarah Sutton interview
68 John Nathan-Turner interview
69 Season Survey results
74 Episode Guide
101 Ron Jones interview
110 Sarah Sutton interview
117 Novelization review
190 Michael Cochrane interview
196 Roger Limb interview
202 Matthew Waterhouse interview
214 Peter Davison interview
215 Video review
235 The John Nathan-Turner Memoirs
298 Archive Feature
338 Gary Downie interview
346 Eric Saward interview

Recording Dates
5-9 October 1981 (Location filming), 20-21 October 1981 (TC3)

Locations
Buckinghamshire Railway Centre and 99 Quainton Road, Buckinghamshire; Buckhurst Park, Withyham, Hartfield, East Sussex

Working Title
The Beast

Factoids
- Stock footage from BBC children's series *God's Wonderful Railway* (1980) was inserted in Part One to show the train departing Cranleigh Station.
- *Black Orchid* was the first purely historical story since *The Highlanders* (31) in 1966/67. It was also the first story to be script edited by Eric Saward, previous script editor Antony Root having already done some work on it before leaving his temporary post for *Juliet Bravo* (1980-85). John Nathan-Turner had planned to direct it himself, but became heavily involved with the pilot episode of *K-9 and Company* and had to reluctantly turn the assignment down.
- Split-screen (two separately recorded images recorded on a locked-off camera and then combined in post-production) was used to show Sarah Sutton as Nyssa and Ann in the same shot. For shots where one character's face was not visible, actress Vanessa Paine was chosen to double Ann or Nyssa, although Sarah Sutton felt the resemblance to her was not strong. Due to changing light conditions on locations, the split-screen shots were only attempted for the studio sessions.
- Stuntman Gareth Milne wore uncomfortable latex make-up, including a false ear and a palate to keep his mouth open, when playing George Cranleigh (or The Unknown as he was listed in the *Radio Times* and on the closing credits of Part One). The flat roof from which he tumbles in Part Two was added to Buckhurst Park's real roof by Tony Burrough's design team. Milne misjudged his fall though, his legs hitting the ground instead of the boxes and

mattresses specially laid out for him. But despite this injury he managed to complete his duties that day and double for the actor Michael Cochrane climbing the drainpipes up to the roof.

Comment
A charming English country house whodunit, *Black Orchid* stands out as being a simple story expertly told. The location filming is lovely, the Cranleigh Halt interiors are excellent (despite being overlit, a common drawback in '80s *Doctor Who*) and there is a delicious atmosphere of nostalgia in the whole production. For the first time, the regulars look like they're actually *enjoying* themselves, with the viewers treated to the Tardis travellers indulging in that rare pursuit - relaxation. The Doctor taking a bath? Who would have thought it. Part Two is weaker than the first, and the cop-out, "Look, here's the Tardis, I must be genuine" scene is a sign of lazy writing. However, the climactic conflagration is an impressive piece of stage management and the last moment, as the Doctor and companions return from George's funeral, is a beautiful touch.
95%

"For some people, small beautiful events are what life is all about." ~ The Doctor

122) Earthshock
Eric Saward

Serial Code: 6B
Original Transmission
Part One
Monday 8 March 1982, 18.55-19.20, 9.1m / 45
Part Two
Tuesday 9 March 1982, 19.05-19.30, 8.8m / 50
Part Three
Monday 15 March 1982, 18.55-19.20, 9.8m / 32
Part Four
Tuesday 16 March 1982, 19.05-19.30, 9.6m / 40
Repeat Transmission
As part of 'Doctor Who and the Monsters' season:
Part One (Part One & Part Two)
Monday 9 August 1982, 19.40-18.30, 4.9m / 83
Part Two (Part Three & Part Four)
Monday 16 August 1982, 19.20-20.10, 5.2m / 79
BBC Archive
All episodes exist as 625-line two-inch PAL colour master videotapes.

Novelization
Doctor Who - Earthshock by Ian Marter (128/10)
Hardback:
May 1983, WH Allen (0491031815 / Photograph)
Paperback:
1. August 1983, Virgin (0426193776 / Photograph)
2. April 1994, Virgin (0426193776 / Alister Pearson)
Video
September 1992 (BBCV 4840 / Andrew Skilleter)
DVD
August 2003, isolated music score, optional CGI effects, film footage, commentary by Peter Davison, Janet Fielding, Matthew Waterhouse and Sarah Sutton (BBCDVD 1153 / Clayton Hickman)
Music and Sound Effects
1. March 1983, *Doctor Who - The Music*, LP (REH 462 / Iain McCaig)
2. March 1983, *Doctor Who - The Music*, cassette (ZCR 462 / Iain McCaig)
3. December 1992, Silva Screen, *Doctor Who - Earthshock*, CD (FILMCD 709 / Alister Pearson)
4. December 1992, Silva Screen, *Doctor Who - Earthshock*, cassette (FILMC 709 / Alister Pearson)
Précis
The Doctor runs into the Cybermen who are out to destroy the Earth any way they can…
Cast
Peter Davison (The Doctor), Matthew Waterhouse (Adric), Sarah Sutton (Nyssa), Janet Fielding (Tegan), James Warwick (Scott), Clare Clifford (Kyle), June Bland (Berger), Beryl Reid (Briggs), Alec Sabin (Ringway), Steve Morley (Walters), Suzi Arden (Snyder), Ann Holloway (Mitchell), Anne Clements (First Trooper), Mark Straker (Second Trooper), David Banks (Cyber Leader), Mark Hardy (Cyber Lieutenant), Jeff Wayne, Peter Gates-Fleming, Steve Ismay, Norman Bradley, Graham Cole, David Bache (Cybermen), Mark Fletcher (First Crewmember), Christopher Whittingham (Second Crewmember), Carolyn Mary Simmonds (Female Android), Barney Lawrence (Male Android), Val McCrimmon, John Towns, David Melbourne, Tim Goodings (Crewmembers), Stephen Whyment (Trooper Brooks), Jonathan Evans (Trooper Marshall)
Crew
Visual Effects Designer Steve Bowman, *Visual Effects Assistant* Martin Bower, *Graphic Designer* Ian Hewitt, *Dave Effects* Dave Chapman, *Technical Manager* Alan Jeffery, *Senior Cameraman* Alec Wheal, *Vision Mixer* James Gould, *Videotape Editor* Rod Waldron, *Studio Lighting* Fred Wright, *Studio Sound* Alan Machin,

Film Cameraman Keith Hopper, *Film Sound* John Gatland, *Film Sound Assistant* John Crossland, *Film Lighting* Paul Evemy, *Film Editor* Mike Houghton, *Properties Buyer* Barbara Horne, *Special Sound* Dick Mills, *Grams Operator* Tony Revell, *Incidental Music* Malcolm Clarke, *Costume Designer* Dinah Collin, *Costume Assistant* Pat Jackson, *Dressers* John Atkins, Heather Williams, Stephen George, Sheila Price, Gale Clarkson, Joanna Dawn, Tony Moore, Ray Davies, *Make-Up Artist* Joan Stribling, *Make-Up Assistants* Linda Burr, Juliet Mayer, Lesley Bond, Demelza Rogers, *Designer* Bernard Lloyd-Jones, *Production Managers* Geoffrey Manton, Elinor Carruthers, *Production Associate* Angela Smith, *Production Assistant* Jane Ashford, *Assistant Floor Manager* Nicholas Laughland, *Director's Assistant* Nick Squires, *Floor Assistant* Sarah Woodside, *Script Editors* Antony Root, Eric Saward, *Producer* John Nathan-Turner, *Director* Peter Grimwade

DWM Index
63 Preview
66 TV review
67 Archive
68 John Nathan-Turner interview
69 Eric Saward interview
    Season Survey results
72 Imagineering interview
88 Episode Guide
91 Richard Gregory interview
94 Eric Saward interview
106 Peter Davison interview
107 Matthew Waterhouse interview
116 Eric Saward - A Retrospective Review
121 Ian Marter Tribute
125 Novelization review
143 David Banks interview
148 Eric Saward interview
182 Those *Radio Times*
191 Video review
195 Malcolm Clarke interview
196 What The Papers Said
202 Matthew Waterhouse interview
214 Peter Davison interview
235 The John Nathan-Turner Memoirs
239 Archive Feature
    Beryl Reid interview
244 David Banks interview
313 Peter Davison interview
332 DVD preview
333 DVD review
346 Eric Saward interview

Recording Dates
29 October 1981 (Location filming), November 1981 (Unknown studio modelwork), 10-12 November 1981 (TC8), 24-26 November 1981 (TC8)

Locations
Springwell Quarry, Rickmansworth, Hertfordshire

Working Titles
Sentinel
Sentenial [sic]
Centenal [sic]

Factoids
- *Earthshock* replaced an abandoned script entitled *The Enemy Within* by Christopher Priest, in which Adric was also written out.
- It was against Writers' Guild rules for a script editor to edit his own scripts, except under exceptional circumstances, and so Eric Saward asked Antony Root to return to his old job briefly to read through Saward's *Earthshock* script. Root therefore received an on-screen credit as script editor, despite the bulk of the work being done by Saward.
- Following the example of *Logopolis* (116), a flashback scene was written for Part Two. Researched by fan adviser Ian Levine, the clips chosen were from *The Tenth Planet* 4 (29), *The Wheel in Space* 6 (43) and *Revenge of the Cybermen* 3 (79).
- Eight new Cybermen costumes were constructed by Richard Gregory of Imagineering. Their bodies were G-suits (as worn by high altitude aircraft pilots) covered in coolant tubes, and they sported fibreglass helmets - with black handles in the case of the Cyber Leader - with transparent lower jaw sections so that the actors' silver-painted chins would be visible. This latter effect was to emphasise the creatures' human origins, although as the production went on, they gradually became more silver and less transparent. New-style hollow fibreglass chest units were designed by Gregory, with boots and motorcycle gloves completing the ensemble, all sprayed silver. The Cybermen actors spoke their lines in real time and then redubbed them in post-production, with sound supervisors deepening their tones and adding reverberation. A ninth costume was sliced up and fixed to a piece of blockboard to represent the fused Cybermen seen in the bulkhead door in Part Three.
- The closing credits on Part Four were rolled in silence against a static shot of Adric's crushed badge for mathematical excellence. This was a technique borrowed by producer John Nathan-Turner from the soap opera *Coronation Street* (1960 - today).

- The reappearance of the Cybermen and the death of Adric were kept secret from fans and the general public alike. To this end, Nathan-Turner refused a *Radio Times* cover and interior article, as this would have given away the baddies' identities. The Cybermen were listed in the magazine as 'Leader' and 'Lieutenant'.

Comment
Some say *Earthshock* is one of the most exciting *Doctor Who* stories ever. Others say it is one of the worst. The truth is, it's both. Peter Grimwade's liquid direction and Rod Waldron's dynamic editing give it the edge over any other story - copycat adventure *Resurrection of the Daleks* (134) doesn't even come close - but there are many plot holes and the story itself is neither well structured nor remotely coherent. But, like a glossily made Hollywood action flick, *Earthshock* does a very good job of entertainment if you're prepared to let your brain take a holiday. Acting is variable - Alec Sabin is good, Clare Clifford is bad and Beryl Reid is…interesting - but the story's aim is about moving from one set piece to another as quickly as possible, and as such, mere acting does not get in the way of this.. The dramatic reintroduction of the Cybermen and the needless death of an unnecessary companion sent shockwaves through fandom on its original transmission, and two decades on it still stands up as a damn good production, but in terms of script and plot it is a backward step. **85%**

"I don't know what English cricket is coming to!" ~ The Doctor

123) Time-Flight
Peter Grimwade

Serial Code: 6C
Original Transmission
Part One
Monday 22 March 1982, 18.55-19.20, 10m / 26
Part Two
Tuesday 23 March 1982, 19.05-19.30, 8.5m / 48
Part Three
Monday 29 March 1982, 18.55-19.20, 8.9m / 46
Part Four
Tuesday 30 March 1982, 18.50-19.15, 8.1m / 64
BBC Archive
All episodes exist as 625-line two-inch PAL colour master videotapes.

Novelization
Doctor Who - Time-Flight by Peter Grimwade (128/10)
Hardback:
January 1983, WH Allen (0491031408 / Photograph)
Paperback:
April 1983, Target (0426192974 / Photograph)
Video
July 2000 (BBCV 6878 / Photomontage)
Précis
Two Concordes are dragged back in time to the Pleistocene age…
Cast
Peter Davison (The Doctor), Sarah Sutton (Nyssa), Janet Fielding (Tegan), Anthony Ainley (The Master/Kalid), Richard Easton (Captain Stapley), Keith Drinkel (Flight Engineer Scobie), Michael Cashman (First Officer Bilton), Nigel Stock (Professor Hayter), John Flint (Captain Urquhart), Hugh Hayes (Anithon), André Winterton (Zarak/Plasmaton Voice), Peter Dahlsen (Horton), Judith Byfield (Angela Clifford/Tannoy Voice), Brian McDermott (Sheard), Peter Cellier (Andrews), Barney Lawrence (Dave Culshaw), Matthew Waterhouse (Adric Phantom), Graham Cole (Melkur Phantom), Chris Bradshaw (Terileptil Phantom), Richard Gregory (Dragon Puppeteer), Graham Jarvis, Steve Fideli, Mykel Mills, Chris Holmes, Kelly Garfield, Nigel Tisdall, Giles Melville, Martin Grant (Plasmatons)
Crew
Visual Effects Designer Peter Logan, *Plasmatons Designer* Unit 22, *Video Effects* Dave Chapman, *Technical Manager* Peter Granger, *Senior Cameraman* Alec Wheal, *Vision Mixer* Nigel Finnis, *Videotape Editor* Rod Waldron, *Studio Lighting* Eric Wallis, *Studio Sound* Martin Ridout, *Film Cameraman* Peter Chapman, *Film Sound* John Gatland, *Film Editor* Mike Houghton, *Properties Buyer* Alan Huxley, *Special Sound* Dick Mills, *Grams Operator* Tony Revell, *Incidental Music* Roger Limb, *Costume Designer* Amy Roberts, *Dressers* Mervin Bezar, Robin Smith, Heather Williams, *Make-Up Artist* Dorka Nieradzik, *Make-Up Assistant* Wendy Freeman, *Designer* Richard McManan-Smith, *Graphic Designer* Ian Hewitt, *Production Manager* Liz Mace, *Production Associate* Angela Smith, *Production Assistant* Joan Elliott, *Assistant Floor Manager* Lynn Richards, *Floor Assistant* Charles Beeson, *Script Editor* Eric Saward, *Producer* John Nathan-Turner, *Director* Ron Jones

DWM Index
63	Preview
65	Richard McManan-Smith interview
66	TV review
68	John Nathan-Turner interview
	Dorka Nieradzik interview
72	Novelization review
88	Episode Guide
91	Janet Fielding interview
101	Ron Jones interview
106	Peter Davison interview
110	Sarah Sutton interview
134	Peter Grimwade interview
	Peter Davison interview
202	Matthew Waterhouse interview
214	Peter Davison interview
218	Sarah Sutton interview
235	The John Nathan-Turner Memoirs
236	Video review (cancelled release)
293	Video review
294	Archive Feature
346	Eric Saward interview

Recording Dates
6-7 January 1982 (Location filming), 11 January 1982 (Location filming), 19-20 January 1982 (TC8), 24 January 1982 (TC8), 1-3 February 1982 (TC8)

Location
Heathrow Airport and Concorde, Hounslow, Middlesex

Working Titles
Zanadin
Xeraphin

Factoids
- Part of author Peter Grimwade's research for *Time-Flight* - which was originally pencilled in to close Season 18 instead of *Logopolis* (116) - was to spend time with a Concorde flight crew and attend training sessions in the British Airways flight simulator at Heathrow.
- *Doctor Who* was the first television drama series to film in and around a genuine Concorde aeroplane. A fee was waived in return for British Airways on-screen product placement.
- Outside contractor Unit 22 made five Plasmaton costumes from expanded polyurethane poured in uneven layers over Post Office mail sacks. These fitted over the bodies of the standing actors and meant that their movement and vision was very restricted.
- The green liquid that spewed from Kalid's face at the end of Part Two nearly choked Anthony Ainley and the sequence was curtailed early for the actor's safety

- Assistant floor manager Val McCrimmon appeared as an extra in the Heathrow concourse scenes (following her more substantial role as a freighter crewmember in *Earthshock*).

Comment
Much as I like to defend poorly received stories, with *Time-Flight* I feel I must go with the majority opinion and say that, yes, it is really pretty terrible. Part One is mildly intriguing, but after that things go downhill very steeply, a bit like the show's budget at the end of the season. Suffice it to say that a combination of terrible effects, lacklustre direction, appalling music and the incomprehensible technobabble that passes for a plot conspire to make this one of the least satisfying *Doctor Who* outings ever. Peter Grimwade is clearly a very talented individual behind the camera, but his storytelling skills leave something to be desired. Add to this a general dearth of talent in all areas of the production, and *Time-Flight*'s fate is sealed. Even the much-hyped Heathrow location scenes may as well have been filmed in a Brentford shopping centre. **22%**

Season 20

"Our duty - if not our conscience - is clear." ~ *Lord President Borusa*

124) Arc of Infinity
Johnny Byrne

Serial Code: 6E
Original Transmission
Part One
Monday 3 January 1983, 18.45-19.10, 7.2m / 74
Part Two
Wednesday 5 January 1983, 18.45-19.10, 7.3m / 66
Part Three
Tuesday 11 January 1983, 18.50-19.15, 6.9m / 89
Part Four
Wednesday 12 January 1983, 18.45-19.10, 7.2m / 82
BBC Archive
All episodes exist as 625-line two-inch PAL colour master videotapes.
Novelization
Doctor Who - Arc of Infinity by Terrance Dicks (117/12)

Hardback:
July 1983, WH Allen (0491030614 / Photomontage)
Paperback:
November 1983, Target (0426193423 / Photomontage)
Video
March 1994 (BBCV 5199 / Pete Wallbank)
Music and Sound Effects
1. March 1983, *Doctor Who - The Music*, LP (REH 462 / Iain McCaig)
2. March 1983, *Doctor Who - The Music*, cassette (ZCR 462 / Iain McCaig)
3. December 1992, Silva Screen, *Doctor Who - Earthshock*, CD (FILMCD 709 / Alister Pearson)
4. December 1992, Silva Screen, *Doctor Who - Earthshock*, cassette (FILMC 709 / Alister Pearson)
Précis
The Time Lord renegade Omega needs the Doctor's body so he can escape from his antimatter world…
Cast
Peter Davison (The Doctor/Omega), Sarah Sutton (Nyssa), Janet Fielding (Tegan), Michael Gough (Councillor Hedin), Leonard Sachs (Lord President Borusa), Ian Collier (The Renegade/Omega), Colin Baker (Commander Maxil), Paul Jerricho (The Castellan), Elspet Gray (Chancellor Thalia), Neil Daglish (Damon), John D Collins (Talor), Andrew Boxer (Robin Stuart), Alastair Cumming (Colin Frazer), Malcolm Harvey (The Ergon), Max Harvey (Cardinal Zorac), Maya Woolfe (Hostel Receptionist), Guy Groen (Second Receptionist), Barbie Denham (Waitress)
Crew
Visual Effects Designer Christopher Lawson, *Graphic Designer* Ian Hewitt, *Video Effects* Dave Chapman, *Technical Manager* Bob Hignett, *Senior Cameraman* Alec Wheal, *Vision Mixers* James Gould, Carol Johnson, *Videotape Editors* Graham Hutchings (1), Rod Waldron (2-4), *Studio Lighting* Don Babbage, *Studio Sound* Trevor Webster, *Film Sound* Bill Wild, *Film Editor* Bernard Ashby, *Properties Buyer* Robert Fleming, *Special Sound* Dick Mills, *Grams Operator* John Downes, *Incidental Music* Roger Limb, *Costume Designer* Dee Robson, *Make-Up Artist* Fran Needham, *Designer* Marjorie Pratt, *Production Manager* Ralph Wilton, *Production Associate* June Collins, *Production Assistant* Diana Brookes, *Assistant Floor Manager* Lynn Richards, *Floor Assistant* Simon Spencer, *Script Editor* Eric Saward, *Producer* John Nathan-Turner, *Director* Ron Jones

DWM Index
73	Preview
	Fashions for Infinity
75	TV review
79	Season 20 Poll Results
88	Episode Guide
91	Janet Fielding interview
100	Archive + Fact File
101	Ron Jones interview
110	Sarah Sutton interview
118	Colin Baker interview
164	John Nathan-Turner interview
169	Johnny Byrne interview
179	Paul Jerricho interview
196	What The Papers Said
197	What The Papers Said
210	Video review
214	Peter Davison interview
218	Sarah Sutton interview
236	The John-Nathan Turner Memoirs
261	Archive Feature
	Ian Collier interview
	Paul Jerricho interview
347	Eric Saward interview

Recording Dates
3-7 May 1982 (Location filming), 17-18 May 1982 (TC1), 31 May-2 June 1982 (TC1)
Locations
Muntplein, 72 Middenweg, Lijnbaansgracht, Nieuwezijds Voorburgwal, Schipol Airport, Leidseplin, Vondelpark Youth Hostel, Herenstraat, Blauwburgwal, Singel, Amstelveld, Prinsengracht, Dam Square, Damrak, Sint Nicolaasstraat, Amstel, Stationsplein - all Amsterdam, Netherlands
Working Title
The Time of Omega
Factoids
- John Nathan-Turner wanted to film overseas again (it had been three years since the Paris jaunt of *City of Death*, 105) and he settled on Amsterdam because the much-derided BBC soap *Triangle* (1981-83) had a production base there. The producer made an unplanned appearance in Part Four when he stepped into shot to keep passersby away from the camera.
- Richard Gregory made Omega's fibreglass mask and costume, incorporating his own initials into the swirling pattern on Omega's chestplate. The Ergon costume was created from casts of various animal bones and had a head based on a pterodactyl skull, worn on top of operator Malcolm Harvey's own head like a hat.

- The chase scenes in Part Four were largely planned 'on the hoof', with Ian Collier playing the role of Omega when Peter Davison was in the same shot as the Doctor. Rice crispies stuck to the actors' faces represented Omega's gradual dissolution.
- Future Doctor Colin Baker appeared as Commander Maxil in the Gallifrey sequences. He was given a helmet with a large plume made from ostrich feathers, but as it was too tall to be worn when entering the Tardis console room, Baker instead wore it under his arm for the duration of the story.
- The Matrix was visualised by placing perspex rods against a black background and shining coloured lights over them. An electronic ripple added to the effect. Actors were superimposed against this background via CSO.
- Tegan's reintroduction was held over until Part Two to create a modicum of suspense. However, those who glanced at the *Radio Times* cast list or remembered the continuity announcer's assurance that Tegan would return next year (spoken over the closing credits of *Time-Flight*), would not have been surprised.

Comment

After the drab finale that was *Time-Flight*, we now get a drab opening story directed in much the same drab way by the very same drab director, Ron Jones. Amsterdam, judging by *Arc of Infinity*, is one of the bleakest places in the universe, although not quite as bleak as the corridors and rooms of early '80s Gallifrey. Everything about this story is tired, unimaginative and bland, which is a great pity because one feels that somewhere there is a promising little story struggling to escape. If bringing Omega back in a completely different costume was a strange decision, then employing a top-notch guest and giving them utter rubbish to say is even stranger. Roger Limb's music is as woeful as ever, but then at least this suits the tone of the story. **19%**

"You won't succeed. In the end, evil never does."
~ *The Doctor*

125) *Snakedance*
Christopher Bailey

Serial Code: 6D
Original Transmission
Part One
Tuesday 18 January 1983, 18.50-19.15, 6.7m / 95
Part Two
Wednesday 19 January 1983, 18.45-19.10, 7.7m / 75
Part Three
Tuesday 25 January 1983, 18.50-19.15, 6.6m / 98
Part Four
Wednesday 26 January 1983, 8.45-19.10, 7.4m / 78
BBC Archive
All episodes exist as 625-line two-inch PAL colour master videotapes.
Novelization
Doctor Who - Snakedance by Terrance Dicks (124/12)
Hardback:
January 1984, WH Allen (0491031513 / Andrew Skilleter, Photograph)
Paperback:
April 1984, Target (0426194578 / Andrew Skilleter, Photograph)
Video
December 1994 (BBCV 5433 / Colin Howard)
Music and Sound Effects
1. March 1983, *Doctor Who - The Music*, LP (REH 462 / Iain McCaig)
2. March 1983, *Doctor Who - The Music*, cassette (ZCR 462 / Iain McCaig)
3. December 1992, Silva Screen, *Doctor Who - Earthshock*, CD (FILMCD 709 / Alister Pearson)
4. December 1992, Silva Screen, *Doctor Who - Earthshock*, cassette (FILMC 709 / Alister Pearson)
Précis
Tegan takes the Tardis to Manussa where the Mara is about to stage a re-entry into this world…
Cast
Peter Davison (The Doctor), Sarah Sutton (Nyssa), Janet Fielding (Tegan), Martin Clunes (Lon), Colette O'Neil (Tanha), John Carson (Ambril), Preston Lockwood (Dojjen), Brian Miller (Dugdale), Johnathon Morris (Chela), George Ballentine (Hawker), Hilary Sester (Fortune Teller), Barry Smith (Puppeteer), Brian Grellis (Megaphone Man), Bob Mills (Lon's Bodyguard), Barney Lawrence (Tanha's Bodyguard), Chris Holmes (Ambril's Attendant), Ray Lavender (Snakedancer)

Crew
Visual Effects Designer Andy Lazell, *Visual Effects Assistant* Steve Lucas, *Graphic Designer* Ian Hewitt, *Video Effects* Dave Chapman, *Technical Manager* Derek Thompson, *Senior Cameramen* Alec Wheal, Geoff Clark, *Vision Mixer* Carol Johnson, *Videotape Editor* Rod Waldron, *Studio Lighting* Henry Barber, *Studio Sound* Martin Ridout, *Film Cameraman* John Baker, *Film Sound* Ron Blight, *Film Editor* Alastair Mackay, *Properties Buyer* Pamela Hoffman, *Special Sound* Dick Mills, *Incidental Music* Peter Howell, *Costume Designer* Ken Trew, *Make-Up Artist* Marion Richards, *Designer* Jan Spoczynski, *Production Manager* Margot Hayhoe, *Production Associates* Angela Smith, June Collins, *Production Assistant* Rita Dunn, *Assistant Floor Manager* Maggy Campbell, *Floor Assistant* Kate Power, *Script Editor* Eric Saward, *Producer* John Nathan-Turner, *Director* Fiona Cumming

DWM Index
73   Preview
76   TV review
79   Season Survey results
87   Novelization review
88   Episode Guide
91   Janet Fielding interview
94   Eric Saward interview
127 Archive + Fact File
129 Fiona Cumming interview
173 Fiona Cumming interview
194 Peter Howell interview
215 Peter Davison interview
222 Video review
227 Archive Feature
236 The John Nathan-Turner Memoirs
346 Eric Saward interview

Recording Dates
31 March 1982 (EFS), 12-14 April 1982 (TC6), 26-28 April 1982 (TC6)

Working Title
Snake Dance

Factoids
- This sequel to *Kinda* had been commissioned as early as September 1981, and, like the earlier story, was intended to be totally studio-bound. Unlike *Kinda* though, a day's filming was conducted at Ealing with live snakes - a luxury not afforded the first Mara tale. Three non-poisonous snakes were used: two garter snakes and a tree snake, provided by 'animal actors' firm Janimals.
- On 18 March 1982, shortly before production on *Snakedance* began, Peter Davison was confronted by Eamonn Andrews in Trafalgar Square for an edition of *This Is Your Life*. The programme was transmitted a week later on 25 March 1982.
- New costumes were provided for Sarah Sutton and Janet Fielding, following complaints about the 'uniform' look of the previous season.
- Two future sitcom stars made appearances in *Snakedance*. Martin Clunes would star in *No Place Like Home* (1983-87) and, more famously, *Men Behaving Badly* (1992-99), while Johnathon Morris would become a fixture of Liverpuddlian comedy *Bread* (1986-91).
- Four different snake props were made for this story. One was a perfect replica of a garter snake for the scene in which the Doctor is bitten, the second was a large snake skull with an articulated jaw which was overlaid over shots of Tegan's reflection in the hall of mirrors, the third was the intermediate snake prop used in Part Four of *Kinda*, which was carried at the head of the carnival procession, and the fourth and biggest was a hydraulically operated latex head and neck section seen at the climax to the story.
- Various set elements, including the spiral staircase in Lon's suite, were reused from a recently transmitted *Song for Europe* programme, precursor to the annual *Eurovision Song Contest* in May 1982.

Comment
Snakedance's chief fault is that it literalises the psychological menace of *Kinda* into a conventional story of alien possession. It's rather like watching a sequel to *The Mind Robber* (45) in which UNIT is up against deadly Toy Soldiers. Eschewing the reality of *Kinda*'s Dome environment, *Snakedance* is also one of the stagiest *Doctor Who* stories ever, with the generally heightened acting style combining with the artificial-looking sets to produce a serial that seems to belong more to the theatre than the small screen. That said, there are some effective moments of horror - in particular the crystal ball shattering at the end of Part One - but the sluggish pace and over-reliance on dialogue make this sequel consistently inferior to its illustrious progenitor. The story is lifted from the run-of-the-mill by good performances from the guest cast and a frenetic turn by the Doctor as he vainly tries to convince all and sundry of the dangers of the Mara's reawakening - to no avail. **69%**

"The Doctor and the Tardis - well, how could I ever forget?" ~ *Brigadier Lethbridge-Stewart*

126) Mawdryn Undead
Peter Grimwade

Serial Code: 6F
Original Transmission
Part One
Tuesday 1 February 1983, 18.50-19.15,
6.5m / 103
Part Two
Wednesday 2 February 1983, 18.45-19.10,
7.5m / 83
Part Three
Tuesday 8 February 1983, 18.50-19.15, 7.4m / 84
Part Four
Wednesday 9 February 1983, 18.45-19.10,
7.7m / 78
BBC Archive
All episodes exist as 625-line two-inch PAL colour master videotapes.
Novelization
Doctor Who - Mawdryn Undead by Peter Grimwade (119/8)
Hardback:
August 1983, WH Allen (0491030916 / Photograph)
Paperback:
1. January 1984, Target (0426193938 / Photograph)
2. March 1992, Target (0426193938 / Alister Pearson)
Video
November 1992 (BBCV 4874 / Andrew Skilleter)
Music and Sound Effects
1990, Julian Knott, *Doctor Who - The Corridor of Eternity*, cassette (JPD1)
Précis
The Doctor fears something terrible has happened when the Brigadier can't remember him...
Cast
Peter Davison (The Doctor), Sarah Sutton (Nyssa), Janet Fielding (Tegan), Mark Strickson (Turlough), Nicholas Courtney (Brigadier Lethbridge-Stewart), David Collings (Mawdryn), Valentine Dyall (Black Guardian), Angus MacKay (Headmaster), Stephen Garlick (Ibbotson), Roger Hammond (Dr Runciman), Sheila Gill (Matron), Peter Walmsley (First Mutant), Brian Darnley (Second Mutant), Nick Gillard (Double for Turlough), Paul Heasman (Double for Ibbotson), Mark McBride (Van Driver), Richard Sheekey (Double for Brigadier Lethbridge-Stewart), Lucy Baker (Nyssa as a Child), Sian Pattenden (Tegan as a Child), Robert Smythe (Police Constable), John Cannon (Police Sergeant)

Crew
Stuntmen Nick Gillard, Paul Heasman, Mark McBride, *Visual Effects Designer* Stuart Brisdon, *Graphic Designer* Ian Hewitt, *Video Effects* Robin Lobb, *Technical Manager* Alan Arbuthnott, *Senior Cameraman* Robin Barnes, *Vision Mixer* Carol Johnson, *Videotape Editor* Rod Waldron, *Studio Lighting* Don Babbage, *Studio Sound* Martin Ridout, *Film Cameraman* Godfrey Johnson, *Film Sound* Ron Brown, *Film Lighting* Dennis Kettle, *Film Editor* Chris Woolley, *Properties Buyer* Chris Ferriday, *Special Sound* Dick Mills, *Grams Operator* John Downes, *Incidental Music* Paddy Kingsland, *Costume Designers* Amy Roberts (studio), Richard Croft (location), *Dressers* Beverley Jasper, Arthur Funge, Malcolm Morris, Brian Baker, *Make-Up Artists* Sheelagh Wells (studio), Carolyn Perry (location), *Make-Up Assistants* Lesley Holmes, Karen Turner, *Designer* Stephen Scott, *Production Manager* Ann Aronsohn, *Production Associate* June Collins, *Production Assistant* Valerie Letley, *Assistant Floor Manager* Ian D Tootle, *Director's Assistant* Deborah Knight, *Floor Assistant* Lesley Fowler, *Script Editor* Eric Saward, *Producer* John Nathan-Turner, *Director* Peter Moffatt

DWM Index
72	Introducing Mark Strickson
	Nicholas Courtney interview
74	Preview
76	Mark Strickson interview
77	TV review
79	Season Survey results
89	Episode Guide
102	Mark Strickson interview
110	Archive + Fact File
	Sarah Sutton interview
111	Nicholas Courtney interview
133	Peter Grimwade interview
166	Sheelagh Wells interview
177	David Collings interview
182	Those *Radio Times*
194	Video review
196	What The Papers Said
205	Paddy Kingsland interview
215	Peter Davison interview
227	Mark Strickson interview
229	Nicholas Courtney interview
234	Archive Feature
236	The John Nathan-Turner Memoirs
253	Peter Moffatt interview
329	David Collings interview
347	Eric Saward interview

Recording Dates
24-27 August 1982 (Location filming), 8-9 September 1982 (TC6), 22-24 September 1982 (TC8)
Locations
Middlesex Polytechnic and campus, Trent Park, Cockfosters, London N14
Working Title
As broadcast
Factoids
- Peter Grimwade's first idea had been to feature original companion Ian Chesterton, hence the school setting. Unfortunately, William Russell proved unavailable, as did Ian Marter (who played Harry Sullivan, early companion to the Fourth Doctor). However, Nicholas Courtney, the third choice, was available and happy to reprise his role as the Brigadier.
- Fan adviser Ian Levine warned John Nathan-Turner that the traditional dating of the UNIT stories (as being in the late 1970s or early 1980s) was not generally consistent with having the Brigadier retired by 1977, but the producer insisted that the familiar date be kept.
- Along with Quantel 5000, a new piece of image-manipulation equipment called Tipsy was used for the Tardis dematerialization in Part Four.
- 'Mawdryn' is the Welsh word for 'undead', so the story's title is tautological.
- 21-year-old Mark Strickson had previously appeared in *Angels* (1975-83) and *Juliet Bravo* (1980-85). His naturally blond hair was tinted orange so it didn't clash with Peter Davison's.
- Eight mutant costumes were created by Amy Roberts. Their long floor length gowns were inspired by the Georgian State Dancers, with the actors' small, shuffling steps making them appear to glide across the floor. (Years earlier, Terry Nation had used these dancers as inspiration for his Daleks.) Latex headpieces were applied to the mutant actors to suggest that their brains were bulging out of their skulls. A metal band across their foreheads hid the visible join.
- A sepia-tinted flashback sequence in Part Two consisted of the following UNIT clips: a younger Brigadier (*The Three Doctors*, 65), a Yeti (*The Web of Fear*, 41), a Cyberman (*The Invasion*, 46), Patrick Troughton (*The Three Doctors*, 65), an Axon (*The Claws of Axos*, 57), the Gold Dalek (*Day of the Daleks*, 60), Jon Pertwee (*Spearhead from Space*, 51), William Hartnell (*The Three Doctors*, 65), the K1 Robot (*Robot*, 75), a Zygon (*Terror of the Zygons*, 80), Tom Baker (ditto) and finally a reprise of the first clip.

Comment
Endless running from one place to another characterises this poor excuse for a story. Characterization and dialogue is trite, and the motivation for why the various characters do things is often unclear. Part One's contrived car-crash has horribly intrusive 'incidental music' and the special effects are cheap and nasty throughout (especially the pattern behind the Black Guardian's head). There is no core to the plot and no emotional involvement, unless you count the Doctor's lives being taken away to allow the mutants to die - although this just comes over as another continuity-obsessed piece of technobabble. Individually, the guest cast perform well, with David Collings providing much-needed gravitas as the tortured mutant Mawdryn, and Nicholas Courtney doing the best he can with an incomprehensible script. Mark Strickson is really too mannered to be believable, and is certainly far too old to be a public schoolboy. Soporific nonsense. **50%**

"This is where the lazars come to die!" ~ Olvir

127) Terminus
Steve Gallagher

Serial Code: 6G
Original Transmission
Part One
Tuesday 15 February 1983, 18.55-19.20, 6.8m / 86
Part Two
Wednesday 16 February 1983, 18.45-19.10, 7.5m / 75
Part Three
Tuesday 22 February 1983, 18.55-19.20, 6.5m / 97
Part Four
Wednesday 23 February 1983, 18.45-19.10, 7.4m / 80
BBC Archive
All episodes exist as 625-line two-inch PAL colour master videotapes.
Novelization
Doctor Who - Terminus by John Lydecker [pen-name for Steve Gallagher] (159/0)

Hardback:
June 1983, WH Allen (0491031319 / Photomontage)
Paperback:
September 1983, Target (0426193857 / Photomontage)
Video
January 1993 (BBCV 4890 / Andrew Skilleter)
Précis
The Doctor must stop one of Terminus' engines exploding or it will destroy the Universe…
Cast
Peter Davison (The Doctor), Sarah Sutton (Nyssa), Janet Fielding (Tegan), Mark Strickson (Turlough), Liza Goddard (Kari), Dominic Guard (Olvir), Andrew Burt (Valgard), Martin Potter (Eirak), Tim Munro (Sigurd), Peter Benson (Bor), RJ Bell (The Garm), Valentine Dyall (Black Guardian), Rachel Weaver (Inga), Martin Muncaster (Tannoy Voice)
Crew
Fight Arranger John Waller, *Visual Effects Designer* Peter Pegrum, *Graphic Designer* Ian Hewitt, *Video Effects* Dave Chapman, *Technical Manager* Jeff Jeffery, *Senior Cameraman* Alec Wheal, *Vision Mixers* Carol Johnson, Mary Kellehar, Nigel Finnis, *Videotape Editor* Rod Waldron, *Studio Lighting* Sam Barclay, *Studio Sound* Scott Talbott, *Film Cameraman* Remi Adefarasin, *Film Sound* Graham Hare, *Film Editor* Frances Parker, *Properties Buyers* David Privett, Dave Morris, *Special Sound* Dick Mills, *Grams Operator* Ian Tomlin, *Incidental Music* Roger Limb, *Costume Designer* Dee Robson, *Make-Up Artist* Joan Stribling, *Designer* Dick Coles, *Production Manager* Steve Goldie, *Production Associate* June Collins, *Production Assistant* Rena Butterwick, *Assistant Floor Manager* Polly Davidson, Adrian Heywood, *Director's Assistant* Mel O'Toole, *Floor Assistants* Kate Power, Roz Stock, *Script Editor* Eric Saward, *Producer* John Nathan-Turner, *Director* Mary Ridge
DWM Index
74 Preview
77 TV review
79 Season Survey results
89 Episode Guide
91 Janet Fielding interview
102 Mark Strickson interview
110 Sarah Sutton interview
137 Archive + Fact File
139 Stephen Gallagher interview
196 Roger Limb interview
    Video review
215 Peter Davison interview
218 Sarah Sutton interview
227 Mark Strickson interview
236 The John Nathan-Turner Memoirs
291 Archive Feature
295 Stephen Gallagher interview
329 Lisa Goddard interview
347 Eric Saward interview

Recording Dates
28 September 1982 (TC Presentation Studio B modelwork), 29-30 September 1982 (EFS), 11-12 October 1982 (TC6), 25-27 October 1982 (TC8), 18 December 1982 (TC1)

Working Title
As broadcast

Factoids
- Many of the concepts used in this serial came from history and mythology. The Vanir were Norse fertility gods (also used by JRR Tolkien in his history of Middle Earth, *The Silmarillion*, published posthumously in 1977) and the Garm was inspired by a Scandinavian dog-headed figure that guarded the gates of Hell. 'Lazer's disease' was a fictitious illness taken from an archaic word for leprosy derived from the Biblical figure of Lazarus. The design of the Vanir's armour came from Middle Age woodcuts, with five costumes being made by outside contractor Richard Gregory of Unit 22. The Lazar sufferers wore shrouds in the style of Black Death victims.
- Various problems occurred during the studio recording of *Terminus*, resulting in some scenes having to be remounted in December. This meant that Sarah Sutton had to return to record one shot five weeks after she had 'officially' left the series. The remount upset director Mary Ridge, whose extra hour in which to finish the story at the end of the final studio session had been promised but then cancelled at the last minute.
- When Liza Goddard and Dominic Guard blast onto the passenger liner in Part One, the explosive charge was considerably louder than either had expected, leading to Goddard swearing on camera. This was later cut from the soundtrack.
- A post-production 'patch' was applied to a scene in Part Two in which Peter Davison could be seen standing on a stairway after finishing his scene. Unfortunately, the inserted image was rather inexpertly applied and drew even more attention to the error.
- Complaints were received from the British Leprosy Association concerning the programme's treatment of that disease, and

also from Tannoy Ltd who criticised the BBC for using their registered trademark in the closing captions for Parts One, Two and Four.
- The original explanation for Nyssa shedding her skirt in Part Three was so that she could relieve pressure on her distended stomach. This was not made clear in the transmitted episode.
- In Part One, actress Kathy Burke stood in for a friend of hers (using her friend's name) and played a Lazar victim. She later became famous as Perry to Harry Enfield's Kevin in *Harry Enfield's Television Programme* (1990-92) and *Harry Enfield and Chums* (1994-97) and the snobbish Linda La Hughes in BBC sitcom *Gimme, Gimme, Gimme* (1999-2001). She was also nominated for a BAFTA Award for her role as an abused wife in *Nil by Mouth* (1997).

Comment
Another dull runaround (or rather, walk- and crawlaround) in yet more corridors in yet another spaceship. Yawn. The fact that these corridors and rooms are deliberately grey and faceless hardly adds to the excitement of this improbable and unconvincing story. The acting throughout is wooden (most notably Liza Goddard and Andrew Burt) and the scaffolding and plastic sheeting that represents Terminus has to be one of the production team's less successful attempts at conjuring up an alien setting. It is, of course, impossible to take the Garm seriously. And the shock revelation that the engines of this boring old spaceship somehow created the Big Bang is one of *Doctor Who*'s silliest concepts and should have been scrubbed from Gallagher's first draft. Depressing. **35%**

"What is love?" ~ Marriner

128) *Enlightenment*
Barbara Clegg

Serial Code: 6H
Original Transmission
Part One
Tuesday 1 March 1983, 18.55-19.20, 6.6m / 89
Part Two
Wednesday 2 March 1983, 18.45-19.10, 7.2m / 76
Part Three
Tuesday 8 March 1983, 18.55-19.20, 6.2m / 99
Part Four
Wednesday 9 March 1983, 18.45-19.10, 7.3m / 68
BBC Archive
All episodes exist as 625-line two-inch PAL colour master videotapes.
Novelization
Doctor Who - Enlightenment by Barbara Clegg (127/9)
Hardback:
February 1984, WH Allen (0491031327 / Andrew Skilleter, Photograph)
Paperback:
May 1984, Target (042619537X / Andrew Skilleter, Photograph)
Video
February 1993 (BBCV 4891 / Andrew Skilleter)
Music and Sound Effects
1. May 1983, *The Soundhouse: Music from the BBC Radiophonic Workshop*, LP (REC 467 / Photomontage)
2. May 1983, *The Soundhouse: Music from the BBC Radiophonic Workshop*, cassette (ZCR 467 / Photomontage)
3. February 1985, *Doctor Who - The Music II*, LP (REH 552 / Photomontage)
4. February 1985, *Doctor Who - The Music II*, cassette (ZCR 552 / Photomontage)
5. November 1992, Silva Screen, *Doctor Who - The Five Doctors*, CD (FILMCD 710 / Alister Pearson)
Précis
The Doctor and his companions find themselves guests of the pleasure-seeking Eternals…
Cast
Peter Davison (The Doctor), Janet Fielding (Tegan), Mark Strickson (Turlough), Keith Barron (Striker), Christopher Brown (Marriner), Tony Caunter (Jackson), Leee John (Mansell), Lynda Baron (Wrack), Valentine Dyall (Black Guardian), Cyril Luckham (White Guardian), James McClure (First Officer), Clive Kneller (Collier), Richard Bonehill, Tim Oldroyd (First Officers on *The Shadow*), John Cannon (Helmsman on *The Shadow*), Pat Gorman (Grogan), Byron Sotiris (Critas), Lloyd Williams, Jerry Judge (First Officers on *The Buccaneer*)
Crew
Visual Effects Designer Mike Kelt, *Visual Effects Assistants* Stuart Murdoch, Bill Pearson, Robert Thomas, *Video Effects* Dave Chapman, *Technical Manager* Alan Jeffery, *Senior Cameraman* Alec Wheal, *Vision Mixer* Paul Wheeler, *Videotape Editor* Rod Waldron, *Studio Lighting* Fred Wright, *Studio Sound* Martin Ridout, *Film Cameramen* John Walker, Paul Hellings-Wheeler, *Film Camera*

Assistant Paul Godfrey, *Film Sound* Jim McAllister, *Film Editors* Michael Boyd, Ian McKendrick, *Properties Buyers* Judy Ducker, Alan Mansey, *Special Sound* Dick Mills, *Grams Operator* John Downes, *Incidental Music* Malcolm Clarke, *Costume Designer* Dinah Collin, *Make-Up Artists* Carolyn Perry, Jean Seward, *Designer* Colin Green, *Production Manager* Jennie Osborn, *Production Associate* June Collins, *Production Assistant* Patricia O'Leary, *Assistant Floor Managers* Ian D Tootle, Val McCrimmon, *Floor Assistant* Stephen Moore, *Script Editor* Eric Saward, *Producer* John Nathan-Turner, *Director* Fiona Cumming

DWM Index
79   Season Survey results
81   TV review
87   Novelization review
89   Episode Guide
91   Janet Fielding interview
102   Mark Strickson interview
116   Eric Saward - A Retrospective Review
121   Archive + Fact File
129   Fiona Cumming interview
173   Fiona Cumming interview
186   Fiona Cumming interview
      Mike Kelt storyboards
      Tony Caunter interview
      Archive Feature
195   Malcolm Clarke interview
197   Video review
      What The Papers Said
215   Peter Davison interview
227   Mark Strickson interview
236   The John Nathan-Turner Memoirs
267   Barbara Clegg interview
347   Eric Saward interview

Recording Dates
3-5 November 1982 (EFS and modelwork), 17-18 January 1983 (TC1), 30 January-2 February 1983 (TC1)

Working Title
The Enlighteners

Factoids
- Industrial action by electricians' union EEPTU meant that *Enlightenment*'s studio sessions were delayed from November 1982 to early 1983, thus losing space allocated to Dalek season finale *The Return*.
- The model ships - based on research visits to the Maritime Museum at Greenwich - were mounted on rods attached to a wheeled platform, allowing smooth movement. Sequences involving them were based on detailed storyboards drawn by Mike Kelt and filmed in 35mm, rather than the normal 16mm, at Ealing. Spacesuits and backpacks were made by Imagineering.
- Peter Sallis and David Rhule had been contracted to play Striker and Mansell respectively, but when the studio dates were shifted back, neither were available, and so their roles were taken by Keith Barron and Leee John (the latter from pop group *Imagination*).

Comment
A pirate story in space, *Enlightenment* is easily the most imaginative story to come out of this wilderness of a season. Part One is sparkling with mystery and intrigue, and the cliffhanger is one of the finest for a long time. Malcolm Clarke's music is - oddly for this composer - unobtrusive and hauntingly atmospheric, complementing Mary Ridge's evocative direction. It is also good to see Janet Fielding get out of her clothes for a change (and into a low-cut ballgown, I hasten to add). Keith Barron is eerily otherworldly and Christopher Brown makes a great job of a part that could easily have been embarrassingly clichéd. Lynda Barron, on the other hand, seems to think she is performing in a Christmas pantomime at Skegness. Set design, costume and period detail are the story's main assets, once the initial premise has worn off. Turlough's dilemma at the end, despite the obvious outcome, is milked for all its worth, and rightly so. **85%**

"Oh my dear Doctor, you have been naïve" ~ *The Master*

129) *The King's Demons*
Terence Dudley

Serial Code
6J
Original Transmission
Part One
Tuesday 15 March 1983, 18.55-19.20, 5.8m / 107
Part Two
Wednesday 16 March 1983, 18.45-19.10, 7.2m / 66
Repeat Transmission
Part One
Friday 6 July 1984, 18.55-19.20, 3.3m / 80
Part Two
Friday 13 July 1984, 18.55-19.20, 5m / 603

BBC Archive
All episodes exist as 625-line two-inch PAL colour master videotapes.
Novelization
Doctor Who - The King's Demons by Terence Dudley (153/10)
Hardback:
February 1986, WH Allen (0491036426 / David McAllister)
Paperback:
July 1986, Target (0426202279 / David McAllister)
Video
November 1995, in limited edition box with *The Five Doctors* special edition (BBCV 5733/ Colin Howard)
Music and Sound Effects
1. February 1985, *Doctor Who - The Music II*, LP (REH 552 / Photomontage)
2. February 1985, *Doctor Who - The Music II*, cassette (ZCR 552 / Photomontage)
3. November 1992, Silva Screen, *Doctor Who - The Five Doctors*, CD (FILMCD 710 / Alister Pearson)
Précis
The Master is attempting to interfere with the signing of the Magna Carta...
Cast
Peter Davison (The Doctor), Janet Fielding (Tegan), Mark Strickson (Turlough), Frank Windsor (Ranulf), Gerald Flood (King John/Kamelion Voice), Isla Blair (Isabella), Anthony Ainley (The Master/Sir Gilles Estram), Christopher Villiers (Hugh), Michael J Jackson (Geoffrey), Peter Burroughs (Jester), Paul Bowes (Hugh's Squire), Terry Sachs (Sir Gilles' Squire), Stephen Butler (Hugh's Page), Wayne Harvey (Sir Gilles' Page), Henry Roberts (Marshall), Brian Bowes (Stunt Double for Sir Gilles/Knight/Carter), Nick Wilkinson (Stunt Double for Hugh/Knight), David Cole (Beggar), Darren Mango (Carter's Boy), Phil Murray (Sir Geoffrey's Squire), Tony Annis (Gaoler)
Crew
Fight Arranger John Waller, *Stuntmen* John Waller, *Visual Effects Designer* Tony Harding, *Kamelion Operators* Chris Padmore, *Video Effects* Dave Chapman, *Technical Manager* Tony Troughton, Malcolm Martin, *Senior Cameraman* Alec Wheal, *Vision Mixer* Nigel Finnis, Paul Wheeler, *Videotape Editor* Rod Waldron, *Studio Lighting* Peter Smee, *Studio Sound* Martin Ridout, *Film Cameraman* Remi Adefarasin, *Film Sound* Simon Wilson, *Film Editor* Mike Robotham, *Properties Buyer* Dave Morris, *Special Sound* Dick Mills, *Grams Operator* John Downes, *Incidental Music* Jonathan Gibbs, Peter Howell, *Lute Player* Jakob Lindberg, *Costume Designer* Colin Lavers, *Make-Up Artists* Elizabeth Rowell, Frances Hannon, *Designer* Ken Ledsham, *Design Assistant* Gilly Page, *Production Managers* Jeremy Silberston, Jenny Osborn, *Production Associate* June Collins, *Production Assistant* Sue Upton, *Assistant Floor Manager* Sue Hedden, *Director's Assistant* Gilly Page, *Floor Assistant* Stephen Moore, *Script Editor* Eric Saward, *Producer* John Nathan-Turner, *Director* Tony Virgo

DWM Index
75 Preview
79 Season Survey results
81 TV review
89 Episode Guide
94 Eric Saward interview
102 Mark Strickson interview
110 Novelization review
215 Peter Davison interview
232 Video review
236 The John Nathan-Turner Memoirs
269 Archive Feature
    Tony Virgo interview
    Christopher Villiers interview
347 Eric Saward interview

Recording Dates
5-7 December 1982 (Location filming), 19-20 December 1983 (TC1), 17 January 1983 (TC1)
Locations
Bodiam Castle, Bodiam, East Sussex
Working Titles
The Android
The Demons
A Knight's Tale
Demons Keeper [sic]
Factoids
- Kamelion was a semi-working automaton designed by software designer Mike Power and Chris Padmore of CP Cybernetics. It was produced as a promotional tool to advertise cars, but when the advertising company chose not to use the robot in their campaign - largely because it wasn't capable of walking yet - its creators began looking for funding from the entertainment industry to continue its development. Padmore and colleague Richard Gregory of Imagineering gave two demonstrations of the robot's capabilities to John Nathan-Turner, who then asked Terence Dudley to pen a script introducing the creature as a new companion. It was Dudley who coined the name Kamelion and invented the idea of the robot's transformational powers, which would allow it to be played by real

actors if necessary. But while Kamelion could mime lip movements to pre-recorded dialogue, all its other movements had to be programmed in advance and the information fed down a cable from a computer in the recording studio. This was very time-consuming to organise (a week per episode), and meant that actors had to say their lines at exactly the right speed in order to match Kamelion's pre-planned movements. It was also still not capable of walking. Unfortunately in the spring of 1983 Mike Power was killed in a boating accident, and many of the secrets of operating and maintaining Kamelion went with him.

- In keeping with the Master's previous roles, Sir Gilles Estram's surname was an anagram of 'Master'. The *Radio Times* credited the actor playing this character as 'James Stoker', an anagram of 'Master's Joke'.
- Technical problems plagued the story, and a further studio day was assigned in January 1983 at the start of *Enlightenment*'s remounted recording sessions. (This remount in turn meant that Eric Saward's planned season finale, *The Return*, which would have seen the reintroduction of the Daleks, was postponed. It would resurface in Season 21 as *Resurrection of the Daleks*, 134.)

Comment
Like *The Horns of Nimon*, this particular adventure was never intended to end the season. However, unlike *The Horns of Nimon*, *The King's Demons* isn't really strong enough to stand up as a story in its own right. While it has some nice location filming and generally polished production values, it's hard to see it as anything other than a 'blink or you'll miss it' breathing space between two more accomplished stories (one of which never made it to the screen). The Master's inclusion seems odd - from attempting to control the whole Universe in *Logopolis* (116) to fiddling about with the Magna Carta here is a bit of a jump - and Kamelion is clearly not a viable new member of the Tardis crew, even if he had been working properly. Didn't John Nathan-Turner learn anything with K-9? **39%**

Anniversary Special

"A man is the sum of his memories, you know - a Time Lord even more so." ~ The Doctor

130) The Five Doctors
Terrance Dicks

Serial Code: 6K
Original Transmission
Friday 25 November 1983, 19.20-20.50, 7.7m / 54
Repeat Transmission
Part One
Tuesday 14 August 1984, 18.15-18.40, 4.7m / 88
Part Two
Wednesday 15 August 1984, 18.15-18.40, 4.5m / 93
Part Three
Thursday 16 August 1984, 18.15-18.40, 3.7m / 107
Part Four
Friday 17 August 1984, 18.15-18.40, 4m / 102
BBC Archive
All episodes exist as 625-line two-inch PAL colour master videotapes.
Novelization
Doctor Who - The Five Doctors by Terrance Dicks (128/12)
Hardback:
November 1983, WH Allen (0491030525 / Andrew Skilleter)
Paperback:
1. November 1983, Target (0426195108 / Andrew Skilleter)
2. February 1991, Target (0426195108 / Alister Pearson)
Video
1. September 1985, edited (BBCV 2020 / Andrew Skilleter)
2. September 1985, Betamax, edited (BBCB 2020 / Andrew Skilleter)
3. July 1990 (BBCV 4387 / Alister Pearson)
4. November 1995, Special Edition in limited edition box with *The King's Demons* (BBCV 5734 / Colin Howard)
DVD
November 1999, Special Edition, isolated music score, Dolby 5.1 sound mix (BBCDVD 1006 / Colin Howard)
Music and Sound Effects
1. February 1985, *Doctor Who - The Music II*, LP (REH 552 / Photomontage)

205

2. February 1985, *Doctor Who - The Music II*, cassette (ZCR 552 / Photomontage)
3. November 1992, Silva Screen, *Doctor Who - The Five Doctors*, CD (FILMCD 710 / Alister Pearson)
4. July 1993, *Doctor Who: 30 Years at the Radiophonic Workshop*, CD (BBCCD 871 / Photomontage)

Précis
Doctors and companions are taken from their time streams and dumped in Gallifrey's Death Zone…

Cast
Peter Davison, Tom Baker, Jon Pertwee, Patrick Troughton, Richard Hurndall (The Doctors), Janet Fielding (Tegan), Mark Strickson (Turlough), Carole Ann Ford (Susan), Frazer Hines (Jamie McCrimmon), Wendy Padbury (Zoe), Elisabeth Sladen (Sarah), Lalla Ward (Romana II), Caroline John (Liz Shaw), John Leeson (K-9 Voice), Nicholas Courtney (Brigadier Lethbridge-Stewart), Richard Franklin (Captain Yates), Anthony Ainley (The Master), David Savile (Colonel Crichton), Ray Float (Sergeant), Philip Latham (Lord President Borusa), Paul Jerricho (The Castellan), Dinah Sheridan (Chancellor Flavia), Richard Mathews (Rassilon), Roy Skelton (Dalek Voice), John Scott Martin (Dalek), Stephen Meredith (Technician), John Tallents (Guard), David Banks (Cyber Leader), William Kenton (Cyber Scout), Mark Hardy (Cyber Lieutenant), Stuart Blake (Commander), Lee Woods, Richard Naylor, Mark Whincup, Gilbert Gillan, Emyr Morris Jones, Stuart Fell, Graham Cole, Alan Riches, Ian Marshall-Fisher, Mark Bessenger (Cybermen), Keith Hodiak (Raston Robot), Johnnie Mack, Frederick Wolfe, Charles Milward (Immortalised Time Lords)

Crew
Armourer Tony Chilton, *Stuntman* Stuart Fell, *Visual Effects Designers* John Brace, *Visual Effects Assistant* Mike Kelt, *Graphic Designer* Ian Hewett, *K-9 Operator* John Brace, *Video Effects* Dave Chapman, *Technical Manager* Derek Thompson, *Senior Cameraman* Alec Wheal, *Vision Mixer* Shirley Coward, *Videotape Editor* Hugh Parson, *Studio Lighting* Don Babbage, *Studio Sound* Martin Ridout, *Film Cameraman* John Baker, *Film Sound* John Gatland, *Film Editor* MAC Adams, *Properties Buyer* Robert Flemming, *Special Sound* Dick Mills, *Grams Operator* John Downes, *Incidental Music* Peter Howell, *Costume Designer* Colin Lavers, *Costume Assistant* Peter Halston, *Dressers* Carl Levy, Philip Winter, Camilla Gavin, *Make-Up Artist* Jill Hagger, *Make-Up Assistants* Naomi Donne, Fay Hammond, *Designer* Malcom Thornton, *Design Assistant* Steve Fawcett, *Design Effects* Jean Peyre, *Production Manager* Jeremy Silberston, *Production Associate* June Collins, *Production Assistant* Jean Davis, *Assistant Floor Manager* Pauline Saeger, *Floor Assistant* Chris Stanton, *Script Editor* Eric Saward, *Producer/Second Unit Director* John Nathan-Turner, *Directors* Peter Moffat, Pennant Roberts

Special Edition Crew
Video Effects Dave Chapman, Jo McGrogan, Alison Rickman, Steve Roberts, *Graphics Consultants* Steve Broster, Ralph Montagu, *Videotape Editor* Paul Vanezis, *Dubbing Mixers* Benedict Peissel, Andy Freeth, *Music Rescoring* Peter Howell, *Programme Consultant* Ian Levine, *Research* Richard Molesworth, *Post Production Liaison* Shirley O'Mara, *Executive Producer* Sue Kerr, *Producer* Paul Vanezis

DWM Index
80	Preview
85	TV review
86	Carole Ann Ford interview
87	Deborah Watling interview
89	Elisabeth Sladen interview
	Episode Guide
91	Janet Fielding interview
92	Tom Baker interview
94	Eric Saward interview
95	Terrance Dicks interview
96	Archive + Fact File
100	Robert Holmes interview
102	Mark Strickson interview
106	Peter Davison interview
107	Andrew Skilleter interview
	Video review (edited version)
111	Nicholas Courtney interview
113	Jon Pertwee interview
114	Caroline John interview
116	John Leeson interview
117	Mervyn Haisman interview
120	Wendy Padbury interview
123	Richard Hurndall Remembered
143	David Banks interview
152	Stuart Fell interview
158	Kevin O'Shea interview
163	Elisabeth Sladen interview
	Comic Assassins
164	Video review
170	Jon Pertwee interview
180	Tom Baker interview
182	Those *Radio Times*
194	Peter Howell interview
197	What The Papers Said
208	Wendy Padbury interview
215	Peter Davison interview

222   Richard Franklin interview
227   Mark Strickson interview
231   Taken Out Of Time (Special Edition)
232   Video review (Special Edition)
237   The John Nathan-Turner Memoirs
243   Frazer Hines interview
244   David Banks interview
254   Peter Moffatt interview
261   Paul Jerricho interview
272   Terrance Dicks interview
286   DVD review
313   Archive Feature
347   Eric Saward interview

Recording Dates
5 March 1983 (Location filming), 7-11 March 1983 (Location filming), 13-15 March 1983 (Location filming), 17 March 1983 (Location filming), 18 March 1983 (EFS), 29-31 March 1983 (TC6)

Locations
Plas Brondanw, Llanforthen, Penrhyndeudraeth, Gwynedd; Carreg Y Foel Grom, near Ffestiniog, Gwynedd; Manod Quarry, Cwt Y Bugail, Ffestiniog, Gwynedd; Cwm Bychan, near Llanbedr, Gwynedd; Halings House and Tilehouse Lane, Denham Green, Buckinghamshire; 2 West Common and bus-stop outside 15 North Common Road, Uxbridge, Middlesex; The Backs, River Cam, Cambridge; Blackmoor Head Yard, Cambridge

Working Title
As broadcast

Factoids
- For this 20th Anniversary adventure, veteran scriptwriter Robert Holmes - championed by script editor Eric Saward - began work on a storyline entitled *The Six Doctors*, in which the First Doctor would be revealed to be a cyborg impostor. However, Holmes found it hard going as he did not like the idea of writing for so many Doctors and companions and disliked having to use the Cybermen. Announcing that he couldn't continue with it in October 1982, fellow veteran Terrance Dicks was quickly given the job instead. Dicks' initial storyline was very similar to the completed programme, although his cast list was continually revised as the availability of companions kept fluctuating. One notable scene dropped from his first draft involved the Third Doctor and Sarah battling the Autons in a ruined city street.
- Tom Baker initially agreed to appear in *The Five Doctors* but then backed out, claiming that he did not want to turn the clock back to past glories. Terrance Dicks had to delete all scenes involving him, with his presence in the finished story represented by film clips of himself and Lalla Ward in Cambridge from the cancelled *Shada* (109).
- In a first for the programme, *The Five Doctors* was co-produced by the Australian television network ABC. In return for co-financing the project, ABC were allowed to air the story for free.
- Cybermen costumes were reused from *Earthshock* (122), modified with silver sprayed jaws and firemen's boots instead of moon boots.
- A brand-new Tardis console was designed by Mike Kelt, incorporating many working electronic components, such as LED displays and a TV monitor. To accompany the console, new interior walls and doors were built by Malcolm Thornton.
- The story began with a sepia-tinted pre-credits clip of William Hartnell, taken from the final episode of *The Dalek Invasion of Earth* (10). For the closing titles, Peter Howell blended his own version of the theme music halfway through the original arrangement by Delia Derbyshire.
- A *Radio Times* cover and feature appeared in the issue dated 19-25 November 1983. A separate *Doctor Who* 20th Anniversary *Radio Times* magazine was also published at the same time.
- A special edition of the story was prepared by Birmingham BBC producer Paul Vanezis in 1995. It changed the order of some scenes and used alternate, often extended, takes for most sequences (all the studio tapes and film recordings having survived intact). New computer-generated effects replaced the old ones and the music was rescored and redubbed into Dolby Digital 5.1 by Peter Howell.

Comment
The fact that *The Five Doctors* is an anniversary story makes it easier for the viewer to accept its threadbare plot and dearth of action. The geriatric cast going through their well-worn routines resembles a particularly starry episode of *Last of the Summer Wine*, and the acting of the guest cast, from the lowliest guard to the loftiest president, is as bland as the faces on Rassilon's tomb. Production design is not especially memorable either - the bog-standard sets for Gallifrey and the Dark Tower are too brightly lit. The Welsh location filming is at times quite atmospheric - despite the fact that the Eye of

Orion is clearly the same place as the Death Zone - but one feels this is more to do with the ambient weather conditions than any skill on the director's part. The best contribution is from composer Peter Howell; his bombastic music does a brilliant job of creating a sense of mystery and excitement otherwise totally lacking in Peter Moffatt's insipid direction. Too many companions, too many monsters, not enough talent. 45%

Season 21

"There should have been another way." ~ *The Doctor*

131) *Warriors of The Deep*
Johnny Byrne

Serial Code:
Original Transmission
Part One
Thursday 5 January 1984, 18.40-19.05, 7.6m / 51
Part Two
Friday 6 January 1984, 18.40-19.05, 7.5m / 52
Part Three
Thursday 12 January 1984, 18.40-19.05, 7.3m / 74
Part Four
Friday 13 January 1984, 18.40-19.05, 6.6m / 87
BBC Archive
All episodes exist as 625-line one-inch PAL colour master videotapes.
Novelization
Doctor Who - Warriors of the Deep by Terrance Dicks (126/12)
Hardback:
May 1984, WH Allen (0491033028 / Andrew Skilleter)
Paperback:
1. August 1984, Target (0426195612 / Andrew Skilleter)
2. August 1992, Target (0426195612 / Alister Pearson)
Talking Book
June 1995, 1 x cassette, abridged, read by Peter Davison (0563388366 / Photomontage)
Video
September 1995 (BBCV 5668 / Colin Howard)

Music and Sound Effects
1. February 1985, *Doctor Who - The Music II*, LP (REH 552 / Photomontage)
2. February 1985, *Doctor Who - The Music II*, cassette (ZCR 552 / Photomontage)
3. November 1992, Silva Screen, *Doctor Who - The Five Doctors*, CD (FILMCD 710 / Alister Pearson)
4. July 1993, *Doctor Who: 30 Years at the Radiophonic Workshop*, CD (BBCCD 871 / Photomontage)
Précis
Sea Base 4 is engaged in a cold war, not helped by the appearance of the Silurians and Sea Devils...
Cast
Peter Davison (The Doctor), Mark Strickson (Turlough), Janet Fielding (Tegan), Tom Adams (Vorshak), Ian McCulloch (Nilson), Ingrid Pitt (Solow), Martin Neil (Maddox), Nigel Humphreys (Bulic), Tara Ward (Preston), Vincent Brimble (Tarpok), Christopher Farries (Sauvix), Nitza Saul (Karina), Norman Comer (Icthar), Stuart Blake (Scibus), James Coombes (Paroli/Sentinel Six Voice), Steve Kelly, Chris Wolff, Jules Walters, Mike Brayburn, Dave Ould (Sea Devil Warriors), Gareth Milne (Double for the Doctor), William Perrie, John Asquith (The Myrka)
Crew
Visual Effects Designer Mat Irvine, *Visual Effects Assistants* Stuart Murdoch, Stan Mitchell, Martin Bower, *Video Effects* Dave Chapman, John Mitchell, *Technical Manager* Alan Arbuthnott, *Senior Cameramen* Bob Baxter, Alec Wheal, *Vision Mixer* Nigel Finnis, *Videotape Editor* Hugh Parson, *Studio Lighting* Peter Smee, *Studio Sound* Martin Ridout, *OB Sound* Chris Holcombe, *OB Cameraman* Alastair Mitchell, *Engineering Manager* Alan Woolford, *Properties Buyer* Roger Wood, *Special Sound* Dick Mills, *Incidental Music* Jonathan Gibbs, *Costume Designer* Judy Pepperdine, *Dressers* Stephen George, Alan Brewer, Richard Bateman, Camilla Gavin, *Make-Up Artist* Jennifer Hughes, *Designer* Tony Burrough, *Design Assistant* Michael Trevor, *Production Manager* Michael Darbon, *Production Associate* June Collins, *Production Assistant* Norma Flint, *Assistant Floor Manager* Adrian Haward, *Script Editor* Eric Saward, *Producer* John Nathan-Turner, *Director* Pennant Roberts
DWM Index
85   Preview
88   TV review
90   Episode Guide
     Novelization review
91   Richard Gregory interview

93	Season Survey results
94	Eric Saward interview
95	Terrance Dicks interview
102	Mark Strickson interview
122	Pennant Roberts interview
126	Archive + Fact File
169	Johnny Byrne interview
199	Archive Feature
	Johnny Byrne interview
	Ingrid Pitt interview
215	Peter Davison interview
230	Video review
238	The John Nathan-Turner Memoirs
248	Pennant Roberts interview
347	Eric Saward interview

Recording Dates
23-24 June 1983 (TC6), 28 June 1983 (Location videotaping), 29-30 June 1983 (Shepperton Studios videotaping), 4-7 July 1983 (Acton Studio modelwork), 13-15 July 1983 (TC6)

Location
Royal Engineers' Diving Establishment, McMullen Barracks, Marchwood, Hampshire

Working Title
As broadcast

Factoids
- Six Sea Devils costumes were constructed by Imagineering, under the aegis of Richard Gregory. The heads, with their Samurai-style helmets, were designed by Mat Irvine using an original John Friedlander mask as reference. Four Silurian costumes were made. Mat Irvine designed a totally new mask for them while Imagineering provided the fibreglass armoured body sections. The Myrka was operated by the people who played the Pantomime Horse in children's series *Rentaghost* (1976-84). Its movement was slower and more cumbersome than anticipated, and the green paint on its body had not had a chance to dry properly.
- Ealing Film Studios had originally been earmarked to film the water-tank sequences, but this was shifted at short notice to Shepperton Studios after the announcement of a General Election in May altered various BBC studio allocations.
- Underwater model sequences were shot on a dry stage with the camera filming through a top-lit water tank. Clever lighting created a rippling water effect.

Comment
Forget the returning old foes, Tony Burrough's fantastic sets are the real stars of *Warriors of the Deep*. Sea Base 4 really is a masterpiece of realistic-looking corridors, airlocks and rooms. The lighting in the corridors is actually quite dim and atmospheric, but even in the main control room the harsh lighting seems entirely reasonable. Clever merging of OB location work and studio recording is virtually undetectable. What lets the story down is not the much-pilloried Myrka but the ridiculously slow and silly Sea Devils, with their lolling heads and snail-like speed. In *The Sea-Devils* (62) they were terrifyingly fast, suddenly popping up from nowhere and zapping people with their explosive charges. Here they're just another identikit monster, their appearance and authority (now slaves of the Silurians) a shadow of their former selves. *Warriors of the Deep* is not as bad as is sometimes said, but with a bit more thought, it could have been so much better. **65%**

"You are about to take part in an event that will change the future of mankind." ~ *Sir George Hutchinson*

132) *The Awakening*
Eric Pringle

Serial Code: 6M
Original Transmission
Part One
Thursday 19 January 1984, 18.40-19.05, 7.9m / 61
Part Two
Friday 20 January 1984, 18.40-19.05, 6.6m / 84
Repeat Transmission
Omnibus
Friday 20 July 1984, 18.50-19.40, 4.4m / 104
BBC Archive
Both episodes exist as 625-line one-inch PAL colour master videotapes. Damage to Part One has been fully repaired using the existing 16mm colour film and the omnibus repeat master tape.
Novelization
Doctor Who - The Awakening by Eric Pringle (144/10)
Hardback:
February 1985, WH Allen (0491031947 / Andrew Skilleter)
Paperback:
1. June 1985, Target (0426201582 / Andrew Skilleter)
2. April 1992, Target (0426201582 / Alister Pearson)

Video
March 1997, twin-pack with *Frontios* (BBCV 6120 / Colin Howard)
Music and Sound Effects
1. February 1985, *Doctor Who - The Music II*, LP (REH 552 / Photomontage)
2. February 1985, *Doctor Who - The Music II*, cassette (ZCR 552 / Photomontage)
3. November 1992, Silva Screen, *Doctor Who - The Five Doctors*, CD (FILMCD 710 / Alister Pearson)
4. November 1992, Silva Screen, *Doctor Who - The Five Doctors*, cassette (FILMC 710 / Alister Pearson)
Précis
In the sleepy village of Little Hodcombe, a Civil War re-enactment is getting out of hand...
Cast
Peter Davison (The Doctor), Mark Strickson (Turlough), Janet Fielding (Tegan), Denis Lill (Sir George Hutchinson), Polly James (Jane Hampden), Glyn Houston (Colonel Wolsey), Keith Jayne (Will Chandler), Jack Galloway (Joseph Willow), Frederick Hall (Andrew Verney), Christopher Saul (First Trooper), Christopher Wenner (Second Trooper), John Kearns (Plague Victim), Nigel Tisdall (Phantom Cavalier/Phantom Roundhead), Scott Free, Sean McCabe (Phantom Roundheads)
Crew
Visual Effects Designer Tony Harding, *Visual Effects Assistants* George Reed, Martin Geeson, *Video Effects* Dave Chapman, Dave Jervis, *Technical Manager* Alan Arbuthnott, *Camera Supervisor* Alec Wheal, *Vision Mixer* Paul Wheeler, *Videotape Editor* Hugh Parson, *Studio Lighting* Peter Catless, *Studio Sound* Martin Ridout, *Film Cameraman* Paul Wheeler, *Film Sound* Bryan Showell, *Film Editor* MAC Adams, *Special Sound* Dick Mills, *Incidental Music* Peter Howell, Dick Mills, *Costume Designer* Jackie Southern, *Make-Up Artist* Ann Ailes, *Designer* Barry Newbery, *Production Managers* Mike Hudson, Liz Trubridge, *Production Associate* June Collins, *Production Assistant* Rosemary Parsons, *Assistant Floor Manager* Marcus DF White, *Script Editor* Eric Saward, *Producer* John Nathan-Turner, *Director* Michael Owen Morris
DWM Index
85 Preview
89 TV review
90 Episode Guide
91 Richard Gregory interview
93 Season Survey results
94 Eric Saward interview
97 Novelization review
102 Mark Strickson interview
116 Eric Saward: A Retrospective Review
148 Eric Saward interview
172 Archive + Fact File
    Eric Pringle interview
194 Peter Howell interview
215 Peter Davison interview
238 The John Nathan-Turner Memoirs
249 Video review
282 Archive Feature
347 Eric Saward interview
Recording Dates
19-22 July 1983 (Location filming), July 1983 (Acton Studios modelwork), 4-6 August 1983 (TC6)
Locations
Tarrant Monkton, Dorset; St Bartholomew's Church, village cross and Bishops Court Farm, Shapwick, Dorset; Village street, ford, village green, Martin Down and Damers Farm, Martin, Fordingbridge, Hampshire
Working Title
War Game
Factoids
- A brief scene involving Kamelion in a Tardis corridor was recorded for Part One, but was cut for timing reasons.
- Three real-life villages represented the fictitious village of Little Hodcombe. A glass-painting of the distant church in Part One helped to foster the illusion.
- Peter Davison gained a new costume from this story. The pullover's V-neck had wider stripes and the shirt had a green inner-lining, rather than red.
- Former *Blue Peter* presenter Christopher Wenner appeared as a non-speaking guard.
- Richard Gregory of Imagineering sculpted the large Malus head from fibreglass and made the puppet from moulded rubber.

Comment
A scary and atmospheric two-parter, *The Awakening* only loses impetus towards the end with some overlong explanatory scenes inside the Tardis. The editing throughout is razor-sharp, and the consistently bright and sunny feel to the location filming and well-matched studio work actually adds to the underlying air of evil, in the same way that the deceptively cheerful village scenes in *The Wicker Man* (1973) make the pagan rituals more disturbing. Keith Jayne would have made an excellent companion too. **80%**

"I came and went like a summer cloud." ~ The Doctor

133) *Frontios*
Christopher H Bidmead

Serial Code: 6N
Original Transmission
Part One
Thursday 26 January 1984, 18.40-19.05, 8m / 58
Part Two
Friday 27 January 1984, 18.40-19.05, 5.8m / 115
Part Three
Thursday 2 February 1984, 18.40-19.05, 7.8m / 59
Part Four
Friday 3 February 1984, 18.40-19.05, 5.6m / 112
BBC Archive
All episodes exist as 625-line one-inch PAL colour master videotapes.
Novelization
Doctor Who - Frontios by Christopher H Bidmead (143/12)
Hardback:
September 1984, WH Allen (0491032536 / Andrew Skilleter)
Paperback:
December 1984, Target (0426197801 / Andrew Skilleter)
Video
March 1997, twin-pack with *The Awakening* (BBCV 6120 / Colin Howard)
Précis
An Earth colony in the far future is being bombarded by meteorites…
Cast
Peter Davison (The Doctor), Mark Strickson (Turlough), Janet Fielding (Tegan), Jeff Rawle (Plantagenet), Peter Gilmore (Brazen), Lesley Dunlop (Norna), William Lucas (Range), Maurice O'Connell (Cockerill), John Beardmore (Captain Revere), John Gillett (Gravis), Richard Ashley (Orderly), George Campbell, Michael Malcolm, Stephen Speed, William Bowen, Hedi Khursandi (Tractators), Raymond Murtagh (Retrograde), Alison Skilbeck (Deputy), Jim Dowdall (Warnsman), Steve Emerson (Fighting Retrograde)
Crew
Visual Effects Designer Dave Harvard, *Visual Effects Assistant* Barry Brahan, *Video Effects* Dave Chapman, *Technical Manager* Alan Arbuthnott, *Camera Supervisor* Alec Wheal, *Vision Mixer* Paul Wheeler, *Videotape Editor* Hugh Parson, *Studio Lighting* John Summers, *Studio Sound* Martin Ridout, *Properties Buyer* Robert Flemming, *Special Sound* Dick Mills, *Grams Operator* Gordon Phillipson, *Incidental Music* Paddy Kingsland, *Costume Designer* Anushia Nieradzik, *Costume Assistant* Peter Halston, *Dressers* Frances Miles, Sue Clayton, Derek Sumner, Philip Winter, Camilla Gavin, *Make-Up Artist* Jill Hagger, *Make-Up Assistants* Damalza Rogers, Susan Kirkham, Helen Johnson, *Designer* David Buckingham, *Design Assistants* Maggie Carroll, Matthew Lorrimer, *Production Manager* Alex Gohar, *Production Associate* June Collins, *Production Assistant* Valerie Letley, *Assistant Floor Managers* Joanna Guritz, Ed Stevenson, *Floor Assistant* Brenda Thomas, *Script Editor* Eric Saward
Producer John Nathan-Turner, *Director* Ron Jones
DWM Index
85   Preview
89   TV review
90   Episode Guide
     Novelization review
93   Season Survey results
94   Eric Saward interview
101 Ron Jones interview
     Archive + Fact File
102 Mark Strickson interview
106 Peter Davison interview
109 Christopher H Bidmead interview
     Novelization review
170 Jeff Rawle interview
205 Paddy Kingsland interview
220 Archive Feature
     William Lucas interview
227 Mark Strickson interview
238 The John Nathan-Turner Memoirs
249 Video review
259 Christopher H Bidmead interview
Recording Dates
24-26 August 1983 (TC6), 7-9 September 1983 (TC6)
Working Titles
The Wanderers
Frotious
The Frontios
Factoids
- The Tractators were based on woodlice. Six costumes were made by an outside contractor, consisting of fibreglass heads, heavy black rubber carapaces and latex-covered Hessian stomachs. Tall dancers were chosen to inhabit the costumes, as director Ron Jones intended to show them first curled into a ball and then uncurling menacingly to trap their victims. However, the unwieldy nature of the costumes made this impracticable. Strips of Front Axial

Projection material called Scotchlite were applied to the Tractators' chests so that they would be seen to glow, but this was only seen occasionally on-screen due to the complex nature of the lighting required.
- The excavating machine was farmed out to Tom Harris of outside props builder Any Effects. Ron Jones was unhappy with the finished product and kept its use to a minimum.
- Peter Arne was originally chosen to play the part of Dr Range, but was murdered in his flat shortly before recording began. Similarly, *Frontios*' original designer Barrie Dobbins had died in tragic circumstances a month earlier.
- For the guards' uniforms, Federation helmets were reused from science fiction series *Blake's 7* (1978-81).

Comment
Very rarely does *Doctor Who* portray a believable culture with a backstory that seems to exist beyond the confines of the television screen. But in *Frontios*, the plight of the Earth colonists in their fragile outpost is astutely and credibly executed, both in terms of scripting and design. Their history and culture are tangibly conjured up by Christopher H Bidmead and the beautifully lit, imaginative set design by David Buckingham is a wonder to behold. Paddy Kingsland's haunting music is also extremely effective. On the downside, the Tractators are rather comical-looking and there is a clumsiness about some of the action scenes, especially when Brazen (Peter Gilmore) 'falls' into the excavating machine. But odd technical fluffs aside, *Frontios*' combination of visual spectacle and disturbing concepts is a real winner. And there's even room for some humour too. **91%**

"A lot of good people have died today." ~ *Tegan*

134) Resurrection of the Daleks
Eric Saward

Serial Code: 6P
Original Transmission
Part One
Wednesday 8 February 1984, 18.50-19.35, 7.3m / 73
Part Two
Wednesday 15 February 1984, 18.50-19.35, 8m / 53

BBC Archive
Both episodes exist as 625-line one-inch PAL colour master videotapes, in their original four-part format and in the re-edited two-part version. A 71 edit also exists for the original Part Two.
Novelization
None
Video
1. November 1993, 4-part version (BBCV 5143 / Bruno Elettori)
2. September 2001, 4-part version in 'The Davros Collection' box set [BBCV 7241 / Photomontage] with the other four Davros stories (BBCV 7253 / Photomontage)
DVD
1. November 2002, 4-part version, isolated music score, optional Dolby 5.1 surround mix, extended and deleted scenes, trailer, Part Two VT clock, production subtitles, photo gallery, commentary by Peter Davison, Janet Fielding and Matthew Robinson (BBCDVD 1100 / Clayton Hickman)
2. October 2003, as part of 'Dalek Collectors Edition' exclusive to WHSmith (- / Photomontage)
Music
1. February 1985, *Doctor Who - The Music II*, LP (REH 552 / Photomontage)
2. February 1985, *Doctor Who - The Music II*, cassette (ZCR 552 / Photomontage)
3. November 1992, Silva Screen, *Doctor Who - The Five Doctors*, CD (FILMCD 710 / Alister Pearson)
4. November 1992, Silva Screen, *Doctor Who - The Five Doctors*, cassette (FILMC 710 / Alister
Précis
The Daleks need Davros to help neutralize a Movellan virus...
Cast
Peter Davison (The Doctor), Janet Fielding (Tegan), Mark Strickson (Turlough), William Sleigh (Galloway), Maurice Colbourne (Lytton), Terry Molloy (Davros), Rodney Bewes (Stien), Rula Lenska (Styles), Del Henney (Colonel Archer), Chlöe Ashcroft (Professor Laird), Philip McGough (Sergeant Calder), Jim Findley (Mercer), Leslie Grantham (Kiston), Sneh Gupta (Osborn), Roger Davenport (Trooper), John Adam Baker, Linsey Turner (Crewmembers), Michael Jeffries, Mike Braben (Policemen), Adrian Scott (Chemist), Pat Judge (Metal Detector Man), Albert Welch (Tramp), Brian Miller, Royce Mills (Dalek Voices), John Scott Martin, Cy Town, Tony Starr, Toby Byrne (Daleks)
Crew
Visual Effects Designer Peter Wragg, *Visual Effects Assistants* Roger Perkins, Stan Mitchell, *Video Effects* Dave Chapman, *Technical Coordinator*

Alan Arbuthnott, *Camera Supervisor* Alec Wheal, *Vision Mixer* Jane Beckett, *Videotape Editor* Hugh Parson, *Studio Lighting* Ron Bristow, *Studio Sound* Scott Talbot, *Film Cameraman* Ian Hunter, *Film Sound* Bob Roberts, *Film Editor* Dan Rae, *Properties Buyer* Alan Huxley, *Special Sound* Dick Mills, *Incidental Music* Malcolm Clarke, *Costume Designer* Janet Tharby, *Costume Assistant* Linda Haysman, *Make-Up Artist* Eileen Mair, *Make-Up Assistant, Designer* John Anderson, *Design Assistant* Kathy Atty, *Production Manager* Corinne Hollingworth, *Production Associate* June Collins, *Production Assistant* Joy Sinclair, *Assistant Floor Manager* Matthew Burge, *Floor Assistant* Anna Campbell, *Script Editor* Eric Saward, *Producer* John Nathan-Turner, *Director* Matthew Robinson

DWM Index

86	Preview
	Set Report
89	TV review
90	Episode Guide
91	Janet Fielding interview
94	Eric Saward interview
102	Mark Strickson interview
106	Peter Davison interview
	Archive + Fact File
109	Terry Molloy interview
116	Eric Saward - A Retrospective Review
117	Michael Wisher interview
183	Those *Radio Times*
194	Lindsay Turner interview
	Archive Feature
195	Malcolm Clarke interview
197	What The Papers Said
206	Video review
214	Janet Fielding interview
215	Peter Davison interview
227	Mark Strickson interview
232	Matthew Robinson interview
236	The John Nathan-Turner Memoirs 1
238	The John Nathan-Turner Memoirs 2
272	Terry Molloy interview
309	Rula Lenska interview
	Video review (Davros box set)
325	DVD review
347	Eric Saward interview
353	Janet Fielding interview

Recording Dates
11-12 September 1983 (Location filming), September 1983 (unknown studio modelwork), 21-23 September 1983 (TC8), 5-7 September 1983 (TC6)

Locations
Curlew Street, Shad Thames, Lafone Street, Butler's Wharf, all Bermondsey, London SE1

Working Titles
Warhead
The Return
The Resurrection

Factoids
- Four working Daleks were used, using components from previous props. A new Davros mask was sculpted by Stan Mitchell.
- Due to the staging of the 1984 Winter Olympics, the story's four 25-minute episodes were condensed into two 45-minute parts, scheduled around live coverage of the event.
- A Part Two sequence involving caption slides of old companions was collated by fan adviser Ian Levine. Leela was inadvertently excluded.
- The model sequences used a state-of-the-art motion-control system, later seen to great effect in Part One of *The Trial of a Time Lord* (144).
- A *Radio Times* cover had been planned for the story but the Olympics precluded its use, and so it appeared instead in John Craven's Back Page (4-10 February 1984).

Comment
This is nothing more than a soulless remake of *Earthshock*, minus its shock value and integrity. Much has been made about *Resurrection*'s violence, but although virtually all the guest cast are killed, there is little drama or horror in their deaths, just a numbing sense of tedium. Matthew Robinson seems unable to control the hordes of extras and the on-screen action is often clumsy and ineffectual. The plotless nature of the narrative adds to the deficiencies of the miscast actors (Rula Lenska, Chlöe Ashcroft and Rodney Bewes appear to have been chosen for their 'star' status rather than their acting skills) and in every way the story lacks cohesion. **33%**

"I am immutably the Master!" ~ The Master

135) Planet of Fire
Peter Grimwade

Serial Code: 6Q
Original Transmission
Part One
Thursday 23 February 1984, 18.40-19.05, 7.4m / 71
Part Two
Friday 24 February 1984, 18.40-19.05, 6.1m / 102

Part Three
Thursday 1 March 1984, 18.40-19.05, 7.4m / 67
Part Four
Friday 2 March 1984, 18.40-19.05, 7m / 74
BBC Archive
All episodes exist as one-inch 625-line PAL colour videotape masters.
Novelization
Doctor Who - Planet of Fire by Peter Grimwade (143/11)
Hardback:
October 1984, WH Allen (0491033230 / Andrew Skilleter)
Paperback:
February 1988, Target (0426199405 / Andrew Skilleter)
Video
September 1998 (BBCV 6567 / Photomontage)
Music
1. February 1985, *Doctor Who - The Music II*, LP (REH 552 / Photomontage)
2. February 1985, *Doctor Who - The Music II*, cassette (ZCR 552 / Photomontage)
3. November 1992, Silva Screen, *Doctor Who - The Five Doctors*, CD (FILMCD 710 / Alister Pearson)
4. November 1992, Silva Screen, *Doctor Who - The Five Doctors*, cassette (FILMC 710 / Alister Pearson)
Précis
The miniaturized Master uses Kamelion to restore his size on the doomed planet of Sarn...
Cast
Peter Davison (The Doctor), Nicola Bryant (Peri Brown), Mark Strickson (Turlough), Gerald Flood (Kamelion Voice), Peter Wyngarde (Timanov), Anthony Ainley (The Master), Dallas Adams (Professor Howard Foster), Barbara Shelley (Sorasta), James Bate (Amyand), Jonathan Caplan (Roskal), Edward Highmore (Malkon), Michael Bangerter (Curt), Simon Sutton (Lookout), Max Arthur (Zuko), John Alkin (Lomand/Voice of Trion Control)
Crew
Visual Effects Designer Christopher Lawson, *Visual Effects Assistant* Roger Turner, *Video Effects* Dave Chapman, *Technical Manager* Alan Arbuthnott, *Camera Supervisors* Alec Wheal, Geoff Clark, *Vision Mixer* Dinah Long, *Videotape Editor* Hugh Parson, *Studio Lighting* John Summers, *Studio Sound* Scott Talbott, *Film Sound Assistant* Don Lee, *Film Cameraman* John Walker, *Assistant Cameraman* Tony Bragg, *Film Sound* John Tellick, *Film Editor* Alistair Mitchell, *Properties Buyer* Paul Woods, *Special Sound* Dick Mills, *Incidental Music* Peter Howell, *Costume Designer* John Peacock, *Dressers* Frances Miles, Ron Simpson, *Make-Up Artist* Elizabeth Rowell, *Make-Up Assistant* Elizabeth Hardiment, *Designer* Malcolm Thornton, *Design Assistant* Dinah Walker, *Production Manager* Corinne Hollingworth, *Production Associate* June Collins, *Production Assistant* Claire Hughes Smith, *Assistant Floor Manager* Rob Evans, *Floor Assistant* Anna Campbell, *Script Editor* Eric Saward, *Producer* John Nathan-Turner, *Director* Fiona Cumming

DWM Index
86	Preview
90	Episode Guide
	TV review
92	Novelization review
93	Season Survey results
94	Eric Saward interview
96	Nicola Bryant interview
102	Mark Strickson interview
116	Eric Saward - A Retrospective Review
119	Nicola Bryant interview
129	Fiona Cumming interview
133	Peter Grimwade interview
165	The Doctor Abroad
194	Peter Howell interview
206	Archive Feature
215	Peter Davison interview
227	Mark Strickson interview
236	Nicola Bryant interview
238	The John Nathan-Turner Memoirs
269	Peter Wyngarde interview
	Video review
347	Eric Saward interview

Recording Dates
14-15 October 1983 (Location filming), 17-19 October 1983 (Location filming), 26-27 October 1983 (TC1), 9-11 November 1983 (TC6)
Locations
Montañas del Fuego, Timanfaya National Park, Lanzarote; Mirador del Rio, Lanzarote; Papagoyo Bay, Lanzarote; Orzola, Lanzarote
Working Title
As broadcast
Factoids
- Lanzarote was chosen as the programme's third foreign sojourn because director Fiona Cumming had sent John Nathan-Turner a postcard from there over Christmas 1982 and he had thought it looked ideal for a future story. Peter Grimwade was assigned to write the story, although he never visited the locale.
- Actress Nicola Bryant was not American in real life - she was born in Guildford, Surrey, although marriage to a Broadway singer

entitled her to dual American/British nationality. When offered the role of Peri, she had yet to acquire her Equity card.
- When Nicola Bryant was pretending to drown in Part One, a naked German swimmer, thinking it was for real, 'rescued' her and brought her back to the beach.

Comment
Considering that Peter Grimwade was given four criteria to fulfil for this story - it had to be set in Lanzarote, it had to introduce Peri, it had to reintroduce and kill off Kamelion, and it had to explain Turlough's origins and see him leave - it's amazing that the story is as coherent as it is. But spectacular scenery and unusually good miniature effects aside, *Planet of Fire* is often insipid and uninspiring. And it's also rather obvious that Lanzarote and Sarn are the same place. That said, the Master's involvement for once springs organically from the story and the effects showing his miniaturization and 'death' are very well done. **49%**

"Is this death?" ~ The Doctor

136) The Caves of Androzani
Robert Holmes

Serial Code: 6R
Original Transmission
Part One
Thursday 8 March 1984, 18.40-19.05, 6.9m / 66
Part Two
Friday 9 March 1984, 18.40-19.05, 6.6m / 75
Part Three
Thursday 15 March 1984, 18.40-19.05, 7.8m / 62
Part Four
Friday 16 March 1984, 18.40-19.05, 7.8m / 62
Repeat Transmission
On BBC2:
Part One
Friday 19 February 1993, 19.15-19.40, 2.1m / 27
Part Two
Friday 26 February 1993, 19.15-19.40, 1.9m / 27
Part Three
Friday 5 March 1993, 19.15-19.40, 1.8m / -
Part Four
Friday 12 March 1993, 19.15-19.40, 1.4m / -
BBC Archive
All episodes exist as 625-line one-inch PAL colour master videotapes.
Novelization
Doctor Who - The Caves of Androzani by Terrance Dicks (135/12)

Hardback:
November 1984, WH Allen (0491034830 / Andrew Skilleter)
Paperback:
1. February 1985, Target (0426199596 / Andrew Skilleter)
2. May 1993, Target (0426199596 / Alister Pearson)
Non-Fiction Book
March 1996, Boxtree, *Classic Who: The Harper Classics* by Adrian Rigelsford, Hardback (0752201883 / Photograph)
Video
January 1992 (BBCV 4713 / Andrew Skilleter)
DVD
June 2001, original trailer, extended scene, studio footage, alternative Part One, isolated music score, production subtitles, photo gallery, commentary by Peter Davison, Nicola Bryant and Graeme Harper (BBCDVD 1042 / Photomontage)
Music and Sound Effects
1. February 1985, *Doctor Who - The Music II*, LP (REH 552 / Photomontage)
2. February 1985, *Doctor Who - The Music II*, cassette (ZCR 552 / Photomontage)
3. November 1992, Silva Screen, *Doctor Who - The Five Doctors*, CD (FILMCD 710 / Alister Pearson)
4. November 1992, Silva Screen, *Doctor Who - The Five Doctors*, cassette (FILMC 710 / Alister Pearson)
5. July 1993, *Doctor Who: 30 Years at the Radiophonic Workshop*, CD (BBCCD 871 / Photomontage)
Précis
The Doctor and Peri are caught in a futile war on Androzani Minor...
Cast
Peter Davison, Colin Baker (The Doctor), Nicola Bryant (Peri), Janet Fielding (Tegan), Mark Strickson (Turlough), Sarah Sutton (Nyssa), Matthew Waterhouse (Adric), Anthony Ainley (The Master), Gerald Flood (Kamelion Voice), Christopher Gable (Sharaz Jek), Maurice Roëves (Stotz), John Normington (Morgus), Robert Glenister (Salateen), Martin Cochrane (Chellak), Roy Holder (Krelper), Barbara Kinghorn (Timmin), David Neal (President), Ian Staples (Soldier/Signals Voice), Colin Taylor (Magma Creature), Keith Harper, Andrew Smith, Stephen Smith (Androids), Gareth Milne (Stunt Double for the Doctor), Gerry O'Brien, Les Conrad, Robert Smythe (Gunrunners)

Crew
Visual Effects Designers Jim Francis, Stuart Brisdon, *Visual Effects Assistant* Simon Fullerlove, *Matte Artist* Jean Peyre, *Graphic Designer* Ian Hewitt, *Video Effects* Dave Chapman, *Technical Co-ordinator* Alan Arbuthnott, *Camera Supervisor* Alec Wheal, *Vision Mixer* Dinah Long, *Videotape Editor* Steve Newnham, *Studio Lighting* Don Babbage, *Studio Sound* Scott Talbott, *Film Cameraman* John Walker, *Film Camera Assistant* John Daley, *Film Sound* Malcolm Campbell, *Film Editor* Roger Guertin, *Properties Buyer* Alan Huxley, *Special Sound* Dick Mills, *Incidental Music* Roger Limb, *Costume Designer* Andrew Rose, *Dressers* Liz Scamell, Philip Falconer, *Make-Up Designers* Jan Nethercot, Shirley Stallard, *Make-Up Assistant* Janet Philips, *Designer* John Hurst, *Design Assistant* Mark Kebby, *Production Managers* Elizabeth Trubridge, Corinne Hollingworth, *Production Associate* June Collins, *Production Assistant* Juley Harding, *Assistant Floor Manager* Susan Hedden, *Floor Assistant* Simon Spencer, *Script Editor* Eric Saward, *Producer* John Nathan-Turner, *Director* Graeme Harper

DWM Index
87   Preview
90   Graeme Harper interview
     Episode Guide
     TV review
91   Richard Gregory interview
92   Novelization review
93   Season Survey results
94   Eric Saward interview
95   Archive + Fact File
96   Nicola Bryant interview
100 Robert Holmes interview
106 Peter Davison interview
110 Sarah Sutton interview
116 Eric Saward: A Retrospective Review
118 Colin Baker interview
119 Nicola Bryant interview
134 Peter Davison interview
166 Nicola Bryant interview
183 Video review
184 Graeme Harper interview
196 Roger Limb interview
197 What The Papers Said
199 TV review (repeat)
202 Matthew Waterhouse interview
215 Peter Davison interview
236 Nicola Bryant interview
238 The John Nathan-Turner Memoirs
255 John Normington interview
265 *Doctor Who Magazine* Awards (3rd)
279 Archive Feature
304 DVD restoration feature
305 DVD review
322 Colin Baker interview
347 Eric Saward interview

Recording Dates
15-17 November 1983 (Location filming), 15-17 December 1983 (TC6), December 1983 (Unknown studio modelwork), 11-12 January 1984 (TC6)

Location
Masters Pit, Gallows Heath, Wareham, Dorset

Working Title
Chain Reaction

Factoids
- Sharaz Jek's mask - a balaclava made of tanned leather and sprayed black and white - was based on a photograph of a Zulu warrior. The costume consisted of a black leather biker's outfit with a cowl at the front to hide the zip. For Part Four, Christopher Gable had prosthetic latex pieces attached to his face to represent his terrible disfigurement.
- The Magma Creature was built by an outside contractor. Although highly detailed, director and producer both thought it was unsuccessful and kept its screen time to a minimum.
- A scenery shifters' strike caused the loss of the first studio session in December. This was rearranged for January, meaning that recording on Colin Baker's debut story *The Twin Dilemma* (137) was put back several weeks.
- The Fifth Doctor's previous companions assembled to record specially shot 'farewells' on the final studio session, the same day that the regeneration was shot. Video effects expert Dave Chapman spent a day's work in post-production adding the howlround effect that accompanies the transformation (inspired by the 1968 film *2001: A Space Odyssey*) and manipulating each of the companion's images with Quantel 5000. The impending regeneration is signposted at the climax to Part Three when a bewildered Doctor sees howlround images start forming on the spaceship's screen.

Comment
It's hardly possible to find a bad word to say about *The Caves of Androzani*. Even the mistakes are effective, such as John Normington inadvertently addressing his asides directly to camera. The cave interiors are the best in the programme's history and the sight of armed extras

fighting heated battles in such a dramatic environment is hard to forget. The violence is unremitting, Graeme Harper's direction and editing is electrifying, and - uniquely - there is not a duff performance in sight. From Jek's 1940s-style underground base to the high-tech simplicity of Morgus' penthouse suite, the story looks simply stunning. Roger Limb's music is uncharacteristically superb too, piling up the tension throughout. The only two conceivable bugbears are the unconvincing Magma Creature and the over-dramatic regeneration (did Peri sees all this, or is it in the Doctor's mind?). A classic, and rightfully so. **97%**

Sixth Doctor: Colin Baker

"Sweet? Effete!" ~ *The Doctor*

137) *The Twin Dilemma*
Anthony Steven

Serial Code: 6S
Original Transmission
Part One
Thursday 22 March 1984, 18.40-19.05, 7.6m / 66
Part Two
Friday 23 March 1984, 18.40-19.05, 7.4m / 71
Part Three
Thursday 29 March 1984, 18.40-19.05, 7m / 59
Part Four
Friday 30 March 1984, 18.40-19.05, 6.3m / 67
BBC Archive
All episodes exist as 625-line one-inch PAL colour master videotapes.
Novelization
Doctor Who - The Twin Dilemma by Eric Saward (138/10)
Hardback:
October 1985, WH Allen (0491031246 / Andrew Skilleter)
Paperback:
1. March 1986, Target (0426201558 / Andrew Skilleter)
2. January 1993, Target (0426201558 / Andrew Skilleter)
Video
May 1992 (BBCV 4783 / Andrew Skilleter)
Précis
A giant slug called Mestor wants to turn his sun supernova and populate the Universe with his eggs...

Cast
Colin Baker (The Doctor/Jocondan Voice), Nicola Bryant (Peri Brown), Dennis Chinnery (Sylvest), Maurice Denham (Edgeworth/Azmael), Kevin McNally (Hugo Lang), Edwin Richfield (Mestor), Seymour Green (Chamberlain), Barry Stanton (Noma), Oliver Smith (Drak), Gavin Conrad (Romulus), Andrew Conrad (Remus), Helen Blatch (Fabian), Dione Inman (Elena), Roger Nott (Prisoner), John Wilson (Jocondan Guard), Steve Wickham, Ridgewell Hawkes (Gastropods)
Crew
Visual Effects Designer Stuart Brisdon, *Video Effects* Dave Chapman, *Technical Manager* Alan Arbuthnott, *Camera Supervisor* Alec Wheal, *Vision Mixer* Dinah Long, *Videotape Editor* Hugh Parson, *Studio Lighting* Don Babbage, *Studio Sound* Scott Talbott, *Film Cameramen* John Baker, John Walker, *Film Sound* Malcolm Campbell, *Film Editor* Iain McKendrick, *Special Sound* Dick Mills, *Incidental Music* Malcolm Clarke, *Costume Designer* Pat Godfrey, *Make-Up Artist* Denise Baron, *Make-Up Assistant* Janet Philips, *Designer* Valerie Warrender, *Production Manager* Michael A Treen, *Production Associate* June Collins, *Production Assistant* Christine Fawsett, *Assistant Floor Managers* Stephen Jeffrey-Poulter, Beth Millward, *Script Editor* Eric Saward, *Producer* John Nathan-Turner, *Director* Peter Moffat
DWM Index
87	Preview
91	Richard Gregory interview
	TV review
93	Season Survey results
94	Eric Saward interview
97	Colin Baker interview
104	Eric Saward interview
	Novelization review
116	Eric Saward: A Retrospective Review
120	Episode Guide
148	Eric Saward interview
182	Those *Radio Times*
187	Video review
195	Malcolm Clarke interview
198	What The Papers Said
236	Nicola Bryant interview
238	The John Nathan-Turner Memoirs
254	Peter Moffatt interview
270	Archive Feature
321	Colin Baker interview
322	Colin Baker interview
348	Eric Saward interview

Recording Dates
24-28 January 1984 (TC8), 7-8 February 1984 (Location filming), February 1984 (Unknown studio modelwork), 14-16 February 1984 (TC3)

Locations
Springwell Quarry, Rickmansworth, Hertfordshire; Gerrards Cross Sand and Gravel Quarry, Gerrards Cross, Buckinghamshire

Working Titles
A Stitch in Time
A Switch in Time

Factoids
- The decisive factor in Colin Baker's casting was that producer John Nathan-Turner saw him entertaining guests at the wedding reception of assistant floor manager Lynn Richards in 1982. Script editor Eric Saward was less happy with the choice of actor but worked alongside the producer to give the new incumbent a darker, more alien, personality than recent Doctors.
- The Sixth Doctor's costume was made by Pat Godfrey. John Nathan-Turner's stipulation was that it be "totally tasteless", something that the experienced costume designer found particularly difficult. The specially made trousers, waistcoat, frock coat and shirt were assembled by tailor Arthur Davey. Colin Baker's first costume photocall was on 10 January 1984.
- The original starfield opening and closing title sequences were modified by Sid Sutton and Terry Handley. Colin Baker's smiling face was added and the sequences were reshot through a prism to give them a multi-coloured tint. A slightly different version of the neon logo was used, along with an extra 'woomph' provided by theme music arranger Peter Howell.
- Richard Gregory of Unit 22 built four Gastropod costumes. One was worn by Edwin Richfield, two were worn by extras, and a fourth was a dummy version for Mestor's death scene.
- Playing the Sylvest twins were Paul and Andrew Conrad, sons of veteran *Doctor Who* extra Les Conrad. Paul had to change his name to 'Gavin' for the story because actors' union Equity already had an actor with his name on their books.

Comment
Oh dear. After all the hard work spent on *The Caves of Androzani*, along comes this lazy, badly-written, appallingly produced joke of a story. What's worse is that for nine months it was the only glimpse viewers would have of Colin Baker, and so the sour taste in the mouth was made ever more unappetising over time. If it had been the first of a season, it would have been easier to overlook. So where to begin? Firstly, the entire cast delivers the sort of performance only their mothers would be proud of; secondly, every aspect of the production is cheap, tacky and poorly visualised; thirdly, the direction is utterly flat, and fourthly, the music is so bad it should have been made illegal to transmit it. On the positive side, the story itself (not the dialogue, heaven forbid) is actually quite engaging in a naïve B-movie kind of way. And I suppose it's a clever idea to get the worst Sixth Doctor story out of the way first. But still... **12%**

Season 22

"The Tardis, when working properly, is capable of many amazing things - not unlike myself!" ~ The Doctor

138) Attack of the Cybermen
Paula Moore (pen-name for Eric Saward and Paula Woolsey, from a story by Ian Levine)

Serial Code: 6T
Original Transmission
Part One
Saturday 5 January 1985, 17.20-18.05, 8.9m / 71
Part Two
Saturday 12 January 1985, 17.20-18.05, 7.2m / 104
BBC Archive
Both episodes exist as 625-line one-inch PAL colour master videotapes. The four original 25-minute episodes also exist in the same format.
Novelization
Doctor Who - Attack of the Cybermen by Eric Saward (140/10)
Paperback:
1. April 1989, Target (0426202902 / Colin Howard)
2. November 1992, Target (0426202902 / Alister Pearson)
Talking Book
August 1995, 1 x cassette, abridged, read by Colin Baker (0563388668 / Photomontage)
Video
November 2000, in 'Cybermen Limited Edition Tin' [BBCV 7030] with *The Tenth Planet* (BBCV 7048 / Photomontage)
Précis
The Cybermen want to divert Halley's Comet so it can crash into the Earth...

Cast
Colin Baker (The Doctor), Nicola Bryant (Peri), Maurice Colbourne (Lytton), Terry Molloy (Russell), Brian Glover (Griffiths), James Beckett (Payne), Jonathan David (Stratton), Michael Attwell (Bates), Sarah Greene (Varne), Sarah Berger (Rost), Esther Freud (Threst), Faith Brown (Flast), David Banks (Cyberleader), Brian Orrell (Cyber Lieutenant), Michael Kilgarriff (Cyber Controller), Stephen Churchett (Bill), Stephen Wale (David), John Ainley, Ian Marshall-Fisher, Roger Pope, Thomas Lucy (Cybermen), Ken Barker (Stunt Cyberman), Pat Gorman (Cyberman/Rogue Cyberman), Michael Braben, Michael Jeffries (Policemen), Ken Pritchard (Cybernised Man), Trisha Clark, Irela Williams, Maggie Lynton (Cryons)

Crew
Visual Effects Designer Chris Lawson, *Visual Effects Assistant* Graham Brown, *Video Effects* Dave Chapman, *Technical Manager* Alan Arbuthnott, *Camera Supervisor* Alec Wheal, *Vision Mixers* Nigel Finnis, Dinah Long, *Videotape Editor* Hugh Parson, *Studio Lighting* Henry Barber, *Studio Sound* Andrew Stacey, *Film Cameraman* Godfrey Johnson, *Film Sound* Barry Tharby, *Film Editor* MAC Adams, *Special Sound* Dick Mills, *Grams Operator* John Doyes, *Incidental Music* Malcolm Clarke, *Costume Designer* Anushia Nieradzik, *Costume Assistant* Juliet Godfrey, *Make-Up Artist* Linda McInnes, *Make-Up Assistant* Sharon Walsh, *Designer* Marjorie Pratt, *Design Assistant* Adele Marolf, *Production Manager* Andrew Buchanan, *Production Associates* June Collins, Sue Anstruther, *Production Assistant* Llinos Wyn Jones, *Assistant Floor Manager* Pennie Bloomfield, *Floor Assistant* Lynda Pannett, *Script Editor* Eric Saward, *Producer* John Nathan-Turner, *Director* Matthew Robinson

DWM Index
91 Richard Gregory interview
92 Location report 1
93 Location report 2
94 Eric Saward interview
96 Preview
    Nicola Bryant interview
100 TV review
104 Eric Saward interview
108 Season Survey results
120 Episode Guide
143 David Banks interview
148 Eric Saward interview
149 Novelization review
152 Ken Barker interview
182 Those *Radio Times*
195 Malcolm Clarke interview
207 Archive Feature
232 Matthew Robinson interview
236 Nicola Bryant interview
239 The John Nathan-Turner Memoirs
244 David Banks interview
272 Terry Molloy interview
297 Sarah Berger interview
298 Video review
322 Colin Baker interview
323 Colin Baker interview
334 Sarah Greene interview
348 Eric Saward interview

Recording Dates
29 May-1 June 1984 (Location filming), 7-8 June 1984 (Acton Studio modelwork), 21-22 June 1984 (TC6), 6-8 July 1984 (TC6)

Locations
Dartmouth Castle pub, Glenthorne Road, London W6; London Scrapyard, 161 Becklow Road, London W12; Davis Road and back alley, London W12; Gerrards Cross Sand and Gravel Quarry, Gerrards Cross, Buckinghamshire; Cameron Scrap Merchant, 36 Birkbeck Road, London W3

Working Titles
Return to Telos
The Cold War

Factoids
- Due to the high ratings for the double-length episodes of last season's *Resurrection of the Daleks* (134), all stories in Season 22 would be 45 minutes long.
- The eight Cybermen costumes from *Earthshock* were reused, complete with modifications from *The Five Doctors*. The Cryons wore white leotards under cellophane jumpsuits impregnated with a sparkling metallic substance. Semi-transparent masks and cellophane ruffs completed the ensemble.
- For this story only, the Tardis exterior changed from a Police Box into a gaudily painted dresser, a pipe organ and a pair of iron gates.
- Many of the Cryon actresses were famous in other walks of life - Sarah Greene was the current presenter of *Blue Peter*, Faith Brown was a prominent impressionist and comedienne, and Esther Freud - now a bestselling novelist - was (and still is) the great-granddaughter of Sigmund Freud and daughter of artist Lucian Freud.

Comment
Ostensibly a sequel to every Cyberman story ever written, the opening story of Season 22 fails for two entirely opposing reasons. On the one hand

it is obsessed with *Doctor Who* continuity - enough to hinge a whole story around an event that happened almost twenty years ago - and on the other, it can't be bothered to get any of the details right. For instance, the tombs in *Attack of the Cybermen* are rubbish and look nothing like the tombs seen in the 1967 story, or even much like tombs at all. The Cybermen can now be killed by anyone wielding a reasonably sharp instrument. As to the Cryons, their backstory makes no sense and their costumes are quite possibly the worst in the programme's history, down there with the Fish People from *The Underwater Menace* (32). It has its moments though, and Colin Baker is slightly more credible here than he was in his debut. He certainly outshines Nicola Bryant, who - breasts aside - contributes little to the story. The plotting is a mess and the out-of-context violence is clearly a cheap shock tactic that convinces no-one. **45%**

"Do you always get the priest parts?" ~ The Doctor

139) Vengeance on Varos
Philip Martin

Serial Code: 6V
Original Transmission
Part One
Saturday 19 January 1995, 17.20-18.05, 7.2m / 110
Part Two
Saturday 26 January 1995, 17.20-18.05, 7m / 108
BBC Archive
Both episodes exist as 625-line one-inch PAL colour master videotapes. The four original 25-minute episodes also exist in the same format.
Novelization
Doctor Who – Vengeance on Varos by Philip Martin (137/16)
Hardback:
January 1988, WH Allen (0491035020 / David McAllister)
Paperback:
1. June 1988, Target (0426202910 / David McAllister)
2. January 1993, Target (0426202910 / Alister Pearson)
Video
May 1993 (BBCV 4962 / Andrew Skilleter)
DVD
October 2001, optional production soundtrack, trailers, extended and deleted scenes, studio footage, outtakes, continuity announcements, production subtitles, photo gallery, commentary by Colin Baker, Nicola Bryant and Nabil Shaban (BBCDVD 1044 / Photomontage)
Talking Book
November 1997, 1 x cassette, abridged, read by Colin Baker (ZBBC 1832 / Photomontage)
Précis
The people of Varos are conditioned to watch hideous executions as entertainment...
Cast
Colin Baker (The Doctor), Nicola Bryant (Peri), Nabil Shaban (Sil), Martin Jarvis (Governor), Jason Connery (Jondar), Forbes Collins (Chief Officer), Sheila Reid (Etta), Stephen Yardley (Arak), Geraldine Alexander (Areta), Owen Teale (Maldak), Nicholas Chagrin (Quillam), Graham Cull (Bax), Keith Skinner (Rondel), Hugh Martin (Priest), Gareth Milne, Roy Alon (Mortuary Attendants), Jack McGuire, Alan Troy (Madmen), Sam Scott, Charles Rayford (Monks), Bob Tarff (Guard/Executioner), Ronnie Cush, Anthony Wellington, Kwabena Monso (Sil's Attendants)
Crew
Visual Effects Designer Charles Jeanes, *Visual Effects Assistant* Julian Fullalove, *Video Effects* Dave Chapman, *Technical Coordinator* Alan Arbuthnott, *Camera Supervisor* Alec Wheal, *Vision Mixers* Nigel Finnis, Jayne Becket, *Videotape Editor* Hugh Parson, *Studio Lighting* Dennis Channon, *Studio Sound* Andy Stacey, *Properties Buyer* Camilla Gavin, *Special Sound* Dick Mills, *Incidental Music* Jonathan Gibbs, *Costume Designer* Anne Hardinge, *Costume Assistant* Jill Taylor, *Dressers* Joanna Dawn, Alan Hatchman, Paul Mayo, Anthony Moore, *Make-Up Artists* Cecile Hay-Arthur, Dorka Nieradzik, *Make-Up Assistant* Juliette Mayer, *Designer* Tony Snoaden, *Design Assistant* Rod McLean, *Production Manager* Margot Eavis, *Production Associate* Sue Anstruther, *Production Assistants* Jane Whittaker, Pat Greenland, *Assistant Floor Manager* Sophie Neville, *Floor Assistant* Brenda Thomas, *Script Editor* Eric Saward, *Producer* John Nathan-Turner, *Director* Ron Jones
DWM Index

94	Eric Saward interview Preview
96	Nicola Bryant interview Preview
100	TV review
101	Ron Jones interview
104	John Nathan-Turner interview
108	Season Survey results
120	Episode Guide

125	Philip Martin interview
129	Novelization review
144	Archive + Fact File
166	Nicola Bryant interview
201	Martin Jarvis interview
	Stephen Yardley interview
236	Nicola Bryant interview
239	John Nathan-Turner interview
288	Nabil Shaban interview
309	Archive Feature
	DVD review
322	Colin Baker interview
326	Martin Jarvis interview
348	Eric Saward interview

Recording Dates
18-20 July 1984 (TC6), 31 July – 2 August 1984 (TC6)

Working Titles
Domain
Planet of Fear

Factoids
- Actor Nabil Shaban was a co-founder of theatre group Graeae, a company that promoted disabled performers. Tim Barlow (Tyssan in *Destiny of the Daleks*, 104) was also a member. Shaban's Sil costume was made from a textured latex body with a maggot-like tail and a separate cowled headpiece. His 'marshminnows' were peaches coloured with green vegetable dye.
- Modified golf buggies were used for the guards' patrol cars. Noisy and slow-moving, they were only just slim enough to navigate the narrow corridors of Varos.
- Martin Jarvis made his third and final appearance in *Doctor Who* (previously he had appeared as Hilio in *The Web Planet*, 13, and Butler in *Invasion of the Dinosaurs*, 71). Stephen Yardley had played the mutant Sevrin in *Genesis of the Daleks* (78) and would go on to star in the up-market BBC soap opera *Howard's Way* (1985-90).
- Peri's transformation into a bird was done in reverse, with the full effect being recorded first and then subsequent stages taped with fewer and fewer feathers (to which, unfortunately, Nicola Bryant was allergic).
- *Radio Times* and *Points of View* featured much critical viewer feedback, most complaining about the violence seen in this story and *Attack of the Cybermen*.

Comment
It's ironic that a story purporting to condemn the antisocial effects of television violence should itself be the subject of intense criticism for its own scenes of wanton violence (especially from the Doctor). But in many ways, *Vengeance on Varos* is a very sanitised representation of the debate, eschewing a realistic setting in favour of clichéd dungeons, masked henchmen and grotesque villains. Of course, in this respect it can also be seen as a spoof of *Doctor Who* itself, with Arak and Etta representing the jaded TV viewers tuning in for the latest instalment of the formulaic adventures of man in a multicoloured coat running around with a bunch of ineffectual rebels while his beautiful companion lies immobile and helpless in the felon's lair. Clever stuff. Unfortunately, the effect is ruined by the wooden and unconvincing performances of the guest cast, most notably Nicholas Chagrin and Forbes Collins. Added to this are some diabolically executed action sequences and a plot that fizzles out well before it should. But there are some things to enjoy, including Nabil Shaban's era-defining performances as the loathsome Sil and the wonderfully self-referential cliffhanger. Just forget the old men in nappies. Please. **58%**

"You can't mistake him. He's mean looking." ~ The Master

140) The Mark of the Rani
Pip and Jane Baker

Serial Code: 6X
Original Transmission
Part One
Saturday 2 February 1985, 17.20-18.05, 6.3m / 111
Part Two
Saturday 9 February 1985, 17.20-18.05, 7.3m / 84
BBC Archive
Both episodes exist as 625-line one-inch PAL colour master videotapes. The four original 25-minute episodes also exist in the same format.
Novelization
Doctor Who – The Mark of the Rani by Pip and Jane Baker (135/22)
Hardback:
January 1986, WH Allen (0491035322 / Andrew Skilleter)
Paperback:
June 1986, Target (0426202325 / Andrew Skilleter)
Video
July 1995 (BBCV 5603 / Colin Howard)

Précis
The Master joins forces with the Rani to extract brain fluids from Luddite mine workers...

Cast
Colin Baker (The Doctor), Nicola Bryant (Peri), Kate O'Mara (The Rani), Anthony Ainley (The Master), Terence Alexander (Lord Ravensworth), Gawn Grainger (George Stephenson), Gary Cady (Luke Ward), Peter Childs (Jack Ward), William Ilkley (Edwin Green), Kevin White (Sam Rudge), Martyn Whitby (Drayman), Richard Steele (Guard), Sarah James (Young Woman), Cordelia Ditton (Older Woman), Leon Laurence, Nick Joseph (Miners), Alan Talbot (Tom), Nigel Johnson (Josh), Tony Dell (Boy)

Crew
Stunt Arranger Bill Weston, *Visual Effects Designer* Dave Barton, *Visual Effects Assistants* George Reed, Tony McKillop, Roger Turner, Tom Davis, *Video Effects* Dave Chapman, *Technical Coordinator* Alan Arbuthnott, *Camera Supervisor* Alec Wheal, *Vision Mixer* Jayne Beckett, *Videotape Editor* Hugh Parson, *Studio Lighting* Don Babbage, *Studio Sound* Keith Bowden, *Film Cameraman* Kevin Rowley, *Film Sound* Barrie Tharby, *Film Editor* Ray Wingrove, *Properties Buyer* Al Huxley, *Special Sound* Dick Mills, *Grams Operator* Ian Tomlin, *Incidental Music* Jonathan Gibbs, *Costume Designer* Dinah Collin, *Costume Assistant* Barry Simmons, *Dressers* Ray Green, Brian Baker, Rachel Gordon, Natalie Harris, Colin May, Terry Pettigrew, Ita Murray, *Make-Up Artist* Catherine Davies, *Make-Up Assistants* Lisa Lubbock, Patricia Tilley, Julie Shephard, *Designer* Paul Trerise, *Design Assistant* Matt Sindall, *Production Manager* Tony Redston, *Production Associate* Sue Anstruther, *Production Assistant* Carolyn Mawdsley, *Assistant Floor Manager* Penny Williams, *Floor Assistant* Helen Greaves, *Script Editor* Eric Saward, *Producer* John Nathan-Turner, *Director* Sarah Hellings

DWM Index
97	Preview
	Colin Baker interview
101	TV review
103	Paul Trerise interview
	Dinah Collin interview
	Catherine Davies interview
	Pip and Jane Baker interview
	Sarah Hellings interview
104	Eric Saward interview
108	Season Survey results
120	Episode Guide
128	Kate O'Mara interview
137	Pip and Jane Baker interview
182	Those *Radio Times*
217	Archive Feature
	Pip and Jane Baker interview
228	Video review
236	Nicola Bryant interview
239	The John Nathan-Turner Memoirs
281	Sarah Hellings interview
298	Kate O'Mara interview
303	Pip and Jane Baker interview
322	Colin Baker interview
323	Colin Baker interview
343	The Fact of Fiction
348	Eric Saward interview

Recording Dates
22-27 October 1984 (Location filming), 29 October – 2 November 1984 (Location filming), 12 November 1984 (Location filming), 18-20 November 1984 (TC1)

Locations
Granville Colliery Spoil Heaps, Donnington, Telford, Shropshire; Blists Hill Open Air Museum, Madelay, Telford, Shropshire; Coalport China Works, Coalport, Telford, Shropshire; Park Wood, Ruislip, Middlesex

Working Titles
Too Clever By Far
Enter the Rani

Factoids
- Pip and Jane Baker had declined former producer Graham Williams' offer to write for the series in the late 1970s. John Nathan-Turner decided to commission them after reading a script for an aborted Williams' produced thriller series called *The Zodiac Factor*.
- Colin Baker performed all his own stunts in this story. For the cliffhanger sequence, visual effects assistant Tom Davis was housed inside the trolley to which Baker was strapped, attempting to steer it as it careered downhill. He was also inside the fake tree that protects Peri in Part Two.
- Kate O'Mara had previously acted opposite Colin Baker in the 1970s series *The Brothers*.
- Because of atrocious weather locations in Shropshire, a remount of the Redfern Dell scenes took place at Park Wood in Ruislip, near the home of Pip and Jane Baker.
- The interior of the Rani's Tardis was designed by David Barton with a circular mushroom-shaped console and two spinning metal hoops in the centre instead of a rising and falling perspex column.

Comment
The Mark of the Rani is a very good example of a story being considerably less than the sum of its parts. It has a clever premise, excellent location

filming and a genuinely classy feel. But because of its dialogue-heavy, meandering plot - nothing much happens in Part Two, for instance - and its insistence on two clichéd villains instead of one, any good points are lost in the general malaise. It is also impossible to take seriously any story that has a moving tree in it (and, yes, that includes Tolkien's *The Two Towers*). If only more had been at stake in narrative terms and Anthony Ainley had been excluded, this could have been very good. **54%**

"I've been butchering all my life - primitive animals don't feel pain in the way that we would." ~ Shockeye

141) The Two Doctors
Robert Holmes

Serial Code: 6W
Original Transmission
Part One
Saturday 16 February 1985, 17.20-18.05, 6.6m / 92
Part Two
Saturday 23 February 1985, 17.20-18.05, 6m / 90
Part Three
Saturday 2 March 1985, 17.20-18.05, 6.9m / 66
BBC Archive
All episodes exist as 625-line one-inch PAL colour master videotapes, with a 71 edit also existing of Part One. The six original 25-minute episodes also exist in the same format.
Novelization
Doctor Who – The Two Doctors by Robert Holmes (159/12)
Hardback:
August 1985, WH Allen (0491035004 / Andrew Skilleter)
Paperback:
December 1985, Target (0426202015 / Andrew Skilleter)
Video
November 1993 (BBCV 5148 / Colin Howard)
DVD
September 2003, clean title sequence and end credits, isolated music score, location film footage, studio footage, *A Fix With Sontarans*, production subtitles, photo gallery, commentary by Colin Baker, Nicola Bryant, Frazer Hines, Jacqueline Pearce and Peter Moffatt (BBCDVD 1213 / Clayton Hickman)

Précis
Sontarans abduct the Second Doctor and take him to Seville to steal his time travel secrets...
Cast
Colin Baker, Patrick Troughton (The Doctors), Nicola Bryant (Peri), Frazer Hines (Jamie McCrimmon), Laurence Payne (Dastari/Computer Voice), John Stratton (Shockeye), Jacqueline Pearce (Chessene), James Saxon (Oscar Botcherby), Carmen Gomez (Anita), Clinton Greyn (Stike), Tim Raynham (Varl), Nicholas Fawcett (Technician), Aimee Delamain (Doña Arana), Fernand Monast (Scientist), Jay McGrath (Dead Androgum), Mercedes Carnegie (Woman on Balcony)
Crew
Visual Effects Designer Steve Drewett, *Visual Effects Assistant* Simon McDonald, *Video Effects* Dave Chapman, *Technical Coordinator* Alan Arbuthnott, *Camera Supervisor* Alec Wheal, *Vision Mixer* Jayne Beckett, *Videotape Editor* Hugh Parson, *Studio Lighting* Don Babbage, *Studio Sound* Keith Bowden, *Film Cameraman* John Walker, *Film Camera Assistant* Paul Carter, *Film Sound* Colin March, *Film Sound Assistant* Jonathan Walker, *Film Editor* Mike Robotham, *Properties Buyer* Leanda Bowden-Smith, *Special Sound* Dick Mills, *Grams Operator* Terry Foote, *Incidental Music* Peter Howell, *Guitar Player* Les Thatcher, *Costume Designer* Jan Wright, *Dressers* Sheila Cullen, Dennis Addoo, *Make-Up Artist/Designer* Catherine Davies, *Make-Up Assistant* Jane Buxton, *Designer* Tony Burrough, *Design Assistant* Colin Blaymires, *Production Manager* Gary Downie, *Production Associate* Sue Anstruther, *Production Assistant* Patricia O'Leary, *Assistant Floor Manager* Isla Rowe, *Floor Assistant* Anna Price, *Script Editor* Eric Saward, *Producer* John Nathan-Turner, *Director* Peter Moffatt
DWM Index
94	Eric Saward interview
96	Nicola Bryant interview
97	Colin Baker interview
	Preview
98	Frazer Hines interview
100	Robert Holmes interview
	Novelization review
101	TV review
102	Patrick Troughton interview
104	Eric Saward interview
	John Nathan-Turner interview
107	Andrew Skilleter interview
108	Season Survey results
118	Anthony Read interview
	Colin Baker interview
119	Nicola Bryant interview

121 Episode Guide
163 The Two Nervous Breakdowns 1
*   (Gary Downie on location filming)*
164 The Two Nervous Breakdowns 2
*   (Gary Downie on location filming)*
182 Clinton Greyn interview
194 Peter Howell interview
195 Archive Feature
*   Laurence Payne interview*
202 Colin Baker interview
204 What The Papers Said
206 Video review
236 Nicola Bryant interview
239 The John Nathan-Turner Memoirs
243 Frazer Hines interview
254 Peter Moffatt interview
322 Colin Baker interview
334 Preview 335   DVD review
338 Gary Downie interview
348 Eric Saward interview

Recording Dates
9-14 August 1984 (Location filming), 16 August 1984 (Location filming), 30-31 August 1984 (TC1), 13-14 September 1984 (TC6), 27-28 September 1984 (TC6)

Locations
Rio Guadiamar, SE521, between Gerena and Aznalcollar, Spain; Dehera Boyar and country road, between Gerena and ElGarrobo, Spain; Seville Cathedral and streets in Santa Cruz, Seville, Spain

Working Titles
The Kraalon Inheritance
The Kraglon Inheritance [sic]
The Androgum Inheritance
The Seventh Augmentation
Parallax
Creation

Factoids
- Producer John Nathan-Turner had originally envisioned *The Two Doctors* taking place in the American city of New Orleans in Louisiana. A script by Los Angeles writer Lesley Elizabeth Thomas called *Way Down Yonder* was rejected and the commission passed to Robert Holmes, who imagined a race of culinary-obsessed aliens called Androgums (an anagram of 'gourmands'). However, this location fell through when American distributor Lionheart pulled out of co-financing the trip. Instead, the Spanish city of Seville was chosen and Holmes set about altering the script to accommodate the new setting.
- Two new Sontaran costumes were made for this serial. Jan Wright recreated the look of the original ones, last seen in *The Invasion of Time* (97), with much thinner, less padded, material (because of the hot climes), while Richard Gregory of Imagineering moulded new masks, collars and helmets. Unfortunately, the less bulky costumes made it harder to attach the collars to them and because they sat lower on the actors' shoulders, more was seen of the masks' necks than was intended.
- To date, *The Two Doctors* was the final six-part length story to be made.
- Between Parts Two and Three of this story, the BBC delivered the bombshell announcement that it would be postponing the next season of *Doctor Who*.
- The expense of location filming (including a remount of a scene involving James Saxon and Carmen Gomez that required them to be specially flown back to Spain from England) meant that the space-station scenes in Part One could not stretch to any extras to make it look inhabited.

Comment
Because *The Two Doctors* is a multi-Doctor tale, it inevitably sets up a lot of expectations - most of them false. It's not an anniversary story, there's no particularly earth-shattering revelations to be had, and the plot is all rather trivial and insular. Added to this, Peter Moffat's directing is extremely lethargic and avoids any obvious suspense-creating techniques. But if you think of it in terms of a light-hearted comedy drama for vegetarians (and, let's face it, how many of *those* have you seen lately?) then it's actually possible to quite enjoy the thing. The location filming is pleasant if unspectacular, the actors positively embrace the theatrical dialogue, and the plotting is easy to follow and satisfying - if, again, unspectacular. On top of it all, the four regulars are clearly having a ball in each other's company. But apart from the pathetic-looking Sontarans, the main note of discord is the tacked-on violence, which, like *Vengeance on Varos*, is problematic for portraying the Sixth Doctor as a wise-cracking thug. **75%**

"The waves of time wash us all clean." ~ The Doctor

142) Timelash
Glen McCoy

Serial Code: 6Y
Original Transmission
Part One
Saturday 9 March 1985, 17.20-18.05, 6.7m / 69
Part Two
Saturday 16 March 1985, 17.20-18.05, 7.4m / 79
BBC Archive
Both episodes exist as 625-line one-inch PAL colour master videotapes. The four original 25-minute episodes also exist in the same format.
Novelization
Doctor Who – Timelash by Glen McCoy (124/12)
Hardback:
December 1985, WH Allen (0491038518 / David McAllister)
Paperback:
May 1986, Target (0426202295 / David McAllister)
Video
January 1998 (BBCV 6229 / Photomontage)
Music and Sound Effects
July 1993, *Doctor Who: 30 Years at the Radiophonic Workshop*, CD (BBCCD 871 / Photomontage)
Précis
On the planet Karfel, those who oppose the Borad are thrown into the Timelash...
Cast
Colin Baker (The Doctor), Nicola Bryant (Peri), Paul Darrow (Tekker), Jeananne Crowley (Vena), Eric Deacon (Mykros), David Chandler (Herbert Wells), Robert Ashby (Borad), Denis Carey (Old Man), David Ashton (Kendron), Dicken Ashworth (Sezon), Dean Hollingsworth (Android), Peter Robert Scott (Brunner), Christine Kavanagh (Aram), Martin Gower (Tyheer), Steven Macintosh (Gazak), James Richardson (Guardolier), Neil Hallett (Maylin Renis), Tracy Louise Ward (Katz), Martin Gower (Bandril Ambassador), Chris Bradshaw (Young Karfelon)
Crew
Visual Effects Designer Kevin Molloy, *Visual Effects Assistant* Paul Mann, Stan Mitchell, *Video Effects* Dave Chapman, *Technical Coordinator* Alan Arbuthnott, *Camera Supervisor* Alec Wheal, *Vision Mixers* Jayne Beckett, Dinah Long, *Videotape Editor* Hugh Parson, *Studio Lighting* Henry Barber, Don Babbage, *Studio Sound* Andy Stacey, *Properties Buyers* Al Huxley, Howard Jones, *Special Sound* Dick Mills, *Incidental Music* Liz Parker, *Guitar Player* Les Thatcher, *Costume Designers* Alun Hughes, Pat Godfrey, *Costume Assistant* Liz Dawson, *Dressers* Liz Dixon, Alan Hatchman, Lesley Bingham, Stephen Smith, John Watts, *Make-Up Artists* Vanessa Poulton, Dorka Nieradzik, *Make-Up Assistant* Wendy Harrison, *Designers* Bob Cove, Alan Spaulding, *Design Assistants* Francis Boyle, Adele Maroff, *Production Managers* Alan Wareing, Michael Cameron, *Production Associates* Sue Anstruther, Angela Smith, *Production Assistants* Jane Whittaker, Elizabeth Sherry, *Assistant Floor Managers* Abigail Sharp, Jo O'Leary, *Floor Assistants* Helen Greaves, Anna Price, *Script Editor* Eric Saward, *Producer* John Nathan-Turner, *Director* Pennant Roberts
DWM Index
98   Preview
99   Set Report
102 TV review
106 Novelization review
108 Season Survey results
118 Colin Baker interview
119 Nicola Bryant interview
121 Episode Guide
122 Pennant Roberts interview
166 Nicola Bryant interview
203 Liz Parker interview
210 Glen McCoy interview
231 Archive Feature
236 Nicola Bryant interview
240 The John Nathan-Turner Memoirs
248 Pennant Roberts interview
260 Video review
322 Colin Baker interview
348 Eric Saward interview
Recording Dates
4-6 December 1984 (TC4), 19-21 December 1984 (TC8), 30 January 1985 (TC8)
Working Title
As broadcast
Factoids
- The Borad's half-mask was sculpted by Stan Mitchell from very fine foam rubber so that it was light to wear and moved realistically with Norman Ashby's facial expressions.
- One plot requirement was that all costumes and sets be made of non-reflective material. Thus the inhabitants of Karfel were decked out in heavily-pleated baggy cream gabardine tunics and trousers.
- The inside of the Timelash was a wall-flat studded with hexagonal rods, some of which were made of wood so that they could hold the actors' weight. Tinsel,

tinfoil and scrunched up plastic film were glued to the wall and illuminated by a disco light.
- Part Two was found to be severely under-running, and so an additional six-minute Tardis scene was written by Eric Saward and recorded during production of *Revelation of the Daleks* (143).
- *Timelash* saw the first use of an image processing system called 'Harry'. Used to create the wobble effect inside the Tardis in Part One, it had a much higher frame-storage memory than its predecessor, Quantel 5000.

Comment
Okay, I admit it - I have a sneaking fondness for *Timelash*. While admitting that it's flawed in areas such as acting and plot, I happen to think that it's superior to some of Season 22's offerings because a) it doesn't take itself too seriously and b) it's never boring. Glen McCoy's plot may be full of holes, but the whole is executed with a certain healthy bravura. Or a lot, in the case of Paul Darrow's Richard III impression. The set design and costumes are imaginative, and the Borad stands out as easily the most convincing monster of Colin Baker's tenure. As to David Chandler, I think he makes a good foil for the Doctor's pomposity, and I like the idea of the grandfather of science-fiction travelling aboard the Tardis. The *Timelash* itself may look rubbish, and the Tardis padding in Part Two should have been scrapped (who cares if the episode runs short - stick a *Tom and Jerry* cartoon on afterwards!), but overall I can always find something to amuse me. Which is more than can be said for many a 1980s story.
68%

"I would rather run away with my mother than own a fawning little creep like you!" ~ *Jobel*

143) Revelation of the Daleks
Eric Saward

Serial Code: 6Z
Original Transmission
Part One
Saturday 23 March 1985, 17.20-18.05, 7.4m / 65
Part Two
Saturday 30 March 1985, 17.20-18.05, 7.7m / 58
Repeat Transmission
On BBC2 in 25-minute instalments:
Part One
Friday 19 March 1993, 19.15-19.40, 1.7m / 28

Part Two
Friday 26 March 1993, 19.15-19.40, 1.8m / -
Part Three
Friday 2 April 1993, 19.15-19.40, 1.6m / 30
Part Four
Friday 9 April 1993, 19.15-19.40, 1.2m / -
BBC Archive
Both episodes exist as 625-line two-inch PAL colour master videotapes, with a 71 edit also existing of Part One. The four original 25-minute episodes also exist in the same format.
Novelization
None
Non-Fiction Book
March 1996, Boxtree, *Classic Who: The Harper Classics* by Adrian Rigelsford, Hardback (0752201883 / Photograph)
Video
1. November 1999, edited, 71 edit of Part Two, in 'Dalek Limited Edition Tin' [BBCV 6875 / Photomontage] with *The Planet of the Daleks* (BBCV 6927 / Photomontage)
2. September 2001, edited, 71 edit of Part Two, in 'The Davros Collection' box set [BBCV 7241 / Photomontage] with the other four Davros stories (BBCV 7255 / Photomontage)
DVD
July 2005, optional Dolby 5.1 surround mix, optional CGI effects, deleted scenes, commentary by Graeme Harper, Nicola Bryant, Eric Saward and Terry Molloy (DVD 1357 / Clayton Hickman)
Précis
On Necros, Davros is posing as the Great Healer and using corpses to make more Daleks...
Cast
Colin Baker (The Doctor), Nicola Bryant (Peri), Clive Swift (Jobel), Jenny Tomasin (Tasembeker), Eleanor Bron (Kara), Hugh Walters (Vogel), Alec Linstead (Arthur Stengos), Terry Molloy (Davros), Alexei Sayle (DJ), William Gaunt (Orcini), John Ogwen (Bostock), Stephen Flynn (Grigory), Bridget Lynch-Blosse (Natasha), Trevor Cooper (Takis), Colin Spaull (Lilt), Ken Barker (Mutant), Penelope Lee (Computer Voice), John Scott Martin, Cy Town, Tony Starr, Toby Byrne (Daleks), Royce Mills, Roy Skelton (Dalek Voices)
Crew
Stuntman Steven Emerson, *Visual Effects Designer* John Brace, *Visual Effects Assistants* George Reed, Tony McKillop, Roger Turner, Andy Lazell, *Video Effects* Dave Chapman, *Technical Coordinator* Alan Arbuthnott, *Camera Supervisor* Alec Wheal, *Vision Mixer* Dinah Long, *Videotape Editor* Steve Newnham, *Studio Lighting* Don Babbage, *Studio Sound* Andy Stacey, *Film Cameraman* John Walker, *Film Sound* Steve Gatland, *Film Editor*

Ray Wingrove, *Properties Buyer* Howard Jones, *Special Sound* Dick Mills, *Incidental Music* Roger Limb, *Costume Designer* Pat Godfrey, *Dresser* John Watts, *Make-Up Artist* Dorka Nieradzik, *Designer* Alan Spalding, *Design Assistant* Adele Marolf, *Production Manager* Michael Cameron, *Production Associate* Angela Smith, *Production Assistant* Elizabeth Sherry, *Assistant Floor Manager* Jo O'Leary, *Floor Assistant* Anna Price, *Script Editor* Eric Saward, *Producer* John Nathan-Turner, *Director* Graeme Harper

DWM Index

98	Preview
102	TV review
104	Eric Saward interview
108	Season Survey results
117	Michael Wisher interview
121	Episode Guide
148	Eric Saward interview
152	Ken Barker interview
166	Nicola Bryant interview
188	Graeme Harper interview Archive Feature
196	Roger Limb interview
201	Repeat review
236	Nicola Bryant interview
240	The John Nathan-Turner Memoirs
272	Terry Molloy interview
284	Video review
304	Eleanor Bron interview
309	Clive Swift interview Video review (Davros box set)
323	Colin Baker interview
348	Eric Saward interview
358	DVD preview
359	The Fact of Fiction DVD review

Recording Dates

7-10 January 1985 (Location filming), January 1985 (Acton Studio modelwork), 17-18 January 1985 (TC1), 30 January-1 February 1985 (TC8)

Locations

Bolinge Hill Farm, Petersfield, Hampshire; Butser Hill and Queen Elizabeth Country Park, Horndean, Hampshire; IBM, Cosham, Portsmouth, Hampshire; Goodwood Estate, Halnaker, West Sussex; Tangmere Aerodrome, West Sussex

Working Title

The End of the Road

Factoids

- Six new cream and gold Daleks were built by the BBC Visual Effects Department.
- Director Graeme Harper had planned for a location sequence involving two flying Daleks being destroyed by Orcini - dummy props packed with explosives were to be launched from a specially made spring-loaded platform at Butser Hill. Unfortunately, a heavy snowfall prevented the vehicles from moving the platform into place and Harper reluctantly dropped the scene.
- A hollow perspex Dalek was constructed in three segments by outside contractor Dennys at Shepherds Bush. Inside sat actor Alec Linstead, heavily made-up as if a liver and kidneys were growing on the side of his head.
- Some set dressings for Tranquil Repose were reused from BBC drama series *By The Sword Divided* (1983-5) and comedy programme *The Little and Large Show* (1978-91).
- A new mask and chair were made for Terry Molloy as Davros, by Dorka Nieradzik and John Brace respectively.
- Colin Baker's last line ended on the word "Blackpool", which would have lead into Season 23's opening story *The Nightmare Fair*, written by Graham Williams and featuring the Celestial Toymaker. However, plans for this season altered as soon as the BBC imposed an eighteen-month break for the programme, and so a freeze-frame was employed (for the first time since 1978) before the final word was uttered.

Comment

The plot of *Revelation of the Daleks* is no better than any other story this season. In fact, it's considerably worse then many, offering as it does a bizarre narrative in which the Doctor and Peri spend the first 45 minutes largely on their own. However - and it's a big however - director Graeme Harper transforms Eric Saward's slavish Robert Holmes pastiche into a great work of art, thanks to his fantastic eye for detail and instinct for dramatic imagery. Everything about the story is stylistically and dramatically over-played, from the acting and characterization to the music and set design. It shouldn't work, but it does. Even Jenny Tomasin's wooden performance seems deliberate. The Daleks barely feature, but when they do, they look magnificent gliding along the smoke-filled catacombs. Terry Molloy really makes the part of their wizened creator his own - the sight of Davros' severed head, swivelling hawk-like from side to side in his glass cylinder, spitting out curses and cackling hysterically is not easily forgotten. Perhaps the music is a little monotonous, and many of the directorial tricks come out of the same bag that *The Caves of*

Androzani (136) used, but the twist here is the maudlin streak of black comedy missing from the earlier story. Sex, swearing, drug abuse, homosexuality, nose picking, necrophilia, double entendres, explicit violence, death - *Revelation of the Daleks* has it all (and should have been broadcast well after teatime). It all gets a bit confused towards the end of Part Two, but nonetheless this is a spectacular production filled with memorable moments. **90%**

Season 23

"Am I late for something?" ~ The Doctor

144a) *The Trial of a Time Lord 1-4*
Robert Holmes

Serial Code: 7A
Original Transmission
Part One
Saturday 6 September 1986, 17.45-18.10, 4.9m / 69
Part Two
Saturday 13 September 1986, 17.45-18.10, 4.9m / 75
Part Three
Saturday 20 September 1986, 17.45-18.10, 3.9m / 98
Part Four
Saturday 27 September 1986, 17.45-18.10, 3.7m / 97
BBC Archive
All episodes exist as 625-line one-inch PAL master videotapes. 71 edits also exist for all four episodes in the same format.
Novelization
Doctor Who – The Mysterious Planet by Terrance Dicks (127/14)
Hardback:
November 1987, WH Allen (0491030967 / Tony Masero)
Paperback:
April 1988, Target (0426203194 / Tony Masero)
Video
November 1993, triple-pack, in *The Trial of a Time Lord* Limited Edition Tardis Tin [BBCV 5008 / Andrew Skilleter] with the other three stories (BBCV 5009 / Alister Pearson)

Précis
Put on trial by the Time Lords, the Doctor is shown a recent adventure by the prosecuting Valeyard…
Cast
Colin Baker (The Doctor), Nicola Bryant (Peri), Michael Jayston (The Valeyard), Lynda Bellingham (The Inquisitor), Tony Selby (Glitz), Joan Sims (Katryca), Glen Murphy (Dibber), Tom Chadbon (Merdeen), Paul McGuinness (Drathro), Roger Brierley (Drathro Voice), David Rodigan (Broken Tooth), Adam Blackwood (Balazar), Timothy Walker (Grell), Sion Tudor Owen (Tandrell), Billy McColl (Humker), Mike Ellis (L1 Service Robot Operator)
Crew
Visual Effects Designer Mike Kelt, *Visual Effects Assistants* Mike Ellis, Mike Tucker, *Video Effects* Danny Popkin, *Technical Coordinator* Alan Arbuthnott, *Camera Supervisor* Alec Wheal, *Vision Mixer* Jim Stephens, *Videotape Editor* Stephen Newnham, *Studio Lighting* Mike Jefferies, *Studio Sound* Brian Clark, *OB Lighting* John Wiggins, *OB Sound* Bill Whiston, *OB Boom Operators* Peter Hales, Ken Gilvear, *OB Cameramen* Paul Harding, John Hawes, *OB Engineering Manager* Bernie Davis, *Properties Buyer* Paul Schrader, *Special Sound* Dick Mills, *Grams Operator* Jean Whippey, *Incidental Music* Dominic Glynn, *Costume Designer* Ken Trew, *Costume Assistant* Barbara Sweyda, *Dressers* Isabelle Foley, Derek Rowe, Dennis Addoo, Lorraine Windus, *Make-Up Artist* Denise Baron, *Make-Up Assistants* Isabel Webley, Lesley Altringham, Adam Beck, Helen Warren, Debbie Taylor, *Designer* John Anderson, *Design Assistant* Adrian Uwalaka, *Production Manager* Clare Graham, *Production Associate* Angela Smith, *Production Assistant* Joy Sinclair, *Assistant Floor Managers* Stephen Jeffery-Poulter, Sally Newman, *Floor Assistant* Yvonne O'Grady, *Script Editor* Eric Saward, *Producer* John Nathan-Turner, *Director* Nicholas Mallett
DWM Index
116   Preview
120   TV review
122   Episode Guide
123   Mike Kelt interview
126   Season Survey results
129   Novelization review
132   Nicholas Mallett interview
134   Tony Selby interview
158   Kevin O'Shea interview
205   What The Papers Said
         Video review
206   Imitating Reality: Colin Baker on Season

23   Dominic Glynn interview
230   Nicholas Mallett interview
237   Nicola Bryant interview
245   The John Nathan-Turner Memoirs
282   Tony Selby interview
284   Michael Jayston interview
289   Archive Feature
324   Colin Baker interview
338   The Accidental Tourist Part 3
346   Lynda Bellingham interview
348   Eric Saward interview

Recording Dates
8-11 April 1986 (Location videotaping), April 1986 (Peerless Studios modelwork), 24-25 April 1986 (TC6), 10-12 May 1986 (TC3), 13 June 1986 (TC6)

Locations
Queen Elizabeth Country Park, Gravel Hill, Hampshire; Butser Ancient Farm Project, Pidham Hill, East Meon, Hampshire

Working Titles
Wasteland
Robots of Ravolox
The Mysterious Planet

Factoids
- After the last season's postponement it was decided that this new, truncated season would reflect the real-life 'on trial' status of the series. Therefore a 14-part story arc was envisioned, consisting of four individual, but interconnected, stories.
- Musician Dominic Glynn composed a new, minimalist arrangement of the *Doctor Who* theme music to a five-day deadline.
- The opening 45-second shot of the six-foot diameter space station (designed by Mike Kelt and detailed by Peter Akass) was the most complex motion-controlled model shot ever attempted in Britain at that time. Shot on 35mm film, it cost £8,000 and took a week to execute at Peerless Studios in Elstree.
- Two new miniature Tardises were built by Visual Effects assistant Mike Tucker, replacing ones lost during the programme's 18-month break.
- The large Drathro robot costume was made from fibreglass and was intended to be worn by actor David Brierley. When Brierley refused to don it for fear it was too claustrophobic, effects assistant Paul McGuinness stepped into the breech, with Brierley delivering his lines off-camera.
- From this story onward (with the exception of the 1996 television movie), all *Doctor Who* location work would be recorded onto videotape, rather than 16mm film.

Comment
There's no doubting the rush of excitement with which fans greeted the first part of this mammoth-length story. The opening model shot is still impressive all these years later, and there's some nice banter between the Doctor and Peri that makes up for the irritating bickering that characterized their relationship in Season 22. However, no amount of surface gloss can hide the fact that the story is really very mundane. Part Four is the worst offender, with unfunny 'comic' moments (such as the food processor sequence and Colin Baker 'losing' his Tardis) and 'bleeped' explanatory dialogue (to disguise shock revelations) that must have left casual viewers equally bemused and dissatisfied. **39%**

"Welcome to your new body!" ~ *Crozier*

144b) The Trial of a Time Lord 5-8
Philip Martin

Serial Code: 7B
Original Transmission
Part Five
Saturday 4 October 1986, 17.45-18.10, 4.8m / 76
Part Six
Saturday 11 October 1986, 17.45-18.10, 4.6m / 87
Part Seven
Saturday 18 October 1986, 17.45-18.10, 5.1m / 87
Part Eight
Saturday 25 October 1986, 17.45-18.10, 5m / 84

BBC Archive
All episodes exist as 625-line one-inch PAL colour master videotapes. 71 edits exist for Parts Five, Six and Seven, with a 72 edit also existing for Part Seven, all in the same format.

Novelization
Doctor Who - Mindwarp by Philip Martin (142/17)
Paperback:
June 1989, Target (0426203356 / Alister Pearson)

Video
November 1993, triple-pack, in *The Trial of a Time Lord* Limited Edition Tardis Tin [BBCV 5008 / Andrew Skilleter] with the other three stories (BBCV 5009 / Alister Pearson)

Précis
On Thoras Beta, Peri is chosen as the new host for the sluglike Kiv's brain…

Cast
Colin Baker (The Doctor), Nicola Bryant (Peri), Michael Jayston (The Valeyard), Lynda Bellingham (The Inquisitor), Patrick Ryecart (Crozier), Brian Blessed (King Yrcanos), Nabil Shaban (Sil), Christopher Ryan (Kiv), Trevor Laird (Frax), Thomas Branch (The Lukoser), Gordon Warnecke (Tuza), Alibe Parsons (Matrona Kani), Richard Henry (Mentor), Russell West (Raak), Deep Roy (Possicar Delegate/Mentor), Ernest Jennings (Llanna), Johnny Clayton (Vern), Ray Charles, Ferdinan Oraka (Bearers), James Dublin (Guard/Bearer)

Crew
Visual Effects Designer Peter Wragg, *Visual Effects Assistant* David Vialls, *Graphic Designer* Clive Harris, *Video Effects* Danny Popkin, *Technical Coordinator* Alan Arbuthnott, *Camera Supervisor* Alec Wheal, *Vision Mixer* Jim Stephens, *Videotape Editor* Hugh Parson, *Studio Lighting* Don Babbage, *Studio Sound* Brian Clark, *OB Lighting* Colin Widgery, *OB Sound* Mike Johnstone, *Properties Buyer* Roger Williams, *Special Sound* Dick Mills, *Grams Operator* Jem Whippey, *Incidental Music* Richard Hartley, *Costume Designer* John Hearne, *Costume Assistant* Susan Moore, *Dressers* Isabelle Foley, Dennis Addoo, Derek Rowe, Leslie Bingham, Paul Mayo, Kevin Rowland, June Hill, Richard Blanchard, *Make-Up Artist* Dorka Nieradzik, *Make-Up Assistants* Sharon Welch, Lesley Smith, *Designer* Andrew Howe-Davies, *Design Assistant* Susan Turner, *Production Manager* Kevan Van Thompson, *Production Associates* Angela Smith, June Collins, *Production Assistant* Karen Jones, *Assistant Floor Manager* Anna Price, *Floor Assistants* Antonia Rubinstein, Julia Thomas, *Script Editor* Eric Saward, *Producer* John Nathan-Turner, *Director* Ron Jones

DWM Index
117   Preview
121   TV review
122   Episode Guide
123   Peter Wragg interview
125   Philip Martin interview
126   Season Survey results
150   Philip Martin interview
       Novelization review
205   Video review
206   Imitating Reality: Colin Baker on Season 23
237   Nicola Bryant interview
245   The John Nathan-Turner Memoirs
249   Archive Feature
284   Michael Jayston interview
288   Nabil Shaban interview
324   Colin Baker interview

Recording Dates
27-29 May 1986 (TC1), 11-13 June 1986 (TC6), 15-16 June 1986 (Location videotaping)

Locations
Telscombe Cliffs, Peacehaven, East Sussex

Working Titles
The Planet of Sil
Mindwarp

Factoids
- Four new Mentor costumes were created by Peter Wragg. Nabil Shaban reused his original Sil costume from *Vengeance on Varos* (139) but with a new, more comfortable, headpiece. For his marshminnows, he ate a prototype Marsh Minnow sweet from Trebor (after John Nathan-Turner had tried to interest them in manufacturing the sweets), dipped in green gelatine.
- Christopher Ryan, previously the 'normal' flatmate in *The Young Ones* (1980-83), had his legs either sticking down through holes in his chair or strapped underneath him when playing Kiv.
- Circular lighting rigs normally suspended above the stage in pop concerts were placed on their side and used as entranceways.
- Intensive use was made of digital image processor 'Harry' (first seen in *Timelash*, 142) to dramatically alter the colour of the sky, sea and beach of Telscombe Cliffs. Electronic mattes created the high ceilings of Crozier's laboratory and the induction centre.
- A remount of the opening space station scene from Part One was recording during the final studio block.

Comment
This second segment is probably the most rewarding one of *The Trial of a Time Lord*, despite more intrusive courtroom scenes and the Doctor's unexplained out-of-character behaviour. The production is atmospherically directed and complemented nicely by one-off composer Richard Hartley's impressive musical score. Revisiting Season 22's fascination with violence and humour, the story stays just the right side of farce, with Patrick Ryecart's po-faced mad genius providing some of the wittiest moments in a lucid and well-written script - judging from script writer Philip Martin's excellent track record, one can't help but feel that the muddled areas of the narrative were the result of the production team's tinkering. The ending is one of the most shocking since, well, *Earthshock* (122) and demonstrates that Colin Baker can act with subtlety and depth when he chooses to. **89%**

"You make delicious coffee, Janet." ~ *Edwardes*

144c) The Trial of a Time Lord 9-12
Pip and Jane Baker

Serial Code: 7C
Original Transmission
Part Nine
Saturday 1 November 1986, 17.45-18.10, 5.2m / 85
Part Ten
Saturday 8 November 1986, 17.45-18.10, 4.6m / 93
Part Eleven
Saturday 15 November 1986, 17.45-18.10, 5.3m / 86
Part Twelve
Saturday 22 November 1986, 17.45-18.10, 5.2m / 89
BBC Archive
All episodes exist as 625-line one-inch PAL colour master videotapes. 71 edits exist for all episodes, and a 72 edit exists for Part Nine, in the same format.
Novelization
Doctor Who – Terror of the Vervoids by Pip and Jane Baker (144/26)
Hardback:
September 1987, WH Allen (0491030568 / Tony Masero)
Paperback:
February 1988, Target (0426203135 / Tony Masero)
Video
November 1993, triple-pack, in *The Trial of a Time Lord* Limited Edition Tardis Tin [BBCV 5008 / Andrew Skilleter] with the other three stories (BBCV 5009 / Alister Pearson)
Précis
Murders occur on a space liner filled with deadly plant-like Vervoids…
Cast
Colin Baker (The Doctor), Bonnie Langford (Melanie Bush), Michael Jayston (The Valeyard), Lynda Bellingham (The Inquisitor), Honor Blackman (Lasky), Michael Craig (Commodore Travers), Denys Hawthorne (Rudge), Tony Scoggo (Hallett/Grenville/Enzu), Malcolm Tierney (Doland), David Allister (Bruchner), Simon Slater (Edwardes), Yolande Palfrey (Janet), Arthur Hewlett (Kimber), Hugh Beverton (First Guard), Hugh Weedon (Second Guard), Sam Howard (Atza), Leon Davis (Ortezo), Mike Mungarvan (Duty Officer), Barbara Ward (Ruth Baxter), Peppi Borza (First Vervoid), Bob Appleby (Second Vervoid), Gess Whitfield, Paul Hillier, Bill Perrie, Jerry Manley (Vervoids), Martin Hyder, Barry Holland (Waste Disposal Operators/Attendants/Loaders)
Crew
Visual Effects Designer Kevin Molloy, *Visual Effects Assistants* Chris Reynolds, John Van Der Pool, Clare Chopping, Briony Keating, *Graphic Designer* Clive Harris, *Video Effects* Danny Popkin, *Technical Coordinator* Alan Arbuthnott, *Camera Supervisor* Alec Wheal, *Vision Mixers* Shirley Coward, Jim Stephens, *Videotape Editor* Hugh Parsons, *Studio Lighting* Don Babbage, *Studio Sound* Brian Clark, *Properties Buyer* Al Huxley, *Special Sound* Dick Mills, *Grams Operator* Jem Whippey, *Incidental Music* Malcolm Clarke, *Costume Designer* Andrew Rose, *Costume Assistant* Chrissie Tucker, *Make-Up Artist* Shaunna Harrison, *Make-Up Assistants* Simon Tytherleigh, Lesley Smith, Issy Webley, *Designer* Dinah Walker, *Production Manager* Ian Fraser, *Production Associates* June Collins, Jenny Doe, *Production Assistant* Jane Wellesley, *Assistant Floor Manager* Karen Little, *Floor Assistants* Yvonne O'Grady, Adam Tandy, *Producer* John Nathan-Turner, *Director* Chris Clough
DWM Index
112 John Nathan-Turner interview
118 Preview
122 Episode Guide
 TV review
123 Kevin Molloy interview
126 Season Survey results
127 Novelization review
131 Bonnie Langford interview
135 Chris Clough interview
137 Pip and Jane Baker interview
158 Kevin O'Shea interview
182 Those *Radio Times*
183 Nostalgia
195 Malcolm Clarke interview
205 Video review
 What The Papers Said
206 Pip and Jane Baker interview
 Imitating Reality: Colin Baker on Season 23
245 The John Nathan-Turner Memoirs
260 Bonnie Langford interview
284 Michael Jayston interview
303 Pip and Jane Baker interview
323 Archive Feature
324 Colin Baker interview
348 Eric Saward interview

Recording Dates
16 July 1986 (TC1), 30 July – 1 August 1986 (TC3), 12-14 August 1986 (TC3)
Working Titles
The Ultimate Foe
The Vervoids
Factoids
- Bonnie Langford was appearing in the title role of *Peter Pan - The Musical* at the Aldwych Theatre, London, when she was offered the role of Melanie by John Nathan-Turner.
- Pip and Jane Baker's *Murder on the Orient Express*-influenced story (with a dash of John Wyndham's *The Day of the Triffids*) was a late replacement for *Paradise Five* by *Sapphire and Steel* scriptwriter Peter J Hammond, itself a replacement for *Pinocotheca* by Christopher H Bidmead which replaced two part-two tales by David Halliwell and Jack Trevor Story.
- Citing artistic differences, Eric Saward left halfway through production, leaving script editing chores to producer John Nathan-Turner.
- Six Vervoid costumes were made from overalls covered with rubber and latex leaves. The masks, based on Venus fly traps, were made of foam latex with broom bristles sticking out at the front. A half-mask was attached to actress Barbara Ward's face for the Part Ten cliffhanger, complete with pulsating veins operated by an off-screen air pump.
- Model ceilings to the *Hyperion III* reception and lounge were added by CSO in post-production.
- For Episode Nine's cliffhanger, Bonnie Langford was asked to scream in the key of F to blend in with the closing theme music.
- Colin Baker was given a new waistcoat and cravat to emphasise the 'future' setting of the serial.

Comment
A perfectly adequate whodunit in space is let down by sets that look and sound as if they're made from MDF, accompanied by performances made out of the same material. Malcolm Clarke's music, although effective at key moments, over-emphasises every vaguely humorous moment and would be more at home on an episode of *The Chuckle Brothers*. Once again, extraneous courtroom material is inserted and the Doctor's uncharacteristic actions are never properly explained. The Vervoids are pleasing though, and the first two cliffhangers are expertly executed. But coming after the strong second segment, this is a blandly made formulaic story that looks amateurish in comparison. **34%**

"There's nothing you can do to prevent the catharsis of spurious morality!" ~ The Valeyard

144d) The Trial of a Time Lord 13-14
Robert Holmes (13) and Pip and Jane Baker (14)

Serial Code: 7C
Original Transmission
Part Thirteen
Saturday 29 November 1986, 17.20-17.45, 4.4m / 98
Part Fourteen
Saturday 6 December 1986, 17.45-18.15, 5.6m / 80
BBC Archive
Both episodes exist as 625-line one-inch PAL colour master videotapes. 71 edits also exist for both episodes, and a 72 edit for Part Fourteen, in the same format.
Novelization
Doctor Who – The Ultimate Foe by Pip and Jane Baker (126/25)
Hardback:
April 1988, WH Allen (0491031068 / Alister Pearson)
Paperback:
September 1988, Target (0426203291 / Alister Pearson)
Video
November 1993, triple-pack, in *The Trial of a Time Lord* Limited Edition Tardis Tin [BBCV 5008 / Andrew Skilleter] with the other three stories (BBCV 5009 / Alister Pearson)
Précis
The Doctor and the Valeyard battle it out in the surreal world of the Matrix...
Cast
Colin Baker (The Doctor), Bonnie Langford (Melanie), Michael Jayston (The Valeyard), Lynda Bellingham (The Inquisitor), Anthony Ainley (The Master), Tony Selby (Sabalom Glitz), Geoffrey Hughes (Mr Popplewick), James Bree (The Keeper of the Matrix).
Crew
Visual Effects Designer Kevin Molloy, *Visual Effects Assistants* Chris Reynolds, John Van Der Pool, Clare Chopping, *Graphic Designer* Clive Harris, *Video Effects* Dave Chapman, Danny

Popkin, *Technical Coordinator* Alan Arbuthnott, *Camera Supervisor* Alec Wheal, *Vision Mixers* Shirley Coward, Jim Stephens, *Videotape Editor* Hugh Parson, *Studio Lighting* Don Babbage, *Studio Sound* Brian Clark, *OB Lighting* John Mason, *OB Sound* Vic Godrich, *OB Cameramen* Mike Winser, John Hawes, Tony Maslen, *Properties Buyer* Al Huxley, *Special Sound* Dick Mills, *Grams Operator* Jem Whippey, *Incidental Music* Dominic Glynn, *Costume Designer* Andrew Rose, *Costume Assistant* Chrissie Tucker, *Dressers* Dennis Addoo, Steven George, Isobel Foley, *Make-Up Artist* Shaunne Harrison, *Make-Up Assistants* Simon Tytherleigh, Lesley Smith, Issy Webley, *Designer* Michael Trevor, *Production Manager* Ian Fraser, *Production Associate* Jenny Doe, *Production Assistant* Jane Wellesley, *Assistant Floor Manager* Karen Little, *Floor Assistant* Yvonne O'Grady, *Script Editor* Eric Saward (13 only), *Producer* John Nathan-Turner, *Director* Chris Clough

DWM Index
118   Preview
122   Episode Guide
123   Kevin Molloy interview
       TV review
126   Season Survey results
134   Tony Selby interview
135   Chris Clough interview
137   Pip and Jane Baker interview
W92   Archive Feature
205   Video review
       What The Papers Said
206   Pip and Jane Baker interview
       Imitating Reality: Colin Baker on Season 23
       Dominic Glynn interview
231   Chris Clough interview
245   The John Nathan-Turner Memoirs
282   Tony Selby interview
284   Michael Jayston interview
304   Pip and Jane Baker interview
       Geoffrey Hughes interview
324   Colin Baker interview
348   Eric Saward interview

Recording Dates
23-24 June 1986 (Location videotaping), 30 June – 4 July 1986 (Location videotaping), 16-17 July 1986 (TC1).

Locations
Camber Sands, Camber, near Rye, East Sussex; Gladstone Pottery Museum, Longton, Stoke-on-Trent, Staffordshire

Working Titles
The Ultimate Foe
Time Inc.

Factoids
- Robert Holmes was commissioned to write the two-part conclusion to *The Trial of a Time Lord* but died on 24 May 1986, leaving the final part unfinished. Using Holmes' outline, Eric Saward completed the story, ending it with the Doctor and the Valeyard engaged in a life or death struggle in the Matrix. When producer John Nathan-Turner insisted on an upbeat conclusion, Saward withdrew his script and resigned from the post of script editor. At very short notice, Pip and Jane Baker wrote a brand-new Part Fourteen, using none of the material in either Robert Holmes' or Eric Saward's versions for copyright reasons and utilising only those sets and actors required for Part Thirteen.
- The cliffhanger ending to Part Thirteen was achieved by digging a double-chambered hole in the sand, placing a hydraulic lift into one of the chambers and covering the excavation with plastic sheeting covered in cork chips. Visual Effects assistants stood in one of the chambers and provided the hands that appeared from beneath the sand, while Colin Baker lay on the hydraulic press which lowered him into the ground.
- An excerpt of the Vervoids' destruction from the previous instalment was shown at the beginning of Part Thirteen, while the 'happy ending' with Peri and King Yrcanos was a brief slow-motion clip taken from Part Eight.
- Because of the complexities inherent in the conclusion of *The Trial of a Time Lord*, Part Fourteen was allowed to air in an extended 30-minute slot.

Comment
There are many excellent aspects to this story - most notably the very effective night filming at the Gladstone Pottery Museum - but as the conclusion to a 14-part epic, it is sadly wanting. Simply put, there's too much technobabble and too few characters to provide any kind of satisfying closure. Holmes' episode is an enjoyably surreal build-up to what promises to be a dynamic dénouement. The Bakers, however, refuse to up the ante, delivering a lacklustre, cheap-looking runaround that (unavoidably) is almost entirely taken up with explanations of previous weeks' events. The intended climax is largely incomprehensible. **36%**

Seventh Doctor: Sylvester McCoy

Season 24

"Just three small points. Where am I? Who am I? And who are *you*?" ~ The Doctor

145) Time and the Rani
Pip and Jane Baker

Serial Code: 7D
Original Transmission
Part One
Monday 7 September 1987, 19.35-20.00, 5.1m / 71
Part Two
Monday 14 September 1987, 19.35-20.00, 4.2m / 85
Part Three
Monday 21 September 1987, 19.35-20.00, 4.3m / 81
Part Four
Monday 28 September 1987, 19.35-20.00, 4.9m / 86
BBC Archive
All episodes exist as 625-line one-inch PAL colour master videotapes. 71 edits of all episodes also exist in the same format.
Novelization
Doctor Who – Time and the Rani by Pip and Jane Baker (143/23)
Hardback:
December 1987, WH Allen (0491031866 / Photograph)
Paperback:
1. May 1988, Target (0426202325 / Photograph)
2. October 1991, Target (0426203313 / Alister Pearson)
Video
July 1995 (BBCV 5617 / Colin Howard)
Music and Sound Effects
1. November 1988, *The Doctor Who 25th Anniversary Album*, LP (REB 707 / Logo)
2. November 1988, *The Doctor Who 25th Anniversary Album*, CD (BBCCD 707 / Logo)
3. November 1988, *The Doctor Who 25th Anniversary Album*, cassette (ZCF 707 / Logo)
4. May 1997, Prestige Records, *Evolution - The Music from Doctor Who*, CD (CDSGP0320 / -)

Précis
The Doctor is captured by the Rani who attempts to use his genius for her own twisted ends…
Cast
Sylvester McCoy (The Doctor), Bonnie Langford (Melanie Bush), Kate O'Mara (The Rani), Donald Pickering (Beyus), Wanda Ventham (Faroon), Karen Clegg (Sarn), Mark Greenstreet (Ikona), Richard Gauntlett (Urak), Peter Tuddenham, Jacki Webb (Special Voices), John Segal (Lanisha), Tom O'Leary (Einstein), Cenydd Joeenz (Pasteur), Helen Garton, Christopher Holmes, Cavid Ianson, Lea Derrick, Karen England, Ian Durrant, Paul Page-Hansen, Ricardo Mullhall, Mark Carroll, Paul Goddard (Genii)
Crew
Visual Effects Designer Colin Mapson, *Visual Effects Assistants* Len Hutton, Stan Mitchell, Mike Tucker, Roger Barham, Jim Lancaster, *Computer Effects* CAL Video, *Video Effects* Dave Chapman, *Technical Coordinator* Richard Wilson, *Studio Camera Supervisor* Alec Wheal, *Vision Mixer* Sue Thorne, *Videotape Editor* Hugh Parson, *Studio Lighting* Henry Barber, *Studio Sound* Brian Clark, *Film Cameraman* William Dudman, *OB Lighting* Ian Dow, *OB Sound* Doug Whittaker, *OB Cameramen* Alastair Mitchell, John Hawes, *Properties Buyer* Francis Smith, *Special Sound* Dick Mills, Keff McCulloch, *Grams Operator* Mike Weaver, *Incidental Music* Keff McCulloch, *Costume Designer* Ken Trew, *Costume Assistant* Philip Crichton, *Dressers* Tom Reeve, Brian Baker, Lena Hansen, *Make-Up Artist* Lesley Rawstorne, *Make-Up Assistants* Elaine Davis, Anne McEwan, Helen Johnson, Wendy Harrison, *Designer* Geoff Powell, *Production Manager* Tony Redston, *Production Associate* Ann Faggetter, *Production Assistant* Joy Sinclair, *Assistant Floor Managers* Joanna Newbury, Christopher Sandeman, *Floor Assistant* Sue Bear, *Script Editor* Andrew Cartmel, *Producer* John Nathan-Turner, *Director* Andrew Morgan
DWM Index
124	Meet Sylvester!
128	Preview
	Kate O'Mara interview
130	Sylvester McCoy interview
	Geoff Powell interview
131	John Nathan-Turner interview
	Bonnie Langford interview
132	TV review
133	Novelization review
137	Season Survey results
	Pip and Jane Baker interview
138	Susan Moore and Stephen Mansfield interview

165   Dave Chapman interview
167   Keff McCulloch interview
172   Episode Guide
182   Those *Radio Times*
198   Archive Feature
      Richard Gauntlett interview
204   Andrew Morgan interview
206   What The Papers Said
216   Keff McCulloch interview
217   Sylvester McCoy interview
224   Andrew Cartmel interview
228   Video review
246   The John Nathan-Turner Memoirs
260   Bonnie Langford interview
266   Donald Pickering and Wanda Ventham
      interview
277   Andrew Morgan interview
298   Kate O'Mara interview
304   Pip and Jane Baker interview
352   The Secret Diary of a Script Editor

Recording Dates
4-8 April 1987 (Location videotaping), April 1987 (Acton Studio modelwork), 20-21 April 1987 (TC8), 3-5 May 1987 (TC1)

Locations
Cloford Quarry, Whatley Quarry and Westdown Quarry, all Frome, Somerset

Working Title
Strange Matter

Factoids
- Colin Baker having been ignominiously sacked in October 1986, 43-year-old Scottish actor Sylvester McCoy (born James Kent-Smith) was chosen to be his replacement in February 1987. Other actors considered included Chris Jury, Ken Campbell, Hugh Futcher, Dermot Crowley and David Fielder.
- The Seventh Doctor's cream-coloured costume was designed by Ken Trew. A question-mark pullover (based on a 1930s golfing design) replaced the question-mark collars. The original tartan scarf was superseded by a Paisley one for his next story, *Paradise Towers*.
- A new title sequence was designed by BBC graphic designer Oliver Elmes and executed using computer generated imagery by Gareth Edwards of CAL Videographics. McCoy's green-tinted face originally appeared only faintly, but John Nathan-Turner insisted it was overlaid with a much sharper image. The original version was mistakenly transmitted on Part Four (and replaced on the video release). To accompany the new titles, a revised version of the theme music was composed by freelance musician Keff McCulloch.
- CAL Videographics also supplied special effects sequences for the story, such as the pre-credits sequence of the Tardis being attacked, the asteroid orbiting Lakertya, and the space scenes on the Rani's monitor screen in Part Four.
- Only one full-size base was built for the Rani's spinning globes. For scenes involving them spinning around the quarry, miniatures were inlayed onto the live-action shots using a digital image manipulation tool called Paintbox. The model of the Rani's citadel was shot on video at the quarry location and in studio on 35mm film for its explosive demise.
- Because Colin Baker refused to return to the programme, Sylvester McCoy donned a curly blonde wig to record the speedy regeneration sequence used in the pre-credits sequence.

Comment
After the continuity-obsessed and introspective *Trial of a Time Lord* season, *Time and the Rani* comes across as a huge breath of fresh air. It's a bright and attractive story that has no qualms about aiming itself straight at a children's audience. Sylvester McCoy gives a likeable debut performance, reinventing the part as a comic mad professor, and Kate O'Mara's impersonation of Mel is wickedly accurate. The Tetraps are a little silly, but this is more than made up for by the spectacular visual effects, especially the superb spinning globes. As a piece of entertainment it's all great fun, although I'd be the first to admit that a whole season like this would be extremely tiresome. **74%**

"All hail the Great Architect!" ~ *The Chief Caretaker and his cohorts*

146) *Paradise Towers*
Stephen Wyatt

Serial Code: 7E
Original Transmission
Part One
Monday 5 October 1987, 19.35-20.00, 4.5m / 88
Part Two
Monday 12 October 1987, 19.35-20.00, 5.2m / 84
Part Three
Monday 19 October 1987, 19.35-20.00, 5m / 79

Part Four
Monday 26 October 1987, 19.35-20.00, 5m / 93
BBC Archive
All episodes exist as 625-line one-inch PAL colour master videotapes. 71 edits also exist for all episodes in the same format.
Novelization
Doctor Who - Paradise Towers by Stephen Wyatt (143/12)
Paperback:
December 1988, Target (0426203305 / Alister Pearson)
Video
December 1995 (BBCV 5686 / Colin Howard)
Music and Sound Effects
1. November 1988, *The Doctor Who 25th Anniversary Album*, LP (REB 707 / Logo)
2. November 1988, *The Doctor Who 25th Anniversary Album*, CD (BBCCD 707 / Logo)
3. November 1988, *The Doctor Who 25th Anniversary Album*, cassette (ZCF 707 / Logo)
4. July 1993, *Doctor Who: 30 Years at the Radiophonic Workshop*, CD (BBCCD 871 / Photomontage)
5. May 1997, Prestige Records, *Evolution - The Music from Doctor Who*, CD (CDSGP0320 / -)
Précis
The Chief Caretaker rules Paradise Towers under the all-seeing presence of Great Architect Kroagnon...
Cast
Sylvester McCoy (The Doctor), Bonnie Langford (Melanie), Richard Briers (Chief Caretaker/Kroagnon Voice), Clive Merrison (Deputy Chief Caretaker), Howard Cooke (Pex), Annabel Yuresha (Bin Liner), Julie Brennon (Fire Escape), Catherine Cusack (Blue Kang Leader), Astra Sheridan (Yellow Kang), Brenda Bruce (Tilda), Elizabeth Spriggs (Tabby), Judy Cornwell (Maddy), Joseph Young (Young Caretaker), Simon Coady (Video Commentary Voice), Ellie Bertram (Stunt Double for Melanie Bush)
Crew
Stunt Arranger Roy Scammell, *Visual Effects Designer* Simon Taylor, *Visual Effects Assistants* Mark Collcutt, *Video Effects* Dave Chapman, *Computer Effects* CAL Video, *Graphic Designer* Oliver Elmes, *Technical Coordinator* Richard Wilson, *Senior Camera Supervisor* Alec Wheal, *Vision Mixer* Shirley Coward, *Videotape Editor* Hugh Parson, *Studio Lighting* Henry Barber, *Studio Sound* Brian Clark, *OB Lighting* Ian Dow, *OB Sound* Doug Whittaker, *OB Sound Assistants* Peter Hales, Dave Roll, *OB Cameramen* Alastair Mitchell, David Hunter, *Properties Buyer* Bob Sutton, *Special Sound* Dick Mills, *Grams*

Operator Mike Weaver, *Incidental Music* Keff McCulloch, *Costume Designer* Janet Tharby, *Dressers* Lena Hausen, Belinda Peters, Lisa Pembroke, Tom Reeve, Leslie Bingham, Liz Scammell, Bob Springett, *Make-Up Artist* Shaunna Harrison, *Make-Up Assistants* Sharon Welsh, Wendy Holmes, Carol Elms, Jules York-Marsh, *Designer* Martin Collins, *Design Assistant* Phil Harvey, *Production Manager* Ian Fraser, *Production Associate* Ann Faggetter, *Production Assistant* Frances Graham, *Assistant Floor Manager* Val McCrimmon, *Floor Assistant* Jane Litherland, *Script Editor* Andrew Cartmel, *Producer* John Nathan-Turner, *Director* Nicholas Mallett
DWM Index
129	Preview
131	John Nathan-Turner interview
	Bonnie Langford interview
132	Nicholas Mallett interview
133	TV review
137	Season Survey results
	Novelization review
146	Stephen Wyatt interview
216	Keff McCulloch interview
217	Sylvester McCoy interview
224	Andrew Cartmel interview
230	Nicholas Mallett interview
	Judy Cornwell interview
231	Video review
246	The John Nathan-Turner Memoirs
260	Bonnie Langford interview
263	Stephen Wyatt interview
308	Clive Merrison interview
326	Archive Feature
	Richard Briers interview
352	The Secret Diary of a Script Editor

Recording Dates
21-22 May 1987 (Location videotaping), 4-5 June 1987 (TC1), 17-19 June 1987 (TC1)
Location
Elmswell House, Chalfont St Giles, Buckinghamshire
Working Title
Paradise Tower
Factoids
- For this story, Stephen Wyatt (whose only previous television commission was the play *Claws*, broadcast on 4 October 1987) was heavily influenced by the 1975 JG Ballard satirical novel *High-Rise*, concerning the social problems arising from a 40-storey tower block in London's Docklands.
- Musician David Snell's original score for *Paradise Towers* was vetoed at the last

minute by producer John Nathan-Turner who decided his music was too monotonous. He turned to regular *Doctor Who* composer Keff McCulloch to provide an alternative score in only six days.
- Excerpts from BBC2 architecture series *The Shock of the New* (1981) were used for the Paradise Towers 'travelogue' seen in several of the episodes.
- The swimming pool at Elmswell House was unheated and caused Bonnie Langford extreme discomfort. The pool cleaner robot was a five-foot long prop operated by off-screen wetsuited visual effects assistants with perspex rods. Veteran stuntman Roy Scammell oversaw its attack on stunt double Ellie Bertram.
- Three fibreglass Cleaner robots were built, one of which was a dummy that could be blown up on cue.

Comment
This is a wonderful story, full of dry wit and marvellous one-liners. The central concept may be unoriginal (JG Ballard got there first), but it's very satisfying to see a *Doctor Who* story set against a believable backdrop and tackling real issues - in this case, urban blight and the rise of teenage gang violence. Then again, it can also be seen as a class comedy or even a comedy of manners - just how *does* a young girl react in the company of geriatric cannibals, for instance? Richard Briers plays the Hitler-moustachioed Chief Caretaker as a picture of frustrated middle management, forever trying to restore order in a system that has long since gone down the pan; Clive Merrison gives great support. Pex is a less successful character, due to the miscasting of Howard Cooke (although there are, pleasingly, shades of TA-obsessed Gareth from BBC2 sitcom *The Office*), and the Kangs are a little too dainty to be entirely credible. But Brenda Bruce and Elizabeth Spriggs shine as the flesh-eating OAPs, and if one ignores Bonnie Langford's over-enthusiasm and the lacklustre swimming pool - couldn't they have chosen somewhere a bit more impressive? - this is a charming production. Sylvester McCoy, in only his second story, has well and truly made the part his own. **85%**

"I haven't had such a shindig since I went buffalo hunting in Africa!" ~ Burton

147) Delta and the Bannermen
Malcolm Kohll

Serial Code: 7F
Original Transmission
Part One
Monday 2 November 1987, 19.35-20.00, 5.3m / 90
Part Two
Monday 9 November 1987, 19.35-20.00, 5.1m / 93
Part Three
Monday 16 November 1987, 19.35-20.00, 5.4m / 87
BBC Archive
All episodes exist as 625-line one-inch PAL colour master videotapes. 71 edits exist for all episodes, and a 72 edit exists for Part Two, held on the same format.
Novelization
Doctor Who - Delta and the Bannermen by Malcolm Kohll (142/34)
Paperback: January 1989, Target (042620333X / Alister Pearson)*
* Titled *Doctor Who - Delta and the Bannerman* on the spine
Video
March 2001 (BBCV 7131 / Photomontage)
Music and Sound Effects
1. November 1988, *The Doctor Who 25th Anniversary Album*, LP (REB 707 / Logo)
2. November 1988, *The Doctor Who 25th Anniversary Album*, CD (BBCCD 707 / Logo)
3. November 1988, *The Doctor Who 25th Anniversary Album*, cassette (ZCF 707 / Logo)
4. July 1993, *Doctor Who: 30 Years at the Radiophonic Workshop*, CD (BBCCD 871 / Photomontage)
5. May 1997, Prestige Records, *Evolution - The Music from Doctor Who*, CD (CDSGP0320 / -)
Précis
Delta, last of the Chimerons, hides from the warlike Bannermen in a 1950s Welsh holiday camp...
Cast
Sylvester McCoy (The Doctor), Bonnie Langford (Melanie), Belinda Mayne (Delta), Don Henderson (Gavrok), David Kinder (Billy), Sara Griffiths (Ray), Stubby Kaye (Jerome K Weismuller), Morgan Deare (Lex Hawk), Richard Davies (Burton), Hugh Lloyd (Goronwy Jones), Johnny Dennis (Murray), Ken Dodd (Tollmaster),

Tim Scott (Chima), Anita Graham (Bollit), Leslie Meadows (Adlon), Brian Hibbard (Keillor), Robin Aspland, Keff McCulloch, Justin Myers, Ralph Salmins (The Lorells), Tracey Wilson, Jodie Wilson (Vocalists), Martyn Geraint (Vinny), Jessica McGough (Baby Chimeron), Amy Osborn (Young Chimeron), Clive Condon (Callon), Richard Mitchley (Arrex), Laura Collins (Young Chimeron/Chimeron Princess), Carley Joseph (Chimeron Princess), Pepsi (Burton's Dog), Roy Scammell (Stunt Double for Gavrok)

Crew
Stunt Arranger Roy Scammell, *Visual Effects Designer* Andy McVean, *Visual Effects Assistant* Paul Mann, *Graphic Designer* Oliver Elmes, *Special Props* Susan Moore, Stephen Mansfield, *Video Effects* Dave Chapman, *Technical Coordinator* Richard Wilson, *Senior Camera Supervisor* Alec Wheal, *Vision Mixer* Shirley Coward, *Videotape Editor* Hugh Parson, *Film Cameraman* William Dudman, *OB Lighting* Ian Dow, *OB Sound* Doug Whittaker, Brian Clark, *OB Cameramen* Alastair Mitchell, Chris Snare, *OB VT Engineer* Martin Perrett, *Engineering Manager* John Wilson, *Properties Buyer* Cathy Cosgrove, *Special Sound* Dick Mills, *Incidental Music* Keff McCulloch, *Costume Designer* Richard Croft, *Costume Assistant* Leigh Archer, *Dressers* Bob Springett, Lena Hausen, Tom Reeve, Kate Hurst, *Make-Up Artist* Gillian Thomas, *Make-Up Assistants* Petrona Winton, Anabela Dellot-Seguro, Jayne Buxton, *Designer* John Asbridge, *Design Assistant* Hilda Liptrott, *Production Manager* Gary Downie, *Production Associate* Ann Faggetter, *Production Assistant* Rosemary Parsons, *Assistant Floor Managers* Christopher Sandeman, Kim Wilcocks, *Script Editor* Andrew Cartmel, *Producer/Second Unit Director* John Nathan-Turner, *Director* Chris Clough

DWM Index
130 Preview
131 John Nathan-Turner interview
134 TV review
135 Chris Clough interview
137 Season Survey results
138 Susan Moore and Stephen Mansfield interview
142 Sylvester McCoy interview
146 Novelization review
167 Keff McCulloch interview
172 Episode Guide
184 Archive Feature
 Morgan Deare interview
216 Sylvester McCoy interview
 Keff McCulloch interview
217 Sylvester McCoy interview
224 Andrew Cartmel interview
231 Chris Clough interview
246 The John Nathan-Turner Memoirs
276 Malcolm Kohll interview
301 Ken Dodd interview
 Sara Griffiths interview
302 Video review
339 Gary Downie interview
352 The Secret Diary of a Script Editor

Recording Dates
24-27 June 1987 (Location videotaping), 29 June-4 July 1987 (Location videotaping), 6-7 July 1987 (Location videotaping), 12 August 1987 (TC3), August 1987 (Acton Studio modelwork)

Locations
Springwell Quarry, Rickmansworth, Hertfordshire; Majestic Holiday Camp, Barry Island, South Glamorgan, Wales; British Tissues Hanger, Llandow, South Glamorgan, Wales; Pysgodlyn Mawr Reservoir, Hensol Forest, South Glamorgan, Wales; Sutton Farm, Fort Road, near Penarth, South Glamorgan, Wales; Coed Y Wallas, Near Castle Upon Alun, Mid Glamorgan, Wales

Working Title
Flight of the Chimeron

Factoids
- With the exception of brief Tardis scenes recorded during *Dragonfire* (148), *Delta and the Bannermen* was the first all-location *Doctor Who* story since *The Sontaran Experiment* (77).
- Keff McCulloch provided cover versions of all the 1950s rock and roll music heard in this serial, as well as incorporating the following famous tunes into his incidental score: *Devil's Gallop* (used as the radio theme for *Dick Barton*), *Calling All Workers* (used on *Workers' Playtime*) and *Children's Favourites* from the radio series of the same name. He also appeared on-screen in the ballroom scenes in Part One, playing in the fictitious band The Lorells.
- Freelance props builders Susan Moore and Stephen Mansfield created the baby Chimeron puppet.
- Welsh actress Lynn Gardner was originally chosen to play the part of Ray, but when she injured her leg during scooter practice she was replaced by the shortlisted candidate Sara Griffiths.
- Amongst the 1950s vehicles required for this story were two old touring coaches, a Morris Minor 1100, a Vespa motor scooter and a 1953 Vincent Rapide motorbike. The

Tardis prop was pressed into service as a bona fide telephone box with the addition of a 1950s telephone.

Comment
Delightfully silly, *Delta and the Bannermen* is the sort of story that one either loves or loathes. In terms of the production, it can hold its head up to any other McCoy tale: the various model effects are well executed, the bright, summery location work is wonderfully evocative of the 1950s and the characterisation is strong. But of course it's the music and Ken Dodd that everyone remembers, and in any other story they'd look very out of place. But *Delta and the Bannermen* is one of a kind (thank goodness, say might some) and as such can accommodate the quirkiest of directorial decisions. Only Weismuller and Hawke seem extraneous to requirements, but the rest of the time this story is a foot-tapping mixture of romance, adventure and nostalgia, with Hugh Lloyd standing out as the mysterious 'more than just a beekeeper' Goronwy. **87%**

"I like women with fire in their bellies." ~ Kane

148) Dragonfire
Ian Briggs

Serial Code: 7G
Original Transmission
Part One
Monday 23 November 1987, 19.35-20.00, 5.5m / 80
Part Two
Monday 30 November 1987, 19.35-20.00, 5m / 96
Part Three
Monday 7 December 1987, 19.35-20.00, 4.7m / 94
BBC Archive
All episodes exist as 625-line one-inch PAL colour master videotapes. 71 edits also exist for all episodes, held on the same format.
Novelization
Doctor Who - Dragonfire by Ian Briggs (144/16)
Paperback:
March 1989, Target (0426203224 / Alister Pearson)
Video
January 1994 (BBCV 5181 / Bruno Elattori)
Music and Sound Effects
July 1993, *Doctor Who: 30 Years at the Radiophonic Workshop*, CD (BBCCD 871 / Photomontage)

Précis
On the frozen planet of Svartos, Kane is seeking the Dragon's treasure...
Cast
Sylvester McCoy (The Doctor), Bonnie Langford (Melanie), Sophie Aldred (Ace), Edward Peel (Kane), Patricia Quinn (Belazs), Tony Osoba (Kracauer), Stephanie Fayerman (McLuhan), Stuart Organ (Bazin), Nigel Miles-Thomas (Pudovkin), Ian Mackenzie (Anderson), Tony Selby (Glitz), Leslie Meadows (Creature), Sean Blowers (Zed), Shirin Taylor (Customer), Miranda Borman (Stellar), Lynn Gardner (Announcer), Chris MacDonnell (Arnheim), Daphne Oxenford (Archivist), Larry Bishop (Sculptor)
Crew
Visual Effects Designer Andy McVean, *Visual Effects Assistants* Sue Moore, Lindsey MacGowan, Mike Tucker, Paul Mann, Paul McGuinness, Jonathan Clarke, *Video Effects* Dave Chapman, *Technical Coordinator* Richard Wilson, *Camera Supervisor* Alec Wheal, *Vision Mixer* Shirley Coward, *Videotape Editor* Hugh Parson, *Studio Lighting* Don Babbage, *Studio Sound* Brian Clark, *Deputy Sound Supervisor* Mike Weaver, *Film Cameraman* William Dudman, *Special Props* Susan Moore, Stephen Mansfield, *Special Sound* Dick Mills, *Incidental Music* Dominic Glynn, *Costume Designer* Richard Croft, *Make-Up Designer* Gillian Thomas, *Make-Up Assistant* Petrona Winton, *Designer* John Ashbridge, *Production Manager* Gary Downie, *Production Associate* Ann Faggetter, *Production Assistants* Rosemary Parsons, Karen King, *Assistant Floor Manager* Christopher Sandeman, *Script Editor* Andrew Cartmel, *Producer* John Nathan-Turner, *Director* Chris Clough
DWM Index

131	Set Report
134	Tony Selby interview
135	TV review
	Chris Clough interview
138	Susan Moore and Stephen Mansfield interview
139	Sophie Aldred interview
142	Sylvester McCoy interview
146	Novelization review
147	Ian Briggs interview
172	Episode Guide
182	Those *Radio Times*
206	Dominic Glynn interview
	What The Papers Said
208	Video review
217	Sylvester McCoy interview
224	Andrew Cartmel interview
231	Chris Clough interview

246   The John Nathan-Turner Memoirs
255   Archive Feature
282   Tony Selby interview
327   The Mary Whitehouse Experience
339   Gary Downie interview
352   The Secret Diary of a Script Editor

Recording Dates
28-30 July 1987 (TC1), 12-13 August 1987 (TC3), August 1987 (Acton studios modelwork)

Working Title
The Pyramid's Treasure

Behind-the-Scenes
- The story originally featured a bounty hunter called Razorback, but on the insistence of producer John Nathan-Turner the character became intergalactic conman Glitz, as seen in *The Trial of a Time Lord* (144).
- *Dragonfire* was actress Sophie Aldred's first television work, and inspiration from her costume came from an edition of trendy style magazine *The Face*. Her two Blue Peter badges are genuine - one was for a letter she sent describing how to make a rocket launcher from a washing up liquid bottle and a garden hose. Her character of Ace was originally to be called 'Alf'.
- The effect of Kane's head dissolving was done by melting a multilayered wax cast of actor Edward Peel's head and then speeding up the result in post-production. A wide shot of Kane collapsing was simply a blow-up sex doll dressed in his costume being deflated off-screen.
- Many of the central characters were named after prominent film critics and media theorists, such as Bela Belazs, Marshall McLuhan and Vsevolod Pudovkin. Dialogue between the Doctor and Arnheim in Part Two was an in-joke reference to media studies book *Doctor Who - The Unfolding Text* (1983).
- The *Radio Times* promoted this story, erroneously, as the 150th *Doctor Who* adventure. (Their numbering system presumably ignored *Mission to the Unknown* [19] and treated the linked segments of the story *The Trial of a Time Lord* [144] as separate entries.)

Comment
With hindsight, this is probably the most ridiculous introduction for a companion ever - a teenage girl from North London is whisked off to an alien planet by a 'time storm' after messing around with home-made explosives, finds a job working in a café, pours a drink over a customer's head and goes off with the Doctor. I mean, I ask you - could that happen? So it's a huge surprise to find that Sophie Aldred's performance here is actually very good, imbuing the cardboard character with enormous energy and screen presence. Mel, playing second fiddle to Ace, becomes consequently less irritating. The production design is a mixture of good (Kane's base) and bad (the ice chamber), but the modelwork is uniformly excellent. Edward Peel gives a genuinely chilling portrayal of Kane and his graphic demise is justly praised as a brilliant piece of visual effects trickery. However, Sylvester McCoy seems to be amusing only himself with his slapstick routines and the Part One cliffhanger is appallingly mismanaged. **70%**

Season 25

"I think I might have miscalculated." ~ The Doctor

149) Remembrance of the Daleks
Ben Aaronovitch

Serial Code: 7H
Original Transmission
Part One
Wednesday 5 October 1988, 19.35-20.00, 5.5m / 78
Part Two
Wednesday 12 October 1988, 19.35-20.00, 5.8m / 78
Part Three
Wednesday 19 October 1988, 19.35-20.00, 5.1m / 91
Part Four
Wednesday 26 October 1988, 19.35-20.00, 5m / 96

BBC Archive
All episodes exist as 625-line one-inch PAL colour master videotapes. 71 edits also exist for all episodes, held on the same format.

Novelization
Doctor Who - Remembrance of the Daleks by Ben Aaronovitch (160/24)
Paperback:
June 1990, Target (0426203372 / Alister Pearson)

Video
1. September 1993, in 'The Daleks Limited Edition Box Set' [BBCV 5005 / Photographs] with *The Chase* (BBCV 5007 / Alister Pearson)
2. September 2001, in 'The Davros Collection' box set [BBCV 7241 / Photomontage] with the other four Davros stories (BBCV 7255 / Photomontage)

DVD
1. February 2001, isolated music score, extended and deleted scenes, trailers, location footage, out-takes, production subtitles, photo gallery, commentary by Sylvester McCoy and Sophie Aldred (BBCDVD 1040 / Photograph)
2. October 2003, as part of 'Dalek Collectors Edition' exclusive to WHSmith (- / Photomontage)

Music and Sound Effects
1. November 1988, *The Doctor Who 25th Anniversary Album*, LP (REB 707 / Logo)
2. November 1988, *The Doctor Who 25th Anniversary Album*, CD (BBCCD 707 / Logo)
3. November 1988, *The Doctor Who 25th Anniversary Album*, cassette (ZCF 707 / Logo)
4. July 1993, *Doctor Who: 30 Years at the Radiophonic Workshop*, CD (BBCCD 871 / Photomontage)
5. May 1997, Prestige Records, *Evolution - The Music from Doctor Who*, CD (CDSGP0320 / -)

Précis
Two rival Dalek factions are after the Hand of Omega in 1963 London…

Cast
Sylvester McCoy (The Doctor), Sophie Aldred (Ace), George Sewell (Ratcliffe), Simon Williams (Group Captain Gilmore), Dursley McLinden (Sergeant Mike Smith), Pamela Salem (Rachel Jensen), Karen Gledhill (Allison Williams), Michael Sheard (Headmaster), Harry Fowler (Harry), Jasmine Breaks (Girl), Peter Halliday (Vicar), Peter Hamilton Dyer (Sergeant Embery), Joseph Marcell (John), William Thomas (Martin), Derek Keller (Private Kaufman), Tracey Eddon (Stunt-double for Ace), Tip Tipping (Stunt-double for the Doctor/Stunt-double for Mike/Exterminated Soldier), Mark Oliver (Driving Double for the Doctor, Ace and Mike), Terry Molloy (Emperor Dalek/Davros), John Evans (Undertaker), Kathleen Bidmead (Mrs Smith), Richie Kennedy (Milkman), Hugh Spight, John Scott Martin, Tony Starr, Cy Town, David Harrison, Norman Bacon, Nigel Wild (Daleks), John Leeson (Battle Computer Voice), Royce Mills, Roy Skelton, Brian Miller (Dalek Voices)

Crew
Armourer Doug Needham, *Stunt Arranger* Tip Tipping, *Visual Effects Designer* Stuart Brisdon, *Visual Effects Assistants* Micky Edwards, Andrew David, Tony Auger, Martin Geeson, Dave Becker, Melvyn Friend, Mike Tucker, *Video Effects* Dave Chapman, *Technical Coordinator* Richard Wilson, *Studio Camera Supervisor* Alec Wheal, *Vision Mixers* Shirley Coward, Fred Law, *Videotape Editor* Hugh Parson, *Studio Lighting* Henry Barber, *Studio Sound* Scott Talbot, *Film Cameraman* William Dudman, *OB Lighting* Ian Dow, *OB Sound* Doug Whittaker, Les Mowbray, *OB Cameramen* Robin Sutherland, Barry Chaston, *OB Senior Engineer* Peter Thomas, *OB VT Engineer* Dave Lees, *Engineering Manager* Brian Jones, *Properties Buyer* Chris Ferriday, *Special Sound* Dick Mills, *Incidental Music* Keff McCulloch, *Costume Designer* Ken Trew, *Costume Assistant* Andrew Duckett, *Dressers* Debbie Roberts, Pippa Rowlandson, Michael Johnson, David Hughes, David Bailey, *Make-Up Designer* Christine Greenwood, *Make-Up Assistants* Lesley Altringham, Jane Cole, Carmel Jackson, *Designer* Martin Collins, *Design Assistant* Brian Sykes, *Production Managers* Ian Fraser, Michael McDermott, *Production Associates* June Collins, Hilary Barratt, *Production Assistant* Rosemary Parsons, *Assistant Floor Managers* Lynn Grant, Val McCrimmon, *Floor Assistants* Louise Percival, Jes Nightingale, *Script Editor* Andrew Cartmel, *Producer* John Nathan-Turner, *Director* Andrew Morgan

DWM Index
140 Preview
    John-Nathan Turner interview
145 TV review
147 Ben Aaronovitch interview
    Season Guide
148 Stuart Brisdon interview
149 Tip Tipping interview
150 Season Survey results
151 Dalek Continuity
160 Novelization review
173 Episode Guide
S93 Archive Feature
204 Video review
210 What The Papers Said
216 Keff McCulloch interview
218 Sylvester McCoy interview
225 Andrew Cartmel interview
247 The John Nathan-Turner Memoirs
265 *Doctor Who Magazine* Awards (6th)
271 Pamela Salem interview
    Karen Gledhill interview
272 Terry Molloy interview

277	Andrew Morgan interview
299	Simon Williams interview
	George Sewell interview
301	DVD review
302	Michael Sheard interview
309	Jasmine Breaks interview
	Video review ('The Davros Collection')
321	Peter Halliday interview
352	The Secret Diary of a Script Editor
352	The Secret Diary of a Script Editor

Recording Dates
4-9 April 1988 (Location OB), 11-12 April 1988 (Location OB), 27-29 April 1988 (TC8)

Locations
Theed Street, London SE1; Kew Bridge Steam Museum, Brentford, Middlesex; Old Oak Common Lane, East Acton, London W3; Kendal Avenue, North Acton, London W3; Willesden Lane Cemetery, London NW6; Territorial Army Hall, Acton, London W3; John Nodes Funeral Services, Ladbroke Grove, London W10; St John's CE Junior and Infants School, Macbeth Street, Hammersmith, London W6; Macbeth Street, Hammersmith, London W6; Windmill Walk, London SE1

Working Title
Nemesis of the Doctor

Factoids
- In order to disguise Davros' presence in the serial, the Dalek Emperor was credited as 'Roy Tromelly' (an anagram of Terry Molloy).
- The four Renegade Daleks were repainted props from previous Dalek serials, while the four Imperial Daleks, with slightly modified sink plunger arms, were specially constructed. The black Dalek Supreme was a BBC Enterprises prop made by Martin Wilkie, son of BBC Visual Effects Department founder Bernard Wilkie.
- The hovering Dalek at the end of Part One was achieved by fixing the prop to a chairlift-like device and painting out the mechanism with a post-production glow around the Dalek's base.
- During location filming close to Waterloo Station on 4 April 1988, the fire brigade were called out after a particularly loud explosion was reported by railway staff as a suspected IRA bomb.

Comment
Seen at the time as a breathless, dynamic action romp that wiped away memories of the previous lightweight season, *Remembrance* today has lost none of its appeal. What delighted then still delights now: the brilliantly executed cliffhangers, the taut editing, the spectacular pyrotechnics and the hugely impressive presence of the Daleks themselves. Keff McCulloch's incidental music score, however, is one of the worst in the series' history (rivalling *Doctor Who and the Silurians* [52] and the third part of *The Trial of a Time Lord* [144c]) and McCoy is even more incoherent than usual. But despite this, and the anally retentive obsession with Dalek continuity, this is one of the most professional action adventures the series ever embarked upon and should delight the most cynical of non-fans. **88%**

"Time to get really depressed." ~ Silas P

150) The Happiness Patrol
Graeme Curry

Serial Code: 7L
Original Transmission
Part One
Wednesday 2 November 1988, 19.35-20.00, 5.3m / 96
Part Two
Wednesday 9 November 1988, 19.35-20.00, 4.6m / 104
Part Three
Wednesday 16 November 1988, 19.35-20.00, 5.3m / 88

BBC Archive
All episodes exist as 625-line one-inch PAL colour master videotapes. 71 edits also exist for all episodes, and 72 edits for Parts One and Three, in the same format.

Novelization
Doctor Who - The Happiness Patrol by Graeme Curry (140/15)
Paperback:
February 1990, Target (0426203399 /Alister Pearson)

Video
August 1997 (BBCV 5803 / Photomontage)

Précis
On a rundown colony world the Doctor and Ace discover that it's sinful to be sad...

Cast
Sylvester McCoy (The Doctor), Sophie Aldred (Ace), Sheila Hancock (Helen A), Ronald Fraser (Joseph C), Harold Innocent (Gilbert M), Lesley Dunlop (Susan Q), David John Pope (Kandy Man), Georgina Hale (Daisy K), Rachel Bell (Priscilla P), Richard D Sharp (Earl Sigma), John Normington (Trevor Sigma), Jonathan Burn (Silas

P), Mary Healey (Killjoy), Tim Barker (Harold V), Philip Neave (Wences), Ryan Freedman (Wulfric), Steve Swinscoe, Mark Carroll (Snipers), Tim Scott (Forum Doorman), Annie Hulley (Newscaster), Cy Town (Execution Victim), Chris Clough (Fifi Voice), Duncan Pettigrew (Billposter)

Crew

Visual Effects Designer Perry Brahan, *Visual Effects Assistants* Paul McGuinness, Mike Tucker, Russell Pritchard, Alan Marshall, *Special Props* Susan Moore, Stephen Mansfield, *Video Effects* Dave Chapman, *Technical Coordinator* Richard Wilson, *Camera Supervisors* Alec Wheal, Geoff Clark, *Vision Mixer* Shirley Coward, *Videotape Editor* Hugh Parson, Malcolm Warner, *Studio Lighting* Don Babbage, *Studio Sound* Scott Talbot, Trevor Webster, *Senior Studio Engineer* Adam Corcoran, *Properties Buyer* John Charles, *Special Sound* Dick Mills, *Grams Operator* Mike Weaver, *Harmonic Player* Adam Burney, *Incidental Music* Dominic Glynn, *Costume Designer* Richard Croft, *Costume Assistant* Leah Archer, *Dressers* Debbie Roberts, Michael Johnson, Robin Smith, *Make-Up Designer* Dorka Nieradzik, *Make-Up Assistants* Jayne Buxton, Sara Ellis, Anna Lubbock, Francoise Cresson, Mark Phillips, *Designer* John Asbridge, *Design Assistant* Philip Harvey, *Production Manager* Gary Downie, *Production Associate* June Collins, *Production Assistant* Jane Wellesley, *Assistant Floor Manager* Lynn Grant, *Floor Assistant* Alex Starr, *Script Editor* Andrew Cartmel, *Producer* John Nathan-Turner, *Director* Chris Clough

DWM Index

140	John Nathan-Turner interview
142	Preview
145	TV review
147	Season Guide
148	Perry Brahan interview
150	Season Survey results
154	Sylvester McCoy interview
	Sophie Aldred interview
158	Novelization review
167	Dominic Glynn interview
173	Graeme Curry interview
	Episode Guide
206	Dominic Glynn interview
210	What The Papers Said
218	Sylvester McCoy interview
225	Andrew Cartmel interview
236	Video review
245	Chris Clough interview
247	The John Nathan-Turner Memoirs
255	John Normington interview
	Georgina Hale interview
	Rachel Bell interview
302	Sheila Hancock interview
	Archive Feature
339	Gary Downie interview

Recording Dates
26-28 July 1988 (TC3), 10-11 August 1988 (TC8)

Working Title
The Crooked Smile

Factoids

- Director Chris Clough intended this story to be shot in a style reminiscent of 1940s *film noir* in which angles were always slightly skewed, but producer John Nathan-Turner vetoed the idea during camera rehearsals as he thought the result might be too distracting.
- Helen A's pet Fifi consisted of three props built by Susan Moore and Stephen Mansfield- a glove puppet, an animatronic version and a static body moved along on a wire.
- The Kandy Man was built by outside contractor Artem using an aluminium exoskeleton covered with fibreglass, polypropylene tubing, latex and foam polyurethane. It was not quite ready for its first studio appearance and so a metal chin-brace was added for the second studio session. After transmission, Bassett Foods plc complained to John Nathan-Turner about its resemblance to their Bertie Bassett sweet character.

Comment

The Happiness Patrol is a brave attempt at doing something new, but unfortunately all the characters come over as just ciphers and there really isn't enough material to fill the running time. The Kandy Man is a fantastic creation though, silly and sinister in equal measure, and Sheila Hancock makes the most of her thinly disguised Margaret Thatcher impression. But the studio-bound cheapness of the sets (albeit deliberate) and the irritatingly arch dialogue provides good reason to turn over and watch something more interesting on the other side. Excellent sound design and direction cannot save this bizarre experiment from the backwaters of popularity. **50%**

"Doctor, who *are* you?" ~ Ace

151) *Silver Nemesis*
Kevin Clarke

Serial Code: 7K
Original Transmission
Part One
Wednesday 23 November 1988, 19.35-20.00, 6.1m / 76
Part Two
Wednesday 30 November 1988, 19.35-20.00, 5.2m / 94
Part Three
Wednesday 7 December 1988, 19.35-20.00, 5.2m / 98
BBC Archive
All episodes exist as 625-line one-inch PAL colour master videotapes. 71 edits also exist for all episodes, and a 72 edit for Part Three, in the same format.
Novelization
Doctor Who - Silver Nemesis by Kevin Clarke (138/11)
Paperback:
1. November 1989, Target (0426203402 / Alister Pearson)
2. September 1993, Target (0426203402 / Alister Pearson)
Video
April 1993, extended version with 'The Making of *Doctor Who*' (BBCV 4888 / Photomontage)
Music and Sound Effects
July 1993, *Doctor Who: 30 Years at the Radiophonic Workshop*, CD (BBCCD 871 / Photomontage)
Précis
Nazis team up with Cybermen to hunt for a statue made of living metal...
Cast
Sylvester McCoy (The Doctor), Sophie Aldred (Ace), Anton Diffring (De Flores), Fiona Walker (Lady Peinforte/Statue), Gerard Murphy (Richard), Metin Yenal (Karl), David Banks (Cyber Leader), Mark Hardy (Cyber Lieutenant), Brian Orrell, Danny Boyd, Paul Barrass, Scott Mitchell, Tony Carlton, Bill Malin (Cybermen), Chris Chering, Symond Lawes (Skinheads), Leslie French (Mathematician), Courtney Pine, Adrian Reid, Ernest Mothle, Frank Tontoh (Jazz Quartet), Dolores Gray (Miss Remington), Martyn Read (Security Guard), Terry Duran (De Flores' Gardener), John Ould, Dave Ould (Walkmen), Paul Heasman (Double for the Doctor/Cyberman), Sylvia Victor, Rosamund Hartley (Ladies in Tearoom), Wendy Florence (Waitress), Christian Fletcher, Daryl Brook, Mike Mungarvan (Policemen), Mary Reynolds (Queen Elizabeth II), Ricardo Mulhall (Hitchhiker), Karen Young (1638 Young Woman)
Crew
Armourer Doug Needham, *Stunt Arrangers* Paul Heasman, Nick Gillard, *Stuntman* Paul Heasman, *Visual Effects Designer* Perry Brahan, *Visual Effects Assistants* Mike Tucker, Paul McGuinness, Russell Pritchard, Alan Marshall, *Computer Animation* CAL Video, *Graphic Designer* Oliver Elmes, *Video Effects* Dave Chapman, Jim McCarthy, *Vision Mixer* Barbara Gainsley, *Videotape Editor* Hugh Parson, *Film Cameraman* William Dudman, *OB Lighting* Ian Dow, *OB Sound* John Nottage, Trevor Webster, Scott Talbott, *OB Cameramen* Barry Chaston, Alan Jessop, *Engineering Manager* Brian Jones, *Properties Buyer* John Charles, *Special Sound* Dick Mills, *Incidental Music* Keff McCulloch, *Costume Designer* Richard Croft, *Costume Assistant* Leigh Archer, *Dressers* Debbie Roberts, Michael Johnson, *Make-Up Artist* Dorka Nieradzik, *Make-Up Assistants* Jayne Buxton, Sara Ellis, *Designer* John Asbridge, *Design Assistant* Philip Harvey, *Production Manager* Gary Downie, *Production Associate* June Collins, *Production Assistant* Jane Wellesley, *Assistant Floor Managers* Lynn Grant, Jeremy Fry, *Script Editor* Andrew Cartmel, *Producer* John Nathan-Turner, *Director* Chris Clough
DWM Index
140	John Nathan-Turner interview
142	Sylvester McCoy interview
143	Preview
	David Banks interview
146	TV review
	Kevin Clarke interview
147	Season Guide
148	On Location
	Perry Brahan interview
149	The Fall Guys
150	Season Survey results
156	Novelization review
173	Episode Guide
182	Those *Radio Times*
196	Sophie Aldred interview
198	The Making of 'The Making of *Doctor Who*'
199	Video review
210	What The Papers Said
216	Keff McCulloch interview
218	Sylvester McCoy interview
225	Andrew Cartmel interview

*244 David Banks interview
Archive Feature
Kevin Clarke interview
245 Chris Clough interview
247 The John Nathan-Turner Memoirs
262 Fiona Walker and Gerard Murphy interview
325 Courtney Pine interview
339 Gary Downie interview*

Recording Dates
22-24 June 1988 (Location videotaping), 26 June-2 July 1988 (Location videotaping), 5 July 1988 (Location videotaping), July 1988 (Elstree Studios car park modelwork)

Locations
Greenwich Gasworks, Greenwich, London SE10; High Street, Tarrant Street, London Road, Arundel Castle and Arundel Estate, all Arundel, West Sussex; Casa Del Mar, Aldsworth Avenue, Goring-by-Sea, West Sussex; St Mary's House, Bramber, West Sussex; Black Jack's Mill Restaurant, Black Jack's Mill, Harefield, Middlesex

Working Titles
The Harbinger
Nemesis

Factoids
- *Silver Nemesis* was originally planned to close Season 25, but in order to have it transmitted on the show's 25th anniversary date, it was swapped with *The Greatest Show in the Galaxy*. A side-effect of this was that Ace already had a gold earring that she acquires in the next story.
- Modified chrome-plated Cybermen helmets and chest pieces were reused from *Earthshock* with WWII parachute G-suits as the bodies, sprayed silver, adorned with hooped metal wire on the arms and legs. Larger silver gloves were also provided. The Cybermen actors spoke their lines live via radio mikes inside their helmets.
- Veteran film actor Anton Diffring had never seen *Doctor Who* before and was persuaded to appear by the offer of tickets to the Wimbledon Tennis Championships on top of his normal fee. He died less than a year later.
- During the Arundel Castle scenes (standing in for Windsor Castle), the following members of the production team made up the tourist party being shown around the grounds - production manager Ian Fraser, directors Fiona Cumming, Andrew Morgan and Peter Moffatt, actors Nicholas Courtney and Kathleen Bidmead, and scriptwriters Kevin Clarke and Stephen Wyatt. *Blake's 7*

producer and director Vere Lorrimer was the tour guide. Kevin Clarke also appeared as a passersby and a car-driver in other Arundel scenes.

Comment
I'll be kind - *Silver Nemesis* is a terrible piece of old tat. In an era in which disparate plot elements often came together to provide an interesting new amalgam, this is one of those stories where nothing sticks. The writing is chiefly to blame, as is the inclusion of many totally unnecessary characters, of whom supposedly famous American 'star' Dolores Gray is the main culprit. Why on earth is she there? The Nazi/Cybermen pairing is effective, but the Doctor's involvement with the Silver Nemesis statue is unclear and the finale is identical to that seen only weeks before in *Remembrance of the Daleks* (149). On the plus side, the location work is quite nice, the Part Two gun battle is certainly dramatic, and the introduction of the Doctor's love of jazz makes perfect sense. But the bad moments far outweigh the good, and *Silver Nemesis* is easily the worst McCoy story. **23%**

"Although I never got to see it in the early days, I know it's not as good as it used to be." ~ Whizzkid

152) The Greatest Show in the Galaxy
Stephen Wyatt

Serial Code: 7J
Original Transmission
Part One
Wednesday 14 December 1988, 19.35-20.00, 5m / 86
Part Two
Wednesday 21 December 1988, 19.35-20.00, 5.3m / 99
Part Three
Wednesday 28 December 1988, 19.40-20.05, 4.8m / 108
Part Four
Wednesday 4 January 1989, 19.35-20.00, 6.6m / 79
BBC Archive
All episodes exist as 625-line one-inch PAL colour master videotapes. 71 edits also exist for Parts One, Two and Three in the same format.
Novelization
Doctor Who - The Greatest Show in the Galaxy by Stephen Wyatt (141/14)

245

Paperback:
December 1989 (0426203410 / Alister Pearson)
Video
January 2000 (BBCV 6798 / Photomontage)
Music and Sound Effects
April 1992, Silva Screen, *Doctor Who: The Greatest Show in the Galaxy*, CD (FILMCD 114 / Alister Pearson)
Précis
The Doctor and Ace have to participate in a sinister talent show at The Psychic Circus...
Cast
Sylvester McCoy (The Doctor), Sophie Aldred (Ace), Ricco Ross (Ringmaster), TP McKenna (The Captain), Jessica Martin (Mags), Chris Jury (Deadbeat), Daniel Peacock (Nord), Ian Reddington (Chief Clown), Christopher Guard (Bellboy), Dee Sadler (Flowerchild), Peggy Mount (Stallslady), Gian Sammarco (Whizzkid), Deborah Manship (Morgana), Janet Hargreaves (Mum/Mum God), David Ashford (Dad/Dad God), Kathryn Ludlow (Girl), Lorna McCulloch (Girl God), Dean Hollingsworth (Bus Conductor/Advertisement Voice/Robot Junk Mail Voice), Alan Rudolph (Clown Driver), Paul Sadler, Philip Sadler, Patrick Ford, Alan Heap, Paul Miller, Nicky Dewhurst, Dave Pumfrett, John Alexander, Karl Magee, Hugh Spight, Jeff Davies, Earth G, Raymond Dunstan (Clowns), Alan Wareing (Voice of Girl God), Jim Lancaster (Robot Operator)
Crew
Armourer Doug Needham, *Stunt Arranger* Tip Tipping, *Magic Consultant* Geoffrey Durham, *Visual Effects Designer* Steve Bowman, *Visual Effects Assistants* Mike Tucker, Biddy Palmer, Dave Wells, Dave Becker, Jim Lancaster, *Computer Animation* CAL Video, *Graphic Designer* Oliver Elmes, *Video Effects* Dave Chapman, *Technical Coordinators* Michael Langley-Evans, Richard Wilson, *Studio Camera Supervisor* Alec Wheal, *Vision Mixers* Barbara Gainsley, Dinah Long, Julie Mann, Fred Law, *Videotape Editor* Hugh Parson, *Studio Lighting* Don Babbage, Henry Barber, *Studio Sound* Scott Talbott, *OB Lighting* Ian Dow, *OB Sound* Doug Whittaker, *OB Cameramen* Barry Chaston, Alan Jessop, *OB VT Engineer* Steve Preston, *Engineering Manager* Brian Jones, *Properties Buyer* Bob Blanks, *Special Sound* Dick Mills, *Incidental Music* Mark Ayres, *Costume Designer* Rosalind Ebbutt, *Costume Assistant* Sarah Jane Laskey, *Dressers* Debbie Roberts, Michael Johnson, Tim Bonstow, Patricia McAuley, Ann Richardson, *Make-Up Artist* Denise Baron, *Make-Up Assistants* Helen Johnson, Mark Phillips, Sunetra Sasty, Lyn Somerville, *Designer* David Laskey, *Production Managers* Suzanna Shaw, Gary Downie, Ian Fraser, *Production Associate* June Collins, *Production Assistants* Alexandra Todd, Hilary Barratt, *Assistant Floor Managers* David Tilley, Duncan McAlpine, *Floor Assistants* Alex Starr, Stephen Morris, *Script Editor* Andrew Cartmel, *Producer* John Nathan-Turner, *Director* Alan Wareing

DWM Index
140	John Nathan-Turner interview
141	Preview
142	Sylvester McCoy interview
146	Stephen Wyatt interview
147	Season Guide
	TV review
148	Steve Bowman interview
	TP McKenna interview
150	Season Survey results
154	Novelization review
161	Alan Wareing interview
173	Episode Guide
186	CD soundtrack review
210	What The Papers Said
211	Archive Feature
	Send In The Clowns
218	Sylvester McCoy interview
220	Mark Ayres interview
225	Andrew Cartmel interview
247	The John Nathan-Turner Memoirs
263	Stephen Wyatt interview
287	Video review
	Jessica Martin interview
339	Gary Downie interview

Recording Dates
14-18 May 1988 (Location videotaping), 6-10 June 1988 (Elstree Studios car park videotaping), 15-16 June 1988 (Elstree Studios car park videotaping), 18 June 1988 (Elstree Studios car park videotaping)
Location
Warmwell Quarry, Warmwell, Dorset
Working Title
As broadcast
Factoids
- An asbestos scare at BBC Television Centre prevented *The Greatest Show in the Galaxy* from using any studios to record its interior scenes. Planned for the beginning and middle of June, these sequences were remounted in a large tent in the car park of the BBC's Elstree Studios (home to *EastEnders*) in Boreham Wood, Hertfordshire.
- For Part Four's climax, a model of the stone amphitheatre was made and destroyed on cue, but unfortunately due to a

communications error, the camera operators were not instructed to record the scene and so no footage was taken. The full-size set was made from jabolite and designed on a computer software package called EUCLID.
- Freelancers Robert Allsopp and Susan Moore built the Gods of Ragnarok costumes from blocks of foam rubber cladding. The Girl God was played by a different child actress, as Kathryn Ludlow had used up her allotted juvenile working hours playing the 'human' version.
- Filmed model shots of the junk mail satellite approaching the Tardis were scrapped because they were considered too poor to use.
- A six-feet long model of the Psychic Circus tent was made by Mike Tucker and erected on location to blend in with the live action sequences. The only full-size element was the entranceway and surrounding fence.

Comment
The Greatest Show in the Galaxy is a cherishably surreal voyage into uncharted territory. Taking as its starting point the oft-repeated maxim that clowns are scary (and they are, as you well know), the story plays with some deliciously bizarre imagery, such as clowns driving a silent hearse, or brightly-coloured kites tracking fleeing prisoners. As a subversion of childhood images of stability and reassurance, it really hits the mark - but it can also be enjoyed as that straightforward SF standby (much used in *Doctor Who*) of an ancient evil about to be unleashed onto an unsuspecting world. Along the way it has time to be a lament for the lost innocence of the 1960s and also a barbed dig at the typically obsessive *Doctor Who* fan. What perhaps lets it down is the transparently archetypal nature of the characters - thus ruling out any naturalistic interpretation of events - and the slightly meandering feel to Parts Three and Four. But these are minor quibbles in a production that boasts so much - among them Mark Ayres' chilling incidental music and Ian Reddington's terrifying performance as the Chief Clown. **91%**

Season 26

"You call me 'my lady' once more and I'll break your nose." ~ *Brigadier Bambera*

153) Battlefield
Ben Aaronovitch

Serial Code: 7N
Original Transmission
Part One
Wednesday 6 September 1989, 19.35-20.00, 3.1m / 102
Part Two
Wednesday 13 September 1989, 19.35-20.00, 3.9m / 91
Part Three
Wednesday 20 September 1989, 19.35-20.00, 3.6m / 95
Part Four
Wednesday 27 September 1989, 19.35-20.00, 4m / 89
Repeat Transmission
Part One
Friday 23 April 1993, 19.20-19.45, 1.6m / -
Part Two
Friday 30 April 1993, 19.10-19.35, 1.2m / -
Part Three
Friday 7 May 1993, 19.20-19.45, 1.3m / -
Part Four
Friday 14 May 1993, 19.20-19.45, 1.2m / -
BBC Archive
All episodes exist as 625-line one-inch PAL colour master videotapes. 71 edits also exist for each episode in the same format.
Novelization
Doctor Who - Battlefield by Marc Platt (172/19)
Paperback:
July 1991, Target (042620350X / Alister Pearson)
Video
March 1998, 71 edit of Parts Two and Three (BBCV 6330 / Photomontage)
Music and Sound Effects
July 1993, *Doctor Who: 30 Years at the Radiophonic Workshop*, CD (BBCCD 871 / Photomontage)
Précis
Knights from another dimension converge on a nuclear missile convoy…
Cast
Sylvester McCoy (The Doctor), Sophie Aldred (Ace), Jean Marsh (Morgaine), Angela Bruce (Brigadier Winifred Bambera), Christopher Bowen

(Mordred), Marcus Gilbert (Ancelyn), Ling Tai (Shou Yuing), Nicholas Courtney (Brigadier Lethbridge-Stewart), Angela Douglas (Doris), June Bland (Elizabeth Rowlinson), Noel Collins (Pat Rowlinson), James Ellis (Peter Warmsly), Marek Anton (The Destroyer), Robert Jezek (Sergeant Zbigniev), Dorota Rae (Flight Lieutenant Lavel), Stefan Schwartz (Knight Commander), Paul Tomany (Major Husak), David Bingham (Voices), Alf Joint (Stunt Double for Brigadier Lethbridge-Stewart)

Crew
Armourer Ken Bond, *Stunt Arranger* Alf Joint, *Stuntmen* Ken Barker, Mark Anthony Newman, Rod Woodruff, *Visual Effects Designer* Dave Bezkorowajny, *Special Props* Susan Moore, Stephen Mansfield, *Video Effects* Dave Chapman, *Technical Coordinator* Richard Wilson, *Camera Supervisor* Geoff Clark, *Vision Mixer* Dinah Long, *Videotape Editor* Hugh Parson, *Studio Lighting* David Lock, *Studio Sound* Scott Talbott, *OB Lighting* Ian Dow, *OB Sound* Martin Broadfoot, *OB Cameramen* Paul Harding, Alan Jessop, *Engineering Manager* Brian Jones, *Properties Buyer* Sara Richardson, *Special Sound* Dick Mills, *Grams Operator* Mike Weaver, *Incidental Music* Keff McCulloch, *Costume Designer* Anushia Nieradzik, *Costume Assistant* Sarah Buckland, *Senior Dresser* Richard Blanchard, *Dressers* Sara Wilkinson, Debbie Clark, Ray Greenhill, Giles Gale, *Make-Up Artist* Juliette Mayer, *Make-Up Assistants* Kate Benton, Renata Strickland-Loeb, *Designer* Martin Collins, *Design Assistant* Sophie Boulez, *Production Manager* Ritta Lynn, *Production Associate* June Collins, *Production Assistant* Rosemary Parsons, *Assistant Floor Managers* Matthew Purves, Julian Herne, Val McCrimmon, *Script Editor* Andrew Cartmel, *Producer* John Nathan-Turner, *Director* Michael Kerrigan

DWM Index
151 Preview
153 John Nathan-Turner interview
154 Sophie Aldred interview
156 Susan Moore and Stephen Mansfield interview
158 Dave Bezkorowajny interview
159 Angela Bruce interview Season Guide
160 Season Survey results TV review
164 Marek Anton interview
165 Dave Chapman interview
175 Novelization review James Ellis interview
182 Those *Radio Times*
184 Marc Platt interview
201 Ben Aaronovitch interview
202 TV review (repeat)
211 What The Papers Said
216 Keff McCulloch interview
218 Sylvester McCoy interview
226 Andrew Cartmel interview
229 Nicholas Courtney interview
237 Jean Marsh interview
248 The John Nathan-Turner Memoirs
262 Video review
275 Marcus Gilbert and Angela Bruce interview
317 Archive Feature
318 Robert Jezek interview

Recording Dates
6-8 May 1989 (Location videotaping), 11 May 1989 (Location videotaping), 13-17 May 1989 (Location videotaping), 30 May-1 June 1989 (TC3)

Locations
Fulmer Plant Park, Little Paston and Black Park, all Fulmer, Buckinghamshire; Dowager House, Stamford, Lincolnshire; Hambleton, Leicestershire; Twyford Woods, near Colsterworth, Lincolnshire; Castle Cement Quarry, Ketton, Lincolnshire

Working Titles
Storm over Avallion
Lake over Avallion
Pool of Avallion
Song of Avallion
Stormtroopers of Avallion
The Battlefield

Factoids
- *Battlefield* was originally scripted as a three-part story before script editor Andrew Cartmel requested it be expanded by an episode. In an early draft, the Brigadier dies.
- Ben Aaronovitch's concept for The Destroyer was that it would look like an ordinary, unthreatening person before transforming into a blue-skinned monster. This would have been too costly to do, and so the idea was dropped. The eventual Destroyer costume was made from fibreglass and foam latex by Susan Moore and Stephen Mansfield, with horns constructed by Robert Allsopp. It was dressed in fibreglass chain mail armour.
- The Tardis interior's walls had inadvertently been destroyed since *The Greatest Show in the Galaxy* (152). For its single short appearance in this story (the only one of the season), a painted sheet was hung up to suggest the roundelled walls and the scene was shot in very dim lighting.

- For Part Two's cliffhanger, the water tank that actress Sophie Aldred was inside suddenly cracked and spilt its contents across the studio floor. The actress was hoisted out of safety just in time, otherwise she could have been seriously injured by the jagged glass. An investigation laid the blame at producer John Nathan-Turner's feet, despite the outside contractor having made the tank with glass that was thinner than specified.
- The sleek, futurist armour called for in Aaronovitch's script could not be provided within the show's budget, and so stock suits of armour were hired from a props supplier, many having been used in John Boorman film *Excalibur* (1981).
- Modelwork was done on video, using a tank of water between camera and model to give the illusion that Arthur's spaceship is actually underwater.

Comment
Clearly *Battlefield* tried to repeat the success of *Remembrance of the Daleks*, but without either the script-editing skill or the budget to visualize writer Ben Aaronovitch's ambitious storyline. What we end up with is comedy knights flying through the air (for all the world like deleted scenes from *Monty Python and the Holy Grail*), a wicked witch shouting pantomime curses, an impressive but immobile reject from *Legend*, and a Doctor who is rubbish at pretending to be angry, although he has to do this for most of the story. Individual sequences impress - Ace pulling the sword from the lake or the Part One cliffhanger - but far too much of this tedious exercise is either amateur, unbelievable or downright silly. **29%**

"Heaven help anyone who's still here after dark."
~ Mrs Grose

154) *Ghost Light*
Marc Platt

Serial Code: 7Q
Original Transmission
Part One
Wednesday 4 October 1989, 19.35-20.00, 4.2m / 94
Part Two
Wednesday 11 October 1989, 19.35-20.00, 4m / 93
Part Three
Wednesday 18 October 1989, 19.35-20.00, 4m / 104
BBC Archive
All episodes exist as 625-line one-inch PAL colour master videotapes.
Novelization
Doctor Who - Ghost Light by Marc Platt (160/12)
Paperback:
September 1990, Target (0426203518 / Alister Pearson)
Video
May 1994 (BBCV 5344 / Colin Howard)
DVD
September 2004, isolated music score, optional Dolby 5.1 surround mix, continuity announcements, deleted and extended scenes, studio footage, production subtitles, photo gallery, commentary by Sophie Aldred, Marc Platt, Andrew Cartmel and Mark Ayres (BBCDVD 1352 / Clayton Hickman)
Music and Sound Effects
June 1993, Silva Screen, *Doctor Who: Ghost Light*, CD (FILMCD 133 / Alister Pearson)
Script Book
July 1993, Titan Books, edited by John McElroy with background notes by Stephen James Walker and an article by Marc Platt (185286477X / Alister Pearson)
Précis
In Victorian England, something very sinister is being kept in the basement of Gabriel Chase...
Cast
Sylvester McCoy (The Doctor), Sophie Aldred (Ace), Ian Hogg (Josiah Smith), Carl Forgione (Nimrod), Sylvia Syms (Mrs Pritchard), Katharine Schlesinger (Gwendoline), Sharon Duce (Control), John Hallam (Light), Michael Cochrane (Redvers Fenn-Cooper), Frank Windsor (Inspector Mackenzie), John Nettleton (Reverend Ernest Matthews), Brenda Kempner (Mrs Grose), Emma Darrell, Vivienne Drake, Diana Frances, Fiona King (Night Maids), Katie Jarrett, Sue Somerset (Day Maids), Keith Harvie (Reptile Husk), Jack Talbot (Insect Husk)
Crew
Stunt Arranger Paul Heasman, *Visual Effects Designer* Malcolm James, *Visual Effects Assistants* Guy Lunn, Paul McGuinness, Mike Tucker, James Davis, *Graphic Designer* Oliver Elmes, *Video Effects* Dave Chapman, *Technical Coordinator* Richard Wilson, *Camera Supervisor* Spencer Payne, *Vision Mixer* Susan Brincat, *Videotape Editor* Hugh Parson, *Studio Lighting* Henry Barber, *Studio Sound* Scott Talbott, Keith Bowden, *VT Engineer* Steve Grayston, *Properties Buyer*

Nick Barnett, *Special Sound* Dick Mills, *Grams Operator* Mike Weaver, *Incidental Music* Mark Ayres, *Pianist* Alasdair Nicolson, *Costume Designer* Ken Trew, *Costume Assistant* Sally Booth-Jones, *Senior Dresser* Riley Clark, *Dressers* Karen Beale, Ray Greenhill, Sara Wilkinson, Lisa Bellingham, *Make-Up Artist* Joan Stribling, *Make-Up Assistants* Christine Wheeler, Helen Johnson, Caroline O'Neil, Christina Webster, Val Sparkes, *Designer* Nick Somerville, *Design Assistant* Paddy Lea, *Production Manager* Gary Downie, *Production Associate* June Collins, *Production Assistant* Valerie Whiston, *Assistant Floor Manager* Stephen Garwood, *Floor Assistant* Eirwen Davies, *Script Editor* Andrew Cartmel, *Producer* John Nathan-Turner, *Director* Alan Wareing

DWM Index
153 Preview
    John Nathan-Turner interview
154 Sophie Aldred interview
    Sylvester McCoy interview
155 Ian Hogg interview
157 Frank Windsor interview
158 Marc Platt interview
    Malcolm James interview
159 Season Guide
160 Season Survey results
    TV review
161 Alan Wareing interview
165 Dave Chapman interview
167 Mark Ayres interview
169 Carl Forgione interview
175 Episode Guide
178 First Call: Sophie Aldred on *Ghost Light*
190 Archive Feature
    Sharon Duce interview
    Michael Cochrane interview
    Frank Windsor interview
204 Script Book review
212 Video review
218 Sylvester McCoy interview
220 Mark Ayres interview
226 Andrew Cartmel interview
248 The John Nathan-Turner Memoirs
306 Marc Platt interview
323 Ian Hogg interview
346 Preview(DVD)
347 DVD review
348 The Fact of Fiction

Recording Dates
21 June 1989 (Location videotaping), 18-19 July 1989 (TC3), 1-3 August 1989 (TC3)

Locations
Stanton Court, 11 Greenhill, Weymouth, Dorset

Working Titles
The Bestiary
Life Cycle

Factoids
- Writer Marc Platt's original storyline, entitled *Lungbarrow*, concerned the Doctor's ancestral home on Gallifrey. It was rejected by John Nathan-Turner, but the story resurfaced in book form as Virgin's penultimate New Adventure in 1997.
- Establishing shots of Gabriel Chase were shot at Weymouth during recording of the previous story in production order, *The Curse of Fenric*.
- The two husks were made by Mike Tucker and Paul McGuinness. Originally scripted were three such creatures - in the form of an insect, a reptile and a fish.
- Sophie Aldred wore a white corseted dress that had previously been made by costume designer Ken Trew for an episode of BBC nautical drama *The Onedin Line* (1971-80).
- To reflect the Doctor's darker persona, Sylvester McCoy gained a new dark brown jacket (although it was used first on *The Curse of Fenric*, recorded before this story).

Comment
There are many wonderful things about *Ghost Light*. The beautifully decorated set, the atmospheric lighting, the surreal and disturbing imagery, the striking visual effects, the haunting music score…but the effect of all these is largely undermined by the fact that the story is an incoherent mess. It's not that I don't like complex stories. It's that *Ghost Light* has, at its core, a very simple story ('alien goes mad because it can't catalogue a changing world') told extremely badly. This is not entirely Platt's fault - much of the blame lies with Andrew Cartmel who, as script editor, should have ironed out the many rough patches and made sure the story was intelligible to a general viewer. The most popular periods in the show's history have been when the producer couldn't give a toss for fandom. For instance, *The Deadly Assassin* (88) upset fans but was a hit with the general public. However, *Ghost Light* is a story made solely for fans (and newspaper critics), and when that happens the show deserves what it gets. Which in this case was cancellation. **17%**

"The wolves of Fenric shall return for their treasure..." ~ Commander Millington

155) The Curse of Fenric
Ian Briggs

Serial Code: 7M
Original Transmission
Part One
Wednesday 25 October 1989, 19.35-20.00, 4.3m / 67
Part Two
Wednesday 1 November 1989, 19.35-20.00, 4m / 68
Part Three
Wednesday 8 November 1989, 19.35-20.00, 4m / 64
Part Four
Wednesday 15 November 1989, 19.35-20.00, 4.2m / 68

BBC Archive
All episodes exist as 625-line one-inch PAL colour master videotapes. 71 edits also exist for all episodes in the same format.

Novelization
Doctor Who - The Curse of Fenric by Ian Briggs (188/21)
Paperback:
November 1990, Target (0426203488 / Alister Pearson)

Video
February 1991, extended version (BBCV 4453 / Alister Pearson)

DVD
October 2003, four-part original and Special Edition with CGI effects and Dolby 5.1 surround mix, clean title sequence with optional Dolby 5.1 surround mix, isolated music score, continuity announcements, Visual Effects location footage, *Take Two* excerpt, production subtitles, photo gallery, commentary by Sylvester McCoy, Sophie Aldred and Nicholas Parsons (BBCDVD 1154 / Clayton Hickman).

Music and Sound Effects
July 1991, Silva Screen, *Doctor Who: The Curse of Fenric*, LP (FILMCD 087 / Alister Pearson)

Précis
On the North Yorkshire coast, Viking legends about Fenric appear to be coming true...

Cast
Sylvester McCoy (The Doctor), Sophie Aldred (Ace), Dinsdale Landen (Dr Judson), Alfred Lynch (Commander Millington), Tomek Bork (Sorin), Nicholas Parsons (Reverend Wainwright), Janet Henfrey (Miss Hardaker), Joann Kenny (Jean), Joanne Bell (Phyllis), Marek Anton (Vershinin), Peter Czajkowski (Sergeant Prozorov), Mark Conrad (Petrossian), Marcus Hutton (Sergeant Leigh), Christien Anholt (Perkins), Anne Reid (Nurse Crane), Stevan Rimkus (Captain Bates), Cory Pulman (Kathleen Dudman), Aaron Hanley (Baby), Raymond Trickett (Ancient Haemovore), John Van Der Pool (Dead Russian Commando), Ian Elliott, Jennifer Crome, Graham Stagg, Perry Evans, Raymond Martin, Tony Ryan, Cy Town, Ann Graham, Jacqui Nolan, Ian Collins (Haemovores), Tracey Eddon (Stunt Double for Ace), Tip Tipping, Paul Heasman (Stunt Haemovores)

Crew
Armourer Ken Bond, *Stunt Arranger* Tip Tipping, *Stuntmen* Tip Tipping, Paul Heasman, *Visual Effects Designer* Graham Brown, *Visual Effects Assistants* Mike Tucker, Alan Marshall, John Van Der Pool, Russell Pritchard, Steve Bland, Dave Vialls, *Graphic Designer* Oliver Elmes, *Special Props* Stephen Mansfield, Susan Moore, *Video Effects* Dave Chapman, *Vision Mixer* Dinah Long, *Videotape Editor* Hugh Parson, *OB Lighting* Ian Dow, *OB Sound* John Nottage, Scott Talbott, *OB Sound Assistants* Peter Hales, Ken Osborne, *OB Cameramen* Paul Harding, Alan Jessop, *Engineering Manager* Brian Jones, *Properties Buyer* Yvonne Alfert, *Special Sound* Dick Mills, *Incidental Music* Mark Ayres, *Costume Designer* Ken Trew, *Costume Assistant* Andrew Duckett, *Dressers* Michael Purcell, Ray Greenhill, Cathy George, Sara Wilkinson, Dennis Addoo, *Make-Up Artist* Denise Baron, *Make-Up Assistants* Helen Johnson, Wendy Harrison, Lyn Somerville, Kathy Harris, *Designer* David Laskey, *Design Assistant* Paddy Lea, *Production Manager* Ian Fraser, *Production Assistant* Winifred Hopkins, *Assistant Floor Manager* Judy Corry, *Script Editor* Andrew Cartmel, *Producer/Second Unit Director* John Nathan-Turner, *Director* Nicholas Mallett

DVD Movie Version Crew
Project Coordinator, Editing and 5.1 Sound Design Mark Ayres, *Dubbing Mixers* Benedict Peissel, Fiona Vooght, *Video Post-Production Supervisors* Steve Roberts, Paul Vanezis, *Colourist* Dave Hawley *Digital Effects* Ian Simpson

DWM Index
152	Preview
153	John Nathan-Turner interview
154	Sophie Aldred interview
157	Crowborough location report
158	Graham Brown interview
159	Dinsdale Landen interview
160	Season Survey results
	Season Guide
	TV review

164	Marek Anton interview
165	Dave Chapman interview
167	Comic Assassins
	Mark Ayres interview
168	Novelization review
171	Video review
	David Jackson interview
	Tomek Bork interview
175	Episode Guide
179	CD review
211	What The Papers Said
218	Sylvester McCoy interview
220	Mark Ayres interview
225	Archive Feature
	Nicholas Parsons interview
226	Andrew Cartmel interview
230	Nicholas Mallett interview
248	The John Nathan-Turner Memoirs
335	Preview (Special Edition)
336	Review

Recording Dates
3-8 April 1989 (Location videotaping), 11-15 April 1989 (Location videotaping), 18-20 April 1989 (Location videotaping)

Locations
Crowborough Training Camp, Crowborough, East Sussex; St Lawrence's Church, Hawkhurst, Kent; Bedgebury Lower School, Roses Farm, Yew Tree Farm, all Hawkhurst, Kent; Lulworth Cove, Dorset

Working Titles
Wolf-Time
The Wolves of Fenric

Factoids
- The Haemovores wore stock costumes from different historical periods, sprayed green, while Susan Moore and Stephen Mansfield made the latex masks in four stages of evolution, starting with quarter-masks and ending up as full head coverings. The Ancient One's mask and body adornments were sculpted by Moore and Mansfield, with Robert Allsopp providing the costume. Bladder mechanisms operated its gills and eyelids, giving it a semblance of movement.
- A vestry was created inside the Hawkhurst church by erecting a fake interior wall across the entrance.
- The sequence of Jean and Phyllis crumbling to death was recorded in a hurry for children's programme *Take Two* (transmitted on 19 April 1989 and contained on the DVD). Considered unconvincing, it was subsequently remounted a few days later.
- In a rare move for *Doctor Who*, underwater photography was sanctioned for scenes showing the Haemovores and their Viking ship. Producer John Nathan-Turner directed these shots, with visual effects assistant John Van Der Pool (made up to appear Caucasian) deputising for visual effects designer and trained diver Graham Brown as the dead Russian commando whose eyes suddenly open.
- Sophie Aldred was doubled by stunt performer Tracey Eddon for her climb down the church spire, but performed her Part Four dive into the freezing water of Lulworth Cove herself.

Comment
Doctor Who does John Carpenter's *The Fog* - and does it very well too. This is a visceral, atmospheric slice of vampirism with a haunting music score from Mark Ayres and a storyline packed with iconic Hammeresque imagery. On the downside, there's at least one too many subplots - a common problem this season - and the scenes become ever more cryptic as the story races towards its conclusion. As to the acting, Nicholas Parsons gives a surprisingly moody portrayal of a vicar who's lost his faith, while Alfred Lynch goes straight to the understated core of his character and Dinsdale Landen makes a menacing Fenric possessee. But it's Ace's story really, and Sophie Aldred proves what a talented actress she is by giving a performance of great strength and also of great sensitivity. There's none of the silly heroics that marked *Battlefield* out as the simplistic no-brainer that it was - here Ian Briggs has a brave stab at portraying a gung-ho girl maturing into a young woman, and for the most part it works. Most memorable, though, are the chilling underwater scenes and the Haemovores' emergence from the depths. Genuinely suspenseful. **77%**

"Run beyond the horizon and catch your hunger!" ~ *Karra*

156) Survival
Rona Munro

Serial Code: 7P
Original Transmission
Part One
Wednesday 22 November 1989, 19.35-20.00, 5m / 89
Part Two
Wednesday 29 November 1989, 19.35-20.00, 4.8m / 96

Part Three
Wednesday 6 December 1989, 19.35-20.00,
5m / 91
BBC Archive
All episodes exist as 625-line one-inch PAL colour master videotapes. 71 edits also exist for all episodes in the same format
Novelization
Doctor Who - Survival by Rona Munro (134/8)
Paperback:
October 1990, Target (0426203526 / Alister Pearson)
Video
October 1995 (BBCV 5687 /Alister Pearson)
Précis
Ace and the Doctor arrive in 1989 Perivale and find that her friends are mysteriously vanishing one by one...
Cast
Sylvester McCoy (The Doctor), Sophie Aldred (Ace), Anthony Ainley (The Master), Julian Holloway (Paterson), Will Barton (Midge), Sean Oliver (Stuart), Lisa Bowerman (Karra), Sakuntala Ramanee (Shreela), Gareth Hale (Harvey), Norman Pace (Len), Kate Eaton (Ange), David John (Derek), Adele Silva (Squeak), Kathleen Bidmead (Woman), Michelle Martin (Neighbour), Damon Jeffrey (Man Washing Car), Muriel Wellesley (Woman at Window), Lee Towsey (Injured Self-Defence Boy/Cheetah), Jack Talot (Milkman), Wayne Michaels (Double for Karra), Basil Peton, Leslie Meadows, Emma Darrell, Samantha Leverette, Adel Jackson, Susan Goode, Damon Jeffrey (Cheetah People)
Crew
Armourer Ken Bond, *Stuntmen* Tip Tipping, Eddie Kidd, Damon Jeffrey, *Stunt Arranger* Paul Heasman, *Visual Effects Designer* Malcolm James, *Visual Effects Assistants* Guy Lunn, Mike Tucker, Paul McGuinness, James Davis, *Video Effects* Dave Chapman, *Vision Mixer* Susan Brincat, *Senior Vision Engineer* Dave Jennings, *Vision Engineers* Dick Barlowe, Anthony Kemp, *Videotape Editor* Hugh Parson, *VT Engineer* Steve Grayson, *Engineering Manager* Brian Jones, *OB Lighting* Ian Dow, *OB Sound* Les Mowbray, Scott Talbot, *Deputy Sound Supervisor* Peter Hales, *OB Cameramen* Paul Harding, Alan Jessop, *Artist Booker* Maggie Anson, *Properties Buyer* Nick Barnett, *Special Sound* Dick Mills, *Grams Operator* Mike Weaver, *Incidental Music* Dominic Glynn, *Guitarist* David Hardington, *Costume Designer* Ken Trew, *Costume Assistant* Sally Booth, *Senior Dresser* Riley Clark, *Dressers* Ray Greenhill, Sara Wilkinson, *Make-Up Designer* Joan Stribling, *Make-Up Assistants* Christine Wheeler, Helen Johnson, Caroline O'Neil, Rebecca Walker, *Designer* Nick Somerville, *Design Assistant* Paddy Lea, *Production Manager* Gary Downie, *Production Assistant* Valerie Whiston, *Assistant Floor Managers* Stephen Garwood, Leigh Poole, *Script Editor* Andrew Cartmel, *Producer* John Nathan-Turner, *Director* Alan Wareing

DWM Index
153	John Nathan-Turner interview
154	Preview
	Sophie Aldred interview
	Sylvester McCoy interview
158	Malcolm James interview
160	Season Guide
	Season Survey results
	TV review
161	Alan Wareing interview
165	Dave Chapman interview
167	Dominic Glynn interview
	Novelization review
175	Episode Guide
189	Rona Munro interview
206	Dominic Glynn interview
211	What The Papers Said
S94	Archive Feature
218	Sylvester McCoy interview
226	Andrew Cartmel interview
231	Will Barton interview
	Julian Holloway interview
	Video review
248	The John Nathan-Turner Memoirs
339	Gary Downie interview

Recording Dates
10-15 June 1989 (Location videotaping), 18-23 June 1989 (Location videotaping)
Locations
Medway Drive, Medway Parade, Colwyn Avenue, Bleasdale Avenue, Woodhouse Avenue, Ealing Central Sports Ground, Horsendon Hill, all Perivale, Middlesex; Drayton Court Public House, The Avenue, London NW5; EYJ Martial Arts Centre, Sudbury Hill, Middlesex; Warmwell Quarry, Warmwell, Dorset
Working Titles
Cat-Flap
Blood-Hunt
The Survival
Factoids
- This would be the final broadcast BBC production of *Doctor Who* for over fifteen years. Knowing that the next season had not been renewed, producer John Nathan-Turner asked for a redubbed epilogue to be inserted at the end of the story (recorded on 23 November 1989, the show's 26th anniversary).

- The 'kitling' that appears during Part One was a combination of three real black cats and an animatronic creation operated by Mike Tucker.
- On the planet of the Cheetah People, fake skeletons made from fibreglass and strips of aluminium sheeting were augmented with real bones and offal from a nearby abattoir.
- A new costume made from black silk was designed for the Master, accompanied by a white silk shirt with winged collar and a turquoise cravat.
- The eight Cheetah People were clothed with costumes originally used for the Outsiders in *The Invasion of Time* (97).

Comment
Part One is a delight. For the first time in the show's history we are treated to a plausible suburban setting peopled with realistic characters. This makes the appearance of the horse-riding Cheetah People even more of a shock - Ace being pursued through a children's playground is a fantastic image. The presentation of big issues - pacifism vs aggression, instinct vs rationality - is a welcome attempt to enlarge the programme's vocabulary, despite the unsubtle way in which it's done. Unfortunately, any credibility is shattered by the Doctor's unscathed survival of a head-on bike collision (perhaps this is the true meaning of the title). Still, the whole thing is visually stunning and features some of the most evocative *Doctor Who* incidental music ever heard. **85%**

Eighth Doctor: Paul McGann

One-Off Special

"I always like to dress for the occasion!" ~ The Master

157) *Doctor Who*
Matthew Jacobs

Serial Code: 83705
Original Transmission
Monday 27 May 1996, 20.30-21.55, 9.1m / 9
Repeat Transmission
On BBC2 as part of 'Doctor Who Night':
Saturday 13 November 1999, 23.05-00.30, 1.4m / -

BBC Archive
This story exists as a 625-line PAL colour D3 digital videotape of the 525-line NTSC colour master videotape.
Novelization
Doctor Who by Gary Russell (223/8)
Paperback:
May 1996 (0563380004 / Photograph)
Non-Fiction Book
Doctor Who - Regeneration by Philip Segal with Gary Russell
Hardback:
October 2000, HarperCollins (007105916 / Photomontage)
Paperback:
August 2001, HarperCollins (0007120257 / Photomontage)
Video
May 1996 (BBCV 5882 / Photograph)
DVD
August 2001, isolated music score, trailers, Jon Pertwee caption, 4 audio tracks, alternate scenes, production subtitles, photo gallery, commentary by Geoffrey Sax (BBCDVD 1043 / Photomontage)
Music and Sound Effects
July 1997, Super Tracks, *Doctor Who*, CD (JDCD 005 / Photomontage)
Talking Book
June 1997, 2 x cassettes, abridged, read by Paul McGann (0563381485 / Photograph)
Script Book
May 1996, *Doctor Who - The Script of the Film* by Matthew Jacobs (056340499X / Photograph)
Précis
The newly regenerated Doctor battles with the Master in 1999 San Francisco...
Cast
Sylvester McCoy, Paul McGann (The Doctor), Eric Roberts (Bruce/The Master), Daphne Ashbrook (Dr Grace Holloway), Yee Jee Tso (Chang Lee), John Novak (Salinger), Michael David Simms (Dr Swift), Catherine Lough (Wheeler), Dolores Drake (Curtis), William Sasso (Pete), Jeremy Radick (Gareth), Eliza Roberts (Miranda), Bill Croft (Motorcycle Policeman), Joel Wirkkunen (Ted), Dave Hurtubise (Professor Wagg), Dee Jay Jackson (Security Guard), Gordon Tipple (The Old Master), Mi-Jung Lee, Joanna Piros (News Anchors), Geoffrey Sax (Dalek Voices), Dean Choe, Michael Ching (Lee's Friends), Ron James (Motorcycle Cop), Bill Stewart (Stunt Cop), Mike Langlois (Stunt Double for the Seventh Doctor), Charles Andre, Jamie Jones (Stunt Double for the Eighth Doctor), Dawn Stouffer (Stunt Double for Dr Grace), Michael Crestjo (Stunt Double for Chang Lee), Fred Perron (Stunt Double for The Master)

Crew
Stunt Coordinators JJ Makaro, Fred Perron, *Visual Effects Producer* Tony Dow, *Visual Effects* Northwest Imaging & FX, *Visual Effects Supervisor* Eric Alba, *Visual Effects Coordinator* Marush Kushniruk, *Special Effects Coordinator* Gary Paller, *Camera Operator* Randal Platt, *First Assistant Camera* Greg Fox, *Second Assistant Camera* Nick Watson, *Location Manager* Ed Nesling, *Editor* Patrick Lussier, *Additional Editing* Daris Ellerman, *Property Master* Dan Sissons, *Sound Mixer* Gordon W Anderson, *Sound Supervisor* Jacqueline Cristianini, *Music* John Debney, *Additional Music* John Sponsler, Louis Serbe, *Costume Designer* Jori Woodman, *Make-Up Artist* Joann Fowler, *Hairstylist* Julie McHaffie, *Director of Photography* Glen MacPherson, *Art Director* Bridget McGuire, *Production Designer* Richard Hudolin, *Set Decorator* Cynthia Lewis, *Head Painter* Barry Kootchin, *Construction Coordinator* Derick MacLeod, *Production Manager* Fran Rosati, *Production Coordinator* Sandra Palmer, *Script Supervisor* Jessica Clothier, *Executive Producers* Alex Beaton, Philip David Segal, *Executive Producer for the BBC* Jo Wright, *Co-Producer* Matthew Jacobs, *Producer* Peter V Ware, *First Assistant Director* Patrice Leung, *Second Assistant Director* David Klohn, *Director* Geoffrey Sax

DWM Index
226   Philip Segal interview
236   Paul McGann - The New Doctor
237   Preview
238   Location report
      Paul McGann interview
      Geoffrey Sax interview
      Daphne Ashbrook interview
239   Sylvester McCoy interview
      Matthew Jacobs interview
      Eric Roberts interview
240   Philip Segal interview
      TV review
      Novelization review
      Script Book review
      Bidding Adieu video review
241   Timelines Extra
242   Class 4G on *Doctor Who*
243   Out of the Tardis: Philip Segal
245   The High Council Special
246   The Mourning After...
      Paul McGann interview
247   The Mourning After...2
      Philip Segal interview
252   Talking Book review
253   1997 Readers' Survey
254   Out of the Tardis: Yee Jee Tso
279   Out of the Tardis: Daphne Ashbrook
283   1995-1999: Come Together
299   *Doctor Who - Regeneration* review
300   Dear Paul...
307   DVD review
320   Yee Jee Tso interview
341   Revenge of the Accidental Tourist (Coda)
351   Daphne Ashbrook and Paul McGann interview

Recording Dates
15-19 January 1996 (Location filming), 22-26 January 1996 (Location filming), 29 January-2 February 1996 (Location filming), 5-7 February 1996 (Location filming), 8-10 February 1996 (Burnaby sound stage), 12-15 February 1996 (Burnaby sound stage), 19-21 February 1996 (Burnaby sound stage)

Locations
222 Keefer Street, Alley between East Georgia Street and Union Street, Waterfront Road, BC Children's Hospital, Rear of 218 East Georgia Street, Golden Crow Centre, 1998 Ogden Street, Hadden Park, Corner of Carrall Street and Keefer Street, Pacific Space Centre and Andy Livingstone Park, all Vancouver, British Columbia, Canada

Working Title
As broadcast

Factoids
- Amongst those auditioning for the role of the Doctor were Mark McGann, Liam Cunningham, Tony Slattery, John Sessions, Rob Heyland, Peter Capaldi and Harry Von Gorkum.
- The story went through many drafts during its development period. John Leekley and Robert DeLaurentis both contributed outlines, but British writer Matthew Jacobs - whose father Anthony had placed Doc Holliday in *The Gunfighters* (25) - was the one finally chosen in May 1995.
- A brand-new Tardis interior was designed by Richard Hudolin, filling the entire sound stage at Burnaby, Vancouver. Hudolin kept the central console shape but created a new, Jules Verne-style feel to the interior décor, with liberal use made of the Gallifreyan symbol designed by Roger Murray-Leach and first seen in *Revenge of the Cybermen* (79).
- Many BBC props were meticulously recreated for the movie, such as the Police Box exterior, the sonic screwdriver (last seen in *The Visitation*, 120), the Tardis key and a neutron ram from *Earthshock* (122), copied from Mark Harris' 1983 book *The Doctor Who Technical Manual*. Other BBC

references included the Doctor's bag of jelly babies and a 900-year diary (a modified version of the Second Doctor's 500-year diary).
- A one-tenth scale model of the Tardis was filmed against a black background and incorporated with CGI effects by Northwest Imaging. This company also created the Master Morphant, the regeneration, the matt shots of the Tardis interior's ceiling and the Doctor passing through Grace's window.
- The Ron Grainer theme music was rescored by John Debney and John Sponsler and played by a 60-piece orchestra.
- The gunfight in the opening scene was heavily trimmed prior to the BBC1 premiere as a reaction to the Dunblane school massacre that had occurred on 13 March 1996, leaving 16 children and one teacher dead. Likewise, the video was also cut in order to bring it down to a 12 certificate. (This extra material has now been added to the DVD release.)
- Redubbing took care of a minor error in which the Doctor states that he has twelve lives - in fact, he has thirteen lives and twelve regenerations.
- *Radio Times* (issue dated 25-31 May 1996) heavily promoted the new story, with a cover, articles and a pull-out supplement on the history of the series.
- *Doctor Who* debuted on the American Fox network on 14 May 1996 at 20.00 EST. It achieved lower viewing figures than Fox had hoped: 8.3m, which was a 9% share of the available audience (it came 75th out of the top 100 shows watched that week). But as 15% was needed to commission a series, the pilot remained a one-off programme.
- Jon Pertwee died in his sleep on 20 May 1996. Marking this, a caption slide was inserted at the end of the UK screening which read, "Dedicated to the memory of Jon Pertwee 1919-1996".

Comment
To get the bad points over with first, the *Doctor Who* TV movie is too obsessed with the television series that spawned it - and often gets the continuity wrong anyway - and has a final act that combines a mystifying amount of technobabble with a thoroughly vapid cop-out ending. On the plus side, it is breathtakingly directed and edited and is one of the glossiest slices of small-screen science fiction action you're likely to see in a long while. Performances are universally excellent, from Paul McGann's perfectly realized Doctor to Daphne Ashbrook's gutsy-yet-feminine Grace, with Eric Roberts providing solid opposition as the Master (although, in fact, he might as well be any baddie). The Tardis interior is spectacular beyond words, and music, photography and location filming are all top-notch. One can't help but feel, though, that the central threat is rather less than coherent and making the Doctor half-human is an unnecessary addition to a crowded narrative. But as a pilot episode, it is better than anyone could have rightfully expected and makes it all the more tragic that a series never followed. **77%**

Ninth Doctor: Christopher Eccleston

Season 27

"The Doctor is a legend woven throughout history. When disaster comes, he's there." ~ *Clive*

158) Rose
Russell T Davies

Original Transmission
Saturday 26 March 2005, 19.00-19.45, 10.8m / 7
Repeat Transmissions
On BBC Three:
Sunday 27 March 2005, 19.00-19.45, 0.6m / -
Sunday 17 July 2005, 19.00-19.45, 0.2m / -
Friday 22 July 2005, 21.00-21.45, 0.1m / -
BBC Archive
This story exists as a 625-line 50 interlaced fields per second Digital Betacam videotape, shot with a Pro-Mist filter and applied with a film-look standards converter outputting 25 progressive frames per second.
DVD
1. May 2005, as part of 'Series 1, Volume 1' (BBCDVD 1755 / Photomontage)
2. November 2005, commentary by Russell T Davies, Julie Gardner and Phil Collinson, as part of the 'The Complete First Series' box set (BBCDVD 1770 / Photograph)
Script Book
October 2005, edited by Russell T Davies, *Doctor Who-The Shooting Scripts* (0563486414 / Photomontage)
Synopsis
The Nestene Consciousness has taken residence in London and plans an all-out invasion...

Cast
Christopher Eccleston (Doctor Who), Billie Piper (Rose Tyler), Camille Coduri (Jackie Tyler), Noel Clarke (Mickey Smith), Mark Benton (Clive), Elli Garnett (Caroline), Adam McCoy (Clive's Son), Alan Ruscoe, David Sant, Paul Kasey, Elizabeth Fost, Helen Otway, Holly Lumsden (Autons), Nicholas Briggs (Nestene Voice), Will Willoughby (Stunt Double for Doctor Who), Alun Jenkins (Neighbour), Maurice Lee, Rod Woodruff (Stunt Doubles for Mickey), Kevin Hudson, Chris Stone (Headless Mickey), Juliette Cheveley (Stunt Double for Rose)

Crew
Stunt Coordinator Rod Woodruff, *Stunt Performers* Holly Lumsden, Paul Kulik, *Choreographer* Ailsa Altena-Berk, *Art Department Coordinator* Gwenllian Llwyd, *Concept Artist* Bryan Hitch, *Supervising Art Director* Stephen Nicholas, *Visual Effects* The Mill, *Visual FX Producer* Will Cohen, *Visual FX Supervisor* Dave Houghton, *Special Effects* Any Effects, *Graphic Artist* Jenny Bowers, *Property Master* Patrick Begley, *Standby Props* Phill Shellard, Adrian Anscombe, *Construction Manager* Andrew Smith, *Colourist* Kai van Beers, *2D VFX Artists* Simon C Holden, David Bowman, Sarah Bennett, Alberto Montanes, Jennifer Herbert, *3D VFX Artists* Andy Howell, Chris Tucker, Jean-Claude Deguara, Mark Wallman, Paul Burton, Chris Petts, Porl Perrot, *Digital Matte Painter* Alex Fort, *Model Unit Supervisor* Mike Tucker, *Prosthetics* Millennium Effects, *Assistant Editor* Ceres Doyle, *Post-Production Supervisor* Marie Brown, *On-Line Editor* Matthew Clarke, *Editor* Mike Jones, *Location Managers* Clive Evans, Lowri Thomas, *Camera Operators* Mike Costelloe, Martin Stephens, *Focus Pullers* Steve Lawes, Mark Isaac, *Grip* John Robinson, *Boom Operator* Damian Richardson, *Gaffer* Mark Hutchings, *Best Boy* Peter Chester, *Casting Associate* Kirsty Robertson, *Casting Director* Andy Pryor, *Production Buyer* Catherine Samuel, *Set Decorator* Peter Walpole, *Sound Recordist* Ian Richardson, *Dubbing Mixer* Tim Ricketts, *Dialogue Editor* Paul McFadden, *Sound FX Editor* Paul Jefferies, *Incidental Music* Murray Gold, *Wardrobe Supervisor* Yolanda Peart-Smith, *Costume Designer* Lucinda Wright, *Make-Up Supervisor* Linda Davie, *Make-Up Designer* Davy Jones, *Make-Up Artist* Sarah Wilson, *Production Designer* Edward Thomas, *Director of Photography* Ernie Vincze, *Finance Manager* Richard Pugsley, *Production Accountants* Debi Griffiths, Kath Blackman, Endaf Emyr Williams, *Production Manager* Tracie Simpson, *Production Coordinator* Dathyl Evans, *Continuity* Sian Prosser, *First Assistant Director* George Gerwitz, *Second Assistant Director* Steffan Morris, *Third Assistant Director* Dafydd Rhys, *Script Editor* Elwen Rowlands, *Associate Producer* Helen Vallis, *Executive Producers* Russell T Davies, Julie Gardner, Mal Young, *Producer* Phil Collinson, *Director* Keith Boak

DWM Index
344	Edward Thomas interview
354	Julie Gardner interview
	Preview
355	Location report
	How to Build a Tardis
	Review
356	Lorraine Heggessey interview
358	Pixel Perfect
359	Russell T Davies interview
	Lucinda Wright interview

Recording Dates
20-22 July 2004 (Location videotaping), 26-30 July 2004 (Location videotaping), 2-3 August 2004 (Location videotaping), 20 August 2004 (Q2), 22-23 August 2004 (Location videotaping), 26 August 2004 (Q2), 1-3 September 2004 (Q2), 6 September 2004 (Q2), 8-9 September 2004 (Location videotaping), 10-11 September 2004 (Q2, location videotaping), 14-16 September 2004 (Kendal Avenue modelwork), 18 October 2004 (Q2, location videotaping), 10 November 2004 (Studio 1, Cardiff)

Locations
Howell's Department Store, Working Street, St Mary's Street, Queen's Arcade, University Hospital of Wales, La Fosse restaurant, The Paper Mill, Cardiff Royal Infirmary, Taff Terrace, Lydstep Flats, all Cardiff; Trafalgar Square, Westminster Bridge, Victoria Embankment, London Eye, Brandon Estate, all London; Skinner Street, Newport

Factoids
- Christopher Eccleston was announced as the Ninth Doctor on 19 March 2004. Born in Salford in 1964, television appearances included *Cracker* (1993-96), *Our Friends in the North* (1996), *Hillsborough* (1996) and *The Second Coming* (2003) amongst many others. Film rôles included *Shallow Grave* (1994), *Jude* (1996), *Elizabeth* (1998), *The Others* (2001) and *28 Days Later* (2002).
- Billie Piper was born in Swindon in 1982. Although trained as an actress, she rose to fame at 15 as a pop singer with the song 'Because We Want To', which debuted at Number One in the UK charts. Previous television appearances included *The Canterbury Tales* (2003) and *Bella and the Boys* (2004), while the British horror film *Spirit Trap*, although made before *Doctor Who*, was finally released in 2005.

- This story featured the Autons' third televised appearance (although they were never mentioned as such on screen), following Third Doctor stories *Spearhead from Space* (51) and *Terror of the Autons* (55). The shop dummies were designed by Neill Gorton while the Nestene Consciousness was a CGI creation courtesy of MillTv. The company's original pitch for the creature was a 3D rendering of Peter Brookes' *Doctor Who and the Terror of the Autons* Target book cover illustration of the monster, complete with crablike claws and single eye.
- A brand-new Police Box prop was constructed by BBC Wales. Consisting of fifteen interlocking pieces (base, roof, four corner struts, four illuminated signs, three walls and two doors), it was larger in size than previous versions and incorporated a different roof lamp. The domed organic-like multilevel Tardis interior was the brainchild of Bryan Hitch and Edward Thomas, with Dan Walker - who also designed the new sonic screwdriver - assisting on the console design. It is currently a permanent standing set at the BBC's Newport studios.
- Swansea-based close-up magician Phil Jay performed the Doctor's card shuffle.
- Much videotaping was conducted in Cardiff to represent various parts of London. Rose Tyler's flat in the fictitious Powell Estate actually consisted of three separate locations: the Brandon Estate, Kennington (London) and the Channel View Flats and Lydstep Flats (Cardiff).
- Costume designer Lucinda Wright decided on the Ninth Doctor's simple costume because she wanted him to blend in wherever he went, but at the same time have a distinctive silhouette. Two battered German leather jackets were acquired (one for Eccleston, and one for his stunt double) while the leather boots came from Timberlands.
- The new CGI opening and closing sequences were created by MillTv, the television arm of visual effects company The Mill. The new elliptical *Doctor Who* logo seen during the 'Next Time' trailer and closing credits was designed by the BBC Wales graphics department, while a simplified version featured in the title sequence itself.
- The *Radio Times* (issue dated 26 March-1 April 2005) promoted the new series with a gatefold cover revealing the new Tardis console room and a glossy pull-out brochure detailing the behind-the-scenes aspects of the series.

Comment
Along with *Spearhead from Space* (51) and *Doctor Who* (157), this story is clearly designed to sell the whole *Doctor Who* concept for a brand new audience. Well, it achieves its aim magnificently. From the opening titles, via the zooming in to Rose' alarm clock, to the archetypal scene of a lone female being stalked in a darkened basement, pretty much everything is exactly as you'd want it. There is *some* continuity with the past, but only in small bite-size chunks, and always seen from Rose' viewpoint. Christopher Eccleston puts in a fantastic performance, balancing edgy panic, childlike enthusiasm and authoritative 'Doctorishness'. Billie Piper has a fascinating screen presence too, and their scenes together are pure magic. Dialogue is fast, funny and purposeful. Most scenes work (the Doctor in Rose's flat, the Autons coming to life, the chase across London), others don't (the burping wheelie bin, plastic Mickey), but the editing is so frenetic - too frenetic in some places - that any minor quibbles are soon forgotten. What is especially clever is in making *Rose* the resolution of a story that's apparently been running for a while now - the Nestene Consciousness already has a foothold on London and the Doctor is stepping up his game to defeat it. The downside is that the Autons' attack and defeat happens all too quickly, with the Doctor's 'anti-plastic' being an obvious indication of the alien's tokenistic appearance. This is a story about character not plot, and it shows. But as a clean-slate reintroduction to the whole *Who* phenomenon, it really is hard to beat. **90%**

"Everything has its time, and everything dies." ~ The Doctor

159) *The End of the World*
Russell T Davies

Original Transmission
Saturday 2 April 2005, 19.00-19.45, 8m / 19
Repeat Transmissions
On BBC Three:
Sunday 3 April 2005, 19.00-19.45, 0.5m / -
Sunday 24 July 2005, 19.00-19.45, 0.2m / -
Friday 29 July 2005, 21.00-21.45, 0.2m / -

BBC Archive
This story exists as a 625-line 50 interlaced fields per second Digital Betacam videotape, shot with a Pro-Mist filter and applied with a film-look standards converter outputting 25 progressive frames per second.
DVD
1. May 2005, as part of 'Series 1, Volume 1' (BBCDVD 1755 / Photomontage)
2. November 2005, commentary by Phil Collinson and Will Cohen, as part of the 'The Complete First Series' box set (BBCDVD 1770 / Photograph)
Script Book
October 2005, edited by Russell T Davies, *Doctor Who-The Shooting Scripts* (0563486414 / Photomontage)
Synopsis
In the year five million an alien delegation watches as the Earth blows up, but a murderer is in their midst...
Cast
Christopher Eccleston (Doctor Who), Billie Piper (Rose Tyler), Simon Day (Steward), Yasmin Bannerman (Jabe), Jimmy Vee (Moxx of Balhoon), Zoë Wanamaker (Cassandra), Beccy Armory (Raffalo), Camille Coduri (Jackie), Sara Stewart (Computer Voice), Silas Carson (Alien Voices), Paul Kasey (Lute), Alan Ruscoe (Coffa), Von Pearce, John Collins (Surgeons), Sarah Franzl (Stunt Double for Jabe)
Crew
Stunt Coordinator Lee Sheward, *Stunt Performers* Jamie Edgell, Sarah Franzl, *Choreographer* Ailsa Altena-Berk, *Art Department Coordinator* Gwenllian Llwyd, *Concept Artist* Bryan Hitch, *Supervising Art Director* Stephen Nicholas, *Visual Effects* MillTv, *Visual FX Producer* Will Cohen, *Visual FX Supervisor* Dave Houghton, *Special Effects* Any Effects, *Graphic Artist* Jenny Bowers, *Property Master* Patrick Begley, *Standby Props* Phill Shellard, Adrian Anscombe, *Construction Manager* Andrew Smith, *Colourist* Kai van Beers, *2D VFX Artists* Sara Bennett, Michael Harrison, Jennifer Herbert, Astrid Busser-Casas, Simon C Holden, Alberto Montanes, Bronwyn Edwards, *3D VFX Artists* Nick Webber, Matt McKinney, Porl Perrot, Joel Meire, Paul Burton, Chris Petts, Andy Howell, *Digital Matte Painter* Alex Fort, *Prosthetics* Millennium Effects, *Assistant Editor* Ceres Doyle, *Post-Production Supervisor* Marie Brown, *On-Line Editor* Matthew Clarke, *Editor* John Richards, *Location Manager* Clive Evans, *Camera Operators* Martin Stephens, Mike Costelloe, *Focus Pullers* Steve Lawes, Mark Isaac, *Camera Assistants* Anna James, David Jones, *Grip* John Robinson, *Boom Operator* Damian Richardson, *Gaffer* Mark Hutchings, *Best Boy* Peter Chester, *Casting Associate* Kirsty Robertson, *Casting Director* Andy Pryor, *Production Buyer* Catherine Samuel, *Set Decorator* Peter Walpole, *Sound Recordist* Ian Richardson, *Dubbing Mixer* Tim Ricketts, *Dialogue Editor* Paul McFadden, *Sound FX Editor* Paul Jefferies, *Incidental Music* Murray Gold, *Wardrobe Supervisor* Yolanda Peart-Smith, *Costume Designer* Lucinda Wright, *Make-Up Designer* Davy Jones, *Production Designer* Edward Thomas, *Director of Photography* Ernie Vincze, *Finance Manager* Richard Pugsley, *Production Accountants* Debi Griffiths, Kath Blackman, Endaf Emyr Williams, *Production Manager* Tracie Simpson, *Unit Manager* Emma Reid, *Production Coordinator* Pamela Joyce, *Continuity* Non Eleri Hughes, *First Assistant Director* Lloyd Elis, *Second Assistant Director* Steffan Morris, *Third Assistant Director* Dan Mumford, *Script Editor* Elwen Rowlands, *Associate Producer* Helen Vallis, *Executive Producers* Russell T Davies, Julie Gardner, Mal Young, *Producer* Phil Collinson, *Director* Euros Lyn

DWM Index
354   Julie Gardner interview
355   Preview
356   Location report
        Review
358   Pixel Perfect
359   Lucinda Wright interview

Recording Dates
7 September 2004 (Q2), 23 September 2004 (Q2), 4-5 October 2004 (Q2), 6-8 October 2004 (Location videotaping), 11-14 October 2004 (Location videotaping), 15 October 2004 (Q2), 18 October 2004 (Q2), 20 October 2004 (Location videotaping), 22 October 2004 (Q2), 9 November 2004 (Location videotaping), 26 November 2004 (Q2), 18 February 2005 (Q2), 19 February 2005 (Location videotaping)

Locations
Temple of Peace and Health, Churchill Way, Queen Street, all Cardiff; Headlands School, Penarth

Factoids
- The majority of the series' effects budget was used up for this episode, because the story required more CGI effects than any other story.
- Cassandra's 'face' was provided by CGI. The idea for the character came from Russell T Davies' reaction to seeing once beautiful actresses with facelifts during the Oscars ceremony.

- The blue staff were played by twenty children (in two alternating groups) and three midgets.
- The entire sequence featuring the plumber Raffalo (Beccy Armoury) was a late addition to the story after a long sequence between Rose and Cassandra was dropped for budgetary reasons.
- The full list of the alien delegates is as follows: Trees from the Forest of Cheam, the Moxx of Balhoon, the Adherents of the Repeated Meme [a word coined by ethologist Richard Dawkins in his 1976 book *The Selfish Gene* and defined by the author as 'a unit of cultural transmission, or a unit of imitation'], the Face of Boe, Ambassadors from the City State of Binding Light, the Brothers Hop Pyleen, Mr and Mrs Pakoo and the chosen scholars of Class 55 from the University of Rago Rago Five Six Rago and Cal 'Spark Plug' MacNannovich.
- Arriving for a political discussion programme called *Dragon's Eye*, the Welsh Assembly's First Minister Rhodri Morgan was mistaken for a Forest of Cheem extra for BBC Wales staff. A spokesman later claimed: "He thought it was really funny."
- The first Bad Wolf reference was in the Moxx of Balhoon's dialogue: "This is the Bad Wolf scenario…"

Comment
The main problem with this episode is one of believability. Firstly, the much touted alien delegates - with the exception of Jabe - just look like extras with silly (and flimsy) masks on. There is none of the animatronic sophistication or artistry of, say, the Destroyer from *Battlefield* (153) or Morbius from *The Brain of Morbius* (84). Secondly, the interior of Platform One is clearly a 20th century Earth building and totally inconsistent with the CGI exterior. Thirdly, the satirical nature of the storyline and the continual in-jokes mitigate against audience involvement. Fourthly, the whole cooling fans sequence - whilst impressively visualised - bears no scrutiny whatsoever (the PS2-style low-tech levers, the blades blocking the access walkway, the fact that wood doesn't spontaneously ignite in the presence of heat etc). Fifthly, no-one really cares whodunit, so when the villain is 'unmasked', it's a big anticlimax. And with Christopher Eccleston gurning away at the aliens (perhaps he didn't believe in them either), it's left to Billie Piper to carry the story. Which she does marvellously at the beginning, acting her socks off as the proverbial stranger in a strange land. But then she's locked in a room for the rest of the story. Ho hum. **28%**

"The stiffs are getting lively again!" ~ Sneed

160) *The Unquiet Dead*
Mark Gatiss

Original Transmission
Saturday 9 April 2005, 19.00-19.45, 8.9m / 15
Repeat Transmission
On BBC Three:
Sunday 10 April 2005, 19.00-19.45, 0.4m / -
Sunday 31 July 2005, 19.00-19.45, 0.2m / -
Friday 5 August 2005, 21.00-21.45, 0.1m / -
BBC Archive
This story exists as a 625-line 50 interlaced fields per second Digital Betacam videotape, shot with a Pro-Mist filter and applied with a film-look standards converter outputting 25 progressive frames per second.
DVD
1. May 2005, as part of 'Series 1, Volume 1' (BBCDVD 1755 / Photomontage)
2. November 2005, commentary by Mark Gatiss, Simon Callow and Euros Lyn, as part of the 'The Complete First Series' box set (BBCDVD 1770 / Photograph)
Script Book
October 2005, edited by Russell T Davies, *Doctor Who-The Shooting Scripts* (0563486414 / Photomontage)
Synopsis
Charles Dickens joins the Doctor and Rose as they investigate walking corpses in 1869 Cardiff…
Cast
Christopher Eccleston (Doctor Who), Billie Piper (Rose Tyler), Simon Callow (Charles Dickens), Alan David (Sneed), Huw Rhys (Redpath), Eve Myles (Gwyneth), Jennifer Hill (Mrs Peace), Wayne Cater (Stage Manager), Meic Povey (Driver), Zoe Thorne (The Gelth), Lucy Allan (Stunt Double for Mrs Peace), Claire Williams, Felicity Boylett (Prostitutes), David Marc Thomas, Bryn Dawes (Tramps), John Pope (Gentleman), Paulette Stansbie (Lady)
Crew
Stunt Coordinator Lee Sheward, *Stunt Performer* Lucy Allan, *Art Department Coordinator* Gwenllian Llwyd, *Concept Artist* Bryan Hitch, *Supervising Art Director* Stephen Nicholas, *Visual Effects* MillTv, *Visual FX Supervisor* Dave Houghton, *Special Effects* Any Effects, *Graphic Artist* Jenny Bowers, *Property Master* Patrick Begley, *Standby Props* Phill Shellard, Adrian Anscombe, *Construction Manager* Andrew Smith, *Colourist* Kai van Beers, *2D VFX Artists* Sara

Bennett, Jennifer Herbert, Simon C Holden, Alberto Montanes, Astrid Busser-Casas, David Bowman, *3D VFX Artists* Chris Petts, Chris Tucker, *Assistant Editor* Ceres Doyle, *Post-Production Supervisor* Marie Brown, *On-Line Editor* Matthew Clarke, *Editor* John Richards, *Location Manager* Clive Evans, *Camera Operators* Mike Costelloe, Martin Stephens, *Camera Assistants* Anna James, David Jones, *Focus Pullers* Steve Lawes, Mark Isaac, *Grip* John Robinson, *Boom Operator* Damian Richardson, *Gaffer* Mark Hutchings, *Best Boy* Peter Chester, *Casting Associate* Kirsty Robertson, *Casting Director* Andy Pryor, *Production Buyer* Catherine Samuel, *Set Decorator* Peter Walpole, *Sound Recordist* Ian Richardson, *Dubbing Mixer* Tim Ricketts, *Dialogue Editor* Paul McFadden, *Sound FX Editor* Paul Jefferies, *Incidental Music* Murray Gold, *Wardrobe Supervisor* Yolanda Peart-Smith, *Costume Designer* Lucinda Wright, *Make-Up Supervisor* Linda Davie, *Make-Up Artist* Sarah Wilson, Claire Pritchard, *Make-Up Designer* Davy Jones, *Production Designer* Edward Thomas, *Director of Photography* Ernie Vincze, *Finance Manager* Richard Pugsley, *Production Accountants* Debi Griffiths, Kath Blackman, Endaf Emyr Williams, *Production Manager* Tracie Simpson, *Unit Manager* Emma Reid, *Production Coordinator* Pamela Joyce, *Continuity* Non Eleri Hughes, *First Assistant Director* Lloyd Ellis, *Second Assistant Director* Steffan Morris, *Third Assistant Director* Dan Mumford, *Script Editor* Helen Raynor, *Associate Producer* Helen Vallis, *Executive Producers* Russell T Davies, Julie Gardner, Mal Young, *Producer* Phil Collinson, *Director* Euros Lyn

DWM Index
352   Phil Collinson interview
353   Mark Gatiss interview
355   Preview
      Simon Callow interview
356   Review
359   Lucinda Wright interview

Recording Dates
19-22 September 2004 (Location videotaping), 23 September 2004 (Q2), 27 September-2 October 2004 (Location videotaping), 19-20 October 2004 (Location videotaping), 22 October 2004 (Q2)

Locations
New Theatre, Cardiff; Cambrian Place, Swansea; Beaufort Arms Court, Church Street, St Mary's Street, all Monmouth; Headlands School, Penarth

Working Title
The Crippingwell Horror

Factoids
- Scriptwriter Mark Gatiss had already penned four *Doctor Who* novels, including *Nightshade* (1992) and *The Last of the Gaderene* (2000), as well as two Big Finish audios. He was also a character actor of some distinction, having starred in, and co-written, three series of the macabre comedy series *The League of Gentlemen* (1999-2002). His debut mainstream novel, *The Vesuvius Club*, was published in 2004.
- Early drafts of the story featured a sequence cribbed from *Pyramids of Mars* (82) in which the Doctor takes Rose to a barren present-day Earth to show what would happen if they didn't try and stop the Gelth in 1869.
- Simon Callow had already played Charles Dickens in the acclaimed one-man play *The Mystery of Charles Dickens*, written by Dickens biographer Peter Ackroyd. Among the many films he had appeared in were *A Room With a View* (1985), *Four Weddings and a Funeral* (1994), *Shakespeare in Love* (1998) and *The Phantom of the Opera* (2004).
- The BBC received several complaints from concerned parents about the supernatural element in the programme, worried that it might affect their offspring. Newspapers referred to the figure as being in the region of fifty, but broadcast regulator OffCom only received two complaints on the subject. In response, the BBC initially said *Doctor Who* was no longer suitable for under-eights, but then quickly relented and claimed that parents should be held responsible for their child's viewing habits.
- The second Bad Wolf reference occurred when Gwyneth is reading Rose' mind and is horrified to see "the big bad wolf".

Comment
This is a beautifully judged Victorian ghost story by a writer who is clearly fascinated with the subject. Location photography is sumptuous and Simon Callow breaths life into a character that could so easily have been a collection of dreary clichés. His verbal tussles with the Doctor are truly wonderful. The most memorable aspect, of course, is the horror - and it's pretty unflinching stuff. The old crone smashing her way out of the coffin is a great opening moment, while the scene where the Gelth turns from angel to demon is particularly chilling. As a parent, it didn't bother me - or my children - but I do appreciate a brief warning would have been appropriate

beforehand ("Scares aplenty now in a brand new ghost story for the Doctor and Rose…"). But quite the best thing in the whole episode was the exquisite performance of Eve Myles as Gwyneth. The first of many strong female guest characters in this series, it was a real tragedy that she got blown up at the end. She would have made a fantastic companion. **94%**

"I'm shaking my booty!" ~ *Margaret Blaine*

161) Aliens of London / World War Three
Russell T Davies

Original Transmission
1) *Aliens of London*
Saturday 16 April 2005, 19.00-19.45, 7.6m / 18
2) *World War Three*
Saturday 23 April 2005, 19.00-19.45, 8m / 20
Repeat Transmissions
On BBC Three:
1) *Aliens of London*
Sunday 17 April 2005, 19.00-19.45, 0.6m / -
Sunday 7 August 2005, 19.00-19.45, 0.2m / -
Friday 12 August 2005, 21.00-21.45, 0.1m / -
2) *World War Three*
Sunday 24 April 2005, 00.05-00.50, 0.2m / -
Sunday 24 April 2005, 19.00-19.45, 0.6m / -
Sunday 14 August 2005, 19.00-19.45, 0.2m / -
Friday 19 August 2005, 21.00-21.45, 0.2m / -
BBC Archive
This story exists as a 625-line 50 interlaced fields per second Digital Betacam videotape, shot with a Pro-Mist filter and applied with a film-look standards converter outputting 25 progressive frames per second.
DVD
1. June 2005, as part of 'Series 1, Volume 2' (BBCDVD 1756 / Photomontage)
2. November 2005, commentary by Julie Gardner, Will Cohen, David Verrey, Phil Collinson, Helen Raynor and Annette Badland, as part of the 'The Complete First Series' box set (BBCDVD 1770 / Photograph)
Script Book
October 2005, edited by Russell T Davies, *Doctor Who-The Shooting Scripts* (0563486414 / Photomontage)
Synopsis
Flatulent aliens are running amok in 10 Downing Street…

Cast
Christopher Eccleston (Doctor Who), Billie Piper (Rose Tyler), Camille Coduri (Jackie Tyler), Noel Clarke (Mickey Smith), Annette Badland (Margaret Blaine), Penelope Wilton (Harriet Jones), Rupert Vansittart (General Asquith), David Verrey (Joseph Green), Eric Potts (Oliver Charles), Andrew Marr (Himself), Matt Baker (Himself), Navin Chowdhry (Indra Ganesh), Steve Speirs (Strickland), Naoko Mori (Doctor Sato), Morgan Hopkins (Sergeant Price), Elizabeth Fost, Alan Ruscoe, Paul Kasey (Slitheens), Corey Doabe (Graffiti Artist), Ceres Jones (Policeman), Jack Tarlton, Lachele Carl (Reporters), Fiesta Mei Ling (Chinese Woman), Basil Chung (Chinese Man), Jimmy Vee (Pig Alien), Roderick Mair (Dead Prime Minister)
Crew
Stunt Coordinator Rod Woodruff, *Art Department Coordinator* Gwenllian Llwyd, *Concept Artist* Bryan Hitch, *Supervising Art Director* Stephen Nicholas, *Visual Effects* MillTv, *Visual FX Producer* Will Cohen, *Visual FX Supervisor* Dave Houghton, *Special Effects* Any Effects, *Graphic Artist* Jenny Bowers, *Property Master* Patrick Begley, *Standby Props* Adrian Anscombe, Phill Shellard, *Construction Manager* Andrew Smith, *Colourist* Kai van Beers, *2D VFX Artists* David Bowman, Simon C Holden, Michael Harrison, Bronwyn Edwards, *3D VFX Artists* Chris Petts, Jean-Claude Deguara, Paul Burton, Porl Perrot, Mark Wallman, Andy Howell, *Model Unit Supervisor* Mike Tucker, *Prosthetics* Millennium Effects, *Assistant Editor* Ceres Doyle, *Post-Production Supervisor* Marie Brown, *On-Line Editor* Matthew Clarke, *Editor* Mike Jones, *Location Managers* Clive Evans, Lowri Thomas, *Camera Operators* Mike Costelloe, Martin Stephens, *Focus Pullers* Steve Lawes, Mark Isaac, *Grip* John Robinson, *Boom Operator* Damian Richardson, *Gaffer* Mark Hutchings, *Best Boy* Peter Chester, *Casting Associate* Kirsty Robertson, *Casting Director* Andy Pryor, *Production Buyer* Catherine Samuel, *Set Decorator* Peter Walpole, *Sound Recordist* Ian Richardson, *Dubbing Mixer* Tim Ricketts, *Dialogue Editor* Paul McFadden, *Sound FX Editor* Paul Jefferies, *Incidental Music* Murray Gold, *Wardrobe Supervisor* Yolanda Peart-Smith, *Costume Designer* Lucinda Wright *Make-Up Supervisor* Linda Davie, *Make-Up Artist* Sarah Wilson, *Make-Up Designer* Davy Jones, *Production Designer* Edward Thomas, *Director of Photography* Ernie Vincze, *Finance Manager* Richard Pugsley, *Production Accountants* Debi Griffiths, Kath Blackman, Endaf Emyr Williams, *Production Manager* Tracie Simpson, *Production*

Coordinator Dathyl Evans, *Continuity* Sian Prosser, *First Assistant Director* George Gerwitz, *Second Assistant Director* Steffan Morris, *Third Assistant Director* Dafydd Rhys Parry, *Script Editor* Elwen Rowlands, *Associate Producer* Helen Vallis, *Executive Producers* Russell T Davies, Julie Gardner, Mal Young, *Producer* Phil Collinson, *Director* Keith Boak

DWM Index
355   Preview
356   Location report
357   Review
358   Pixel Perfect
       Location report
359   Lucinda Wright interview

Recording Dates
18-19 July 2004 (Location videotaping), 25-30 July 2004 (Location videotaping), 3-6 August 2004 (Location videotaping), 8-13 August 2004 (Location videotaping), 16-19 August 2004 (Location videotaping), 20 August 2004 (Q2), 21 August 2004 (BBC Broadcasting House, Cardiff), 26-28 August 2004 (Q2), 30 August 2004-3 September 2004 (Q2), 6 September 2004 (Q2), 8-9 September 2004 (Location videotaping), 11 September 2004 (Location videotaping), 14-16 September 2004 (Ealing modelwork), 4 October 2004 (TC4), 9 November 2004 (Q2), 10 November 2004 (Studio 1, Cardiff), 22 November 2004 (Studio 1, Cardiff), 24 November 2004 (Location videotaping)

Locations
Cardiff Royal Infirmary, University Hospital of Wales, Channel View Flats, West Bute Street, Loudoun Square, all Cardiff; John Adams Street, Victoria Embankment, Brandon Housing Estate, all London; Lower Dock Street, Newport; Hensol Castle, Hensol

Working Title
10 Downing Street (Part Two)

Factoids
- Russell T Davies' inspiration for this story came from watching a Girls Aloud pop video set within 10 Downing Street, as featured in *Love, Actually* (2003).
- The interior of Downing Street was represented by various rooms inside Hensol Castle Conference Centre in Hensol, South Wales, while the exterior used an architecturally similar doorway in John Adams Street, London. A partially demolished building on Lower Dock Street in Newport was used for the destroyed version in *World War Three*.
- Videotaping at the Thames was disrupted when the BBC's motor launch, hired from Poole in Dorset, was apprehended by anti-terrorist officers when it inadvertently sailed into the security zone surrounding the Palace of Westminster.
- *Aliens of London* featured one of Christopher Eccleston's very first scenes for Season 27, in which he ran down a corridor in Cardiff's Royal Infirmary chasing Scottish night-club bouncer Jimmy Vee dressed as a pig in a spacesuit.
- Three fibreglass and latex Slitheen costumes with remote-controlled faces were supplied by Millennium Effects, who also supplied the empty skin suits and forehead zips. MillTv provided CGI versions of the monsters for scenes of them chasing after humans and emerging from their human disguises.
- For the destruction of St Stephen's tower, Mike Tucker opted to construct a 1/14th scale model from plaster overlaid onto a timber frame, which was then partially destroyed by swinging a model spaceship wing into it. The finished shot was actually a reversed image. Although considered cheaper and more effective than a CGI effect, unfortunately the blobs of glue holding the plaster moulds to the timber were visible on screen.
- Matt Baker appeared as himself in a brief insert of a fake *Blue Peter* 'make' shot in Television Centre Studio 4 (using a cake decorated with jelly babies in homage to Tom Baker's Doctor), while BBC political editor Andrew Marr also appeared as himself for scenes shot in John Adams Street.
- The third Bad Wolf reference was when a young boy sprayed it onto the Tardis exterior (which disappeared when the Doctor landed it inside Albion Hospital).

Comment
The most child-friendly story of the season, *Aliens of London* is a wonderfully anarchic romp. Heavy-handed political satire, soldiers with guns, a pig from space, endless running up and down corridors, explosions - it's just like the old days. The farting aliens, of course, is a very naff idea, and seriously overplayed. But the whole story is so full of energy and enthusiasm that it's quite easy to be drawn along even if (especially if?) you leave your brain behind. Unusually, *World War Three* is by far the stronger of the two parts, with tighter plotting and a satisfying (if completely unbelievable) conclusion. Flaws abound - notably the ease with which a member of the public can fire a Polaris missile - but there are lots of

quintessentially *Doctor Who*-ish moments, such as the Doctor's reaction to the pig's death and his confrontation with the Slitheen while ensconced inside the Cabinet Room. The chief drawback of the story is that the combination of humour and drama is at times unbalanced, but there is a notable improvement in the second part when the story proper clicks into place. Penelope Wilton aside, the uniformly childish acting throughout almost adds to the proceedings - it's like a bunch of ten-year-old school children have been let loose on a *Doctor Who* script. And I daresay it probably helps to be that age in order to get the most out of it. **70%**

"What're you going to do? Sucker me to death?"
~ Simmons

162) Dalek
Robert Shearman

Original Transmission
Saturday 30 April 2005, 19.00-19.45, 8.6m / 14
Repeat Transmissions
On BBC Three:
Sunday 1 May 2005, 00.15-01.00, 0.2m / -
Sunday 1 May 2005, 19.00-19.45, 0.5m / -
Sunday 21 August 2005, 19.00-19.45, 0.2m / -
Friday 26 August 2005, 21.00-21.45, 0.1m / -
BBC Archive
This story exists as a 625-line 50 interlaced fields per second Digital Betacam videotape, shot with a Pro-Mist filter and applied with a film-look standards converter outputting 25 progressive frames per second.
DVD
1. June 2005, as part of 'Series 1, Volume 2' (BBCDVD 1756 / Photomontage)
2. November 2005, commentary by Robert Shearman, Dave Houghton, Nick Briggs and Bruno Langley, as part of the 'The Complete First Series' box set (BBCDVD 1770 / Photograph)
Script Book
October 2005, edited by Russell T Davies, *Doctor Who-The Shooting Scripts* (0563486414 / Photomontage)
Synopsis
A billionaire collector has added a 'Metaltron' to his underground collection of alien artefacts...
Cast
Christopher Eccleston (Doctor Who), Billie Piper (Rose Tyler), Corey Johnson (Henry Van Statten), Bruno Langley (Adam), Anna-Louise Plowman (Goddard), Steven Beckingham (Polkowski), Nigel Whitmey (Simmons), John Schwab (Bywater), Jana Carpenter (De Maggio), Joe Montana (Commander), Barnaby Edwards (Dalek), Nick Briggs (Dalek voice)
Crew
Stunt Coordinator Lee Sheward, *Stunt Performers* Stuart Clark, Derek Lea, Neil Finnigan, Tony Luckden, *Art Department Coordinator* Gwenllian Llwyd, *Concept Artist* Bryan Hitch, *Supervising Art Director* Stephen Nicholas, *Visual Effects* MillTv, *Visual FX Producer* Will Cohen, *Visual FX Supervisor* Dave Houghton, *Special Effects* Any Effects, *Graphic Artist* Jenny Bowers, *Property Master* Adrian Anscombe, *Standby Props* Phill Shellard, Trystan Howell, *Construction Manager* Andrew Smith, *Colourist* Kai van Beers, *2D VFX Artists* Simon C Holden, David Bowman, Jennifer Herbert, *3D VFX Artists* Chris Petts, Mark Wallman, Andy Howell, *Digital Matte Painter* Alex Fort, *Model Unit Supervisor* Mike Tucker, *Prosthetics* Millennium Effects, *Assistant Editor* Ceres Doyle, *Post-Production Supervisor* Marie Brown, *On-Line Editor* Matthew Clarke, *Editor* Graham Walker, *Location Manager* Lowri Thomas, *Camera Operator* Martin Stephens, *Focus Puller* Mark Isaac, *Grip* John Robinson, *Boom Operator* Damian Richardson, *Gaffer* Mark Hutchings, *Best Boy* Peter Chester, *Casting Associate* Kirsty Robertson, *Casting Director* Andy Pryor, *Production Buyer* Catherine Samuel, *Set Decorator* Liz Griffiths, *Sound Recordist* Ian Richardson, *Dubbing Mixer* Peter Jefferys, *Dialogue Editor* Paul McFadden, *Sound FX Editor* Paul Jefferies, *Incidental Music* Murray Gold, *Choir* The Crouch End Festival Chorus, *Wardrobe Supervisor* Yolanda Peart-Smith, *Costume Designer* Lucinda Wright, *Make-Up Supervisor* Linda Davie, *Make-Up Artists* Claire Pritchard, Steve Williams, *Make-Up Designer* Davy Jones, *Production Designer* Edward Thomas, *Director of Photography* Ernie Vincze, *Finance Manager* Richard Pugsley, *Production Accountants* Debi Griffiths, Kath Blackman, Endaf Emyr Williams, *Rights Executive* James Dundas, *Production Manager* Tracie Simpson, *Unit Manager* Llyr Morris, *Production Coordinator* Jess van Niekerk, *Continuity* Pam Humphreys, *First Assistant Director* Gareth Williams, *Second Assistant Director* Sean Clayton, *Third Assistant Director* Dan Mumford, *Script Editor* Helen Raynor, *Associate Producer* Helen Vallis, *Executive Producers* Russell T Davies, Julie Gardner, Mal Young, *Producer* Phil Collinson, *Director* Joe Ahearne

DWM Index
349 Robert Shearman interview
352 Phil Collinson interview
356 Diary of a Dalek 1
Preview
Bruno Langley interview
357 Diary of a Dalek 2
Location report
Review
358 Pixel Perfect

Recording Dates
25-30 October 2004 (Location videotaping), 1-3 November 2004 (Location videotaping), 4-5 November 2004 (Q2), 8 November 2004 (Q2), 23 November 2004 (Q2), 26 November 2004 (Q2)

Locations
National Museum of Wales, Millennium Stadium, both Cardiff

Working Titles
Return of the Daleks
Creature of Lies

Factoids
- Robert Shearman's script was loosely based on the premise of his 2003 Big Finish audio play *Jubilee*, in which the Sixth Doctor encounters a lone imprisoned Dalek. Inspiration also came from the Hannibal Lector cell scenes in *Silence of the Lambs* (1991). Shearman was an established playwright who had already written for Radio 4 and BBC1's *Born and Bred* (2002-present). His stage plays *Knights in Plastic Armour* (1999) and *Inappropriate Behaviour* (2001) were produced by Alan Ayckbourn for the Stephen Joseph Theatre in Scarborough.
- Negotiations between the BBC and Tim Hancock, the agent responsible for the estate of Dalek creator Terry Nation, broke down in July 2004 and for a while it looked as if a Dalek would not be able to appear. Shearman subsequently created a new opponent, but then the rights were finally acquired in August and so the Dalek was reinserted into his script.
- It was executive producer Julie Gardner who suggested using a Cyberman head as a museum exhibit. The version chosen was from *Revenge of the Cybermen* (79). Also seen was a Slitheen arm from the previous story.
- The new Dalek was designed by Edward Thomas and Matt Savage, with input from the production team. Two Dalek props were built (before and after its revitalizing energy boost) by Mike Tucker, Scott Wayland, Nick Kool and Melvyn Friend using moulds based on fan-made Daleks made by Dave Brian and Steve Allen. The new 'chunkier' version incorporated the best elements of Dalek design throughout the years, including the Peter Cushing films and the *TV21* comic strip. Every element was updated and given a stronger appearance, with the two most notable changes being the fatal suction action of the plunger and the 360° rotation of the midriff section. The head and eyestalk movement were radio-controlled, rather than being moved by the operator as in previous stories. Neill Gorton made the mutant from silicone rubber, which was then made to move animatronically. Levitation scenes were done in post-production by MillTv.
- Actor Nick Briggs had previously supplied Dalek voices for Big Finish audio plays, as well as appearing as the Doctor himself in *Doctor Who Magazine* comic strip *Wormwood* (a reference to 1980s fan-produced *Doctor Who* audio plays in which he played the title character). He supplied his own ring modulator for the rôle.
- To represent the Utah underground base, shooting was conducted in the lower passageways of Cardiff's Millennium Stadium. The *Blue Peter* team visited on 3 November to make a location report which aired on 29 April 2005.
- The *Radio Times* (30 April-6 May 2005) featured a General Election-themed fold-out Dalek cover - "Vote Dalek!" - in a homage to *The Dalek Invasion of Earth* (10). Along with a four-page feature on the story were details of how to order a free double-sided A1 poster of the creatures.
- The fourth Bad Wolf reference was in the name of Van Statten's helicopter: Bad Wolf One.

Comment
Saddled with a huge burden of responsibility on its shoulders, the makers of *Dalek* come up trumps with this vivid re-engineering of an iconic villain. The Dalek itself is a thing of beauty (although I quickly tired of the machine whine every time it moved its eyestalk or dome) and the scenes of destruction are all brilliantly staged. Possibly the Dalek levitation scene is played a little slowly, but then to most young viewers it would have been a revelation, so I suppose it was understandable it was milked to excess. (But why couldn't the Dalek just rise straight up in the stairwell?) Christopher

Eccleston goes rather overboard on his 'angry' acting, while his gun-toting action figure stance at the end doesn't really convince, but other than that his performance here is exemplary - a lone Time Lord facing an equally lone Dalek. It's a nice piece of dramatic symmetry. The one real problem with the episode - and it's a big one - is the cloyingly sentimental twist at the end. Having established the Dalek as an indestructible war machine, it's then touted as a twee little puppet figure who just wants to feel the sunshine on his face. Ah, how sweet, pass the sick bag. If it wasn't for their triumphal return at the end of the series, this would have felt like a gross betrayal of the whole Dalek concept. **85%**

"We all know what happens to non-entities. They get promoted." ~ The Editor

163) The Long Game
Russell T Davies

Original Transmission
Saturday 6 May 2005, 19.00-19.45, 8m / 17
Repeat Transmissions
Sunday 7 May 2005, 00.10-00.55, 0.2m / -
Sunday 7 May 2005, 19.00-19.45, 0.6m / -
Sunday 28 August 2005, 19.00-19.45, 0.1m / -
Friday 2 September 2005, 21.00-21.45, 0.2m / -
BBC Archive
This story exists as a 625-line 50 interlaced fields per second Digital Betacam videotape, applied with a film-look standards converter outputting 25 progressive frames per second.
DVD
1. June 2005, as part of 'Series 1, Volume 3' (BBCDVD 1757 / Photomontage)
2. November 2005, commentary by Bruno Langley, Brian Grant and Christine Adams, as part of the 'The Complete First Series' box set (BBCDVD 1770 / Photograph)
Script Book
October 2005, edited by Russell T Davies, *Doctor Who-The Shooting Scripts* (0563486414 / Photomontage)
Synopsis
On Satellite Five in the year 200,000, things are not as they should be...
Cast
Christopher Eccleston (Doctor Who), Billie Piper (Rose Tyler), Bruno Langley (Adam Mitchell), Simon Pegg (The Editor), Tamsin Greig (Nurse), Christine Adams (Cathica Santini Cadani), Anna Maxwell-Martin (Suki Macrae Cantrell), Colin Prockter (Head Chef), Judy Holt (Adam's Mum), Grainne Joughin, Chloe Swift, Jamila Akhar, Darren Clarke, Philip Myles, Toby Sperring (Spike Room Journalists)
Crew
Stunt Coordinator Lee Sheward, *Art Department Coordinator* Gwenllian Llwyd, *Concept Artist* Bryan Hitch, *Supervising Art Director* Stephen Nicholas, *Visual Effects* MillTv, *Visual FX Producer* Will Cohen, *Visual FX Supervisor* Dave Houghton, *Special Effects* MTFX, *Graphic Artist* Jenny Bowers, *Property Master* Adrian Anscombe, *Standby Props* Phill Shellard, Trystan Howell, *Construction Manager* Andrew Smith, *Colourist* Kai van Beers, *2D VFX Artists* David Bowman, Simon C Holden, Astrid Busser-Casas, Jennifer Herbert, Alberto Montanes, *3D VFX Artists* Chris Petts, Jean-Claude Deguara, Nick Webber, Mark Wallman, Andy Howell, *Digital Matte Painter* Alexander Fort, *Prosthetics* Millennium Effects, *Assistant Editor* Ceres Doyle, *Post-Production Supervisor* Marie Brown, *On-Line Editor* Matthew Clarke, *Editor* John Richards, *Location Managers* Lowri Thomas, *Camera Operator* Martin Stephens, *Focus Puller* Mark Isaac, *Grip* John Robinson, *Boom Operator* Damian Richardson, *Gaffer* Mark Hutchings, *Best Boy* Peter Chester, *Casting Associate* Kirsty Robertson, *Casting Director* Andy Pryor, *Production Buyer* Catherine Samuel, *Set Decorator* Liz Griffiths, *Sound Recordist* Ian Richardson, *Dubbing Mixer* Tim Ricketts, *Dialogue Editor* Paul McFadden, *Sound FX Editor* Paul Jefferies, *Incidental Music* Murray Gold, *Wardrobe Supervisor* Yolanda Peart-Smith, *Costume Designer* Lucinda Wright, *Make-Up Supervisor* Linda Davie, *Make-Up Artists* Claire Pritchard, Steve Williams, *Make-Up Designer* Davy Jones, *Production Designer* Edward Thomas, *Director of Photography* Ernie Vincze, *Finance Manager* Richard Pugsley, *Production Accountants* Debi Griffiths, Kath Blackman, Endaf Emyr Williams, *Production Manager* Tracie Simpson, *Unit Manager* Llyr Morus, *Production Coordinator* Jess van Niekerk, *Continuity* Pam Humphreys, *First Assistant Director* Gareth Williams, *Second Assistant Director* Steffan Morris, *Third Assistant Director* Dan Mumford, *Script Editor* Elwen Rowlands, *Associate Producer* Helen Vallis, *Executive Producers* Russell T Davies, Julie Gardner, Mal Young, *Producer* Phil Collinson, *Director* Brian Grant
DWM Index
356   Preview
358   Pixel Perfect
          Review

Recording Dates
30 November-3 December 2004 (Q2), 6 December 2004 (Location videotaping), 7 December 2004 (Q2), 8-9 December 2004 (Location videotaping), 10-11 December 2004 (Q2), 13-15 December 2004 (Q2)
Location
Old British Telecom Building, Coryton
Factoids
- Comedy actor Simon Pegg had previously appeared in the 2002 Big Finish audio drama *Invaders from Mars*, and was also recording the narration for BBC Three companion series *Doctor Who Confidential*. He revealed to the *Radio Times* that he had had, understandably, huge problems with the line, "The Mighty Jagrafess of the Holy Hadrojassic Maxarodenfoe".
- As a cost-cutting exercise, several sets were redressed and reused, such as the Spike Room on Floors 139 and 500, and the atrium on Floors 16 and 500. The exterior of Adam's house was actually an unused shot from *Rose*, showing the property next door to Clive's home.
- MillTv visualized the Jagrafess as a totally CGI creation, based on Russell T Davies' description of it as a mass of red meat quivering on the ceiling. Inspiration for the final design came from the shark in *Jaws* (1975).
- The fifth Bad Wolf reference was when the Face of Boe appeared on Bad Wolf TV.

Comment
It's hard to pinpoint the exact problem with this story, but it's probably got something to do with the insubstantial nature of the threat - so what if the human race has been set back by 91 years? The way in which information is disseminated is also somewhat cryptic. What exactly is the *point* of passing all that news through people's brains? Wouldn't it be a lot easier to stick it onto TV so everyone could watch it? As a metaphor about our unthinking acceptance of news media - in a similar vein to the excellent *Brass Eye* series (1997, 2001) - it certainly makes its point, but at the same time there's no real evidence of how *bad* the situation is and exactly why the Doctor feels so desperate to change it. Tamsin Greig gives a delightful cameo, Bruno Langley is marginally less wet than Adric, and Simon Pegg makes the most of an underwritten part. But the real acting honours go to Christine Adams and Anna Maxwell-Martin as the trainee journalists Cathica and Suki. Both are attractive and watchable and help ground the story when it threatens to become too esoteric. Brian Grant's direction is arguably the most polished of the season, helped by intelligent editing and a sharp visual style, aided enormously by dropping the Pro-Mist filter that makes every other episode look like it's in permanent soft focus. Pity about the dire music though. 45%

"I'm so useless I couldn't even die properly." ~ *Pete Tyler*

164) Father's Day
Paul Cornell

Original Transmission
Saturday 14 May 2005, 19.00-19.45, 8.1m / 17
Repeat Transmissions
Sunday 15 May 2005, 00.10-00.55, 0.2m / -
Sunday 15 May 2005, 19.00-19.45, 0.5m / -
Sunday 4 September 2005, 19.00-19.45, 0.2m / -
Friday 9 September 2005, 21.00-21.45, TBA / -
BBC Archive
This story exists as a 625-line 50 interlaced fields per second Digital Betacam videotape, shot with a Pro-Mist filter and applied with a film-look standards converter outputting 25 progressive frames per second.
DVD
1. June 2005, as part of 'Series 1, Volume 3' (BBCDVD 1757 / Photomontage)
2. November 2005, commentary by Paul Cornell, Billie Piper, Shaun Dingwall and Phil Collinson, as part of the 'The Complete First Series' box set (BBCDVD 1770 / Photograph)
Script Book
October 2005, edited by Russell T Davies, *Doctor Who-The Shooting Scripts* (0563486414 / Photomontage)
Synopsis
Rose asks the Doctor to take her back to when her father got run down in 1987...
Cast
Christopher Eccleston (Doctor Who), Billie Piper (Rose Tyler), Camille Coduri (Jackie Tyler), Shaun Dingwall (Pete Tyler), Christopher Llewellyn (Stuart), Frank Rozelaar-Green (Sonny), Natalie Jones (Sarah), Eirlys Bellin (Bev), Rhian James (Suzie), Julia Joyce (Young Rose), Casey Dyer (Young Mickey), Robert Barton (Registrar), Kim McGarrity, Bean Peel (Stunt Doubles for Rose Tyler), Seon Rogers (Stunt Double for Pete Tyler), Lee Griffiths (Vicar), Monique Ennis (Mickey's Mum), Crispin Layfield (Driver), Abigail Nichols, Charlotte Nichols (Baby Rose), Ken Teale (Gardener)

Crew

Stunt Coordinator Lee Sheward, *Stunt Performers* Crispin Layfield, Seon Rogers, Bean Peel, *Art Department Coordinator* Gwenllian Llwyd, *Concept Artist* Bryan Hitch, *Supervising Art Director* Stephen Nicholas, *Visual Effects* MillTv, *Visual FX Producer* Will Cohen, *Visual FX Supervisor* Dave Houghton, *Graphic Artist* Jenny Bowers, *Property Master* Adrian Anscombe, *Standby Props* Phill Shellard, *Trystan Howell, Construction Manager* Andrew Smith, *Colourist* Kai van Beers, *2D VFX Artists* David Bowman, Sara Bennett, Simon C Holden, *3D VFX Artists* Chris Petts, Jean-Claude Deguara, Nicolas Hernandez, Mark Wallman, Andy Howell, *Assistant Editor* Ceres Doyle, *Post-Production Supervisor* Marie Brown, *On-Line Editor* Matthew Clarke, *Editor* Graham Walker, *Location Manager* Lowri Thomas, *Camera Operator* Martin Stephens, *Polecam Operator* Andy Leonard, *Focus Puller* Mark Isaac, *Grip* John Robinson, *Boom Operator* Damian Richardson, *Gaffer* Mark Hutchings, *Best Boy* Peter Chester, *Casting Associate* Kirsty Robertson, *Casting Director* Andy Pryor, *Production Buyer* Catherine Samuel, *Set Decorator* Liz Griffiths, *Sound Recordist* Ian Richardson, *Dubbing Mixer* Tim Ricketts, *Dialogue Editor* Paul McFadden, *Sound FX Editor* Paul Jefferies, *Incidental Music* Murray Gold, *Wardrobe Supervisor* Yolanda Peart-Smith, *Costume Designer* Lucinda Wright, *Make-Up Supervisor* Linda Davie, *Make-Up Artists* Claire Pritchard, Steve Williams, *Make-Up Designer* Davy Jones, *Production Designer* Edward Thomas, *Director of Photography* Ernie Vincze, *Finance Manager* Richard Pugsley, *Production Accountants* Debi Griffiths, Kath Blackman, Endaf Emyr Williams, *Production Manager* Tracie Simpson, *Unit Manager* Llyr Morus, *Production Coordinator* Jess van Niekerk, *Continuity* Pam Humphreys, *First Assistant Director* Gareth Williams, *Second Assistant Director* Sean Clayton, *Third Assistant Director* Dan Mumford, *Script Editor* Elwen Rowlands, *Associate Producer* Helen Vallis, *Executive Producers* Russell T Davies, Julie Gardner, Mal Young, *Producer* Phil Collinson, *Director* Joe Ahearne

DWM Index

352   Paul Cornell interview
354   Julie Gardner interview
356   Preview
358   Shaun Dingwall interview
       Lee Sheward interview
       Pixel Perfect
       Review
359   Lucinda Wright interview

Recording Dates

11-13 November 2004 (Location videotaping), 15-18 November 2004 (Location videotaping), 19 November 2004 (Location videotaping / Studio 1, Cardiff), 22 November 2004 (Location videotaping / Studio 1, Cardiff), 23 November 2004 (Q2), 25-26 November 2004 (Location videotaping)

Locations

St Paul's Church, St Fagans Street, Oakley Place, Llanmales Street, Grange Gardens, all Grangetown, Cardiff; Furniture Land car park, HTV boardroom, Loudoun Square, Heol Trelai, Heol Pennar, all Cardiff

Working Title

Wounded Time

Factoids

- Paul Cornell was a prolific *Doctor Who* writer, having penned stories for books, audio plays and even comic strips. His most recent offering was the 2004 novelization of BBCi's Internet drama *The Scream of the Shalka* featuring 'alternative' Ninth Doctor Richard E Grant. Cornell also worked on various television shows, including *Children's Ward* (1988-2000), *Springhill* (1997) and *Casualty* (1986-present). He also wrote the ITV teen drama *Wavelength* (1997-98).

- Russell T Davies' initial outline was for a monsterless time paradox story along the lines of American anthology series *The Twilight Zone* (1959-65).

- Cornell originally envisaged the Reapers as traditional cowled Death figures complete with scythes. Later drafts likened them to the demonic apparitions seen in *Jacob's Ladder* (1990). The final versions were rendered using CGI by MillTv, based on concept sketches by Bryan Hitch and a small clay maquette sculpted by Alex Fort. The finished design incorporated bat wings, the mouth of a praying mantis and a scythlike tail in homage to Cornell's initial concept.

- St Paul's Church in Grangetown, Cardiff stood in for the fictitious St Christopher's Parish Church in Southwark, with fake road signs reading 'Walterley Street SE15'.

- The sixth Bad Wolf reference was in some fleetingly-seen graffiti across an 'Energize' fly poster at the beginning

Comment
The most intelligent script of the season, *Father's Day* bristles with insight, honesty and humour. It's incredibly fast-moving - note the number of jump cuts - and yet allows itself plenty of time to engage in intimate character moments. Which is where we come to Billie Piper. The promise she showed in *The End of The World* (159) is thoroughly vindicated here; she is quite simply superb. Her scenes with Shaun Dingwell (also superb) are raw, powerful and entirely free of cliché. Unlike the music, sadly, which often sounds like it's come from a straight-to-video Barbara Cartland flick. The central Christian concept of an ordinary man sacrificing his own life in order to save humanity is beautifully underplayed, and the story works on many different levels. There are some unanswered questions (how exactly does the Doctor make the Tardis appear with a charged-up key? why does the hit and run driver keep reappearing, and in a different place to where he originally hit Pete?) and I would've preferred the Reapers to only attack people directly influenced by the time paradox, rather than everyone in the world, but these are small points in a story clearly desperate to do something different. Which it does, magnificently. **88%**

"Go to your room!" ~ The Doctor

165) The Empty Child / The Doctor Dances
Steven Moffat

Original Transmission
1) *The Empty Child*
Saturday 21 May 2005, 18.30-19.15, 7.1m / 21
2) *The Doctor Dances*
Saturday 28 May 2005, 19.00-19.45, 6.9m / 18
Repeat Transmissions
On BBC Three:
1) *The Empty Child*
Sunday 22 May 2005, 00.20-01.05, 0.2m / -
Sunday 22 May 2005, 19.15-20.00, 0.8m / -
Sunday 11 September 2005, 19.30-20.15, TBA / -
Friday 16 September 2005, 21.00-21.45, TBA / -
2) *The Doctor Dances*
Sunday 29 May 2005, 00.15-01.00, 0.2m / -
Sunday 29 May 2005, 19.00-19.45, 0.5m / -
Sunday 11 September 2005, 20.15-21.00, TBA / -
Friday 23 September 2005, 21.00-21.45, TBA / -

BBC Archive
This story exists as a 625-line 50 interlaced fields per second Digital Betacam videotape, shot with a Pro-Mist filter and applied with a film-look standards converter outputting 25 progressive frames per second.
DVD
1. June 2005, as part of 'Series 1, Volume 3' (BBCDVD 1757 / Photomontage)
2. November 2005, commentary by Steven Moffatt, John Barrowman and Dave Houghton, as part of the 'The Complete First Series' box set (BBCDVD 1770 / Photograph)
Script Book
October 2005, edited by Russell T Davies, *Doctor Who-The Shooting Scripts* (0563486414 / Photomontage)
Synopsis
In the midst of a London blitz, an unearthly child wanders amongst the rubble looking for its mummy...
Cast
Christopher Eccleston (Doctor Who), Billie Piper (Rose Tyler), John Barrowman (Captain Jack Harkness), Albert Valentine (The Empty Child/Jamie), Florence Hoath (Nancy), Cheryl Fergison (Mrs Lloyd), Damian Samuels (Mr Lloyd), Luke Perry (Double for The Empty Child/Timothy Lloyd), Richard Wilson (Dr Constantine), Robert Hands (Algy), Joseph Tremain (Jim), Jordan Murphy (Ernie), Brandon Miller (Alf), Noah Johnson (Voice of The Empty Child), Martin Hodgson (Jenkins), Dian Perry (Computer Voice), Vilma Hollingbury (Mrs Harcourt), Kate Harvey (Nightclub Singer), Paul Newbolt (Barman), Kim McGarrity (Stunt Double for Rose Tyler), Tony Lucken (Stunt Double for Captain Jack), James Edgell (Stunt Double for Doctor Who), Mike Smith (Double for Dr Constantine)
Crew
Stunt Coordinator Lee Sheward, *Stunt Performers* Kim McGarrity, Tony Lucken, *Art Department Coordinator* Gwenllian Llwyd, *Concept Artist* Bryan Hitch, *Supervising Art Director* Stephen Nicholas, *Visual Effects* MillTv, *Visual FX Producer* Will Cohen, *Visual FX Supervisor* Dave Houghton, *Special Effects* Any Effects, *Graphic Artist* Jenny Bowers, *Property Master* Adrian Anscombe, *Standby Props* Phill Shellard, Trystan Howell, *Construction Manager* Andrew Smith, *Colourist* Jamie Wilkinson, *2D VFX Artists* David Bowman, Alberto Montanes, Astrid Busser-Casas, Jennifer Herbert, Simon C Holden, Sam Bennett, Michael Harrison, Bronwyn Edwards, *3D VFX Artists* Andy Howell, Matt McKinney, Jean-Claude Deguara, Paul Burton, Chris Petts, Nicolas Hernandez, Nick

Webber, Mark Wallman, *Digital Matte Painter* Alexander Fort, *Prosthetics* Millennium Effects, *Assistant Editors* Ceres Doyle, Jamie Adams, *Post-Production Supervisor* Marie Brown, *On-Line Editors* Matthew Clarke, Zoe Cassey, *Editor* Liana del Guidice, *Location Manager* Llyr Morris, *Camera Operator* Martin Stephens, *Focus Puller* Mark Isaac, *Grip* John Robinson, *Boom Operator* Damian Richardson, *Gaffer* Mark Hutchings, *Best Boy* Peter Chester, *Casting Associate* Kirsty Robertson, *Casting Director* Andy Pryor, *Production Buyer* Catherine Samuel, *Set Decorator* Liz Griffiths, *Sound Recordist* Ian Richardson, *Dubbing Mixer* Tim Ricketts, *Dialogue Editor* Paul McFadden, *Sound FX Editor* Paul Jefferies, *Incidental Music* Murray Gold, *Wardrobe Supervisor* Yolanda Peart-Smith, *Costume Designer* Lucinda Wright, *Make-Up Supervisor* Linda Davie, *Make-Up Artists* Claire Pritchard, Steve Williams, *Make-Up Designer* Davy Jones, *Production Designer* Edward Thomas, *Director of Photography* Ernie Vincze, *Finance Manager* Richard Pugsley, *Production Accountants* Debi Griffiths, Kath Blackman, Endaf Emyr Williams, *Production Manager* Tracie Simpson, *Unit Manager* Justin Gyphion, *Production Coordinator* Jess van Niekerk, *Continuity* Non Eleri Hughes, *First Assistant Director* Jon Older, *Second Assistant Director* Steffan Morris, *Third Assistant Director* Dan Mumford, *Script Editor* Helen Raynor, *Associate Producer* Helen Vallis, *Executive Producers* Russell T Davies, Julie Gardner, Mal Young, *Producer* Phil Collinson, *Director* James Hawes

DWM Index
350   Steven Moffat interview
356   Preview
357   John Barrowman interview
359   Review

Recording Dates
17-18 December 2004 (Q2), 4-7 January 2005 (Location videotaping), 9-14 January 2005 (Location videotaping), 17 January 2005 (Location videotaping), 18-20 January 2005 (Q2), 21 January 2005 (Location videotaping), 23-28 January 2005 (Location videotaping), 31 January 2005 (Q2), 7 February 2005 (Q2), 8 February 2005 (Location videotaping / Kendal Avenue modelwork), 9 February 2005 (Q2 / Kendal Avenue modelwork), 11 February 2005 (Q2), 25 February 2005 (Q2)

Locations
Cardiff Royal Infirmary, Womanby Street, Bargoed Street, Glamorgan House, all Cardiff; Headlands School, Penarth; Vale of Glamorgan Railway, Barry Island; RAF St Athan, Barry

Factoids
- Steven Moffat was primarily known as a comedy writer, having penned the sitcoms *Joking Apart* (1991-95), *Chalk* (1997) and *Coupling* (2001-04). He also penned the 1999 Comic Relief skit *Doctor Who and the Curse of Fatal Death*.
- John Barrowman was the only actor considered for the rôle of Time Agent Jack Harkness. Born in Glasgow but raised in Illinois, Barrowman had made a name for himself in stage musicals, such as *Miss Saigon*, *Sunset Boulevard*, *Phantom of the Opera* and *Chicago*. His television career began inauspiciously as co-presenter of the first series of children's entertainment show *Live and Kicking* (1993-2001), while his film appearances include *De-Lovely* (2004) and *The Producers* (2005), the Hollywood adaptation of the stage musical of Mel Brooks' classic 1968 film. His character was described by Moffat as resembling *Eagle* comic-strip character Dan Dare.
- Scenes of Rose hanging above the London Blitz were mainly achieved through suspending Billie Piper in front of a green-screen on which were added digital matte paintings during post-production. For the shot of her falling, stunt performer Kim McGarrity dropped ten feet onto mattresses, with her image digitally reduced to make the drop seem longer. For some sequences, Piper was videotaped against a real night sky background to add to the realism
- Cardiff's Royal Infirmary was also used as Albion Hospital in *Aliens of London* (161); this was referred to in the script. Barry Island had previously featured in Seventh Doctor story *Delta and the Bannermen* (147). The drinking den scenes, inspired by the Skin Scapes nightclub from Dennis Potter's serial *The Singing Detective* (1986), were videotaped in the basement of Headlands School, the same location used for the majority of *The Unquiet Dead* (160).
- The gasmasks were especially designed for the story, in order to simplify their overall shape (thus making them easier to mass-produce). The size of the eye-holes were increased for maximum effect.
- The production team opted to remove the sound of bones cracking as Dr Constantine's face morphs into a gasmask at the end of *The Empty Child*. Newspaper suggestions that it was cut by higher powers at the BBC because it was too horrific were

unfounded, although the alleged 'scoop' undoubtedly attracted more publicity for the episode.
- The seventh Bad Wolf reference was stencilled onto the Nazi bomb right at the end: 'Schlecter Wolf'. However, 'Schlecter' (which should be 'schlecte' anyway) actually means 'worse'. A more accurate version would be 'Böse Wolf'.

Comment
Surprising that televised *Doctor Who* had rarely touched on the Second World War before, because to judge by this story the two genres are made for each other. It helps to have excellent production values, of course, and *The Empty Child* is probably the best looking story this season. Impressive enough to set an entire 100 minute storyline at night time, even more impressive to fill it with German bombers, searchlights, rubble-strewn streets, barrage balloons and explosions. It is also, without a shadow of a doubt, the scariest *Doctor Who* story since *Horror of Fang Rock* (92). Shamelessly stealing the nightmarish Matrix imagery of *The Deadly Assassin* (88), it succeeds in creating an iconic monster by just sticking a gasmask onto a 'possessed' child. This would be unsettling enough on its own, but suggest that the mask has somehow grown out of the child's own face (and then go and show it in an unprecedented moment of explicit body horror) and I'm surprised that the entire juvenile population of Great Britain weren't immediately traumatized for life. The resolution is extremely clever, answering all the clues in a satisfyingly coherent way but without being predictable. And it's a happy ending too. The scariest *Who* in decades and it ends on a high - how wonderful is that? John Barrowman, although extraneous to the mix, does wonders with a potentially irritating character and the Rose/Doctor dynamic is notched up several gears as soon as he steps onto the scene. I only have two reservations: the overt nature of the sex references, which at times seem rather forced, and the tacked-on and rather silly ending with the bomb, resulting in one of the most embarrassing sequences ever made for the show - the Doctor dancing. **96%**

"Dinner in bondage - works for me." ~ Margaret Blaine

166) Boom Town
Russell T Davies

Original Transmission
Saturday 4 June 2005, 19.00-19.45, 7.7m / 18
Repeat Transmissions
On BBC Three:
Sunday 5 June 2005, 00.20-01.05, 0.2m / -
Sunday 5 June 2005, 19.00-19.45, 0.5m / -
Sunday 18 September 2005, 19.00-19.45, TBA / -
Friday 30 September 2005, 21.00-21.45, TBA / -
BBC Archive
This story exists as a 625-line 50 interlaced fields per second Digital Betacam videotape, shot with a Pro-Mist filter and applied with a film-look standards converter outputting 25 progressive frames per second.
DVD
1. June 2005, as part of 'Series 1, Volume 4' (BBCDVD 1758 / Photomontage)
2. November 2005, commentary by Annette Badland, Phil Collinson and John Barrowman, as part of the 'The Complete First Series' box set (BBCDVD 1770 / Photograph)
Script Book
October 2005, edited by Russell T Davies, *Doctor Who-The Shooting Scripts* (0563486414 / Photomontage)
Synopsis
A lone Slitheen is planning to blow up Cardiff, and then the world...
Cast
Christopher Eccleston (Doctor Who), Billie Piper (Rose Tyler), John Barrowman (Captain Jack), Noel Clarke (Mickey Smith), Annette Badland (Margaret Blaine), William Thomas (Cleaver), Aled Pedrick (Idris Hopper), Mali Harries (Cathy), Alan Ruscoe (Slitheen), Tina Maskell (Stunt Double for Margaret), Tony Lucken (Stunt Double for Captain Jack), Kim McGarrity (Stunt Double for Rose Tyler), Lucy Allen (Stunt Tea Lady), Kirsty-Ann Green (Secretary), Sarah Franzl (Stunt Secretary), Paul Battenburgh (Double for Captain Jack)
Crew
Armourers Faujja Singh, Wilbur Wright, *Stunt Coordinator* Lee Sheward, *Stunt Performers* Kim McGarrity, George Cottle, Tina Maskell, Tony Lucken, Lucy Allen, *Art Department Coordinator* Gwenllian Llwyd, *Concept Artist* Bryan Hitch, *Supervising Art Director* Stephen Nicholas, *Visual Effects* MillTv, *Visual Effects Designer*, *Visual*

Effects Assistants, Visual FX Producer Will Cohen, *Visual FX Supervisor* Dave Houghton, *Special Effects* Any Effects, *Graphic Artist* Jenny Bowers, *Properties Buyer* Joelle Rumbelow, *Property Master* Adrian Anscombe, *Standby Props* Phill Shellard, Trystan Howell, *Construction Manager* Andrew Smith, *Colourist* Paul Harrison, *2D VFX Artists* Simon C Holden, Jennifer Herbert, Astrid Busser-Casas, *3D VFX Artists* Joel Moire, Matthew McKinney, Jean-Claude Deguara, *Prosthetics* Millennium Effects, *Assistant Editor* Ceres Doyle, *Post-Production Supervisor* Marie Brown, *On-Line Editor* Matthew Clarke, *Editor* Graham Walker, *Location Manager* Gareth Lloyd, *Camera Operator* Martin Stephens, *Focus Puller* Mark Isaac, *Grip* John Robinson, *Boom Operator* Damian Richardson, *Gaffer* Mark Hutchings, *Best Boy* Peter Chester, *Casting Associate* Kirsty Robertson, *Casting Director* Andy Pryor, *Production Buyer* Joelle Rumbelow, *Set Decorator* Catherine Samuel, *Sound Recordist* Ian Richardson, *Dubbing Mixer* Tim Ricketts, *Dialogue Editor* Paul McFadden, *Sound FX Editor* Paul Jefferies, *Incidental Music* Murray Gold, *Wardrobe Supervisor* Yolanda Peart-Smith, *Costume Designer* Lucinda Wright, *Make-Up Supervisor* Linda Davie, *Make-Up Artists* Claire Pritchard, Steve Williams, *Make-Up Designer* Davy Jones, *Production Designer* Edward Thomas, *Director of Photography* Ernie Vincze, *Finance Manager* Richard Pugsley, *Production Accountants* Debi Griffiths, Kath Blackman, Endaf Emyr Williams, *Production Manager* Tracie Simpson, *Unit Manager* Lowri Thomas, *Production Coordinator* Jess van Niekerk, *Continuity* Dorothy Friend, *First Assistant Director* Howard Arundel, *Second Assistant Director* Steffan Morris, *Third Assistant Director* Dan Mumford, *Script Editor* Elwen Rowlands, *Associate Producer* Helen Vallis, *Executive Producers* Russell T Davies, Julie Gardner, Mal Young, *Producer* Phil Collinson, *Director* Joe Ahearne

DWM Index
357 Preview
       John Barrowman interview
358 Noel Clarke interview

Recording Dates
19 January 2005 (Location videotaping), 1-2 February 2005 (Location videotaping), 3 February 2005 (Q2), 4 February 2005 (Location videotaping), 5 February 2005 (Q2), 8 February 2005 (Location videotaping), 10 February 2005 (Q2), 11 February 2005 (Location videotaping), 14-15 February 2005 (Location videotaping), 18 February 2005 (Q2)

Locations
Mermaid Quay, Glamorgan House, Millennium Centre Square, Cardiff Railway Station, all Cardiff

Working Title
Dining with Monsters

Factoids
- This episode was intended to be written by prolific scriptwriter Paul Abbott, but he was too busy on his award-winning C4 drama *Shameless* (2004-05) to contribute
- Annette Badland's inclusion was a late decision after Russell T Davies saw her in *Aliens of London* (161) and considered her character much underused. His initial concept of the episode was based around the restaurant scene (shot at Bistro 10 in Cardiff Bay), hence his original working title.
- William Thomas (Cleaver) became the first actor to have appeared in the original BBC series and the relaunched 2005 version. He played the undertaker Martin in *Remembrance of the Daleks* (149).
- The eighth Bad Wolf reference was the name of the nuclear power station, Blaidd Drwg ('Bad Wolf' in Welsh).

Comment
The worst episode of Season 27 by far, this is probably one of the silliest, most boring 45 minutes of *Doctor Who* ever transmitted. Promoted as a disaster story, it is only a disaster in the sense that it just doesn't really work on any level. The Slitheen is an uninteresting alien race, Margaret Blaine is a one-dimensional pantomime villain, the comedy moments are embarrassingly overplayed (witness Eccleston's gurning in the restaurant scenes), the characterization is universally bland and the ending is as crass and twee as it is inexplicable. We'd already had a 'character piece' with *Father's Day* - we didn't need another one, and especially not one like this. **15%**

"I cultivated pure and blessed Dalek!" ~ *Emperor Dalek*

167) Bad Wolf / The Parting of the Ways
Russell T Davies

Original Transmission
1) *Bad Wolf*
Saturday 11 June 2005, 19.00-19.45, 6.8m / 19
2) *The Parting of the Ways*
Saturday 18 June 2005, 19.00-19.45, 6.9m / 17
Repeat Transmissions
On BBC Three:
1) *Bad Wolf*
Saturday 11 June 2005, 22.55-23.40, 0.3m / -
Sunday 12 June 2005, 19.00-19.45, 0.7m / -
Friday 17 June 2005, 21.00-21.45, 0.2m / -
Sunday 25 September 2005, 19.30-20.15, TBA / -
Friday 7 October 2005, 21.00-21.45, TBA / -
2) *The Parting of the Ways*
Saturday 18 June 2005, 22.50-23.35, 0.3m / -
Sunday 19 June 2005, 19.00-19.45, 0.7m / -
Sunday 25 September 2005, 20.15-21.00, TBA / -
Friday 14 October 2005, 21.00-21.45, TBA / -
BBC Archive
This story exists as a 625-line 50 interlaced fields per second Digital Betacam videotape, shot with a Pro-Mist filter and applied with a film-look standards converter outputting 25 progressive frames per second.
DVD
1. June 2005, as part of 'Series 1, Volume 4' (BBCDVD 1758 / Photomontage)
2. November 2005, commentary by Russell T Davies, John Barrowman, Julie Gardner, Phil Collinson and Billie Piper, as part of the 'The Complete First Series' box set (BBCDVD 1770 / Photograph)
Script Book
October 2005, edited by Russell T Davies, *Doctor Who-The Shooting Scripts* (0563486414 / Photomontage)
Synopsis
The Doctor and his companions are plunged into bizarre reality TV shows, while behind the scenes the Daleks plan a massed invasion of Earth...
Cast
Christopher Eccleston, David Tennant (Doctor Who), Billie Piper (Rose Tyler), John Barrowman (Captain Jack), Camille Coduri (Jackie), Noel Clarke (Mickey Smith), Anne Robinson (Ann Droid Voice), Alan Ruscoe (Ann Droid/Trine-E), Paul Kasey (Zu-Zana), Davina McCall (Davinadroid Voice), Trinny Woodall (Trine-E Voice), Susannah Constantine (Zu-Zana Voice), Martha Cope (Controller), Jo Joyner (Lynda), Jamie Bradley (Strood), Abi Eniola (Crosbie), Paterson Joseph (Rodrick), Dominic Burgess (Agorax), Karren Winchester (Fitch), Kate Loustau (Colleen), Jo Stone Fewings (Male Programmer), Nisha Nayar (Female Programmer), Barnaby Edwards, Nicholas Pegg, David Hankinson (Daleks), Nicholas Briggs (Dalek Voices), Jenna Russell (Floor Manager), Sebastian Armesto (Broff), Sam Callis (Security Guard), Tony Lucken (Stunt Double for Captain Jack/Stunt Security Guard), Stuart Clarke (Stunt Security Guard), Paul Newbolt (Double for Doctor Who), Maurice Lee (Stunt Double for Mickey), Jamie Edgell (Stunt Double for Programmer), Ian Hilditch, Kyle Davies (Security Guards)
Crew
Stunt Coordinator Jamie Edgell, *Stunt Performers* Tony Luckall, Maurice Lee, Stuart Clarke, Derek Lea, *Art Department Coordinator* Gwenllian Llwyd, *Concept Artist* Bryan Hitch, *Supervising Art Director* Stephen Nicholas, *Visual Effects* MillTv, *Visual FX Producer* Will Cohen, *Visual FX Supervisor* Dave Houghton, *Special Effects* Any Effects, *Graphic Artist* Jenny Bowers, *Property Master* Adrian Anscombe, *Standby Props* Phill Shellard, Trystan Howell, *Construction Manager* Andrew Smith, *Colourist* Paul Harrison, *2D VFX Artists* David Bowman, Simon C Holden, Jennifer Herbert, Bronwyn Edwards, Astrid Busser-Casas, Richard Roberts, Ched Meire, *3D VFX Artists* Chris Petts, Andy Howell, Paul Burton, Matt McKinney, Nick Webber, Mark Wallman, Nicolas Hernandez, Jean-Claude Deguara, *Digital Matte Painter* Alexander Fort, *Model Unit Supervisor* Mike Tucker, *Model Unit Director of Photography* Peter Tyler, *Prosthetics* Millennium Effects, *Assistant Editor* Ceres Doyle, *Post-Production Supervisor* Marie Brown, *On-Line Editor* Matthew Clarke, *Editor* Graham Walker, *Location Manager* Llyr Morris, *Camera Operator* Martin Stephens, *Focus Puller* Mark Isaac, *Grip* John Robinson, *Boom Operator* Damian Richardson, *Gaffer* Mark Hutchings, *Best Boy* Peter Chester, *Casting Associate* Kirsty Robertson, *Casting Director* Andy Pryor, *Production Buyer* Catherine Samuel, *Set Decorator* Liz Griffiths, *Sound Recordist* Ian Richardson, *Dubbing Mixer* Tim Ricketts, *Dialogue Editor* Paul McFadden, *Sound FX Editor* Paul Jefferies, *Incidental Music* Murray Gold, *Wardrobe Supervisor* Yolanda Peart-Smith,

Costume Designer Lucinda Wright, *Make-Up Supervisor* Linda Davie, *Make-Up Artists* Claire Pritchard, Steve Williams, *Make-Up Designer* Davy Jones, *Production Designer* Edward Thomas, *Director of Photography* Ernie Vincze, *Finance Manager* Richard Pugsley, *Production Accountants* Debi Griffiths, Kath Blackman, Endaf Emyr Williams, *Rights Executive* James Dundas, *Production Manager* Tracie Simpson, *Production Coordinator* Jess van Niekerk, *Production Runners* Anna Evans, Tim Hodges, Debbie Meldrum, *Continuity* Non Eleri Hughes, *First Assistant Director* Peter Bennett, *Second Assistant Director* Steffan Morris, *Third Assistant Director* Dan Mumford, *Script Editor* Helen Raynor, *Associate Producer* Helen Vallis, *Executive Producers* Russell T Davies, Julie Gardner, Mal Young, *Producer* Phil Collinson, *Director* Joe Ahearne

DWM Index
357 Preview
358 Pixel Perfect
359 David Tennant interview
     Russell T Davies interview

Recording Dates
16-17 February 2005 (Location videotaping), 18-19 February 2005 (Q2), 22-24 February 2005 (Q2), 25 February 2005 (Newport City Live Arena), 28 February 2005 (Newport City Live Arena), 1-4 March 2005 (Q2), 5 March 2005 (Enfys TV studio, Cardiff), 7 March 2005 (Enfys TV studio, Cardiff), 8-9 March 2005 (Q2), 10-11 March 2005 (Location videotaping), 12 March 2005 (Q2), 14 March 2005 (Q2), 22-23 March 2005 (Kendal Avenue modelwork), 21 April 2005 (Q2)

Locations
Severn Square, Loudoun Square, both Cardiff

Factoids
- The Emperor Dalek had first appeared on 6 February 1965 in a full-colour comic strip in *TV Century 21*. Drawn by Richard Jennings, it consisted of an enormous golden globe, surmounted by a dozen or more 'indicator lights', with an eyestalk, atop a truncated Dalek skirt. Its first television appearance was in *The Evil of the Daleks* (36) in which Michaeljohn Harris and Peter Day designed it as a large, stylized immobile Dalek figure with two globes as 'eyes', an inverted conelike head and several cables coming off it. For its third appearance, in *Remembrance of the Daleks* (149), Mike Tucker designed the Dalek Emperor as a deliberate copy of its comic strip forbear, this time with a white globe on a normal Dalek skirt section, two 'indicator lights' and no eyestalk. For this, its final appearance (to date), the Emperor was in the form of a gigantic 30-40 feet high Dalek with an 'exploded' skirt section revealing a tentacled mutant in its glass biosphere. The five-foot high model was designed by Edward Thomas and built by Mike Tucker, Nick Kool and Alan Brannan and combined with live action footage, CGI Daleks and a digital matte painting of the Dalek spaceship interior.
- Only three Daleks were used in the story (including the one seen in *Dalek*, 162), with split-screen effects and CGI versions swelling their ranks.
- Television shows parodied included *The Weakest Link* (2000-present), *Big Brother* (2000-present), *What Not To Wear* (2001-present), *Call My Bluff* (1965-88, 1996-present), *Countdown* (1982-present), *Ground Force* (1988-2005), *Stars in Their Eyes* (1990-present) and *Wipeout* (1995-2003). Most were BBC productions, but special permission had to be sought from Endemol for using *Big Brother*.
- Various sets were reused from *The Long Game*, specifically the medical centre (for *What Not To Wear*), Floor 500, the spike room (for Archive Six) and the observation deck. The same set, redressed, was used for Floors 56, 407, 499 and 500.
- Christopher Eccleston and Billie Piper shot the special Season 27 trailer ("Do you wanna come with me?") on 26 and 27 February 2005. The fireball sequence was videotaped in the underpass of the Newport High Street railway station.
- In order to maintain secrecy, the lead-up to the regeneration scene was recorded with various alternate sections of dialogue, including a 'fake' ending, as circulated in bogus copies of Episode 13. Scenes with David Tennant were shot almost six weeks later.
- David Tennant was officially announced as the Tenth Doctor on 16 April 2005, shortly after the BBC admitted that Christopher Eccleston would only be staying for one series. Tennant had already featured in the Big Finish audio plays *Medicinal Purposes* (2004) and *Colditz* (2001) as well as the 2003 Internet drama *The Scream of the Shalka*. Recent television work included *He Knew He Was Right* (2004), *Blackpool* (2004), a live broadcast of *The Quatermass*

Experiment (2005) and Russell T Davies' *Casanova* (2005). Filmwork includes *Jude* (1996, with Christopher Eccleston), *Bright Young Things* (2003) and *Harry Potter and the Goblet of Fire* (2005).

Comment
A game of two halves, *Bad Wolf* is played as a biting satire on reality TV shows while *The Parting of the Ways* is a straightforward 'base under siege' runaround. In terms of plotting, the first part is undoubtedly more interesting, and has much more to say, than the second. The presence of the huge Dalek army gives the final part a dramatic weight that it doesn't deserve. Their total destruction in the last few seconds comes not from the ingenuity or heroism of the few Game Station survivors, but from an essentially magical property of the Tardis, never before glimpsed in the programme. (For the record, its effect in *Boom Town* produced a quite different result from that seen here.) And Rose's overlong exile on Earth seems a waste of a strong character, even though it does ultimately leads to her rescuing the Doctor (yet again). But the whole story rattles along in fine style and the Daleks look fabulous. As to the Emperor Dalek, I can't help thinking it would have been much more impressive if it had begun looking like the version from *The Evil of the Daleks* (36) and then slowly opened up like its minion in *Dalek* (162) to reveal the creature inside. As it is, it's simply too static. But Christopher Eccleston exudes energy in his final hour (and a half) and his final scene is delivered in typically boisterous fashion. Probably the most audience-friendly story of the season - despite the disappointingly anodyne explanation of Bad Wolf - it's a great climax to a hugely successful relaunch. **93%**

Television Spin-Offs
This list excludes sketches, documentaries and fan-produced videos.

"She's like a butterfly - never in one place long enough to lick a stamp." ~ Aunt Lavinia

1) K-9 and Company
Terence Dudley

Original Transmission
A Girl's Best Friend
Monday 28 December 1981, 17.45-18.35, 8.4m / -
Repeat Transmission
On BBC2:
A Girl's Best Friend
Friday 24 December 1982, 17.40-18.30, 2.1m / -
BBC Archive
The story exists as a 625-line two-inch PAL colour master videotape.
Novelization
The Companions of Doctor Who - K-9 and Company by Terence Dudley (160/15)
Paperback:
October 1987, Target (0426203097 / Peter Kelly)
Video
August 1995 (BBCV 5635 / Andrew Skilleter)
Music and Sound Effects
February 1982, Solid Gold Records, theme music single (SGR117 / Photograph)
Précis
Sarah and K-9 Mk III, a present from the Doctor, foil the machinations of a local witches' coven…
Cast
Elisabeth Sladen (Sarah Jane Smith), John Leeson (K-9 III Voice), Bill Fraser (Bill Pollock), Ian Sears (Brendan Richards), Colin Jeavons (George Tracey), Mary Wimbush (Aunt Lavinia), Linda Polan (Juno Baker), Gillian Martell (Lilly Gregson), John Quarmby (Henry Tobias), Neville Barber (Howard Baker), Nigel Gregory (Vince Wilson), Sean Chapman (Peter Tracey), Stephen Oxley (PC Carter), Susie Brown (Double for Sarah Jane Smith), Bruno (Dog)
Crew
Visual Effects Designer Mat Irvine, *Visual Effects Assistants* Charlie Lumm, Tony Auger, *Graphic Designer* Bob Cosford, *Video Effects* Nick Moore, *K-9 Operator* Mat Irvine, *Technical Manager* Barry Chatfield, *Senior Cameraman* Phil Wilson, *Vision Mixer* Mark Kershaw, *Videotape Editor* John Burkill, *Studio Lighting* Barry Hill, *Studio Sound* David Hughes, *Film Cameraman* Michael

Williams, *Film Sound* Dave Brinicombe, *Film Editor* Michael Lomas, *Properties Buyer* Michael Preece, *Special Sound* Dick Mills, *Grams Operator* Richard Hetherington, *Incidental Music* Peter Howell, *Costume Designer* Ann Arnold, *Costume Assistant* Sally Pearson, *Dressers* Tessa Murray, Nick Eastwood, *Make-Up Artist* Susie Bancroft, *Make-Up Assistant* Carole Brady, *Designer* Nigel Jones, *Design Assistant* Bob Farr, *Production Managers* Robert Gabriel, Matthew Kuipers, *Production Associate* Angela Smith, *Production Assistant* Yvonne Collins, *Assistant Floor Manager* Sue Hedden, *Floor Assistant* Di Hughes, *Script Editors* Eric Saward, Antony Root, *Producer* John Nathan-Turner, *Director* John Black

DWM Index
- 60   Preview
- 62   TV review
- 68   John Nathan-Turner interview
- 89   Elisabeth Sladen interview
- 116 Eric Saward: A Retrospective Review John Leeson interview
- 163 Elisabeth Sladen interview
- 194 Peter Howell interview
- 228 John Leeson interview
- 229 Video review
- 346 Eric Saward interview

Recording Dates
9 November 1981 (Location filming), 12-17 November 1981 (Location videotaping), 29-30 November 1981 (PM A)

Locations
Old church, North Woodchester, Gloucestershire; Crossroads, Sapperton, Gloucestershire; Barnsley House, Barnsely, Gloucestershire; Miserden Petrol Station, St Andrew's Church and Miserden Park Estate, Miserden, Gloucestershire; Wishanger Farm, Wishanger, Gloucestershire; Police Station and Post Office, Bisley, Gloucestershire; Daneway, Gloucestershire

Working Title
Sarah and K-9

Factoids
- *A Girl's Best Friend* was the pilot episode of a mooted six-part series of movie-length stories for the 1982/83 period. Due to low ratings (caused in part by a massive blackout affecting North-West England), more shows were not commissioned.
- John Nathan-Turner reduced Season 19 from 28 episodes to 26, and used the extra money to finance this spin-off story.
- Production was delayed from summer 1981 until November so that Elisabeth Sladen would be free to take part. Because no London studios were available at this later date, studio recording was carried out at Birmingham's Pebble Mill Studios (as it had been for *Horror of Fang Rock*, 92).
- Specially composed theme music was written by Ian Levine and Fiachre Trench and realized by Peter Howell of the BBC Radiophonic Workshop. A fast-moving title sequence was devised in the style of American drama series *Hart to Hart*.

Comment
In many ways, *K-9 and Company* is all that *Doctor Who* wasn't in the early 1980s. It had a realistic Earth setting, naturalistic performances from the guest cast, a charming companion (who was now the central character), beautifully lit studio interiors and a tangible sense of place. The story is just enough to last the 50 minutes and there are many delightfully observed moments along the way. On the negative side, Sarah's kung-fu at the end is risible and the faux Doctor replacement Brendan is more irritating than Adric. But on the whole this is a lovingly made vehicle for K-9 with a cosy, Christmassy feel to it. **75%**

"You've been selected for *The Ultimate Challenge!*" ~ The Doctor

2) Search Out Space

Lambros Atteshlis, Berry-Anne Billingsley and Robin Mudge

Original Transmission
On BBC2:
Wednesday 21 November 1990, 10.15-10.35, -/-
Repeat Transmission
On BBC2:
Wednesday, 28 November 1990, 10.05-10.35, -/-
Précis
The Doctor tasks his companions with finding out about space...
Cast
Sylvester McCoy (The Doctor), Sophie Aldred (Ace), John Leeson (K-9 Voice), Stephen Johnson (Cedric).
Crew
Visual Effects Designer Mat Irvine, *Videotape Editor* Dave Austin, *Lighting* John Collins, *Sound* Dave Brinicombe, *Cameraman* Mike Dauncey, *Assistant Cameraman* Paul Cox, *Researcher*

Teresa Griffiths, *Designer/Assistant Producer* Peter Findley, *Unit Manager* Valerie Booth, *Production Assistant* Eve Lucas, *Assistant Floor Manager/Properties Buyer* Crispin Avon, *Producer* Lambros Atteshlis, *Series Producer* Robin Mudge, *Director* Berry-Anne Billingsley

DWM Index
170   Feature

Recording Dates
14-15 May 1990 (Location videotaping), 18 May 1990 (Location videotaping), 21 May 1990 (Location videotaping), 20 May 1990 (EFS modelwork), 25 May 1990 (EFS modelwork)

Locations
Avalon Travel Agency and The Danish Kitchen, Ealing, London; London Underground Foot Tunnel, Shepherd's Bush Station, London; Jodrell Bank Observatory, Cheshire; Lloyds Building, London, EC2

Factoids
- This programme formed the 'Earth' segment for children's education series *Search Out Science*.
- The scenes in Cedric's spaceship were shot overnight in a disused London Underground foot tunnel.
- The original Delia Derbyshire theme music was heard at the beginning, while Keff McCulloch's version featured over the closing titles.
- A small feature promoted the programme in the *Radio Times*, issue dated 17-23 November 1990.

Comment
Nice to see the Doctor and Ace back again, and some of the effects are actually quite good, but ultimately the show proffers more questions than answers (which, I suppose, is the point of a teaching aid). **37%**

"Boo!" ~ *Gareth Jenkins*

3) A Fix with Sontarans
Eric Saward

Original Transmission
Saturday 23 February 1985, 18.05-18.40*, - / -
(*Duration refers to *Jim'll Fix It*)

DVD
September 2003, as an extra on *The Two Doctors* (BBCDVD 1213 / Clayton Hickman)

Précis
Tegan and Gareth Jenkins help the Doctor to defeat two Sontarans aboard the Tardis...

Cast
Colin Baker (The Doctor), Gareth Jenkins (Himself), Janet Fielding (Tegan), Clinton Greyn (Group Marshall Nathan), Tim Raynham (Sontaran), Jimmy Saville OBE (Himself)

Crew
Special Sound Dick Mills, *Studio Lighting* Peter Wesson, *Studio Sound* Richard Chamberlain, *Designer* Gwen Evans, *Producer* Roger Ordish, *Director* Marcus Mortimer

DWM Index
195   Archive Feature
323   Colin Baker interview

Recording Date
20 February 1985 (TC8)

Factoids
- This nine-minute segment on wish-fulfilment TV show *Jim'll Fix It* (1975-94) followed a request by eight-year-old Gareth Jenkins to appear in *Doctor Who*, his grandmother having made him a Sixth Doctor costume. It was recorded in front of a live studio audience, except for the Sontarans' grisly demise which was taped earlier in the day.
- Nicola Bryant was on holiday, so Janet Fielding was contracted to resume her old role of Tegan.
- Adopting Jon Pertwee's acting technique, some of Jenkins' lines were written out for him on the Tardis console.

Comment
A dialogue-heavy long Tardis scene with two poorly realized Sontarans - just like Season 22 then. **42%**

"I can hear the heartbeat of a killer!" ~ *The Doctor*

4) Dimensions in Time
John Nathan-Turner and David Roden

Original Transmission
Part One
Friday 26 November 1993, 20.07-22.15, 13.8m / 15
Part Two
Saturday 27 November 1993, 19.23-19.28, 13.6m / 10

Précis
The Rani has imprisoned the Doctor and his assistants in the London suburb of Walford…
Cast
Jon Pertwee, Tom Baker, Peter Davison, Colin Baker, Sylvester McCoy (The Doctor), Kate O'Mara (The Rani), Sophie Aldred (Ace), Bonnie Langford (Melanie Bush), Carole Ann Ford (Susan Foreman), Elisabeth Sladen (Sarah Jane Smith), Nicola Bryant (Peri Brown), Sarah Sutton (Nyssa), Caroline John (Liz Shaw), Richard Franklin (Captain Yates), Nicholas Courtney (Brigadier Lethbridge-Stewart), Lalla Ward (Romana II), Deborah Watling (Victoria Waterfield), Louise Jameson (Leela), John Leeson (K-9 Voice), Gillian Taylforth (Kathy Beale), Adam Woodyatt (Ian Beale), Alan Cave (Ruffian), Mike Reid (Frank Butcher), Ross Kemp (Grant Mitchell), Steve McFadden (Phil Mitchell), Letitia Dean (Sharon Mitchell), Nicola Stapleton (Mandy), Wendy Richard (Pauline Fowler), Pam St Clement (Pat Butcher), Sam West (Cyrian), Tony Kirke, David Miller (Cybermen), Andrew Beech (Time Lord), Deepak Verma (Sanjay), Shobu Kapoor (Gita), Derek Handley (Ogron), John Frank Rosenbaum (Vanir), Martin Wilkie (Tractator/Tetrap/Zog, Dragon), Stephen Mansfield (Fifi Operator), Philip Newman (Kiv), Anthony Clark (Vervoid), Paul Lunn (Mawdryn Mutant), Stephen Coates (Mogarian), Mike Fillis (Sea Devil), Ilona McDonald (Voc Robot), Tim Packham (Plasmaton), Andy Hopkinson (Argolin), Terry Walsh (Double for the Doctor)
Crew
Visual Effects Designer Mike Tucker, *K-9 Operator* Mat Irvine, *Video Effects* Dave Chapman, *Technical Manager* David Spencer, *Studio Coordinator* Mark Ball, *Lighting* Dave Wells, Alan Rixon, *Sound* Peter Ball, Barry Bonner, *Cameramen* Tommy Beiger, Nigel Saunders, *Incidental Music* Keff McCulloch, *Costume Designer* Ken Trew, *Make-Up Artist* Leslie Smith, *Designer* Derek Evans, *Production Manager* Gary Downie, *Production Assistant* Gary Broadhurst, *Programme Coordinator* Maggie Greenhalgh, *Assistant Floor Manager* Jenny Drewett, *EastEnders Producer* Leonard Lewis, *Producer* John Nathan-Turner, *Director* Stuart McDonald, *Children In Need Editor* Nick Handel
DWM Index
209 Mike Tucker on *Dimensions in Time* TV review
212 Deborah Watling interview
214 Janet Fielding interview
215 Louise Jameson interview
216 Keff McCulloch interview
217 Lalla Ward interview
218 Sarah Sutton interview
  Sylvester McCoy interview
219 Caroline John interview
222 Richard Franklin interview
229 Nicholas Courtney interview
237 Nicola Bryant interview
249 The John Nathan-Turner Memoirs
250 Elisabeth Sladen interview
298 Kate O'Mara interview
308 Deborah Watling interview
324 Archive Extra
325 Colin Baker interview
339 Gary Downie interview
Recording Dates
21 September 1993 (Fountain Studios), 22-23 September 1993 (Elstree Studios *EastEnders* lot), 24 September 1993 (Location videotaping)
Locations
Cutty Sark, Royal Naval College and National Maritime Museum, all Greenwich, London SE10
Working Titles
3-Dimensions of Time
The Dimensions of Time
Factoids
- This was a special 30th anniversary story to raise funds for the BBC charity 'Children in Need' which has run telethons every November since 1980.
- *Dimensions in Time* used a 3D technique called the Pulfrich Effect which worked on the principle that action moving from right to left, when seen through different coloured lenses for each eye, appeared to have a three-dimensional quality. Static shots exhibited no 3D effect.
- The first episode was broadcast during the actual 'Children in Need' telethon, while the second, edited-down episode, aired on the following day's *Noel's House Party* (1991-94) and was introduced by Jon Pertwee. Viewers could vote for whether they wanted Mandy or Big Ron to rescue the Doctor. Mandy won, raising £101,000 in the process.
- Cast and crew worked for free - the proviso being that the production is never repeated or released commercially in any form. Thank goodness.

Comment
This could have worked had it been vaguely humorous in tone, but the po-faced seriousness of the whole garbled mess merely makes the 'story' one big embarrassment from start to finish. Still, the 3D effect is nice and it's all for charidee, so that's okay. **12%**

"Say hello to the sofa of reasonable comfort." ~ *The Doctor*

5) Doctor Who and the Curse of Fatal Death
Steven Moffat

Original Transmission
Part One
Friday 12 March 1999, 20.11-20.16, 9.8m / -
Part Two
Friday 12 March 1999, 20.36-20.41, 9.4m / -
Part Three
Friday 12 March 1999, 21.39-21.44, 5.8m / -
Part Four
Friday 12 March 1999, 22.08-22.15, 8.7m / -
Video
September 1999, with documentary and other televised spoofs (BBCV 6889 / Photomontage)
Précis
The Master joins forces with the Daleks to defeat the Doctor and bring about his final regenerations...
Cast
Rowan Atkinson, Richard E Grant, Jim Broadbent, Hugh Grant, Joanna Lumley (The Doctor), Julia Sawalha (Emma), Jonathan Pryce (The Master), Andrew Beech, Chris Kirk, Dave Clarke, Mike Mungarvan, Stephen Cranford, Ashley Nealfuller, Wendy Addicott, Antonia Moss, David J Ross, Dave Chapman (Daleks), Roy Skelton, Dave Chapman (Dalek Voices), Gabe Cronnelly (Stunt Double for The Master)
Crew
Stuntmen Gabe Cronnelly, *Visual Effects Designer* Andy McVean, *Post-Production Effects* Liz Browne, Dave Houghton, Ben Turner, *Vision Engineer* Simon Lyon, *Offline Editor* Nick Arthurs, *Dubbing Editors* Glenn Calder, Philip Meehan, *Studio Lighting* Colin McCarthy, *Studio Sound* John Midgley, *Cameramen* Martin Foley, Jamie Harcourt, *Assistant Cameramen* Stuart Clayton, David Hedges, *Camera Trainee* Sarah Welsh, *Crane Operator* Dave Foster, *Production Buyer* Bobby Warans, *Props Master* Paul Emerson, *Music Consultant* Mark Ayres, *Costume Designer* Rebecca Hale, *Wardrobe Supervisor* Clare Grant, *Make-Up Artists* Jan Sewell, Julie Dartnell, Mandy Gold, *Art Director* Sarah Milton, *Designer* Simon Kimmel, *Director of Photography* Chris Howard, *Stage Manager* Mark Palmer, *Production Manager* Alison McPhail, *Production Assistant* Debbie Somerville, *Executive Producer* Richard Curtis, *Producer* Sue Vertue, *First Assistant Director* Tim Lewis, *Second Assistant Director* Sharon Ricketts, *Director* John Henderson

DWM Index
278   Studio report
279   Comic Relief raffle
282   Video review
328   Archive Extra
350   Steven Moffat interview
Recording Dates
22-24 February 1999 (Pinewood Studios)
Working Title
As broadcast
Factoids
- *The Curse of Fatal Death* aired as part of Red Nose Day 1999, an evening's entertainment to help raise funds for Comic Relief, a charity established in 1985 to help underprivileged people worldwide.
- The Tardis walls and console had been made by fans for a video production called *Devious*. Seven Daleks were used in total - three from the BBC and five on loan from fans.
- The programme used a truncated version of the first Tom Baker title sequence to introduce each of its four episodes. On the video release, these were compiled into two episodes.
- The *Radio Times* (6-12 March 1999) featured an article on the show with a full-page photograph of Rowan Atkinson as the Doctor.
- Incidental music was orchestrated by composer Mark Ayres, sourcing material from his own scores for the programme (*The Greatest Show in the Galaxy*, *The Curse of Fenric* and *Ghost Light*) as well as various Radiophonic Workshop ones from the 1980s. He wrote just two new pieces - 'Zectronic Beam Machine' and 'Doctor Hugh'.
- Other suggested actors to play the Doctor included Alan Rickman, Colin Firth, Mel Smith, Lee Evans and Robson Green.

Comment
Probably the only spoof to accurately capture the spirit of *Doctor Who*, *The Curse of Fatal Death* is an unalloyed joy from start to finish. Schoolboy fart gags aside, it gently mocks core elements of the show without resorting to the clichéd targets of wobbling walls and cheap monsters. In short, it satirises a typical *Doctor Who* storyline rather than the way it was actually brought to the screen - and thus is timeless in its appeal and considerably more witty than any of the other spoofs we've been subjected to over the years (with the possible exception of *The Web of Caves* sketch on 1999's 'Doctor Who Night'). Of all the

Doctors to appear here, Hugh Grant is by far the best, playing the role utterly straight and providing one of the *Doctor Who*'s most moving 'death scenes'. **81%**

2: AUDIO

LP recordings, radio programmes and Big Finish audio adventures

Record

"Even my goosepimples have goosepimples." ~ Sarah Jane Smith

Doctor Who and the Pescatons
Victor Pemberton

Details
1. August 1976, Argo/Decca Records, LP (LPZSW 564 / Laurie Richards)
2. August 1976, Argo/Decca Records, cassette (CZSW 564 / Laurie Richards)
3. April 1985, London Records, LP (414 4591 / Laurie Richards)
4. April 1985, London Records, cassette (414 4594 / Laurie Richards)
5. December 1991, Silva Screen, CD (FILMCD 707 / Pete Wallbank)
6. December 1991, Silva Screen, cassette (FILMC 707 / Pete Wallbank)
7. November 1993, PolyGram, cassette (8443644 / Pete Wallbank)
8. January 2005, plus Elisabeth Sladen interview, 2 x CDs (0563527641 / Max Ellis)

Novelization
Doctor Who - The Pescatons by Victor Pemberton
Paperback:
September 1991 (0426203291 / Pete Wallbank)

Précis
The Doctor and Sarah stop the shark-like Pescaton leader Zor from invading London…

Cast
Tom Baker (The Doctor), Elisabeth Sladen (Sarah Jane Smith), Bill Mitchell (Zor)

Crew
Incidental Music Kenny Clayton, *Studio Manager* Harley Usill, *Engineers* Kevin Daley, Robert Parker, Brian Hodgson, *Producer/Director* Don Norman

DWM Index
179 Book Review
186 CD review
287 Thrilling Adventures in Time and Space
318 Victor Pemberton interview
352 CD review (reissue)

Recording Date
Early 1976 (Argo Studios)

Factoids
- Victor Pemberton was script editor for *Tomb of the Cybermen* (37) and wrote the story *Fury from the Deep* (42). The latter was a clear inspiration for this one-off LP recording.

Comment
Because of the effective use of crowd sound effects, it's hard to imagine there are only three actors in this atmospheric two-parter. The opening scene on the deserted beach is fabulously eerie and Baker and Sladen are so comfortable with their characters it's a delight to listen to them perform together. The story's silly at times, but always fun, and the quality of the production is excellent throughout. **79%**

Radio

"We're getting loster and loster!" ~ Sarah Jane Smith

1) Exploration Earth: The Time Machine
Bernard Venables

Original Transmission
On Radio 4:
Monday 4 October 1976, 14.00-14.20

Soundtrack
July 2001, CD, with *Genesis of the Daleks* (0563478578 / Max Ellis)

Cast
Tom Baker (The Doctor), Elisabeth Sladen (Sarah Jane Smith), John Westbrook (Megron)

Crew
Special Sound Dick Mills, *Producers* Mike Howarth, David Lyttle

Précis
The Doctor has to stop Megron from endangering Mankind's first appearance on Earth…

DWM Index
287 Thrilling Adventures in Time and Space
308 CD review
349 Archive Extra

Recording Date
27 April 1976 (BH unknown studio)
Factoids
- This 20-minute programme was the third in a BBC schools' radio series looking at the geography of our planet.

Comment
The dialogue is appalling throughout - especially Elisabeth Sladen's tortuous one-liners - but as an educational show about the formation of the Earth it does its job as well as can be expected. John Westbrook gives a powerful performance as the Megron and Dick Mills' sound effects are surprisingly effective (ie loud). **32%**

"Look at my pustules grow!" ~ *Captain Slarn*

2) *Slipback*
Eric Saward

Original Transmission
On Radio 4:
Episode One
Thursday 25 July 1985, 10.08-10.18
Episode Two
Thursday 25 July 1985, 11.44-11.54
Episode Three
Thursday 1 August 1985, 10.20-10.30
Episode Four
Thursday 1 August 1985, 11.26-11.36
Episode Five
Thursday 8 August 1985, 09.44-09.54
The Final Episode
Thursday 8 August 1985, 11.36-11.48
Novelization
Doctor Who - Slipback by Eric Saward
Hardback:
August 1986, WH Allen (0491037937 / Paul Mark Tams)
Paperback:
January 1987, Target (0426202635/ Paul Mark Tams)
Soundtrack
November 1988, 2 x cassettes, with *Genesis of the Daleks* (0563225572 / Photomontage)
Précis
The Doctor has to stop a schizoid computer from destroying the Universe…
Cast
Colin Baker (The Doctor), Nicola Bryant (Peri Brown), Jane Carr (Computer voice), Jon Glover (Shellingbourne Grant), Nick Revell (Mr Bates), Valentine Dyall (Captain Slarn), Ron Pember (Seedle), Alan Thompson (Mutant/Maston/Steward/Barton/Time Lord)
Crew
Incidental Music Jonathan Gibbs, *Special Sound* Dick Mills, *Studio Managers* Colin Duff, Wilfredo Acosta, Sarah Rosewarne, *Producer* Paul Spencer, *Pirate Radio 4 Producer* Jonathan James Moore
DWM Index
104 Feature
178 Archive + Fact File
287 Thrilling Adventures in Time and Space
300 CD review
323 Colin Baker interview
348 Eric Saward interview
349 Archive Extra
Recording Date
10 June 1985 (BH B11)
Factoids
- This six-part radio series was broadcast as part of three three-hour morning shows entitled 'Pirate Radio 4' hosted by DJ Steve Blacknell. A short-lived experiment to attract teenage listeners to Radio 4, it was deemed a failure by critics and the BBC alike.
- Valentine Dyall, more famous to *Doctor Who* viewers as the Black Guardian, died a fortnight after recording this story.
- A *Radio Times* feature (dated 20-26 July 1985) in 'John Craven's Back Pages' accompanied the first two parts of *Slipback*.

Comment
We learn something from this story. We learn that Eric Saward is not Douglas Adams. **9%**

"Appearances are not always deceptive." ~ *The Doctor*

3) *The Paradise of Death*
Barry Letts

Original Transmission
On BBC Radio 5:
Part One
Friday 27 August 1993, 18.30-19.00
Part Two
Friday 3 September 1993, 18.30-19.00
Part Three
Friday 10 September 1993, 18.30-19.00
Part Four
Friday 17 September 1993, 18.30-19.00
Part Five
Friday 24 September 1993, 18.30-19.00

Repeat Transmission
On BBC Radio 2:
Part One
Tuesday 12 April 1994, 19.00-19.30
Part Two
Tuesday 19 April 1994, 19.00-19.30
Part Three
Tuesday 26 April 1994, 19.00-19.30
Part Four
Tuesday 3 May 1994, 18.30-19.00
Part Four (transmitted in error)
Tuesday 10 May 1994, 19.00-19.30
Part Five
Tuesday 17 May 1994, 19.00-19.30
Novelization
Doctor Who - The Paradise of Death by Barry Letts
Paperback:
April 1994, Doctor Who (0426203534 / Alister Pearson)
Soundtrack
1. November 1993, 2 x cassettes (ZBBC 1494 / Photomontage)
2. June 2002, 2 x CDs (0563553235 / Max Ellis)
Music and Sound Effects
July 1993, *Doctor Who: 30 Years at the Radiophonic Workshop*, CD (BBCCD 871 / Photomontage)
Précis
UNIT is called in to investigate a horrific death at Hampstead's new Space World theme park…
Cast
Jon Pertwee (The Doctor), Elisabeth Sladen (Sarah Jane Smith), Nicholas Courtney (Brigadier Lethbridge-Stewart), Peter Miles (Tragan), Harold Innocent (Freeth), Richard Pearce (Jeremy Fitzoliver), Maurice Denham (President), Jane Slavin (Onya), Jonathan Tafler (Waldo), Andrew Wincott (Crestin/Bill/Radio Voice/Ambulance Man/ Man), Dominic Letts (Nobby/Kitson/Wilkins/Soldier), Brian Hall (Grebber/ Reporter), Jillie Meers (Clorinda/ Secretary General of the UN), John Hardwood (General Commanding Unit), John Fleming (Odun/Patrol Leader), Jonathan Tafler (Captain Waldo Rudley), Jane Slavin (Onya), Emma Myant (Greckle), Michael Onslow (Rasco Heldal), David Holt (Medan/Hunter), Julian Rhind Tutt (Echo-Location Operator/Lexhan), Trevor Martin (Kaido/Guard 2/Ungar/Custodian of Data Store/Jenhegger), Philip Anthony (Yallett/Officer of the Day)
Crew
Special Sound Alison Carter, *Spot Effects* Colin Guthrie, *Incidental Music* Peter Howell, *Studio Manager* John Whitehall, *Production Assistant* Dawn Ellis, *Director* Phil Clarke
DWM Index
204   Radio Who: Cast interviews
        Radio review
205   Radio Who: Studio report
212   Novelization review
229   Nicholas Courtney interview
251   Elisabeth Sladen interview
287   Thrilling Adventures in Time and Space
292   CD review
335   Peter Miles interview
349   Archive Extra
Recording Dates
21 May 1993 (MV 7), 24-27 May 1993 (MV 6)
Factoids
- The story was written by Barry Letts, who, as well as being the producer of almost every Jon Pertwee television story, had also co-written *The Dæmons* (59) with Robert Sloman in 1971.
- The CD soundtrack contained slighter more material than the radio broadcast.

Comment
A promising first episode soon descends into a muddled plot riddled with trite, clichéd dialogue and an irritating extra companion in the form of unfunny snob Jeremy Fitzoliver (Richard Pearce). Touted as a slice of '70s nostalgia, it doesn't feel remotely like a Pertwee television story, with the star himself sounding decidedly elderly. Peter Miles and Harold Innocent excel, but somewhere along the line the magic *Doctor Who* ingredient has fallen by the wayside. **50%**

"I had a happy childhood…" ~ Susan Foreman

4) Whatever Happened to…Susan?
Adrian Mourby

Original Transmission
On BBC Radio 4:
Saturday 9 July 1994, 10.00-10.30
DVD
June 2003, on *The Dalek Invasion of Earth* (BBCDVD 1156 / Clayton Hickman)
Précis
The further adventures of the Doctor's granddaughter Susan Foreman…

283

Cast
Jane Asher (Susan), James Grout (Ian Chesterton), June Barrie (Barbara Wright), Eva Haddon (Jo Jones), Andrew Sachs (Temmosus), Peter Woodthorpe (Joey), Becky Harrison (Researcher), Claire Rayner (Herself)
Crew
Producer Brian King
DWM Index
351 Archive Extra
Recording Date
17 May 1994 (BBC Broadcasting House, Bristol)
Factoid
- This was the penultimate episode in a six-part 'mockumentary' series for BBC Radio 4 which featured the hidden sides of such fictional characters as Billy Bunter and Little Lord Fauntleroy.

Comment
Rather odd and not terribly funny spoof documentary. *Doctor Who* anoraks aside, its intended audience is a mystery. **25%**

"An awful lot of nonsense is spoken by people about the Fourth Dimension." ~ *The Doctor*

5) *The Ghosts of N Space*
Barry Letts

Original Transmission
On BBC Radio 2:
Part One
Saturday 20 January 1996, 19.00-19.30
Part Two
Saturday 27 January 1996, 19.00-19.30
Part Three
Saturday 3 February 1996, 19.00-19.30
Part Four
Saturday 10 February 1996, 19.00-19.30
Part Five
Saturday 17 February 1996, 19.00-19.30
Part Six
Saturday 24 February 1996, 19.00-19.30
Repeat Transmission
On BBC Radio 2:
Part One
Tuesday 17 December 1996, 20.30-21.00
Part Two
Tuesday 24 December 1996, 20.30-21.00
Part Three
Tuesday 7 January 1997, 20.30-21.00
Part Four
Tuesday 14 January 1997, 20.30-21.00
Part Five
Tuesday 21 January 1997, 20.30-21.00
Part Six
Tuesday 28 January 1997, 20.30-21.00
Novelization
Doctor Who - The Ghosts of N-Space by Barry Letts (264/16)
Paperback:
February 1995, Doctor Who (0426204344 / Alister Pearson)
Soundtrack
1. February 1996, 2 x cassettes (0563388838 / Photomontage)
2. August 2002, 2 x CDs (0563477016 / Max Ellis)
Précis
The Doctor investigates evil ghost sightings at the Brigadier's great-uncle's Sicilian castle...
Cast
Jon Pertwee (The Doctor), Elisabeth Sladen (Sarah Jane Smith), Nicholas Courtney (Brigadier Lethbridge-Stewart), Richard Pearce (Jeremy Fitzoliver), Stephen Thorne (Max), Sandra Dickinson (Maggie), Harry Towb (Mario), Jonathan Tafler (Clemenza), Don McCorkindale (Don Fabrizzio), David Holt (Nico), (Maggie), Harry Towb (Mario), Deborah Berlin (Louisa), Peter Yapp (Umberto), Joanne Sergeant (Maid), Paul Brooke (Paolo), Gavin Muir (Barone), Jillie Meers (Baronessa/Marcella), Jonathan Keeble (Roberto), Jim Sweeney (Guido)
Crew
Special Sound Alison Carter, *Spot Effects* Colin Guthrie, *Incidental Music* Peter Howell, *Studio Manager* John Whitehall, *Production Assistant* Dawn Ellis, *Director* Phil Clarke
Recording Dates
6-13 November 1994 (MV 6)
DWM Index
222 Studio report
229 Nicholas Courtney interview
237 Cassettes review
251 Elisabeth Sladen interview
287 Thrilling Adventures in Time and Space
293 CD review
351 Archive Extra
Factoid
- When asked to provide a sequel to *The Paradise of Death*, Barry Letts was in the middle of writing his novel *The Ghosts of N-Space* for Virgin Publishing's Missing Adventures series, so he decided to adapt this into the required radio serial.

Comment
If *The Paradise of Death* wasn't exactly perfect, then *The Ghosts of N-Space* fails spectacularly. Its

over-riding fault is in the central concept - ghosts have never existed in the world of *Doctor Who*, and certainly not in the rational-scientific Pertwee era. Secondly, the whole story is just ridiculously convoluted and badly written, and the once-familiar characters are shadows of their former selves, with especial damage being done to the character of the Brigadier, now reduced to the comic sidekick of a Sicilian Mafia boss. Terrible. **15%**

Big Finish Audio Adventures

All double CD releases unless otherwise stated. Producers Gary Russell, Jason Haigh-Ellery, Jacqueline Rayner, and John Ainsworth. Titles listed in release order.

Fifth Doctor: Peter Davison

1) *Phantasmagoria*
Mark Gatiss

Details
October 1999 (1903654092 / James Arnott)
Cast
Peter Davison (The Doctor), Mark Strickson (Turlough), David Walliams (Quincy Flowers), Jonathan Rigby (Edmund Carteret), Mark Gatiss (Jasper Jeake), Jez Fielder (Poltrot), David Ryall (Sir Nikolas Valentine), Steven Wickham (Dr Samuel Holywell), Julia Dalkin (Hannah Fry)
Crew
Music Alistair Lock, *Director* Nicholas Briggs
Précis
The Doctor investigates odd disappearances in 17th century London…
DWM Index
283   Review
333   Mark Gatiss interview
Comment
Clichéd historical adventure played for all its worth by an energetic cast. **80%**

2) *Land of the Dead*
Stephen Cole

Details
January 2000 (1844350649 / Peri Godbold)
Cast
Peter Davison (The Doctor), Sarah Sutton (Nyssa), Andrew Fettes (Gaborik), Lucy Campbell (Monica Lewis), Christopher Scott (Shaun Brett), Neil Roberts (Tulung), Alistair Lock (Supplier)
Crew
Music Nicholas Briggs, *Director* Gary Russell
Précis
A long-dead evil resurfaces in a strange house in Alaska…
DWM Index
288   Review
Comment
Atmospheric runaround hampered by some unconvincing dialogue and a rushed explanation. **53%**

3) *Red Dawn*
Justin Richards

Details
May 2000 (1903654173 / Clayton Hickman)
Cast
Peter Davison (The Doctor), Nicola Bryant (Peri), Robert Jezek (Commander Forbes), Maureen Oakeley (Susan Roberts), Georgia Moffatt (Tanya Webster), Stephen Fewell (Paul Webster), Matthew Brenher (Commander Zzarl), Hylton Collins (Sub-Commander Sstast)
Crew
Music Russell Stone, *Director* Gary Russell
Précis
NASA astronauts encounter a terrible secret in a Martian tomb…
DWM Index
291   Preview
292   Review
Comment
Clunky Ice Warrior potboiler that only warms up towards the end. **43%**

4) Winter For The Adept
Andrew Cartmel

Details
July 2000 (1903654173 / Clayton Hickman)
Cast
Peter Davison (The Doctor), Sarah Sutton (Nyssa), Peter Jurasik (Lieutenant Peter Sandoz), Sally Faulkner (Miss Tremayne), Liz Sutherland (Alison Speers), India Fisher (Peril Bellamy), Hannah Dickinson (Mlle Maupassant), Christopher Webber (Harding Wellman)
Crew
Music Russell Stone, *Director* Gary Russell
Précis
1963, and Nyssa is being haunted by a poltergeist in a snowbound Swiss girls' school...
DWM Index
293 Preview
294 Review
304 India Fisher interview
Comment
An effective blending of *The Amityville Horror* and *Picnic at Hanging Rock*, although there are some deeply silly moments. **59%**

5) Dalek Empire - Part Three: The Mutant Phase
Nicholas Briggs

Details
December 2000 (1903654211 / Clayton Hickman)
Cast
Peter Davison (The Doctor), Sarah Sutton (Nyssa), Christopher Blake (Professor Ptolem), Jared Morgan (Commander Ganatus), Mark Gatiss (Roboman/Professor Karl Hendryk), Andrew Ryan (Albert), Sara Wakefield (Delores), Alistair Lock, Nicholas Briggs (Dalek Voices)
Crew
Music/Director Nicholas Briggs
Précis
In the far future, the Doctor must save the Daleks from their cannibalistic mutated selves...
DWM Index
299 Preview
301 Review
326 Nicholas Briggs interview
Comment
Technically brilliant, this tale of Dalek evolution gone bad falls to pieces in its second half. **65%**

6) Loups-Garoux
Marc Platt

Details
May 2001 (1903654297 / Clayton Hickman)
Cast
Peter Davison (The Doctor), Mark Strickson (Turlough), Nicky Henson (Pieter Stubbs), Sarah Gale (Rosa Caiman), Eleanor Bron (Ileana De Santos), Jane Nurke (Inez), Burt Kwouk (Dr Hayashi), David Hankinson (Anton Lichtfuss), Derek Wright (Jorge), Barnaby Edwards (Victor)
Crew
Music Alistair Lock, *Director* Nicholas Pegg
Précis
At the Rio de Janeiro carnival, the Doctor is shocked to discover werewolves prowling the city...
DWM Index
304 Preview
306 Marc Platt interview
307 Review
Comment
Extremely effective werewolf tale with an exotic backdrop. **80%**

7) The Eye Of The Scorpion
Iain McLaughlin

Details
September 2001 (1903654491 / Clayton Hickman)
Cast
Peter Davison (The Doctor), Peri (Nicola Bryant), Harry Myers (Yanis), Caroline Morris (Erimem), Jonathan Owen (Antranak), Jack Gallagher (Fayum), Steve Perring (Horemshep), Daniel Brennan (Kishik), Mark Wright (Slave)
Crew
Music David Darlington, *Director* Gary Russell
Précis
Landing in Ancient Egypt, the Doctor and Peri come to the aid of Pharoah-to-be Erimem...
DWM Index
308 Preview
311 Review
Comment
Well-paced debut for Erimem. **70%**

8) Primeval
Lance Parkin

Details
November 2001 (1903564513 / Clayton Hickman)
Cast
Peter Davison (The Doctor), Sarah Sutton (Nyssa), Stephen Greif (Kwundar), Susan Penhaligon (Shayla), Ian Hallard (Sabian), Billy Miller (Narthex), Romy Tennant (Anona), Mark Woolgar (Hyrca), Rita Davies (Janneus)
Crew
Music Russell Stone, *Director* Gary Russell
Précis
Nyssa is taken to Traken millennia before she was born, but there's a serpent in this particular paradise…
DWM Index
311   Preview
313   Review
Comment
Quietly accomplished drama, albeit rather sluggish. **58%**

9) Excelis Dawns
Paul Magrs

Details
February 2002 (1903654637 / Lee Binding)
Cast
Peter Davison (The Doctor), Anthony Stewart Head (Lord Grayvorn), Katy Manning (Iris Wildthyme), Patricia Leventon (Mother Superior), Posy Miller (Sister Jolene), Billy Miller (Zombie King)
Crew
Music David Darlington, *Director* Gary Russell
Précis
The Doctor and Iris search the swamp world of Artaris for a mysterious holy relic…
DWM Index
316   Review
319   Excelis Exposed
Comment
Odd BBC Books crossover that's never quite as amusing as it thinks. **35%**

10) Spare Parts
Marc Platt

Details
July 2002 (1903654734 / Clayton Hickman)
Cast
Peter Davison (The Doctor), Sarah Sutton (Nyssa), Sally Knyvette (Doctorman Allan), Pamela Binns (Sisterman Constant), Derren Nesbitt (Thomas Dodd), Paul Copley (Dad), Kathryn Guck (Yvonne Hartley), Jim Hartley (Frank Hartley), Nicholas Briggs (Cyberleader Zheng)
Crew
Music Russell Stone, *Director* Gary Russell
Précis
The Doctor arrives on Mondas to witness the birth of the Cybermen…
DWM Index
320   Preview
322   Review
Comment
Genesis of the Cybermen, beautifully written, with breathtaking sound design. **94%**

11) The Church And The Crown
Cavan Scott and Mark Wright

Details
November 2002 (1903654750 / Clayton Hickman)
Cast
Peter Davison (The Doctor), Nicola Bryant (Peri), Caroline Morris (Erimem), Andrew Mackay (King Louis XIII), Michael Shallard (Cardinal Richelieu), Marcus Hutton (Duke of Buckingham), Peter John (Delmarre), Andy Coleman (Rouffet), Wendy Abiston (De Chevreuse), Robert Curbishley (Captain Morand)
Crew
Music Russell Stone, *Director* Gary Russell
Précis
The Tardis arrives in 17th century Paris amidst skirmishes between Louis XIII and Cardinal Richelieu…
DWM Index
324   Preview
326   Review
Comment
Tongue-in-cheek swashbuckler. **82%**

12) Nekromanteia
Austen Atkinson

Details
February 2003 (1844350231 / Lee Binding)
Cast
Peter Davison (The Doctor), Nicola Bryant (Peri), Caroline Morris (Erimem), Gilly Cohen (Jal Dor Kal), Glyn Owen (Harlon), Kerry Skinner (Cochrane), Ivor Danvers (Marr), Kate Brown (Tallis), Nigel Fairs (Rom), Andrew Fettes (Salaysian), Simon Williams (Paul Addison)
Crew
Music and Sound Design David Darlington, *Director* John Ainsworth
Précis
The Tardis crew become embroiled in a war for an immensely powerful relic on the planet Talderun...
DWM Index
327 Preview
329 Review
Comment
Unoriginal occultic tale with muddled ideas. **38%**

13) Creatures of Beauty
Nicholas Briggs

Details
May 2003 (1844350266 / Paul Burley)
Cast
Peter Davison (The Doctor), Sarah Sutton (Nyssa), David Daker (Gilbrook), David Mallinson (Brodlik), Jemma Churchill (Lady Forleon), Nigel Hastings (Quain), Michael Smiley (Seedleson), Philip Wolff (Murone), Emma Manton (Veline), Nicholas Briggs (The Koteem)
Crew
Music and Sound Design/Director Nicholas Briggs
Précis
Nyssa has not gone unnoticed on Veln, a planet whose populace is suffering a disfiguring disease...
DWM Index
331 Preview
333 Review
Comment
Basic morality tale told in reverse. **70%**

14) Omega
Nev Fountain

Details
August 2003 (1844350290 / Clayton Hickman)
Cast
Peter Davison (The Doctor), Ian Collier (Omega), Caroline Munro (Sentia), Patrick Duggan (Professor Ertikus), Hugo Myatt (Daland), Conrad Westmaas (Tarpov), Jim Sangster (Zagreus), Faith Kent (Maven), Anita Elias (Glinda)
Crew
Music and Sound Design ERS, *Director* Gary Russell
Précis
A sightseeing tour to the Sector of Forgotten Souls soon encounters an old enemy...
DWM Index
334 Preview
337 Review
Comment
Whimsically iconoclastic 'comedy' that trivialises an arch-villain for no good reason. **40%**

15) The Axis of Insanity
Simon Furman

Details
April 2004 (1844350940 / Lee Binding)
Cast
Peter Davison (The Doctor), Nicola Bryant (Peri), Caroline Morris (Erimem), Roy North (Overseer), Garrick Hagon (Jester), Marc Danbury (Tog), Stephen Mansfield (Bird Trader), Daniel Hogarth (Carnival Barker)
Crew
Music Andy Hardwick, *Sound Design* Gareth Jenkins, *Director* Gary Russell
Précis
Axis has been stabilising the Universe for aeons, but now its control is failing...
DWM Index
342 Preview
346 Review
Comment
Celestial Toymaker-style shenanigans in a brilliantly realized audio nightmare. **85%**

16) The Roof of the World
Adrian Rigelsford

Details
August 2004 (1844350975 / Lee Binding)
Cast
Peter Davison (The Doctor), Nicola Bryant (Peri), Caroline Morris (Erimem), Edward de Souza (Lord Mortimer Davey), William Franklyn (Pharoah Amenhotep II), Sylvester Morand (General Bruce), Alan Cox (John Matthews)
Crew
Sound Design Gareth Jenkins, *Director* Gary Russell
Précis
The Himalayas, 1917, and a mysterious entity is lying in wait for the Doctor…
DWM Index
346 Preview
349 Review
Comment
Episodic runaround which compares unfavourably with the similar, but more effective, television Yeti stories. **45%**

17) The Game
Darin Henry

Details
February 2005 (1844351009 / Lee Binding)
Cast
Peter Davison (The Doctor), Sarah Sutton (Nyssa), Ursula Burton (Faye Davis), Robert Curbishley (Ockle Dirr), Gregory Donaldon (Bela Destry), Christopher Ellison (Morian), Andrew Lothian (Hollis Az), Jonathan Pearce (Garny Diblick), William Russell (Lord Darzil Carlisle), Dickon Tolson (Sharz Sevix)
Crew
Music and Sound Design ERS, *Director* Gary Russell
Précis
The planet Cray's entire future depends on a single game of Naxy…
DWM Index
353 Preview
Comment
Overlong but enjoyable sporting hokum. **67%**

18) Three's a Crowd
Colin Brake

Details
May 2005 (1844351440 / Stuart Manning)
Cast
Peter Davison (The Doctor), Nicola Bryant (Peri), Caroline Morris (Erimem), Deborah Watling (Auntie), Richard Gauntlett (General Makra'Thon), Charles Pemberton (Butler), Lucy Beresford (Bellip), Richard Unwin (Vidler), Daniel Hogarth (Laroq), Sara Carver (Khellian Queen)
Crew
Music and Sound Design David Darlington, *Director* Gary Russell
Précis
Things look bleak for the inhabitants of Earth Colony Phoenix…
DWM Index
357 Preview
Comment
Clichéd 'base under siege' story with generic monsters. **40%**

Sixth Doctor: Colin Baker

1) Whispers of Terror
Justin Richards

Details
November 1999 (1844350649 / James Arnott)
Crew
Colin Baker (The Doctor), Nicola Bryant (Peri), Lisa Bowerman (Beth Pernell), Matthew Brehner (Visteen Krane), Nick Scovell (Detective Berkeley), Peter Miles (Curator Gantman), Steffan Boje (Hans Stengard), Hylton Collins (Computer Voice), Mark Trotman (Miles Napton), Rebecca Jenkins (Car Computer)
Crew
Incidental Music Nicholas Briggs, *Director* Gary Russell
Précis
In the Museum of Aural Antiquities, a politician's death heralds the start of a terrifying manifestation…
DWM Index
286 Review
Comment
Eerie ghost story with excellent sound design makes this a perfect story for audio. **78%**

2) The Marian Conspiracy
Jacqueline Rayner

Details
March 2000 (1903654173 / Clayton Hickman)
Cast
Colin Baker (The Doctor), Maggie Stables (Evelyn Smythe), Sean Jackson (George Crow), Gary Russell (John Wilson), Jez Fielder (William Leaf), Jo Castleton (Lady Sarah), Anah Ruddin (The Queen), Nicholas Pegg (Reverend Thomas), Barnaby Edwards (Francois de Noailles), Alistair Lock (Royal Guard)
Crew
Incidental Music Alistair Lock, *Director* Gary Russell
Précis
The Doctor travels back to Elizabethan London to restore Evelyn's fading time-line...
DWM Index
290   Review
Comment
Talky discourse on the true nature of Queen Elizabeth I, with a plot liberally borrowed from *Back to the Future*. **45%**

3) The Spectre Of Lanyon Moor
Nicholas Pegg

Details
June 2000 (1844350711 / Clayton Hickman)
Cast
Colin Baker (The Doctor), Maggie Stables (Evelyn), Nicholas Courtney (Brigadier), Susan Jameson (Mrs Moniyhan), Barnaby Edwards (Philip Ludgate), Toby Longworth (Professor Morgan), James Bolam (Sir Archibald Flint), Helen Goldwyn (Nikki), Nicholas Pegg (Captain Ashforde)
Crew
Music Alistair Lock, *Director* Nicholas Pegg
Précis
The Doctor finds strange creatures stalking the windswept moors near a remote Cornish village...
DWM Index
292   Preview
       Studio Report
293   Review
Comment
More than a hint of *Terror of the Zygons* in a chilling tale with strong performances. **80%**

4) Dalek Empire - Part Two: The Apocalypse Element
Stephen Cole

Details
August 2000, (1903654025 / Clayton Hickman)
Cast
Colin Baker (The Doctor), Lalla Ward (Romana II), Maggie Stables (Evelyn Smythe), Michael Wade (The President), Anthony Keetch (Coordinator Vansell), Andrew Fettes (Vrint/Commander Reldath), Karen Henson (Monitor Trinkett), James Campbell (Assistant Officer Ensac), Andrea Newland (Commander Vorna), Toby Longworth (Monan Host), Nicholas Briggs, Alistair Lock (Dalek Voices)
Crew
Incidental Music/Director Nicholas Briggs
Précis
The Daleks invade Gallifrey...
DWM Index
294   Preview
295   Review
326   Nicholas Briggs interview
Comment
A noisy, attention-seeking mess, although sporadically entertaining. **43%**

5) The Holy Terror
Robert Shearman

Details
November 2000 (1903654106 / Clayton Hickman and Chris Gregory)
Cast
Colin Baker (The Doctor), Robert Jezek (Frobisher), Dan Hogarth (Captain Sejanus), Sam Kelly (Eugene Tacitus), Roberta Taylor (Berengaria), Helen Punt (Livilla), Peter Guinness (Childeric), Stefan Atkinson (Pepin), Peter Sowerbutts (Clovis), Bruce Mann (Arnulf)
Crew
Music Russell Stone, *Director* Nicholas Pegg
Précis
In the bizarre medieval fiefdom of Pepin VII, Frobisher is mistaken for an emissary from heaven...
DWM Index
298   Preview
299   Review
318   Robert Jezek interview
349   Robert Shearman interview

Comment
A typically witty script by Shearman, somewhat let down by an unnecessarily surreal conclusion. **77%**

6) Bloodtide
Jonathan Morris

Details
June 2001 (1903654327 / Clayton Hickman)
Cast
Colin Baker (The Doctor), Maggie Stables (Evelyn Smythe), Miles Richardson (Charles Darwin), George Telfer (Captain Fitzroy), Julian Harries (Governor Lawson), Daniel Hogarth (S'rel Tulok), Helen Goldwyn (Scientist Sh'vak), Jez Fielder (Lokan), Jane Goddard (Greta Rodriguez)
Crew
Music Alistair Lock, *Director* Gary Russell
Précis
In 1835, an exiled Silurian turns up on the Galapagos Islands at the same time as Charles Darwin…
DWM Index
305 Preview
308 Review
Comment
Extremely effective Silurian tale with intelligent characterization and vivid sound design. **90%**

7) Project: Twilight

Cavan Scott and Mark Wright
Details
August 2001 (1903654459 / Clayton Hickman)
Cast
Colin Baker (The Doctor), Maggie Stables (Evelyn Smythe), Holly de Jong (Amelia Doory), Rob Dixon (Reggie Mead), Rosie Cavaliero (Cassie), Stephen Chance (Nimrod), Rupert Booth (Dr William Abberton), Kate Hadley (Nurse), Mark Wright (Mr Deeks), Daniel Wilson (Eddie)
Crew
Music Jane Elphinston and Jim Mortimore, *Director* Gary Russell
Précis
The Doctor discovers vampires in South London…
DWM Index
307 Preview
309 Review

Comment
The Sweeney meets *Ultraviolet* with predictably gruesome results. **67%**

8) The One Doctor
Gareth Roberts and Clayton Hickman

Details
December 2001 (1903654564 / Clayton Hickman)
Cast
Colin Baker (The Doctor), Bonnie Langford (Melanie Bush), Christopher Biggins (Banto Zame), Clare Buckfield (Sally-Anne Stubbins), Matt Lucas (The Cylinder), Adam Buxton (Assembler One), Stephen Fewell (Councillor Potikol), Nicholas Pegg (Mentos), Jane Goddard (The Questioner), Mark Wright (Guard)
Crew
Music Alister Lock, *Director* Gary Russell
Précis
A conman and his girlfriend are masquerading as the Doctor and his lovely assistant…
DWM Index
312 Preview
314 Review
Comment
Gloriously funny pantomime with masses of perfectly judged jokes. **97%**

9) Excelis Rising
David A McIntee

Details
April 2002 (1903654645 / Lee Binding)
Cast
Colin Baker (The Doctor), Anthony Stewart Head (Reeve Maupassant), Charles Kay (The Curator), James Lailey (Minister Pryce), Nicky Goldie (Inquisitor Danby), Patricia Leventon (Mother Superior), Rupert Laight (Solomon), Toby Walton (Thief)
Crew
Music David Darlington, *Director* Edward Salt
Précis
On Artaris, mysterious deaths are caused by a holy relic at the Imperial Museum…
DWM Index
318 Review
319 Excelis Exposed
343 David A McIntee interview

Comment
The Sixth Doctor is on fine form in this somewhat so-so effort. **50%**

10) ...ish
Philip Pascoe

Details
August 2002 (1903654734 / Clayton Hickman)
Cast
Colin Baker (The Doctor), Nicola Bryant (Peri), Moray Treadwell (Book), Marie Collett (Professor Osefa), Chris Eley (Warren), Oliver Hume (Cawdrey)
Crew
Music Neil Clappison, *Director* Nicholas Briggs
Précis
A professor is murdered at an intergalactic lexicographical conference...
DWM Index
321 Preview
Comment
Deliberately overplayed essay on the evolution of language; startlingly effective. **88%**

11) *The Sandman*
Simon A Forward

Details
October 2002 (1903654769 / Lee Binding and Chris Gregory)
Cast
Colin Baker (The Doctor), Maggie Stables (Evelyn Smythe), Anneke Wills (Director Nrosha), Ian Hogg (General Voshkar), Robin Bowerman (Mr Mordecan), Stephanie Colburn (Nintaru), Mark Donovan (Orchestrator Shol), Mark Wharton (Commander Brel)
Crew
Music Russell Stone, *Director* Jason Haigh-Ellery
Précis
The Doctor's appearance rekindles an ancient fear in the lizard-like Galyari...
DWM Index
322 Anneke Wills interview
323 Preview
      Ian Hogg interview
325 Review
Comment
The Sixth Doctor as evil manipulator - hardly a surprise. **50%**

12) *Jubilee*
Rob Shearman

Details
January 2003 (1844350223 / Clayton Hickman)
Cast
Colin Baker (The Doctor), Maggie Stables (Evelyn Smythe), Martin Jarvis (Rochester), Rosalind Ayres (Miriam), Steven Elder (Farrow), Kai Simmons (Lamb), Jane Goddard, Robert Shearman (TV Presenters), Jack Galagher, Georgina Carter (Movie Stars), Nicholas Briggs (Dalek Voices)
Crew
Music and Sound Design Nicholas Briggs, *Directors* Nicholas Briggs, Robert Shearman
Précis
The Doctor lands in the Tower of London and finds the Daleks have perverted the course of history...
DWM Index
326 Preview
      Martin Jarvis interview
      Nicholas Briggs interview
328 Review
349 Robert Shearman interview
Comment
Precursor to Season 27's *Dalek* with annoyingly loopy characters and situations. **65%**

13) *Doctor Who And The Pirates*
(Or: *The Lass That Lost A Sailor*)
Jacqueline Rayner

Details
April 2003 (1884435024X / Lee Binding)
Cast
Colin Baker (The Doctor), Maggie Stables (Evelyn Smythe), Bill Oddie (Red Jasper), Dan Barratt (Jem), Helen Goldwyn (Sally), Nicholas Pegg (Swan), Mark Siney (Mr Merryweather), Timothy Sutton (Mate/Sailor/Pirate)
Crew
Music Timothy Sutton (with apologies to Arthur Sullivan), *Sound Design* David Darlington, *Director* Barnaby Edwards
Précis
The Doctor and Evelyn cheer up a student by spinning her a swashbuckling tale of piratical daring-do...

DWM Index
329 Preview
332 Review
Comment
Strangely affecting Gilbert and Sullivan pastiche with psychological overtones. **89%**

14) Project: Lazarus
Cavan Scott and Mark Wright

Details
June 2003 (1844350274 / Lee Binding)
Cast
Colin Baker (The Doctor), Maggie Stables (Evelyn Smythe), Sylvester McCoy (The Doctor), Stephen Chance (Nimrod), Rosie Cavaliero (Cassie), Emma Collier (Oracle), Adam Woodroffe (Sergeant Frith), Ingrid Evans (Dr Crumpton), Vidar Magnussen (Professor Harket)
Crew
Music Andy Hardwicke, *Director* Gary Russell
Précis
A secret research facility on Dartmoor is conducting dangerous experiments with alien technology…
DWM Index
332 Preview
335 Review
Comment
Belated sequel to *Project: Twilight* which cleverly subverts expectations. **77%**

15) Davros
Lance Parkin

Details
September 2003 (1844350304 / Clayton Hickman)
Cast
Colin Baker (The Doctor), Terry Molloy (Davros), Arnold Baynes (Bernard Horsfall), Lorraine Baynes (Wendy Padbury), Eddie de Oliveira (Willis), Ruth Sillers (Kimberly Todd), Katarina Olsson (Shan)
Crew
Music and Sound Design Jim Mortimore, *Director* Gary Russell
Précis
A new era beckons for humanity, provided a certain crippled genius can help…

DWM Index
335 Preview
338 Review
Comment
Brilliant character study of Davros before and after the accident that crippled him. **92%**

16) The Wormery
Stephen Cole and Paul Magrs

Details
November 2003 (1844350339 / Lee Binding)
Cast
Colin Baker (The Doctor), Katy Manning (Iris Wildthyme), Bianca (Maria McErlane), Paul Clayton (Paul), Jane McFarlane (Mickey), James Campbell (Allis & Ballis), Mark Donovan (Sturmer), Ian Brooker (Barman)
Crew
Music Jason Loborik, *Sound Design* Ian Potter, *Director* Gary Russell
Précis
In Bianca's nightclub, the Doctor joins Iris Wildthyme on a (drunken) secret mission…
DWM Index
337 Preview
340 Review
Comment
Fans of Iris Wildthyme and Katy Manning will lap this up; others may be less keen. **45%**

17) Arrangements for War
Paul Sutton

Details
May 2004 (1844350959 / Lee Binding)
Cast
Colin Baker (The Doctor), Maggie Stables (Evelyn Smythe), Gabriel Woolf (Governor Rossiter), Philip Bretherton (Suskind), Geoffrey Leesley (Minister Mortund), Katarina Olsson (Princess Krisztina), Lewis Rae (Corporal Reid), Kraig Thornber (Commander Pokol)
Crew
Music and Sound Design Steve Foxon, *Director* Gary Russell
Précis
The Doctor unknowingly upsets an arranged marriage between two warring states…

DWM Index
343 Preview
347 Review
Comment
Mills and Boon love story with a feeble script and lifeless performances. **20%**

18) Medicinal Purposes
Robert Ross

Details
August 2004 (1844350983 / Lee Binding)
Cast
Colin Baker (The Doctor), Maggie Stables (Evelyn Smythe), Leslie Phillips (Dr Robert Knox), David Tennant (Daft Jamie), Glenna Morrison (Mary Patterson), Kevin O'Leary (William Burke), Tom Farrelly (Billy Hare), Janie Booth)
Crew
Music and Sound Design David Darlington, *Director* Gary Russell
Précis
Edinburgh, 1827, and Burke and Hare are busy at their work…
DWM Index
347 Preview
351 Review
Comment
Atmospheric Victorian melodrama with a plot that doesn't bear close scrutiny. **70%**

19) The Juggernauts
Scott Alan Woodard

Details
January 2005 (1844351017 / Lee Binding)
Cast
Colin Baker (The Doctor), Bonnie Langford (Melanie Bush), Terry Molloy (Davros), Bindya Solanki (Sonali), Klaus White (Geoff), Peter Forbe (Kryson), Paul Grunert (Brauer), Julia Houghton (Loewen), Nick Briggs (Mechonoid Voices/Dalek Voices)
Crew
Music and Sound Design Steve Foxon, *Director* Gary Russell
Précis
On the colony world of Lethe, Davros is creating a new race of robots…

DWM Index
352 Preview
354 Review
Comment
Intense continuity-fest but, albeit done with real enthusiasm. **85%**

20) Catch-1782
Alison Lawson

Details
April 2005 (1844351351 / Lee Binding)
Cast
Colin Baker (The Doctor), Bonnie Langford (Melanie Bush), Keith Drinkel (Henry Hallam), Jillie Meers (Mrs McGregor), Michael Chance (Dr Wallace), Ian Fairbairn (Professor David Munro), Rhiannon Meades (Rachel), Derek Benfield (John Hallam)
Crew
Music Russell Stone, *Sound Design* ERS, *Director* Gary Russell
Précis
Strange things are happening with time at a Berkshire scientific institute…
DWM Index
355 Preview
357 Review
Comment
Slow-moving time paradox tale, but quite well played. **45%**

Seventh Doctor: Sylvester McCoy

1) The Fearmonger
Jonathan Blum

Details
February 2000 (1844350444 / Clayton Hickman)
Cast
Sylvester McCoy (The Doctor), Sophie Aldred (Ace), Jack Gallagher (Alexsandr Karadjic), Mark McDonnell (Walter Jacobs), John Ainsworth (Hospital Tannoy Voice), Jonathan Clarkson (Paul Tanner), Hugh Walters (Roderick Allingham), Vince Henderson (Mick Thompson), Jacqueline Pearce (Sherilyn Harper)

Crew
Music Alistair Lock, *Director* Gary Russell
Précis
The New Britannia Party has infected Britain with its racial hatred, and awoken an ancient evil...
DWM Index
289   Review
Comment
Dreary and formulaic 'what if?' scenario with a heavy-handed anti-racist message. **41%**

2) Dalek Empire - Part One: The Genocide Machine
Mike Tucker

Details
April 2000 (184435069X / Clayton Hickman)
Cast
Sylvester McCoy (The Doctor), Sophie Aldred (Ace), Louise Falkner (Bev Tarrant), Bruce Montague (Chief Librarian Elgin), Nicholas Briggs (Cataloguer Prink), Daniel Gabriel (Rappell)
Crew
Music/Director Nicholas Briggs
Précis
The Daleks invade a state-of-the art data storage facility on the planet Kar-Charrat...
DWM Index
288   Return of the Daleks
291   Review
326   Nicholas Briggs interview
330   Mike Tucker and Robert Perry interview
Comment
Rather unlikely tale of a water-based filing system redeemed by vibrant Dalek action and excellent sound design. **85%**

3) The Fires Of Vulcan
Steve Lyons

Details
September 2000 (1903654025 / Clayton Hickman)
Cast
Sylvester McCoy (The Doctor), Bonnie Langford (Melanie Bush), Gemma Bissix (Aglae), Nicky Goldie (Valeria Hedone), Andy Coleman (Popidius Celsinus), Lisa Hollander (Eumachia), Steven Wickham (Murranus), Robert Curbishly (Tibernus), Anthony Keetch (Professor Scarlini), Karen Henson (Captain Muriel Frost)
Crew
Music Alistair Lock, *Director* Gary Russell
Précis
The Tardis lands in Pompeii prior to the eruption of Vesuvius...
DWM Index
295   Preview
296   Review
Comment
Potentially exciting story spoilt by mundane history lessons and an unnecessary time paradox subplot. **35%**

4) The Shadow Of The Scourge
Paul Cornell

Details
October 2000 (1903654203 / Clayton Hickman)
Cast
Sylvester McCoy (The Doctor), Sophie Aldred (Ace), Lisa Bowerman (Bernice Summerfield), Michael Piccarilli (Dr Michael Pembroke), Holly King (Annie Carpenter), Nigel Fairs (Gary Williams), Lennox Greaves (Brian Hughes), Caroline Burns-Cook (Mary Hughes), Peter Trapani (Scourge Leader)
Crew
Music Alistair Lock, *Director* Gary Russell
Précis
A temporal experiment in a Kent hotel leads to the arrival of the fearsome insectoid Scourge...
DWM Index
296   Preview
297   Review
Comment
New Adventures crossover with the usual gore and guilt. **70%**

5) Dust Breeding
Mike Tucker

Details
July 2001 (1903654297 / Clayton Hickman)
Cast
Sylvester McCoy (The Doctor), Sophie Aldred (Ace), Louise Faulkner (Bev Tarrant), Ian Ricketts (Guthrie), Caroline John (Madame Salvadori), Mark Donovan (Klemp), Geoffrey Beevers (The Master), Johnson Willis (Damien Pierson)
Crew
Music Russell Stone, *Director* Gary Russell

Précis
The Krill are set to rampage through an artists' colony on the dust-world of Duchamp 331...
DWM Index
306   Preview
307   Review
311   Geoffrey Beevers interview
330   Mike Tucker and Robert Perry interview
Comment
An impressive audio debut for Geoffrey Beevers' Master, less so for the Krill. **82%**

6) Colditz
Steve Lyons

Details
October 2001 (1903654475 / Clayton Hickman)
Cast
Sylvester McCoy (The Doctor), Sophie Aldred (Ace), Tracey Childs (Klein), Nicholas Young (Bill Gower), Toby Longworth (Julius Schäfer), David Tennant (Feldwebel Kurtz), Peter Rae (Timothy Wilkins)
Crew
Music Toby Richards, *Director* Gary Russell
Précis
Soon after D-Day, the Tardis materializes in the courtyard of Colditz Castle...
DWM Index
310   Preview
312   Review
Comment
Lazy story covering well-trodden ground. **28%**

7) Excelis Decays
Craig Hinton

Details
June 2002 (1903654653 / Lee Binding)
Cast
Sylvester McCoy (The Doctor), Anthony Stewart Head (Lord Vaughan Sutton), Ian Collier (Commisar Erco Sallis), Yee Jee Tso (Major Jal Brant), Patricia Leventon (Mother Superior), Stuart Piper (Mattias), Penelope McDonald (Jancis)
Crew
Music David Darlington, *Director* Gary Russell
Précis
A vicious totalitarian regime is at war with the planet Artaris...

DWM Index
319   Excelis Exposed
321   Review
Comment
Orwellian dystopia of a rather predictable kind. **53%**

8) The Rapture
Joseph Lidster

Details
September 2002 (1903654742 / Clayton Hickman)
Cast
Sylvester McCoy (The Doctor), Sophie Aldred (Ace/McShane), Tony Blackburn (DJ), Matthew Brenher (Jude), Neil Henry (Gabriel), Carlos Riera (Gustavo), David John (Liam), Anne Bird (Caitriona), Daniel Wilson (Brian), Jeremy James (Bouncer)
Crew
Music Jim Mortimore and Jane Elphinston with Simon Robinson and Feel Summery, *Director* Jason Haigh-Ellery
Précis
Youthful clubbers on the holiday island of Ibiza are unaware of the terrible danger they're in...
DWM Index
322   Preview
324   Review
Comment
A fantastic premise spoilt by banal characters, dubious casting and terrible acting. **43%**

9) Bang-Bang-A-Boom!
Gareth Roberts and Clayton Hickman

Details
December 2002 (1903654777 / Clayton Hickman)
Cast
Sylvester McCoy (The Doctor), Bonnie Langford (Melanie Bush), Sabina Franklyn (Dr Eleanor Harcourt), Graeme Garden (Professor Ivor Fassbinder), Vidar Magnussen (Lieutenant Strindberg), Nickolas Grace (Mr Loozly), Patricia Quinn (Queen Angvia), Anthony Spargo (Nicky Newman), Jane Goddard (Geri), David Tughan (Commentator Logan)

Crew
Music Andy Hardwicke, *Sound Design* Andy Hardwicke and Gareth Jenkins, *Director* Nicholas Pegg
Précis
Murder stalks the giant space station *Dark Space 8*, venue of the Intergalactic Song Contest…
DWM Index
325 Preview
327 Review
Comment
Vaguely disappointing parody of the Eurovision Song Contest, not a patch on the authors' *The One Doctor*. **72%**

10) The Dark Flame
Trevor Baxendale

Details
March 2003 (1844350258 / Lee Binding)
Cast
Sylvester McCoy (The Doctor), Sophie Aldred (Ace), Lisa Bowerman (Bernice Summerfield), Michael Praed (Slyde), Andrew Westfield (Remnex), Hannah Smith (Lomar), Steven Wickham (Joseph/Victor), Toby Longworth (Broke)
Crew
Music Gareth Jenkins, *Sound Design* Andy Hardwick, *Director* Jason Haigh-Ellery
Précis
On Orbos, the moon of Marren Alpha, the long-dormant Dark Flame cult is very much alive…
DWM Index
328 Preview
331 Review
Comment
New Adventures homage along predictable lines. **65%**

11) Flip-Flop
Jonathan Morris

Details
July 2003 (1844350282 / Lee Binding and Chris Gregory)
Cast
Sylvester McCoy (The Doctor), Bonnie Langford (Melanie Bush), Richard Gibson (Mitchell), Pamela Miles (Bailey), Francis Magee (Stewart), Audrey Schoellhammer (Reed), Trevor Littledale (Potter), Trevor Martin (Professor Capra), Daniel Hogarth (Slithergees)

Crew
Music and Sound Design David Darlington, *Director* Gary Russell
Précis
Two Christmas Eves on the colony world of Puxatornee, and two completely different histories…
DWM Index
333 Preview
336 Review
Comment
Clever-clever time paradox tale with no beginning, middle or end that rewards repeated listening. **87%**

12) Master
Joseph Lidster

Details
October 2003 (1844350312 / Clayton Hickman)
Cast
Sylvester McCoy (The Doctor), Geoffrey Beevers (Dr John Smith/The Master), Philip Madoc (Victor Schaeffer), Anne Ridler (Jacqueline Schaeffer), Daniel Barzotti (Man), Charlie Hayes (Jade), Joe Bassett (Child)
Crew
Music and Sound Design David Darlington, *Director* Gary Russell
Précis
Dr John Smith invites his two closest friends to dinner, but the evening ends in disaster…
DWM Index
336 Preview
339 Review
Comment
An atmospheric Edwardian ghost story with Geoffrey Beevers on fine form. **90%**

13) The Harvest
Dan Abnett

Details
June 2004 (1844350967 / Lee Binding)
Cast
Sylvester McCoy (The Doctor), Sophie Aldred (Ace), Philip Olivier (Hex), Janie Booth (System), William Boyde (Subject One), Richard Derrington (Dr Richard Farrer), Mark Donovan (Polk), Paul Lacoux (Dr Mark Mathias), David Warwick (David Garnier)

Crew
Music and Sound Design David Darlington, *Director* Gary Russell
Précis
Strange experiments are taking place in a futuristic London hospital…
DWM Index
344 Preview
348 Review
Comment
A good introduction for Hex in a neat, comic-strip-style adventure with some great twists. **78%**

14) Dreamtime
Simon A Forward

Details
March 2005 (184435136X / Lee Binding)
Cast
Sylvester McCoy (The Doctor), Sophie Aldred (Ace), Philip Olivier (Hex), Tamzin Griffin (Vresha), Jef Higgins (Whitten), Brigid Lohrey (Wahn), Josephine Mackerras (Toomey), Andrew Peisley (Mulyan), Steffan Rhodri (Korshal), John Scholes (Baiame)
Crew
Music and Sound Design Steve Foxon, *Director* Gary Russell
Précis
An ancient city travels through space, inhabited by stone ghosts…
DWM Index
354 Preview
357 Review
Comment
Unsuccessful blend of SF and magic with resistible performances. **30%**

15) Unregenerate!
David A McIntee

Details
June 2005 (1844351580 / Lee Binding)
Cast
Sylvester McCoy (The Doctor), Bonnie Langford (Melanie Bush), Jennie Linden (Professor Klyst), Hugh Hemmings (Johannes Rausch), Gail Clayton (Rigan), Jamie Sandford (Louis), John Aston (Louis 2), Sam Peter Jackson (Shokra), Toby Longworth (Cabbie)

Crew
Music and Sound Design Ian Potter, *Director* John Ainsworth
Précis
You don't have to be mad to be in the Klyst Institute, but it helps…
DWM Index
358 Preview
Comment
Disturbing psychological drama from the same writing school as *Ghost Light*. **70%**

Eighth Doctor: Paul McGann

1) Storm Warning
Alan Barnes

Details
January 2001 (1903654246 / Clayton Hickman)
Transmission
On BBC Radio 7:
6-27 August 2005, 18.30-19.00
Cast
Paul McGann (The Doctor), India Fisher (Charley), Gareth Thomas (Lord Tamworth), Nicholas Pegg (Lieutenant-Colonel Frayling), Barnaby Edwards (Rathbone), Hylton Collins (Chief Steward Weeks), Helen Goldwyn (The Triskele)
Crew
Music Alistair Lock, *Director* Gary Russell
Précis
On the maiden voyage of a giant airship in 1930, the Doctor is attacked by creatures from the Vortex…
DWM Index
294 Studio Report
300 Preview
302 Review
304 India Fisher interview
Comment
After an uncertain start, the Eighth Doctor's first audio adventure soon falls into its stride. **84%**

2) Sword Of Orion
Nicholas Briggs

Details
February 2001 (1903654157 / Clayton Hickman)
Transmission
On BBC Radio 7:
3-24 September 2005, 18.30-19.00
Cast
Paul McGann (The Doctor), India Fisher (Charley), Michelle Livingstone (Deeva), Bruce Montague (Grash), Helen Goldwyn (Chev), Ian Marr (Ike), Hylton Collins (Vol), Toby Longworth (Kelsey), Nicholas Briggs, Alistair Lock (Cybermen)
Crew
Music Nicholas Briggs, *Director* Nicholas Briggs
Précis
The crew of a Garazone salvage ship make an unpleasant discovery on a deserted star destroyer...
DWM Index
301 Preview
303 Review
304 India Fisher interview
Comment
Based on an old fan-produced audio adventure, this is standard seen-it-all-before Cyber fare. **65%**

3) The Stones Of Venice
Paul Magrs

Details
March 2001 (1903654254 / Clayton Hickman)
Transmission
On BBC Radio 7:
1-22 October 2005, 18.30-19.00
Cast
Paul McGann (The Doctor), India Fisher (Charley), Michael Sheard (Duke Orsino), Nick Scovell (Churchwell), Barnaby Edwards (Pietro), Elaine Ives-Cameron (Ms Lavish), Mark Gatiss (Vincenzo)
Crew
Music Russell Stone, *Director* Gary Russell
Précis
Under the dictatorship of Duke Orsino, 23rd century Venice is about to be swept beneath the waves...
DWM Index
302 Preview
    Michael Sheard interview
304 Review

Comment
Talky discourses on art and culture dominate an inappropriately dry story. **50%**

4) Minuet In Hell
Alan W Lear and Gary Russell

Details
April 2001 (190365405X / Clayton Hickman)
Cast
Paul McGann (The Doctor), India Fisher (Charley), Nicholas Courtney (Brigadier Lethbridge-Stewart), Robert Jezek (Brigham Elisha Dashwood), Morgan Deare (Senator Waldo Pickering), Helen Goldwyn (Becky Lee), Maureen Oakeley (Dr Dale Pargeter), Nicholas Briggs (Gideon Crane)
Crew
Music William Allen, *Director* Nicholas Briggs
Précis
The Doctor is locked up in a mental asylum in the 51st American state of Malebolgia...
DWM Index
294 Studio Report
303 Preview
305 Review
Comment
Strangely compelling, if overlong, character study with a well-crafted storyline. **85%**

5) Invaders From Mars
Mark Gatiss

Details
January 2002 (1903654572 / Clayton Hickman)
Transmission
On BBC Radio 7:
29 October-19 November 2005, 18.30-19.00
Cast
Paul McGann (The Doctor), India Fisher (Charley Pollard),Simon Pegg (Don Chaney), Jessica Stevenson (Glory Bee), David Benson (Orson Welles), Paul Putner (Bix Biro), Jonathan Rigby (John Houseman), John Arthur (Cosmo Devine), Mark Benton (Ellis), Ian Hallard (Mouse)
Crew
Music Alistair Lock, *Director* Gary Russell
Précis
Arriving on Broadway on the eve of WWII, the Doctor judges that an alien invasion is taking place...

DWM Index
313 Preview
315 Review
333 Mark Gatiss interview
335 Mark Gatiss interview
Comment
Neat concept, extremely well done. **85%**

6) *The Chimes Of Midnight*
Robert Shearman

Details
February 2002 (1903654580 / Clayton Hickman)
Cast
Paul McGann (The Doctor), India Fisher (Charley Pollard), Louise Rolfe (Edith), Lennox Greaves (Mr Shaughessy), Sue Wallace (Mrs Baddeley), Robert Curbishley (Frederick), Juliet Warner (Mary)
Crew
Music Russell Stone, *Director* Barnaby Edwards
Précis
The Doctor and Charley arrive in a seemingly deserted Edwardian house on Christmas Eve…
DWM Index
314 Preview
316 Review
349 Robert Shearman interview
Comment
Superlative sound design and a crackling script makes this the creepiest audio to date. **99%**

7) *Seasons Of Fear*
Paul Cornell & Caroline Symcox

Details
March 2002 (1903654599 / Clayton Hickman)
Cast
Paul McGann (The Doctor), India Fisher (Charley Pollard), Stephen Perring (Sebastian Grayle), Stephen Fewell (Marcus), Robert Curbishley (Lucillius), Lennox Greaves (Edward the Confessor), Sue Wallace (Edith), Justine Mitchell (Lucy Martin)
Crew
Music Jane Elphinston, *Director* Gary Russell
Précis
Moving between three time periods on Earth, the Doctor battles the immortal Sebastian Grayle…
DWM Index
315 Preview
317 Review

Comment
Overwritten tale of time meddling redeemed by the reappearance of the Nimons. **80%**

8) *Embrace The Darkness*
Nicholas Briggs

Details
April 2002 (1903654602 / Clayton Hickman)
Cast
Paul McGann (The Doctor), India Fisher (Charley Pollard), Nicola Boyce (Orllensa), Lee Moone (Ferras), Mark McDonnell (Haliard), Ian Brooker (ROSM/Chimmerian), Nicholas Briggs (Chimmerian)
Crew
Music Jim Mortimore, *Director* Nicholas Briggs
Précis
A Throxillian base on Cimmerian IV is attacked by natives of the planet, plunging it into darkness…
DWM Index
316 Preview
318 Review
Comment
Traditional tale enlivened by excellent sound effects and creepy voices. **70%**

9) *The Time Of The Daleks*
Justin Richards

Details
May 2002 (1903654592 / Clayton Hickman)
Cast
Paul McGann (The Doctor), India Fisher (Charley Pollard), Dot Smith (General Mariah Learman), Nicola Boyce (Viola), Julian Harries (Major Ferdinand), Jem Bassett (Kitchen Boy), Mark McDonnell (Priestly), Lee Moone (Hart), Ian Brooker (Professor Osric), Nicholas Briggs, Clayton Hickman (Dalek Voices)
Music/Director Nicholas Briggs
Précis
The Daleks arrive in a Shakespeare-free New Britain…
DWM Index
317 Preview
319 Review
326 Nicholas Briggs interview
Comment
Splendid time paradox tale; the Daleks reciting Shakespeare is oddly chilling. **90%**

10) Neverland
Alan Barnes

Details
June 2002 (1903654629 / Clayton Hickman)
Cast
Paul McGann (The Doctor), India Fisher (Charley Pollard), Lalla Ward (President Romana), Anthony Keetch (Co-ordinator Vansell), Dot Smith, Jonathan Rigby, Ian Hallard (Matrix Voices), Peter Trapani (Kurst), Holly King (Levith), Lee Moone (Under-Cardinal), Mark McDonnell (Rorvan), Nicola Boyce (Taris)
Crew
Music Nicholas Briggs, *Sound Design* Alistair Lock, *Director* Gary Russell
Précis
The President of Gallifrey tracks the Tardis so she can explore the strange dimension of Anti-Time…
DWM Index
318   Preview
321   Review
Comment
Occasionally muddled plotting, heavy on info-dumping, but with a fantastic cliffhanger. **77%**

11) Zagreus
Alan Barnes and Gary Russell

Details
October 2003, 3 x CDs (1844350320 / Clayton Hickman)
Cast
Paul McGann (The Doctor), India Fisher (Charley Pollard), Sophie Aldred, Colin Baker, Lisa Bowerman, Nicola Bryant, Nicholas Courtney, Peter Davison, Stephen Fewell, Louise Jameson, Robert Jezek, Bonnie Langford, John Leeson, Sylvester McCoy, Caroline Morris, Stephen Perring, Jon Pertwee, Miles Richardson, Elisabeth Sladen, Maggie Stables, Mark Strickson, Sarah Sutton, Lalla Ward, Don Warrington, Conrad Westmaas (Various)
Crew
Music Andy Hardwick, *Sound Design* Gareth Jenkins, *Director* Gary Russell
Précis
When the Doctor is possessed by the Anti-Time force Zagreus, anything can happen…
DWM Index
337   Studio report
340   Review
341   Lalla Ward interview

Comment
Bewildering and self-indulgent anniversary party to which the casual listener is not invited. **22%**

12) Scherzo
Robert Shearman

Details
December 2003 (1844350355 / Steve Johnson)
Cast
Paul McGann (The Doctor), India Fisher (Charley Pollard)
Crew
Music and Sound Design Gareth Jenkins, Andy Hardwick, *Director* Gary Russell
Précis
Alone and frightened, the Doctor and Charlie have only each other for company…
DWM Index
338   Preview
341   Review
349   Robert Shearman interview
Comment
Fascinating (yet somewhat pretentious) duologue that throws up more questions than answers. **45%**

13) The Creed of the Kromon
Philip Martin

Details
January 2004 (1844350363 / Steve Johnson)
Cast
Paul McGann (The Doctor), India Fisher (Charley Pollard), Conrad Westmaas (C'rizz), Brian Cobby (The Oroog), Stephen Perring (The Kro'ka/Kromon Voices), Jane Hills (L'da), Daniel Hogarth (Kromon Voices)
Crew
Music and Sound Design David Darlington, *Director* Gary Russell
Précis
The Doctor loses his Tardis in the arid world of the Kromons' Alpha Sphere…
DWM Index
339   Preview
341   Review
Comment
Aimless runaround punctuated by unlikely dialogue and formulaic situations. **28%**

14) The Natural History of Fear
Jim Mortimore

Details
February 2004 (184435038X / Steve Johnson)
Cast
Paul McGann, India Fisher, Conrad Westmaas, Geoff Serle, Alison Sterling, Sean Carlsen, Wink Taylor, Jane Hills, Ben Summers (Various)
Crew
Music and Sound Design Jim Mortimore, *Director* Gary Russell
Précis
Blandness is obligatory in Light City…
DWM Index
340 Preview
342 Review
Comment
Complex Orwellian fantasy, intriguing and irritating in equal measure. **76%**

15) The Twilight Kingdom
Will Shindler

Details
March 2004 (1844350371 / Steve Johnson)
Cast
Paul McGann (The Doctor), India Fisher (Charley), Conrad Westmaas (C'rizz), Stephen Perring (The Kro'ka), Anna Carus-Wilson (Vayla), Stephen Fewell (Deral), Dale Ibbotson (Quillian), Jeremy James (Bryn), Michael Keating (Colonel Koth), Vivien Parry (Tysus), Alan Rothwell (Janto), Alison Sterling (Tarrith)
Crew
Music and Sound Design ERS, *Director* Gary Russell
Précis
Lost in an alien jungle, the Doctor prepares for a bitter conflict…
DWM Index
341 Preview
343 Review
Comment
A sort of *Heart of Darkness* with SF overtones, full of menace. **77%**

16) Faith Stealer
Graham Duff

Details
September 2004 (1844351033 / Steve Johnson)
Cast
Paul McGann (The Doctor), India Fisher (Charley Pollard), Conrad Westmaas (C'rizz), Stephen Perring (The Kro'ka), Christian Rodska (Laan Carder), Tessa Shaw (The Bordinan), Jenny Coverack (Miraculite), Ifan Huw Dafydd (Bishop Parrash), Helen Kirkpatrick (Jebdal), Neil Bett (Director Garfolt), Chris Walter-Evans (Assistant), John Dorney (Bakoan), Jane Hills (L'Da)
Crew
Music Russell Stone, *Sound Design* Gareth Jenkins, *Director* Gary Russell
Précis
The Multihaven appears to offer the perfect sanctuary for the Doctor and his friends…
DWM Index
348 Preview
352 Review
Comment
Overblown religious satire that never seems to gel satisfactorily. **40%**

17) The Last
Gary Hopkins

Details
October 2004 (1844351025 / Steve Johnson)
Cast
Paul McGann (The Doctor), India Fisher (Charley pollard), C'rizz (Conrad Westmaas), Stephen Perring (The Kro'ka), Ian Brooker (Minister Voss), Richard Derrington (Landscar), John Dorney (Make-Up Assistant), Tom Eastwood (Requiem), Jane Hills (Nurse), Robert Hines (Minister Tralfinial), Carolyn Jones (Excelsior)
Crew
Music and Sound Design David Darlington, *Director* Gary Russell
Précis
Trapped on the desolate planet of Bortresoye, The Doctor faces the real enemy…
DWM Index
349 Preview
353 Review
Comment
Funereal post-apocalyptic story with powerful characters. **87%**

18) Caerdroia
Lloyd Rose

Details
November 2004 (1844351041 / Steve Johnson)
Cast
Paul McGann (The Doctor), India Fisher (Charley Pollard), C'rizz (Conrad Westmaas), Stephen Perring (The Kro'ka)
Crew
Music and Sound Design Steve Foxon, *Director* Gary Russell
Précis
On a bizarre alien world, the Kro'ka at last reveals his plans for the Doctor…
DWM Index
350 Preview
353 Review
Comment
Disappointingly vacuous psychodrama, although McGann excels. **54%**

19) The Next Life
Alan Barnes and Gary Russell

Details
December 2004, 3 x CDs (184435105X / Steve Johnson)
Cast
Paul McGann (The Doctor), India Fisher (Charley Pollard), Conrad Westmaas (C'rizz), Don Warrington (Rassilon), Stephen Perring (The Kro'ka), Daphne Ashbrook (Perfection), Stephane Cornicard (Daqar Keep), Paul Darrow (Guidance), Jane Hills (L'Da), Anneke Wills (lady Louisa Pollard)
Crew
Music and Sound Design ERS, *Director* Gary Russell
Précis
The Doctor is washed up on the beach of a paradise island…
DWM Index
351 Preview
Daphne Ashbrook and Paul McGann interview
353 Review
Comment
A strong cast give it their all in this overlong culmination of the Divergents story arc. **79%**

Miscellaneous

The Sirens of Time
Nicholas Briggs

Details
July 1999 (1903654289 / Gary Gillatt and James Arnott)
Cast
Peter Davison, Colin Baker, Sylvester McCoy (The Doctor), Maggie Stables (Ruthley), Andrew Fettes (Commander Raldeth/Schmidt), Anthony Keetch (Coordinator Vansell), Michael Wade (The President), Sarah Mowat (Elenya/Helen/Ellie/Knight Commander Lyena), Colin McIntyre (Sancroff), Nicholas Pegg (Delegate), John Wadmore (Commandant/Lieutenant Zentner/Pilot Azimendah/Sub-Commander Solanec), Mark Gatiss (Captain Schwieger/Captain/Knight 2), Nicholas Briggs (The Temperon)
Crew
Music/Director Nicholas Briggs
Précis
The Fifth, Sixth and Seventh Doctors defend Gallifrey against the Knights of Valeshya…
DWM Index
280 Review
Comment
Solid multi-Doctor adventure with effective sound design. **90%**

3: Cinema Films

"We could be anywhere in the Universe and at any time - rather exciting, isn't it?" ~ *Doctor Who*

1) Dr. Who and the Daleks
Milton Subotsky, based on the BBC television series by Terry Nation

Details
UK Premiere: 24 June 1965, Technicolor, 85m, an Aaru Production for Regal International
Cine Film
1. 1977, Walton Sound and Film Services, 8 x 200ft reels, Super 8 colour/sound (F740 / Artwork)
2. 1977, Walton Sound and Film Services, 2 x 200ft reels, Super 8 colour/sound (A848, A849 / Artwork)
Video
1. 1982, Thorn EMI, 4:3 (TVC 9005952 / Film poster artwork)
2. 1982, Thorn EMI, Betamax, 4:3 (TXC 9005954 / Film poster artwork)
3. June 1988, Warner Home Video, 4:3 (PES 38024 / Photomontage)
4. 1993, Warner Home Video, with *Daleks' Invasion Earth 2150AD*, 4:3 (PES 38328 / Photomontage)
5. February 1996, Beyond Vision, widescreen (SO388354 / Photomontage)
DVD
July 2002, Warner [box-set with *Daleks' Invasion Earth 2150 A.D.*], widescreen, commentary by Jonathan Southcott, Jennie Linden and Roberta Tovey, trailer, CD-Rom campaign book, *Dalekmania* documentary (D038470 / Photomontage)
Comic Strip
1966, Dell Comics
Précis
Ian accidentally sends Dr Who and his friends to the planet Skaro where they meet the Daleks...
Cast
Peter Cushing (Dr Who), Roy Castle (Ian), Jennie Linden (Barbara), Roberta Tovey (Susan), Barrie Ingham (Alydon), Michael Coles (Ganatus), Geoffrey Toone (Temmosus), Mark Peterson (Elyon), John Brown (Antodus), Yvonne Antrobus (Dyoni), Robert Jewell, Kevin Manser, Gerald Taylor (Daleks), David Graham, Peter Hawkins (Dalek Voices).

Crew
Special Effects Ted Samuels, *Special Electronic Effects* Les Hillman, *Camera Operator* David Harcourt, *Camera Grip* Ray Jones, *Sound* Buster Ambler, *Sound Supervisor* John Cox, *Sound Editors* Tom Priestley, Roy Hyde, *Construction Manager* Bill Waldron, *Set Decorator* Scott Slimon, *Director of Photography* John Wilcox, *Art Director* Bill Constable, *Assistant Art Director* Ken Ryan, *Make-Up* Jill Constable, *Wardrobe* Jackie Cummins, *Hairdresser* Henry Montsash, *Music* Malcolm Lockyear, *Electronic Music* Barry Gray, *Continuity* Pamela Davies, *Production Manager* Ted Lloyd, *Editor* Oswald Hafenrichter, *Executive Producer* Joe Vegoda, *Producer* Max J Rosenberg, *Assistant Director* Anthony Waye, *Director* Gordon Flemying
DWM Index
84	The Dalek Movies
193	Roy Castle interview
197	Allan Bryce interview
211	Roberta Tovey interview
218	Peter Cushing: The Forgotten Doctor Roy Castle Tribute
238	Video review
300	Time Team
315	Screen Test
321	DVD review
CC9	Comic Strip
353	Archive Extra

Filming Dates
8 March-April 1965 (Shepperton Studios)
Factoids
- The character of Doctor Who was changed from a mysterious alien to an eccentric human experimenting with time travel in his back garden. Although the Police Box prop was retained, the Tardis interior was radically altered in a bid to make it larger and more colourful for the big screen. The entire film was made within Shepperton Studios.
- Peter Cushing has the necessary international appeal to play the title role, while rising star Roy Castle made only his second film appearance as the accident-prone Ian.
- Eight new fibreglass Daleks were built by designer Bill Constable, incorporating thick

rubber bumpers and larger flashing lights. Amongst their operators were the same people who had operated them for the BBC television series. The Daleks' lights had flashed randomly during the filming, and it was only in post-production that it was realized that they should have flashed in synch with their dialogue - hence redubbing was required to have the words match the lights. This accounts for the sudden speeding up or slowing down of the Daleks' dialogue.

- Flame-throwers were considered for the Daleks' exterminators, but deemed too violent for a U rating, they became standard CO_2 fire extinguishers.
- This film and its follow up, *Daleks' Invasion Earth: 2150AD*, were both made entirely by Amicus, with Aaru receiving a sole credit as part of a co-finance deal.

Comment
Espousing the gritty drama of the television series, *Dr. Who and the Daleks* is a particularly anodyne form of entertainment. It all looks lovely and colourful (albeit, a bit too colourful), there are some great matte paintings and the music is often impressive, but ultimately it's an inferior remake of its small-screen progenitor. **65%**

"Rebels of London! This is your final warning!" ~ Red Dalek

2) Daleks' Invasion Earth 2150 A.D.

Milton Subotsky with additional material by David Whitaker, based on the BBC television series by Terry Nation

Details
UK Premiere: 22 July 1966, Technicolor, 84m, an Aaru Production for Regal

Cine Film
1. 1977, Walton Sound and Film Services, 8 x 200ft reels, Super 8 colour/sound (F741 / Artwork)
2. 1977, Walton Sound and Film Services, 2 x 200ft reels, Super 8 colour/sound (A850, A851 / Artwork)

Video
1. 1982, Thorn EMI, 4:3 (TVC 9006882 / Film poster artwork)
2. 1982, Thorn EMI, Betamax, 4:3 (TXC 9006884 / Film poster artwork)
3. June 1988, Warner Home Video, 4:3 (PES 38025 / Photomontage)
4. 1993, Warner Home Video, with *Daleks' Invasion Earth 2150AD*, 4:3 (PES 38328 / Photomontage)
5. February 1996, Beyond Vision, widescreen (SO388353 / Photomontage)

DVD
July 2002, Warner [box-set with *Dr. Who and the Daleks*], widescreen, trailer, CD-Rom campaign book, (D038470 / Photomontage)

Précis
The Tardis lands on Earth in 2150AD to find that the Daleks have laid waste to London...

Cast
Peter Cushing (Dr Who), Roberta Tovey (Susan), Jill Curzon (Louise), Bernard Cribbins (Tom Campbell), Ray Brooks (David), Andrew Keir (Wyler), Roger Avon (Wells), Keith Marsh (Conway), Philip Madoc (Brockley), Geoffrey Cheshire (Roboman), Eddie Powell (Thompson), Godfrey Quigley (Dortmun), Kenneth Watson (Craddock), Steve Peters (Roboman Leader), Sheila Steafel, Eileen Way (Women in Wood), Robert Jewell (Dalek), Bernard Spear (Man With Carrier Bag), David Graham, Peter Hawkins (Dalek Voices).

Crew
Special Effects Ted Samuels, *Camera Operator* David Harcourt, *Camera Grip* Ray Jones, *Sound* A Ambler, *Sound Supervisor* John Cox, *Sound Editor* John Poyner, *Construction Manager* Bill Waldron, *Set Decorator* Maurice Pelling, *Director of Photography* John Wilcox, *Art Director* George Provis, *Assistant Art Director*, *Make-Up* Bunty Phillips, *Wardrobe* Jackie Cummins, *Hairdresser* Bobbie Smith, *Music* Bill McGuffie, *Electronic Music* Barry Gray, *Continuity* Pamela Davies, *Production Manager* Ted Wallis, *Unit Manager* Tony Wallis, *Editor* Ann Chegwidden, *Executive Producer* Joe Vegoda, *Producers* Milton Subotsky, Max J Rosenberg, *Assistant Director* Anthony Waye, *Director* Gordon Flemying

DWM Index
84	The Dalek Movies
197	Allan Bryce interview
211	Roberta Tovey interview
218	Peter Cushing: The Forgotten Doctor
240	Video review
300	Time Team
315	Screen Test
321	DVD review
349	Archive Extra (Radio Abridgement)
354	Archive Extra (Film)

Filming Dates
31 January-22 March 1966 (Shepperton Studios)
Locations
Jetty, Battersea Church Road, Battersea, London SW11; Bendy Toys Factory, Ashford, Middlesex; River Ash Footbridge, Littleton Park, Littleton, Middlesex; Shepperton Studios backlot, Littleton, Middlesex
Factoids
- Because of the success of the first Dalek film, this hastily produced sequel was afforded a bigger budget and extensive location filming in and around London.
- Ted Samuels designed the impressive Dalek spacecraft. The three-feet long model was suspended on wires and filmed against a real sky backdrop. It later reappeared in the low-budget UK science-fiction film *The Body Stealers* (1968).
- The film was co-financed by the makers of Sugar Puffs, accounting for several posters of said product appearing throughout the film.
- A lower than expected turnout for *Daleks' Invasion Earth 2150AD*, stalled plans for a third film. This would either have been an adaptation of the third Dalek television serial, *The Chase* (16) or a new story entitled *Doctor Who's Greatest Adventure* in which two Doctors teamed up to fight giant monsters.

Comment
It's hard for me to be objective about this film because it remains such a vivid memory from my childhood, but in terms of its great production design and atmospheric location filming, it's streets ahead of the earlier film and far more impressive a production than its woefully cheap small-screen counterpart. The Dalek saucer, with its concentrically turning platforms, is one of the finest spaceships in cinema history and the various scenes of Daleks gliding about a ruined London are brilliantly executed. Call me mad, but I even like Bernard Cribbins. **90%**

4: Comic Strips

Stories marked by an asterisk indicate an invented title, many coined by Jeremy Bentham for an article in *Doctor Who Monthly* 62. Those without asterisks are either explicitly stated - either on the strip or in the previous week's announcement - or are on the author's script. For reasons of space, comic strips from sources other than weekly comics or monthly magazines have been excluded. *NB: Format entry is as follows: colour or b&w / instalments / total page count.*

First Doctor: William Hartnell

1) The Klepton Parasites*
Unknown author

Artist
Neville Main
Publication
TV Comic 674-683 (14 November 1964-16 January 1965)
Format
B&W / 10 / 20
Companions
John, Gillian
Précis
John and Gillian take a ride with the mysterious Doctor Who and find that in the 30th century the peaceful Thains are being attacked by the sinister Kleptons…
Reprint
Doctor Who Classic Comics 2 (colourized)
Verdict
Ambitious storyline with impressive visuals. **75%**

2) The Therovian Quest*
Unknown author

Artist
Neville Main
Publication
TV Comic 684-689 (23 January-27 February 1965)
Format
B&W / 5 / 10
Companions
John, Gillian
Précis
Grig seeks the Tardis travellers' help in collecting a healing moss from the dangerous ice planet Ixon…
Reprint
Doctor Who Classic Comics 12 (colourized)
Comment
Childish adventure tale with corny monsters. **30%**

3) The Hijackers of Thrax *
Unknown author

Artist
Neville Main
Publication
TV Comic 690-692 (6-20 March 1965)
Format
B&W / 3 / 6
Companions
John, Gillian
Précis
Doctor Who must stop Captain Anastas Thrax from seizing vital Earth supply ships from Venus…
Reprint
Doctor Who Classic Comics 13 (colourized)
Comment
Piratical high-jinks of the most puerile kind. **20%**

4) Doctor Who on The Web Planet
Unknown author
Artist
Neville Main
Publication
TV Comic 693-698 (27 March-1 May 1965)
Format
B&W / 6 / 12

Companions
John, Gillian
Précis
On Vortis, the Menoptra are once again under threat from the Zarbi...
Reprint
Doctor Who Classic Comics 13 (colourized)
Comment
Phallic mushrooms, fake Zarbis and a *Goldfinger* moment - it's mad stuff. **65%**

5) The Gyros Injustice*
Unknown author

Artist
Neville Main
Publication
TV Comic 699-704 (8 May-12 June 1965)
Format
B&W / 6 / 12
Companions
John, Gillian
Précis
Humanoid survivors of a terrible plague are being subjugated by the robotic Spyros...
Reprint
Doctor Who Classic Comics 17 (colourized)
Comment
Your standard tale of Man vs Space Hopper. **37%**

6) Challenge of the Piper *
Unknown author

Artist
Neville Main
Publication
TV Comic 705-709 (19 June-17 July 1965)
Format
B&W / 5 / 10
Companions
John, Gillian
Précis
Doctor Who must free the Hamelin children from the wily Pied Piper...
Reprint
Doctor Who Classic Comics 20 (colourized)
Comment
Mind Robber-style antics in a 'magic wonderland' - strangely beguiling. **70%**

7) Moonshot *
Unknown author

Artist
Neville Main
Publication
TV Comic 710-712 (24 July-8 August 1965)
Format
B&W / 3 / 6
Companions
John, Gillian
Précis
In 1970, the first astronauts on the Moon are amazed to discover a Police Box already there...
Reprint
Doctor Who Classic Comics 22 (colourized)
Comment
A thinly disguised science lesson, but woefully inaccurate. **28%**

8) Time in Reverse *
Unknown author

Artist
Neville Main
Publication
TV Comic 713-715 (14-28 August 1965)
Format
B&W / 3 / 6
Companions
John, Gillian
Précis
Arriving at the end of their adventure, the Tardis crew find that time appears to be running backwards...
Reprint
Doctor Who Classic Comics 22 (colourized)
Comment
Shades of *Memento* in this brilliantly inventive story of time going backwards. **95%**

9) Lizardworld*
Unknown author

Artist
Neville Main
Publication
TV Comic 716-719 (4-25 September 1965)
Format
B&W / 4 / 8

Companions
John, Gillian
Précis
Doctor Who and his friends are captured by a race of giant lizards…
Reprint
Doctor Who Classic Comics 23 (colourized)
Comment
Back to banalities with another simplistic kiddies' adventure. **17%**

10) The Ordeals of Demeter
Unknown author

Artist
Bill Mevin
Publication
TV Comic 720-723 (2-23 October 1965)
Format
Colour / 4 / 8
Companions
John, Gillian
Précis
The planet Demeter is being torn apart by terrible vibrations from the neighbouring world of Bellus…
Reprint
Doctor Who Classic Comics 7
Comment
Colourful *Dan Dare*-style heroics, imaginatively drawn. **65%**

11) Enter: The Go-Ray*
Unknown author

Artist
Bill Mevin
Publication
TV Comic 724 -727 (30 October-20 November 1965)
Format
Colour / 4 / 8
Companions
John, Gillian
Précis
On the planet Go-Ray, the wheeled inhabitants blame the Tardis crew for the loss of their power…
Reprint
Doctor Who Classic Comics 7
Comment
Silly story, patchy art. **23%**

12) Shark Bait*
Unknown author

Artist
Bill Mevin
Publication
TV Comic 728-731 (27 November-18 December 1965)
Format
Colour / 4 / 8
Companions
John, Gillian
Précis
Doctor Who helps a race of intelligent frogs to fight off a giant shark and meets the Ancient Mariner…
Reprint
Doctor Who Classic Comics 10
Comment
Even very young children would feel patronized by this twee rubbish. **11%**

13) A Christmas Story*
Unknown author

Artist
Bill Mevin
Publication
TV Comic 732-735 (25 December 1965-15 January 1966)
Format
Colour / 4 / 8
Companions
John, Gillian
Précis
Santa Claus' toy-making activities are disrupted by the malicious Demon Magician…
Reprint
Doctor Who Classic Comics 15
Comment
Mind-altering drugs could not have made this weird story any weirder. **42%**

14) The Didus Expedition*
Unknown author

Artist
Bill Mevin
Publication
TV Comic 736-739 (22 January-12 February 1966)
Format
Colour / 4 / 8
Companions
John, Gillian
Précis
Doctor Who, John and Gillian try and rescue the Didus from some jungle savages…
Reprint
Doctor Who Classic Comics 24
Comment
Quaint tale of a Dodo, a space-age zoo and some terribly non-PC natives. **35%**

15) Space Station Z-7*
Unknown author

Artist
Bill Mevin
Publication
TV Comic 740-743 (19 February-12 March 1966)
Format
Colour / 4 / 8
Companions
John, Gillian
Précis
Doctor Who must thwart some fanatical rebels who have taken control of a giant space-station…
Comment
Formulaic adventure story. **45%**

16) Plague of the Black Scorpi *
Unknown author

Artist
Bill Mevin
Publication
TV Comic 744-747 (19 March-9 April 1966)
Format
Colour / 4 / 8
Companions
John, Gillian

Précis
A plantation owner on a parched planet is struggling against a plague of locust-like insects…
Comment
A lame and plotless trek across desert wastelands with much padding. **32%**

17) The Trodos Tyranny*
Unknown author

Artist
John Canning
Publication
TV Comic 748-752 (16 April-14 May 1966)
Format
Colour / 5 / 10
Companions
John, Gillian
Précis
On the planet Trodos, the evil robot Trods and their ruler, Super-Trod, have subjugated the population…
Reprint
Doctor Who Classic Comics 8
Comment
Fun story with energetic artwork and imaginative Dalek-style robots. **63%**

18) The Secrets of Gemino*
Unknown author

Artist
John Canning
Publication
TV Comic 753-757 (21 May-16 June 1966)
Format
Colour / 5 / 10
Companions
John, Gillian
Précis
Doctor Who must unlock the Vault of Plenty on Gemino or its citizens will starve to death…
Comment
Stylish artwork lifts a typically humdrum story. **55%**

19) On The Haunted Planet
Unknown author

Artist
John Canning
Publication
TV Comic 758-762 (25 June-23 July 1966)
Format
Colour / 5 / 10
Companions
John, Gillian
Précis
The Doctor and his friends are sentenced to death by Zentor, Master of the Abode of the Supernatural…
Comment
Effective moments early on give way to a silly resolution. **45%**

20) The Hunters of Zerox*
Unknown author

Artist
John Canning
Publication
TV Comic 763-767 (30 July-27 August 1966)
Format
B&W / 5 / 10
Companions
John, Gillian
Précis
Doctor Who must fight to the death in an alien arena…
Comment
Predictable hokum with a plethora of convenient gadgets. **38%**

21) The Underwater Robot*
Unknown author

Artist
John Canning
Publication
TV Comic 768-771 (3-24 September 1966)
Format
B&W / 4 / 8
Companions
John, Gillian
Précis
Doctor Who must stop two insane inventors from plundering ships with their undersea walking robot…
Comment
Lightweight undersea shenanigans with some clever touches. **65%**

22) Return of the Trods*
Unknown author

Artist
John Canning
Publication
TV Comic 772-775 (1-22 October 1966)
Format
B&W / 4 / 8
Companions
John, Gillian
Précis
The Tardis is drawn back to Trodos where a space traveller has reactivated the deadly robot Trods…
Reprint
Doctor Who Classic Comics 8 (colourized)
Comment
Dalek-inspired action with a surprisingly callous Doctor. **75%**

23) The Galaxy Games*
Unknown author

Artist
John Canning
Publication
TV Comic 776-779 (29 October-19 November 1966)
Format
B&W / 4 / 8
Précis
John enters the Galaxy Games but is snatched by the Klondites…
Comment
Simplistic fare with a modicum of SF trappings. **50%**

24) The Experimenters*
Unknown author

Artist
John Canning
Publication
TV Comic 780-783 (26 November-17 December 1966)

Format
B&W / 4 / 8
Companions
John, Gillian
Précis
The Master Race uses the Tardis crew as test pilots for their prototype space rocket…
Comment
So-so conclusion to the regular run of Hartnell strips. **45%**

25) Food for Thought
Nick Briggs

Artist
Colin Andrew
Publication
Doctor Who Magazine 218-220 (26 October-21 December 1994)
Format
B&W / 3 / 21
Companions
Ben, Polly
Précis
The Tardis arrives in an automated city that has been attacked by an alien parasite…
Comment
A clever pre-*Matrix* plot with good characterizations all round. **73%**

26) Operation Proteus
Gareth Roberts

Artist
Martin Geraghty
Publication
Doctor Who Magazine 231-233 (25 October-20 December 1995)
Format
B&W / 3 / 21
Companion
Susan
Précis
The British government is using a stranded alien to develop its chemical weapons technology…
Comment
Gory conspiracy tale with excellent artwork but often poor likenesses of the leads. **80%**

Second Doctor: Patrick Troughton

1) The Extortioner*
Unknown author

Artist
John Canning
Publication
TV Comic 784-787 (24 December 1966-14 January 1967)
Format
B&W / 4 / 8
Companions
John, Gillian
Précis
A powerful megalomaniac threatens to launch rockets at every country from the safety of his volcano…
Reprint
Doctor Who Classic Comics 3 (colourized)
Comment
Rough-and-ready tale about a Mussolini lookalike. **45%**

2) Doctor Who and the Daleks…The Trodos Ambush*
Unknown author

Artist
John Canning
Publication
TV Comic 788-791 (21 January-11 February 1967)
Format
Colour covers, b&w / 4 / 12
Companions
John, Gillian
Précis
Doctor Who intends to make peace with the Trods, but the Daleks have got there first…
Reprint
Doctor Who Classic Comics 8 (colourized)
Comment
Plenty of strong Dalek action in this, their first comic strip appearance. **82%**

3) Doctor Who and the Daleks...The Doctor Strikes Back*
Unknown author

Artist
John Canning
Publication
TV Comic 792-795 (18 February-11 March 1967)
Format
Colour covers, b&w / 4 / 12 (colourized)
Companions
John, Gillian
Précis
Doctor Who infiltrates a Dalek stronghold inside a 'home made' Dalek...
Reprint
Doctor Who Classic Comics 11
Comment
Doctor Who's demolition of a massive Dalek army all in his own is a little far-fetched. **60%**

4) Doctor Who and the Daleks...The Zombies
Unknown author

Artist
John Canning
Publication
TV Comic 796-798 (18 March-1 April 1967)
Format
Colour cover, b&w / 3 / 9
Précis
Doctor Who must free the population of London from the hypnotic powers of the Zagbors...
Reprint
Doctor Who Classic Comics 17 (colourized)
Comment
Avengers-style silliness with a ridiculous conclusion. **25%**

5) Doctor Who and the Daleks...Master of Spiders!
Unknown author

Artist
John Canning
Publication
TV Comic 799- 802 (8-29 April 1967)
Format
Colour cover, b&w / 4 / 12
Companions
John, Gillian
Précis
On a jungle planet, Doctor Who encounters a group of hostile giant spiders...
Reprint
Doctor Who Classic Comics 18 (colourized)
Comment
Doctor Who's ray gun saves the day in this corny insect tale. **33%**

6) Doctor Who and the Daleks...The Exterminator*
Unknown author

Artist
John Canning
Publication
TV Comic 803-806 (6-27 May 1967)
Format
Colour cover, b&w / 4 / 12
Companions
John, Gillian
Précis
Doctor Who derails a Dalek express train carrying a deadly giant gun that could destroy the Earth...
Reprint
Doctor Who Classic Comics 20 (colourized)
Comment
Rollicking Dalek adventure with many exciting moments. **70%**

7) Doctor Who and the Daleks...The Monsters from the Past!
Unknown author

Artist
John Canning
Publication
TV Comic 807-811 (3 June-1 July 1967)
Format
Colour covers, b&w (807-809) + b&w (810-811) / 5 / 13
Companions
John, Gillian

Précis
In 1960s New York, Doctor Who battles against dinosaurs brought back to life by a mad professor…
Reprint
Doctor Who Classic Comics 22 (colourized)
Comment
Prescient *Invasion of the Dinosaurs*-style story with plenty of incident. **76%**

8) The Tardis Worshippers!
Unknown author

Artist
John Canning
Publication
TV Comic 812-815 (8-29 July 1967)
Format
B&W / 4 / 8
Companions
John, Gillian
Précis
Doctor Who, Gillian and John are mistaken for Gods by a South American tribe…
Reprint
Doctor Who Classic Comics 24 (colourized)
Comment
TV Comic's version of *The Aztecs* - with predictable results. **30%**

9) Space War Two!
Unknown author
Artist
John Canning
Publication
TV Comic 816-819 (5-26 August 1967)
Format
B&W / 4 / 8
Companions
John, Gillian
Précis
On Verno, Doctor Who must halt the production of deadly robot troops…
Reprint
Doctor Who Classic Comics 25 (colourized)
Comment
Increasingly slapdash artwork populated with Trod-like robots. **24%**

10) Egyptian Escapade!
Unknown author

Artist
John Canning
Publication
TV Comic 820-823 (2-23 September 1967)
Format
B&W / 4 / 8
Companions
John, Gillian
Précis
The Nile Delta 1880, and Doctor Who is caught between the British garrison and Mahadi soldiers…
Reprint
Doctor Who Classic Comics 26 (colourized)
Comment
First historical comic strip, done with some style too. **70%**

11) Return of the Cybermen*
Unknown author

Artist
John Canning
Publication
TV Comic 824-827 (30 September-21 October 1967)
Format
Colour / 4 / 8
Companions
John, Gillian
Précis
Aboard a spaceship on the planet Minot, Doctor Who discovers a Cyberman bomb…
Reprint
Doctor Who Classic Comics 26 (colourized)
Comment
Doctor Who's on his own against *Tenth Planet*-style Cybermen in this well-drawn adventure. **83%**

12) The Faithful Rocket Pack!
Unknown author

Artist
John Canning
Publication
TV Comic 828-831 (28 October-18 November 1967)

Format
Colour / 4 / 8
Companions
John, Gillian
Précis
American jet fighters from an Arizona air base are being pulled off course by a magnetic force...
Comment
Run-of-the-mill techno-thriller with alien overtones. **50%**

13) Flower Power!
Unknown author

Artist
John Canning
Publication
TV Comic 832-836 (25 November-23 December 1967)
Format
Colour / 5 / 10
Companions
John, Gillian
Précis
Doctor Who and his friends rescue butterfly-mad Professor Gnat from the Cybermen...
Reprint
Doctor Who Magazine 307
Comment
Cybermen can now be defeated by the scent of flowers. I suppose it's as daft as gold. **40%**

14) The Witches!
Unknown author

Artist
John Canning
Publication
TV Comic 837-841 (30 December 1967-27 January 1968)
Format
Colour / 5 / 10
Companions
John, Gillian
Précis
On the planet Vargo, Doctor Who interrupts a gathering of witches...
Reprint
Doctor Who Magazine 308-312
Comment
Preposterous slice of supernatural whimsy. **38%**

15) Cyber-Mole*
Unknown author

Artist
John Canning
Publication
TV Comic 842-845 (3-24 February 1968)
Format
Colour / 4 / 8
Companions
John, Gillian
Précis
Cybermen steal a Doomsday Bomb and threaten to destroy the Earth...
Comment
Slick Cyber adventure with an anti-nuclear message. **60%**

16) The Sabre Toothed Gorillas
Unknown author

Artist
John Canning
Publication
TV Comic 846-849 (2-23 March 1968)
Format
Colour / 4 / 8
Companions
John, Gillian
Précis
Doctor Who protects a mad scientist who has developed a rubber substance called Squidge...
Comment
It's all as daft as it sounds. **27%**

17) The Cyber Empire!
Roger Noel Cook

Artist
John Canning
Publication
TV Comic 850-853 (30 March-20 April 1968)
Format
Colour / 4 / 8
Companions
John, Gillian
Précis
The Cybermen are using Earthmen as slave labour to build a huge city in honour of their Controller...

Comment
Unlikely Cybermen activity in a pretty unlikely story. **35%**

18) The Dyrons!
Roger Noel Cook

Artist
John Canning
Publication
TV Comic 853-858 (27 April-25 May 1968)
Format
Colour / 5 / 10
Companions
John, Gillian
Précis
Giant black land squids menace shipwrecked schoolchildren on a volcanic planet…
Comment
Workaday 'monsters of the week' story with no added frills. **25%**

19) Dr. Who and the Space Pirates!
Roger Noel Cook

Artist
John Canning
Publication
TV Comic 859-863 (1-29 June 1968)
Format
Colour / 5 / 10
Companions
John, Gillian
Précis
Doctor Who helps Zarcus, leader of the planet Neon, to repel space pirate Captain Burglass…
Comment
Far more exciting than the later TV version, but still rubbish. **18%**

20) Car of the Century!
Roger Noel Cook

Artist
John Canning
Publication
TV Comic 864-867 (6-27 July 1968)
Format
Colour / 4 / 8
Companions
John, Gillian
Précis
Doctor Who builds an indestructible car which a criminal mastermind promptly steals…
Comment
More like *The Avengers* than *Doctor Who*, but good fun all the same. **45%**

21) The Jokers!
Roger Noel Cook

Artist
John Canning
Publication
TV Comic 868-871 (3-24 August 1968)
Format
Colour / 4 / 8
Companions
John, Gillian
Précis
On planet Comedy, the Tardis travellers meet four gnomes who delight in playing tricks on them…
Comment
One of the low spots of the series thus far. **15%**

22) Invasion of the Quarks!
Roger Noel Cook

Artist
John Canning
Publication
TV Comic 872-876 (31 August-28 September 1968)
Format
Colour / 5 / 10
Companions
Gillian, John, Jamie
Précis
Enrolling John and Gillian at university, the Doctor joins Jamie in Scotland to fight a Quark invasion…
Comment
A real television companion at last - but a very odd choice of foe. **70%**

23) The Killer Wasps*
Roger Noel Cook

Artist
John Canning
Publication
TV Comic 877-880 (5-26 October 1968)
Format
Colour / 4 / 8
Companion
Jamie
Précis
The Quarks despatch giant wasps to kill Doctor Who and Jamie on the battle-scarred planet Gano…
Comment
Barmy nonsense. **23%**

24) Ice Cap Terror
Roger Noel Cook

Artist
John Canning
Publication
TV Comic 881-884 (2-23 November 1968)
Format
B&W / 4 / 8
Companion
Jamie
Précis
When aliens detonate a bomb at the South Pole, they release a savage race of Ice Apes…
Comment
Substitute Yetis feature in this reasonably well-written runaround. **68%**

25) Jungle of Doom!
Roger Noel Cook

Artist
John Canning
Publication
TV Comic 885-889 (30 November-28 December 1968)
Format
B&W / 4 / 8
Companion
Jamie

Précis
With the Tardis buried under a rockfall, Doctor Who must defend himself against the deadly Quarks…
Comment
The cute-looking robots appear once more to minimum effect. **40%**

26) Father Time
Roger Noel Cook

Artist
John Canning
Publication
TV Comic 890-893 (4-25 January 1969)
Format /
B&W / 4 / 8
Companion
Jamie
Précis
Doctor Who and Jamie are punished for encroaching upon the domain of Father Time…
Comment
Surreal escapade, only slightly better than *A Christmas Story* (Hartnell, 13). **45%**

27) Martha the Mechanical Housemaid
Roger Noel Cook

Artist
John Canning
Publication
TV Comic 894-898 (1 February-1 March 1969)
Format
B&W / 5 / 10
Companion
Jamie
Précis
The Quarks reprogramme Doctor Who's robot maids to attack the population of New York…
Comment
An extraordinarily unDoctorish Doctor masquerades as a mad professor in this silly froth. **45%**

28) The Duellists
Roger Noel Cook

Artist
John Canning
Publication
TV Comic 899-902 (8-29 March 1969)
Format
B&W / 4 / 8
Précis
Quarks and cruel Regency duellists oppose the Doctor on the planet Hekton...
Reprint
TV Comic 1386-1389 (with Tom Baker's face replacing Patrick Troughton's)
Comment
A odd combination of elements that almost works. **60%**

29) Eskimo Joe
Roger Noel Cook

Artist
John Canning
Publication
TV Comic 903-906 (5-26 April 1969)
Format
B&W / 4 / 8
Précis
Pursued by a group of Cybermen on skis, Doctor Who seeks the aid of an Eskimo's robot gulls...
Comment
Just when you thought things couldn't get much worse. **20%**

30) Peril at 60 Fathoms
Roger Noel Cook

Artist
John Canning
Publication
TV Comic 907-910 (3-24 May 1969)
Format
B&W / 4 / 8
Précis
On the watery world of Nook, a crashed spaceship is receiving the unwanted intentions of a giant squid...
Comment
Reasonable underwater adventure. **55%**

31) Operation Wurlitzer!
Roger Noel Cook

Artist
John Canning
Publication
TV Comic 911-915 (31 May-28 June 1969)
Format
B&W / 5 / 10
Précis
Doctor Who assembles a crack team to rescue Jason Wurlitzer, held captive by dog-faced dwarves...
Comment
Fairly engaging kidnap caper. **60%**

32) Action in Exile
Roger Noel Cook

Artist
John Canning
Publication
TV Comic 916 - 920 (5 July-2 August 1969)
Format
B&W / 5 / 10
Précis
On the run from the Time Lords, Doctor Who helps three children escape from nuclear fuel thieves...
Comment
Sans Tardis, Doctor Who is now to be found in a London hotel acting like a hired detective. **52%**

33) The Mark of Terror
Roger Noel Cook

Artist
John Canning
Publication
TV Comic 921-924 (9-30 August 1969)
Format
B&W / 4 / 8
Précis
The sight of the Doctor's chest tattoo sparks off the tale of his encounter with the Nazi-like Blenhims...
Comment
Very strange flashback story with delusions of grandeur. **35%**

34) The Brotherhood
Roger Noel Cook

Artist
John Canning
Publication
TV Comic 925-928 (6-27 September 1969)
Format
B&W / 4 / 8
Précis
The Doctor is abducted by Mafia-types who want him to help unearth buried treasure in Mexico…
Comment
Time-serving treasure hunt story with no extraterrestrial element. **30%**

35) U.F.O.
Roger Noel Cook

Artist
John Canning
Publication
TV Comic 929-933 (4 October-1 November 1969)
Format
B&W / 5 / 10
Précis
Doctor Who and a young radio ham rendezvous with a Quotron spaceship in the Arizona desert…
Comment
Vaguely intriguing mystery with a promising young companion figure. **65%**

36) The Night Walkers*
Roger Noel Cook

Artist
John Canning
Publication
TV Comic 934-936 (8-22 November 1969)
Format
B&W / 3 / 6
Précis
Scarecrow servants of the Time Lords abduct Doctor Who and force him to complete his exile…
Comment
Strangely compelling hokum with a very neat tie-in to The War Games (50). **78%**

37) Land of the Blind
Warwick Scott Gray

Artist
Lee Sullivan
Publication
Doctor Who Magazine 224-226 (12 April-7 June 1995)
Format
B&W / 3 / 21
Companions
Jamie, Zoe
Précis
The Doctor finds the legal system somewhat harsh on the planet Denossus…
Comment
Echoes of Logan's Run in this stylish morality tale. **70%**

Third Doctor: Jon Pertwee

1) The Arkwood Experiments*
Roger Noel Cook

Artist
John Canning
Publication
TV Comic 944-949 (17 January-21 February 1970)
Format
B&W / 6 / 12
Companion
Brigadier
Précis
Child genius Cedric Matthews has invented a gas that turns quiet schoolboys into rampaging monsters…
Reprint
Doctor Who Classic Comics 4 (colourized)
Comment
Wonderfully inept artwork complements a bizarre Winker Watson-style storyline. **30%**

2) The Multi-Mobile!
Roger Noel Cook

Artist
John Canning
Publication
TV Comic 950-954 (28 February-28 March 1970)
Format
B&W / 5 / 10
Companion
Brigadier
Précis
A military tank is stolen by enemy agents who want to attack a nuclear defence centre...
Comment
Little explanation is given for the enemy's actions in this workaday adventure. **38%**

3) Insect*
Unknown author

Artist
John Canning
Publication
TV Comic 955-959 (4 April-2 May 1970)
Format
B&W / 5 / 10
Companion
Brigadier
Précis
Giant insects are roaming the countryside after being sprayed with a freak insecticide...
Comment
Yet another giant monsters story with little or no plot. **35%**

4) The Metal Eaters*
Alan Fennell

Artist
John Canning
Publication
TV Comic 960-964 (9 May-6 June 1970)
Format
B&W / 5 / 10
Companions
Brigadier, Liz
Précis
Intelligent iron filings from a crashed meteorite threaten an aeroplane laden with schoolchildren...
Comment
Spearhead from Space-style plot, done with a tad more intelligence than usual. **55%**

5) The Fishmen of Carpantha*
Alan Fennell

Artist
John Canning
Publication
TV Comic 965-969 (3 June-11 July 1970)
Format
B&W / 5 / 10
Companions
Brigadier, Liz
Précis
An underwater race called the Carpanthans are being disturbed by UNIT depth charges...
Comment
Forerunner to The Sea Devils and with a similar message about peaceful coexistence. **60%**

6) Doctor Who and the Rocks from Venus
Alan Fennell

Artist
John Canning
Publication
TV Comic 970-976 (18 July-29 August 1970)
Format
B&W / 7 / 14
Companions
Brigadier, Liz
Précis
Doctor Who finds that Venusian rock samples brought back by Professor Logan are fake...
Comment
A tale about human greed and deception, obviously inspired by The Ambassadors of Death. **75%**

7) Doctor Who and the Robot
Alan Fennell
Artist
John Canning
Publication
TV Comic 977-984 (5 September-24 October 1970)

Format
B&W / 8 / 16
Précis
Professor Readon's emotional robot goes berserk and rampages across the countryside…
Comment
Back to basics with this childish 'giant monster' runaround. **35%**

8) Trial of Fire*
Alan Fennell

Artist
John Canning
Publication
TV Comic 985-991 (31 October-12 December 1970)
Format
B&W / 6 / 12
Précis
Professor Vinter plans to decimate the human race with the help of the underground Fire People…
Comment
Preposterous story, ridiculous monsters; a bit like an underground version of *The Underwater Menace*. **22%**

9) The Kingdom Builders*
Alan Fennell

Artist
John Canning
Publication
TV Comic 992-999 (19 December 1970-6 February 1971)
Format
B&W / 8 / 16
Précis
Journeying in a prototype time machine, Doctor Who finds the Earth torn apart by two rival kingdoms…
Comment
The final *TV Comic* strip - for now - sees a particularly well characterized Third Doctor becoming arbitrator between two warring factions. **72%**

10) Gemini Plan
Dennis Hooper

Artist
Harry Lindfield
Publication
Countdown 1-5 (20 February-20 March 1971)
Format
Colour / 5 / 10
Précis
The Doctor has to stop Rudolph Steiner deflecting the orbit of Venus and thus destroying the Earth…
Reprint
Doctor Who Classic Comics 1
Comment
New comic, glossy artwork, exciting storyline - a real shot in the arm for the series. **88%**

11) Timebenders
Dennis Hooper

Artist
Harry Lindfield
Publication
Countdown 6-13 (27 March-15 May 1971)
Format
Colour / 8 / 16
Précis
1942 Germany, and the Doctor finds that a scientist's invention might help the Nazis win the war…
Reprint
Doctor Who Classic Comics 1
Comment
A gritty war story, genuinely suspenseful, with excellent artwork throughout. **94%**

12) The Vogan Slaves
Dennis Hooper

Artist
Harry Lindfield
Publication
Countdown 15-22 (29 May-17 July 1971)
Format
Colour / 8 / 17
Précis
On a starship, Doctor Who attempts to free a race of people from slavery by the evil Vogans…

Reprint
Doctor Who Classic Comics 1-2
Comment
Beautiful artwork in the early instalments, but the story and monsters (Mekon clones) are derivative. **65%**

13) The Celluloid Midas
Dennis Hooper

Artist
Harry Lindfield
Publication
Countdown 23-32 (24 July-25 September 1971)
Format
B&W, colour / 10 / 21
Précis
In the quiet village of Puddlesfield, the cast of a daytime soap opera have been turned into plastic...
Reprint
Doctor Who Classic Comics 3 (partly colourized)
Comment
Photographic reference material shot on location during *The Dæmons* makes this ingenious story very similar in tone to its television counterpart. **93%**

14) BackTime
Dick O'Neill

Artist
Frank Langford
Publication
Countdown 33-39 (2 October-13 November 1971)
Format
Colour (33-34), b&w (35-39) / 7 / 14
Companion
Charlie Fisher
Précis
The Tardis is stolen in America at the time of the Gettysburg Address...
Reprint
Doctor Who Classic Comics 3-4
Comment
Uninteresting historical melodrama, rather poorly drawn, with an irritating Artful Dodger assistant in tow. **45%**

15) The Eternal Present
Dennis Hooper

Artists
Harry Lindfield (40-41), Gerry Haylock (42-46)
Publication
Countdown 40-45, *Countdown for TV Action* 46 (20 November 1971-1 January 1972)
Format
Colour / 7 / 14
Companion
Theophillus Tolliver
Précis
The Doctor and a Victorian time-traveller are captured by the ruler of New Britain...
Reprint
Doctor Who Classic Comics 4-5
Comment
Smashing story and great artwork, especially the scenes inside St Paul's Cathedral. **96%**

16) *Sub Zero
Dennis Hooper

Artist
Gerry Haylock
Publication
Countdown for TV Action 47-54 (8 January-26 February 1972)
Format
Colour / 8 / 16
Companion
Lieutenant Davis
Précis
The Daleks launch a nuclear attack on Sydney from their secret armada of ice ships...
Reprint
Doctor Who Classic Comics 5
Comment
Impressive attention to detail in this strangely titled epic; the Daleks look gorgeous. **85%**

17) The Planet of the Daleks
Dennis Hooper
Artist
Gerry Haylock
Publication
Countdown for TV Action 55-57, *TV Action in Countdown* 58, *TV Action + Countdown* 59-62 (4 March-22 April 1972)

Format
Colour (55-58), colour cover, b&w (59-62) / 8 / 20
Companion
Finney
Précis
The Tardis is drawn to Skaro where the Doctor is turned into a humanoid Dalek…
Reprint
Doctor Who Classic Comics 6 (partly colourized)
Comment
Great colour artwork (less so the b/w stuff), a promising temporary companion and loads of Dalek vs Dinosaur action. **80%**

18) A Stitch in Time
Dennis Hooper

Artist
Gerry Haylock
Publication
TV Action + Countdown 63-70 (29 April-17 June 1972)
Format
Colour cover, b&w / 8 / 24
Companion
Brod
Précis
Doctor Who lands in the year 5000 and is taken away in an airship controlled by mutants…
Reprint
Doctor Who Classic Comics 7 (colourized)
Comment
Another Dystopia the Doctor must set right - this time featuring six-legged camels and giant airships. **70%**

19) The Enemy from Nowhere
Dennis Hooper

Artist
Gerry Haylock
Publication
TV Action + Countdown 71-78 (24 June-12 August 1972)
Format
Colour cover, b&w / 8 / 24
Companion
David Jenkins
Précis
Doctor Who fears a devastating space war after the Zerons destroy an Earth missile platform…
Reprint
Doctor Who Classic Comics 12 (colourized)
Comment
Pacy if overlong alien invasion story with one or two twists on the way. **73%**

20) The Ugrakks
Dennis Hooper

Artist
Gerry Haylock
Publication
TV Action + Countdown 79-88 (19 August-21 October 1972)
Format
Colour cover, b&w / 10 / 30
Companion
Professor Lammers
Précis
The elephantine Ugrakks want to use the Doctor's Tardis to escape from the giant Zama flies…
Reprint
Doctor Who Classic Comics 13-14 (colourized)
Comment
The Ugrakks are given a fascinating backstory but, alas, the story isn't really strong enough for ten parts. **58%**

21) Steel Fist
Dennis Hooper

Artist
Gerry Haylock
Publication
TV Action + Countdown 89-93 (28 October-25 November 1972)
Format
Colour cover, b&w / 5 / 15
Précis
Doctor Who investigates the abduction of nuclear physicist Simon Trent by a dangerous gang…
Reprint
Doctor Who Classic Comics 15 (colourized)
Comment
A cleverly written tale of kidnapping and deception with a villain who escapes at the end, never to return. **77%**

22) Zeron Invasion
Dennis Hooper

Artist
Gerry Haylock
Publication
TV Action + Countdown 94-100 (2 December 1972-13 January 1973)
Format
Colour cover, b&w / 7 / 21
Companions
Nick Willard, Jed Felix
Précis
Doctor Who and his friends help stop the Zerons bombarding the Earth with their mind-control ray…
Reprint
Doctor Who Classic Comics 15-16 (colourized)
Comment
Great London action sequences, groovy cover art, and - hooray - some black faces at last. **90%**

23) Deadly Choice
Dennis Hooper

Artist
Gerry Haylock
Publication
TV Action 101-103 (20 January-3 February 1973)
Format
Colour / 3 / 6
Précis
A mad Abbott gases and kidnaps a group of top scientists at a conference…
Reprint
Doctor Who Classic Comics 18
Comment
Shades of Tintin adventure *Flight 714*; a promising set-up but the story ends very abruptly. **40%**

24) Who is the Stranger
Dennis Hooper

Artist
Gerry Haylock
Publication
TV Action 104 (10 February 1973)
Format
B&W / 1 / 7
Précis
The Doctor lands in Nazi-occupied Paris during WWII…
Reprint
1. *1977 Doctor Who Winter Special* (with Tom Baker drawn over Jon Pertwee by John Canning)
2. *Doctor Who Classic Comics* 19 (colourized)
Comment
Formulaic WWII yarn. **25%**

25) The Glen of Sleeping
Dick O'Neill

Artist
Gerry Haylock
Publication
TV Action 107-11 (3-31 March 1973)
Format
Colour / 5 / 10
Précis
The Master steals a Polaris submarine aided by Highland warriors, asleep since 1745…
Reprint
Doctor Who Classic Comics 20
Comment
Bizarre premise but it almost works. Slick artwork. **72%**

26) The Threat from Beneath
Dick O'Neill

Artist
Gerry Haylock
Publication
TV Action 112 (7 April 1973)
Format
B&W / 1 / 7
Précis
The Daleks take control of a submarine from their undersea base…
Reprint
1. *1977 Doctor Who Winter Special*, renamed *Invasion* (with Tom Baker drawn over Jon Pertwee by John Canning)
2. *Doctor Who Classic Comics* 23 (colourized)
Comment
Yet *another* submarine story - this time a sort of Dalek version of *The Sea Devils*. **45%**

27) kcaB to the Sun
Dennis Hooper

Artist
Gerry Haylock
Publication
TV Action 116-119 (5-26 May 1973)
Format
Colour / 4 / 8
Companion
Roger Perritt
Précis
The director of a Welsh solar-energy plant wants to turn the Earth into a raging inferno…
Reprint
Doctor Who Classic Comics 24
Comment
Very similar set-up to the yet-to-be-aired The Green Death, this is a good story well told and drawn. **80%**

28) The Labyrinth
Dennis Hooper

Artist
Gerry Haylock
Publication
TV Action 120 (2 June 1973)
Format
B&W / 1 / 7
Précis
Doctor Who undergoes many gruelling tests by a gorilla-like monster…
Reprint
1. 1977 Doctor Who Winter Special (with Tom Baker drawn over Jon Pertwee by John Canning)
2. Doctor Who Classic Comics 25 (colourized)
Comment
Primitive storytelling and a cop-out ending. **32%**

29) The Spoilers
Dick O'Neill

Artist
Gerry Haylock
Publication
TV Action 123 (23 June 1973)
Format
B&W / 1 / 7
Précis
On the polluted planet Farraf, Lord Soton plans on invading his idyllic neighbouring planet Raffar…
Reprint
1. 1977 Doctor Who Winter Special (with Tom Baker drawn over Jon Pertwee by John Canning)
2. Doctor Who Classic Comics 27 (colourized)
Comment
Heavy-handed morality tale with little inherent interest. **30%**

30) Dr. Who in the Vortex
Dennis Hooper

Artist
Gerry Haylock
Publication
TV Action 125-129 (7 July-4 August 1973)
Format
Colour / 5 / 10
Companion
Tom Phipps
Précis
Doctor Who and his friend are deposited in a specimen-collecting computer by a space tornado…
Reprint
Doctor Who Classic Comics 27
Comment
Claws of Axos meets Twister in this imaginatively illustrated adventure. **75%**

31) The Unheard Voice
Unknown

Artist
Gerry Haylock
Publication
TV Action 131 (18 August 1973)
Format
B&W / 1 / 7
Précis
Earth's animals are driven wild by high-frequency transmissions from a faulty satellite…
Reprint
1. 1977 Doctor Who Winter Special (with Tom Baker drawn over Jon Pertwee by John Canning)
2. Doctor Who Classic Comics 27 (colourized)
Comment
The last TV Action (formerly Countdown) strip is an effective homage to The Birds (1963). **68%**

32) Children of the Evil Eye
Unknown

Artist
Gerry Haylock
Publication
TV Comic plus TV Action 1133-1138 (1 September-6 October 1973)
Format
B&W / 6 / 12
Companion
Arnold
Précis
Children rule future Earth, and their leader Oswald uses his electronic eye to probe the Doctor's mind...
Comment
Reasonably sophisticated take on an unoriginal premise. **55%**

33) Nova
Unknown

Artist
Gerry Haylock
Publication
TV Comic plus TV Action 1139-1147 (13 October-8 December 1973)
Format
B&W / 9 / 18
Companion
Arnold
Précis
The Doctor finds a terrifying world inhabited by giant spiders and bloodthirsty dinosaurs...
Comments
More dinosaurs, more ape creatures, more dull running around. **22%**

34) The Amateur
Unknown

Artist
Gerry Haylock
Publication
TV Comic plus TV Action 1148-1149, TV Comic 1149-1154 (15 December 1973-26 January 1974)
Format
B&W / 7 / 14
Companion
Tobias Philby

Précis
Doctor Who and a Victorian time-traveller land on a German battlefield during WWI...
Reprint
TV Comic 1390-1396 (with Tom Baker drawn over Jon Pertwee by John Canning)
Comment
A simplistic digression on scientific responsibility. **36%**

35) The Disintegrator
Unknown

Artist
Gerry Haylock
Publication
TV Comic 1155-1159 (2 February-2 March 1974)
Format
B&W / 5 / 10
Précis
Doctor Who investigates a daring bank raid, only to find the Daleks behind it...
Comment
The Daleks' involvement in a petty bank robbery goes unexplained in this thinly plotted tale. **44%**

36) Is Anyone There?
Unknown

Artist
Gerry Haylock
Publication
TV Comic 1160-1169 (9 March-11 May 1974)
Format
B&W / 10 / 20
Précis
An Australian scientist's accelerated radio transmissions cause havoc with the world's weather...
Comment
An effective scientific thriller with an interesting race of aliens. **67%**

37) Size Control
Unknown

Artist
Gerry Haylock

Publication
TV Comic 1170-1176 (18 May-29 June 1974)
Format
B&W / 7 / 14
Précis
Doctor Who is taken prisoner by the giant Mantis who want his Tardis to escape from the Tyrryxians…
Reprint
TV Comic 1424-1430 (with Tom Baker drawn over Jon Pertwee by John Canning)
Comment
B-movie nonsense with a surfeit of technobabble. **40%**

38) The Magician!
Unknown

Artist
Gerry Haylock
Publication
TV Comic 1177-1181, *TV Comic plus Tom and Jerry Weekly* 1182-1183 (6 July-17 August 1974)
Format
B&W / 7 / 14
Précis
Landing in the Middle Ages, Doctor Who is captured by a villainous lord and locked in his dungeon…
Reprint
TV Comic 1397-1403 (with Tom Baker drawn over Jon Pertwee by John Canning)
Comment
Fairly interesting historical featuring unexplained magical overtones. **55%**

39) The Metal-Eaters!
Unknown

Artist
Gerry Haylock
Publication
TV Comic plus Tom and Jerry Weekly 1184-1190 (24 August-5 October 1974)
Format
B&W / 7 / 14
Précis
Professor McTurk and his daughter Catriona's metal-eating insects threaten to lay waste to Blackpool…
Reprint
TV Comic 1409-1415 (with Tom Baker drawn over Jon Pertwee by John Canning)
Comment
Remake of the other *The Metal Eaters* (4) from earlier in the Third Doctor's run, this time more *Terror of the Autons* than *Spearhead from Space*. **75%**

40) Lords of the Ether!
Unknown

Artist
Gerry Haylock
Publication
TV Comic plus Tom and Jerry Weekly 1191-1198 (12 October-30 November 1974)
Format
B&W / 8 / 16
Companion
Harry Gordino
Précis
Astronauts on the Moon discover a tunnel leading to the burial chamber of an ancient race…
Reprint
TV Comic 1416-1423 (renamed *Moon Exploration*, with Tom Baker drawn over Jon Pertwee by John Canning)
Comment
Fairly accurate Apollo adventure with a well thought-out plot. **70%**

41) The Wanderers
Unknown

Artist
Gerry Haylock
Publication
TV Comic plus Tom and Jerry Weekly 1199-1201, *TV Comic* 1202-1203 (7 December 1974-4 January 1975)
Format
B&W / 5 / 10
Précis
The Thusion race is in suspended animation aboard a huge spaceship and desperate to find an uninhabited world to settle on…
Reprint
TV Comic 1404-1408 (with Tom Baker drawn over Jon Pertwee by John Canning)

Comment
A neatly written adventure marking the final Third Doctor strip for *TV Comic*. **82%**

42) Change of Mind
Kate Orman

Artist
Barrie Mitchell
Publication
Doctor Who Magazine 221-223 (18 January-15 March 1995)
Format
B&W / 3 / 21
Companions
Brigadier, Liz
Précis
In Cambridge, an ex-UNIT employee is using his psychokinetic powers to kill people...
Comment
Charmless artwork aside, this is a clever story with sequences reminiscent of previous strip *Deadly Choice* (23). **55%**

43) Target Practice
Gareth Roberts

Artist
Adrian Salmon
Publication
Doctor Who Magazine 234 (17 January 1996)
Format
B&W / 1 / 7
Companions
Brigadier, Jo, Sergeant Benton
Précis
Posing as a UNIT corporal, a Kremlin agent attempts to kidnap the Doctor...
Comment
Wistful pastiche of the 1970s TV series and comic strip. **75%**

Fourth Doctor: Tom Baker

1) Death Flower!
Unknown

Artist
Gerry Haylock
Publication
TV Comic 1204-1214 (11 January-22 March 1975)
Format
B&W / 11 / 22
Companion
Sarah
Précis
In the village of Suffingham, the Vegpro Corporation is creating a hybrid species of plant-life...
Reprint
Doctor Who Classic Comics 5-6 (colourized)
Comment
Prescient *Seeds of Death* plot with poor artwork and an over-reliance on BBC reference photos. **38%**

2) Return of the Daleks!
Unknown

Artist
Martin Asbury
Publication
TV Comic 1215-1222 (29 March-17 May 1975)
Format
B&W / 8 / 16
Companion
Sarah
Précis
Renegade Time Lord Shazer joins up with the Daleks to steal Doctor Who's Tardis...
Reprint
Doctor Who Classic Comics 17 (colourized)
Comment
Excellent plot full of continuity references, saddled with appallingly rushed artwork. **50%**

3) The Wreckers!
Dennis Hooper

Artist
Martin Asbury
Publication
TV Comic 1223-1231 (24 May-19 July 1975)
Format
B&W / 9 / 18
Companion
Sarah
Précis
On one of the moons of Gorgas, the Vogans are causing spacecraft to be pulled to their doom…
Reprint
Doctor Who Classic Comics 19
Comment
A rare bit of internal continuity as the return of an old enemy last seen in *The Vogan Slaves* (1971) breathes life into this somewhat daft tale of vanished spaceships and alien horses. **60%**

4) The Emperor's Spy!
Unknown

Artist
John Canning
Publication
TV Comic 1232-1238 (26 July-6 September 1975)
Format
B&W / 7 / 14
Companion
Sarah
Précis
In 19th century England, Doctor Who designs a prototype submarine to fight in the Napoleonic Wars…
Comment
Convincing historical detail aside, there isn't much to write home about here. **35%**

5) The Sinister Sea!
Unknown

Artist
John Canning
Publication
TV Comic 1239-1244 (13 September-18 October 1975)
Format
B&W / 6 / 12
Companion
Sarah
Précis
In the North Sea, an alien spaceship is sending out destructive tidal waves…
Comment
Submarines *again* in this run-of-the-mill alien invasion story. **45%**

6) The Space Ghost!
Unknown

Artist
John Canning
Publication
TV Comic 1245-1250 (25 October-29 November 1975)
Format
B&W / 6 / 12
Companion
Sarah
Précis
On the lonely Yorkshire moors, Doctor Who encounters spectral wraiths in a space tracking centre…
Comment
Atmospheric ghost story; a foretaste of Mark Gatiss' creepy 1992 *Doctor Who* novel *Nightshade*. **80%**

7) The Dalek Revenge!
Unknown

Artist
John Canning
Publication
TV Comic 1251-1258 (6 December 1975-24 January 1976)
Format
B&W / 8 / 16
Companion
Sarah
Précis
The Daleks plan to turn the planet Ercos into a gigantic missile aimed at Earth…
Comment
The Daleks have never looked better in this, their last appearance in *TV Comic*. **85%**

8) Virus*
Unknown

Artist
John Canning
Publication
TV Comic 1259-1265 (31 January-13 March 1976)
Format
B&W / 7 / 14
Companion
Sarah
Précis
The Doctor and Sarah accidentally kill a Bandriggen survey team with a seemingly innocuous virus...
Comment
Intriguing storyline centring around extraterrestrial language difficulties. **76%**

9) Treasure Trail*
Unknown

Artist
John Canning
Publication
TV Comic 1266-1272 (20 March-1 May 1976)
Format
B&W / 7 / 14
Companion
Sarah
Précis
Doctor Who is despatched to prevent Italian artwork falling into German hands during WWII...
Comment
The Doctor is an unlikely lackey of the Time Lords in this trivial tale of art theft. **30%**

10) Hubert's Folly
Unknown

Artist
John Canning
Publication
TV Comic 1273-1279 (8 May-19 June 1976)
Format
B&W / 7 / 14
Companion
Sarah
Précis
Julian Hubert unearths a powerful force from beneath his ancestral seat...
Comment
Declining artwork combined with a forgettable plot. **25%**

11) Counter-Rotation*
Unknown

Artist
John Canning
Publication
TV Comic 1280-1286 (26 June-7 August 1976)
Format
B&W / 7 / 14
Companion
Sarah
Précis
A Martian called Scartig launches an orbital device that will stop the Earth moving on its axis...
Comment
Silly nonsense not helped by more bad artwork. **28%**

12) Mind Snatch
Unknown

Artist
John Canning
Publication
TV Comic 1287-1290 (14 August-4 September 1976)
Format
B&W / 4 / 8
Companion
Sarah
Précis
Meekle, Lord of the Goblins, sets out to possess the Doctor's mind...
Comment
Feeble story stretched to breaking point. **20%**

13) The Hoaxers*
Unknown

Artist
Paul Canning
Publication
TV Comic 1291 (11 September 1976)
Format
B&W / 1 / 2
Companion
Sarah
Précis
Doctor Who and Sarah pretend to be aliens to squeeze out a charitable donation from a wealthy miser…
Comment
Deliberately humorous little tale, quite nicely done. **65%**

14) The Mutant Strain*
Unknown

Artist
John Canning
Publication
Mighty TV Comic 1292-1297 (18 September-23 October 1976)
Format
B&W / 6 / 6
Précis
Doctor Who must stop Professor Braun and his giant mutated pets…
Comment
Yet another unoriginal 'giant monsters on the loose' adventure. **38%**

15) Double Trouble*
Unknown

Artist
John Canning
Publication
Mighty TV Comic 1298-1304 (30 October-11 December 1976)
Format
B&W / 7 / 7
Précis
The evil Varthecs use a double of Doctor Who and frame him for some dastardly crimes…
Comment
The Doctor on trial by the Time Lords again in a reasonably entertaining story. **55%**

16) Dredger
Geoff Cowan

Artist
John Canning
Publication
Mighty TV Comic 1305-1311 (18 December 1976-29 January 1977)
Format
B&W / 7 / 7
Companion
Sarah
Précis
Doctor Who tries to avert a war between the US Navy and the Craytons…
Comment
Sarah briefly returns, and nice to see the Season 14 wooden console room in the strip. **70%**

17) The False Planet
Unknown

Artist
John Canning
Publication
Mighty TV Comic 1312-1317 (5 February-12 March 1977)
Format
B&W / 6 / 6
Précis
Doctor Who has trouble finding the Diloons a new planet for their power source…
Comment
Uninteresting quest to save a dying race. **45%**

18) The Fire Feeders
Unknown

Artist
John Canning
Publication
Mighty TV Comic 1318-1325 (19 March-7 May 1977)

Format
B&W / 8 / 8
Précis
A Zandan invasion force wants to destroy the Earth with their deadly heat projector gun...
Comment
Forgettable yarn with innumerable SF clichés. **28%**

19) Kling Dynasty
Unknown

Artist
John Canning
Publication
Mighty TV Comic 1326-1333 (14 May-2 July 1977)
Format
B&W / 8 / 16
Précis
On the planet Earthos, Doctor Who helps the Braggen slaves defeat the Shogun-like Klings...
Comment
Interesting Oriental angle which quickly descends into fairytale. **35%**

20) The Orb
Unknown

Artist
John Canning
Publication
Mighty TV Comic 1334-1340 (9 July-20 August 1977)
Format
B&W / 7 / 14
Companion
Leela
Précis
Inside a hollow asteroid, a Stracton invasion force prepares to attack the Earth...
Comment
Excellent characterization of Leela in an otherwise bog standard invasion yarn. **40%**

21) The Mutants
Unknown

Artist
John Canning
Publication
Mighty TV Comic 1341-1347 (27 August-8 October 1977)
Format
B&W / 7 / 14
Companion
Leela
Précis
Doctor Who helps the Meerags to defeat mutant insects caused by pollution...
Comment
Vaguely meaningful message-type story about caring for the environment. Or something. **34%**

22) The Devil's Mouth
Unknown author

Artist
John Canning
Publication
Mighty TV Comic 1348-1352 (15 October-12 November 1977)
Format
B&W / 5 / 10
Companion
Leela
Précis
A comatose potholer is suddenly transformed into a lizardlike Vrakon...
Comment
Possibly the only point of interest here is that Leela has slipped out of her leather costume and is now wearing jeans. **30%**

23) The Aqua-City
Geoff Cowan

Artist
John Canning
Publication
TV Comic 1353-1360 (19 November 1977-7 January 1978)
Format
B&W / 8 / 16

Companion
Leela
Précis
On a distant planet, Doctor Who and Leela are attacked by the Atlanteans' Cyeran robots…
Comment
The final Leela story, otherwise business as usual. **28%**

24) The Snow Devils
Unknown

Artist
John Canning
Publication
TV Comic 1361-1365 (14 January-11 February 1978)
Format
B&W / 5 / 10
Précis
Tibetan monks are being terrorized by fierce Himalayan creatures…
Comment
Tired Yeti-less rip-off of *The Abominable Snowmen*. **20%**

25) The Space Garden
Unknown

Artist
John Canning
Publication
TV Comic 1366-1370 (18 February-18 March 1978)
Format
B&W / 5 / 10
Précis
A huge mutated plant, servant of the space pirates, is attacking the peaceful Dovans…
Comment
Oh look, it's the Pathetic Vegetable Monster. How scary. **18%**

26) The Eerie Manor
Unknown

Artist
John Canning
Publication
TV Comic 1371-1372 (25 March-1 April 1978)
Format
B&W / 2 / 4
Précis
In creepy Darke Manor, the mediaeval suits of armour are coming to life…
Comment
A rational explanation is of course found for this *Scooby Doo*-style mystery. **20%**

27) Guardian of the Tomb / The Living Mist! †
Unknown

Artist
John Canning
Publication
TV Comic 1373-1379 (8 April-20 May 1978)
Format
B&W / 7 / 14
Précis
An alien space tomb releases a deadly mind-controlling mist…
Comment
Fairly atmospheric spookiness gives way to the usual running around. **40%**
(† *final episode title only*)

28) The Image Makers
Unknown

Artist
John Canning
Publication
TV Comic 1380-1385 (27 May-1 July 1978)
Format
B&W / 6 / 12
Précis
Stranded on the planet of the Bukats, the Turags use image-projecting devices to protect themselves…
Comment
It had to end sometime - thank goodness. **35%**

NB: Reprints of Second and Third Doctor stories continued - with Tom Baker's likeness appended onto the actors' faces and bodies courtesy of John Canning - until issue 1430 (12 May 1979)

29) Doctor Who and the Iron Legion
Pat Mills and John Wagner

Artist
Dave Gibbons
Publication
Doctor Who Weekly 1-8 (17 October-5 December 1979)
Format
B&W / 8 / 34
Companions
Morris, Vesuvius
Précis
The Doctor must overthrow the alien rulers of a parallel Earth where the Roman Empire never fell…
Reprints
1. *Marvel Premiere* (US) 57-58
2. *Doctor Who 1980 Summer Special*
3. *Doctor Who 1985 Summer Special Classic* (colourised)
4. *Doctor Who Volume 1: The Iron Legion*
Comment
Exciting, funny epic with spectacular artwork; it really *feels* like proper *Doctor Who*. **90%**

30) City of the Damned
Pat Mills and John Wagner

Artist
Dave Gibbons
Publication
Doctor Who Weekly 9-16 (12 December 1979-30 January 1980)
Format
B&W / 8 / 30
Précis
In the City of the Damned, all emotion is forbidden…
Reprints
1. *Marvel Premiere* (US) 57-58 (renamed *City of the Cursed*)
2. *Doctor Who Volume 1: The Iron Legion*
Comment
Full of black humour, this is a surprisingly mature story with some great visual images. **95%**

31) Timeslip
Dez Skinn and Paul Neary

Artist
Paul Neary
Publication
Doctor Who Weekly 17-18 (6-13 February 1980)
Format
B&W / 2 / 8
Companion
K-9
Précis
A hungry space amoeba forces the Doctor back through his own incarnations…
Reprints
1. *The Very Best of Doctor Who* 1981
2. *Doctor Who* (US) 18
3. *Doctor Who Classic Comics* 27
4. *Doctor Who Volume 3: The Tides of Time*
Comment
Despite every frame being copied from reference photos, this is a neat little story with a striking visual look. **75%**

32) Doctor Who and the Star Beast
Pat Mills and John Wagner

Artist
Dave Gibbons
Publication
Doctor Who Weekly 19-26 (20 February-9 April 1980)
Format
B&W / 8 / 34
Companions
K-9, Sharon
Précis
Terrifying Wrath warriors hunt down the cuddly alien Meep in the rain-soaked streets of Blackcastle…
Reprints
1. *Doctor Who* (US) 1-2 (colourised)
2. *Doctor Who Classic Comics* 25-26
3. *Doctor Who Volume 1: The Iron Legion*
Comment
A witty Season 17-style adventure with beautiful artwork, smashing jokes and a wonderful villain. **96%**

33) Doctor Who and the Dogs of Doom
John Wagner and Pat Mills

Artist
Dave Gibbons
Publication
Doctor Who Weekly 27-34 (16 April-5 June 1980)
Format
B&W / 8 / 34
Companions
K-9, Sharon, Brill
Précis
The Daleks and their Werelok henchmen are laying waste to the New Earth planetary system...
Reprints
1. *Doctor Who* (US) 3-4 (colourized)
2. *Doctor Who Volume 1: The Iron Legion*
Comment
Well-written space opera with sympathetic characters, enlivened enormously by the Daleks' dramatic entrance. **88%**

34) Doctor Who and the Time Witch
Steve Moore

Artist
Dave Gibbons
Publication
Doctor Who Weekly 35-38 (12 June-3 July 1980)
Format
B&W / 4 / 17
Companions
K-9, Sharon
Précis
A voluptuous witch uses her powers to keep the Doctor and Sharon hostage inside her black hole...
Reprints
1. *Doctor Who* (US) 5 (colourized)
2. *Doctor Who Volume 1: The Iron Legion*
Comment
Lightweight fairytale, silly rather than funny. **45%**

35) Dragon's Claw
Steve Moore

Artist
Dave Gibbons
Publication
Doctor Who Weekly 39-43, Doctor Who 44-45 (10 July-October 1980)
Format
B&W / 7 / 34
Companions
K-9, Sharon
Précis
A plague of violence in a 16th century Chinese monastery is the work of the Sontarans...
Reprints
1. *Doctor Who* (US) 6-7 (colourized)
2. *Doctor Who Volume 2: Dragon's Claw*
Comment
Intriguing story let down by bland artwork. **60%**

36) The Collector
Steve Moore

Artist
Dave Gibbons
Publication
Doctor Who 46 (November 1980)
Format
B&W / 1 / 8
Companions
K-9, Sharon
Précis
On a barren asteroid, an anthropologist is kept imprisoned by his obsessive computer...
Reprints
1. *Doctor Who* (US) 8 (colourized)
2. *Doctor Who Volume 2: Dragon's Claw*
Comment
Simplistic short story with a cop-out ending. **38%**

37) Dreamers of Death
Steve Moore

Artist
Dave Gibbons
Publication
Doctor Who 47-48 (December 1980-January 1981)

Format
B&W / 2 / 16
Companions
K-9, Sharon
Précis
On Uniceptor IV, telepathic Slinth creatures have been feeding off people's dreams…
Reprint
1. *Doctor Who* (US) 8 (colourized)
2. *Doctor Who Volume 2: Dragon's Claw*
Comment
Inventive premise, but the giant monster is a little hackneyed. **64%**

38) *The Life Bringer! / Life-Bringer†*
Steve Moore

Artist
Dave Gibbons
Publication
Doctor Who 49-50 (February-March 1981)
Issues / Instalments / Format
B&W / 2 / 16
Companion
K-9
Précis
The Doctor rescues Prometheus and meets the Gods of Olympus…
Reprints
1. *Doctor Who* (US) 9 (colourized)
2. *Doctor Who Volume 2: Dragon's Claw*
Comment
Gorgeous artwork although the story itself is rather hard to take seriously. **55%**
(† second episode title only)

39) *War of the Words*
Steve Moore

Artist
Dave Gibbons
Publication
Doctor Who 51 (April 1981)
Format
B&W / 1 / 9
Companion
K-9

Précis
For almost half a century, the Vromyx and Garynths wage war over the library planet of Biblios…
Reprints
1. *Doctor Who* (US) 10 (colourized)
2. *Doctor Who Volume 2: Dragon's Claw*
Comment
Succinct satire on the importance of your local lending library. **70%**

40) *Spider-God*
Steve Moore

Artist
Dave Gibbons
Publication
Doctor Who 52 (May 1981)
Format
B&W / 1 / 8
Précis
A human survey party kills a giant spider, unaware of what it will turn into…
Reprints
1. *Star-Lord Special Edition* 1982 (colourized)
2. *Doctor Who* (US) 10 (colourized)
3. *Doctor Who Magazine* 182
4. *Doctor Who Volume 2: Dragon's Claw*
Comment
Effective morality tale, inspired perhaps by the previous year's *Full Circle*. **80%**

41) *The Deal*
Steve Parkhouse

Artist
Dave Gibbons
Publication
Doctor Who 53 (June 1981)
Format
B&W / 1 / 8
Précis
A mercenary killer uses the Doctor to forestall his inevitable death…
Reprints
1. *Doctor Who* (US) 11 (colourized)
2. *Doctor Who Volume 2: Dragon's Claw*
Comment
Pretentious twaddle about the nature of machismo. **20%**

42) End of the Line
Steve Parkhouse

Artist
Dave Gibbons
Publication
Doctor Who 54-55 (July-August 1981)
Format
B&W / 2 / 16
Précis
The Doctor tries to help a group of people escape from their industrialised city...
Reprint
1. Doctor Who (US) 11-12 (colourized)
2. Doctor Who Volume 2: Dragon's Claw
Comment
Sketchy artwork aside, this is quite possibly the most devastating comic strip ever written. **99%**

43) Doctor Who and the Free-Fall Warriors
Steve Parkhouse

Artist
Dave Gibbons
Publication
Doctor Who 56-57 (September-October 1981)
Format
B&W / 2 / 16
Companion
Dr Isaac Asimoff
Précis
The Doctor takes part in a dangerous space race...
Reprints
1. Doctor Who (US) 12 (colourized)
2. Doctor Who Volume 2: Dragon's Claw
Comment
Pilot story for the Freefall Warriors in which the Doctor plays little part, but Dr Asimoff is charming. **33%**

44) Junk-Yard Demon
Steve Parkhouse

Artist
Mike McMahon and Adolfo Buylla
Publication
Doctor Who 58-59 (November - December 1981)
Format
B&W / 2 / 16
Companions
Flots, Jets
Précis
Two eccentric junk dealers accidentally reactive a Cyberman...
Reprints
1. Doctor Who 1983 Summer Special
2. Doctor Who (US) 13 (colourized)
3. Doctor Who Volume 2: Dragon's Claw
Comment
An extraordinarily surreal excursion complemented by mad, brilliant artwork. Quite wonderful. **85%**

45) The Neutron Knights
Steve Parkhouse

Artist
Dave Gibbons
Publication
Doctor Who 60 (January 1982)
Format
B&W / 1 / 8
Précis
Merlin takes the Doctor to a future Earth in which King Arthur battles the great mutant Catavolcus...
Reprint
1. Doctor Who (US) 14 (colourized)
2. Doctor Who Classic Comics 9 (colourized)
3. Doctor Who Volume 2: Dragon's Claw
Comment
Brilliantly realized, if annoyingly fragmentary, prologue to the Fifth Doctor epic The Tides of Time. **85%**

46) Victims
Dan Abnett

Artist
Colin Andrew
Publication
Doctor Who Magazine 212-214 (11 May-6 July 1994)
Format
B&W / 3 / 24
Companion
Romana II
Précis
Arriving on the fashion planet of Kolpasha, the Doctor finds beauty is only skin-deep...

Comment
Inconsequential satire with so-so artwork. **35%**

47) Black Destiny
Gary Russell

Artists
Martin Geraghty and Bambos Georgiou
Publication
Doctor Who Magazine 235-237 (14 February-10 April 1996)
Format
B&W / 3 / 21
Companions
Sarah, Harry
Précis
At a 21st century Russian cultural centre, the Direktor is less human than he seems…
Comment
Heavy-handed parable about nuclear power with much soul-searching about Chernobyl. **45%**

48) Doctor Who and the Fangs of Time
Sean Longcroft

Artist
Sean Longcroft
Publication
Doctor Who Magazine 243 (25 September 1996)
Format
B&W / 1 / 7
Companion
Sarah
Précis
A prospective *Doctor Who* author gets a life-changing visit from the Fourth Doctor…
Comment
Utterly charming aside on *Doctor Who*'s effect on its fan: sad, funny and true. **90%**

Fifth Doctor: Peter Davison

1) The Tides of Time
Steve Parkhouse

Artist
Dave Gibbons
Publication
Doctor Who Monthly 61-67 (February-August 1982)
Format
B&W, colour (66: centrespread) / 7 / 57
Companions
Justin, Shayde
Précis
The Doctor must hunt down and defeat the demon Melanicus who has stolen the Event Synthesiser…
Reprints
1. *Doctor Who* (US) 15-18 (colourised)
2. *Doctor Who Classic Comics* 10-11 (colourised)
3. *Doctor Who Volume 3: The Tides of Time*
Comment
A masterpiece of graphic art, even though the story itself is largely incoherent. **88%**

2) Stars Fell on Stockbridge
Steve Parkhouse

Artist
Dave Gibbons
Publication
Doctor Who Monthly 68-69 (September-October 1982)
Format
B&W / 2 / 15
Companion
Maxwell Edison
Précis
The Doctor and an eccentric Ufologist explore a derelict spaceship haunted by a mysterious presence…
Reprints
1. *Doctor Who* (US) 19 (colourised)
2. *Doctor Who Classic Comics* 18 (colourised)
3. *Doctor Who Volume 3: The Tides of Time*
Comment
Inconclusive, but heavy on atmosphere and character, and with an ending to die for **75%**

3) The Stockbridge Horror
Steve Parkhouse

Artists
Steve Parkhouse and Paul Neary (70-71), Steve Parkhouse (72), Mick Austin and Paul Neary (73-74), Mick Austin (75)
Publication
Doctor Who Monthly 70-75 (November 1982-April 1983)
Format
B&W / 6 / 48
Précis
The Tardis becomes possessed by the elemental spirit of a deserted spaceship…
Reprints
1. *Doctor Who* (US) 20-22 (colourized)
2. *Doctor Who Classic Comics* 21-23 (colourized)
3. *Doctor Who Volume 3: The Tides of Time*
Comment
Misguided attempt to match the success of *The Tides of Time*, doomed by rubbish artwork. **20%**

4) Lunar Lagoon
Steve Parkhouse

Artist
Mick Austin
Publication
Doctor Who Monthly 76-77 (May - June 1983)
Format
B&W / 2 / 16
Précis
The Doctor befriends a lone Japanese soldier on Pacific island in a WWII…
Reprints
1. *Doctor Who* (US) 23 (colourized)
2. *Doctor Who Volume 3: The Tides of Time*
Comment
Sombre two-hander that's a bit too maudlin for its own good. **55%**

5) 4-Dimensional Vistas
Steve Parkhouse

Artist
Mick Austin
Publication
Doctor Who Monthly 78-83 (July - December 1983)
Format
B&W / 6 / 48
Companion
Gus
Précis
The Doctor engages in a deadly battle of wits with the Meddling Monk and the Ice Warriors…
Reprint
Doctor Who Volume 3: The Tides of Time
Comment
Messy concoction of old foes and muddled plotting. **40%**

6) The Moderator
Steve Parkhouse

Artist
Steve Dillon
Publication
Doctor Who Monthly 84, *The Official Doctor Who Magazine* 86-87 (January, March-April 1984)
Format
B&W / 3 / 24
Companion
Gus
Précis
Toadish tycoon Josiah W Dogbolter has his eyes set on acquiring the Tardis - at all costs…
Reprint
Doctor Who Volume 3: The Tides of Time
Comment
Finely honed satire with an unexpectedly tragic ending. **85%**

7) The Lunar Strangers
Gareth Roberts

Artist
Martin Geraghty
Publication
Doctor Who Magazine 215-217 (3 August-28 September 1994)
Format
B&W / 3 / 21
Companions
Tegan, Turlough
Précis
Seemingly innocent bovine aliens infiltrate their way into a Moonbase…

Comment
Amusing *TV Comic* pastiche done with panache. **67%**

8) The Curse of the Scarab
Alan Barnes

Artist
Martin Geraghty
Publication
Doctor Who Magazine 228-230 (2 August-27 September 1995)
Format
B&W / 3 / 21
Companion
Peri
Précis
1938 Hollywood, and a new Mummy movie unearths an ancient evil…
Comment
Gorier cousin of *Pyramids of Mars* with some eye-catching artwork. **72%**

Sixth Doctor: Colin Baker

1) The Shape Shifter
Steve Parkhouse

Artist
John Ridgway
Publication
The Official Doctor Who Magazine 88-89 (May-June 1984)
Format
B&W / 2 / 16
Companion
Frobisher
Précis
The Doctor and Frobisher relieve Josiah W Dogbolter of a small fortune in universal credits…
Reprints
1. *Doctor Who Collected Comics* (colourized)
2. *Doctor Who: Voyager* graphic novel (colourized)
3. *Doctor Who Marvel Adventure Comics* 5 (colourized)
Comment
Light-hearted sequel to Fifth Doctor strip *The Moderator* which introduces a great new companion. **67%**

2) Voyager
Steve Parkhouse

Artist
John Ridgway
Publication
The Official Doctor Who Magazine 90-94 (July-November 1984)
Format
B&W / 5 / 40
Companion
Frobisher
Précis
The Doctor finds a strange old man called Astrolabus in a lighthouse at the edge of the world…
Reprints
1. *Doctor Who: Voyager* graphic novel (colourized)
2. *Doctor Who Marvel Adventure Comics* 6 (parts 4 & 5 only, colourized)
Comment
Another attempt to emulate *The Tides of Time* with added mysticism; often funny but rarely coherent. **78%**

3) Polly the Glot
Steve Parkhouse

Artist
John Ridgway
Publication
The Official Doctor Who Magazine 95-97 (December 1984-February 1985)
Format
B&W / 3 / 24
Companions
Frobisher, Dr Isaac Asimoff
Précis
The Doctor helps Dr Asimoff stop the hunting of the Glots, but Frobisher is kidnapped by Astrolabus…
Reprint
1. *Doctor Who Collected Comics* (colourized)
2. *Doctor Who: Voyager* graphic novel (colourized)
Comment
Loose follow-up to *Voyager* with many good jokes. **74%**

4) Once Upon a Time-Lord
Steve Parkhouse

Artist
John Ridgway
Publication
The Official Doctor Who Magazine 98, *The Doctor Who Magazine* 99 (March-April 1985)
Format
B&W / 2 / 16
Companion
Frobisher
Précis
Going to the aid of Frobisher, the Doctor engages in a surreal chase after Astrolabus…
Reprints
1. *Doctor Who: Voyager* graphic novel (colourized)
2. *Doctor Who Marvel Adventure Comics* 4 (colourized)
Comment
The Mind Robber on acid; a bamboozling 'conclusion' to the *Voyager* storyline. **82%**

5) War-Game
Alan McKenzie

Artist
John Ridgway
Publication
The Doctor Who Magazine 100-101 (May-June 1985)
Format
B&W / 2 / 16
Companion
Frobisher
Précis
The Doctor becomes involved with a feud between a stranded Draconian warlord and a primitive king…
Reprint
Doctor Who Marvel Adventure Comics 3 (colourized)
Comment
Mundane sword-and-sorcery. **40%**

6) Funhouse
Max Stockbridge (pen-name for Alan McKenzie)

Artist
John Ridgway
Publication
The Doctor Who Magazine 102-103 (July-August 1985)
Format
B&W / 2 / 16
Companion
Frobisher
Précis
A malevolent creature living in the Vortex joins with the Tardis and threatens the Doctor's very lives…
Reprint
Doctor Who Marvel Adventure Comics 2 (colourized)
Comment
Intelligent oddness, with more than an echo of old *Doctor Who Weekly* strip *Timeslip*. **79%**

7) Kane's Story / Abel's Story / The Warrior's Story / Frobisher's Story
Max Stockbridge (pen-name for Alan McKenzie)

Artist
John Ridgway
Publication
The Doctor Who Magazine 104-106, *Doctor Who Magazine* 107 (September-December 1985)
Format
B&W / 4 / 32*
Companions
Frobisher, Peri
Précis
Six experts from various alien races are brought together to defeat the Skeletoids…
Reprint
Doctor Who Classic Comics 19-22 (colourized)
Comment
Fragmentary and slow-moving, with little obvious point. **30%**
* Pages in the final instalment were printed out of sequence

8) Exodus / Revelation! / Genesis!
Alan McKenzie

Artist
John Ridgway
Publication
Doctor Who Magazine 108-110 (January-March 1986)
Format
B&W / 3 / 24
Companions
Frobisher, Peri
Précis
On Sylvaniar, a mad scientist is attempting to brings some stranded Cybermen to life...
Reprints
1. Doctor Who Marvel Adventure Comics 1 (last 2 parts, colourized)
2. Doctor Who Classic Comics 16 (colourized)
Comment
Unengaging storyline which even the Cybermen can't enliven. **24%**

9) Nature of the Beast!
Simon Furman

Artist
John Ridgway
Publication
Doctor Who Magazine 111-113 (April-June 1986)
Format
B&W / 3 / 24
Companions
Frobisher, Peri
Précis
On a paradisiacal world, a savage wolf creature is on the loose...
Comment
A thinly disguised fairytale with little sophistication. **35%**

10) Time Bomb
Jamie Delano

Artist
John Ridgway
Publication
Doctor Who Magazine 114-116 (July-September 1986)
Format
B&W / 3 / 24
Companions
Frobisher, Peri
Précis
The Hedrons dispose of their unwanted genetic waste by sending it back to primeval Earth...
Reprint
The Incomplete Death's Head 9
Comment
A preposterous 'time loop' storyline, inexpertly plotted. **28%**

11) Salad Daze
Simon Furman (with apologies to Lewis Carroll)

Artist
John Ridgway
Publication
Doctor Who Magazine 117 (October 1986)
Format
B&W / 1 / 8
Companion
Peri
Précis
The Doctor has a cunning plan to dissuade Peri from giving him a vegetarian diet...
Comment
Twee anti-vegetarian polemic, nicely drawn. **55%**

12) Changes
Grant Morrison

Artist
John Ridgway
Publication
Doctor Who Magazine 118-119 (November-December 1986)
Format
B&W / 2 / 16
Companions
Frobisher, Peri
Précis
The Tardis has been invaded by a malevolent shape-changing alien...
Comment
Bizarre tale set in the Tardis' version of a *Star Trek* holodeck; the script is subservient to the images. **45%**

13) Profits of Doom!
Mike Collins

Artist
John Ridgway
Publication
Doctor Who Magazine 120-122 (January-March 1987)
Format
B&W / 3 / 24
Companions
Frobisher, Peri, Kara
Précis
The mercenary profiteers of Ephte are plundering an Earth colony ship on its way to Arcadia…
Comment
Cluttered artwork in a rehash of *The Sun Makers* for a less discerning audience. **33%**

14) The Gift
Jamie Delano

Artists
123-125: John Ridgway; 126: John Ridgway (Pencils), Tim Perkins (Inks)
Publication
Doctor Who Magazine 123-126 (April-July 1987)
Format
B&W / 4 / 32
Companions
Frobisher, Peri
Précis
On the jazz-loving planet Zazz, the Doctor battles against a horde of replicating robotic scavengers…
Comment
Stupid story not helped by the dramatically declining artwork. **20%**

15) The World Shapers
Grant Morrison

Artists
John Ridgway (Pencils), Tim Perkins (Inks)
Publication
Doctor Who Magazine 127-129 (August-October 1987)
Format
B&W / 3 / 24
Companions
Frobisher, Peri, Jamie
Précis
The Doctor discovers the Voord are using a Worldshaper machine to turn themselves into Cybermen…
Comment
Fascinating revision of *Doctor Who* lore, hampered by poor art. **50%**

16) Emperor of the Daleks! (Part One)
Paul Cornell

Artist
Lee Sullivan
Publication
Doctor Who Magazine 197 (17 March 1993)
Format
B&W / 1 / 8
Companion
Peri
Précis
The Doctor saves Davros from extermination…
Comment
Rough artwork spoils this exciting prelude to the main Seventh Doctor story in issues 198-202. **55%**

17) "…Up Above the Gods…"
Richard Alan

Artist
Lee Sullivan
Publication
Doctor Who Magazine 227 (5 July 1995)
Format
B&W / 1 / 7
Précis
The Doctor persuades Davros to transform the Dalek army on Spiridon into a force for good…
Comment
A well-written, if slight, two-hander that acts as a very late epilogue to *Emperor of the Daleks* from issues 197-202. **45%**

Seventh Doctor: Sylvester McCoy

1) A Cold Day in Hell!
Simon Furman

Artists
John Ridgway (Pencils), Tim Perkins (Inks)
Publication
Doctor Who Magazine 130-133 (November 1987-February 1988)
Format
B&W / 4 / 31
Companions
Frobisher, Olla
Précis
The Ice Warriors have transformed the pleasure planet A-Lux into an iceworld…
Comment
Good to see some old enemies back, but the script is often undercut by lazy artwork. **60%**

2) Redemption!
Simon Furman

Artists
Kev Hopgood and Tim Perkins
Publication
Doctor Who Magazine 134 (March 1988)
Format
B&W / 1 / 8
Companion
Olla
Précis
Olla is revealed to be a heat vampire, on the run from her former master…
Comment
Rushed exit of an unworkable companion in an otherwise unmemorable tale. **32%**

3) The Crossroads of Time
Simon Furman

Artist
Geoff Senior
Publication
Doctor Who Magazine 135 (April 1988)
Format
B&W / 1 / 8
Précis
The Doctor bumps into a bounty hunter called Death's Head…
Reprints
1. *The Incomplete Death's Head* 1
2. *Bumper Comic Holiday Special* 1988
Comment
Cartoonish slapstick pilot story for a spin-off superhero. **19%**

4) Claws of the Klathi!
Mike Collins

Artists
Kev Hopgood and Dave Hine
Publication
Doctor Who Magazine 136-138 (May - July 1988)
Format
B&W / 3 / 24
Précis
Aliens in Victorian London want to use the Great Exhibition's crystal fountain to power their ship…
Reprint
Marvel Bumper Comic 1-6
Comment
A well-crafted mystery story set against a lovingly detailed Victorian backdrop. **78%**

5) Culture Shock!
Grant Morrison

Artist
Bryan Hitch
Publication
Doctor Who Magazine 139 (August 1988)
Format
B&W / 1 / 8
Précis
The Doctor comes to the aid of a stranded sea creature on an alien beach…
Reprint
Marvel Bumper Comic 9
Comment
Bold artwork (courtesy of Season 27's conceptual artist), wafer-thin story. **35%**

6) Keepsake
Simon Furman

Artist
John Higgins
Publication
Doctor Who Magazine 140 (September 1988)
Format
B&W / 1 / 8
Précis
A scavenger called Keepsake helps the Doctor rescue a busty medic from an alien encampment...
Reprints
1. The Incomplete Death's Head 4-5
2. Marvel Bumper Comic 7-8
Comment
Strong artwork and a likeable story. **55%**

7) Planet of the Dead
John Freeman

Artist
Lee Sullivan
Publication
Doctor Who Magazine 141-142 (October-November 1988)
Format
B&W / 2 / 16
Précis
On the dead planet of Adeki, the Gwanzulum try to cadge a lift off the Doctor by devious means...
Reprint
Doctor Who Classic Comics 14
Comment
Ingenious story with good likenesses of the old Doctors (but not the current one!). **70%**

8) Echoes of the Mogor!
Dan Abnett

Artist
John Ridgway
Publication
Doctor Who Magazine 143-144 (December 1988-January 1989)
Format
B&W / 2 / 16
Précis
The Foreign Hazard Duty team come up against a vicious race memory from the past...
Comment
Aliens rip-off with mediocre artwork. **45%**

9) Time and Tide
Richard Alan and John Carnell

Artists
Dougie Braithwaite and Dave Elliott
Publication
Doctor Who Magazine 145-146 (February-March 1989)
Format
B&W / 2 / 16*
Précis
The Doctor helps a pregnant male Tojanan to escape from his doomed civilization...
Comment
Flat artwork and sentimental philosophising. **23%**
* pages in the final instalment were printed out of sequence

10) Follow That Tardis!
John Carnell

Artists
Andy Lanning, John Higgins, Kev Hopgood, Dougie Braithwaite and Dave Elliott
Publication
Doctor Who Magazine 147 (April 1989)
Format
B&W / 1 / 8
Précis
The Doctor and the Sleaze Brothers chase the Meddling Monk through Earth's history...
Comment
High-jinks across time and space - what The Chase should have been but wasn't. **79%**

11) Invaders from Gantac!
Alan Grant

Artists
Martin Griffiths and Cam Smith
Publication
Doctor Who Magazine 148-150 (May-July 1989)
Format
B&W / 3 / 24

Companion
Alex 'Leapy' Trench
Précis
In 1992, the Gantacs invade London on behalf of their master, the Great Yaga...
Comment
Dated and amateurishly drawn B-movie with a Jabba the Hut lookalike. **35%**

12) Nemesis of the Daleks
Richard Alan and Steve Alan

Artist
Lee Sullivan
Publication
Doctor Who Magazine 152-155 (September-December 1989)
Format
B&W / 4 / 32
Companion
Abslom Daak
Précis
The Doctor joins forces with Dalek slayer Abslom Daak to confront the Emperor Dalek...
Reprint
Abslom Daak - Dalek Killer graphic novel
Comment
Now this is more like it! Mind-blowing Dalek artwork coupled with an epic storyline. **91%**

13) Stairway to Heaven
Paul Cornell and John Freeman

Artists
Gerry Dolan (Pencils), Rex Ward (Inks)
Publication
Doctor Who Magazine 156 (January 1990)
Format
B&W / 1 / 7
Précis
Genetic sculptor Garg Ardoniquist has created an entire species doomed to die for his 'art'...
Comment
Portentous musings on the nature of evolution. **40%**

14) Hunger From the Ends of Time!
Dan Abnett

Artist
John Ridgway
Publication
Doctor Who Magazine 157-158* (February-March 1990)
Format
B&W / 2 / 10
Précis
An FHD team is trying to stop bugs eating the stored knowledge of the Universe on the planet Catalog...
Comment
Slim tale of killer insects. **45%**
* reprinted from 'The Incredible Hulk Presents' 2-3

15) Train-Flight
Andrew Donkin and Graham S Brand

Artist
John Ridgway
Publication
Doctor Who Magazine 159-161 (April-June 1990)
Format
B&W / 3 / 21
Companion
Sarah
Précis
The Doctor and Sarah are transmatted to a living spaceship in Earth orbit inhabited by Kalik hunters...
Reprint
The Mark of Mandragora graphic novel (colourized)
Comment
Undemanding fare with Sarah reintroduced very effectively. **62%**

16) Doctor Conkerer!
Ian Rimmer

Artist
Mike Collins
Publication
Doctor Who Magazine 162 (July 1990)
Format
B&W / 1 / 5

Précis
The Doctor teaches Saxon villagers how to play conkers…
Reprint
The Mark of Mandragora graphic novel (colourized)
Comment
Fine for children aged 4-6, otherwise avoid. **15%**

17) Fellow Travellers
Andrew Cartmel

Artist
Arthur Ranson
Publication
Doctor Who Magazine 164-166 (8 September-31 October 1990)
Format
B&W / 3 / 21
Companion
Ace
Précis
The Doctor meets a body-snatching entity called a Hitcher inside a sinister old house…
Reprint
The Mark of Mandragora graphic novel (colourized)
Comment
Wonderfully dark and atmospheric tale, very scary, with lustrous noir artwork. **94%**

18) Darkness, Falling / Distractions / The Mark of Mandragora
Dan Abnett

Artists
Lee Sullivan (Pencils), Mark Farmer (Inks)
Publication
Doctor Who Magazine 167-172 (28 November 1990-17 April 1991)
Format
B&W / 6 / 34
Companion
Ace
Précis
It is 1999 and in a London nightclub the Mandragora Helix is about to be released onto the world…

Reprint
The Mark of Mandragora graphic novel (colourized)
Comment
Rather over-promoted sequel to *The Masque of Mandragora* but undeniably exciting. **85%**

19) Party Animals
Gary Russell

Artists
Mike Collins (Pencils), Steve Pini (Inks)
Publication
Doctor Who Magazine 173 (15 May 1991)
Format
B&W / 1 / 7
Companion
Ace
Précis
The Doctor meets companions, enemies and even a future incarnation at Bonjaxx' party on Maruthea…
Reprint
The Incomplete Death's Head 12
Comment
Numerous friends and foes are shoehorned into this single poorly drawn 'celebration', including the first appearance of Nick Briggs, later to feature more prominently in the Eighth Doctor strip *Wormwood* (issues 266-271). **20%**

20) The Chameleon Factor
Paul Cornell

Artists
Lee Sullivan (Pencils), Mark Farmer (Inks)
Publication
Doctor Who Magazine 174 (12 June 1991)
Format
B&W / 1 / 5
Companion
Ace
Précis
The Doctor's old ring interferes with the Tardis' chameleon circuits…
Comment
Nice throwback to the Second Doctor, although it's all pretty inconsequential. **40%**

21) The Good Soldier
Andrew Cartmel

Artist
Mike Collins (Pencils), Steve Pini (Inks)
Publication
Doctor Who Magazine 175-178 (10 July-2 October 1991)
Format
B&W / 4 / 28
Companion
Ace
Précis
In Pleasant Valley, Nevada, a 1950s American diner is transported to a giant Cybermen mothership...
Comment
Excellent Cyberman adventure, showcasing their inhumanity to devastating effect. **85%**

22) A Glitch in Time
John Freeman

Artist
Richard Whitaker
Publication
Doctor Who Magazine 179 (30 October 1991)
Format
B&W / 1 / 7
Companion
Ace
Précis
The Tardis lands in the Cretaceous Period at a nexus point in Earth's history...
Comment
Unashamed pastiche of Ray Bradbury's short story *A Sound of Thunder* with added technobabble. **50%**

23) Evening's Empire (Part One)
Andrew Cartmel

Artist
Richard Piers Rayner
Publication
Doctor Who Magazine 180 (27 November 1991)
Format
B&W / 1 / 7
Companion
Ace
Précis
In Middlesbrough, Ace is kidnapped and transported to another world by a strange young man...
Reprint
Doctor Who Classic Comics Autumn Holiday Special 1993 (complete story)
Comment
The best comic strip we never had (until it was completed two years later); incredibly stylish artwork and a real sense of menace. **96%**

24) The Grief
Dan Abnett

Artists
Vincent Danks (Pencils), Adolfo Buylla (Inks, 185), Robin Riggs (Inks, 186-187)
Publication
Doctor Who Magazine 185-187 (15 April-10 June 1992)
Format
B&W / 3 / 21
Companion
Ace
Précis
Space marines unleash a terrible genetic weapon on the dead world of Sorsha...
Comment
Ripped off *Aliens* action-fest done in a very basic style. **29%**

25) Ravens
Andrew Cartmel

Artists
Brian Williamson (Pencils), Cam Smith (Inks)
Publication
Doctor Who Magazine 188-190 (8 July-2 September 1992)
Format
B&W / 3 / 21
Companion
Ace
Précis
A vicious gang causes terror at a service station on the M2...
Comment
Rather unsavoury *New Adventures*-style violence dressed up as something important. **35%**

26) Memorial
Warwick Gray

Artist
John Ridgway
Publication
Doctor Who Magazine 191 (30 September 1992)
Format
B&W / 1 / 7
Companion
Ace
Précis
An elderly war veteran is the unknowing carrier of an alien life essence…
Comment
Charming story, beautifully illustrated. **85%**

27) Cat Litter
Marc Platt

Artist
John Ridgway
Publication
Doctor Who Magazine 192 (28 October 1992)
Format
B&W / 1 / 8
Companion
Ace
Précis
The Tardis does a spot of architectural reconfiguration…
Comment
All style, no content (and very similar in tone to the author's own *Cat's Cradle*), but visually stunning. **60%**

28) Pureblood
Dan Abnett

Artist
Colin Andrew
Publication
Doctor Who Magazine 193-196 (25 November 1992-17 February 1993)
Format
B&W / 4 / 2
Companion
Bernice
Précis
The Doctor finds himself in the middle of a war between two breeds of Sontaran…
Comment
Sontarans vs Klingon lookalikes in a serviceable space opera. **70%**

29) Emperor of the Daleks (Part Two - Part Six)
Paul Cornell and John Freeman

Artist
Lee Sullivan
Publication
Doctor Who Magazine 198-202 (14 April-4 August 1993)
Format
B&W, colour (200) / 5 / 41
Companions
Bernice, Abslom Daak
Précis
Abslom Daak captures the Doctor, who then helps the Daleks to find Davros on Spiridon…
Comment
Continuity-obsessed bridge between the previous two televised Dalek stories, full of great moments. **91%**

30) Final Genesis
Warwick Gray

Artist
Colin Andrew
Publication
Doctor Who Magazine 203-206 (1 September-24 November 1993)
Format
B&W / 4 / 32
Companions
Bernice, Ace
Précis
The Tardis arrives in a parallel world in which Silurians and humans live uneasily side by side…
Comment
New Adventures-inspired reworking of Silurian mythology, quite well handled. **75%**

31) Time and Time Again
Paul Cornell

Artist
John Ridgway
Publication
Doctor Who Magazine 207 (22 December 1993)
Format
Colour / 1 / 10
Companions
Bernice, Ace
Précis
The Doctor and his companions must find once more the six segments of the Key to Time...
Comment
Self-indulgent 30th Anniversary celebration, but done with some style. **68%**

32) Cuckoo
Dan Abnett

Artist
John Ridgway
Publication
Doctor Who Magazine 208-210 (19 January-16 March 1994)
Format
B&W / 1 / 24
Companions
Bernice, Ace
Précis
The presence of an alien fossil in 1855 could lead to Darwin never writing his Theory of Evolution...
Comment
Evocative and atmospheric *Ghost Light*-style tale with splendid artwork. **84%**

33) Uninvited Guest
Warwick Gray

Artist
John Ridgway
Publication
Doctor Who Magazine 211 (13 April 1994)
Format
B&W / 1 / 8
Précis
The Doctor presents a special gift to a party of Eternals...

Comment
Admirably concise in script and execution. **78%**

34) Ground Zero
Scott Gray

Artists
Martin Geraghty (Pencils), Bambos Georgiou (Inks)
Publication
Doctor Who Magazine 238-242 (8 May-28 August 1996)
Format
B&W / 5 / 35
Companions
Ace, Peri, Sarah, Susan
Précis
The Doctor tries to save his companions from the giant spiders of Mankind's collective unconscious...
Comment
Hugely impressive final regular Seventh Doctor story that ties up many loose ends from earlier strips and segues nicely into the Paul McGann TV movie and comic strip. **93%**

35) The Last Word
Gareth Roberts

Artist
Lee Sullivan
Publication
Doctor Who Magazine 305 (27 June 2001)
Format
Colour / 1 / 7
Companions
Ace, Bernice
Précis
The Doctor remembers when he defeated the Timewyrm...
Comment
Inexplicable 'celebration' of a *New Adventures* concept best forgotten. **17%**

Eighth Doctor: Paul McGann

1) Endgame
Alan Barnes

Artists
Martin Geraghty (Pencils), Robin Riggs (Inks, p1), Robin Smith (Inks)
Publication
Doctor Who Magazine 244-247 (23 October 1996-15 January 1997)
Format
B&W / 4 / 29
Companions
Max, Izzy
Précis
The Doctor finds the Celestial Toymaker has taken control of the village of Stockbridge…
Comment
Dynamic opener for the Eighth Doctor, deliberately reminiscent of *The Tides of Time*. **87%**

2) The Keep
Alan Barnes

Artists
Martin Geraghty (Pencils), Robin Smith (Inks)
Publication
Doctor Who Magazine 248-249 (12 February-12 March 1997)
Format
B&W / 2 / 14
Companion
Izzy
Précis
On a barren 51st century Earth, a wizened scientist has constructed the nucleus of an artificial sun…
Comment
Pseudo-scientific potboiler with a typically downbeat ending. **57%**

3) A Life of Matter & Death
Alan Barnes

Artists
Sean Longcroft and Martin Geraghty
Publication
Doctor Who Magazine 250 (9 April 1997)
Format
B&W / 1 / 7
Companion
Izzy
Précis
The Tardis is attacked by a parasite that starts consuming all its memories…
Comment
An extremely silly 250th Anniversary tale featuring a plethora of old comic strip characters. **30%**

4) Fire and Brimstone
Alan Barnes

Artists
Martin Geraghty (Pencils), Robin Smith (Inks)
Publication
Doctor Who Magazine 251-255 (7 May-27 August 1997)
Format
B&W / 5 / 37
Companion
Izzy
Précis
Icarus Falling, one of six satellites surrounding Crivello's artificial sun, is attacked by the Daleks…
Comment
Giant killer wasps, massed Dalek armies and the introduction of the Threshold - it's all here! **90%**

5) By Hook or by Crook
Scott Gray

Artist
Adrian Salmon
Publication
Doctor Who Magazine 256 (24 September 1997)
Format
B&W / 1 / 7
Companion
Izzy

Précis
In the city-state of Tor-Ka-Nom, the Doctor and Izzy are arrested for murder...
Comment
Humorous episode that puts Izzy centre stage. **65%**

6) Tooth and Claw
Alan Barnes

Artists
Martin Geraghty (Pencils), Robin Smith (Inks)
Publication
Doctor Who Magazine 257-260 (22 October 1997-14 January 1998)
Format
B&W / 4 / 28
Companions
Izzy, Fey
Précis
Terrifying incidents plague the guests of a 1930s dinner party on an island in the Indian Ocean...
Comment
Sultry tropical adventure with full-on vampiric action. (The lesbian stuff would come later.) **80%**

7) The Final Chapter
Alan Barnes

Artists
Martin Geraghty (Pencils), Robin Smith (Inks)
Publication
Doctor Who Magazine 262-265 (11 March-3 June 1998)
Format
B&W / 4 / 29
Companions
Izzy, Fey, Shayde
Précis
Izzy and Fey take the Doctor back to Gallifrey to be healed, but the Elysians have other ideas...
Comment
Preposterous but action-packed return to Gallifrey, more *Tides of Time* references, and a truly audacious finale. **85%**

8) Wormwood
Scott Gray

Artists
Martin Geraghty (Pencils), Robin Smith (Inks)
Publication
Doctor Who Magazine 266-271 (1 July-18 November 1998)
Format
B&W / 6 / 43
Companions
Izzy, Fey, Shayde
Précis
In a lunar Wild West town, the temporarily regenerated Doctor meets the creator of The Threshold...
Comment
Nick Briggs *is* the Doctor! A weird and wonderful adventure unfettered by a rational plot. **70%**

9) Happy Deathday
Scott Gray

Artist
Roger Langridge
Publication
Doctor Who Magazine 272 (16 December 1998)
Format
B&W / 1 / 7
Companion
Izzy
Précis
The Beige Guardian plucks the Doctors from their time streams to do battle with their arch-enemies...
Comment
Another anniversary story, yet more old monsters; but at least this time it's just for laughs. **75%**

10) The Fallen
Scott Gray

Artists
Martin Geraghty (Pencils), Robin Smith (Inks)
Publication
Doctor Who Magazine 273-276 (13 January-7 April 1999)
Format
B&W / 4 / 29

Companions
Izzy, Grace
Précis
As youths disappear from Brixton, the Doctor faces an insane scientist with mutated DNA…
Comment
A reasonably well executed tale that's really only memorable for its shock ending. **56%**

11) The Road to Hell
Scott Gray

Artists
Martin Geraghty (Pencils), Robin Smith (Inks)
Publication
Doctor Who Magazine 278-282 (2 June-22 September 1999)
Format
B&W / 5 / 36
Companion
Izzy
Précis
Alien creatures take control of a ruling Chinese family in the 17th century…
Comment
Extremely clever take on the commercial/mystical dichotomy that is Japan. **88%**

12) TV Action!
Alan Barnes

Artist
Roger Langridge
Publication
Doctor Who Magazine 283 (20 October 1999)
Format
B&W / 1 / 8
Companion
Izzy
Précis
The Tardis materializes at the BBC Television Centre in 1979…
Comment
Another year, *another* celebratory comic strip. Thirty-somethings will find much to amuse them, though. **75%**

13) The Company of Thieves
Scott Gray

Artists
Adrian Salmon (Pencils), Fareed Choudhury (Inks)
Publication
Doctor Who Magazine 284-286 (17 November 1999-12 January 2000)
Format
B&W / 3 / 23
Companions
Izzy, Kroton
Précis
The Doctor is captured by Grast Horstrogg and his band of fearsome space pirates…
Comment
Crudely drawn tale of piracy in outer space; unmemorable. **23%**

14) The Glorious Dead
Scott Gray

Artists
Martin Geraghty (Pencils), Robin Smith (Inks)
Publication
Doctor Who Magazine 287-296 (9 February-18 October 2000)
Format
B&W / 10 / 75
Companions
Izzy, Kroton
Précis
On Paradost, Cardinal Morningstar wants to ride the Universe of heretics - including the Doctor…
Comment
The longest ever comic strip, full of inventive cliffhangers and subversive storytelling, but ultimately it's just too fragmentary for its own good. **79%**

15) The Autonomy Bug
Scott Gray

Artist
Roger Langridge
Publication
Doctor Who Magazine 297-299 (15 November 2000-10 January 2001)
Format
B&W / 3 / 21

Companion
Izzy
Précis
The Doctor investigates a case of robot abuse at an institute for maladjusted machines...
Comment
Charming and surprisingly poignant left-field cartoon story, perfectly suited to the artist. **87%**

16) Ophidius
Scott Gray

Artists
Martin Geraghty (Pencils), Robin Smith (Inks & Colours)
Publication
Doctor Who Magazine 300-303 (7 February-2 May 2001)
Format
Colour / 4 / 28
Companions
Izzy, Destrii
Précis
The Tardis is swallowed by a vast sentient zoo, and Izzy and Destrii swap bodies...
Comment
Appropriately garish first regular colour outing, but the story's nothing special. **60%**

17) Beautiful Freak
Scott Gray

Artists
Martin Geraghty (Pencils), Robin Smith (Inks & Colours)
Publication
Doctor Who Magazine 304 (30 May 2001)
Format
Colour / 1 / 7
Companion
Izzy
Précis
The Doctor helps Izzy adjust to her new form...
Comment
Delightful character piece tinged with real emotion. **78%**

18) The Way of All Flesh
Scott Gray

Artists
Martin Geraghty (Pencils), Robin Smith (Inks & Colours)
Publication
Doctor Who Magazine 306, 308-310 (25 July 2001, 19 September-14 November 2001)
Format
Colour / 4 / 28
Companion
Izzy
Précis
The Mexican Day of the Dead provides perfect cover for an invasion of flesh-drinking skeletal fiends...
Comment
Effectively horrific story set against a very evocative backdrop. **90%**

19) Children of the Revolution
Scott Gray

Artists
Lee Sullivan (Pencils & Inks), Adrian Salmon (Colours)
Publication
Doctor Who Magazine 312-317 (9 January-29 May 2002)
Format
Colour / 6 / 42
Companion
Izzy
Précis
The crew of a submarine are dragged down to the underwater city of a race of peace-loving Daleks...
Comment
Fascinating follow up to The Evil of the Daleks with stunning Dalek art. **93%**

20) Me and My Shadow
Scott Gray

Artists
John Ross (Pencils & Inks), Roger Langridge (Colours)
Publication
Doctor Who Magazine 318 (26 June 2002)

Format
Colour 1 / 7
Companions
Fey, Shayde
Précis
The Doctor makes contact with Fey, who has melded with the mysterious figure known as Shayde…
Comment
Doctorless breathing space before the main action begins. **55%**

21) Urobos
Scott Gray

Artists
John Ross (Pencils & Inks), Adrian Salmon (Colours)
Publication
Doctor Who Magazine 319-322 (24 July-16 October 2002)
Format
Colour / 4 / 29
Companions
Fey, Shayde, Destrii
Précis
The Doctor uses Fey-Shayde to track down Izzy to Ophidius, but instead they find Destrii in her body…
Comment
Marginally more interesting follow up to *Ophidius*. **70%**

22) Oblivion
Scott Gray

Artists
Martin Geraghty (Pencils), David A Roach (Inks), Adrian Salmon (Colours)
Publication
Doctor Who Magazine 323-328 (13 November 2002-2 April 2003)
Format
Colour / 6 / 43
Companions
Fey, Shayde, Izzy, Destrii
Précis
The Doctor finds Izzy before she faces combat to the death and a high-powered royal marriage…
Comment
The One With The Lesbian Kiss. After a weak start, it just gets better and better. **90%**

23) Where Nobody Knows Your Name
Scott Gray

Artists
Roger Langridg (Pencils & Colours), David A Roach (Inks)
Publication
Doctor Who Magazine 329 (30 April 2003)
Format
Colour / 1 / 7
Companion
Frobisher
Précis
Feeling lonely after Izzy has gone back home, the Doctor drowns his sorrows in a bar…
Comment
Bittersweet *Cheers* parody with a lovely ending. **67%**

24) Doctor Who and the Nightmare Game
Gareth Roberts

Artists
Mike Collins (Pencils), David A Roach (Inks), Dylan Teague (Colours)
Publication
Doctor Who Magazine 330-332 (28 May-23 July 2003)
Format
Colour / 3 / 21
Précis
1977, and the new owners of Delchester United are actually hideous shape-changing aliens in disguise…
Comment
Doctor Who Weekly meets *Roy of the Rovers* in a deliberately self-conscious spoof. **70%**

25) The Power of Thoueris!
Scott Gray

Artist
Adrian Salmon
Publication
Doctor Who Magazine 333 (20 August 2003)
Format
Colour / 1 / 7

Précis
The Doctor fights a hippo-faced Osirian on the banks of the River Nile...
Comment
An amiable mickey take of *Pyramids of Mars* and a chance to see the Eighth Doctor topless. **60%**

26) The Curious Tale of Spring-Heeled Jack
Scott Gray

Artists
Anthony Williams (Pencils), David A Roach (Inks), Adrian Salmon (Colours)
Publication
Doctor Who Magazine 334-336 (17 September-12 November 2003)
Format
Colour / 3 / 21
Companion
Penny Chapman
Précis
The devilish Victorian serial killer may not be a legend after all...
Comment
Richly satisfying SF retelling of a well-known myth, in full *Talons* mode. **80%**

27) The Land of Happy Endings
Scott Gray

Artists
Martin Geraghty (Pencils), Faz Choudhury (Inks, 1-6), David A Roach (Inks, 7), Daryl Joyce (Colours, 1-6), Adrian Salmon (Colours, 7)
Publication
Doctor Who Magazine 337 (10 December 2003)
Format
Colour / 1 / 7
Précis
The Doctor saves the peaceful Darbodians from the evil scientist Wargonn...
Comment
Beautiful pastiche of Neville Main's *TV Comic* stories with a heart-rending final page. **95%**

28) Bad Blood
Scott Gray

Artists
Martin Geraghty (Pencils), David A Roach (Inks), Adrian Salmon (Colours)
Publication
Doctor Who Magazine 338-342 (7 January-28 April 2003)
Format
Colour / 5 / 35
Précis
Dakota, 1875, and American colonists and Indians are facing attacks by werewolves...
Comment
Wonderful evocation of history and horror with some fantastic cliffhangers. **85%**

29) Sins of the Fathers
Scott Gray

Artists
John Rose (Art), Adrian Salmon (Colours)
Publication
Doctor Who Magazine 343-345 (26 May-21 July 2004)
Format
Colour / 3 / 21
Précis
The Doctor takes Destrii to a space hospital which is attacked by hostile ape creatures...
Comment
Essentially one long (colourful) fight, but enjoyable nonetheless. **75%**

30) The Flood
Scott Gray

Artists
Martin Geraghty (Pencils), David A Roach (Inks), Adrian Salmon (Colours)
Publication
Doctor Who Magazine 346-353 (18 August 2004-2 March 2005)
Format
Colour / 8 / 65
Précis
Invading Cybermen manipulate humanity's guilt - with rain...

Comment
Smartly redesigned villains, fantastic artwork, a huge emotional canvas - easily the Eighth's Doctor's finest comic strip adventure. **95%**

Ninth Doctor: Christopher Eccleston

1) *The Love Invasion*
Gareth Roberts

Artists
Mike Collins (Pencils), David A Roach (Inks), Dylan Teague (Colours)
Publication
Doctor Who Magazine 355-357 (27 April-22 June 2005)
Format
Colour / 3 / 27
Précis
Someone is interfering with the timeline of 1960s Earth…
Comment
Unengaging light entertainment with risible likenesses of the new Tardis duo. **33%**

2) *Art Attack*
Mike Collins

Artists
Mike Collins (Pencils), Kris Justice (Inks), Dylan Teague (Colours)
Publication
Doctor Who Magazine 358 (20 July 2005)
Format
Colour / 1 / 10
Précis
The Doctor and Rose meet a mad performance artist in a trans-dimensional art gallery…
Comment
Silly, lightweight froth. **30%**

5: Books

The Missing Adventures (Virgin)

All titles published by Doctor Who Books, a division of Virgin Publishing, and listed in publication order.

First Doctor: William Hartnell

1) *Venusian Lullaby*
Paul Leonard

Details
October 1994 (0426204247 / Alister Pearson)
Companions
Ian, Barbara
Précis
Landing on Venus, the Tardis crew become embroiled in the inhabitants' peculiar funereal customs…
DWM Index
219 Review
221 Paul Leonard interview
Comment
Challenging alienness in the style of *The Web Planet*, only much more so. **65%**

2) *The Sorcerer's Apprentice*
Christopher Bulis

Details
July 1995 (0426204476 / Paul Campbell)
Companions
Susan, Ian, Barbara
Précis
The Tardis lands in the kingdom of Avalon, a place where science, religion and folktales all coexist…
DWM Index
222 Christopher Bulis interview
228 Review
Comment
Clever blend of sword-and-sorcery and hard SF with a characteristically grumpy First Doctor. **80%**

3) *The Empire of Glass*
Andy Lane

Details
November 1995 (0426204573 / Paul Campbell)
Companions
Vickie, Steven
Ebook
www.bbc.co.uk/cult/doctorwho/ebooks/empireofglass/index.shtml
Précis
Venice, 1609, and the Doctor has been chosen to mediate at an intergalactic peace conference…
DWM Index
232 Review
Comment
Slow-moving tale of alien intervention; largely plot-driven. **58%**

4) *The Man in the Velvet Mask*
Daniel O'Mahony

Details
February 1996 (0426204611 / Alister Pearson)
Companion
Dodo
Précis
In Paris, the Marquis de Sade's adopted son is conducting grotesque experiments on a severed head…
DWM Index
235 Review
Comment
Macabre and brutalised narrative, very well done, but quite out of keeping with the era. **66%**

361

5) The Plotters
Gareth Roberts

Details
November 1996 (0426204883 / Alister Pearson)
Companions
Ian, Barbara, Vicki
Précis
The Tardis lands in London just as Guy Fawkes is about to blow up Parliament...
DWM Index
244   Review
292   Gareth Roberts interview
Comment
Somewhat plot heavy (pun intended), though undeniably accurate, historical. **65%**

Second Doctor: Patrick Troughton

1) The Menagerie
Martin Day

Details
May 1995 (0426204492 / Paul Campbell)
Companions
Jamie, Zoe
Précis
The Doctor is forced to help the Knights of Kuabris in finding the fabled Menagerie of Ukkazaal...
DWM Index
226   Review
Comment
Weakly written, generic *Doctor Who* adventure with unsympathetic characters. **31%**

2) Invasion of the Cat-People
Gary Russell

Details
August 1995 (0426204409 / Colin Howard)
Companions
Ben, Polly
Précis
The Cat-People are hunting the ancient Euterpians, who crash-landed in Australia 4000 years ago...

DWM Index
222   Gary Russell interview
229   Review
Comment
Strong characterization lifts a convoluted story with bland aliens. **60%**

3) Twilight of the Gods
Christopher Bulis

Details
September 1996 (0426204808 / Alister Pearson)
Companions
Jamie, Victoria
Précis
The Doctor returns to Vortis and finds it under the control of the fiercely divided Rhumons...
DWM Index
242   Review
Comment
Benign, if somewhat dreary, sequel to *The Web Planet*. **39%**

4) The Dark Path
David A McIntee

Details
March 1997 (0426205030 / Alister Pearson)
Companions
Jamie, Victoria
Précis
An old Earth Empire colony attracts the attention of Koschei, a future arch-enemy of the Doctor...
DWM Index
249   Review
343   David A McIntee interview
Comment
Accurate rendering of the Second Doctor in a gently simmering story that's thankfully more readable than normal. **66%**

Third Doctor: Jon Pertwee

1) The Ghosts of N-Space
Barry Letts

Details
February 1995 (0426204344 / Alister Pearson)
Companions
Sarah, Jeremy, Brigadier
Précis
On an Italian island, the Doctor has to stop horrifying inhuman spectres taking over the world…
DWM Index
223   Review
Comment
Depressingly accurate adaptation of the radio serial. **9%**

2) Dancing the Code
Paul Leonard

Details
April 1995 (0426204417 / Paul Campbell)
Companions
Jo, UNIT
Précis
A powerful alien force lies beneath the sands of the African state of Kebiria…
DWM Index
221   Paul Leonard interview
225   Review
Comment
Clever UNIT story with much to enjoy. **80%**

3) The Eye of the Giant
Christopher Bulis

Details
April 1996 (0426204697 / Paul Campbell)
Companions
Liz, UNIT
Précis
Giant mutated insects from a crashed alien spaceship start appearing on a remote South Pacific island…
DWM Index
237   Review
Comment
Formulaic UNIT story which presents its threat in a very credible manner. **70%**

4) The Scales of Injustice
Gary Russell

Details
July 1996 (0426204778 / Andrew Skilleter)
Companions
Liz, UNIT
Ebook
www.bbc.co.uk/cult/doctorwho/ebooks/scalesofinjustice/index.shtml
Précis
Silurians and Sea Devils need human scientists to help them cure a genetic disease…
DWM Index
240   Review
287   Everything You Ever Needed to Know About…*The Scales of Injustice*
Comment
Atmospheric conspiracy tale that even makes the Myrka look good. **83%**

5) Speed of Flight
Paul Leonard

Details
October 1996 (0426204875 / Alister Pearson)
Companions
Jo, Mike Yates
Précis
The Tardis lands in an artificial world whose inhabitants pilot steam engines through the air…
DWM Index
243   Review
Comment
Cleverly imagined take on a strange inside-out world with persuasive detail throughout. **65%**

Fourth Doctor: Tom Baker

1) *Evolution*
John Peel

Details
September 1994 (0426204220 / Alister Pearson)
Companion
Sarah
Précis
On Dartmoor, a deranged scientist is conducting experiments that could alter human evolution…
DWM Index
217   Review
Comment
Clunkily written prose, obvious plotting and an out-of-character Fourth Doctor. **18%**

2) *The Romance of Crime*
Gareth Roberts

Details
January 1995 (0426204352 / Alister Pearson)
Companions
Romana II, K-9 II
Précis
Aided by gangsters and Ogrons, a criminal genius is brought back to life on the Rock of Judgement…
DWM Index
221   Gareth Roberts interview
222   Review
292   Gareth Roberts interview
Comment
Spot-on Season 17 entry with wonderful characters and an exciting, funny, thrilling page-turner of a story. **98%**

3) *System Shock*
Justin Richards

Details
June 1995 (042620445X / Martin Rawle)
Companions
Sarah, Harry
Précis
In 1998, the Doctor faces the Voracians, aliens that exists inside any kind of digital technology…
DWM Index
227   Review
294   Justin Richards interview
Comment
Gadget-obsessed technological thriller, quite well done. **77%**

4) *Managra*
Stephen Marley

Details
September 1995 (0426204530 / Paul Campbell)
Companion
Sarah
Précis
The Doctor and Sarah land in the Sistine Chapel and are blamed for the murder of a pope…
DWM Index
230   Review
291   Everything You Ever Needed to Know…
Comment
Convoluted theatrical saga with literary pretensions. **40%**

5) *The English Way of Death*
Gareth Roberts

Details
March 1996 (0426204662 / Alister Pearson)
Companions
Romana II, K-9 II
Précis
A fearsome entity called Zodaal brings terror to the peaceful seaside town of Nutchurch in the 1930s…
DWM Index
236   Review
292   Gareth Roberts interview
Comment
Slightly disappointing Season 17 comedy; the author has done better. **72%**

6) *The Shadow of Weng-Chiang*
David A McIntee

Details
August 1996 (0426204794 / Alister Pearson)
Companions
Romana, K-9 II

Précis
Li H'sen Chang's daughter tries to prevent Magnus Greel's time cabinet from ever landing...
DWM Index
241   Review
343   David A McIntee interview
Comment
Obvious sequel with the usual overblown prose and endless descriptions. **35%**

7) *A Device of Death*
Christopher Bulis

Details
February 1997 (0426205014 / Alister Pearson)
Companions
Sarah, Harry
Précis
The Tardis crew find themselves scattered across three different planets in the midst of a space war...
DWM Index
248   Review
Comment
Genesis of the Dalek rip-off, boringly written. **40%**

8) *The Well-Mannered War*
Gareth Roberts

Details
April 1997 (0426205065 / Alister Pearson)
Companions
Romana II, K-9 II
Ebook
www.bbc.co.uk/cult/doctorwho/ebooks/well_mannered_war/index.shtml
Précis
K-9 stands for election on a planet that has been poised on the brink of war for centuries...
DWM Index
250   Review
292   Gareth Roberts interview
Comment
A glorious culmination of the *Missing Adventures* series with an ending that cocks a snook at all future stories **90%**

Fifth Doctor: Peter Davison

1) *Goth Opera*
Paul Cornell

Details
July 1994 (0426204182 / Alister Pearson)
Companions
Tegan, Nyssa
Précis
In present-day Manchester, vampires await the ascension of their Vampire Messiah...
DWM Index
215   Review
221   Paul Cornell interview
Comment
Chilling *Near Dark*-style contemporary urban updating of the vampire myth. **88%**

2) *The Crystal Bucephalus*
Craig Hinton

Details
November 1994 (0426204298 / Alister Pearson [and photograph])
Companions
Tegan, Turlough, Kamelion
Précis
The Doctor's promising career as a restaurateur is spoilt by the resurrection of the 'Messiah' Lazarus...
DWM Index
220   Review
Comment
Ghastly soap opera mess with an infuriatingly aimless plot. **12%**

3) *Lords of the Storm*
David A McIntee

Details
December 1995 (0426204603 / Alister Pearson)
Companion
Turlough
Précis
Sontarans invade the human colony of Raghi...
DWM Index
233   Review
343   David A McIntee interview

Comment
Endless descriptive passages mire a (probably) fascinating story about Sontaran ethics. **44%**

4) The Sands of Time
Justin Richards

Details
May 1996 (0426204727 / Alister Pearson)
Companions
Tegan, Nyssa
Ebook
www.bbc.co.uk/cult/doctorwho/ebooks/sandsoftime/index.shtml
Précis
The Doctor arrives at the 19th century Kenilworth House where he is confronted by robotic Mummies…
DWM Index
238 Review
283 Everything You Ever Need to Know…
294 Justin Richards interview
Comment
Over-complicated sequel to *Pyramids of Mars* with all the familiar ingredients. **68%**

5) Cold Fusion
Lance Parkin

Details
December 1996 (0426204891 / Alister Pearson)
Doctor and Companions
Seventh Doctor, Adric, Tegan, Nyssa, Roz, Chris
Précis
On an Earth colony world, rebel freedom fighters are engaged in a bitter fight with Imperial forces…
DWM Index
246 Review
Comment
Revisionist and quotation heavy self-styled epic, written to explain rather than entertain. **55%**

Sixth Doctor: Colin Baker

1) State of Change
Christopher Bulis

Details
December 1994 (042620431X / Alister Pearson)
Companion
Peri
Précis
The Tardis arrives in Ancient Rome, but appearances can be deceptive…
DWM Index
221 Review
222 Christopher Bulis interview
Comment
Promising alternative history story with an unlikely resolution. **60%**

2) Time of Your Life
Steve Lyons

Details
March 1994 (0426204387 / Paul Campbell)
Précis
The Doctor has to sort out a few problems behind the scenes at the Meson Broadcasting Service…
DWM Index
223 Steve Lyons interview
224 Review
Comment
The author's usual heavy-handed blend of fiction and reality, this time with the media as its target. **43%**

3) Millennial Rites
Craig Hinton

Details
October 1995 (0426204557 / Alister Pearson)
Companion
Mel
Précis
The Doctor must stop a dangerous computer bug being released on New Year's Eve 1999…
DWM Index
231 Review
Comment
Mel gets her introductory story here, told enthusiastically rather than skilfully. **36%**

4) Killing Ground
Steve Lyons

Details
June 1996 (0426204743 / Alister Pearson)
Companion
Grant Markham
Précis
Cybermen are processing the young male inhabitants of a human colony on the planet Agora…
DWM Index
239 Review
Comment
Traditional Cyberman adventure that tries, daringly, to explain away *Revenge of the Cybermen*. **68%**

5) Burning Heart
Dave Stone

Details
January 1997 (0426204980 / Alister Pearson)
Companion
Peri
Précis
The Adjudicators allow primitive beliefs to take over their thinking - with terrible consequences…
DWM Index
247 Review
Comment
The larger-than-life prose style is as you'd expect, but at least the story is a few degrees this side of believable for a change. **43%**

Miscellaneous

Downtime
Marc Platt

Details
January 1996 (042620462X / Paul Campbell)
Companions
Victoria, Sarah, Brigadier
Précis
At the New World University, the Yeti are once more on the prowl…
DWM Index
234 Review

Comment
Based on a fan video, this is a continuity-laden Yeti story, pleasingly straightforward in tone. **72%**

The New Adventures (Virgin)

All titles published by Doctor Who Books, an imprint of Virgin Publishing, and listed in publication order.

Seventh Doctor: Sylvester McCoy

1) Timewyrm: Genesys
John Peel

Details
June 1991 (0426203550 / Andrew Skilleter)
Companion
Ace
Précis
The Doctor lands in Ancient Mesopotamia and meets legendary god-king Gilgamesh…
DWM Index
175 Prologue
     John Peel introduction
177 Review
Comment
Clumsy sex references shoehorned into a generic fantasy tale. **33%**

2) Timewyrm: Exodus
Terrance Dicks

Details
August 1991 (0426203577 / Andrew Skilleter)
Companion
Ace
Précis
The Tardis materializes in 1951 and finds Europe under Nazi control…
DWM Index
178 Review
     Terrance Dicks interview
183 Peter Darvill-Evans interview
275 Terrance Dicks interview

Comment
Crisply written Nazi thriller with strong characterization. **80%**

3) Timewyrm: Apocalypse
Nigel Robinson

Details
October 1991 (0426203593 / Andrew Skilleter)
Companion
Ace
Précis
On the planet Kirith, gifted members of the community never return from visiting the Kandasi...
DWM Index
178   Nigel Robinson interview
180   Review
Comment
A straightforward, excitingly-paced adventure story. **76%**

4) Timewyrm: Revelation
Paul Cornell

Details
December 1991 (0426203607 / Andrew Skilleter)
Companion
Ace
Précis
The Doctor visits a sentient church on the Moon and the Timewyrm makes its final play...
DWM Index
178   Paul Cornell interview
181   Review
267   Paul Cornell interview
293   Everything You Ever Needed To Know...
Comment
Pretentious, self-obsessed angst with occasional effective moments. **20%**

5) Cat's Cradle: Time's Crucible
Marc Platt

Details
February 1992 (0426203658 / Peter Elson)
Companion
Ace
Précis
The Tardis is destroyed by the Process and Ace finds herself wandering amidst a surreal grey city...
DWM Index
183   Peter Darvill-Evans interview
184   Review
        Marc Platt interview
205   Marc Platt interview
Comment
Hugely fragmented and pointless exercise in circuitous writing. **15%**

6) Cat's Cradle: Warhead
Andrew Cartmel

Details
April 1992 (0426203674 / Peter Elson)
Companion
Ace
Précis
Ace joins a group of Kurdish rebels to overthrow an evil future Earth corporation...
DWM Index
183   Peter Darvill-Evans interview
185   Andrew Cartmel interview
186   Review
Comment
Extremely articulate, albeit totally plot-driven, anti-globalisation rant. **82%**

7) Cat's Cradle: Witch Mark
Andrew Hunt

Details
June 1992 (0426203682 / Peter Elson)
Companion
Ace
Précis
Creatures from legends and fairytales are appearing in the Welsh countryside...
DWM Index
183   Peter Darvill-Evans interview
185   Andrew Hunt interview
188   Review
Comment
Woolly fantasy adventure verging on the twee. **30%**

8) Nightshade
Mark Gatiss

Details
August 1992 (0426203763 / Peter Elson)
Companion
Ace
Précis
An elderly actor finds himself being haunted by monsters from his televised past…
DWM Index
183 Peter Darvill-Evans interview
190 Prelude
    Review
    Mark Gatiss interview
222 Mark Gatiss interview
332 Mark Gatiss interview
Comment
A masterclass in *Doctor Who* storytelling, achingly atmospheric, and written with great skill and love for the subject. Only the tacked-on ending disappoints. **99%**

9) Love and War
Paul Cornell

Details
October 1992 (0426203852 / Lee Sullivan)
Companions
Ace, Bernice
Précis
The planet Paradise is not as peaceful as its name suggests…
DWM Index
183 Peter Darvill-Evans interview
192 Prelude
    Review
    Travelling Companions: Bernice Summerfield
Comment
Strong story and good character development make this an effective introduction for promising new companion Bernice Summerfield. **78%**

10) Transit
Ben Aaronovitch

Details
December 1992 (0426203844 / Peter Elson)
Companion
Bernice, Kadiatu Lethbridge-Stewart
Précis
Things are going terribly wrong on the Mars hyperspace transport system…
DWM Index
195 Prelude
    Review
201 Ben Aaronovitch interview
Comment
Incoherently paced and plotted admixture of explicit sex and SF gadgetry; largely impenetrable. **8%**

11) The Highest Science
Gareth Roberts

Details
February 1993 (0426203771 / Peter Elson)
Companion
Bernice
Précis
Humans, galactic rock fans and tortoise-like Chelonians are struggling to survive on Sakrat…
DWM Index
196 Prelude
    Review
208 Gareth Roberts interview
292 Gareth Roberts interview
Comment
Charmingly imaginative adventure with much to amuse and entertain. **88%**

12) The Pit
Neil Penswick

Details
March 1993 (042620378X / Peter Elson)
Companion
Bernice
Précis
The Doctor meets William Blake on a disintegrating planet…
DWM Index
197 Prelude
    Review
Comment
Dull, incident-free storyline, stuck in first gear throughout. **12%**

13) Deceit
Peter Darvill-Evans

Details
April 1993 (0426203879 / Luis Rey)
Companions
Bernice, Ace
Précis
The Doctor meets up with a battle-hardened, older Ace...
DWM Index
198 Prelude
    Review
209 Peter Darvill-Evans interview
Comment
Ace returns - unfortunately - in an enthusiastically penned tale of space warfare. **72%**

14) Lucifer Rising
Andy Lane and Jim Mortimore

Details
May 1993 (0426203887 / Lee Brimmicombe-Wood)
Companions
Bernice, Ace
Précis
An extra-dimensional being called Legion hampers a murder enquiry on a space-station...
DWM Index
199 Prelude
    Review
208 Andy Lane interview
    Jim Mortimore interview
Comment
Confusingly written whodunit with implausible characters and situations. **45%**

15) White Darkness
David A McIntee

Details
June 1993 (042620395X / Peter Elson)
Companions
Bernice, Ace
Précis
On the island of Haiti, the Doctor comes up against a horde of zombies...
DWM Index
201 Prelude
    Review
209 David A McIntee interview
343 David A McIntee interview
Comment
Good ideas spoilt by dreadfully overwritten prose. **23%**

16) Shadowmind
Christopher Bulis

Details
July 1993 (0426203941 / Christopher Bulis)
Companions
Bernice, Ace
Précis
The Doctor hunts down armed replicas of prominent members of the Tairngire population...
DWM Index
201 Review
202 Prelude
209 Christopher Bulis interview
Comment
Intelligent and fast-moving space opera with many exciting set-pieces. **85%**

17) Birthright
Nigel Robinson

Details
August 1993 (0426203933 / Peter Elson)
Companions
Bernice, Ace
Précis
Stranded without the Doctor, Bernice faces a Jack the Ripper style murderer in Victorian London...
DWM Index
203 Prelude
    Review
209 Nigel Robinson interview
Audio Adaptation
February 1999, Big Finish, CD (190365436X / Peter Elson)
Comment
Experimental Doctorless story that doesn't quite work. **55%**

18) Iceberg
David Banks

Details
September 1993 (0426203925 / Andrew Skilleter)
Précis
At the North Pole, Cybermen await the arrival of the SS Elysium…
DWM Index
204   Prelude
         Review
Comment
Slickly realized protagonists, but the storyline is somewhat far-fetched. **60%**

19) Blood Heat
Jim Mortimore

Details
October 1993 (0426203992 / Jeff Cummins)
Companions
Bernice, Ace, Jo, Liz, Brigadier
Précis
The Tardis is sucked into a tar pit on an alternative Earth in which the Silurians and Sea Devils rule…
DWM Index
205   Prelude
         Review
208   Jim Mortimore interview
279   Everything You Ever Needed To Know…
Comment
Excellent 'alternate future' story with effective John Wyndham-style scenes of devastated London. **80%**

20) The Dimension Riders
Daniel Blythe

Details
November 1993 (0426203976 / Jeff Cummins)
Companions
Bernice, Ace
Précis
An ancient horror has been unleashed from the Matrix…
DWM Index
206   Prelude
         Review
208   Daniel Blythe interview

Comment
Complicated three-way plot brought to life impressively, but with many clichés towards the end. **70%**

21) The Left-Handed Hummingbird
Kate Orman

Details
December 1993 (0426204042 / Pete Wallbank)
Companions
Bernice, Ace
Précis
In Mexico City, the Doctor searches desperately for the identify of a bloodthirsty entity called the Blue…
DWM Index
207   Prelude
208   Review
         Kate Orman interview
328   Kate Orman interview
Comment
Mature examination of the nature of madness, with much violence and drug-taking. **75%**

22) Conundrum
Steve Lyons

Details
January 1994 (0426204085 / Jeff Cummins)
Companions
Bernice, Ace
Précis
When Doctor Nemesis appears, The Adventure Kids discover Arandale is not such a cosy place to be…
DWM Index
208   Prelude
         Review
223   Steve Lyons interview
Comment
Slavish copy of *The Mind Robber*. **28%**

23) No Future
Paul Cornell

Details
February 1994 (0426204093 / Pete Wallbank)
Companions
Bernice, Ace
Précis
London, 1977: Bernice sings in a punk band while the Doctor tracks down an old enemy...
DWM Index
209   Prelude
210   Review
267   Paul Cornell interview
Comment
Self-indulgent, whimsical satire on *Doctor Who* and the 1970s. **65%**

24) Tragedy Day
Gareth Roberts

Details
March 1994 (0426204107 / Jeff Cummins)
Companions
Bernice, Ace
Précis
The government on the planet Olleril dishes out a particularly brutal form of annual justice...
DWM Index
210   Prelude
       Review
221   Gareth Roberts interview
Comment
Blandly written comedy with limited potential. **40%**

25) Legacy
Gary Russell

Details
April 1994 (0426204123 / Peter Elson)
Companions
Bernice, Ace
Précis
Fifty years on, the Doctor returns to Peladon for the King's restatement of his vows...
DWM Index
211   Prelude
212   Review
222   Gary Russell interview
Comment
Lame follow-up to the televised Peladon stories; the intended humour is unsuccessful. **25%**

26) Theatre of War
Justin Richards

Details
May 1994 (042620414X / Jeff Cummins)
Companions
Bernice, Ace
Précis
A play unearthed on the planet Menaxus proves disastrous for the theatre-obsessed Heletian Empire...
DWM Index
212   Prelude
       Review
221   Justin Richards interview
294   Justin Richards interview
Comment
Heavy-handed theatrical referencing in an otherwise bog-standard story. **45%**

27) All-Consuming Fire
Andy Lane

Details
June 1994 (0426204158 / Jeff Cummins)
Companions
Bernice, Ace
Précis
When people start bursting into flames, Holmes, Watson and the Doctor investigate...
DWM Index
213   Prelude
214   Review
221   Andy Lane interview
Comment
Conan Doyle pastiche done with consummate flare. **85%**

28) Blood Harvest
Terrance Dicks

Details
July 1994 (0426204174 / Bill Donohoe)
Companions
Bernice, Ace

Précis
In 1930s prohibition Chicago, a mysterious figure is causing internecine warfare between rival gangs…
DWM Index
214 Prelude
215 Review
275 Terrance Dicks interview
Comment
Simplistic vampire story with one-dimensional baddies. **55%**

29) Strange England
Simon Messingham

Details
August 1994 (0426204190 / Paul Campbell)
Companions
Bernice, Ace
Précis
Twisted and bizarre incidents upset the tranquillity of a Victorian house and garden…
DWM Index
215 Prelude
216 Review
223 Simon Messingham interview
Comment
Wannabe *Ghost Light* contender devoid of much interest. **20%**

30) First Frontier
David A McIntee
Details
September 1994 (0426204212 / Tony Masero)
Companions
Bernice, Ace
Précis
Landing in America in 1957, the Doctor comes across a crashed UFO in a military base…
DWM Index
216 Prelude
217 Review
222 David A McIntee interview
343 David A McIntee interview
Comment
Murky prose obscures what is probably quite a good story. **35%**

31) St Anthony's Fire
Mark Gatiss

Details
October 1994 (0426204239 / Paul Campbell)
Companions
Bernice, Ace
Précis
On the planet Betrushia, the warring Cutch and Ismetch await the coming of the mythical Keth…
DWM Index
217 Prelude
219 Review
222 Mark Gatiss interview
332 Mark Gatiss interview
Comment
Disappointing religious satire with frustratingly undeveloped themes. **45%**

32) Falls the Shadow
Daniel O'Mahony

Details
November 1994 (0426204271 / Kevin Jenkins)
Companions
Bernice, Ace
Précis
The Doctor is trapped in a bizarre house called Shadowfell…
DWM Index
218 Prelude
220 Review
223 Daniel O'Mahony interview
Comment
Sapphire and Steel on acid; a messy book but enlivened by many memorable scenes. **75%**

33) Parasite
Jim Mortimore

Details
December 1994 (0426204255 / Paul Campbell)
Companions
Bernice, Ace
Précis
The Tardis lands inside a giant space ammonite called Artifact…
DWM Index
220 Prelude
221 Review
222 Jim Mortimore interview

Comment
Big ideas, but rather short on narrative progression. **39%**

34) Warlock
Andrew Cartmel

Details
January 1995 (0426204336 / Tony Masero)
Companions
Bernice, Ace
Précis
In Canterbury, the Doctor is worried about a designer drug, while Ace joins the animal activists...
DWM Index
221   Prelude
222   Review
Comment
Excellent environmental thriller, albeit rather unlike *Doctor Who* as we know it. **77%**

35) Set Piece
Kate Orman

Details
February 1995 (0426204360 / Tony Masero)
Companions
Bernice, Ace, Kadiatu
Précis
The Doctor and his companions face an ancient cult and a horde of marauding robots...
DWM Index
222   Prelude
223   Review
328   Kate Orman interview
Comment
Ace's final story is a somewhat confused melée of ideas fighting for attention. **58%**

36) Infinite Requiem
Daniel Blythe

Details
March 1995 (0426204379 / Barry Jones)
Companion
Bernice

Précis
The Doctor must stop the Sensopaths from causing bloodshed in three time zones...
DWM Index
223   Prelude
224   Review
Comment
Above average follow-up to *The Dimension Riders* lumbered with humdrum villains. **64%**

37) Sanctuary
David A McIntee

Details
April 1995 (0426204395 / Peter Elson)
Companion
Bernice
Précis
In 13th century France, Bernice is holed up in a sanctuary from the Inquisition...
DWM Index
222   David A McIntee interview
225   Review
        Prelude
343   David A McIntee interview
Comment
Weighty history lesson in dire need of editing. **29%**

38) Human Nature
Paul Cornell

Details
May 1995 (0426204433/ Bill Donohoe)
Companion
Bernice
Ebook
www.bbc.co.uk/cult/doctorwho/ebooks/human_nature/index.shtml
Précis
The Doctor is enjoying a normal human life as a teacher in an English boarding school...
DWM Index
221   Paul Cornell interview
226   Prelude
        Review
Comment
Intriguing fairytale premise with Christian overtones, bogged down at times by a prosaic narrative style. **86%**

39) Original Sin
Andy Lane

Details
June 1995 (0426204441 / Tony Masero)
Companions
Bernice, Roz, Chris
Précis
A wave of anarchy is engulfing the floating cities of the future Earth Empire…
DWM Index
227 Review
Comment
Skilfully realized future world with a cast of well-drawn supporting characters and an impressive villain. **88%**

40) Sky Pirates!
Dave Stone

Details
July 1995 (0426204468 / Jeff Cummins)
Companions
Bernice, Roz, Chris
Précis
The Tardis finds itself in the System, a bizarre planetary network apparently driven by clockwork…
DWM Index
228 Review
Comment
Not entirely successful attempt at 'zany', but intermittently funny. **37%**

41) Zamper
Gareth Roberts

Details
August 1995 (0426204506 / Tony Masero)
Companions
Bernice, Roz, Chris
Précis
Workers on Zamper spend their entire lives selling advanced battleships to the highest bidder…
DWM Index
229 Review
292 Gareth Roberts interview
Comment
Unambitious comedy drama in the author's usual style. **75%**

42) Toy Soldiers
Paul Leonard

Details
September 1995 (0426204522 / Peter Elson)
Companions
Bernice, Roz, Chris
Précis
After the end of the First World War, children all across Europe are being mysteriously abducted…
DWM Index
230 Review
Comment
Shocking wartime horror story written with style and authority. **84%**

43) Head Games
Steve Lyons

Details
October 1995 (0426204549 / Bill Donohoe)
Companions
Bernice, Roz, Chris, Mel
Précis
On the planet Detrios, the Doctor faces a fearsome foe - Dr Who and his young assistant Jason…
DWM Index
223 Steve Lyons interview
231 Review
288 Everything You Ever Needed to Know…
Comment
More *Mind Robber* escapades, very much in the style of the author's *Conundrum*. **41%**

44) The Also People
Ben Aaronovitch

Details
November 1995 (0426204565 / Tony Masero)
Companions
Bernice, Roz, Chris
Précis
On an inside-out world, the Doctor starts talking to God…
DWM Index
232 Review
284 Everything You Ever Needed To Know…
Comment
A more controlled effort than *Transit*, but still suffering from delusions of grandeur. **39%**

45) Shakedown
Terrance Dicks

Details
December 1995 (042620459X / Peter Elson)
Companions
Bernice, Roz, Chris
Précis
Pursuing a fleeing Rutan scout ship, the Sontarans steal aboard the solar yacht Tiger Moth...
DWM Index
233   Review
275   Terrance Dicks interview
Comment
Novelization of a fan-produced video, this is simple storytelling at its most effective. **82%**

46) Just War
Lance Parkin

Details
January 1996 (0426204638 / Nik Spender)
Companions
Bernice, Roz, Chris
Précis
Early in WWII, the Doctor and his companions land in the middle of Nazi-controlled Berlin...
DWM Index
234   Review
Audio Adaptation
June 1999, Big Finish, CD (1903654351 / Nik Spender)
Comment
Wartime adventure story, crisply written and energetically plotted. **90%**

47) Warchild
Andrew Cartmel

Details
February 1996 (0426204646 / Jeff Cummins)
Companions
Bernice, Roz, Chris
Précis
On a future Earth, packs of bloodthirsty dogs are driving Britain into a state of emergency...
DWM Index
235   Review

Comment
The culmination of the trilogy begun with *Warhead*; bloody and involving, but we've seen it all before. **67%**

48) Sleepy
Kate Orman

Details
March 1996 (0426204654 / Mark Wilkinson)
Companions
Bernice, Roz, Chris
Précis
The emergence of telepathy threatens the stability of a newly settled Earth colony on Yemaya 4...
DWM Index
236   Review
328   Kate Orman interview
Comment
Angst-ridden tale which posits many questions but few answers. **67%**

49) Death and Diplomacy
Dave Stone

Details
April 1996 (0426204689 / Bill Donohoe)
Companions
Bernice, Roz, Chris, Jason Kane
Précis
The Doctor has been abducted by the Hollow Gods to act as arbiter in some alien peace negotiations...
DWM Index
237   Review
Comment
Unhappily self-indulgent comedy relying on its readers being as anally retentive as its author. **45%**

50) Happy Endings
Paul Cornell

Details
May 1996 (0426204700 / Paul Campbell)
Companions
Bernice, Roz, Chris, Jason
Précis
The Doctor returns to the village of Cheldon Boniface for the wedding of Bernice and Jason...

DWM Index
238   Review
267   Paul Cornell interview
Comment
Backslapping 50th Anniversary novel which is almost solely soap opera. **40%**

51) GodEngine
Craig Hinton

Details
June 1996 (0426204735 / Peter Elson)
Companions
Roz, Chris
Précis
On 22nd century Mars, Chris and Roz encounter Ice Warriors at the planet's North Pole…
DWM Index
239   Review
Comment
Appallingly banal and boring soap opera trivialization of a once noble race; unforgivable. **15%**

52) Christmas on a Rational Planet
Lawrence Miles

Details
July 1996 (042620476X / Mike Posen)
Companions
Roz, Chris
Précis
The American town of Woodwicke is visited by an embodiment of the Time Lords' chaotic past…
DWM Index
240   Review
Comment
Edgy, bonkers storytelling that somehow works, although it's hard to say why. **75%**

53) Return of the Living Dad
Kate Orman

Details
August 1996 (0426204824 / Mark Wilkinson)
Companions
Roz, Chris, Bernice, Jason

Précis
Bernice returns to enlist the Doctor's help in tracking down her long-lost father in 1980s Berkshire…
DWM Index
241   Review
328   Kate Orman interview
Comment
Surprisingly fun tale about fatherhood, written with real insight. **68%**

54) The Death of Art
Simon Bucher-Jones

Details
September 1996 (0426204816 / Jon Sullivan)
Companions
Roz, Chris
Précis
The Quoth, an alien race from another dimension, break through into 19th century Paris…
DWM Index
242   Review
Comment
Inventively staged psychological warfare in a historical setting. **72%**

55) Damaged Goods
Russell T Davies

Details
October 1996 (0426204832 / Bill Donohoe)
Companions
Roz, Chris
Précis
A 1980s British housing estate is rife with drugs, teenage prostitution and gang warfare…
DWM Index
243   Review
Comment
Unrelentingly grim view of modern urban culture, but written with much insight and honesty. **85%**

56) Bad Therapy
Matthew Jones

Details
December 1996 (0426204905 / Mark Salwowski)
Companion
Chris
Précis
In 1950s London, the Doctor uses a police officer to help him unravel a mystery at a mental hospital...
DWM Index
246   Review
Comment
This post-Roz wake airs plenty of contentious issues about homosexuality and freedom in 1950s Britain, but at times the author's apparent lack of empathy works against it. **74%**

57) Eternity Weeps
Jim Mortimore

Details
January 1997 (0426204972 / Peter Elson)
Companions
Bernice, Jason, Chris, Liz Shaw
Précis
Turkey 2003, and two rival archaeological groups set out to find the remains of Noah's Ark...
DWM Index
248   Review
Comment
A pleasing first person narrative for a book that equates ambition with success. **45%**

58) The Room With No Doors
Kate Orman

Details
February 1997 (0426205006 / Jon Sullivan)
Companion
Chris
Précis
Landing in 16th century China, Chris is suffering from claustrophobic nightmares...
DWM Index
248   Review
328   Kate Orman interview
Comment
Angst-ridden storyline riddled by various eccentric characters whose exact purpose remains a mystery. **35%**

59) Lungbarrow
Marc Platt

Details
March 1997 (0426205022 / Fred Gambino)
Companions
Chris, Ace, Leela, Romana II, K-9, K-9 II
Ebook
www.bbc.co.uk/cult/doctorwho/ebooks/lungbarrow/index.shtml
Précis
The Doctor returns to his ancestral home on Gallifrey...
DWM Index
249   Review
305   Marc Platt interview
Comment
Oddly enough, despite it resembling a ten-part version of *Ghost Light*, this is a strangely compelling mystery of tour of a book, some of it explicable. **78%**

60) So Vile a Sin
Ben Aaronovitch and Kate Orman

Details
April 1997 (0426204840 / Jon Sullivan)
Companions
Roz, Chris
Précis
Roz returns to her roots to find her family, but it will be the last trip she makes...
DWM Index
251   Review
328   Kate Orman interview
Comment
Planned to follow *Damaged Goods*, this offers a memorable blend of cyberpunk and sentiment in equal measure. **74%**

Eighth Doctor: Paul McGann

The Dying Days
Lance Parkin

Details
April 1997 (0426205049 / Fred Gambino)
Companions
Bernice, Brigadier
Ebook
www.bbc.co.uk/cult/doctorwho/ebooks/dyingdays/index.shtml
Précis
The first British manned landing on Mars presages the Ice Warriors' arrival in present-day London…
DWM Index
250   Review
272   Lance Parkin interview
Comment
Good old-fashioned adventure story with the Ice Warriors back on form. **85%**

Miscellaneous

Who Killed Kennedy
James Stevens and David Bishop

Details
April 1996 (0426204670 / Slatter-Anderson)
Companions
Dodo, Liz Shaw, Brigadier, Mike
Précis
Investigative journalist James Stevens probes the secrets of UNIT, C19 and the Glasshouse, with tragic results…
DWM Index
237   Review
Summary
Sharply observed satire on conspiracy books with deft intertwining of reality and fiction; only the ludicrous ending disappoints. **80%**

Past Doctor Adventures (BBC)

All books published by BBC Books, a division of BBC Worldwide, and listed in publication order.

First Doctor: William Hartnell

1) The Witch Hunters
Steve Lyons

Details
March 1998 (0563405791 / Black Sheep)
Companions
Susan, Ian, Barbara
Précis
The Tardis lands in the frenzied atmosphere of Salem, Massachusetts in 1692…
DWM Index
263   Review
Comment
Doctor Who meets *The Crucible* in a weighty historical drama with plenty of gripping scenes. **79%**

2) Salvation
Steve Lyons

Details
January 1999 (0563555661 / Black Sheep)
Companions
Steven, Dodo
Précis
The Doctor faces the might of the extraterrestrial Gods in 1960s New York…
DWM Index
274   Review
Comment
Effective First Doctor story set in an unusual environment. **69%**

3) City at World's End
Christopher Bulis

Details
September 1999 (0563555793 / Black Sheep)
Companions
Susan, Ian, Barbara
Précis
The moon is on a collision course with the city of Arkhaven…
DWM Index
282   Review
Comment
Perfectly imagined B-movie take on the First Doctor's era. **85%**

4) Bunker Soldiers
Martin Day

Details
February 2001 (0563538198 / Black Sheep)
Companions
Steven, Dodo
Précis
In the 13th century, the city of Kiev is about to be attacked by a descendant of Genghis Khan…
DWM Index
300   Preview
302   Review
Comment
Thoroughly engaging historical with a large rôle for Steven. **75%**

5) Byzantium!
Keith Topping

Details
July 2001 (0563538368 / Black Sheep)
Companions
Ian, Barbara, Vicki
Précis
The Tardis crew, stranded in 64AD Byzantium, face religious and political upheaval on all sides…
DWM Index
306   Preview
308   Review
Comment
Brutal portrayal of a bloody period in history, exactingly done. **78%**

6) Dying in the Sun
Jon de Burgh Miller

Details
October 2001 (0563538406 / Black Sheep)
Companions
Ben, Polly
Précis
The Doctor is suspected of murdering a rich movie producer in 1940s Hollywood…
DWM Index
308   Preview
311   Review
Comment
Shallow antics in Hollywood, entirely unsuited to the Second Doctor. **44%**

7) Ten Little Aliens
Stephen Cole

Details
June 2002 (0563538538 / Black Sheep)
Companions
Ben, Polly
Précis
Ten elite soldiers arrive on a desolate planetoid where they are killed off one by one…
DWM Index
318   Preview
320   Review
Comment
Interactive whodunit with inventive plotting. **85%**

8) The Eleventh Tiger
David A McIntee

Details
May 2004 (0563486147 / Black Sheep)
Companions
Ian, Barbara, Vicki
Précis
The Tardis lands in 19th century China - a time of bandits, rebellion and foreign oppression…
DWM Index
343   David A McIntee interview
347   Review
Comment
Less hard-going than previous McIntee stories, this is a decent historical with cryptic supernatural overtones. **67%**

Second Doctor: Patrick Troughton

1) The Murder Game
Steve Lyons

Details
July 1997 (0563405651 / Black Sheep)
Companions
Ben, Polly
Précis
At a role-playing murder mystery aboard an orbiting space casino, a real murder is committed…
DWM Index
254 Review
    Steve Lyons interview
Comment
So-so whodunit with a surfeit of interchangeable characters. **40%**

2) The Roundheads
Mark Gatiss

Details
November 1997 (0563405678 / Black Sheep)
Companions
Ben, Polly, Jamie
Précis
The Tardis arrives in 1648 London where Oliver Cromwell and Charles I are at bitter loggerheads…
DWM Index
259 Review
333 Mark Gatiss interview
Comment
Pure historical, deliciously written, with spot-on characterization of the regulars. **88%**

3) Dreams of Empire
Justin Richards

Details
August 1998 (0563405988 / Black Sheep)
Companions
Jamie, Victoria

Précis
The Tardis arrives in the middle of a civil war enacted like a giant chess game…
DWM Index
268 Review
    Justin Richards interview
294 Justin Richards interview
Comment
Generally effective wartime drama with many life-or-death scenarios. **62%**

4) The Final Sanction
Steve Lyons

Details
July 1999 (056355584X / Black Sheep)
Companions
Jamie, Zoe
Précis
The Tardis lands on the planet Kayala amidst a pitched battle between the Selachians and the Terrans…
DWM Index
280 Review
    Steve Lyons interview
Comment
Powerful anti-war polemic, albeit rather obvious in places. **69%**

5) Heart of Tardis
Dave Stone

Details
June 2000 (0563555963 / Black Sheep)
Doctor and Companions
Fourth Doctor, Jamie, Victoria, Romana, UNIT
Précis
The Second Doctor's visit to Lychburg is linked with the Fourth Doctor's investigation of a US scientific project…
DWM Index
292 Review
Comment
The author's usual weirdness, this time unusually fragmentary and incoherent. **48%**

6) Combat Rock
Mick Lewis

Details
July 2002 (0563538554 / Black Sheep)
Companions
Jamie, Victoria
Précis
The Tardis sets down in the cannibal-infested jungles of Jenggel...
DWM Index
319   Preview
321   Review
Comment
Violent gore-fest; unpleasant but extremely well written. **80%**

7) The Colony of Lies
Colin Brake

Details
July 2003 (0563486066 / Black Sheep)
Companions
Jamie, Zoe
Précis
In the 26th century, the Tardis lands in what appears to be a Wild West town on Axista 4 ...
DWM Index
232   Preview
236   Review
Comment
Supremely dull and clichéd storyline hampered by tedious prose. **25%**

8) The Indestructible Man
Simon Messingham

Details
November 2004 (0563486236 / Black Sheep)
Companions
Jamie, Zoe
Précis
While SILHOUETTE protects Earth against the Myloki, all is not what it seems...
DWM Index
350   Preview
352   Review
Comment
Affectionate Gerry Anderson pastiche, surprisingly bleak in tone. **85%**

Third Doctor: Jon Pertwee

1) The Devil Goblins from Neptune
Keith Topping and Martin Day

Details
June 1997 (0563405643 / Black Sheep)
Companions
Liz, UNIT
Précis
1970, and hordes of Waro, aliens from Neptune's moon Triton, are invading the Earth...
DWM Index
252   Review
        Keith Topping and Martin Day interview
Comment
Austin Powers spoof of '70s culture, amusingly done, and with a proper plot too. **86%**

2) The Face of the Enemy
David A McIntee

Details
January 1998 (0563405805 / Black Sheep)
Companions
UNIT, Ian, Barbara
Précis
UNIT has to deal with the Master's reappearance on their own...
DWM Index
260   Review
Comment
Doctorless adventure with a recognizable villain and generally lucid prose. **68%**

3) Catastrophea
Terrance Dicks

Details
May 1998 (0563405848 / Black Sheep)
Companion
Jo
Précis
The telepathic natives of the Earth colonised planet of Catastrophea are revolting...

DWM Index
265   Review
275   Terrance Dicks interview
Comment
Achingly obvious British Empire satire, in the style of *The Mutants*. **45%**

4) *The Wages of Sin*
David A McIntee

Details
February 1999 (056355567X / Black Sheep)
Companions
Jo, Liz
Précis
The Doctor meets Rasputin in 1916 St Petersburg…
DWM Index
276   Review
343   David A McIntee interview
Comments
Obvious set-up but done with a certain amount of style. **65%**

5) *Interference Book Two: The Hour of the Geek*
Lawrence Miles

Details
August 1999 (0563555823 / Black Sheep)
Doctor and Companions
Third Doctor, Sam, Fitz, Sarah, K-9 II, Compassion
Précis
The Third Doctor dies on Dust and Fitz is stranded on the Remote's homeworld of Anathema…
DWM Index
281   Review
282   Lawrence Miles interview
Comment
Ultimately unrewarding sequel to the Eighth Doctor *Interference* book with calculated shock moments. **60%**

6) *Last of the Gaderene*
Mark Gatiss

Details
January 2000 (0563555874 / Black Sheep)
Companions
Jo, UNIT
Précis
In the quiet village of Culverton, strange things are happening at the nearby WWII aerodrome…
DWM Index
287   Review
333   Mark Gatiss interview
Comment
Brilliant evocation of the Third Doctor era without resorting to spoof or pastiche. **87%**

7) *Verdigris*
Paul Magrs

Details
April 2000 (0563555920 / Black Sheep)
Companions
Jo, UNIT, Iris Wildthyme
Précis
In the groovy 1970s, the Doctor pits his wits against teenage superheroes Children of Destiny…
DWM Index
289   Paul Magrs: Bafflement and Devotion
290   Review
Comment
The Tomorrow People meets *Top of the Pops* via a particularly silly episode of *The Goodies*. I liked it. **79%**

8) *Rags*
Mick Lewis

Details
March 2001 (0563538260 / Black Sheep)
Companions
Jo, UNIT
Précis
On a tour of pagan sites in South West England, a punk band leaves violence and terror in its wake…
DWM Index
301   Preview
303   Review

Comment
Bloody set pieces galore in a chilling tale of all-out horror. **90%**

9) *Amorality Tale*
David Bishop

Details
April 2002 (0563538503 / Black Sheep)
Companion
Sarah
Précis
Shoreditch 1952, and the Doctor gets himself involved with a bit of gangland thuggery…
DWM Index
315   Preview
317   Review
Comment
Unlikely Third Doctor story with some decidedly one-dimensional characters. **36%**

10) *The Suns of Caresh*
Paul Saint

Details
August 2002 (0563538589 / Black Sheep)
Companion
Jo
Précis
Chichester, 1999, and a bald-headed alien falls in love with a science fiction fan…
DWM Index
320   Preview
323   Review
Comment
Vibrant prose disguises a rather loose plot, but the Third Doctor is perfectly judged. **78%**

11) *Deadly Reunion*
Terrance Dicks and Barry Letts

Details
November 2003 (0563486104 / Photomontage)
Companions
Jo, UNIT
Précis
A huge pop concert causes problems for the Doctor and Jo in the village of Hob's Haven…

DWM Index
337   Preview
340   Review
Comment
A cosily familiar UNIT pastiche - depending on your viewpoint, either 'archetypal' or 'unoriginal'. **56%**

Fourth Doctor: Tom Baker

1) *Eye of Heaven*
Jim Mortimore

Details
February 1998 (0563405783 / Black Sheep)
Companion
Leela
Précis
A young 18th century explorers flees from unnamed horrors on Easter Island…
DWM Index
222   Jim Mortimore interview
262   Review
Comment
Dramatic events seen through Leela's eyes, spoilt by a narrative that tries too hard to be different. **63%**

2) *Last Man Running*
Chris Boucher

Details
September 1998 (0563405945 / Black Sheep)
Companion
Leela
Précis
The Tardis lands in a hostile jungle with a rescue squad chasing an absconded weapons designer…
DWM Index
269   Review
Comment
Formulaic runaround that improves as it goes on. **68%**

3) Millennium Shock
Justin Richards

Details
May 1999 (0563555866 / Black Sheep)
Companion
Harry
Précis
The Voracians have a special microchip that will cause chaos for computers on 1 January 2000…
DWM Index
278 Review
294 Justin Richards interview
Comment
Technobabble-heavy IT plot that nonetheless moves along at a cracking pace. **76%**

4) Corpse Marker
Chris Boucher

Details
November 1999 (0563555750 / Black Sheep)
Companion
Leela
Précis
The Robots are on the warpath again on the streets of Kaldor…
DWM Index
284 Review
Chris Boucher interview
Comment
Stodgy and slow-moving sequel to *The Robots of Death*. **39%**

5) Tomb of Valdemar
Simon Messingham

Details
February 2000 (0563555912 / Black Sheep)
Companions
Romana, K-9 II
Précis
The Doctor is sidetracked by cult leader Paul Neville's obsession to penetrate a fabled tomb…
DWM Index
288 Review
Comment
Stylish quest story plonked in the middle of the Key to Time season. **80%**

6) Festival of Death
Jonathan Morris

Details
September 2000 (0563538031 / Black Sheep)
Companions
Romana II, K-9 II
Précis
A theme park ride called The Beautiful Death gives you an all-too real experience of mortality…
DWM Index
295 Preview
296 Review
344 Jonathan Morris interview
Comment
Witty Season 17 froth spoilt by unnecessary pseudo-science. **67%**

7) Asylum
Peter Darvill-Evans

Details
May 2001 (0563538333 / Black Sheep)
Companion
Nyssa
Précis
The Doctor and Nyssa investigates a murder in a 13th priory…
DWM Index
303 Preview
305 Review
Comment
Historical murder mystery with unnecessary aliens and mismatched protagonists. **30%**

8) Psi-ence Fiction
Chris Boucher

Details
September 2001 (0563538147 / Black Sheep)
Companion
Leela
Précis
In the University of East Wessex, the students are terrified by paranormal incidents…
DWM Index
308 Preview
310 Review

Comment
Moderately successful ghost story enlivened by a good characterization of Leela. **55%**

9) Drift
Simon A Forward

Details
February 2002 (0563538290 / Black Sheep)
Companion
Leela
Précis
A New Hampshire town is in the grip of something far more frightening than a freezing winter...
DWM Index
313   Preview
325   Review
Comment
Fargo-style snowbound mystery with plenty of atmospheric chills. **87%**

10) Wolfsbane
Jacqueline Rayner

Details
September 2003 (0563486090 / Photomontage)
Companions
Sarah, Harry, Eighth Doctor
Précis
The Doctor and Sarah find that Harry has been killed after being mistaken for a werewolf...
DWM Index
334   Preview
338   Review
Comment
Effective and exciting recreation of the early Fourth Doctor era with many spooky scenes. **90%**

11) Match of the Day
Chris Boucher

Details
January 2005 (056348618X / Black Sheep)
Companion
Leela

Précis
The Tardis arrives on a world where fighting to the death is considered family entertainment...
DWM Index
352   Preview
355   Review
Comment
The usual macho posturing, but this time at least there's a decent story to go with it. **60%**

Fifth Doctor: Peter Davison

1) The Ultimate Treasure
Christopher Bulis

Details
August 1997 (0563405635 / Black Sheep, Colin Howard)
Companion
Peri
Précis
On the hidden world of Gelsandor, various parties are seeking a legendary lost treasure...
DWM Index
255   Review
Comment
Puzzles aplenty in this extremely shallow representation of mid-'80s *Who*. **27%**

2) Zeta Major
Simon Messingham

Details
July 1998 (056340597X / Black Sheep)
Companions
Tegan, Nyssa
Précis
The Doctor revisits the Morestran Empire and now finds it involved in a corrupt and violent papal war...
DWM Index
267   Review
Comment
Thankless *Planet of Evil* sequel; as well as could be expected. **67%**

3) Deep Blue
Mark Morris

Details
March 1999 (0563555718 / Black Sheep, Colin Howard)
Companions
Tegan, Turlough, UNIT
Précis
A 1970s summer holiday at Tayborough Sands is spoilt by the arrival of the insectoid Xaranti…
DWM Index
276   Review
Comment
Seamless blending of the UNIT years and the Fifth Doctor era, with a tangible sense of place. **90%**

4) Divided Loyalties
Gary Russell

Details
October 1999 (0563555785 / Black Sheep)
Companions
Adric, Nyssa, Tegan
Précis
The Celestial Toymaker's originals are at last explained…
DWM Index
283   Review
Comment
Continuity-obsessed but entertaining sequel to *The Celestial Toymaker*. **70%**

5) Imperial Moon
Christopher Bulis

Details
August 2000 (0563538015 / Black Sheep)
Companions
Turlough, Kamelion
Précis
Victorian rocketeers find a strange city inhabited by Amazonian women on the Moon…
DWM Index
294   Preview
295   Review
Comment
Gloriously affectionate pastiche of HG Wells and Jules Verne, without whom… **93%**

6) The King of Terror
Keith Topping

Details
November 2000 (0563538023 / Black Sheep)
Companions
Tegan, Turlough, Brigadier
Précis
On the eve of the 21st century, a millionaire is stealing large quantities of plutonium…
DWM Index
297   Preview
298   Review
Comment
Supposedly set in 1999, this is in fact just a highly derivative '70s parody. **38%**

7) Superior Beings
Nick Walters

Details
June 2001 (0563538309 / Black Sheep)
Companion
Peri
Précis
A battle for supremacy is being fought between the vulpine Valethske and the humanoid Eknuri…
DWM Index
305   Preview
308   Review
Comment
Workmanlike story with undelineated characters. **63%**

8) Warmonger
Terrance Dicks

Details
May 2002 (056353852X / Black Sheep)
Companion
Peri
Précis
When Morbius kidnaps Peri, the Doctor is assigned by the Time Lords to lead an army against him…
DWM Index
317   Preview
319   Review
Comment
Trite, clichéd prequel to *The Brain of Morbius*. **40%**

9) Fear of the Dark
Trevor Baxendale

Details
January 2003 (0563538651 / Black Sheep)
Companions
Tegan, Nyssa
Précis
On one of the moons of Akoshemon, the Bloodhunter is engaged in an orgy of killing…
DWM Index
325   Preview
328   Review
Comment
Effective horror story written to a strict formula. **73%**

10) Empire of Death
David Bishop

Details
March 2004 (0563486155 / Black Sheep)
Companion
Nyssa
Précis
Scotland 1863, and after the death of Adric, the Doctor has to face his own ghosts…
DWM Index
340   Preview
344   Review
Comment
Promising central premise spoilt by unengaging prose. **45%**

Sixth Doctor: Colin Baker

1) Business Unusual
Gary Russell

Details
September 1997 (0563405759 / Black Sheep)
Companions
Mel, The Brigadier
Précis
Mel meets the Doctor for the first time amidst strange things going on in the IT industry…
DWM Index
256   Review

Comment
Breathless techno-thriller laced with the author's typical obsession with continuity. **65%**

2) Mission: Impractical
David A McIntee

Details
June 1998 (0563405929 / Black Sheep)
Companions
Frobisher, Sabalom Glitz
Précis
The Doctor returns a stolen artefact to the Veltrochni to avoid further bloodshed with the Tzun…
DWM Index
266   Review
      David A McIntee interview
343   David A McIntee interview
Comment
Comic strip storyline with a cast of irritatingly unfunny characters. **35%**

3) Players
Terrance Dicks

Details
April 1999 (0563555734 / Black Sheep)
Companion
Peri
Précis
The Doctor meets Churchill and the mysterious Players influence the Great War for their own ends…
DWM Index
275   Terrance Dicks interview
278   Review
Comment
Simply told, but effective, sequel to *The War Games*, with intriguing enemies. **77%**

4) Grave Matter
Justin Richards

Details
May 2000 (056355598X / Black Sheep)
Companion
Peri

Précis
Arriving on the island of Dorsill, the Doctor finds the insular community harbouring a terrible secret…
DWM Index
291   Review
294   Justin Richards interview
Comment
Archetypal old-fashioned *Doctor Who*, suitably scary. **88%**

5) The Quantum Archangel
Craig Hinton

Details
January 2001 (0563538244 / Black Sheep)
Companion
Mel
Précis
The Master attempts to use the power source of the Chronovores to alter history itself…
DWM Index
299   Preview
301   Review
Comment
Car-crash sequel to *The Time Monster*; best avoided. **20%**

6) The Shadow in the Glass
Justin Richards and Stephen Cole

Details
April 2001 (0563538384 / Black Sheep)
Companion
Brigadier
Précis
The abandoned town of Turelhampton holds the key to the final destiny of the Third Reich…
DWM Index
302   Preview
304   Review
Comment
Written to plug a gap in the schedule, this is a surprisingly gripping Nazi thriller. **75%**

7) Instruments of Darkness
Gary Russell

Details
November 2001 (0563538287 / Black Sheep)
Companions
Mel, Evelyn, Jeremy
Précis
The accidental death of a UNIT soldier leads to a meeting with mysterious Magnate organization…
DWM Index
311   Preview
312   Review
Comment
Episodic and incoherent sequel to some of the author's previous books; equally mystifying and dull. **11%**

8) Palace of the Red Sun
Christopher Bulis

Details
March 2002 (056353848X / Black Sheep)
Companion
Peri
Précis
The Doctor goes to the aid of a usurped ruler on the garden planet of Aldermar…
DWM Index
314   Preview
316   Review
Comment
Trite and predictable tale of alien royalty with the usual twists. **40%**

9) Blue Box
Kate Orman

Details
March 2003 (0563538597 / Black Sheep)
Companion
Peri
Précis
An organic computer has fallen into the hands of an ambitious computer programmer…
DWM Index
328   Kate Orman interview
*   Preview*
330   Review
Comment
Surprisingly enthralling tale of computer hacking, 1980s style. **75%**

10) Synthespians™
Craig Hinton

Details
July 2004 (0563486171 / Black Sheep)
Companion
Peri
Précis
In the 111th century, the Autons are preparing once again to attack humanity...
DWM Index
345 Preview
349 Review
Comment
Plot-heavy Auton adventure of a rather predictable kind. **55%**

Seventh Doctor: Sylvester McCoy

1) Illegal Alien
Mike Tucker and Robert Perry

Details
October 1997 (0563405708 / Black Sheep)
Companion
Ace
Précis
London in the Blitz, and a group of Nazis are after Cyber-technology to fulfil their destiny...
DWM Index
257 Review
285 Everything You Ever Need To Know...
330 Mike Tucker and Robert Perry interview
Comment
Faithful recreation of the Seventh Doctor's era. **80%**

2) The Hollow Men
Martin Day and Keith Topping

Details
April 1998 (0563405821 / Black Sheep, Colin Howard)
Companion
Ace
Précis
The Doctor finds a strange curse hanging over the village of Hexen Bridge...
DWM Index
264 Review
    Martin Day and Keith Topping interview
Comment
Fairly well-written evocation of the era, let down by unnecessary in-jokes. **70%**

3) Matrix
Robert Perry and Mike Tucker

Details
October 1998 (0563405961 / Black Sheep)
Companions
Ace, Ian, Barbara
Précis
On an alternative Earth, Jack the Ripper's influence has tainted the course of 20th century history...
DWM Index
270 Review
330 Mike Tucker and Robert Perry interview
Comment
Impressive journey through an alternative 1963 London highlighted by memorable character studies. **84%**

4) Storm Harvest
Robert Perry and Mike Tucker

Details
June 1999 (0563555777 / Black Sheep, Mike Tucker)
Companion
Ace
Précis
The Doctor investigates a mysterious shipwreck on the ocean world of Coralee...
DWM Index
279 Review
    Mike Tucker interview
330 Mike Tucker and Robert Perry interview
Comment
Monsters aplenty in another accurate pastiche of the early Seventh Doctor stories. **68%**

5) Prime Time
Mike Tucker

Details
July 2000 (0563555971 / Black Sheep, Mike Tucker)
Companion
Ace
Précis
The Doctor and Ace become unwitting stars of Channel 400's new docusoap…
DWM Index
293   Review
330   Mike Tucker and Robert Perry interview
Comment
Undisciplined amalgam of the author's previous works, but fun nevertheless. **73%**

6) Independence Day
Peter Darvill-Evans

Details
October 2000 (056353804X / Black Sheep)
Companion
Ace
Précis
The Doctor tries to avert an inter-colony war between Mendebs Two and Three…
DWM Index
296   Preview
297   Review
Comment
Straightforward story made memorable by its bleak resolution. **55%**

7) Bullet Time
David A McIntee

Details
August 2001 (0563538341 / Black Sheep)
Companion
Sarah
Précis
The Doctor joins Sarah in her investigation of Triad gangsters in Hong Kong…
DWM Index
307   Preview
309   Review
Comment
Clinically written self-styled Hollywood blockbuster with few memorable scenes. **35%**

8) Relative Dementias
Mark Michalowski

Details
January 2002 (0563538449 / Black Sheep)
Companion
Ace
Précis
In the Scottish village of Muirbridge, residents of an old people's home are mysteriously vanishing…
DWM Index
312   Preview
314   Review
Comment
Great concepts and great characterization in a solid story well told. **89%**

9) Heritage
Dale Smith

Details
October 2002 (0563538643 / Black Sheep)
Companion
Ace
Précis
Colonists on the backwater planet of Heritage are hiding a terrible secret…
DWM Index
322   Preview
326   Review
Comment
Rather depressing small-scale murder story with much introspection. **40%**

10) Loving the Alien
Mike Tucker and Robert Perry

Details
May 2003 (056348604X / Black Sheep)
Companion
Ace
Précis
While battling giant ants in 1959 London, the Doctor does all he can to prevent Ace's tragic death…
DWM Index
330   Mike Tucker and Robert Perry interview
333   Review
Comment
Slick storytelling compromised by a cop-out ending. **77%**

11) *The Algebra of Ice*
Lloyd Rose

Details
August 2004 (056348621X / Black Sheep)
Companions
Ace, Brigadier
Précis
Edgar Allan Poe is caught in a time anomaly that threatens the Universe..
DWM Index
347   Preview
351   Review
Comment
Excellent characterization in this superior tribute to Virgin's New Adventures series. **85%**

Miscellaneous

The Infinity Doctors
Lance Parkin

Details
November 1998 (0563405910 / Black Sheep, Colin Howard)
Précis
On Gallifrey, 'The Doctor' deals with alien invasions and social upheavals…
DWM Index
271   Review
272   Lance Parkin interview
Comment
Brilliant, archetypal *Doctor Who* story full of memorable characters and stunning imagery. **93%**

Eighth Doctor Novels (BBC)

All titles are published by BBC Books, a division of BBC Worldwide, and are listed in publication order.

DWM Index
305   The (New) Adventure Game

1) *The Eight Doctors*
Terrance Dicks

Details
June 1997 (0563405635 / Black Sheep)
Companion
Samantha Jones
Précis
The Tardis takes an amnesia-suffering Doctor to meet his previous incarnations…
DWM Index
252   Review
275   Terrance Dicks interview
Comment
Terrible old tosh masquerading as a memory jolt for new readers. **35%**

2) *Vampire Science*
Jonathan Blume and Kate Orman

Details
July 1997 (056340566X / Black Sheep)
Companion
Sam
Précis
The Doctor comes across a coven of vampires in present-day San Francisco…
DWM Index
254   Review
328   Kate Orman interview
Comment
Buffy inspired schlock of a rather bland variety. **65%**

3) *The Bodysnatchers*
Mark Morris

Details
August 1997 (0563405686 / Black Sheep)
Companion
Sam, Litefoot

Précis
The Zygons are abroad in fog-shrouded Victorian London…
DWM Index
255   Review
       Mark Morris interview
Comment
The wonderful opening chapters give way to a limp plot with little or no tension. **50%**

4) Genocide
Paul Leonard

Details
September 1997 (0563405724 / Black Sheep)
Companion
Sam
Précis
The ox-like Tractites attempt to wipe out Stone Age man so that they can inhabit the Earth…
DWM Index
256   Review
       Paul Leonard interview
Comment
A straightforward story rattles along with the emphases firmly on suspense and scares. **78%**

5) War of the Daleks
John Peel

Details
October 1997 (0563405716 / Black Sheep)
Companion
Sam
Précis
The Doctor and Sam are captured by Thals, who take them to Davros…
DWM Index
257   Review
       John Peel interview
Comment
Not so much a book, more a list of old Dalek stories haphazardly strung together. **25%**

6) Alien Bodies
Lawrence Miles

Details
November 1997 (0563405775 / Black Sheep)
Companion
Sam
Précis
In the 21st century rainforest of Borneo lurks a Gallifreyan Voodoo cult called Faction Paradox…
DWM Index
258   Review
282   Lawrence Miles interview
       Everything You Ever Need to Know…
Comment
Open-ended introduction to Faction Paradox, with a cast of memorably weird characters. **70%**

7) Kursaal
Peter Anghelides

Details
January 1998 (0563405783 / Black Sheep)
Companion
Sam
Précis
Terrorists disrupt plans to turn the rain-soaked planet Saturnia Regna into a vast theme park…
DWM Index
260   Review
       Peter Anghelides interview
Comment
Intelligent *Blade Runner*-style werewolf tale with plenty of atmosphere. **75%**

8) Option Lock
Justin Richards

Details
February 1998 (056340588X / Black Sheep, Colin Howard)
Companion
Sam
Précis
The Doctor visits a country house in which intelligence operatives are trained by hypnosis…
DWM Index
262   Review
       Justin Richards interview
294   Justin Richards interview

Comment
Slickly written psychological drama played out against a world teetering on the brink of nuclear war. **84%**

9) Longest Day
Michael Collier

Details
March 1998 (0563405805 / Colin Howard)
Companion
Sam
Précis
On the barren world of Hirath, different time zones exist in different time periods…
DWM Index
263   Review
Comment
Weakly written and plotted fantasy which fails totally. **18%**

10) Legacy of the Daleks
John Peel

Details
April 1998 (0563405740 / Black Sheep)
Companions
Sam, Susan
Précis
The Doctor revisits Susan on a future Earth, only to find an old enemy among the ruins…
DWM Index
264   Review
Comment
Contrived and artless sequel to *The Dalek Invasion of Earth*. **40%**

11) Dreamstone Moon
Paul Leonard

Details
May 1998 (0563405856 / Black Sheep)
Companion
Sam
Précis
The Doctor explores a planet rich in dream-enhancing gems…

DWM Index
265   Review
Comment
Fitfully impressive one-note action story. **58%**

12) Seeing I
Jonathan Blume and Kate Orman

Details
June 1998 (0563405864 / Black Sheep)
Companion
Sam
Précis
Sam is stranded on Ha'olam, a colony world settled by Middle East émigrés…
DWM Index
266   Review
328   Kate Orman interview
Comment
Sam is allowed to develop nicely despite the concept-heavy plot. **75%**

13) Placebo Effect
Gary Russell

Details
July 1998 (0563405872 / Black Sheep)
Companions
Sam, Stacey, Ssard
Précis
The Wirrn arrive on the eve of the Galactic Olympics and disrupt the wedding of Stacey and Ssard…
DWM Index
267   Review
      Gary Russell interview
272   Gary Russell interview
Comment
Reworking of various *Doctor Who* elements in the author's typically frenetic style. **41%**

14) Vanderdeken's Children
Christopher Bulis

Details
August 1998 (0563405902 / Colin Howard)
Companion
Sam

Précis
The Tardis materializes inside a huge abandoned space vessel...
DWM Index
268   Review
Comment
Rendezvous with Rama with knobs on. **70%**

15) The Scarlet Empress
Paul Magrs

Details
September 1998 (0563405953 / Black Sheep)
Companions
Sam, Iris Wildthyme
Précis
The Doctor meets an old flame on the planet Hyspero...
DWM Index
269   Review
280   Everything You Ever Needed To Know..
289   Paul Magrs: Bafflement and Devotion
Comment
Full-bodied but cripplingly self-referential campery. **54%**

16) The Janus Conjunction
Trevor Baxendale

Details
October 1998 (0563405996 / Black Sheep)
Companion
Sam
Précis
On the war-torn planet of Janus Prime, the giant spider population is being ruthlessly harnessed...
DWM Index
270   Review
Comment
Straightforward and unpretentious adventure tale, easy to read and easier to enjoy. **88%**

17) Beltempest
Jim Mortimore

Details
November 1998 (0563405937 / Black Sheep)
Companion
Sam

Précis
The Bel planetary system is under attack by planet-sized aliens...
DWM Index
271   Review
272   Jim Mortimore interview
Comment
Uninvolving 'hard SF' with limited appeal. **55%**

18) The Face-Eater
Simon Messingham

Details
January 1999 (0563555696 / Black Sheep)
Companion
Sam
Précis
Colonists in Proxima Centauri are powerless against a hostile entity that literally eats their memories...
DWM Index
274   Review
Comment
Carefully plotted, albeit slow, monster tale with clever detail. **76%**

19) The Taint
Michael Collier

Details
February 1999 (0563555688 / Black Sheep)
Companions
Sam, Fitz
Précis
In a large country house in the 1960s, the Doctor is privy to some disturbing tales from its inmates...
DWM Index
272   Steven Cole interview
276   Review
Comment
Low-key introduction of Fitz, but the story never really gets going. **36%**

20) Demontage
Justin Richards

Details
March 1999 (0563555726 / Black Sheep)
Companions
Sam, Fitz
Précis
An outbreak of sabotage upsets the quiet running of the Vega Station leisure complex…
DWM Index
272   Justin Richards interview
276   Review
Comment
Arch comedy spoofing the movie absurdities of James Bond, amongst others. **60%**

21) Revolution Man
Paul Leonard

Details
April 1999 (056355570X / Black Sheep)
Companions
Sam, Fitz
Précis
The Doctor and his friends hurry to avert a time anomaly from destroying the Earth in 1969…
DWM Index
277   Review
Comment
International spy thriller perfectly fitted for the Eighth Doctor. **82%**

22) Dominion
Nick Walters

Details
May 1999 (0563555742 / Black Sheep)
Companions
Sam, Fitz
Précis
In Sweden, an alien invasion heralds the disappearance of Sam…
DWM Index
278   Review
Comment
Clear-cut prose and a generally intriguing plot make up for an ineffectual ending. **70%**

23) Unnatural History
Jonathan Blume and Kate Orman

Details
June 1999 (0563555769 / Black Sheep)
Companions
Sam, Fitz
Précis
Faction Paradox return in 21st century San Francisco, along with two versions of Sam…
DWM Index
279   Review
328   Kate Orman interview
Comment
A bizarre concoction of sex and impenetrable prose, but the Eighth Doctor has never looked better. **70%**

24) Autumn Mist
David A McIntee

Details
July 1999 (0563555831 / Black Sheep)
Companions
Sam, Fitz
Précis
The Tardis lands on the German front in 1944 and Fritz disguises himself as an SS officer…
DWM Index
280   Review
343   David A McIntee interview
Comment
Disappointingly twee fairytale with roots in *The Hobbit* amongst others. **45%**

25) Interference Book One: Shock Tactic
Lawrence Miles

Details
August 1999 (0563555807 / Black Sheep)
Doctor and Companions
Third Doctor, Sam, Fitz, Sarah, K-9 III, Compassion
Précis
Gallifrey's history is reinvented by Faction Paradox, while the Remote look on…
DWM Index
281   Review
282   Lawrence Miles interview

Comment
Frenetic open-ended adventure, mysterious and dynamic in equal measure. **87%**

26) *The Blue Angel*
Paul Magrs and Jeremy Hoad

Details
September 1999 (0563555815 / Black Sheep)
Companions
Fitz, Compassion, Iris Wildthyme
Précis
The Doctor and Iris visit the fantastical world of the Enclave dimension…
DWM Index
282   Review
       Iris Wildthyme interview
289   Paul Magrs: Bafflement and Devotion
Comment
Barbarella-style fantasy with a meandering storyline. **37%**

27) *The Taking of Planet 5*
Simon Bucher-Jones and Mark Clapham

Details
October 1999 (0563555793 / Black Sheep)
Companions
Fitz, Compassion
Précis
An expedition to Antarctica unearths a demonic alien presence…
DWM Index
283   Review
Comment
Lovecraftian horror tale with a few too many convoluted ideas thrown in. **62%**

28) *Frontier Worlds*
Peter Anghelides

Details
November 1999 (0563555890 / Black Sheep)
Companions
Fitz, Compassion
Précis
On Drebnar, the Doctor searches for the insane scientist responsible for deadly alien vegetation…
DWM Index
285   Review
       Peter Anghelides interview
Comment
Ambitious eco-thriller bristling with big targets. **75%**

29) *Parallel 59*
Natalie Dallaire and Stephen Cole

Details
January 2000 (0563555904 / Black Sheep)
Companions
Fitz, Compassion
Précis
The government of the planet Skale wants no-one to know the secret of 'The Project'…
DWM Index
287   Review
       Stephen Cole interview
Comment
Depressing and somewhat redundant clone of *Nineteen Eighty-Four*. **43%**

30) *The Shadows of Avalon*
Paul Cornell

Details
February 2000 (0563555882 / Black Sheep)
Companions
Fitz, Compassion, The Brigadier
Précis
A nuclear missile is hijacked and a warrior queen appears from another dimension…
DWM Index
288   Review
       Paul Cornell interview
Comment
A reworked *Battlefield*, with considerably more impact. **68%**

31) *The Fall of Yquatine*
Nick Walters
Details
March 2000 (0563555947 / Black Sheep)
Companions
Fitz, Compassion

Précis
The Marquis of Yquatine has to chose between his love for a woman and his responsibilities as ruler…
DWM Index
289 Review
Comment
Slushy soap opera piffle with attendant teenage angst. **25%**

32) Coldheart
Trevor Baxendale

Details
April 2000 (056355955 / Black Sheep)
Companions
Fitz, Compassion
Précis
The frozen planet of Eskon is home to hideous mutations called Slimers…
DWM Index
290 Review
Comment
Good, old-fashioned storytelling with a satisfying, if over-familiar, plot. **76%**

33) The Space Age
Steve Lyons

Details
May 2000 (0563538007 / Black Sheep)
Companions
Fitz, Compassion
Précis
On a 1960s inspired 21st century Earth, gang warfare is the order of the day…
DWM Index
291 Review
Comment
The author's ingeniously described 'retro' future world is a real accomplishment. **72%**

34) The Banquo Legacy
Andy Lane and Justin Richards
Details
June 2000 (0563538082 / Black Sheep)
Companions
Fitz, Compassion

Précis
In a Victorian manor house, an experiment involving electricity and telepathy goes horrifying awry…
DWM Index
292 Review
294 Justin Richards interview
Comment
Endless running around inside a stately home is no substitute for a story. **15%**

35) The Ancestor Cell
Peter Anghelides and Stephen Cole

Details
July 2000 (0563538090 / Black Sheep)
Companions
Fitz, Compassion
Précis
A colossal bone structure appears in the skies above Gallifrey…
DWM Index
293 Review
     Peter Anghelides and Stephen Cole interview
Comment
As a resolution to the questions posed in *Interference*, it almost works - as a novel in its own right it is rather unwelcoming. **36%**

36) The Burning
Justin Richards

Details
August 2000 (0563538120 / Black Sheep)
Précis
Stranded on Earth, the Doctor seeks to regain his memories in the 19th century village of Middletown…
DWM Index
294 Justin Richards interview
295 Review
Comment
Timely re-invention of the Eighth Doctor, ditching all extraneous baggage for a brand new start. **95%**

37) Casualties of War
Steve Emmerson

Details
September 2000 (056353805 / Black Sheep)
Précis
An experimental new treatment at a psychiatric hospital causes dead WWI soldiers to reappear…
DWM Index
295   Preview
296   Review
Comment
Slick and exciting storytelling which concentrates on character and location to great effect. **92%**

38) The Turing Test
Paul Leonard

Details
October 2000 (0563538066 / Black Sheep)
Précis
At the end of WWII, the Doctor meets novelist Graham Greene and computer genius Alan Turing…
DWM Index
296   Preview
297   Review
Comment
Intelligent wartime drama split into three distinct first-person narratives. **76%**

39) Endgame
Terrance Dicks

Details
November 2000 (0563538228 / Black Sheep)
Précis
In 1951 London, the Players are interfering with Cold War history…
DWM Index
297   Preview
298   Review
Comment
Sequel to *The Players* with limited characterization. **50%**

40) Father Time
Lance Parkin

Details
January 2001 (0563538104 / Black Sheep)
Précis
In the 1980s village of Greyfirth, the Doctor is shocked to discover that he has an adopted daughter…
DWM Index
299   Preview
301   Review
Comment
Wry satire on the 1980s with intriguing character development for the Doctor. **84%**

41) Escape Velocity
Colin Brake

Details
February 2001 (0563538252 / Black Sheep)
Companions
Fitz, Anji Kapoor
Précis
During the Kulan invasion of Earth, the Doctor starts regaining his memories…
DWM Index
300   Preview
302   Review
Comment
Banal conclusion to the 'trapped on Earth' arc. **60%**

42) EarthWorld
Jacqueline Rayner

Details
March 2001 (0563538279 / Black Sheep)
Companions
Fitz, Anji
Précis
The Doctor discovers the dark side of the EarthWorld theme park on New Jupiter…
DWM Index
301   Preview
303   Review
Comment
Enjoyable debut for Anji in this *Jurassic Park*-style hokum. **68%**

43) Vanishing Point
Stephen Cole

Details
April 2001 (0563538384 / Black Sheep)
Companions
Fitz, Anji
Précis
The populace of an alien planet face a tough task in getting into the afterlife...
DWM Index
302   Preview
304   Review
Comment
Promising material too hung up on an endless DNA science lesson. **44%**

44) Eater of Wasps
Trevor Baxendale

Details
May 2001 (0563538325 / Black Sheep)
Companions
Fitz, Anji
Précis
A dentist in the 1930s village of Marpling finds something strange in his vegetable patch...
DWM Index
303   Preview
305   Review
Comment
Beautifully written horror story, strong on grotesque imagery. **95%**

45) The Year of Intelligent Tigers
Kate Orman

Details
June 2001 (0563538317 / Black Sheep)
Companions
Fitz, Anji
Précis
The cool, music-loving cats of paradise island Hitchemus may not be as friendly as they seem...
DWM Index
305   Preview
307   Review
328   Kate Orman interview
Comment
Partially successful change of pace blessed with intriguing feline aliens. **45%**

46) The Slow Empire
Dave Stone

Details
July 2001 (056353835X / Black Sheep)
Companions
Fitz, Anji
Précis
The Doctor accidentally disrupts a teleport experiment in the vast, far-flung Shakrath Empire...
DWM Index
306   Preview
308   Review
Comment
Dreary travelogue liberally interspersed with the author's own brand of humour. **25%**

47) Dark Progeny
Steve Emmerson

Details
August 2001 (0563538376 / Black Sheep)
Companions
Fitz, Anji
Précis
The city-machine of Ceres Alpha might not be such a good solution to Earth's overcrowding after all...
DWM Index
307   Preview
309   Review
Comment
Unfocused futuristic horror story with ecological leanings. **58%**

48) The City of the Dead
Lloyd Rose

Details
September 2001 (0563538392 / Black Sheep)
Companions
Fitz, Anji
Précis
The Doctor lands in present-day New Orleans, the home to a sinister Voodoo cult...

DWM Index
308 Preview
310 Review
Comment
Fascinating blend of magic and science, imaginatively written. **77%**

49) Grimm Reality
Simon Bucher-Jones and Kelly Hale

Details
October 2001 (0563538414 / Black Sheep)
Companions
Fitz, Anji
Précis
The Doctor lands in a world where fairytales come true - at a cost…
DWM Index
309 Preview
311 Review
Comment
Crazy fairytale in true, unfettered *Mind Robber* style. **76%**

50) The Adventuress of Henrietta Street
Lawrence Miles

Details
November 2001 (0563538422 / Black Sheep)
Companions
Fitz, Anji
Précis
The Doctor makes his headquarters in a brothel as a being called Sabbath is summoned to England…
DWM Index
310 Preview
312 Review
Comment
Sublime re-imagining of many sacred *Doctor Who* cows. **83%**

51) Mad Dogs and Englishmen
Paul Magrs

Details
January 2002 (0563538457 / Black Sheep)
Companions
Fitz, Anji
Précis
A race of talking poodles gatecrashes an interplanetary science fiction conference…
DWM Index
312 Preview
314 Review
Comment
Silly, bright, fun, frenetic - in other words, the author's usual mixture. **65%**

52) Hope
Mark Clapham

Details
February 2002 (0563538465 / Black Sheep)
Companions
Fitz, Anji
Précis
In a frightening futuristic city, Anji is given the chance to resurrect her long-dead boyfriend…
DWM Index
313 Preview
315 Review
Comment
Solidly written close-up on Anji. **70%**

53) Anachrophobia
Jonathan Morris

Details
March 2002 (0563538503 / Black Sheep)
Companions
Fitz, Anji
Précis
The Tardis lands on a space station in the midst of a time war between the Plutocrats and the Defaulters…
DWM Index
314 Preview
316 Review
344 Jonathan Morris interview
Comment
Unremittingly grim horror with an annoyingly unresolved conclusion. **68%**

54) Trading Futures
Lance Parkin

Details
April 2002 (0563538481 / Black Sheep)
Companions
Fitz, Anji
Précis
The Doctor is up against a Russian conman and the rhinoceros-like Onihr…
DWM Index
315   Preview
317   Review
Comment
Supposed spoof of the James Bond movies that just seems like mediocre storytelling. **44%**

55) The Book of the Still
Paul Ebbs

Details
May 2002 (0563538511 / Black Sheep)
Companions
Fitz, Anji
Précis
On the planet of Lebenswelt, the Doctor is imprisoned for a crime he may just have committed…
DWM Index
317   Preview
319   Review
Comment
Circular storyline with much inventive detail. **78%**

56) The Crooked World
Steve Lyons

Details
June 2002 (0563538562 / Black Sheep)
Companions
Fitz, Anji
Précis
When the Doctor lands in a cartoon world he meets some very familiar characters…
DWM Index
318   Preview
320   Review
Comment
The same brand of 'fiction as fact' this author normally peddles, redeemed by humour. **75%**

57) History 101
Mags L Halliday

Details
July 2002 (0563538546 / Black Sheep)
Companions
Fitz, Anji
Précis
A powerful alien observer called the Absolute wants to change the outcome of the Spanish Civil War…
DWM Index
319   Preview
321   Review
Comment
Intriguing essay on historicity, albeit somewhat padded. **67%**

58) Camera Obscura
Lloyd Rose

Details
August 2002 (0563538570 / Black Sheep)
Companions
Fitz, Anji
Précis
An eccentric Victorian time machine has the power to split its observers into multiple personalities…
DWM Index
320   Preview
322   Review
Comment
Engaging Victorian whimsy with good scenes between the Doctor and Sabbath. **66%**

59) Time Zero
Justin Richards

Details
September 2002 (056353866X / Black Sheep)
Companions
Fitz, Anji
Précis
Carnivorous dinosaurs from another dimension are on the loose in Siberia…
DWM Index
321   Preview
323   Review
Comment
Clever thriller spoilt by occasionally incomprehensible science. **75%**

60) The Infinity Race
Simon Messingham

Details
November 2002 (0563538635 / Black Sheep)
Companions
Fitz, Anji
Précis
The Tardis lands on an eerily deserted yacht on the ocean planet of Selonart…
DWM Index
324   Preview
325   Review
Comment
Unadventurous story with a misjudged first person narrative. **56%**

61) The Domino Effect
David Bishop

Details
February 2003 (0563538694 / Black Sheep)
Companions
Fitz, Anji
Précis
The Doctor arrives in 21st Edinburgh to find its inhabitants don't even know what a computer is…
DWM Index
326   Preview
329   Review
Comment
Over-egged romp with little subtlety and even weaker characterization. **52%**

62) Reckless Engineering
Nick Walters

Details
April 2003 (0563486031 / Black Sheep)
Companions
Fitz, Anji
Précis
On an alternate Earth, the Doctor is hunted down by the Wildren in the ruins of Bristol…
DWM Index
329   Preview
332   Review
Comment
A lovingly created alternate Bristol is the star of this stark and depressing work. **85%**

63) The Last Resort
Paul Leonard

Details
June 2003 (0563486058 / Black Sheep)
Companions
Fitz, Anji
Précis
As aliens conquer an alternative Earth, Anji has to stop Good Times Inc from damaging this one…
DWM Index
331   Preview
335   Review
Comment
High concept SF yarn which builds on the 'changed history' arc to great effect. **82%**

64) Timeless
Stephen Cole

Details
August 2003 (0563486074 / Black Sheep)
Companions
Fitz, Anji, Beatrix 'Trix' MacMillan
Précis
The Doctor becomes embroiled in the workings of the mysterious Timeless organisation…
DWM Index
333   Preview
335   Review
Comment
Burdened with too many plot requirements, this is still an intelligent, if unwieldy, read. **79%**

65) Emotional Chemistry
Simon A Forward

Details
October 2003 (0563486082 / Black Sheep)
Companions
Fitz, Trix
Précis
The Kremlin, 2024, and Fitz is under arrest for a fire which has apparently killed the Doctor…
DWM Index
336   Preview
339   Review
Comment
Analytical rather than emotional, Forward's well constructed plot is short on human interest. **38%**

66) Sometime Never...
Justin Richards

Details
January 2004 (0563486112 / Black Sheep)
Companions
Fitz, Trix
Précis
The Council of Eight discovers a dangerous rogue element in the Time Vortex...
DWM Index
338   Justin Richards interview
341   Review
Comment
Disappointingly lifeless and unappealing resolution to the 'changed history' arc. **55%**

67) Halflife
Mark Michalowski

Details
April 2004 (0563486139 / Black Sheep)
Companions
Fitz, Trix
Précis
The Doctor's gone and lost his memory - again...
DWM Index
341   Preview
347   Review
Comment
Confident and absorbing tale with a nice slant on new(ish) companion Trix. **88%**

68) The Tomorrow Windows
Jonathan Morris

Details
June 2004 (0563486163 / Black Sheep)
Companions
Fitz, Trix
Précis
The Tate Modern's newest acquisition is a device that can look into the future...
DWM Index
344   Jonathan Morris interview
348   Review
Comment
Whimsical Douglas Adams pastiche that's never less than hugely entertaining. **87%**

69) The Sleep of Reason
Martin Day

Details
August 2004 (0563486201 / Black Sheep)
Companions
Fitz, Trix
Précis
A suicidal woman has strange dreams of an old building surrounded by sinister ghostly dogs...
DWM Index
346   Preview
349   Review
Comment
Satisfyingly doom-laden horror story with a marvellous sense of place. **79%**

70) The Deadstone Memorial
Trevor Baxendale

Details
September 2004 (0563486228 / Black Sheep)
Companions
Fitz, Trix
Précis
In an ordinary house, in an ordinary street, nightmares have taken on a life of their own...
DWM Index
348   Preview
351   Review
Comment
Explicitly violent and horrific tale of alien possession - the sort of thing this author does so well. **82%**

71) To The Slaughter
Stephen Cole

Details
February 2005 (0563486252 / Black Sheep)
Companions
Fitz, Trix
Précis
With the aid of some cosmic feng-shui, the solar system is getting a spring-clean...
DWM Index
353   Preview
355   Review
Comment
A plotless satire that misses as many targets as it hits. **52%**

72) The Gallifrey Chronicles
Lance Parkin

Details
June 2005 (0563486244 / Black Sheep)
Companions
Fitz, Trix
Précis
Gallifrey has been destroyed and the culprit lured to Earth in 2005…
DWM Index
358   Preview
Comment
The Eighth Doctor goes out with a bang in this epic *fin de siècle* adventure. **95%**

Ninth Doctor: Christopher Eccleston

1) The Clockwise Man
Justin Richards

Details
May 2005 (0563486287 / Photomontage)
Companion
Rose Tyler
Précis
The Doctor and Rose hunt for a mysterious killer in 1920s London…
DWM Index
357   Justin Richards interview
358   Review
Comment
Rather formulaic historical mystery that gets better as it goes on. **80%**

2) The Monsters Inside
Stephen Cole

Details
May 2005 (0563486295 / Photomontage)
Companion
Rose Tyler
Précis
Rose is trapped in a teenage borstal with some flatulent monsters…
DWM Index
357   Stephen Cole interview
358   Review
Comment
Aimless runaround with no vestige of excitement or tension. **25%**

3) Winner Takes All
Jacqueline Rayner

Details
May 2005 (0563486279 / Photomontage)
Companions
Rose Tyler, Mickey
Précis
In present-day London, video gamers are mysteriously going missing…
DWM Index
357   Jacqueline Rayner interview
358   Review
Comment
Bright, breezy and unpretentious adventure story with charmingly odd aliens. **85%**

Novellas

These titles are published by Telos in standard hardback (£10) and deluxe leather-bound (£25) editions, with frontispiece illustrations in the latter by a variety of well-known fantasy and science fiction artists. The company lost its licence to produce this range in 2004.

1) Time and Relative
Kim Newman (foreword by Justin Richards)

Details
November 2001 (Hardback 1903889022, Deluxe 1903889030 / Bryan Talbot)
Précis
Easter 1963, and Susan is keeping a diary of her time on Earth and wondering why it is so cold…
DWM Index
311   Preview
313   Review
Comment
Stylish interpretation of a pre-*An Unearthly Child* Doctor with a great villain. **96%**

2) Citadel of Dreams
Dave Stone (foreword by Andrew Cartmel)

Details
March 2002 (Hardback 1903889049, Deluxe 1903889057 / Lee Sullivan)
Précis
A street urchin has nightmares that his sprawling city is under attack - and then the Doctor appears...
DWM Index
315 Preview
317 Review
Comment
Reigned-in hokum with clever twists. **72%**

3) Nightdreamers
Tom Arden (foreword by Katy Manning)

Details
May 2002 (Hardback 1903889065, Deluxe 1903889073 / Martin McKenna)
Précis
The Doctor and Jo encounter a royal love triangle on the forest moon of Verd...
DWM Index
318 Preview
319 Review
Comment
Fey Shakespearian comedy with arbitrary *Doctor Who* elements. **30%**

4) Ghost Ship
Keith Topping (foreword by Hugh Lamb)

Details
1. August 2002 (Hardback 1903889081, Deluxe 190388909X / Dariusz Jasiczak)
2. November 2003 (Paperback 1903889324)
Précis
1963, and something horrible is lurking aboard the ocean liner *The Queen Mary*...
DWM Index
321 Preview
322 Review
Comment
Clichéd story with an inadequate first person narrative from the Fourth Doctor. **20%**

5) Foreign Devils
Andrew Cartmel (foreword by Mike Ashley)

Details
1. November 2002 (Hardback 1903889103, Deluxe 1903889111 / Mike Collins)
2. November 2003 (Paperback 1903889332)
Précis
The Doctor's search for his companions leads to a meeting with a famous paranormal investigator...
DWM Index
324 Preview
325 Review
Comment
Marvellous Victorian melodrama with great characters. **85%**

6) Rip Tide
Louise Cooper (foreword by Steve Gallagher)

Details
February 2003 (Hardback 190388912X, Deluxe 1903889138 / Fred Gambino)
Précis
A Cornish murder points to a solitary red-headed stranger who wanders the beach at night...
DWM Index
327 Preview
329 Review
Comment
Quiet character piece set against a beautifully descriptive Cornish backdrop.

7) Wonderland
Mark Chadbourn (foreword by Graham Joyce)

Details
April 2003 (Hardback 1903889146, Deluxe 1903889154 / Dominic Harman)
Précis
In 1960s San Francisco, a new drug called Moonbeams is literally making people vanish into thin air...
DWM Index
329 Preview
330 Review
Comment
Psychedelic shenanigans perfectly suited to the Second Doctor. **80%**

8) Shell Shock
Simon A Forward (foreword by Guy N Smith)

Details
June 2003 (Hardback 1903889162, Deluxe 1903889170 / Bob Covington)
Précis
The Doctor meets some genetically-modified crabs while Peri's mind is absorbed by a sea sponge…
DWM Index
331 Preview
332 Review
Comment
Emotionally draining character study, equally brilliant and disturbing. **87%**

9) The Cabinet of Light
Daniel O'Mahony (foreword by Chaz Brenchley)

Details
July 2003 (Hardback 1903889189, Deluxe 1903889197 / John Higgins)
Précis
Time sensitive Honoré Lechasseur hunts for the Doctor in 1949 London…
DWM Index
232 Preview
233 Review
Comment
Promising start to an intended spin-off series. **83%**

10) Fallen Gods
Jonathan Blum and Kate Orman (foreword by Storm Constantine)

Details
August 2003 (Hardback 1903889200, Deluxe 1903889219 / Daryl Joyce)
Précis
In ancient Akrotiri, a young girl learns mysteries from a tutor who fell from the skies…
DWM Index
334 Preview
335 Review
336 Review
Comment
Slow-moving foray into Greek mythology; also an alleged metaphor for 9/11. **67%**

11) Frayed
Tara Samms (foreword by Stephen Laws)

Details
October 2003 (Hardback 1903889227, Deluxe 1903889235 / Chris Moore)
Précis
The Doctor and Susan find themselves in the middle of a war they cannot understand…
DWM Index
336 Preview
337 Review
Comment
Formula 'base under siege' story with sinister undertones. **75%**

12) Eye of the Tyger
Paul J McAuley (foreword by Neil Gaiman)

Details
November 2003 (Hardback 1903889243, Deluxe 1903889251, Special Edition 1903889340 / Walter Howarth, Andrew Skilleter, Fred Gambino [Special Edition], Jim Burns)
Précis
A religious cult inhabiting an Earth colony ship is trapped in orbit around a black hole…
DWM Index
338 Preview
341 Review
Comment
Variable *Beauty and the Beast* reworking, with good set-pieces. **72%**

13) Companion Piece
Mike Tucker and Robert Perry (foreword by Rev Colin Midlane)

Details
December 2003 (Hardback 190388926X, Deluxe 1903889278 / Allan Bednar)
Précis
The Doctor and Catherine find themselves on a world where time travellers are persecuted as witches…
DWM Index
339 Preview
342 Review
Comment
A full-blown satire on Roman Catholicism that hits its target square on. **80%**

14) Blood and Hope
Iain McLaughlin (foreword by John Ostrander)

Details
January 2004 (Hardback 1903889286, Deluxe 1903889294 / Walter Howarth)
Précis
The Fifth Doctor, Peri and Erimem arrive during the American Civil War…
DWM Index
340 Preview
344 Review
Comment
Engaging history lesson with serious points about slavery and racism. **83%**

15) The Dalek Factor
Simon Clark (foreword by Christopher Fowler)

Details
March 2004 (Hardback 1903889308, Deluxe 1903889316 / Graham Humphreys)
Précis
Thals and Daleks fight to the death on a hostile swamp world…
DWM Index
341 Preview
346 Review
Comment
Dalek-by-numbers adventure that's as exciting as it is unoriginal. **90%**

6: Internet Webcasts

All webcasts take place on the BBC's official *Doctor Who* website at www.doctorwho/cult/doctorwho.co.uk

1) Death Comes to Time
Colin Meek

Details
12 July 2001-30 May 2002, 5 episodes
Soundtrack
October 2002, 3 x CDs (0563528230 / Lee Sullivan)
Cast
Sylvester McCoy (The Doctor), Sophie Aldred (Ace), John Culshaw (Golcrum/Senator Hawk/President), Jacqueline Pearce (Admiral Mettna), Kevin Eldon (Antimony), David Evans (Pilot), Leonard Fenton (Casmus), Stephen Fry (Minister of Chance), John Sessions (General Tannis), Richard Garraty (Senator/Soldier/Civilian), Britta Gartnet (Senator Sala), Benjamin Langley (Fighter Pilot), Huw Thomas (President), Murray Treadwell (Captain), Anthony Stewart Head (St Valentine), Dave Hill (Nessican), Charlotte Palmer (Dr Cain), Stephen Brody (Speedwell), Gareth Jones (Campion), Nicholas Courtney (Brigadier Lethbridge-Stewart), John Humphrys (Himself)
Crew
Illustrations Lee Sullivan, *Music* Nik Romero, *Script Editor* Nev Fountain, *Producer/Director* Dan Freedman
Précis
The Doctor arrives on Santiny in the middle of a war, while Ace is guided by the mysterious Casmus…
DWM Index
298 Pilot Ready for Take-off! (Nev Fountain)
303 Sylvester McCoy interview
306 Preview
314 Dan Freedman and Nev Fountain interview
315 Studio Report
    Stephen Fry interview
319 Webcast review
347 MP3-CD review
351 Archive Extra

Comment
Hugely fragmentary ragbag of clichéd SF and misplaced satire, voiced by an extraordinary cast. **38%**

2) Real Time
Gary Russell

Details
2 August-6 September 2002, 6 episodes
Soundtrack
December 2002, Big Finish, 2 x CDs (1903654785 / Lee Sullivan)
Cast
Colin Baker (The Doctor), Maggie Stables (Evelyn Smythe), Nicholas Briggs (Professor Osborn), Robert Curbishley (President), Jane Goddard (Doctor Nicola Savage), Andrew Hair (Fantham), Richard Herring (Taylor Renchard), William Johnston (Lieutenant Kreuger), Stewart Lee (Ryan Carey), Alistair Lock (Hoyer), Christopher Scott (Administrator David Isherwood), Yee Jee Tso (Doctor Reece Goddard), Mark (Dean)
Crew
Illustrations Lee Sullivan, *Producers* Gary Russell, Jason Haigh-Ellery, *Executive Producer for BBC Worldwide* Jacqueline Rayner, *Executive Producer for BBCi Drama and Entertainment* Martin Trickey, *Associate Producer for BBCi Drama and Entertainment* James Goss, *Director* Gary Russell
Précis
On the planet Chronos, an archaeological team uncover a long-forgotten temple…
DWM Index
321 Studio Report
    Colin Baker interview
    Nicholas Briggs interview
324 Review

Comment
Proudly traditional Cyberman adventure, solidly plotted. **80%**

409

3) *The Scream of the Shalka*
Paul Cornell

Details
November 2003, 6 episodes
Novelization
The Scream of the Shalka by Paul Cornell (288/14)
Paperback:
February 2004 (0563486198 / Steve Maher)
Cast
Richard E Grant (The Doctor), Derek Jacobi (The Master), Sophie Okonedo (Alison Cheney), Jim Norton (Thomas Kennett), Craig Kelly (Joe), Diana Quick (Prime), Anna Calder Marshall (Mathilda), Andrew Dunn (Max), Connor Moloney (Sergeant Graves), David Tennant, Ben Morrison (Caretakers), Derek Jacobi (The Master)
Crew
Animators Cosgrove Hall, *Director* Wilson Milam
Précis
A Lancashire town is under siege from mysterious forces...
DWM Index
336 Studio report
Paul McGann interview
338 Preview
339 Preview (Book)
340 Webcast review
343 Book review
352 Paul Cornell interview
Comment
An unsympathetic Doctor in an otherwise enjoyably old-fashioned yarn. **77%**

7: Stage Plays

1) The Curse of the Daleks
David Whitaker

Details
21 December 1965-3 January 1966, Wyndham's Theatre, Charing Cross Road, London WC2
Cast
Nicholas Hawtrey (Redway), Colin Miller (Sline), John Line (Ladiver), John Moore (Professor Vanderlyn), Nicholas Bennett (Dexion), Suzanne Mockler (Ijayna), Hilary Tindall (Marion), Edward Gardener (Rocket)
Crew
Director Gillian Howell, *Designer* Hutchinson Scott, *Producers* John Gale & Ernest Hecht
Précis
The spaceship *Starfinder* makes an emergency landing on Skaro where the Daleks are waiting...
DWM Index
147   GG: Who's On Stage!
200   What The Papers Said Feature
279   Thrilling Adventures in Time and Space
339   Archive Extra
Factoids
- The Doctor or his companions did not appear in this production.
- Four special Dalek props were built by Shawcraft Models.
- The play is credited to David Whitaker and Terry Nation, although it was in fact solely written by Whitaker.

Comment
Judging from contemporary reports, this was a rather stilted production only enlivened by the appearance of the Daleks themselves. It's also a moot point whether the absence of the Doctor and his companions was a particularly clever idea.

2) Doctor Who and the Daleks - Seven Keys to Doomsday
Terrance Dicks

Details
16 December 1974-12 January 1975, Adelphi Theatre, Strand, London WC2
Cast
Trevor Martin (The Doctor), Wendy Padbury (Jenny), James Mathews (Jimmy), Simon Jones (Master of Karn), Ian Ruskin (Jedak), Patsy Dermott (Tara), Peter Jolley, Mo Kiki, Peter Whitting (Clawrantulars)
Crew
Director Mick Hughes, *Designer* John Napier, *Producers* Robert de Wynter, Anthony Pye-Jeary
Précis
Two teenagers help the regenerated Doctor collect seven crystal keys that form a powerful weapon...
DWM Index
147   GG: Who's On Stage!
191   What The Papers Said
208   Wendy Padbury interview
273   Terrance Dicks interview
279   Thrilling Adventures in Time and Space
339   Archive Extra
Factoids
- The show's monsters were designed by James Acheson and constructed by prop builder Alistair Bowtell. Elements of the plot, such as the Clawrantulars and the Karn setting, later inspired the Terrance Dicks story *The Brain of Morbius* (84).
- A giant screen above the stage was used to show Jon Pertwee regenerating into Trevor Martin at the start of the show.
- Actors James Matthews and Wendy Padbury were secreted in the auditorium and ran onto the stage, as if from the audience, to help the Doctor in his quest.
- An IRA bombing campaign put many people off journeying into the West End, and the producers reluctantly decided to cancel a mooted regional tour.

Comment
This sounds as if it was a really wonderful production with all the latest state-of-the-art technical gubbins put to good use. Trevor Martin's Hartnellish Doctor must have been intriguing and the monsters and sets look groovy, man. **86%**

3) Recall UNIT: The Great T-Bag Mystery
Richard Franklin and George A Cairns

Details
20-25 August 1984, Moray House Theatre, Edinburgh
Cast
Graham Smith (Alistair), Lene Lindewell (Miss Bergo), Paul Holness (Silent Stephen), Richard Franklin (Captain Mike Yates), David Roylance (Hamish), Liam Rudden (Jimmy), Kevin Philpotts (Tim), Glynn Dack (Stallion), John Levene (Sergeant Benton), Richard Kettles (Major Molesworth), Nicholas Courtney (Voice of Brigadier Lethbridge-Stewart), John Scott Martin (Supreme Dalek)
Crew
Director Richard Franklin, *Designer* James Helps
Précis
UNIT has to rescue PM Margaret Thatcher who has been imprisoned in a tea-bag...
DWM Index
95   Review
279   Thrilling Adventures in Time and Space
341   Archive Extra
Factoids
- This satire on the Falklands War began with Richard Franklin and John Levene as themselves before changing into their UNIT costumes and assuming their fictive alter egos.
- When Jon Pertwee was unable to appear in a cameo role, John Scott Martin stepped in as a 'plain-clothes' Supreme Dalek.
- The supporting cast was made up of members of the Edinburgh and Lothian *Doctor Who* Local Group.

Comment
By all accounts a rather wet satire that probably only appealed to Lefties or rabid *Who* fans. **40%**

4) Doctor Who - The Ultimate Adventure
Terrance Dicks

Details
23 March-1 April 1989, Wimbledon Theatre, London SW19. A tour followed until 19 August 1989.
Cast
Jon Pertwee (The Doctor, 23 April-3 June 1989), Colin Baker (The Doctor, 5 June-19 August 1989), David Banks (The Doctor, 29 April 1989), Graeme Smith (Jason, to 15 July 1989 excluding 22-23 April 1989), Rebecca Thornhill (Crystal), Judith Hibbert (Delilah/Mrs T), David Banks (Karl, excluding 29 April 1989), Chris Beaumont (US Envoy, excluding 29 April 1989/Karl, 29 April 1989/Dalek Voices), David Bingham (MC, to 15 July 1989/Jason, from 17 July 1989), Wolf Christian (Cyberleader), Stephanie Colburn (Zog), Oliver Gray (Dalek/MC, from 17 July 1989/Cybermen, to 24 June 1989), Deborah Hecht (Waitress), Claudia Kelly (Ant-Person), Alison Reddihough (Mercenary), Paula Tappenden (Chief Dalek/Cyberman), Terry Walsh (Duelling Guard), Troy Webb (Emperor Dalek/Dalek Voices)
Crew
Director Carole Todd, *Designer* Paul Staples, *Musical Director/Composer* Steven Edis, *Creative Consultant* John Nathan-Turner, *Producer* Mark Furness
Précis
The PM asks the Doctor to stop the Daleks and Cybermen sabotaging a peace conference...
Factoids
- Andrew Cartmel and Ben Aaronovitch's original storyline proved too ambitious to stage, and so Terrance Dicks was called on to furnish a more practical alternative.
- Lasers were used throughout the production, with a large screen projecting video images for key scenes, such as a meteor bombardment.
- Producer Mark Furness' original choices for the Doctor's companions were *Neighbours* stars Kylie Minogue and Jason Donovan.
- David Banks played the Doctor for two performances in the Alexandra Theatre, Birmingham, when Jon Pertwee fell ill.
- Zog's costume was made by Susan Moore, Stephen Mansfield and Clare Pratt.

DWM Index

147	GG: Who's On Stage!
149	Photo Special
	In Rehearsal / Cast List
	Review (Jon Pertwee)
151	GG: David Banks as the Doctor
152	Review (Colin Baker)
155	Last Word On The Ultimate Tour?:
	David Banks' Diary
	Cast List
244	David Banks interview
273	Terrance Dicks interview
279	Thrilling Adventures in Time and Space
325	Colin Baker interview
341	Archive Extra

Comment

Lively, fun pantomime adventure with some smashing laser effects. Jon Pertwee returned to the rôle as if he'd never been gone and performances generally were excellent, especially David Banks and Graeme Smith. And let's face it, it's the only time you were ever going to see Cybermen and Daleks in the same story! Pity about the songs though - 'Business is Business' still haunts me to this day... **95%**

If you would like to correspond with the author, please contact him via his website, www.skonnos.homechoice.co.uk, email him at mark.campbell10@virgin.net or write to him through the publisher.